A DICTIONARY OF GREEN IDE

Vocabulary for a sane and sustainable future

A DICTIONARY OF GREEN IDEAS

Vocabulary for a sane and sustainable future

John Button

'Colourless green ideas sleep furiously'
Noam Chomsky

Routledge
London

First published in 1988 by Routledge
11 New Fetter Lane, London EC4P 4EE

Set in 9 on 10½pt Century Light
by the author and Saxon Printing Ltd,
and printed in Great Britain
by The Guernsey Press Co. Ltd.

British Library Cataloguing in Publication Data

Button, John
A dictionary of green ideas : vocabulary
for a sane and sustainable future.
1. Subculture — Dictionaries
I. Title
306'.1'0321 HM73

ISBN 0-415-00231-1

Acknowledgements

I could not have undertaken this project without the help and support of many friends within and on the fringes of the green movement. This is especially true of the entries covering different oppressions, and the need for the perspectives of people who have had very different life experiences from my own. I thank particularly the following people, who have helped by making suggestions and comments, reading all or part of the manuscript, and being ruthless and sensitive critics: Isiaka Amodu, Diana Becker, Simon Burton, Yarrow Cleaves, Emily Driver, Margaret Elphinstone, Roz Elphinstone, Paul Evenson, Clare Hill, Sandy Irvine, Geoff Kaplan, Mirka Knaster, Sandra Kramer, Bernard Little, Ian MacPherson, Tony Mercer, Jennifer Outhwaite, Walt Patterson, Jan Resnick, John Rowan, Mary Simister, Ian Simmons, Joyce Treuherz, Sasha Treuherz, Roberta Urbani and Jon Wynne-Tyson. My thanks too to Wendy Morris and Andrew Delahunty at Routledge, for their faith and encouragement.

Introduction

The way that can be spoken of is not the constant way;
The name that can be named is not the constant name.

A Dictionary of Green Ideas is designed to bring together concepts from a landscape of distinct but intimately linked green fields, which together form an area rapidly becoming populated with day-trippers and longer-term visitors. Each field has a name, sometimes more than one: there is ecology, conservation, peace studies, feminism, humanistic psychology, the politics of food and nutrition, spirituality, development studies, green politics, appropriate and alternative technology, holistic healing and complementary medicine, alternative education, the communes movement, new economics. What all of these subjects have in common is an approach that is increasingly coming to be called 'green'.

Each part of the landscape has been explored in more or less detail, and some already have excellent gazetteers — Cheris Kramerae and Paula Treichler's *Dictionary of Feminism* stands out as a model — but as yet there has been no map of the whole territory. As Peter Bunyard and Fern Morgan-Grenville say at the end of *The Green Alternative*,

> The way forward into a new land requires the creation of a map. We who call ourselves Green are standing on the high ground of environmental awareness and trying to make out the shape of the land which lies ahead. There is much which is obscure, much to be found out. But one thing is clear: if we do not go the right way forward we shall perish from the combined effects of all the environmentally destructive ways of living which increasingly characterise this age.

Taking 'environmentally destructive' in its widest sense to include everything that operates to deaden the variety, sparkle and joy of life on earth, I fully agree, and hope that this volume will go some way to rectifying this state of affairs.

The green approach is eclectic, and draws its ideas from a wide range of disciplines, but above all it acknowledges that any person or party that claims absolute rightness is immediately suspect: anybody so presumptuous as to write a dictionary would do well to keep the above words of the Taoist teacher Lao Tzû in mind. People who consult dictionaries are usually looking for accurate and precise meanings, but this dictionary recognises that meaning is often in the eye of the beholder, and that the same word can mean precisely opposite things in different mouths, at different times, and in different places. 'Development' in the mind of a nuclear engineer is very different from 'development' in the mind of a central African villager or the mind of a gestalt group leader in San Francisco. 'Discrimination' for a black South African is not the same 'discrimination' as that of the stockbroker choosing a diamond engagement ring. Dictionaries are never 'objective' and this one is no exception — it is my dictionary just as much as *The Dictionary of Ortho-Rhino-Laryngology* is someone else's, no matter how sterile and objective it may look on the library shelf.

Hence the layout and approach of *A Dictionary of Green Ideas*. Under each idea you will find some 'facts' — its first recorded use in the sense of my definition, and the pre-modern English origins of the word(s). Then there is either a definition or, where that proved impossible, a commentary on the idea. While I have attempted to be as accurate as possible in my 'green definitions', especially those that describe a specific thing or idea (like WIND ENERGY or NEW INTERNATIONAL ECONOMIC ORDER), defining an idea like FACT or TRUTH is not so easy. I gave up altogether on REALITY. Thus what follows in each case is a combination of what I hope is thought-provoking and informative text together with a large number of quotations, which together illustrate the points I am making. Within and at the end of an entry you will often find suggestions about other related ideas you might like to explore — these are given in SMALL CAPITAL letters. Where I give the date of the first recorded use of an idea, remember that this is only the first time I have found it under this name — the idea itself is usually much older. Dates given as '12c' or '15c' tell you in which century the word or term was first used, when this is before about 1750; *c.*1900 means 'about (*circa*) 1900'. When I say 'in this sense' it means that the word has earlier uses, but this is the earliest I have found it in the sense in which I use it. *L* means Latin and *Gk* Greek; otherwise I have given the language of origin in full.

Defining the boundaries of what to include as 'green' has turned out to be easier than I imagined, though some edges were hazier than others. I have deliberately left out most specific therapies and techniques in healing and therapy, though some make it by virtue of their wider application, like GESTALT, HOMEOPATHY and COUNSELLING — if you want to know more about these areas I would recommend Stephen

Fulder's *The Handbook of Complementary Medicine* for healing, and Sue Walrond-Skinner's *Dictionary of Psychotherapy* for therapy.

The boundaries within spirituality were more of a problem, and I admit to working on personal whim in some cases. If I had to explain my policy, I would say that I have included everything that I can relate to as a practical green sort of person, and left out the ones I have problems with. Thus AFFIRMATION, ATTUNEMENT and MEDITATION make it, and 'guidance', 'manifestation' and 'power points' don't (if you want to know more about them you'll need a book like David Harvey's *Complete Guide to Alternative Living*). Likewise as a geography graduate I can just handle EARTH MYSTERIES, but have drawn the line at 'landscape temple' and 'ley line'.

Some authors seem to find it impossible to write without coining new words and concepts on every line — Buckminster Fuller (*see* JARGON), William Irwin Thompson, Erich Jantsch and Gregory Bateson spring immediately to mind. If I had included every word that every green-hued writer had ever coined, this dictionary would be at least twice as long as it is. As an exercise, I have made a collection of all the ECO-words I have found (99 at the last count), which gives you just a taste of what greenoglots can get up to when they try. My policy on new coinings has been to ignore them unless (1) they have been picked up by other writers and become part of fairly standard green usage, or (2) they seem to be particularly useful. One word I have coined, because I couldn't think of an alternative, is 'green-thinker' (though I suspect I'm not the first to use it): a green-thinker is someone who holds a fair selection of green ideas, and who thinks and lives — as far as possible — along green lines.

In an attempt to be universal, I hope I have succeeded in being transatlantic (and transpacific too) without drowning in mid-ocean. My policy has been to put things under the heading that most people will look under and cross-reference them from their equivalents — thus TRUCK is cross-referenced from LORRY, and WASTE from GARBAGE. I have used British spelling in the parts I have written, since I am British, but all quotations have been left exactly as they were written. Each quotation is identified by its author(s) and date; the sources can be found at the end of the book by looking up the last name of the author. In the list of sources I have given only author, title and date of the first publication of each book; this should always be sufficient to find the relevant volume.

This is a dictionary, and not an encyclopedia. You will not find individual people's names in the alphabetical lists, nor individual countries, continents (with the exception of ANTARCTICA) or cities. I have kept fairly strictly to 'green ideas', but this does not mean an avoidance of concrete examples — a flip into any part of the text should confirm this.

In line with green thinking on ownership, trusteeship and commonwealth, I have avoided putting emphasis on exactly who originated many of these 'green ideas'. On the other hand, where an idea is traceable to a particular author, a quotation from that author will almost always be included in the entry.

What I have tried to do above all is explain things simply and clearly without being simplistic and condescending. If green-thinkers, with their faith in the simple and the clear, can't get basic ideas across, there is little hope for the future of human communication. As Charlene Spretnak and Fritjof Capra say in their (otherwise) ground-breaking book *Green Politics*: 'A core problem of the new-paradigm politics is that accessible language sufficient to present the long-term goals dynamically and persuasively has yet to be developed' (*see* CORE, PROBLEM, PARADIGM, POLITICS, LANGUAGE, SUFFICIENCY, GOAL, DYNAMIC and DEVELOPMENT in this dictionary). Perhaps *A Dictionary of Green Ideas* will go some way to help!

I hope that this will be an early step on the way to creating a green vocabulary that will help us speak to each other, and will help people who are new to green thinking to understand us. I'd like to think of it sitting on the White House and Downing Street bookshelves so it can be pulled out whenever a strange new idea is floated that they have vaguely heard of but haven't quite understood. And I would appreciate your help too. If you have any thoughts, ideas or misgivings about what is included, or about what might be included in future editions, do please let me know by writing to me care of the publishers.

Happy reading!

John Button

Laurieston, February 1988

Aa

Abiotic

[1893. *Gk a- + biotikos*, not living]

A substance which, while not 'alive' in scientific terms, is necessary for the existence of LIFE. First used widely in the 1950s by biologists to describe basic organic and inorganic compounds forming part of an ECOSYSTEM. 'For example, the quantity of chlorophyll per unit area of land or water surface and the quantity of dissolved organic matter in water are two items of great ecological interest' (Eugene Odum, 1963). In recent years the distinction between 'living' (BIOTIC) and 'non-living' (abiotic) substances has become blurred: 'We would like to think that we are different from stones because we are living and they are not, but there is no way we can prove our position' (Gary Zukav, 1979).

Abortion

[*c*.1800 in this sense. *L abortus*, miscarried]

The ending of the life of a human foetus, either by miscarriage ('spontaneous abortion'), or because the mother has decided that it would be inappropriate for her to give birth to the child. In the relative absence of reliable forms of BIRTH CONTROL, abortion has been carried out for centuries, and until recently took a heavy toll on women's lives. There are still some risks, but if a deliberate abortion is carried out under good and experienced supervision the risks today are very slight. Some people believe that deliberate abortion offends against moral and religious principles, and many more feel that it should only be used if all other contraceptive techniques have failed; even in countries where abortion is freely available it is not generally thought of as a method of CONTRACEPTION. One of the early demands of the women's liberation movement was that any woman should be free to make decisions about her own body, including the foetus inside her womb, and 'a woman's right to choose' is an important part of many people's philosophy. The question of abortion can raise two contradictory considerations from a green point of view: 'On the one hand [is] the right of women and men to self-determination, on the other hand [the protection] of human life in all areas. Protection of life, and human life above all . . . means making sure that the new life can grow up in a future as happy and humane as possible. This possibility must not depend simply on the resources of the individual family, but requires comprehensive measures of social and state support. Termination of a pregnancy is a question of morality and personal circumstances, and must not be subject to legal prosecution. It should be made unnecessary through sex education and social assistance, as well as by introducing new methods of birth control' (Die Grünen, 1983). 'The quality of the debate in Green parties over abortion has more integrity than that currently being waged in American politics precisely because all aspects of the issue are considered. In our country half the debate often seems to be missing: women's suffering' (Charlene Spretnak, 1986). *See also* REPRODUCTIVE RIGHTS.

Abundance
[14c. *L abundans*, abounding]
The existence of things or qualities in copious amounts. A two-edged and potentially dangerous idea: the abundance of flora and fauna in the Amazon rainforest, for example, means very different things to an ecologist, a mineral prospector and a native villager. Yet there are things and qualities which are more abundant than most people acknowledge, and an important distinction can be made between things which seem abundant but are strictly limited, like oil and iron ore; things which are abundant but can only be used to the extent that they remain in EQUILIBRIUM with other parts of the ecosystem, like SOLAR ENERGY and running water; and qualities which are unlimited, like LOVE and UNDERSTANDING. 'We . . . pursue the holy grail of economic abundance by living — more or less unwittingly — according to the advertiser's cliché: "Hurry, quantities are limited. Get yours now!" ' (William Catton, in Michael Tobias (ed), 1985). 'Most people think the word abundance means total overflowing, whereas it is a magnificent word that says everything is there in perfect timing and proportion to what one needs. It's very exciting to realise that we are part of a universe that can supply us perfectly' (Lionel Fifield, in Mary Inglis and Sandra Kramer (ed), 1985).

Access
[*L accessus*, an approach]
(1) [14c] Providing people with the freedom to use resources which are part of their birthright, both individually and communally. One of these rights is access to land, particularly open land — some countries, like Sweden, have a right of common access, and green-thinkers believe that this right should be extended worldwide: 'We need a change from a

system that treats presence on rural land as trespass except in special circumstances, to one that presumes a public right to walk on the land except in circumstances where there are good reasons why it should be withheld' (Marion Shoard, 1987). Part of providing access is ensuring that everybody, particularly people with physical disabilities, can go wherever they would like to — in recent years awareness has grown about the need for easy access to public buildings and communal facilities, and while a lot has been done, there is a great deal of room for improvement.
(2) [*c*.1950] Helping the flow of ideas and information by opening new channels and simplifying ways of finding things out. '*Maggie's Farm* is an access magazine servicing a diverse network of citizen initiative groups and emerging new lifestyles' (*Maggie's Farm* magazine, Australia, 1986).

Accident
[14c. *L accidere*, to happen]
An unplanned (yet not unexpected) event, usually with harmful and far-reaching consequences. Many accidents are the result of the application of dangerous and untested TECHNOLOGY — the Three Mile Island and Chernobyl nuclear accidents, the chemical leaks at Seveso in Italy and Bhopal in India, the quarter of a million people killed each years on the world's roads — yet we are still told that technologies are safe, that accidents won't happen. 'When an "accident" occurs, like the one at Seveso or the Morhange talcum powder incident, we are expected to believe that it is an isolated incident, a mistake. Obviously that is wrong. As things are, it is *impossible* for accidents *not* to happen *all* the time' (Léonie Caldecott and Stephanie Leland (ed), 1983). SAFETY precautions are all very well (when they are applied), but cannot deal with the very many inappropriate technologies — particularly toxic CHEMICALS and the NUCLEAR industry — which incorporate accidents just waiting to happen, worldwide.

Acid Rain
[1872]
(*also* 'acid deposition')
Rain and other precipitation which is more acid than it would naturally be because it carries an excess quantity of airborne pollutants, particularly sulphur. Through its corrosive properties, acid rain wears down both the natural and artificial environment, causing excessive acidification of land and groundwater. The term was coined in 1872 by Robert Angus Smith in a book called *Air and Rain: The Beginnings of a Chemical Climatology*, but it was not until the 1960s that scientists became fully aware of the problem of dying trees, crumbling buildings and asphyxiated fish, and only very recently that the general public has

become concerned about what is happening. 'Acid rain is a consequence of the combustion of coal and oil on an enormous scale, either for the production of electricity or in certain industrial processes. The by-products from this massive conflagration of fossil fuels are released untreated into the air, and eventually they return to earth and distort natural cycles' (Steve Elsworth, 1984). 'Scientists and doctors have noticed that where the air is contaminated by acidic and other poisonous gases released from power stations, heavy industry and vehicle exhausts . . . more people suffer from chronic respiratory ailments such as bronchitis and lung cancer. . . When people drink the water, these poisons build up in their bodies. One poison in particular — aluminium — finds its way into the brain. In Norway and Sweden where there is now aluminium in the water, scientists have found high incidences of Alzheimer's disease. This disease causes symptoms of extreme senility in relatively young people. Victims become deranged and helpless. In most cases death ensues within 10 years of symptoms appearing' (Greenpeace leaflet, 1987). 'All this should frighten us. Our forests and fish, cathedrals and crops, lichen and lungs — are all under attack. Today's air pollution is every bit as lethal as the black smogs it has replaced. And it is everywhere' (Fred Pearce, 1987). *See also* ATMOSPHERIC POLLUTION, PHOTOCHEMICAL SMOG, WALDSTERBEN.

Action
[*c*.1949 in this sense. *L actio*, a happening or performance]
An event, usually involving a number of people, designed to draw attention to an important environmental, social, political or economic issue. Hence 'citizen action', 'industrial action', 'nonviolent action', 'peace action', 'protest action'. 'Strategic, often public, behaviour which functions practically or symbolically to challenge the conditions of women's oppression and other forms of injustice' (Cheris Kramerae and Paula Treichler, 1985). 'In political terms nonviolent action is based on a very simple postulate: people do not always do what they are told to do, and sometimes they do things which have been forbidden to them' (Gene Sharp, 1973). *See also* ACTIVISM, DIRECT ACTION, NONVIOLENT DIRECT ACTION.

Active Birth
(*see* NATURAL CHILDBIRTH)

Active Solar
[*c*.1960]
A method of heating which uses the heat of the sun to generate energy within a system around which water is pumped, thus distributing heat throughout the building or heating scheme. Some people, particularly in the USA, extend the term to embrace any system which uses energy

from solar radiation to do work at a distance, including wind turbines and biofuel furnaces. See also PASSIVE SOLAR, SOLAR ENERGY.

Activism
[1915 in this sense. *L actio*, a happening or performance]
A doctrine and policy which advocates the taking of DIRECT ACTION in order to publicise and achieve desired goals. 'Nobody made a greater mistake than he [or she] who did nothing because he [or she] could only do a little' (Edmund Burke, 1729-97, quoted in *Resurgence*, Jan/Feb 1982).

Adaptation
[1859 in this sense. *L adaptare*, to fit]
Modifications by which a living organism or species is able to thrive more easily in a particular environment. Originally a biological term, later taken into ecology. 'Adaptation is necessary for the historical continuity of all living things. While it is true that organisms living in a stable, mature, natural environment may not need to adapt to survive, just as human beings in a stable cultural situation do not have to change very much, this certainly is not the situation we find ourselves in now. In a number of ways, the present world is far from a state of equilibrium. More than any single factor, the quality of the future will depend on the effectiveness of our adaptation to the forces of change that are at work in our world today — the wisdom and creativity that we put into finding a new balance' (Warren Johnson, 1979).

Addiction
[*c*.1600. *L addicere*, to give as a slave]
Being so dependent on one particular sort of stimulant that you feel you cannot live without it. Some substances are known to cause a chemical change in the body, which leads the taker to crave yet more of it to maintain that changed state. Other stimulants — PAIN, SEX, TELEVISION or VIOLENCE — are more subtly addictive, but the addiction can be just as strong. Addiction is usually a result of unmet emotional needs becoming projected on to activities which bring temporary relief. Withdrawal from the addiction is difficult partly because of the physical craving, and partly because of the knowledge that these unmet needs will resurface — anybody 'coming off' an addiction therefore needs a great deal of emotional support. There is some evidence (from CLINICAL ECOLOGY, for example) that people often crave the very thing they are allergic or sensitive to, and as a result of taking it can suffer a range of symptoms from headaches to hallucinations. Some humanistic psychologists describe destructive behaviour patterns in terms of addiction: 'When we use the word "addiction," we will be referring to something

we tell ourselves we must have to be happy. . . An addiction is an emotion-backed demand . . . or expectation' (Ken Keyes, 1979).

Additive

[1872 in this sense. *L addere*, to add]

A substance which is added to something and which changes its characteristics; most frequently used as shorthand for 'food additives', a range of substances added by the food-processing industry which help to make FOOD yield larger profits, appear more 'attractive', and keep longer. It is true that certain additives can improve food without harming its nutritional value or the consumer, but this is rarely the real reason why additives are used — most additives are used to replace flavours and colours destroyed by processing, disguise second-rate (and sometimes bad) food, and turn basic and relatively cheap ingredients into costly 'convenience' foods. Some additives are harmless — many are made from natural food sources — but some are known to be health risks, among them the azo coal tar dyes used for colouring (particularly the yellow dye Tartrazine, numbered E102 in Europe — the other azo colours are E104-133, 142, 151 and 154-155), the benzoate preservatives (E210-213) and the purine flavour enhancers (627-635). 'The benefits to the industry from its use of additives are substantial, and substantially outweigh any benefits which their use may confer on consumers. If there are risks which arise from the use of additives, these risks are borne almost entirely by consumers, and not by the manufacturing companies' (Erik Millstone, 1986). Although it is difficult to avoid additives completely, especially when eating out, it is neither difficult nor expensive to reduce consumption of processed foods and eat more fresh, varied, organically-grown produce. As a result of rapidly-shifting public pressure, many manufacturers have reduced their use of additives, and you can help this process by checking labels and insisting on foodstuffs without artificial colourings, flavourings, shelf-life extenders, fortifiers, sweeteners, improvers and preservatives.

Adultism

[1975]

The systematic OPPRESSION of YOUNG PEOPLE by older people. 'Part of the special oppression of children and young people consists . . . of enforced dependency, the lack of resources, the lack of finances, the organized interference in their being in charge of their own lives, their not being allowed to set their own goals. [Condescension and oversimplification deny them the] understanding they need. They are more ready to grasp the whole picture, in general, than are adults' (Harvey Jackins, 1978). Adultism is the universal oppression — everybody has been oppressed as a child, even people whose only role now seems to be that of oppressor. Adultism can in fact be seen as the training ground for oppressive behaviour, and many green-thinkers believe that if young people were not oppressed, they would not learn how to oppress. *See also* EDUCATION, SCHOOL.

Advertising
[1762. *Old French a(d)vertir*, to turn the attention]
(US: 'advertizing')
Notices or announcements designed to sell a product or service. Freedom of INFORMATION is an important aspect of green thinking, and although some advertising is information, most is persuasion, insinuation, subtle blackmail, and clever combinations of half-truth and misrepresentation. 'Advertisements are one of the most important cultural factors moulding and reflecting our life today. They are ubiquitous, an inevitable part of everyone's lives: even if you do not read a newspaper or watch television, the images posted over our urban surroundings are inescapable. . . Obviously [advertising] has a function, which is to sell things to us. But it has another function, which I believe in many ways replaces that traditionally fulfilled by art or religion. It creates structures of meaning. . . Advertisements are selling us something else besides consumer goods: in providing us with a structure in which we, and those goods, are interchangeable, they are selling us ourselves. . . Thus instead of being identified with what they produce, people are made to identify themselves with what they consume' (Judith Williamson, 1978).

Advocacy
[*c*.1970 in this sense. *L advocare*, to summon to the aid of another person]
The active support of a particular cause, often the upholding of individual, community or minority rights; usually used in phrases like 'advocacy journalism' and 'advocacy planning'. 'Advocacy planning emerged first in the USA and describes the practice of professional planners voluntarily helping underprivileged sections of society to give expression to their hopes for a better environment' (Graham Ashworth, 1973). 'In trying to achieve a pluralist society through advocacy there is an attempt to balance off the interests of those with financial power, who can buy planning expertise and the material goods they want, such as better housing and better schools, against those who can only ask for what they want. If those who already control the economy and the government are *willing* to share power, then of course the problem would be one of *articulating* and arguing the needs of different interest groups. But within the present economic structure of our society, simply giving the poor more access to planning expertise

doesn't basically change their chances of getting the same goods and services as wealthier citizens. What it gives them is more power to compete among themselves for the government's welfare products' (Robert Goodman, 1972). *See also* PLANNING.

Aetiology
[*c*.1600 *Gk aetiologia*, giving a cause]
(*also* 'etiology')
The study of the causes of ill health. The word also has an earlier and more general meaning, 'the study of causes'.

Affinity Group
[1976]
A small group of people trained in nonviolent methods taking part in an ACTION, each of which appoints a spokesperson by CONSENSUS to take part in larger group decision-making. An organisational method first used at the Seabrook anti-nuclear action in the USA in 1977. *See also* NONVIOLENCE.

Affirmation
[15c. *L affirmare*, to make strong]
A statement of the existence of the TRUTH of something, or the making of such a statement. Affirmation has two meanings in green thinking:
(1) Making positive statements which contradict the generally negative and destructive view of the world asserted by many people.
(2) A statement of personal POWER, CREATIVITY or INTELLIGENCE, which enables the person making the affirmation to take RESPONSIBILITY for themself and their surroundings. 'Affirmations work by replacing the negative programme . . . by a positive, life-affirming one. Once you have started bringing awareness to your life and uncovering your self-limiting [and self-destructive patterns], you are ready to use affirmations to cancel them out. . . Examples of affirmations [are:] I deserve to enjoy radiant health; . . I love and accept myself totally, just the way I am; . . I can express myself freely and with confidence' (Swami Anand Samarpan, 1983). Always watch for the fine line between affirmations, LIES, and power trips. *See also* APPRECIATION, CELEBRATION.

Affirmative Action
[1965]
Action by an individual or a group of people which shows clearly and positively that they are working to overturn DISCRIMINATION, not only by employing people regardless of race, sex or religion, but also by actively encouraging such PARTICIPATION. 'Companies, universities and other institutions which do business with the [US] government or receive federal funding . . . shall take affirmative action to ensure that applicants

are employed, and that employees are treated during their employment, without regard to their race, color, religion, sex or national origin' (US Executive Order 11375, 1976). *See also* POSITIVE DISCRIMINATION.

Affluence
[17c. *L affluens*, flowing towards]
Owning large amounts of personal possessions, often far more than you need. 'Most people in rich countries have little idea how very expensive their lifestyles are in terms of materials and energy... We can only go on being as affluent as we are because we are using up more than our share of world resources, and we can only go on being as affluent as we are if most people in the world remain poor' (F.E. Trainer, 1985). 'If we are to enjoy this planet for a long time, we may as well face the fact that trying to perpetuate the affluent society is going to be an uphill struggle. . . Affluence will grow less comfortable, and there will be less peace and security in it' (Warren Johnson, 1979). *See also* GROWTH, POSSESSION, POVERTY, PROGRESS, PROPERTY, WEALTH.

Ageism
[1970]
(*also* 'agism')
The systematic OPPRESSION of older people by younger people. 'Given the "ageism" in our society paid employment is not always easy to find for people who have . . . been made "redundant" ' (Mary Stott, 1981). The main tools of ageism are segregation and silencing, a marked contrast to the role of ELDERS in most traditional societies. 'Ageism' has also been used (mostly in the 1970s) to mean the oppression of any group of people because of their age, including children, though the oppression of young people is now usually called ADULTISM.

Age Structure
[1932]
The distribution of people of different ages and sexes within the POPULATION of a community or region. While individual needs are also vital, a knowledge of age structure can help to ascertain what general level of help and facilities that community needs. 'Alarmingly, about 37% of the people now on this planet are under 15. . . These young people are the broad base of the world age structure and represent the even greater population explosion to come' (G. Tyler Miller and Patrick Armstrong, 1982). 'When a tremendous population momentum has been created, it takes from 50 to 70 years . . . after its family size has been reduced to the replacement level of just two before natural increase comes to an end' (Rufus Miles, 1976). *See also* OVERPOPULATION.

Aggression
[*c*.1600. *L aggredi*, to attack]
Behaviour marked by unnecessary and often unprovoked VIOLENCE; often confused with ANGER or ASSERTIVENESS. Aggression is usually thought of as typically 'male' behaviour (*see* MAN, MASCULINE, WAR). Both animal and human behaviourists have debated endlessly whether aggression is instinctive and uncontrollable, or learned and controllable, often drawing parallels between animal and human behaviour. 'There cannot be any doubt, in the opinion of any biologically-minded scientist, that intraspecific fighting is in Man [*sic*], just as much of a spontaneous instinctive drive as in most other higher vertebrates' (Konrad Lorenz, 1966). 'The extension of the findings of biology and psychology into the international relationship is probably false; but as an analogy it could be useful to point out that in animals and in man [more *sic*], aggressiveness is a non-passive response to the perception of a threat, or to the experience of frustration. Political leaders of states who accuse other states of being aggressive, would then know where the responsibility for aggression finally lies' (John Burton, quoted in Robert Ardrey, 1967).

Agreement
[15c. *Middle English agreen*, to be pleasing to]
A consciously negotiated settlement made so that two or more people can work together on a project. It may be made legally binding, but need not be. The important point about an agreement is that each person who is party to the agreement has negotiated from a position of personal POWER, and has not been manipulated or forced into agreeing to something that does not benefit them. *See also* MEDIATION, NEGOTIATION.

Agribusiness
[1955. From 'agri[culture]' + 'business']
AGRICULTURE which is run along exploitative industrial lines on large-scale intensive farms, with little or no long-term interest in the health of the LAND, the livestock or the workers. The aim of agribusiness is to make money for the owner, so PRODUCTIVITY is paramount. Agribusinesses are often owned by essentially non-agricultural corporations, who install managers and accountants and ask few questions as long as profits remain high. They have few qualms about using chemicals to boost short-term production, or about the displacement of rural population. In the USA and many parts of the Third World, agribusiness is often owned by food processing companies wanting to maintain absolute control over their raw materials; elsewhere this is less common, though agribusinesses may have contractual arrangements with food processing companies.

Agricide
[1983]
The acknowledgement that if current mainstream agricultural practices are continued, the ability of land to support healthy life will deteriorate so drastically that all life will be threatened. 'If the structure and practice of agriculture [are] not quickly changed, and made ecologically more sound, health-inducing, humane, and equitable, the next generation will face inevitable agricide' (Michael Fox, 1986). *See also* AGRICULTURE.

Agriculture
[15c. *L agricultura*, tillage of the land]
Using LAND and the LIFE it supports wisely and sensitively in order to yield healthy FOOD for human beings. Agriculture is what keeps most of us alive, and in traditional cultures almost everybody is — among other things — a farmer, or perhaps more accurately, a gardener (*see* GARDEN). The distinction is an important one, since until the Neolithic Revolution around ten thousand years ago there was no agriculture. Some pre-agricultural societies, both historical and contemporary, adhere to a basic belief that it is sacrilege to till the earth with ploughs or to fell trees. The beginnings of agriculture probably marked the most profound of all changes in the relationship of people with land and NATURE, and green-thinkers are aware that all agriculture freezes nature into artificial moulds, always resulting in a loss of ecological DIVERSITY. 'Most analyses of problems *in* agriculture do not deal with the problem *of* agriculture. Most talk is about the ways farming is done . . . not the threat *of* agriculture to the biosphere itself' (Wes Jackson, 1985). In the West 'agriculture', highly mechanised and specialised, provides very few people with their main livelihood — less than 4% of the working population of the USA works on the land, and in Britain it is nearer 2%. 'We have an unprecedentedly large urban population that has no land to grow food on, no knowledge of how to grow it, and less and less knowledge of what to do with it after it is grown. That this population can continue to eat through shortage, strike, embargo, riot, depression, war . . . is not a certainty or even a faith; it is a superstition' (Wendell Berry, 1981). It comes as little surprise to green-thinkers and ecologists that the intensive agriculture of South-East Asia can produce nine or ten times the calories per acre of US agriculture, with perhaps a hundred times the input of human labour. This is because traditional cultures use high-yield and labour-intensive but sustainable methods with a large variety of crops (*see* PERMACULTURE, POLYCULTURE), while Western agriculture is increasingly based on methods of MONOCULTURE which use large amounts of NON-RENEWABLE RESOURCES instead of human labour. This may make it 'efficient' in money terms, but at enormous

environmental, ecological and social cost. The adverse global balance of the TECHNOLOGICAL FIX of Western agriculture is becoming increasingly obvious. Not only are SOIL EROSION, SALINISATION and DESERTIFICATION increasing rapidly, but even after the so-called GREEN REVOLUTION of the late 1960s world agriculture is still often not providing the food that people need: 'Since 1971, gains in output have barely kept pace with population growth; production per person has fluctuated widely but shown little real increase. Indeed, per capita grain production of 324 kilograms in 1980, an unusually poor harvest, was actually lower than the 330 kilograms of 1971. As food prices have climbed, diets have deteriorated in some Third World countries, especially among landless labourers and the urban poor' (Lester Brown, 1981). Yet this global shortage overlooks vast inter-regional inequalities, and Europeans who hear about the vast food mountains in storage (twenty million tonnes of cereals; five years' supply of milk powder) might well wonder what the fuss is all about. The fact is that these surpluses have resulted only from a system of agricultural subsidy which has further impoverished already degraded farmland and put large sums of money into the pockets of a few large-scale farmers. It has done nothing to put agriculture on a sustainable footing, and in ecological terms is part of a one-off bonanza which cannot be repeated: 'Under the existing economic accounting system, food production can soar even while the agricultural practices followed are consuming the resource base on which future production depends' (Lester Brown, in *Worldwatch* 1987). Not only is land being degraded; Western-style agriculture is highly energy-intensive and depends on large quantities of fertilizers and PESTICIDES which hurt the soil, poison crops, harm human health and use up valuable non-renewable resources. 'Maximum crop yields depend upon massive inputs of artificial fertilizers. But these, in turn, create ideal conditions for pests and diseases. . . While scientists develop new crop varieties and new pesticides, modern chemical-intensive farming methods actually encourage the evolution of resistant pests and diseases. Despite pesticides with names such as Commando, Missile, Trident and Avenge, it is an "arms race" which nature is bound to win' (Jonathon Porritt (ed), 1987). The only sustainable way forward is to return to APPROPRIATE, ORGANIC, traditional, small-scale agriculture. In the West this means listening to farmers who know what the land needs; in the Third World it means learning from traditional methods which have fed people adequately for centuries. 'In the short term [present agricultural methods] benefit only a few powerful people. In the longer term they spell ecological, social and economic disaster. . . The agricultural question is one of survival' (Bernard Little and Stewart Biggar, 1987).

Agroforestry
(*see* FORESTRY)

Aid
[1940 in this sense. *L adjutare*, to help]
Helping poor people, particularly in the THIRD WORLD, to become SELF-RELIANT in FOOD, HEALTH, EDUCATION, APPROPRIATE TECHNOLOGY and livelihood. This, however, is not the nature of most 'aid', which is in the nature of 'grants with strings' — we will give you this if: if you buy from us; if you take our advice; if you do it our way. Even aid of this sort represents a tiny amount — less than half a per cent — of the income of the rich world, and the rich world still, as it has always done, gets the best bargain. For every pound or dollar given in Third World aid, nearly twice that amount is returned from the Third World in produce, purchases from the rich world, or debt repayment (*see* DEBT CRISIS). 'The poor of the world are subsidising us' (Green Party, 1987). 'Aid is one of the links that bind the system together, and propaganda like the Brandt Report that treats it just as a sort of international welfare benefit is dangerously misleading. . . Even those donors, such as the Swedes, who concentrate aid on few "good" governments, are, through that very policy, deeply paternalistic' (Dudley Seers, 1982, in Victoria Brittain and Michael Simmons (ed), 1987). 'In both relative and absolute numbers, there are more hungry people in the world today — with an undue proportion of them in Africa — than there were before "aid" was ever invented' (Marcus Linear, 1985). *See also* DELINKING, DEVELOPMENT, TRADE.

AID
(1) [1948. Abbreviation of 'artificial insemination by donor'] A way that a woman can conceive without having sexual intercourse; the donor's semen is inserted through a tube passed through the woman's vagina into the uterus. Originally developed to allow a married woman to have a child if her husband was sterile, it has become widely used by lesbians who want to have a child without the direct participation of a man. (2) [1961] The acronym of the US Agency for International Development, an important AID agency.

AIDS
[1982. Abbreviation of 'acquired immune-deficiency syndrome']
A viral syndrome (set of symptoms) which first infected people in the late 1970s, involving a weakening of the body's immune system so the body cannot cope with otherwise minor infections, thus leading to death in apparently all cases. By late 1986 about 50,000 people had died from AIDS, and about ten million people all over the world were thought to be carrying the virus. As it is such a new disease, relatively

little is known about its origins and long-term effects, but it is clear that it is spread mostly through sexual intercourse, with the transfer of infected blood being another important channel. In the West, many sufferers are gay men, though both women and men are at risk; this has however led to the stigmatisation of GAY men. Similarly, because the disease appeared in Africa at much the same time as in the USA, Africans have been unfairly blamed for the spread of AIDS. The truth is that Africans and gay men have been prominent among the early sufferers of AIDS, but are intrinsically no more or less at risk than anybody else. Because AIDS is related to two of our most taboo subjects — SEX and DEATH — it appears to threaten people on many levels, but it has had the positive effect of making most people think very hard about their attitudes to both subjects. Not surprisingly, AIDS has given many moralist reactionaries abundant material for blame and self-righteousness, which must be resisted. The secrecy and exploitation hidden by conventional patterns of relationships are far more conducive to the spread of AIDS than openly-discussed and safe sexual experimentation. There are many safe and satisfying alternatives to conventional intercourse, and clear communication does not detract from sensual pleasure. 'It changes what is possible in sex, but that does not mean sex is simply going to get worse. People may decide that, instead of business as usual plus condom, they may get more physical and emotional pleasure by giving more time and care to their relationships. Restrictions on sexual freedom could lead to a world of lifeless partnerships held together by fear and a resurgent conservatism, in which purity and virgins are at a premium. They could also encourage people to value friendship more highly, and to reconsider the code of sexual precedence which holds that only heterosexual fucking counts, and that anything else is either juvenile or perverse. Wouldn't it be better to try and create a new world out of the disaster, rather than letting the old one take over?' (Marek Kohn, *The Face* magazine, May 1987).

Air
(*see* ATMOSPHERE)

Air Pollution
(*see* ATMOSPHERIC POLLUTION)

Albedo
[1859. *L albedo*, whiteness]
The ratio of the intensity of light reflected from the surface of the earth to the amount of sunlight falling on it. This affects the amount of heat absorbed by the earth's surface, and the vegetation growing on it. Large areas of artificial surface can distort local albedo enormously. An understanding of albedo is useful in the design of solar heating systems (*see* SOLAR ENERGY).

Alienation
[14c. *L alienus*, belonging to another person or place]
The inability to relate to yourself, other people, or your environment. Many psychologists and sociologists (following the lead of Karl Marx) see the apparent meaninglessness of alienation as a result of the dehumanisation of human beings in an artificial industrial and technological environment. 'Alienation' also implies being an outsider in society, being ignored and devalued, to the extent that you yourself feel powerless and worthless. Too many psychologists and social workers see their task as the reintegration of such people into an essentially inhuman world, then wonder why their 'failure' rate is so high. *See also* REALITY.

Allergy
[1911. *Gk allos*, other, different + *ergon*, effect]
A sensitivity of the human body to small amounts of particular foods, chemicals or other substances. Some allergies, like hay fever, have been acknowledged for years, but many people now believe that symptoms from headaches to arthritis could be the result of the increasing POLLUTION of our environment, including our food, the air we breathe, and the water we drink. Background levels of pollution must have some effect on human bodies that have developed over thousands of years in a pollution-free environment, and it would be surprising if we had no reaction to the high levels of lead, sulphur, ozone, nitrates, chemical additives and so on that we take in all the time. CLINICAL ECOLOGY believes that exposure to these substances can easily take us over the tolerance threshold for natural irritants like pollen and dust, and that many allergic reactions may be due to a number of substances (allergens) acting on the body at once. The conventional medical response has been to prescribe drugs, but these too often cause yet further allergic reactions. The most commonly prescribed anti-allergens, the antihistamines, simply shut down all of the body's mucus production, dealing with the problem by pure overkill. What really needs to be done in relation to allergy is to reduce levels of pollutants in the environment. Those with a vested interest in ill health and the status quo, however, especially the pharmaceutical companies and the polluters, not only ignore the problem but deny its very existence. Sufferers are often blamed for being so sensitive; meanwhile people continue to experience pains they can't understand, blinding headaches, eczema and depression, find it hard to sleep and then wake up sweating. 'At the risk of sounding cynical, I would suggest that perhaps the only way the situation of allergic people will gain the widespread publicity it deserves is for people in high places to lose their tolerance for the world in which we live' (Vicky Rippere, 1983).

Alliance
[1977 in this sense. *L alligare*, to bind to]
(*also* 'coalition')
The coming together of groups of people interested in a common cause and with similar ideas, to support and work alongside each other. The first green alliances were the 1970s anti-nuclear groupings in the USA — Clamshell, Shad, Abalone and Catfish — followed by similar alliances in other parts of the world, such as the Torness Alliance in Scotland. More widely-based alliances are now common in the green movement, such as the British Green Alliance, which works to further green ideas within the existing political structure.

Allopathy
[*c*.1840. *Gk allos* + *patheia*, differently-suffering]
The attempt to alleviate DISEASE by the use of a CURE not directly related to that disease (as opposed to HOMEOPATHY — 'same-suffering'). 'Allopathy' is used more generally to describe the currently prevailing system of MEDICINE with its emphasis on drugs, surgery and technological solutions. Allopathic medicine is also sometimes called 'conventional medicine' or 'mainstream medicine' to distinguish it from 'alternative medicine', though it is important to remember how very recently allopathic treatment became the conventional mainstream. 'Holistic healing' or COMPLEMENTARY MEDICINE are the most commonly-used terms to describe a philosophy of healing which embraces both allopathic and alternative approaches.

Ally
[15c. *L alligare*, to bind to]
A person who has a special bond with another, particularly a person who is not a member of an oppressed group who chooses to interrupt the OPPRESSION of that group whenever it arises. This can best be done by examining your own conditioning (*see* CONSCIOUSNESS-RAISING), LISTENING carefully to the EXPERIENCE and wishes of members of the oppressed group, changing your own behaviour to be non-oppressive, and taking action to support members of that group whenever you are aware of them being the object of oppression. In the parlance of international politics, by contrast, it means putting even more people at risk of ANNIHILATION: 'How do you get the war on European soil? By having on European soil sufficiently attractive targets, and how do you get that? By persuading so-called allies to take on the maximum of the nuclear load. The key function of [the US siting of missiles] in Britain is not to be fired. It could be that its major function is to be hit' (Johan Galtung, *Resurgence*, March/April 1981). Some ally.

Alternative

[16c. *L alternativus*, one thing done after another, from *alter*, other]
Choosing to live your life or an aspect of your life in a different way from the majority of contemporary society, because it is more harmonious, fulfilling and ecologically sound to do it in that way. 'Above all else, [these ventures] represent attempts by people to develop patterns of living different from those conventionally considered "normal" by the majority of folk. All of them are, in a very real sense, seeking to create alternatives to the largely unquestioned and taken-for-granted routines that guide and channel the lives of most of us' (Andrew Rigby, 1974). Hence 'alternative community' (*see* COMMUNE, COMMUNITY), 'alternative education' (sometimes called 'education otherwise'; *see also* DESCHOOLING, FREE SCHOOL), 'alternative lifestyle', 'alternative medicine' (*see also* COMPLEMENTARY MEDICINE, HEALING). 'Alternative' can be used indiscriminately as a justification for any sort of individualistic behaviour, and for some people 'being alternative' has become an excuse for excessive selfishness, irresponsibility and introspection. 'The alternative fringe' has frequently been the butt of much REACTIONARY criticism, although 'alternative' has gradually become more accepted among the mainstream as more people try different ways of living some aspect of their life, whether it be changing their diet or taking part in community action. 'Time was when the term "alternative" had a valid connotation, as being indicative of the explosion of new thought on the environment, human relations and other issues. . . But time and perceptions move on. As the "alternative scene" became more familiar in the public consciousness and as elements of it became absorbed into the mainstream, the distinction between what was alternative and what was not became blurred and less relevant. I believe it is now time to move away from this now divisive and alienating perception to an era in which ideas and advances can be considered on their own merits . . . If the future cannot accommodate all of us, it may fail to accommodate any of us' (Michael Barker, 1986).

Amenity

[*c*.1910 in this sense. *L amœnitas*, pleasantness]
Originally meaning 'the quality of being pleasant or agreeable', 'amenity' was institutionalised in the early 1900s to mean whatever was considered by those in power to be pleasant for people. By the time the word was taken into PLANNING jargon in the 1950s it had become a very confusing idea, and is now best avoided. 'Amenity: the quality which makes a desirable residence desirable, a favoured locality favoured, or enchanting views in all directions enchanting' (HMSO, 1951.)

Anarchism

[16c. *Gk anarchia*, without a ruler]

The refusal to accept forced AUTHORITY, especially governmental authority. From its very earliest use, the term was subverted by those in authority to mean a state of disorder and chaos, thought to result from the failure or absence of government. 'Anarchism, if it means anything at all, is trying to remove coercive authority from human relationships' (Alan Albon, *Green Anarchist*, June/July 1986). Like SOCIALISM or MARXISM, 'anarchism' covers a wide range of viewpoints, and can mean anything from visionary communalism to anti-state terrorism: 'Anarchism simply cannot be viewed as a homogeneous or even coherent philosophy. . . At one extreme is the romantic, egotistical and reactionary anarchism of that revolting character, Stirner [Max Stirner, the so-called 'individualistic anarchist' of the early nineteenth century] (who . . . judged "everything ruthlessly from the viewpoint of his own well-being"). At the other end is anarchist-socialism, represented by, for example, anarcho-syndicalism (the "guild socialism" which Bertrand Russell advocated) or by anarcho-communists like Kropotkin [Peter Kropotkin, nineteenth century Russian visionary, author of the influential *Fields, Factories and Workshops* (1899) — a 'small is beautiful' manifesto a hundred years before its time]' (David Pepper, letter to *Green Line*, April 1987). Whether or not it is called anarchism, a belief in individual FREEDOM and RESPONSIBILITY and the right not to be coerced by arbitrary authority is central to green thinking.

Anarcho-Pacifism

[1968]

A philosophy and lifestyle which combines the refusal to accept unwanted external authority with a belief in the importance of peaceful coexistence. 'In a series of editorials that appeared early in 1968 . . . *Peace News* tried to spell out its developing position, one best depicted as anarcho-pacifism: a fusion of the anarchist critique of the state and the pacifist critique of violence as a means of revolutionary transformation' (Gail Chester and Andrew Rigby (ed), 1986).

Androcentrism

[1903. *Gk andro-* + *-centrikos*, man-centred]

A view of the world which believes that male human beings are the most important things that exist. 'The androcentric theory is the view that the male sex is primary and the female secondary in the organic scheme, that all things center, as it were, about the male' (Lester Brown, 1903). The inevitable result of the coming together of ANTHROPOCENTRISM and PATRIARCHY. *See also* MAN, MASCULINE.

Androgyny
[17c. *Gk andro- + gune*, man-woman]
Incorporating and integrating the strengths and virtues traditionally associated with both women and men. Androgyny has been the subject of much questionable debate about male and female essences, energy balancing and sexual chemistry, but it is clear to most green-thinkers that women and men must learn strengths and awarenesses from each other, and that as a result the false distinctions between male and female will tend to disappear. At the same time, we live in a patriarchal world in which traditionally female strengths and wisdoms are demeaned, a bias which needs to be acknowledged. The usefulness of the idea has been questioned by several feminist writers, who point out that it can easily be used to support an inflexible and limiting position, which argues either that women should be more like men, or that women alone understand the mysteries of the universe. 'There is a paradox inherent in the ideal of androgyny, namely that, while it calls for the elimination of the sexual stereotyping of human virtues, it is itself formulated in terms of the discredited concepts of masculinity and femininity which it ultimately rejects' (Mary Anne Warren, 1980, quoted in John Rowan, 1987). *See also* FEMININE, MASCULINE, WOMEN'S SPIRITUALITY, YIN/YANG.

Anger
[13c. *Old Norse angr*, trouble, affliction]
Justifiable and passionate rage resulting from the recognition that something is wrong in the world. 'And so her anger grew. It swept through her like a fire. She was more than shaken. She thought she was consumed. But she was illuminated with her rage; she was bright with fury. And though she still trembled, one day she saw that she had survived this blaze. And after a time she came to see this anger-that-was-so-long-denied as a blessing' (Susan Griffin, 1984). 'Anger' is often used synonymously with AGGRESSION or VIOLENCE, but this is a confusing misunderstanding. 'Anger is an *emotion* and violence is a *behavior*. Anger is a healthy emotion. It is normal and natural that throughout life there will be times when you feel irritated, annoyed, angry or even enraged. Violence, on the other hand, is just one expression of anger. In addition, it has a long list of negative consequences. It may mean losing a relationship or being arrested, and it definitely means not liking yourself very much' (Daniel Sonkin and Michael Durphy, 1982). Some green-thinkers reject the link between anger and violence, seeing anger as powerful but not in itself destructive; they see violence as the result of FEAR, the expression of which, being thought cowardly (particularly in men), is suppressed and instead becomes channelled into defensive and destructive behaviour (*see* DEFENCE, THREAT).

Animal
[14c. *L animal*, living creature]
Any living creature, with a common right to be respected, a capacity for contentment and for pain, and an important place in the WEB OF LIFE. An essential part of green philosophy is that life — in its widest sense — should never be thoughtlessly destroyed or damaged, yet we live in a society which in general rates animals so low on the scale of importance that we are wiping out whole species in the quest for human expansion and growth. To justify our actions, we conveniently categorise animals into pets (which we sometimes treat better than we do other people, yet can also abandon them when they have served their usefulness), farm animals (which are 'only bred for eating anyway'), wildlife (which can be romanticised but ignored when it gets in the way of progress), and humans (which are usually thought to be much more special within the biosphere than they obviously are). 'We suppose the term "animal-lover" has gathered to itself more than a little opprobrium, but it need not imply the sentimental drooling one sees over dogs and cats, while the owner, blissfully unconscious of the fact that a cow is also an animal, gnaws part of a Friesian's rib. In its best application it might mean one who appreciates and cherishes life in all its forms' (Geoffrey Rudd, 1966, quoted in Jon Wynne-Tyson (ed), 1985). 'That we have a duty to animals is as hard for governments to understand as it was hard for slave traders to realise that their commodity had rights' (Robert Waller, 1982).

Animal Rights
[*c*.1960]
The rights of animals to be protected from exploitation and abuse by human beings. 'The animal liberation movement . . . is not saying that all lives are of equal worth or that all interests of humans and other animals are to be given equal weight, no matter what those interests may be. It *is* saying that where animals and humans have similar interests — we might take the interest in avoiding physical pain as an example, for it is an interest that humans clearly share with other animals — those interests are to be counted equally, with no automatic discounts just because one of the beings is not human. A simple point, no doubt, but nevertheless part of a far-reaching ethical revolution' (Peter Singer, 1985). Hence also 'animal liberation' [1977], 'animal rights group', 'animal rights lobby', 'animalist' (in the sense of someone concerned with animal rights).

Annihilation
[*c*.1965 in this sense. *L annihilare*, to reduce to nothing]
Complete destruction, the blotting out of existence; widely used follow-

ing the recognition that the use of nuclear weapons would annihilate, not merely destroy, LIFE as we know it on the PLANET. 'The annihilation of the belligerent nations would be a catastrophe beyond anything in history, but it would not be the end of the world. The destruction of human civilization, even without the biological destruction of the human species, may perhaps rightly be called the end of the world, since it would be the end of that sum of cultural achievements and human relationships which constitutes what many people mean when they speak of "the world." The biological destruction of [hu]mankind would, of course, be the end of the world in a stricter sense. As for the destruction of all life on the planet, it would not be merely a human but a planetary end — the end of the earth. And although the annihilation of other forms of life could hardly be of concern to human beings once they themselves had been annihilated, this more comprehensive, planetary termination is nevertheless full of sorrowful meaning for us as we reflect on the possibility now, while we still exist. We not only live on the earth but also are of the earth, and the thought of its death, or even of its mutilation, touches a deep chord in our nature' (Jonathan Schell, 1982).

Anorexia
[1873. *Gk anorexis*, without appetite]
(also 'anorexia nervosa')
A social disease, experienced mostly by young women, characterised by an obsession with FOOD. Long periods of starvation (which can result in death) are typically interspersed with eating binges. Some people recognise different 'sorts' of anorexia, such as bulimia, compulsive eating and compulsive dieting, but all are agreed that they are variations on an overall theme, which is women's relationship with food. Many 'theories' of anorexia have been put forward; what is clear is that it has a great deal to do with patriarchal expectations of a woman's physical appearance, with the DOUBLE STANDARD in our society which puts women in the very physical role of food-provider while stressing wraith-like slimness and ethereal BEAUTY; with suppressed ANGER; and with the guilt which often accompanies an awareness of the destructiveness of over-consumption (*see* AFFLUENCE, OBESITY). 'One reason men do not develop eating disorders and open themselves to that oral helplessness and vulnerability and rage is quite simply that they have available to them a far more reassuring form of obsessive attack upon the female body in their actual and imagined sexual relationship to women' (Kim Chernin, 1985).

Another Development
[1975]
An alternative approach to world economic DEVELOPMENT, based on work done by the Dag Hammarskjöld Foundation in Sweden. Unlike the conventional economic foundations (greed and profit first) of mainstream 'development', 'another development' looks at the real needs of local communities. Its main features are:
— it is based on what communities really need.
— it stems from the cultural and social values of the community.
— it is self-reliant, depending upon locally-available skills and resources as far as possible.
— it is ecologically sound.
— it is related closely to changes in society.
'Another Development means liberation' (Paul Ekins, 1986).

Antarctica
[14c]
The continent which surrounds the South Pole, consisting largely of a vast icesheet with mountain ranges pushing through it; the exception in this dictionary to the principle of not including particular places, and for a very good reason. So far, Antarctica has been the one large area of the world where human beings have restrained themselves from rushing in to take all the realisable wealth they can lay their hands on. 'The vast ice continent of Antarctica, the last great wilderness on Earth, is a unique wildlife habitat, the feeding ground for millions of whales, seals, penguins and birds, and plays a key role in regulating our climate and the ocean ecosystem' (Lee Durrell, 1986). Since 1959, the Antarctic Treaty, signed by the seven nations who claim sovereign rights over the continent and twelve others, has recognised 'that it is in the interest of all [hu]mankind that Antarctica shall continue forever to be used exclusively for peaceful purposes and shall not become the scene or object of international discord'. The same signatories have negotiated, but not ratified, agreements about Antarctic wildlife. Many conservationists are concerned that in the absence of any agreement about mineral exploitation, demands for minerals could threaten the unique status of the continent. The Antarctic and Southern Ocean Coalition, an alliance of environmental organisations set up in 1978, wants to see Antarctica designated a 'World Park'.

Anthropocentrism
[1863. *Gk anthropos + kentron*, human-centred]
A world view which sees human beings as being at the centre of all creation. Anthropocentrism is taken for granted by most Westerners, but is a recent invention, and one we need to dismantle as quickly as

possible. 'Our deepest folly is the notion that we are in charge of the place, that we own it and can somehow run it. We are a living part of Earth's life, owned and operated by the Earth, probably specialized for functions on its behalf that we have not yet glimpsed' (Lewis Thomas, 1986). 'It is *hubris* to declare that humans are the central figures of life on Earth and that we are in control. In the long run, *Nature* is in control' (Charlene Spretnak, 1986).

Antic
[16c. *L antiquus*, age-old, used to describe fantastic or grotesque sculptures in ancient ruins]
A practical joke used to point out the apparent absurdity of someone's behaviour. 'For a man's antics are ego-protecting and dull the mind and body whereas a woman's antics are hilarious and resound with intelligent laughter' (Jenny James, 1986). *See also* INTERRUPTION.

Anti-Nuclear
[1958]
Opposing the use of NUCLEAR ENERGY and NUCLEAR WEAPONS.

Anti-Party
[*c*.1980]
An acknowledgement of the paradox of working within a party political system and having to organise activities as a PARTY, while at the same time believing that such an organisation is largely antithetical to green thinking. Hence green parties (following the lead of the West German Greens, die Grünen) sometimes call themselves the 'anti-party party'. *See also* POLITICS.

Anti-Racist
[*c*.1960]
Behaviour which interrupts RACISM, either by an individual (*see also* ALLY), or by a group of people following a collectively-agreed policy. 'Anti-racist' is a humbler and more realistic idea than 'non-racist', acknowledging the deep roots of racism within our society.

Anti-Sexist
[*c*.1971]
Behaviour which interrupts SEXISM, either by an individual (*see also* ALLY), or by a group of people following a collectively-agreed policy. Many feminists claim that men often fail to see sexist oppression in action, and since it is mostly men who give themselves the label 'anti-sexist', the epithet is frequently suspect. *See also* NON-SEXIST, POST-PATRIARCHAL.

Apartheid
[1930. *Afrikaans apartheid*, separateness]
The official South African policy of enforcing racial segregation in order to maintain white supremacy, now the most important feature of South African society. It is as well to remember that the present system dates only from the 1948 Group Areas Act and subsequent legislation. Although 'reform' has been promised by some South African politicians and there are now many white as well as black South Africans risking their lives and freedom for the abolition of apartheid, racial hatred of blacks by whites is rampant. After a long period of indifference fuelled by economic interests in South Africa's mineral wealth, other countries are now listening to popular concern and applying pressure on the South African government. Change will have to come; it remains to be seen whether white South Africans value their lives above their principles. 'None of us was prepared for the full reality of apartheid. As a contrivance of social engineering, it is awesome in its cruelty. It is achieved and sustained only through force, creating human misery and deprivation and blighting the lives of millions . . . The living standards of South Africa's white cities and towns must rank with the highest anywhere; those of the black townships which surround them defy description in terms of "living standards". Apartheid creates and separates them; black and white live as strangers in the same land' (*Mission to South Africa*, 1986). 'There is no way we can avoid violence. The police and the army who are in the townships are violent. You can get arrested for just walking in the street. . . There will be no end to violence in the townships until the army is removed. Only when this violent government is removed will violence end' (Lehlohonolo Mokoena, *New Internationalist*, May 1986). 'I find it ironic . . . that South African black men express so much agony and distress about the oppression they suffer at the hands of the apartheid régime without realising that, to a limited extent, they cause similar anguish and suffering to their womenfolk without flinching at all. For it is urgent that this community taps the potential of women, men and youth able to contribute to the advancement of black people. The foremost need at this point is to close ranks — to start to know and understand one another and thus reduce suspicion and fear. This is a precondition if black people are to move forward as a united front, liberating themselves from the discrimination they have suffered for more than 300 years in this, the land of their birth' (Ellen Kuzwayo, *New Internationalist*, May 1986). 'Apartheid' has also been used to describe similar segregationist policies elsewhere, particularly between rich suburbs and poor welfare-dependent urban neighbourhoods, creating 'a new form of publicly sanctioned, publicly subsidised apartheid' (Peter Hall, 1973).

Apathy
[*c*.1600 *Gk apatheia*, without feeling]
Being numbed to the point of not seeming to care what happens. 'Apathy is the inability or refusal to experience pain . . . The pain of awareness in this planet-time . . . pertains not just to loss of wealth, health, reputation or loved ones, but to the extinction of life itself. It is hardly surprising that we often prefer not to feel or even acknowledge it' (Joanna Macy, 1983). Yet go through the feeling we must, empowering ourselves to act against the structures and machinery that threaten all life. *See also* EMPOWERMENT.

Appreciation
[*L appretiare*, to evaluate]
(1) [*c*.1600] Consciously enjoying your surroundings and circumstances.
(2) [1963] The clear and unequivocal validation of a person's strengths and virtues, either by that person (SELF-APPRECIATION) or by someone else.

Appropriate
[15c. *L appropriare*, to make one's own]
(1) Something which is entirely fitting, such as an action which takes the circumstances into account and achieves the desired goal, or a building or TOOL which exactly achieves what is intended of it without causing unnecessary human hurt or environmental damage. *See also* ELEGANT.
(2) To take something away from somebody else, or from nature, usually with implications of violence and domination.

Appropriate Technology
[*c*.1970]
Technological concepts and innovations which work efficiently and produce the desired results without exploiting people or resources. Such technologies:
'1 are low in capital cost;
2 use local materials wherever possible;
3 create jobs, employing local skills and labour;
4 are small enough in scale to be affordable by a small group of farmers [or other people];
5 can be understood, controlled and maintained by villagers wherever possible, without a high level of Western-style education;
6 can be produced out of a small metal-working shop, if not in a village itself;
7 suppose that people can and will work together to collectively bring improvements to their communities . . .;

8 involve decentralized renewable energy sources . . .;
9 make technology understandable to the people who are using it and thus suggest ideas that could be used in further innovations;
10 are flexible so that they can continue to be used or adapted to fit changing circumstances;
11 do not involve patents, royalties, consultant fees, import duties, shipping charges, or financial wizards' (Ken Darrow and Rick Pam, 1978).

Approval
[*L approbare*, to approve]
(1) [*c*.1700] A favourable opinion of yourself ('self-approval') or somebody else. A two-edged idea: in green thinking, complete approval (APPRECIATION) of yourself is necessary for self-empowerment; at the same time, many people (especially members of oppressed groups) are taught that they should modify their behaviour in order to gain the approval of others at the expense of their own integrity. 'Depending less and less upon male approval, recognizing that such approval is more often than not a reward for weakness, we approve of our Selves' (Mary Daly, 1978).
(2) [1948] The agreement by local or central goverment to a building project or change of land use (also called 'planning approval').

Aquaculture
[1929. *L aqua + cultura*, water cultivation]
The cultivation of freshwater and marine resources to provide food and other materials beneficial to human beings. Fish have been reared in ponds and plant crops in flooded fields for centuries, especially in southern and eastern Asia; in the last couple of decades many projects have been developed to improve the efficiency of aquaculture harvests, such as trout hatcheries using artificial fertilisation techniques, the breeding of shrimps in controlled conditions, and producing and harvesting algae for food, fertilisers and drugs. As with agriculture there is the ever-present danger of a TECHNOFIX mentality and of the squandering of sustainability to maximise short-term gain; wisely conserved, however, aquatic resources can provide a substantial and sustainable yield. 'Aquaculture' is sometimes also used as an alternative name for HYDROPONICS.

Aquarian Conspiracy
[*c*.1977]
A brave attempt to name the growing awareness of the need for a new direction in human affairs, and the people involved in this movement. 'While outlining a not-yet-titled book about the emerging social alter-

natives, I thought again about the peculiar form of this movement: its atypical leadership, the patient intensity of its adherents, their unlikely successes. It suddenly struck me that in their sharing of strategies, their linkage, and their recognition of each other by subtle signals, the participants were not merely cooperating with each other. They were in collusion. "It" — this movement — was a conspiracy! . . . Conspire, in its literal sense, means "to breathe together". It is an intimate joining. To make clear the benevolent nature of this joining, I chose the word *Aquarian*. Although I am unaquainted with astrological lore, I was drawn to the symbolic power of the pervasive dream in our popular culture: that after a dark, violent age, the Piscean, we are entering a millennium of love and light — in the words of the popular song, "The Age of Aquarius," the time of "the mind's true liberation." Whether or not it was written in the stars, a different age seems to be upon us; and Aquarius, the waterbearer in the ancient zodiac, symbolizing flow and the quenching of an ancient thirst, is an appropriate symbol' (Marilyn Ferguson, 1981).

Archetype
[1919. *Gk arkhetypon*, a first stamp or impression]
A pervasive idea, image or symbol which forms part of our collective UNCONSCIOUS. An idea popularised by the psychologist Carl Jung, though he drew heavily on mythology and ancient imagery, both Western and Eastern.

Architecture
[16c. *Gk arkhitekton*, master builder]
The design and building of appropriate structures for human occupation. 'Architecture established itself independently of building when the ancient world began to produce grandiose public buildings that demanded forethought and measurement, [but] there was always a tendency to invest the lesser project with something of the glory of the greater. . . Even when Victorian villadom achieved an advance into individuality, it was still often invested with significance in the form of details drawn from the cathedrals or fortresses of the past' (Alice Coleman, 1985). Appropriateness and participation are the keys to a green architecture, and some architects (often architect/builders) are exploring and building structures which are ecologically-sound, beautiful and inspiring, and do what their inhabitants want of them (*see* ADVOCACY, ARCOLOGY, AUTONOMY, BIOECOLOGICAL BUILDING, BIOSHELTER, GEODESIC, INSULATION, PASSIVE COOLING, PASSIVE SOLAR, SELF-BUILD, SOLAR ENERGY, UNDERGROUND BUILDING). Yet inappropriate, energy intensive, standardised and overly professionalised architecture (*see* EXPERT) continues to have a stranglehold on Western building, and is rapidly

doing its best to stifle individuality and appropriate traditional building techniques the world over. Even lower-class housing has been taken completely out of the hands of its 'clients': 'By making the visual environment of the poor and lower middle class a phenomenon for stylish aesthetic titillation, isolated from the social values that produced this environment, it is easier for an intellectual elite to tolerate both the causes and the effects. What is normally considered "ugly" has been analyzed and explained as a "good" method for producing architecture. It becomes a cultural phenomenon that can be seen in architectural books and art museums. You can study it in art-appreciation courses and you can talk about it at cocktail parties. . . Along . . . has come a new battery of social science experts to help the architects. Complaining of the traditional architect's intuitive approach untested by the experimental method, these experts have called for more "scientific" information about the way people use space. For some architects, teaming up with social scientists . . . is seen as a way to resolve the contradiction of dealing with the building's financial developer, instead of the people who actually use the buildings. But the use of "data" is at best a way of ameliorating the contradiction rather than resolving it. At worst it can lead to some dangerous conclusions about how places should be designed' (Robert Goodman, 1972). And we are living with these conclusions. There have been some brave attempts at 'advocacy architecture', 'community architecture', 'ecotecture', 'integral architecture' (Keith Critchlow, *East/West* magazine, February 1987), 'organic architecture', 'sacred architecture', and even 'guerrilla architecture', but as with PLANNING, only the active participation of the people who actually inhabit the structures being designed will put power back into the hands of the people. With a very few exceptions, alternative structures are actively discouraged in Western countries: 'Jeff Gale, an architect living in Exeter [England], submitted plans for a self-built ecological community to be built on a two-acre orchard. The scheme included vegetable gardens, fruit trees, methane digestors, solar panels, windmills, etc. It was turned down in favour of 23 Georgian-style terrace houses with integral garages — sold at £19,000 each. All the fruit trees were bulldozed' (Herbert Girardet (ed), 1976). *See also* HOUSING.

Arcology

[*c*.1968. Abbreviation of 'arc[hitectural ec]ology]

ARCHITECTURE which is in line with ecological principles. A useful idea, it has unfortunately been narrowly appropriated by the philosopher-guru who coined it, Paolo Soleri, to mean structures designed and explained by himself. This is a pity, because his prototype 'city', Arcosanti in Arizona, incorporates many exciting features and ideas, and would benefit further if its founder could add humility to his many talents. 'If we could settle on the name arcology, relax about the fact that Soleri originated it and that we can't all agree with all that Soleri says and believes, then we could have a quickly clarifying tool of enormous and very human power in our hands. We could use it to focus and articulate notions about a meaningful and healthy future — and to build it too' (Richard Faust Register, 1978).

Ark

[*c*.1970 in this sense. *L arca*, chest or coffer]

By analogy with Noah's ark (*The Bible*, Genesis 5-9), a useful image for the earth in danger from the 'deluge' of pollution and exploitation. Used by John and Nancy Todd of the New Alchemy Institute in Massachusetts, who under the title of 'ocean arks' have planned and built small prototypes of craft which will transport samples of flora and fauna to endangered habitats; by Dennis Pirages and Paul Ehrlich in *Ark II: Response to Environmental Imperatives* (1974); by Norman Myers in *The Sinking Ark* (1979); and by Lee Durrell in *The State of the Ark* (1986).

Arms

[13c. *L arma*, weapons, tools]

Equipment made especially to hurt and kill people, and to put money in the pockets of arms dealers. The international arms trade, worth in the order of $30,000,000,000 every year and rising, keeps the world at WAR at the same time as blinkered politicians explain how the nuclear 'deterrent' has 'kept the peace'. The green line is unequivocally that nobody should be able to profit from death and destruction, yet arms sales continue to add to the gross (and how gross can you be?) national product of Western nations — our 'wealth'. 'Armaments, primarily from the United States and the Soviet Union, have been unloaded in such quantity onto the world market that there is hardly a self-respecting guerilla army let alone sovereign state which does not have its arsenal of M-16s, Armalites, Kalatchnikov assault rifles or Katyusha rockets, to say nothing of more "serious" hardware' (Mark Levene, in Joe Weston (ed), 1986). While the nuclear threat is all too real and demands our attention, it is the manufacture, sale and use of 'conventional' weapons that is currently killing and maiming people — this is an important understanding which peace campaigners (who often have not experienced the horrors of war at first hand) need to remember. Green-minded women have made a useful play on the two meanings of the word 'arms' with anti-militarist slogans like 'Arms are for Hugging' and 'Arms are for Linking', while 'Arms Round the Base' and 'Arms Across Scotland [or wherever]' campaigns have drawn attention to the widespread distribution of the arms trade. *See also* DISARMAMENT, MILITARISM, NUCLEAR WEAPONS.

Arms Race
[1936]
The potentially disastrous result of seeing the buildup of ARMS, particularly NUCLEAR WEAPONS, as a competition which has to be won at any cost. 'World expenditure on the arms race is over $1,000 million per day. Countless children are condemned to illiteracy, disease, starvation and death by the massive diversion of resources (natural and human) to the arms race. The cost of one tank would supply equipment for 520 classrooms and the cost of one destroyer could provide electrification for three cities and nineteen rural zones. . . We must realize that it is only *we* who can stop the arms race, for the multinational companies in the nuclear plant and arms business will not, the politicians will not and the negotiators of INF and START will not' (Petra Kelly, 1984).

Artificial
[*c*.1930 in this sense. *L artificium*, something which is made or manufactured]
Something which does not occur naturally (*see* NATURAL), and is often made in imitation of a natural product, as in 'artificial colourings and flavourings'. Many green-minded people try to use as few artificial products as possible, though some are obviously useful, efficient and affordable, where the equivalent natural product may be in short supply, endangered (as with certain timbers, for example), or too expensive. 'Artificial' is a more accurate and non-sexist alternative to 'man-made'.

Artificial Insemination
(*see* AID)

Asbestosis
[1927]
A disease of the lungs, caused by the inhalation of asbestos particles. An example of an environmental hazard which can easily be avoided by the adoption of safe working practices and the use of alternative materials, but which continues to kill people in their thousands because governments refuse to heed the evidence and resist the pressures of an industry that profits from death and disease. 'Official estimates in the USA put the potential death toll from asbestos exposure amongst workers alone at two million. In Britain it is possible that some 500,000 workers will die from asbestos-related diseases over the next 30 years. If that proves the case then, as Alan Dalton of the British Society for Social Responsibility in Science remarks: "Asbestos exposure will kill

more people in Britain than were killed in the armed forces during the Second World War" ' (Angela Singer, in Edward Goldsmith and Nicholas Hildyard (ed), 1986). Though there are some controls on the use of asbestos in Western countries, mining companies in Africa and India continue to make profits and endanger their workers.

As If . . . Mattered
[1974]
Another by-product of Fritz Schumacher's influential book *Small is Beautiful: A Study of Economics as if People Mattered*. Since then there has been a rash of politics/housing/technology/design/growth/you name it as-if-people-mattered. Most green-minded people now have the message that people do matter, and the phrase is in danger of being overworked. My favourites to date are a book called *Behaving As If The God In All Life Mattered: A New Age Ecology* (Machaelle Small Wright, 1983), and the 1987 Ananda Mela Festival of Bliss in Australia, entitled 'Spirituality As If The Planet Matters'.

Assertiveness
[1949 in this sense. *L asserere*, to join to yourself, claim]
The art of clear, honest and direct COMMUNICATION from a basis of complete self-respect. 'Assertiveness is defined as a strong appropriate response to another human being that is neither submissive nor aggressive' (Sue Walrond-Skinner, 1986). 'Being assertive to me means taking myself and my needs seriously, taking risks in my personal relationships in order to be more honest, feeling the insecurity about changing, and discovering that I can be powerful without aggression or violence' (Fiona, quoted in Anne Dickson, 1982).

Assumption
[17c in this sense. *L assumere*, to take up]
Something you believe to be true though you have not made any special effort to check it. We make an assumption each time we fail — because of fear or embarrassment — to QUESTION something that needs questioning, and every time we make an assumption we LIMIT what is POSSIBLE. 'It is an unproved assumption that the domination of the planet by our own species is a desirable thing, which must give satisfaction to its creator' (W.R. [Dean] Inge, quoted in J.M. and M.J. Cohen, 1980). 'We have come to see that part of what allows the forces causing needless suffering to continue is a web of assumptions so banal that most of us aren't even aware of them, much less challenging them. Built up over generations, these assumptions make the most outrageous injustices appear "normal" and, therefore, acceptable. . . We must examine the assumptions and habits woven into our day-to-day lives that, all added together, accept that normality. And then, we must ask

how we can, piece by piece, target those assumptions' (Frances Moore Lappé, Joseph Collins and David Kinley, 1980). '[The] passionate debate about the politics of heterosexuality and lesbianism . . . has made me think again about how many sexual assumptions the [women's] movement still takes for granted . . . 1 That relationships with men means sexual relationships; 2 That the only feminists who have relationships with men are "heterosexuals" . . . 4 That all heterosexuals fuck . . . 15 That radical feminists don't have relationships (*cf* Assumption No. 1) with men; 16 That each radical feminist in a "relationship" with a man is Doing It Her Way . . . and last — 23 That all our sex lives were much easier before we joined the women's movement!!! It probably goes without saying that all these assumptions are highly conservative and have no place in a movement that's aiming to transform human relationships' (Amanda Sebestyen, in Scarlet Friedman and Elizabeth Sarah (ed), 1982). 'Let us assume/that the basic assumptions/are wrong/ . . . let us/turn those assumptions/on their heads/ till they rattle and groan/and beg for mercy/and for our/forgiveness' (Viv Wynant, in Alice Cook and Gwyn Kirk, 1983).

Atmosphere

[17c. *Gk atmos* + *sphaira*, vapour sphere]

The gaseous mantle surrounding the EARTH, providing the balance of gases necessary for LIFE, and now thought by many people to be sustained as part of the living system of the planet (*see* GAIA). 'Our results convinced us that the only feasible explanation of the Earth's highly improbable atmosphere was that it was being manipulated on a day-to-day basis from the surface, and that the manipulator was life itself' (James Lovelock, 1979). 'Like the feathers of a bird, the 9 or 10 layers of the atmosphere provide equable surface temperatures, shield life from the "rain" of cosmic particles, and block lethal ultraviolet radiation' (Norman Myers, 1985). One of the planet's COMMONS, the atmosphere is too often treated as a dump for the gaseous wastes of our inefficient technologies (*see* ATMOSPHERIC POLLUTION).

Atmospheric Pollution

[1934]

(*also* 'air pollution')

The contamination of the ATMOSPHERE with substances which, because of their nature or quantity, cannot be absorbed by the natural flows and cycles within the global atmospheric circulation. Smoke pollution, being the most obvious form of air pollution both in its appearance and effects, has been reduced enormously in the last three decades in most parts of the world, although in some Third World urban areas the problem is increasing. Three other major pollutants — sulphur, nitrates and carbon dioxide — are also causing a great deal of concern to environmentalists. Sulphur and nitrogen oxides produced mostly from power stations are carried hundreds of miles from the tall chimneys such stations are now required to have, falling as ACID RAIN and killing trees and wildlife. The nitrogen oxides from vehicle exhausts react with sunlight to create ozone-laden PHOTOCHEMICAL SMOG, dangerous to all life. Carbon dioxide concentration in the atmosphere is increasing quite markedly as we continue to burn fossil fuels, and although it may be too small a change to affect life directly, some people have expressed their concern about the possibility of major climatic change if carbon dioxide levels continue to rise: 'Given the timescale for making decisions and the lifetime of power stations once constructed, there seems very little prospect of avoiding a build up of carbon dioxide in the atmosphere sufficient to produce noticeable changes in climate and agriculture' (John Gribbin (ed), 1986). *See also* GREENHOUSE EFFECT, OZONE, POLLUTION.

Atomism
[17c. *Gk atomos*, indivisible]
The belief that the universe consists ultimately of minute and indivisible particles. A commonly-held belief until the atom was first 'split', and still held by many people — especially scientists — in the (sometimes subconscious) belief that small parts of any system can be treated as though they were separate and different from all the other parts. *See also* REDUCTIONISM.

Attention
[*L attendere*, to apply the mind to]
(1) [14c] Total concentration on the task in hand.
(2) [1970] The process by which a person taking on the role of therapist or counsellor listens to, takes account of, and is completely present for their client; this is sometimes called 'free attention'. 'The counsellor is strictly discouraged from identifying or reacting emotionally. She is advised to offer clear loving attention, a powerful and validating form of support for the client. She will make as few interventions as possible, unless the client asks her to play a more active role and this is clearly agreed at the start of the session. Her interventions will be geared simply to keeping the client in touch with her feelings ("Can you repeat that?", "Louder!", "Who would you like to say that to?"). She offers feedback but not interpretation. Her clear attention and sensitive interventions create the space for the client to re-experience past hurts and to allow the discharge of feeling which is central to the co-counselling therapy process' (Sheila Ernst and Lucy Goodison, 1981). The giving of this kind of attention is valued in many areas of inter-personal relationship, including negotiation, MEDIATION, the sharing of experiences, and helping people in CRISIS situations.

Attunement
[*c*.1965 in this sense. *L ad-* + *tonus*, to tune to]
Listening and reacting appropriately to the needs of yourself, other people, and your surroundings, thus ensuring that everyone has their needs and skills fully taken into account. 'Attunement' sometimes has transcendental connotations as in 'spiritual attunement'; some communal and alternative groups use the word 'attunement' instead of 'meeting' to stress the mutuality of the process. 'Attunement is like "tuning up" an orchestra, so that each individual's sound will complement and harmonize with the others. Here, balance is sought between the interests, needs and talents of all members of the group. Most attunement processes engage all workers in the opportunity either verbally (through various consensus methods) or intuitively (through visualization or meditation) to express their unique viewpoints about how the group should achieve its goals and about their desired role in the group' (Susan Campbell, 1983).

Authority
[13c. *L auctoritas*, from *auctor*, author]
The POWER given to or taken by a person to judge and control the actions of others, with or without their consent. 'Authority has always reigned through ignorance and deceit. . . Authority is never justified — it's only rationalized. It must avoid *reality* at all costs, because the fact of its true uselessness and tyranny would be exposed. When authority tampers with reality, it creates dislocations in individual and social harmony. It then proclaims as its purpose the correcting or stabilizing of these dislocations. Authority projects onto "human nature" the power, greed, violence and impulsiveness of its *own* nature. It then proclaims as its purpose the necessity of protecting people from the evils of "human nature"' (Su Negrin, 1972).

Autogenic
[*Gk autos* + *genikos*, self-induced]
(1) [1890] Self-induced HEALING. 'Johannes Schultz, a German neurologist [working in Berlin in the 1930s], had experimented with hypnotism and noted the changed perception of bodily states, feelings of heaviness, warmth and deep relaxation, that could be induced. He wondered to what extent people could be taught to induce these feelings themselves through a process of self-hypnosis, or as Wolfgang Luthe, one of his students, was to call it, autogenic training' (David Harvey, 1986).
(2) [1931] An aspect of a HABITAT created by the indigenous vegetation. 'The accumulation of humus . . . is a direct reaction of the plant community itself upon its habitat (autogenic factor)' (A.G. Tansley, 1946).

Automobile
(*see* CAR)

Autonomy
[mid 17c. *Gk autonomos*, self-ruling]
Another word for SELF-RELIANCE, used both of people, communities and technologies, particularly regarding housing: 'The autonomous house . . . is defined as a house operating independently of any inputs apart from those of its immediate environment. . . The autonomous house uses the life-giving properties of the Earth but in so doing provides an environment for the occupants without interfering with or altering these properties' (Brenda and Robert Vale, 1975). One of the most important aims of PSYCHOTHERAPY is to encourage a person to move from definition by other people to autonomous self-definition.

Awareness
[before 12c. *Old English gewœr*, aware]
The state of being fully conscious of what is going on within yourself ('self-awareness'), in your immediate surroundings, and in the world. Most often used in a religious or spiritual context until recently, when it has been widened to include a knowledge and understanding of political and social issues. Related to 'wary' and 'beware', in the sense of being watchful. Awareness is a key concept in GESTALT therapy, where it is often related to CREATIVITY and spontaneity.

Bb

Backfitting
(*see* RETROFITTING)

Back To The Land
[1894]
(*also* 'new settlers', RURAL RESETTLEMENT)
Originally meaning the exodus of people from crowded urban areas into the country, the back-to-the-land idea now embraces a range of life-styles and practices which have in common a practical and everyday relationship between people and their living environment, whether as rural resettlers, allotment gardeners, or conservation volunteers. 'I believe that the Back to the Land idea is a long-term goal; no-one now living will live to see it fully developed. It will be a long, slow movement . . . not, I hope, toward an Earthly paradise, urban or rural, but toward a new nativity of our people in the real world and in the scheme of things' (Wendell Berry, quoted in Richard Merrill, 1976). *See also* RURAL RESETTLEMENT.

Balance
[13c. *L bilanx*, having two scales]
EQUALITY, EQUILIBRIUM, HARMONY, STABILITY, steadiness. 'What matters most is the aspiration to live in balance with nature, walk lightly on the land, treat earth as mother' (Ernest Callenbach, 1970). An ancient and many-faceted word, originally meaning a pair of scales. 'Balance of nature' is a favourite expression, though it is important to recognise the difference between static balance and dynamic balance (*see* HOMEOSTASIS), the latter being a more realistic and less mechanistic concept. The same dynamism is essential in all attempts to maintain or regain balance; enforced and rigid balance is a contradiction. The concept of balance can also be used to perpetuate more or less extreme 'opposites' — male and female, left and right, industry and nature — where it

would be more accurate and useful to recognise a continuum of interests and possibilities. Beware too of claims of 'balance' from powerful people with vested interests; 'media balance' and 'political balance' are almost certainly suspect: 'And to ensure a balanced and impartial discussion of the latest government measures, I have with me a government spokesman and a wild-eyed Trot from the lunatic fringe' (Glasgow University Media Group, 1982).

Barefoot Doctor
[1970. Literal translation of *Chinese chijiao yisheng*]
Somebody trained to work in rural areas who has basic medical skills, both modern and traditional. Pioneered in China, and popularised in the West by translations of *A Barefoot Doctor's Manual*. 'Barefoot' has recently become a popular epithet, with 'barefoot businessmen', 'barefoot economists', 'barefoot gardeners', 'barefoot geologists', 'barefoot technologists' and 'barefoot vets' blistering their soles on newly-blazed paths; there is now even a 'barefoot microchip' (Marilyn Carr (ed), 1985). Ironically, China has meanwhile moved noticeably towards a more Western model of health care.

Barter Economy
[*c*.1930]
An economy in which many goods and services are exchanged without money changing hands. When more things are available within the local economy, rather than being imported with the attendant transport costs, barter becomes an obvious way of conducting a great deal of everyday business. The present emphasis on money value rather than inherent value (and the apparent value of money itself) may make it hard for some people to accept that transactions in a barter economy are more real than in a money economy, not less.

Basic Income
(*see* SOCIAL WAGE)

Basic Needs
[*c*.1960]
(*also* 'rational needs' [1974])
Things that all human beings need for a happy and healthy life, and which should therefore be their right. Compiling lists of such rights is a difficult but necessary task, since although needs obviously vary from time to time and place to place, basic needs remain basic needs for all people in all cultures. Without such an awareness it is too easy for relatively rich people to disidentify with the poor, claiming that wants which they often take for granted (a television, a washing machine, privacy, financial security) are fundamental needs and demanding

them at the expense of the real basic needs of the world's poor. Many people have attempted to list basic needs, agreeing in general that people have material and non-material needs, and that needs are interconnected, not independent of each other. Most go on to point out that basic needs do not vary: 'First: fundamental human needs are finite, few and classifiable. Second: fundamental human needs are the same in all cultures and all historical periods. What changes, both over time and through cultures, is the form or the means by which these needs are satisfied' (Manfred Max-Neef, in Paul Ekins (ed), 1986). Beyond this, different lists of basic needs usually include some combination of the following:

— breathable air / drinkable water / exercise / movement / rest / sleep / solitude
— subsistence/food/shelter
— protection/physical security
— love/closeness/affection/warmth/touch
— communication/understanding/recognition/participation
— creativity/meaning/purpose/identity
— freedom/self-determination

'Basic needs' are often discussed by people involved in international development, following a 1976 World Employment Conference, in which one of the contributors proposed to achieve 'basic needs satisfaction' by the year 2000. 'By the late 1970s, "basic needs" had become the foremost buzzword in international development circles. . . "Basic needs" strategy for economic development supposedly seeks to make the poor majority the *direct* targets of the development goals. . . Implied in the statements of top policymakers is that "basic needs" can be met, without a fundamental restructuring of control over resources, through a shift in priorities and greater assistance from industrial countries' (Frances Moore Lappé, Joseph Collins and David Kinley, 1980) (*see also* AID, SELF-RELIANCE). 'The most basic human need of all is the need to be human, which, in an age of scarcity, means being in psychological and biological harmony with the rest of creation' (Richard Barnet, 1980).

Baubiologie
(*see* BIOECOLOGICAL BUILDING)

Beanstalk Principle
[1980]
The principle that there is an optimal size for everything, and that it can be dangerous to exceed that size. The name comes from an illustration by Kirkpatrick Sale in his book *Human Scale* (1980) in which he points out that the giant in the story 'Jack and The Beanstalk' would never have been able to support his own weight, since the strength of his legs

increases by the square of his increased height while his weight increases by the cube. 'For every animal, object, institution or system, there is an optimal limit beyond which it ought not to grow. Beyond this optimal size, all other elements of an animal, object, institution or system will be affected adversely' (Kirkpatrick Sale, 1980). *See also* HUMAN SCALE.

Beauty
[14c. *Old French bealté*, beauty]
The combination of all the qualities of a person or thing that delight the senses and please the mind. An important and useful word to describe the wonder of things that reach our deepest feelings of connectedness and joy, but also a frequently debased word used in patronising and oppressive ways, often applied to women (rarely to men) who satisfy currently prevailing fashions in physical appearance. 'The exclusive identification of women with beauty occurred at the same time that men stopped being sex objects [around the end of the 1830s]' (Shirley Morahan, 1981). 'The beauty of strong, creative women is "ugly" by misogynist standards of "beauty" to those who fear us' (Mary Daly, 1978).

Behaviour
[15c. *Middle English behaven*, to hold yourself in a certain way]
(US: 'behavior')
The way in which we conduct ourselves, live our lives, and respond to situations that we experience. Psychologists often distinguish between innate or instinctive behaviour (over which we supposedly have no control), and learned behaviour. Green-thinkers generally believe that far more of our behaviour is learned (and can therefore be unlearned and modified) than is often thought, and that 'I can't help it, it's just the way I am' is too often an unnecessary excuse for refusing to change (*see, for example*, RAPE and VIOLENCE). Because the word 'behaviour' is often used in a mechanistic way by academic psychologists, some green-thinkers prefer to use the words 'action' or 'conduct'.

Behaviourism
[1913]
(US: 'behaviorism')
A school of psychology, initiated by John Broadus Watson in 1913, which proposed that psychology should only be concerned with the observation of behaviour and ways in which it could be modified, and not with attempts to understand why human beings respond in the ways they do. This would have little to do with green thinking if the influential behaviourist psychologist Burrhus Skinner, author of *Science and Human Behavior* (1953), had not also written a book

called *Walden Two* (1948; *Walden* is the famous book by Henry Thoreau) about a hypothetical behaviourist community. *Walden Two* inspired several communal groups in the late 1960s and early 1970s, including Twin Oaks in Virginia, East Wind in Tennessee, and Dandelion in Ontario, which pioneered many practical systems of communal living and appropriate technology. Be careful of the distinction between 'behaviourism' and 'behaviouralism' [1951], the latter being an approach which supposedly takes into account the true complexities of human behaviour.

Being
[*Old English beon*, to come to be]
(1) [*c*.1700] Anything that is living; the word implies a recognition of and respect for both physical form and spirit. Joanna Macy, the founder of the despair and empowerment Interhelp network, has proposed a 'Council of All Beings', in which the voices of all living things might be heard.
(2) [*c*.1970] The antithesis of 'doing'; based in consciousness rather than in action, the present rather than the past or future, 'being here now'. 'It is a kind of deliberate unfocusing, as is well described in the Taoist literature . . . where we enter what Maslow [in *The Farther Reaches of Human Nature*, 1973] calls the 'realm of Being'. Instead of grasping and grabbing the world, we find ourselves allowing the world to come in to us, so that we can then flow out and become that world, losing our usual boundaries' (John Rowan, 1983).
(3) [1976] The antithesis of 'having'. 'To have or to be?' (Erich Fromm, 1976). 'Those who stand for the transition from Having to Being must make it clear that this means a change in values such as can only succeed through what up till now has been described as a religious experience' (Rudolf Bahro, 1986).

Belief
[before 12c. *Old English geleafa*, belief (related to *lief*, love)]
An IDEA or principle accepted as being true, often without the need of proof. Belief is often seen as an absolute: either you do or you don't, and once you have decided it's difficult to change your mind; while greenthinkers do have strong beliefs, rigidity and inflexibility are not compatible with a holistic approach. 'Our fear of the unknown keeps us jammed in the known. The unknown unnerves; ambiguity causes anxiety. So the game of projecting our narrow, well-tried beliefs onto every situation and having them comfortably reconfirmed goes on. We need to recognize how our fear-filled urge to protect our old beliefs may be stopping us from opening up to new visions. We need to be prepared to take the risk of hearing whispers from other camps which may shake our mental

edifices' (Anuradha Vittachi, *New Internationalist*, April 1987). 'Generally the theories we believe we call facts, and the facts we disbelieve we call theories' (Felix Cohen, quoted in Laurence Peter (ed), 1977). Beware the fine distinctions between belief, opinion and ASSUMPTION; and between belief, faith, TRUST and HOPE.

Bender
[*c*.1980 in this sense]
A temporary living structure made of bent branches covered with tarpaulins and other weatherproof materials. 'Out of all canvas and tarp[aulin] structures featured, none are as cheap or as easy to erect as the bender. Benders have been used by travellers for generations and nowadays this semi-permanent structure is commonly seen at peace camps, festival sites, and other gatherings where quick and simple shelter is needed' (*Ideal Home*, 1986).

Benefit
[*L bene facere*, to do well]
(1) [14c] Something which improves a situation for somebody; often set against 'cost' (*see* COST-BENEFIT ANALYSIS, SOCIAL COSTS AND BENEFITS). Though difficult to imagine in our competitive society, many green-thinkers believe that given good communication and the clear statement of needs, a solution can always be found which benefits all parties to an apparent conflict (*see* MEDIATION).
(2) [1802] A performance (of music, drama, etc.) held to raise money for a cause.
(3) [1875] A WELFARE payment or other financial assistance from the STATE.

Benign
[14c. *L benignus*, well-born]
Not wishing any harm. The patriarchal view of NATURE as a potentially terrifying force to be overcome has no place in green thinking. While nature does not go out of its way to benefit one individual or species at the expense of others, the natural flows and balances within a healthy ecosystem ensure the overall wellbeing of every part of that system. *See also* REALITY.

Benthamite Calculus
[1977. After Jeremy Bentham, 1748-1832]
A pseudo-mathematical method of supposedly maximising human happiness. Jeremy Bentham was the founder of the philosophical school of UTILITARIANISM, in which self-interest is considered to be the driving force of society, and in which the role of social policy is to provide the greatest good (measured as the amount of happiness) for

the greatest number of people. Seen by many environmentalists as the mistaken foundation for our materialist society, and a method of calculation which can only lead to disaster. 'Can Bentham's goal of "the greatest good for the greatest number" be realised? No — for two reasons, each sufficient by itself. The first is a theoretical one. It is not mathematically possible to maximize for two (or more) variables at the same time... The second reason springs directly from biological facts... If our goal is to maximize population it is obvious what we must do: we must make the work calories per person approach as close to zero as possible... I think everyone will grant that, without argument or proof, maximizing population does not maximize goods. Bentham's goal is impossible' (Garrett Hardin, 1964). 'With no intrinsic values other than human happiness, conceived indiscriminately as the wholesale satisfaction of perceived individualistic human wants and desires, ... warnings of ecologists on the necessity of maintaining the integrity of the biosphere, of protecting the species of the planet, and of applying basic ecological principles such as "carrying capacity" to human populations usually fall on deaf ears. Ecological integrity is subjectively traded away' (George Sessions, *Journal of Environmental Education*, 1983). Greens see 'the greatest good' in a much wider context.

Bias
[17c in this sense. *Old French biais*, oblique]
A tendency or deliberate decision to display personal preferences or prejudices when making public or private pronouncements, usually about political or economic issues. Bias often extends to misrepresentation, DISCRIMINATION and OPPRESSION. 'On 2 April 1981 the Glasgow [University Media] Group wrote to the BBC and the IBA pointing formally to the existence of bias in television. The letter cited the recently published 'More Bad News' as evidence of the serious imbalance in the coverage of industrial and economic affairs. It was also signed by over 100 university professors, trade union leaders and MPs' (Glasgow University Media Group, 1982).

Bicycle
[1868. *L bi-* + *Gk kuklos*, two wheels]
(*also* 'bike' [1882] and 'cycle' [1870])
A vehicle, usually designed for one person, with a tubular metal frame mounted on two wheels, driven by foot pedals and steered by handles attached above the front wheel. After a post-war slump, the sale of bicycles rose enormously during the 1970s in response to an increasing interest in healthy exercise and environmental issues. In some places, notably Holland and Denmark, the rate of bicycle use is very high, especially in urban areas — pollution has thus been reduced and special cycle tracks built to segregate bicycle traffic from motor

vehicles. 'The world will pedal into the twenty-first century on billions of bicycles. From remote semi-arid high plains to teeming cities the bicycle has emerged as the most efficient, convenient and pleasant form of personal transport' (Richard Ballantine, 1975).

Biocentric Equality
[1971. *Gk bios + kentron*, life-centred]
(*also* 'ecocentrism')
Regarding LIFE in general (rather than human life alone) as centrally important to existence; believing that all life-forms, including the PLANET itself, have a continuing right to be themselves without unnecessary intervention from human beings. 'The intuition of biocentric equality is that all things in the biosphere have an equal right to live and blossom and reach their own individual forms of unfolding and self-realization' (Bill Devall and George Sessions (ed), 1985).

Biocide
[1947. *Gk bios + L caedere*, life-destroying]
The indiscriminate use of chemical pesticides, threatening all life forms; the human-led suicide of whole ecosystems. 'Can anyone believe it is possible to lay down such a barrage of poisons on the surface of the earth without making it unfit for all life? They should not be called "insecticides", but "biocides"' (Rachel Carson, 1962).

Biocoenesis
[1883. *Gk bios + koine*, common life]
The varied forms of INTERDEPENDENCE between organisms within an ECOSYSTEM. '[Symbiosis] ranges from the mutually indispensable association of algae and fungi in lichens, to the less intimate but no less vital inter-dependence of animals, plants and bacteria in ecological communities (biocoenesis)' (Arthur Koestler, 1967].

Biodegradable
[*c*.1960. *Gk bios + L degradare*, to disperse by biological means]
Used to describe a substance which can be broken down by the decomposing action of living organisms, particularly bacteria. Despite the claims of manufacturers, many substances, especially PLASTICS, described as 'biodegradable' are not (and certainly not in the quantities in which they are deposited in LANDFILL sites), or cause serious pollution problems as they degrade. 'Many problems still surround the use of biodegradable plastics . . . Although some plastics, particularly those used in packaging, are advertised as biodegradable, this is only a matter of degree. Some plastics which bear the label "biodegradable" actually release undesirable by-products into the environment, so it is best to steer clear of plastics as far as you can' (Jonathon Porritt (ed), 1987). On the other hand, up to 30% of household WASTE is organic matter,

which is easily degraded into valuable COMPOST; whenever this is not done, nutrients are taken from the soil to be replaced by yet more petroleum-based artificial fertiliser.

Biodynamics
[*Gk bios* + *dynamikos*, biologically powerful]
(1) [1924] A method of gardening initiated by Rudolf Steiner and the philosophy of anthroposophy, in which strictly ORGANIC gardening is supplemented by an awareness of planetary and seasonal cycles. 'In practice, this knowledge told the farmer what properties were necessary in the soil to bring out the unique characteristics of the plant under cultivation. Thus biodynamic gardening aims to stimulate, or inhibit, those aspects of the plant which the farmer wishes to control, not simply according to its physical requirements but on the basis of its cosmic or earthly properties' (David Harvey, 1986).
(2) [1945] A branch of biology that deals with the energy production of organisms (more often called BIOENERGETICS).
(3) [*c*.1970] The name of various methods of PSYCHOTHERAPY, including a type of massage developed by Gerda Boyesen, and an attempt (J. Masserman, 1980) to understand the need to integrate a client's physical, social and psychological needs.

Bioecological Building
[*c*.1979]
(*also* 'Baubiologie', the original German term)
The design and construction of buildings which work in line with ecological principles, using natural materials and traditional techniques, and blending with their site. ' "Baubiologie" can be roughly translated as "architectural biology" or "biological architecture". It incorporates elements of *feng shui* [the oriental practice of building in harmony with the environment], the use of natural fabric clothing, bioelectric theory, and Deep Ecology into its outlook' (*East/West* magazine, January 1987). *See also* ARCHITECTURE, HOUSING.

Bioenergetics
[*Gk bios* + *energeia*, biological activity]
(1) [1945] The study of energy production and flow within and between organisms (sometimes called BIODYNAMICS).
(2) [1975] A body-based THERAPY which builds on the work of Wilhelm Reich, named and developed by Alexander Lowen in his book *Bioenergetics* (1975), which concentrates on the importance of grounding yourself in your body and its relationship to the earth. 'Bioenergetics is a therapeutic technique to help a person get back together with [their] body and to help [them] enjoy to the fullest degree possible the life of the body. This emphasis on the body includes sexuality [a preoccupa-

tion of Wilhelm Reich], which is one of its basic functions. But it also includes the even more basic functions of breathing, moving, feeling and self-expression. A person who doesn't breathe deeply reduces the life of [their] body. If [they do not] feel fully, [they narrow] the life of [their] body. And if [their] self-expression is constricted, [they limit] the life of [their] body' (Alexander Lowen, 1975). *See also* BODYWORK.

Bioenergy
(*see* LIFE FORCE)

Biofeedback
[1971]
Techniques for monitoring events (such as heartbeat or rate of breathing) in the body to enable you to regulate your own body functions. The apparatus used is usually electronic, and an awareness of the body thus gained can help to maintain healthy pulse and breathing, even in stressful situations (*see also* FEEDBACK).

Biofuel
[*c*.1960]
A shortened form of 'biomass fuel' (*see* BIOMASS ENERGY).

Biogeochemical Cycle
[1938]
The cyclical flow of elements passing between organisms and their environment. 'The more or less circular paths of the chemical elements passing back and forth between organisms and environment are known as biogeochemical cycles. "Bio" refers to living organisms and "geo" to the rocks, soil, air and water of the earth. Geochemistry is an important physical science, concerned with the chemical composition of the earth and the exchange of elements between different parts of the earth's crust and its oceans, rivers, etc. Biogeochemistry is thus the study of the exchange . . . of materials between living and nonliving components of the biosphere' (Eugene Odum, 1963). *See also* CYCLE.

Biological Oxygen Demand
[*c*.1967]
The amount of oxygen needed in water to allow the healthy life of aquatic organisms and the natural degradation of subaquatic material (*see also* EUTROPHICATION).

Biology
[1802. *Gk bios* + *logos*, writing about life]
The study of living things; by extension, the plant and animal life of a particular area, or the physical qualities of life (usually human life) set against the social or spiritual. As a SCIENCE, biology has suffered from

the DUALISM of the scientific method; perhaps more than the other sciences, since its field of interest is LIFE itself. Biology — more than any other science with the exception of psychology — has tended to reflect its oppressive and patriarchal bias, choosing its subjects with care to 'prove' what it already believed, both about animals and human beings: 'For instance, among billions of animal species, why have certain ones been studied repeatedly and in great detail, while others have been ignored? . . . Could this be because it has been easy to stereotype baboon social behaviour as hierarchical, with relatively rigid sex roles? . . . Is it an accident that among millions of insect species, those whose social behaviour easily conforms to rigid roles are the ones that have caught the imaginations of naturalists . . .? Ant and bee societies still contain slaves and queens, as well as workers and soldiers. . . Turning to our own species, is it an accident that scientists have been primarily interested in exploring contraceptive techniques that tamper with the *female* reproductive system, following the curious logic that because "fertility in women depends upon so many finely balanced factors . . . it should be easy to interfere with the process at many different stages . . ." [Clive Wood, 1969]? Would it not be more sensible to conclude that it is more difficult and riskier to tamper with a woman's reproductive system than a man's *because* the woman's system is made up of "so many finely balanced factors"?' (Ruth Hubbard, in Dale Spender (ed), 1981). 'Biology is not destiny', a phrase first used in the women's movement in the early 1970s, is a repudiation of Freud's (1897) statement that 'anatomy is destiny'; while the practice may be harder than the theory, green-thinkers see biology — including GENDER — as potential rather than destiny. ECOLOGY, once the poor relation of biology, is seen by greens as the way forward in the study of life in its myriad forms and connections, though it still needs to rid itself of many of the unnecessary shackles of scientism.

Biomass
[1934]
(1) The total weight of organic subtances found in a sample area. 'The standing crop can be expressed in terms of the number per unit area or in terms of biomass, that is, organism mass. Biomass can be measured as living weight, dry weight, ash-free dry weight, carbon weight, Calories, or any other unit that may be useful for comparative purposes' (Eugene Odum, 1963).
(2) A renewable source of energy (*see* BIOMASS ENERGY).

Biomass Energy
[1976]
ENERGY created from readily-renewable organic sources, such as wood, straw and methanol (made from sugar cane); such sources are called

'biomass fuels' or 'biofuels'. 'I am astonished that the ERDA [Energy Research and Development Association] suspects electric cars or synfuelled [synfuel is a by-product of the coal industry] cars: this suggests a serious lack of information on biomass conversion and feedstocks. . . It appears that pending better information, ERDA is *assuming* that electricity and synfuels are the cheapest long-run transport fuels . . . and thus continuing the comparative neglect of the biomass alternative' (Amory Lovins, 1979). By far the most important biomass fuel at present is wood, which provides heating and cooking for most people in the Third World and a growing number in the West. Half of the world's timber harvest is used for this purpose, and demand for wood is causing rapid DEFORESTATION and SOIL EROSION in many areas, especially in Africa and southern Asia. Much biomass energy can be retrieved from the controlled burning of domestic, industrial and agricultural WASTE; there is an ever-present danger of the TECHNOFIX of growing crops specifically as biofuels, thus taking land out of food production and perpetuating land degradation.

Biome
[*c*.1916. *Gk bios* + *-ome*, body or group of life]
A major ecological COMMUNITY, extending over a large area and usually defined by its main vegetation type, such as RAINFOREST, desert, or savannah grassland.

Bioregion
[1974]
(*also* 'biotic province' [1940], 'biogeographic province' [1975])
A large area (though smaller than a BIOME) which, while being diverse in detail, has a degree of ecological coherence. 'Bioregion' implies a broader range of defining characteristics than the earlier terms, and has become the preferred concept, particularly in the USA, which is large enough to embrace a large number of bioregions. 'A bioregion can be determined initially by use of climatology, physiography, animal and plant geography, natural history, and other descriptive natural sciences. The boundaries of a bioregion are best described by people who have lived within it, through human recognition of the realities of living in a place. All life on the planet is interconnected in a few obvious ways and in many more that remain barely explored. But there is a distinct resonance among living things and the factors which influence them that occurs specifically within each separate place on the planet. Discovering and describing that resonance is a way to describe a bioregion' (Peter Berg, 1978). *See also* REGION.

Bioregionalism
[1974]
The belief that environmental (and, where appropriate, social, economic and political) policies should be worked out and implemented taking into account the ecological integrity of BIOREGIONS, rather than the frequently arbitrary divisions created by STATE and district boundaries. By extension, a system of social and economic organisation based on bioregions. 'The most fully developed bioregional organization is probably the Ozark Area Community Congress (OACC), founded in 1976 and based on the principle of "political ecology," by which the Congress means that political consciousness must be bioregionally oriented and must operate as an extension of natural or ecological laws. The Congress, which considers itself an alternative representative body for the Ozarks, is committed to achieving regional self-reliance and sustainable economics by using renewable resources and respecting the integrity of the environment. By late 1983 OACC had held four congresses, attracting not only scores of regional enterprises and groups but also participants from national and international organizations' (Fritjof Capra and Charlene Spretnak, 1984). 'Bioregionalism means learning to become native to place, fitting ourselves to a particular place, not fitting a place to our pre-determined tastes' (Judith Plant, *Green Line*, January 1986). 'Bioregionalism begins by acting responsibly at home. Welcome home!' (Kirkpatrick Sale, 1985). The first North American Bioregional Congress was held in Kansas in 1984. *See also* REGIONALISM.

Biorhythms
[1973 *Gk bios* + *rhuthmos*, life rhythm, life flow]
(1) Regularly recurring patterns in nature, such as the alpha brainwave pattern in animals or the circadian (24-hour, from *L circa dies*, about a day) rhythms of many organisms. *See also* CYCLE.
(2) A number of theories which suggest that human beings are subject to cyclical influences, ranging from the mounting evidence that circadian and lunar cycles influence our bodies, to the notion (emanating from the German doctor, Willhelm Fleiss, author of *The Rhythm of Life* (1887) and the Swiss Alfred Tetschler) that human beings operate on rigid cycles (a 23-day physical cycle, a 28-day emotional cycle, and a 30-day intellectual cycle are the favourites).

Bioshelter
[1979]
A cross between a large greenhouse and a small self-contained ECOSYSTEM. 'A bioshelter is similar to a greenhouse, but several steps further along in evolutionary development. . . It has one or more translucent surfaces . . . with orgone gas between them, . . . and like a

greenhouse it admits light and solar heat and provides an environment for plants to grow. [But] to turn a greenhouse into a bioshelter you need some material that absorbs and holds solar heat. The Todds [John and Nancy Todd of the New Alchemy Institute in Massachusetts] . . . designed fiberglass cylinders [which] doubled as fishtanks. . . So a working bioshelter is a mimic of a natural pond ecosystem in which water and vegetation and fish each have certain functions that contribute to the life of the whole' (Walter Truett Anderson, *New Age Journal*, November 1984).

Biosource
[*c*.1980]
Another name for 'biomass fuel' (*see* BIOMASS ENERGY).

Biosphere
[1875. *Gk bios* + *sphaira*, life sphere]
The parts of the earth's crust and atmosphere inhabited by living organisms, though modified by the GAIA hypothesis to include much of the atmosphere and sub-surface geology formerly thought of as ABIOTIC. By extension, the whole living ENVIRONMENT.

Biota
[1901. *Gk biote*, way of life]
The plant and animal life of a particular area or region.

Biotechnology
[1941. *Gk bios* + *tekhnologia*, biological skills]
Those areas of TECHNOLOGY concerned with the use of living organisms in industrial and agricultural processes, and in human REPRODUCTIVE TECHNOLOGY. Scientists and businessmen have become very excited about the possibilities of 'biotech', as well they might, since it is predicted that it could be worth $20 billion by the year 2000. The basic idea is the genetic transformation of micro-organisms, which are then implanted within living cells to 'reprogramme' the growth process of the host organism — scientists have predicted quick-growing, high-yield, disease-resistant CROPS, POLLUTION and WASTE digestion, DRUGS for cancer and AIDS, and all sorts of surrogate childbearing. While there may be sound reasons for the use of biotechnology in some applications — after all, processes like the fermentation of beer and the raising of bread are examples of applied biotechnology — green-thinkers are very concerned that big business is blundering on in the name of technological PROGRESS, with little thought for the ecological and social consequences of its actions, or for more holistic approaches to the issues which biotechnology is addressing. '[Biotechnology] represents the ultimate negation of nature, . . . a final testimonial that . . . all of the physical and biological world has been put there for our exclusive use

. . . Never before in history has such complete power over life been a possibility. The problem is that biotechnology has a beginning but no end. . . It is this radical new concept of life . . . that legitimises the idea of crossing all species' barriers and undermines the inviolability of discrete, recognisable species in nature. All of life becomes reduced to a chemical level and becomes available for manipulation. It is the first experiment that legitimises the process' (Jeremy Rifkin, 1985).

Biotic

[1868. *Gk biotikos*, pertaining to life]
Relating to living organisms, especially in their natural environment. Those parts of the biosphere not generally thought to be 'alive' (*see* LIFE) are called ABIOTIC.

Birth

[13c. *Old Norse byrth*, birth]
The coming into existence or beginning of something, especially new life. Childbirth in Western society is often a paradoxical event, a mix of rare and unique JOY, PAIN, ALIENATION and FRUSTRATION, and personal and cultural expectations. 'Work in a capitalist society is an alienation of labour in the making of a social product which is confiscated by capital. But it can still sometimes be a real act of creation, purposive and responsible, even in conditions of the worst exploitation. Maternity is often a caricature of this' (Juliet Mitchell, *New Left Review*, 1966). Birth is too often taken over by the patriarchal 'expertise' of high-tech medicine, denying both mother and baby the responsibility and the experience, the joy and the pain. 'Who gives [birth]? And to whom is it given? Certainly it doesn't feel like giving, which implies a flow, a gently handing over, no coercion. . . Maybe the phrase was made by someone viewing the result only. . . Yet one more thing that needs to be renamed' (Margaret Atwood, 1977). Many green-minded women believe that it is vitally important to reclaim birth from the 'experts', give choices back to mothers, and acknowledge birth as part of the cycle of life and death, rather than treating it as a social disease (*see* NATURAL CHILDBIRTH). 'Birth' is a favourite metaphor for NEW AGE philosophers (e.g. David Spangler, *Revelation: The Birth of a New Age*, 1976; *Emergence: The Rebirth of the Sacred*, 1984); 'rebirthing' [1977] is a therapy related to primal (*see* BIRTH TRAUMA) and expounded in *Rebirthing in the New Age* (Leonard Orr and Sondra Ray, 1977).

Birth Control

[1914]
Ways of preventing the conception of unwanted children. Coined by Margaret Sanger, the American feminist and publisher. 'The expression "birth control" was devised in my little paper of advanced feminism, *The*

Woman Rebel, as one of the fundamental rights of the emancipation of working women. The response to this idea of birth control was so immediate and so overwhelming that a league was formed — the first birth control league in the world,' she wrote in 1923. Birth control has always been practised, but Margaret Sanger's naming brought the subject into the public arena. It became a subject of interest among ecologists and environmentalists in the 1960s, when uncontrolled POPULATION growth became a major concern. Garrett Hardin's influential anthology, *Population, Evolution and Birth Control* (1964), and later the Club of Rome's *The Limits to Growth* (1972), emphasised what they saw as a need for massive measures of population control. Feminists of the same period, like Shulamith Firestone, also warned of the dangers of OVERPOPULATION. It was realised that human population policies were not a simple matter, though it remained for feminist writers to point out that CONTRACEPTION was still almost exclusively a male TECHNOLOGY forced upon women's bodies. Nevertheless, the right of women to control their own reproduction was incorporated into the 1968 NOW [National Association of Women] Bill of Rights in the USA, and the 1970 List of Demands at the 1970 conference of the Women's Liberation Movement in Britain. The question of birth control in developing countries, and in those countries such as Ireland where it is still not readily available, is a matter of great importance to greens. Birth control has recently become associated with many related aspects of our sexual behaviour, from ideas about the family to sexual health in the age of AIDS. *See also* ABORTION, REPRODUCTIVE RIGHTS, SEX.

Birthing
[*c*.1975]
A sensitive and caring approach to childbirth; 'birthing' conveys an active involvement in the BIRTH process, rather than the passive lying-back-and-having-it-done-to-you approach of conventional medicine. For the same reason, 'birthing' is preferred to 'giving birth'. Virtually synonymous with NATURAL CHILDBIRTH. Alternative 'birthing centers' have been set up in several places in the USA.

Birth Trauma
[1929]
Anxiety experienced by a child at BIRTH, thought by some psychologists (starting with Otto Rank, *The Trauma of Birth*, 1929) to be the prototype of all subsequent anxiety in a person's life. This idea forms the basis of the related therapies of 'primal therapy' (Arthur Janov, *The Primal Scream*, 1970) and 'rebirthing' (*see* BIRTH). Many people believe that the circumstances in which children are born in a conventional hospital setting are indeed very traumatic, both for the mother and for the child, and have explored alternatives to this method of childbirth (*see* NATURAL CHILDBIRTH).

Black

[13c. *Old English blœc*, black]

Somebody whose cultural and family roots, wherever they now live, can be traced to Southern Asia or Africa; black people usually (though not always) have a relatively dark skin colour, and have in common, as part of their historical and cultural experience, the fact of being the object of RACISM. ' "Black" is defined by blacks themselves not only by skin colour and hair but also through a specific configuration of life experiences that are distinctly different from those of all other racial and ethnic groups. Surviving and prospering in a hostile milieu, blacks having these life experiences require psychological skill' (Faye Gary-Harris, quoted in Cheris Kramerae and Paula Treichler (ed), 1985). Such skills and strengths have resulted in an important and distinctive identity which is constantly negated in the wider social context. Some blacks prefer the word to be capitalised to emphasise their solidarity and separate identity, others argue that to capitalise the word simply perpetuates the perceived differences which result in discrimination. *See also* COLOUR, RACE, RACISM.

Black Economy

[*c*.1975]

Any sort of cash transaction that does not appear in official economic statistics. An 'official' name, which is why it is called 'black' to distinguish it from the pure 'white' economy of cash income which is faithfully recorded in income returns. Hazel Henderson (1981) prefers to call this the UNDERGROUND ECONOMY, and to distinguish it from unpaid or voluntary work, and the important and unquantified contribution that nature makes to our economic system. Important though it may be to many people in the West, the black economy is the main livelihood of most urban Third Worlders.

Blame

[13c. *L blasphemare*, to reproach, blaspheme]

The belief that someone has deliberately and maliciously done something to hurt you or others, and should therefore accept the guilt of that action and (frequently) that they should be punished for it. Many green-thinkers make the distinction between 'fault' and RESPONSIBILITY, preferring the latter with its positive and powerful connotations. Some go even further, seeing blame as totally futile and unnecessary: 'Every single human being at every moment of the past, if the entire situation is taken into account, has always done the very best he or she could do, and so deserves neither blame nor reproach' (Harvey Jackins, 1983). This approach stresses that we are all responsible for what happens in the world, and that much behaviour — whether it be the atrocities of the Third Reich or a sexual assault on a child — which is commonly seen as 'evil' or 'criminal', while reprehensible, cannot be 'blamed' on any one individual. It is OPPRESSION, not innate 'fault', that leads people to inhuman behaviour. At the same time, to deny fault is not to deny responsibility — Adolf Hitler was uniquely responsible for his actions, as is the man who assaults a child, as we all are. Such antisocial behaviour cannot be tolerated, but it is only understanding and the fulfilment of basic needs that will help a person to change, not punishment and revenge. In a green and oppression-free society, however, there must always be the space to make individual mistakes, mistakes which are important lessons and which do not deserve blame: 'I have the right to make mistakes' (Anne Dickson, 1982). Blame is the perfect way of not dealing with your own FEELINGS, and in a society where feelings are denied it is hardly surprising that blame is so rampant. Blame frequently results from the PROJECTION of ANGER, FEAR and FRUSTRATION, and the confusion between blame and responsibility is so rife in our society that even the most aware of people often prefer to blame anything and anybody rather than acknowledge their own feelings, their own responsibility, and their own power. The blame can even be couched in apparently RIGHT ON political terms, designed to 'prove' the rightness of the blamer and the inevitable guilt of the blamed. When the denial of responsibility joins forces with the denial of feelings, the result is VICTIM-blaming, a pernicious aspect of oppression particularly apparent in the rising tide of VIOLENCE against women. Thus prostitutes are fined, not their 'clients'; rape survivors are told it was their own fault for being out at night.

Blip Culture
[1980]
A CULTURE, like our own, characterised by its dependence on small and unrelated experiences, with little attempt at SYNTHESIS or overall UNDERSTANDING. 'We are besieged and blitzed by fragments of imagery, contradictory or unrelated, that shake up our old ideas and come shooting at us in the form of broken or disembodied "blips". We live, in fact, in a "blip culture"' (Alvin Toffler, 1980).

Block
[*Old French bloc*, a block of stone]
(1) [1849] A large building, often rather ugly and badly-designed.
(2) [1931] An emotional DISTRESS pattern which gets in the way of clear and creative thinking; another way of describing the apparent split between two essentially integrated parts of a person's being. 'The real self, then . . . is the innermost and truest part of the separate individual, seen still as a separate individual . . . and as such it offers a centre for the full integration of the person . . . What this means is that the usual splits which are found in so many people, between body and mind,

intellect and emotions, duty and inclination, top-dog and underdog and all the rest, can now be healed very simply. It may take a little time to work through all the implications of this healing of the splits, and there may be some painful choices to be made along the way, but the essential blocks to full integration have been removed . . .' (John Rowan, 1983). While the results of psychological blocking are all around us, only the possessor of the block can do anything about it; it is too easy to BLAME someone for their blocks, or to believe that anyone who does not agree with you must therefore have a block against accepting the truth.

Blood

[before 12c. *Old Norse bloth*, blood]

The reddish fluid which in vertebrates moves around the body, carrying oxygen, nutrients and waste products. The killing and injuring (spilling the blood) of oppressed peoples, particularly of women and of native peoples, has made blood into a potent image whenever something precious to life is threatened. Cyclical bleeding is an important part of the experience of being a WOMAN, another aspect of women's lives largely influenced by patriarchal attitudes ('menstruation is unclean') and capitalist enterprise ('so let's hide it and pretend it doesn't happen'). Token blood-sharing ceremonies have linked friends to each other, and people to their land, for centuries. The transmission of disease, particularly AIDS, through blood has given it a new significance.

Blueprint For Survival

[1972]

An early 'green manifesto', published in an early issue of the magazine *The Ecologist* and later in book form. Outlining a GREEN strategy for Britain, it was a pioneer document in that it looked very carefully at how and where change might be achieved, and covered areas like education, relationships between people and spirituality as well as more obviously environmental topics. While it lacked some of the political depth of later manifestos, it made it very clear that we could not go on as we are: 'The principal defect of the industrial way of life with its ethos of expansion is that it is not sustainable. Its termination within the lifetime of someone born today is inevitable' (*The Ecologist*, 1972).

Body

[before 12c. *Old English bodig*, body]

The physical structure of an animal, including that of a human being. One element of the traditional threesome — MIND, body and SPIRIT — each of which is often considered separately in most present-day thinking, but which in the thinking of HOLISM are seen as inextricably interlinked. The body is the part of ourselves which experiences our environment directly, and what it tells us is often not clearly enough apprehended. Mainstream medicine concentrates on the physical body, often failing to recognise that healing must take place in the mind and spirit too, and that illness in the physical body frequently arises from dis-ease in mind and spirit. 'The aim is a body that is organized to move with minimum effort, not through muscular strength, but increased consciousness of how it works' (Moshe Feldenkrais, 1986). Despite popular patriarchal belief, one person's body cannot be owned by another, and each individual body deserves respect, a respect often disregarded in the name of teasing, fun, threat or force (*see* HARASSMENT, RAPE). The body/EXPLOITATION theme is found in AGRICULTURE too: 'Putting virgin soil under cultivation initiates a breakdown of what may be called the "body" of the soil' (William Albreht, quoted in Susan Griffin, 1984). 'Body politics' describes how non-verbal language is often used to maintain power relationships, especially between women and men (Nancy Henley, 1977). 'Body armour' is a term used in some sorts of BODYWORK to describe the way in which the human body becomes tense and rigid in the process of constantly defending itself and repressing feelings (the original but now rarer 'character armour' was first coined by Wilhelm Reich in 1926).

Bodywork
[*c*.1976]
(*also* 'body therapy', 'body work')
Any THERAPY which concentrates on the role of the BODY in both physical and psychological HEALING, including MASSAGE, chiropractic, BIOENERGETICS and YOGA. Usually used in the combination 'bodywork therapy' or 'bodywork technique', though not always. 'With the development of holistic medicine and natural therapies, interest in bodywork has increased dramatically in recent years' (Nevill Drury, 1984).

Bootstrap Approach
[From the expression 'to lift yourself up by your own bootstraps']
(1) [1926] Doing something with minimal resources and without outside assistance (*see* SELF-RELIANCE).
(2) [1962] (*also* 'bootstrap philosophy') An approach to subatomic physics — though with many wider applications — which accepts the different models provided by QUANTUM THEORY and integrates whatever happens to work within a particular application, rather than trying to find the *one* theory which will explain everything. 'A physicist who is able to view any number of different partially successful models without favouritism is automatically a bootstrapper' (Geoffrey Chew, quoted in Fritjof Capra, 1982). 'Bootstrap' has come to mean any systems approach to understanding reality, and has been used in psychology, medicine, and the social sciences. *See also* MODEL.

Bottom-Up Approach
[*c*.1970]
(*also* 'bottom-up development', 'bottom-up economics')
An approach to economic and social change in which individual and GRASSROOTS needs are seen as vitally important. The idea is that benefits should gradually spread 'up' through the system as a result of this priority. 'Bottom-up' is sometimes used in antithesis to the TRICKLE-DOWN development theories propounded by post-war politicians and industrialists. The idea of bottom-up development has been expanded, especially in the 1975 *What Now?* report of the Dag Hammarskjöld Foundation, into the concept of ANOTHER DEVELOPMENT. On a local scale, a good example of bottom-up development is the growth of COMMUNITY BUSINESSes.

Boycott
[1880. After Charles Boycott, an English land agent in Ireland who was ostracised for refusing to reduce rents]
(*also* 'sanctions' [1956 in this sense])
The refusal to have dealings with an organisation or state in order to express disapproval with some aspect of their policy. Such actions are often organised by a group of people in support of a political goal, such as the ending of apartheid in South Africa, or persuading a company to re-examine their employment policy. Boycott actions frequently involve the withholding and redistribution of money (*see* PEACE TAX).

Brain
[before 12c. *Old English brægen*, brain]
The part of the body which organises and coordinates the rest, and where most people believe that what we call THINKING happens. Scientists often like to think of it as a very complex computer, but this technocentric viewpoint is much too simplistic: 'If the brain were so simple we could understand it, *we* would be so simple we couldn't!' (Lyall Watson, quoted in Marilyn Ferguson, 1981).

Brainstorming
[*c*.1955]
A group problem-solving technique which involves the spontaneous contribution of ideas from all the members of the group, without comment or criticism.

Brainwashing
[*c*.1950. Literal translation of the *Chinese xi nao*]
Originally used to describe the methods of drugging and deprivation used in south-east Asia to force people to accept a doctrinaire system of beliefs; has subsequently often been used to describe the methods

used by people in POWER to persuade those who are relatively powerless to agree with their view of the world.

Branch Economy
[*c*.1973]
(*also* 'branch plant economy')
A local economy with a large degree of external economic control. 'In the peripheral regions of advanced industrial economies there will be found what are popularly known as branch plant economies, economies characterised by high levels of external control' (H.D. Watts, 1981). The North-East of England, dependent on the Japanese auto industry, and large parts of the Canadian economy, are good examples of branch economies. Such areas are usually the first to suffer when the 'parent' companies start to contract. *See also* NEW LOCAL ECONOMIC ORDER.

Breath
[before 12c. *Old English brœth*, breath]
The movement of air; a word with many subtle shades of meaning. Breathing, being crucial to human life and health, is both a potent symbol and a vital function of life; the right of all organisms to breathe clean air is fundamental to green philosophy. 'Breath' is a cognate of the *L spiritus*, breath or spirit, which gives us SPIRIT, 'inspiration' (a breathing in), 'conspire' (to breathe with), and 'expire', to breathe out. Breath is a central concept in Eastern lifestyles and philosophies — the Chinese *chi* and Hindu *prana* each relate breath and the importance of breathing to both the physical and spiritual aspects of life. 'Ordinary day-to-day breathing is fine, having the charm of novelty inasmuch as every lungful is slightly different, and deep breathing alright for some situations, and meditational breathing okay if you like meditation, but what I am talking about is the awareness of breathing. . . I *love* breathing. Damn, but am I going to do it hard when I stop' (Keri Hulme, 1987). The emerging concept of the earth as an organism (the GAIA hypothesis) expands the idea of breath to global dimensions: *The Breathing Planet* (John Gribbin (ed), 1986).

Breeder Reactor
[1948]
(*also* 'breeder', 'fast breeder')
A nuclear reactor designed to create more new fissionable material than it consumes. Twenty years ago it was fashionable to see breeder reactors as the way round the problem of finite energy resources; now we are more wary of the nuclear chain and its dangers. 'The only safe fast breeders are rabbits' (Badge slogan, *c*.1970).

Briarpatch Network
[1974]
An informal association of people and co-operative businesses, each of which believes in honesty, the sharing of skills and information, and economic openness. The original Briarpatch was set up in California in 1974 and now has over 300 active members; similar networks function in Canada, Sweden, Finland and Japan. 'The association takes its name from the briarpatch in the folk tales of Uncle Remus, where the hero, Brer Rabbit, led a happy, safe life. The gentle rabbit was protected from predators by its humble and seemingly inhospitable home of thorns. Briar business people feel that, likewise, by keeping their lives simple and their businesses open and honest they will be protected from the problems of larger society. . . . Members of the Briarpatch fervently believe that business is a way to serve others. This value separates them from many other small businesses which exist to make money. Because of their environmental values, Briars engage only in businesses that preserve resources that allow the owners to seek simple life-styles and to enjoy their work' (Paul Ekins, 1986).

Bridge
[*c.*1940 in this sense. *Old English brycg*, bridge]
A symbol of the links that need to be made between people for real UNDERSTANDING to come about, and used to describe such attempts to link people, especially from different backgrounds. 'Building bridges between our divisions,/I reach out to you as you reach out to me;/With all of our voices and all of our visions,/Sisters, we can make such a sweet harmony' (chant, *c.*1976). 'Women from Green Gate [at Greenham Common Peace Camp] begin the bridge building with Pacific women' (*Women's Peace Alliance Newsletter*, December 1986).

Brother
[before 12c. *Old English brothor*, brother]
A MAN who expresses SUPPORT for and SOLIDARITY with other people, often though not necessarily with other men. A word frequently used in socialist and trades union circles, though a comparison with its apparent equivalent SISTER shows that 'brother' has with rare exceptions never had — and possibly never will have — the same implications of closeness and loving solidarity. 'Brotherhood' is still sometimes used to describe the need for international peace and understanding, but it rings rather hollow in a world which should know about non-sexist language.

Bulldozer Technology
[1977]
Large-scale TECHNOLOGY which attacks the environment like an enor-

mous bulldozer: '[Its] characteristics . . . are its dependence on fossil fuel and other non-renewable or man-made resources, its linearity and lack of integration with natural processes, its dominating scale, and its narrow concept of rationality and efficiency' (William Ophuls, 1977).

Bureaucracy
[1818. *L burrus*, red woollen cloth used to cover desks (via *bureau*, desk) + *Gr kratia*, rule. Thus 'rule by people sitting behind desks'] A system of administration marked by excessive division of functions and insistence on rules and regulations, so beset by outmoded practices, inter-departmental rivalry and petty regulations that it has become inefficient and self-destructive, and cannot possibly serve the people it purports to be helping; a condition more or less common to most present-day governmental systems, and which makes real change in the world virtually impossible unless the systems can be bypassed. A green approach to administration stresses DECENTRALISATION, real PARTICIPATION, and simple and efficient GRASSROOTS solutions; in the meantime, learning how to use the system (*see* SUBVERSION) or upset it using its own shortcomings (*see* NONVIOLENT DIRECT ACTION) are sometimes necessary short-term expedients. 'Like corporate bureaucracies, the government bureaucracies which dole out economic assistance are fundamentally disempowering. . . It is . . . true that disempowerment is common to many different kinds of bureaucracies, but there is a different magnitude and scope of powerlessness for people who must rely on the "benevolence" of a bureaucratic organization to satisfy their basic material needs' (Steven Wineman, 1984). 'Bureaucracy defends the status quo long past the time when the quo has lost its status' (Laurence Peter (ed), 1977).

By-Product
(*see* PRODUCTION)

Cc

Campaign

[*c*.1880. *L campania*, countryside]

A programme of coordinated activities designed to achieve a political goal. Taken from military use to describe US electoral campaigns in the late nineteenth century; now used to describe any goal-oriented action designed to influence authority. 'You can change some aspects of your environment yourself . . . but often you'll realise that you can't do it all on your own. Be it stopping a nuclear power station being built or getting a zebra crossing down your street, there are times when you need friends and allies . . . As you build your campaign you'll find unexpected allies in many places, and don't be afraid to come to Friends of the Earth or any other pressure group for assistance. Every environmental disaster starts in someone's back yard, and that's the best place to start fighting it' (Jonathon Porritt (ed), 1987).

Capitalism

[1854. *L capitale*, of the head, important, chief]

An economic, political and social system in which the amassing of private PROPERTY and WEALTH and the creation of private PROFIT are given a high priority. An idea whose details vary from commentator to commentator, but within which eminently praiseworthy ideals like the importance of the individual and the need to look after your own interests come face to face with green non-starters like the belief that everything can be given a cash value, that 'healthy competition' can benefit everybody, and that economic GROWTH can solve every problem. Hence the dilemma faced within the green movement when some advocates of the NEW ECONOMICS talk about 'green capitalism': 'A new breed of environmental entrepreneur is emerging around the world. New companies [selling natural products, wholefoods, etc.] are appearing which are run by what John Elkington [1987] . . . has dubbed 'the green capitalists' (*Earthlife News*, Summer 1986). Then there is the socialist line: '[Greens] must first accept that it is capitalism . . . which lies behind the environmental problems they tackle. They must also see this capitalist system in its true international context — not as some kind of organized conspiratorial system, but as the chaotic economic force that it is. A force which, with the advent of microtechnology — and the resulting ability of transnational corporations to fragment production and seek out the cheapest source of labour — has permeated the whole globe' (Joe Weston (ed), 1986). Many green-thinkers, while acknowledging that capitalism has exacerbated many of our current problems, cannot agree that capitalism and only capitalism is the culprit — after all, they say, look at the massive environmental problems in socialist societies. And again, modern capitalism has only been with us for less than a century and a half — many destructive trends (PATRIARCHY, ANTHROPOCENTRISM, local OVERPOPULATION and OVERGRAZING) were well-established long before that. Yet even 'balanced' discussions about capitalism as it is today recognise that its days are numbered, if only because it is so apparent, especially from US experience, that capitalism is not working. 'Modern capitalism originated in the force and fraud which drove the English workers off the land into the factories created by the Industrial Revolution. . . . Even after the initial harshness of industrialism was mitigated by rising real wages, union pressure and social reform, income and wealth continued to be far more inequitably distributed than considerations of efficency and incentive required. Throughout its history, capitalism has been an unstable, disorderly mode of organization in which business cycles have periodically disrupted the lives of workers and bankrupted farmers and small businessmen. Even in the eyes of its defenders, capitalism has been deficient in two major regards. There are very few competitive markets of the sort envisaged by Adam Smith and his followers. To an increasing degree, capitalist economies are directed by the entirely visible hands of monopolists, multinational giants and domestic oligopolists. And finally, the argument that competition, even where it is to be found, must enhance the public good is deflated by the ever-increasing environmental damage inflicted by externalities' (Robert Lekachman, 1981).

Car

[1895 in this sense. *L carrus*, wagon]

(*also* 'automobile', 'motor car')

A wheeled vehicle primarily designed to carry a small number of people, which runs on ROADS, is fuelled by non-renewable FOSSIL FUEL petroleum, creates widespread congestion, NOISE and POLLUTION, and kills more than a quarter of a million people worldwide every year. 'About thirty million cars are made every year. Each one will offer its owner complete freedom of movement. In exchange it will get through about three tonnes of petrol, will grossly pollute the atmosphere, will kill wildlife and perhaps pedestrians, and will offer the driver a chance to kill him or herself into the bargain. It may not sound like a very good bargain, but it is the one that has been struck' (John Seymour and Herbert Girardet, 1987). Green-thinkers believe that people should be free to move around, but that in most cases privately-owned petrol-driven cars are not the answer — some research has been done on vehicles which run on solar power or on hydrogen, both of which could be both cheap and pollution-free, and the potential for integrated public transport systems is enormous. BICYCLES or WALKING are ideal for most short-distance travel (nearly 30% of car journeys are distances of less than two miles), purpose-built electric vehicles should be available for all disabled people who need them, and RAILWAYS are the obvious choice for longer distances. *See also* OZONE, PHOTOCHEMICAL SMOG, TRANSPORT, TRAVEL.

Carcinogen
[1936. *Gk karkinos* (literally, 'crab') + *-gen*, cancer-forming]
Any substance implicated in the development of cancer; of particular concern because many of the unseen and untastable residues left in and on food from PESTICIDES and herbicides — many of which have been implicated with cancer — are something we often have little choice other than to consume. '"In most circumstances, occasional exposure to higher-than-average levels of pesticide in a foodstuff has no public health significance." These were the reassuring words of the [UK] Ministry of Agriculture's most recent report on pesticide residues [1982]. To be sure, most but not all of the pesticide residues found on foods in Britain appear in minute, almost undetectable quantities. But then, so do the carcinogens . . . in individual cigarettes. And the Environmental Protection Agency in the United States, which regulates pesticide safety, says there is "no safe level" of known or suspected carcinogens' (James Erlichman, 1986). One of the most widespread carcinogens is the tar inhaled as a result of smoking tobacco (*see* SMOKING).

Caring
[*c*.1780 in this sense. *Old English cearu*, to mourn or sorrow]
Looking after and being responsible for something or someone. A word with many shades of meaning; and although a useful and important word, open to much manipulation. Use of the word boomed in the 1960s, when social work and similar provision became 'the caring professions', newly-institutionalised children were 'taken into care', those looking after people 'in care' became 'caretakers' (until then the

word had mostly been used in relation to buildings), and care became a vogue word, spawning homecare, housecare, autocare, Mothercare, and an abundance of CHILDCARE facilities and childcarers. Yet there is no precise synonym for 'caring', with its connotations of EMPATHY, RESPONSIBILITY, RESPECT and concern, so it needs to be reclaimed to mean precisely those qualities of care-taking. 'Our aims are to provide a forum for discussion and exchange of ideas and experiences for parents seeking to bring up their children to live in harmony with nature and to become caring and responsible future generations of Earth and her creatures, aware of the spiritual interconnectedness of all life' (*Pagan Parenting Network Newsletter*, 1986). In a patriarchal society where caring is very much a 'second-rate' activity, rarely warranting acknowledgement let alone reward, women are assumed to be 'natural carers' and then discriminated against; thus nurses are extremely poorly paid, it is never assumed that a man will give up his job to care for a sick child or parent, and most caring is not considered to be 'work' at all. Everybody has a capacity for caring, and green-thinkers would like caring to be an essential and respected aspect of everyone's lives. Hence 'care group', an informal support group for people involved in world-changing activities: 'Local care group will be taking place in the Shrewsbury area in February to give each other the space to relax and scream and strengthen ourselves in our life and work' (*Threads*, Winter 1986/87).

Carrying Capacity
[1930 in this sense]
The POPULATION of animals (and by extension, any living organism, including human beings) that a HABITAT can sustain without resulting in environmental degradation. Originally used by livestock farmers to estimate the number of animals a particular area would support, the term was taken into geography in 1958: 'By relating actual to potential use the capability of the land to support population — that is, its 'carrying capacity' — can be measured' (L. Dudley Stamp, *Geographical Review*, 1958); thence into ecology in the early 1960s: 'The concept of carrying capacity has been elaborated by Dasmann [*Wildlife Biology*, 1964], who suggests that firstly there is a survival capacity where there is food enough for survival but not for vigour nor optimum growth, and where slight changes in ambient conditions can be disastrous. An optimum capacity appears superior since there is adequate nutrition and individual growth except perhaps for a few individuals. A third type is based largely on density, and is the tolerance capacity or the level at which territorial considerations . . . force surplus individuals to migrate. . . . Some parallel with the human population may be seen if we equate the survival and tolerance capacity groups with the poorer nations and the optimum capacity with areas like North America and

Western Europe' (Ian Simmons, 1974). Extended discussion about the human 'carrying capacity' of the earth formed part of the 'ecological crisis' debate in the 1960s, including J.H. Fremlin's spirited article 'How Many People Can The World Support' in the *New Scientist* in 1964, where he estimated that a human population of 60,000 million million people was feasible before the problem of waste heat disposal became insuperable. Most green-thinkers, however, believe that the earth passed its optimum human carrying capacity a long time ago, and that if we do not heed the relevance of basic ecological principles we shall be faced with massive OVERSHOOT problems on a global scale such as led to the collapse of the Inca civilisation in the fifteenth century or the population of Easter Island in the eighteenth, both of which are usually attributed to human agency but were essentially due to excessive pressure on the resource base. 'If those who do not or cannot conceive of human carrying capacity in sustainable terms have their way, mankind will repeat the tragic failures of the past' (R.L. Wisniewski, *Humboldt Journal of Social Relations*, Spring/Summer 1980). 'The optimum is almost always less than the maximum' (Eugene Odum, *Current History*, June 1970).

Cartel
[*c.*1900 in this sense. *Old Italian cartello*, placard]
A group of companies or nations which agree to set mutually acceptable prices and production QUOTAS for a particular product. Being against the perceived spirit of CAPITALISM, cartels are currently illegal in the USA, but they have had some success (particularly oil cartels agreed by OPEC — the Organisation of Petroleum Exporting Countries) in reducing production of raw materials to a level which more closely approximates to current demand.

Cartesian Paradigm
[*c.*1975. After René Descartes (1596-1650), philosopher and mathematician]
A model of the world based on a distinction between the MIND of the individual human being and the world external to the human mind, the result of which is to set people against and apart from the natural world. Descartes' famous dictum, 'I think, therefore I am', sees human beings as creatures of mind alone, not as living beings who combine mental and physical attributes, thus linking us directly with our environment. Many people believe that many of our current problems, ecological, psychological and spiritual, arise from this DUALISM. 'Descartes was one of the founders of the New Science — what we now call modern science — and his schema for launching it involved a peculiar split between consciousness and the external world. The mind schematizes Nature for quantitative purposes — for measurement and calculation, with the

ultimate purpose of *manipulating* Nature — and at the same time the consciousness doing all that, the human subject, is set off against Nature. What emerges, then, is a very striking dualism between mind and the external world' (William Barrett, in Bryan Magee (ed), 1978).

Cash Crop
[1868]
A CROP grown primarily for sale, rather than being grown to provide food for the population of the area where it is being grown. The term usually refers to a crop grown in a poor country for export to the richer parts of the world, seen in conventional economics as the only way for poorer countries to earn their living, but in fact a treadmill instigated in the eighteenth century which impoverishes vast amounts of land to provide unnecessary luxuries and turns millions of people into dependent wage-slaves. The export of cash crops has turned many poor countries into one- and two-product producers, constantly at the mercy of fluctuating prices and with the ever-present threat of bankruptcy if a harvest or a market fails. Many cash crops (tobacco, opium, coffee, sugar) not only deprive the Third World of the yield of valuable land, but also do the eventual human consumer and the land no good either. 'A large part of our world farm — often the best acres in the neediest countries — is used for cash-crops, either for dietary frivolities, such as cocoa, or for animal feed. If the producers of these commodities instead concentrated on producing staples for their own people, then clearly they would have little or nothing to offer the west agriculturally, and the world farm idea would break down. But so long as they do produce these fripperies, then they contribute to the profligacy. If we think we can afford this extravagance, it is because we are insulated from the physical realities' (Colin Tudge, 1977). 'With all cash crops, the evil lies in the way the rich world consumes too much, pays too little for it, and ruins the environment to get it' (Ann Cullen, *New Internationalist*, June 1986).

Catastrophe
[16c. *Gk katastrephein*, to overturn]
A momentous and shattering event.
(1) What some people fear may happen as a result of human abuse of the earth.
(2) A method by which some see the earth healing itself following excessive human intervention.
(3) [1869] An integral part of the formation of the planet in geological time, thought by the geologist Thomas Huxley (who coined the term 'catastrophism' in 1869) and others to explain certain geological and biological phenomena, such as the end of the age of dinosaurs. Catastrophism makes periodic come-backs, and is sometimes contrasted with

uniformitarianism — the belief that everything in history can be explained by processes we can see at work today, or incrementalism — the belief that everything follows logically and by small steps from what has gone before.

Catharsis
[*c*.1890 in this sense. *Gk kathairein*, to cleanse or purge]
The RELEASE of repressed FEELINGS in appropriate sounds and actions, resulting in feelings of well-being and relief. A term which was originally used to signify the cleansing or purging effect both of medical remedies and of moving experiences; adopted by Sigmund Freud in 1893 to describe the part of the therapeutic process associated with the release of suppressed feelings. 'If the client is crying, and seems to need encouragement to go deeper, it is often good to reach out and give a light hold to the shoulder or upper back. This gives reassurance of the therapist's presence and support without interrupting the flow of feelings . . . Let the emotional discharge build to a climax and resolve itself through catharsis' (John Rowan, 1983).

Celebration
[*L celebrare*, to frequent, fill, celebrate]
(1) [15c] The observation of a special event or holiday with festivities.
(2) [*c*.1960] The aware and joyful recognition of human creativity, an idea given impetus by Ivan Illich's *Call to Celebration* (1967): 'I and many others, known and unknown to me, call upon you: To celebrate our joint power to provide all human beings with the food, clothing and shelter they need to delight in living. To discover, together with us, what we must do to use [hu]mankind's power to create the humanity, the dignity and the joyfulness of each one of us. To be responsibly aware of your personal ability to express your true feelings and to gather us together in their expression. . . . The call is to live the future. Let us join together joyfully to celebrate our awareness that we can make our life today the shape of tomorrow's future'.
(3) [*c*.1972] The validation of your own or another person's strength, intelligence and creativity (*see also* APPRECIATION).

Celibacy
[17c. *L caelebs*, unmarried]
The conscious decision not to marry, or, more recently [*c*.1900], not to engage in sexual relationships. Conventionally seen as a denial of baser instinct, usually for religious ends; more recently seen, especially by some women, as a way of using time and effort for more important things. 'For early feminists, given the difficulties of birth control, celibacy was one sure way of maintaining a single life, ensuring the possibility of self-definition and a life devoted to work or friendship or a

cause not dictated by connection to one man. During the second wave of feminism, the modern view of sexuality meant that celibacy was usually perceived as a denial of needs or the refusal to accept lesbianism. But by the mid 1970s celibacy began to be seen once again as a meaningful option for the feminist who felt no sexual desire for women yet wished to detach herself from men and devote her energies and emotions to women' (Lisa Tuttle, 1986). *See also* RELATIONSHIP, SEX.

Censorship
[*c*.1600 *L censere*, to assess, judge]
The denial, usually by a STATE and its apparatus, of the freedom to say, write, read and broadcast whatever anybody wants to say. Only seventeen of the world's 229 states have anything approaching freedom of speech, one of the planks of the United Nations Declaration of Human Rights (Charles Humana, 1986). Censorship is most often used to silence views contrary to those of tyrannical governments, though in most Western countries it is popularly associated with the censorship of displays of violence and overt sexuality. While Greens would never encourage the capitalist exploitation of the most antisocial aspects of our culture, the way of developing a more caring and responsible society must be increasing openness and FREEDOM: 'Pornography has little intrinsic merit — its value is inflated only by scarcity. Censorship inflates the value' (Beatrice Faust, 1980).

Centre
[*L centrum*, the centre of a circle, from *Gk kentron*]
(US: center)
(1) [14c] The one place where everything important seems to be happening, and where people at the periphery find it difficult to get to.
(2) [14c] The 'place' within a human being reached at times of heightened awareness, as during meditation.
(3) [*c*.1959] A building where a range of life-enhancing activities is offered, such as the Open Centres in London and New York, or the Centre for Alternative Technology in Wales.

Chain Reaction
[*c*.1902]
A rapidly-occurring series of events in which each acts as the trigger for the next. Nuclear fission and fusion are physical chain reactions; in human systems we always have the option of stopping to think before acting like lemmings (an anthropocentric and speciesist analogy!).

Challenge
[*c*.1950 in this sense. *L calumnia*, trickery, false accusation]
A new, stimulating and interesting set of circumstances which calls for

creative solutions. Sometimes used by green-thinkers instead of PROBLEM, to stress the positive aspects of CHANGE.

Change
[13c. *L cambire*, to exchange]
The quality of FLOW in events; the constantly-altering nature of circumstances. An important word with a wide range of implications. In Chinese philosophy, particularly in taoism, change is seen as the one unchanging aspect of the universe; its most important text, the *I Ching* (pronounced 'yee jing'), treats change in all its aspects — the title translates as *The Book of Change*. 'No matter what names are applied to these forces [yin and yang; firm and yielding], it is certain that the world of being arises out of their change and interplay. Thus change is conceived of partly as the continuous transformation of the one force into the other and partly as a cycle of complexes of phenomena, in themselves connected, such as day and night, summer and winter. Change is not meaningless — if it were there could be no knowledge of it — but subject to the universal law — tao' (Richard Wilhelm, 1951). Two main types of change can be identified: gradual change or EVOLUTION and sudden change or REVOLUTION (*see also* CATASTROPHE, REFORMISM). Western society does acknowledge change, but all too often subverts it to its own brand of one-way rapid technology-led PROGRESS; in fact change can happen so quickly that it results in what Alvin Toffler calls 'future shock' (*see* FUTURE). Social change needs to be understandable, integrated, and linked with the changes of the natural world; for this to happen, change needs to be truly radical: 'Yes, we need change, but change so fundamental and far-reaching that even the concepts of revolution and freedom must be expanded beyond all earlier horizons' (Murray Bookchin, 1981). 'Real, slow-growing, long-lasting, hard-standing changes, like trees, never come up and pat you on the head and say, "You did it, kid, you made me possible, and you're terrific and I'm grateful as hell"' (Anne Herbert, in Art Kleiner and Stewart Brand (ed), 1986).

Chemical
[1747. *Medieval L alchymia*, alchemy]
A substance obtained by the transformation of naturally-occurring elements and compounds. On one level — as food technologists and agrochemists are fond of pointing out — the whole world is made up of chemicals, so why should we worry about them? Yet human beings have developed ways of synthesising thousands of substances which are not found in nature; although some of these have beneficial properties and some do not react with their environment, the possible side effects of many artificial chemicals are virtually unknown, and when they are mixed (as they almost invariably are), they form millions of combina-

tions which would defy the 'safety tests' of the most ardent scientist. Thus we share our world with a staggering number of different artificial chemical compounds in the form of industrial chemicals, food additives, agrochemicals, pharmaceuticals — chemicals which ecosystems (including the human body) have no way of absorbing, and many of which are known (and many more suspected) to cause harm to living organisms (*see* CARCINOGEN, MUTAGEN). It is hardly surprising that many green-thinkers tend towards the belief that all chemicals which do not occur naturally are suspect. The problem of chemical pollution of the environment was brought to widespread attention by Rachel Carson's book, *Silent Spring* (1962): 'The chemicals to which life is asked to make its adjustment are no longer merely the calcium and silica and copper and all the rest of the minerals washed out of the rocks and carried in rivers to the sea; they are the synthetic creations of man's inventive mind, brewed in his laboratories, and having no counterparts in nature. To adjust to these chemicals would require time on the scale that is nature's; it would require not merely the years of a man's life but the life of generations. And even this, were it by some miracle possible, would be futile, for the new chemicals come from our laboratories in an endless stream; almost five hundred annually find their way into actual use in the United States alone. The figure is staggering and its implications are not easily grasped — five hundred new chemicals to which the bodies of men [of both sexes] and animals are required somehow to adapt each year, chemicals totally outside the limits of biologic experience.' (*see also* AGRICULTURE, POLLUTION). Many of these chemicals find their way into our FOOD, being sprayed and injected in enormous quantities. 'There are . . . a lot of us . . . who would like to know why we and our children have, unwittingly, become the first generations to be fed a diet of chemicals concealed in the basic foods we eat' (James Erlichman, 1986). We are told that chemical storage facilities are regularly inspected and monitored, then have the terrible evidence of the dioxin leak at Seveso in Italy in 1976, the Bhopal pesticide accident in 1984, the killing of the Rhine by a chemical leak in Switzerland in 1986. We are told that all the chemicals being used are subject to extensive safety checks. The truth is that 'even under laboratory conditions, it is difficult to *prove* for certain that a chemical is 100 per cent safe. . . All we can hope to establish is the *probability* that a chemical is harmful, and that should be regarded as sufficient evidence to act upon. Were such an approach to be adopted, however, very few of the chemicals we use today would be permitted' (Edward Goldsmith and Nicholas Hildyard (ed), 1986). 'Chemical warfare' [1917] is the use of chemicals, usually gases, but also DEFOLIANTS, to destroy or damage an ENEMY. *See also* ADDITIVE, DUMPING, WASTE.

Chi
(*see* BREATH, LIFE FORCE)

Child
[before 12c. *Old English cild*, child]
A young human being, somewhere between babyhood and adulthood. Often considered to be inferior to an adult as a result of being dependent, possessing less experience, and being physically smaller, and thus frequently oppressed by adults (*see* ADULTISM). 'The development of the modern family meant the breakdown of a large, integrated society into small, self-centred units. The child within these conjugal units now became important; for he [or she] was a product of that unit, the reason for its maintenance. It became desirable to keep one's children at home for as long as possible, to bind them psychologically, financially and emotionally to the family unit until such time as they were ready to create a new family unit. . . . The concept of childhood dictated that children were a species different not just in age, but in kind, from adults' (Shulamith Firestone, 1971). Childhood is thought by some people to be a relatively recent 'invention', resulting from the rise of the middle class and the advent of universal education in the period from the seventeenth to the nineteenth century. 'The invention of childhood as separate state corresponds with the transition from feudalism to capitalism. The first modern children were middle-class and male' (Martin Hoyles, 1979). Thinking about the concept of 'child' has several important implications for green-thinkers:
— Children are important human beings, and thus deserve respect.
— Children can often show adults ways of being and acting that adults have forgotten about or repressed (*see* GAMES, PLAY).
— The child's excitement at experiencing new things for the first time is always somewhere within every adult, and can be rediscovered if the adult allows him/herself to be more childlike; an idea sometimes referred to as 'the child within' or 'the inner child'.
— The company of children can remind adults of both the good and not-so-good aspects of their own childhood.
As children have been oppressed, so 'childish' has come to mean 'stupid, overly-dependent, immature, not worth listening to' — some green-thinkers use 'childlike' instead, to stress the important things that adults can learn from children. Some people prefer to call children 'young people' or 'little people', thus consciously acknowledging that children *are* indeed human; these expressions can easily, however, become as patronising as those they replace.

Child Abuse
[*c*.1930]
(*also* 'child battering')
The ill-treatment of a CHILD by the adult or adults responsible for its welfare; it may involve physical, sexual or emotional abuse, cruelty or neglect. Child abuse results from prevailing attitudes, beliefs and misconceptions about childhood, the FAMILY and sexuality. 'There are many misconceptions about parents who beat their children: that they are poor and uneducated, that they are unpredictably violent and "mad", that they don't love their children. None of these is true. Child battering occurs in all social classes and income brackets; it occurs in predictable circumstances which can come to be understood; and the parents involved often love their children profoundly. Child battering is part of a larger system of family and personal stress and may involve people who are still struggling with issues from their own childhood which interfere with the job of parenting' (Michèle Cohen and Tina Reid, 1981). *See also* INCEST, RAPE.

Childcare
[1915]
Looking after and being responsible for a CHILD or children. *See also* CARING.

Child-Centred
[1962]
Facilities and activities provided for children which aim to reflect what the children themselves want rather than solely what adults think might be good for them.

China Syndrome
[1977]
The complete meltdown of the core of a nuclear reactor, resulting in a mass of radioactive material burrowing into the ground under a nuclear installation (towards China from the USA, whence the name). The title of an influential fictional account (1979) and film about such a meltdown in a nuclear reactor on the Californian coast. Although a complete meltdown has never yet occurred, partial and devastating meltdowns have happened throughout the history of nuclear power generation, from the world's first source of nuclear electricity, the USA's EBR-1, in 1955, to Chernobyl in 1986.

Choice
[13c. *Old French choisir*, to choose]
The freedom to select an alternative that is most appropriate to your circumstances. Choice is frequently limited by lack of resources and

information, and by discrimination and bureaucratic red tape, but hardly ever do people have no choice at all. Another obstacle to expanding choices is lack of imagination, vision, and faith that radical change is possible. *See also* DECISION.

CHP
(*see* CO-GENERATION)

Circle
[12c. *L circus*, ring]
A closed curve on which every point is the same distance from the centre; a configuration symbolic of the shape of the earth and its orbit around the sun, and many other features of the natural world. By analogy with CYCLE, it mirrors and symbolises the cycles of nature. It is the shape which contains the largest area within the shortest circumference, and so is a symbol of wholeness and, according to Jung, an archetype representing the SELF. It is also much used in traditional building (especially of sacred buildings); many early sacred sites, particularly in Europe, were circular (Stonehenge, Avebury, Silbury). This mathematical attribute also makes the circle an efficient way of arranging a group of people for meetings and celebrations, hence 'opening circle', 'closing circle', 'circle dancing' (a form of dancing where the participants move, often holding hands, in a circle): 'Let the circle be unbroken' (anti-nuclear chant, 1970s). Used by several green-minded authors in book titles: *The Closing Circle* (Barry Commoner, 1971), *The Expanding Circle: Ethics and Sociobiology* (Peter Singer, 1981) and *The Extended Circle* (Jon Wynne-Tyson (ed), 1985). 'Everything the Power of the World does is done in a circle. The sky is round, and I have heard that the earth is round like a ball, and so are all the stars. The wind, in its greatest power, whirls. Birds make their nests in circles, for theirs is the same religion as ours. The sun comes forth and goes down again in a circle. The moon does the same, and both are round. Even the seasons form a great circle in their changing, and always come back again to where they were. The life of a [human being] is a circle from childhood to childhood, and so it is in everything where power moves' (John Neihardt, 1932).

Citizens' Movement
[*c*.1955]
A popular movement of ordinary people who work together for a common cause.

Citizen's Wage
(*see* SOCIAL WAGE)

City
(*see* URBANISATION)

Civil Disobedience
[1849]
Nonviolent methods of political protest, such as refusing to pay taxes, enlist for compulsory national service, or obey oppressive laws. The concept was named by Henry Thoreau and expounded in some detail in his *Yankee in Canada* (1866); the greatest exponent of civil disobedience was probably Mahatma Gandhi (1869-1948), who was frequently imprisoned by the British occupying force for acts of civil disobedience. *See also* NONVIOLENT DIRECT ACTION.

Civilisation
[1772. *L civilis*, relating to the life of citizens]
(US: 'civilization')
A type of human society which is urban-based, highly literate and underpinned by a sophisticated technology, and is generally assumed to be intrinsically 'better' than any other sort; by extension sometimes used as a synonym for CULTURE or SOCIETY. 'Civilisation' is a very emotive idea, always invoked when the breakdown of existing structures of society is threatened, but civilisation is not an all-or-nothing package — we can always choose to keep what we want and reject the rest. 'The promise of the industrial age has been tempered by many disappointments, but none so devastating as the growing belief that our civilization is out of control' (Richard Barnet, 1980). 'Many highly advanced civilisations, of great sophistication and intellectual accomplishment, survived quite nicely without ever stumbling upon an invention as simple as the wheel. What a civilisation discovers depends upon the conceptual framework it chooses to live by. In the West we choose to live by a world view that has led to the nuclear bomb and the engineering of the genetic blueprints of life' (Jeremy Rifkin, 1985). 'True civilization may be looked at as a positive-sum game between human beings and the rest of nature in which both emerge as winners' (Ignacy Sachs, *Resurgence*, May 1983). 'Is civilization progress? The challenge, I think, is clear; and, as clearly, the final answer will be given not by our amassing of knowledge, or by the discoveries of our science, or by the speed of our aircraft, but by the effect our civilized activities as a whole have upon the quality of our planet's life — the life of plants and animals as well as that of men [and women]' (Charles Lindbergh, quoted in Laurence Peter, 1977).

Civil Liberties
[1644]
FREEDOMS to which all people have a right, especially freedom from

arbitrary governmental interference. 'Emphases vary, but most lists of basic civil liberties will include freedom of speech, freedom of religion and of thought, freedom of movement, freedom of association, the right to a fair trial and freedom of the person' (David Robertson, 1985). These freedoms are supposedly guaranteed in the USA by the Bill of Rights of 1798; in other countries, including the UK, they are assumed to be part of the law of the land. In many countries there exist pressure groups to defend civil liberties, such as the American Civil Liberties Union, and the National Council for Civil Liberies in Britain. *See also* BASIC NEEDS, CIVIL RIGHTS.

Civil Rights
[1721]
The personal rights of individual human beings within society, especially the right to fair and decent treatment, and the right to participate in political affairs. More specifically, 'civil rights' covers the right not to be discriminated against, the right to protection against unlawful arrest and police brutality, the right to form or join a trade union (or, in some cases, not to), and to protest in public against official policy. 'Civil rights' were an important rallying-point for protest in the USA in the 1960s, when black demands for equal rights were the main issue, hence 'civil rights movement', 'civil rights worker'. While acknowledging the importance of civil rights, green-thinkers see 'civil responsibilities' as equally important (*see* RESPONSIBILITY). *See also* BASIC NEEDS.

Claimant
[*c.*1960 in this sense. *L clamare*, to call]
A person receiving money from the STATE (usually called 'benefit' following the use of the term in the UK 1911 National Insurance Act, or 'social security' following the use of the term in a US programme of 1935 and its subsequent use in the UK). Claimants often suffer from inefficient BUREAUCRACY and DISCRIMINATION, but with rapidly-increasing numbers of claimants, their collective voice is becoming a strong force for political change. 'Since 1948, there have been several changes in both the size and composition of the claimant population. At the end of 1948, the scheme [British National Assistance] had just over 1 million claimants. Since then, the number of claimants has increased to over 4 million' (*Social Trends*, 1986). Hence 'claimants' union', a trades union style organisation which works to protect the rights of claimants.

Clarity
[14c *L claritas*, clarity]
(1) Clearness of communication, essential to creative and decisive action. 'Everything that can be thought at all can be thought clearly.

Everything that can be said can be said clearly' (Ludwig Wittgenstein, quoted in Rudolf Flesch, 1968).
(2) Purity of water and air, both essential to life.

Classism
[1842. *L classis*, a group of citizens]
The OPPRESSION of the members of one social class of people by those of another, usually the oppression of the working classes by the 'upper' classes, or more recently the oppression of women as a class by men as a class (one interpretation of SEXISM). Some people make the distinction between 'owning class' and 'working class' to replace the traditional lower (working/manual labouring)/middle (bourgeois/commercial/service)/upper (leisured/monied) class distinction. Classism was the first oppression to be identified and named — by Karl Marx (*see* MARXISM) — and later thinking on oppression owes a great deal to his work on class. '[Classism] represents a specific oppression where the rules, values, mores, and ideals of one class are imposed upon another, within the hierarchy of class values. Within feminism it filters through from middle class to working class women, denying them language, banning them from self-expression, labelling them ignorant, stupid, coarse, bombastic, rough, uneducated, ineffectual' (Marlene Packwood, quoted in Cheris Kramerae and Paula Treichler, 1985). In contemporary society people often have class roots which are at variance with their present status, which can create problems in identity and relationships. Most sociologists still follow the oppressive practice of automatically defining women and children as the same class as their male 'protector'; this is simplistic, disrespectful and inaccurate.

Clear Felling
[1922]
(*also* 'clear cutting')
Cutting down and removing all the trees in a particular area, a practice which can leave the soil surface unprotected, often causing massive SOIL EROSION and LEACHING. *See also* DEFORESTATION, FORESTRY.

Client
[*c.*1930 in this sense. *L cluere*, to follow, obey]
(1) Used by many people involved in HEALING and THERAPY to replace the term PATIENT, with its connotations of conventional ideas about illness. In PSYCHOTHERAPY, the 'client' is the person in a therapeutic situation who is 'working' (being given ATTENTION and space to express their thoughts and feelings) at any given time. Hence 'client-centred therapy' [1942], therapy in which the client for the most part directs the course of the therapeutic process. Insofar as it is the client who is most intimate with his or her feelings, this approach to psychotherapy is the

one preferred by people who would rather be assisted in their own personal growth rather than be told what is best for them; it is also the approach used by many people in self-help groups.
(2) To seek therapeutic attention in an unaware way, without first ensuring that the person you are seeking it from is willing to give it; hence 'clienting'. Some people believe that unaware clienting is the cause of much of the miscommunication and inefficiency in group situations.

Climate
[*c*.1860 in this sense. *Gk klima*, latitude, sloping land surface]
A description of the average weather conditions of a particular place, conditions which have enormous significance for the plant and animal life found there. 'Even though the changes of the weather are proverbial, it is nevertheless possible at every place to arrive at a generalization and a composite of these variations. One speaks then of the climate of the region' (B. Haurwitz and J.M. Austin, 1944). Weather conditions have now been monitored for more than 150 years in some places, and these long-term records have given many scientists cause to ponder: 'Unprecedented temperature decreases have occurred in northern regions, such as Iceland, along with many other unfamiliar manifestations, such as modified wind systems and rainfall distributions. Many explanations of these climate trends have been put forward. Some mechanism that either reduces the amount of the Sun's radiation reaching the Earth or increases the amount radiated is required. Ecologists, not unexpectedly, place the blame on the products of [human] activities. Increasing dustiness of the atmosphere, nuclear explosions, supersonic aircraft have all been proposed and considered, but within our admittedly limited theoretical understanding of what goes on, none has stood up well to criticism. Another possibility that we are exploring is that one of the trace gas emissions such as that of nitrous oxide serves as a biological climate regulator. Nitrous oxide is produced naturally by soil micro-organisms at a rate of hundreds of millions of tons annually. The output varies, however, as a result of agriculture, particularly the use of nitrogenous fertilisers. We do not know how nitrous oxide could modify the climate, but the evidence suggests that it has been increasing in concentration and it is known to penetrate the stratosphere where its decomposition products could affect the ozone layer. This climatic trend may be "just another fluctuation" of the kind that has happened before and will cure itself. This tends to be the meteorologists' view but the uncomfortable thought remains that none of the earlier occurrences has been explained. Perhaps some unidentified [human] activity . . . has been the common factor and nowadays there are a good deal more people about, active in

many more ways. The consequences this time could well be much more serious and prolonged. We await developments somewhat uneasily' (James Lovelock and Sidney Epton, in John Gribbin (ed), 1986).

Climax
[1915 in this sense. *Gk klimax*, ladder]
The final and stable plant community in a series of stages of development, which is self-sustaining and in EQUILIBRIUM with its environment. The closer to the climax the vegetation of a region is, the slower it changes (and the longer it takes to regenerate once destroyed). 'Potential climax' describes the vegetation that ecologists have deduced would grow in a location if it were allowed to regenerate without human influence (for Manhattan this is mixed oak forest, for Westminster broad-leaved floodplain forest). 'Monoclimax' describes a single vegetational response to a particular set of climatic and geomorphological circumstances; 'polyclimax' a number of alternative and parallel responses — the more usual situation. Some green-thinkers believe that the 'climax' idea can be extended to economic activities.

Clinical Ecology
[*c*.1950]
Medicine which attempts to take the patient's physical environment into account, particularly diet and exposure to environmental hazards. Practitioners of clinical ecology (who are mostly allopathically-trained doctors) believe that many so-called 'allergies' are in fact reactions to food additives, pesticides, and industrial pollutants. 'Athough it remains controversial, clinical ecology is gaining increasing support, particularly in the UK. A number of rigorous trials have been conducted in response to scepticism from medical science which substantiate the basic claims. In 1978, *The Lancet* carried a report entitled "Food allergy: fact or fiction?" which revealed the carefully conducted trials in a London hospital showing conclusively that the effect of food allergies was real, demonstrable and certainly not all in the mind, as some sceptics suggested' (David Harvey, 1986). *See also* ALLERGY, POLLUTION.

Closet
[*c*.1600. *Old French clos*, enclosure]
A small cupboard; a symbol of the isolation that many people (who hitherto felt they were odd and alone in their choices and visions) are breaking out of.

Clothes
[before 12c. *Old English clathas*, cloths]
Cut, shaped and stitched-together pieces of cloth that human beings cover themselves (and occasionally their dogs and horses) with.

Clothes fulfil an enormous variety of functions: warmth, comfort, decoration, protection, revelation, and a whole range of non-verbal messages about who we are and who we want to present ourselves as: 'Who said that clothes make a statement? What an understatement that was. Clothes never shut up. They gabble on endlessly' (Susan Brownmiller, 1986). While questioning the basis of fashion and conspicuous consumption in clothes, especially in the more obviously-exploitative areas of animal furs and sweated labour, Greens uphold the right of anyone to dress how they want, especially when this adds variety, colour and creativity to the way people look and behave. You cannot pretend, however, that you can easily escape the expectations and pressures of our culture, however noble the cause: 'To the extent that a feminist style does exist, it has to be understood as a sub-theme of the general fashion discourse. Boiler suits and dungarees are after all fashion garments, not just a feminist uniform. They are commercially marketed items of casual chic; and the contortions necessary in the lavatory, and the discomfort in cold weather of having to undress completely in order to relieve oneself, should prove conclusively that this form of dress is not worn to promote rational apparel, but to announce the wearer's feminism in public' (Elizabeth Wilson, 1985). 'Green bloomers? — Oh, no — green is a lovely shade. Any shade that is near to nature is dear to me' (Ruth Draper, 1913). *See also* NAKED.

Club Of Rome
[1968]
A small elitist group of scientists, teachers, economists and industrialists who met on a regular basis from April 1968 onwards to examine and report on the 'predicament of mankind' (the name comes from the fact that the group met first in Rome). The most influential aspect of their work has been the book *The Limits to Growth* (1972), based on an elaborate computer modelling of the inter-relatedness of such aspects of growth as human population, food, resources, industrial output and pollution. The group had rather grandiose plans for 'a controlled, orderly transition from growth to global equilibrium', but the overall message that there are indeed limits to growth was heard by many influential people. *See also* GROWTH, LIMIT.

Coalition
(*see* ALLIANCE)

Co-Counselling
(*see* COUNSELLING)

Co-Creation
[*c*.1972]
Creating something together with the thing being created. Gardening is a good example, where nature works for the gardener just as much as the gardener works with the garden: 'To co-create with nature will result in a garden which embodies the vision of the gardener fused with the essence of the place. As an entity the garden takes on a life of its own. Its character is particular to itself, distinct from its surroundings without ceasing to be a part of them. While remaining an embodiment of nature, it is as objective as any work of art. It is unique as the fused substance of a person and a place' (Margaret Elphinstone and Julia Langley, 1987).

Co-Evolution
[1965]
Things and ideas which evolve together. A term first used in ecology to describe the reciprocal relationship between two species or groups of organisms, and later in green-tinted philosophy and the NEW PHYSICS: 'As individuals we live, so to speak, in co-evolution with ourselves, with our own mental products. At the moment in which the evolutionary process . . . has become concentrated with us . . . it also concentrates spatially within us. The self-reflexive mind not only relates the whole world to the individual, it also relates the individual to the whole world' (Erich Jantsch, 1980). For many people their main association with co-evolution is the magazine *Co-Evolution Quarterly*, published in California from Spring 1974 to the end of 1984, before incorporating *The Whole Earth Software Catalog* and becoming *Whole Earth Review*.

Co-Generation
[1978]
(*also* 'CHP', 'combined heat and power')
The simultaneous production of electricity and low-grade heat from power stations sited near residential and industrial consumers. As well as being much more efficient than electricity-only generating stations (typically returning 70-80% of the energy input, compared with 35% in an ordinary power station), they can easily use domestic waste as a fuel source. Major CHP installations have been built in Berlin, Birmingham (England), Budapest, Copenhagen, Hamburg, Helsinki, Milan, Moscow, Munich, New York, Odense, Oslo, Paris, Rotterdam, Stockholm, Vienna and Warsaw, and many more are planned. *See also* MINICHIP.

Cohabitation
[16c. *L cohabitare*, to live together]
Living together. 'Cohabitation' usually refers to two people who live

together as a COUPLE, usually assumed to be a woman and a man who have chosen not to be married. Cohabitation is rapidly becoming more popular as a preferred alternative to marriage, and is rapidly losing its social stigma, yet it too often perpetuates all the limitations of marriage, sometimes without the legal protection of individual (especially women's) rights that marriage confers (though the rights conferred on women by marriage, such as joint ownership and inheritance rights, can be offset by the rights that marriage takes away, such as tax and welfare benefit rights, and the right not to be assaulted by the man you live with). 'There are many jokes about what you call your unmarried partner — consort, companion, special friend or meaningful associate — but no universal term. This is perhaps a reflection of the diversity of relationships which flourish, but it may also be that the language needs to catch up with the changes that are taking place. We have used a variety of words — lover, partner, the person you live with, cohabitant. We prefer "cohabitant" to the more popular "cohabitee", since the latter seems to bear a more passive connotation. And we hope that [especially] for women, the move away from marriage is a positive step' (Rights of Women, 1981).

Collective
[1919. *L colligere*, to gather together]
A cooperative project. The term is most often applied to cooperative farms, after such farms were established in the Soviet Union after the First World War. 'A collective is a business, a non-profit or cottage "industry" where: workers hold all property and/or assets in common; workers share consensually in the key decisions affecting their lives and the direction of the enterprise; and a certain proportion of surpluses are used to help enrich community life rather than expand profits or markets' (Susan Campbell, 1983). *See also* COOPERATIVE.

Collective Self-Reliance
[1975]
The concept that even projects which aim at SELF-RELIANCE are not locally isolated, and that links with other similar projects must be made so that each complements all the others. *See also* BRIARPATCH NETWORK, DELINKING.

Collective Unconscious
(*see* UNCONSCIOUS)

Collusion
[*c*.1958 in this sense. *L colludere*, to play a game, deceive together]
An unconscious process in which one person supports the DISTRESS of another in the mistaken belief that a situation can thereby be improved.

This can be very draining and counter-productive in relationships and group activities, and especially in therapy sessions: 'Collusion between therapist and patient occurs when the therapist unconsciously allies with dysfunctional, defensive aspects of the patient's self in order to avoid dealing with areas that would be threatening to either the patient or the therapist' (Sue Walrond-Skinner, 1986).

Colonialism
[1853 *L colonus*, farmer, settler]
The domination of an indigenous people by people from elsewhere. A particular feature of the eighteenth and nineteenth centuries, when the European nations carved the world up into empires, only letting go of direct control when the problems, both economic and military, started to outweigh the advantages. Fifty-nine countries are still colonies or protectorates of Western countries; most are small (though not all, including Greenland and Namibia), and most have chosen to remain dependent for the present (though not all, including Estonia, Latvia and Lithuania). While ex-colonies are technically independent, all suffer from a capitalist hierarchy imposed by the occupying élite, and all continue to suffer from colonialism in its new guise — NEOCOLONIALISM.

Colonisation
[1903 in this sense. *L colonus*, farmer, settler]
(US: 'colonization')
The estabishment of an ecological community in an area which previously had little biotic activity, such as a seashore or lava flow. For the relationship between colonisation and colonialism, *see* COLONIALISM.

Colour
[1938 in this sense. *L color*, colour]
(US: 'color')
Having a skin colour which is not 'white'. 'People of colour' and 'women of colour' are terms which recognise that not-being-white is what links most people who are the objects of RACISM, and especially in the early 1980s were preferred descriptions by some people who felt that 'black' did not adequately explain their position. Others believe that they are not convincing terms, and bear too much similarity to the conventional usage of 'coloured people', with its oppressive history of use by 'liberal' racists, especially in South Africa and the USA. A less pejorative and more political term still needs to be found to describe people who have in common the experience of being subject to racism. Green-thinkers generally believe that whatever term is chosen by a group of people to describe themselves should be respected (*see also* NATIVE PEOPLES).

Combined Heat And Power
(*see* CO-GENERATION)

Coming Out
[*c*.1975 in this sense]
The process of acknowledging to yourself and to the world that you want to think and behave in a radically different way from most of the people around you; the phrase is most often used to declare a person's gayness, but by extension it can mean any form of openly-declared acknowledgement: 'Gay people have a special kind of loosening up; an act of self-affirmation we call "coming out". Philosophically speaking "coming out" means Free To Be I and Thou. It means the promise of Freedom, Justice, and Dignity. . . . So I was wondering, Mr. President [Reagan]: why don't you "come out"? Come out of Central America. Come out of the Caribbean. Yes, and while you're at it, why don't you try coming out of the Arms Race?' (Susie Day, 1984, in Cheris Kramerae and Paula Treichler, 1985).

Commensalism
[1870. *L commensalis*, at the same table]
A close association between two species which is beneficial to at least one species and harmful to neither. *See also* PARASITE, SYMBIOSIS.

Committees Of Correspondence
[1985 in this sense]
The main co-ordinating organisation of green politics in North America, founded in 1985 to provide a link between BIOREGIONAL and GREEN groups across the continent. 'The major Green political organization in the US, the Committees of Correspondence (which was the name for grassroots political networks in the American Revolutionary Era and several times since then), is not a third party but, rather, a regionally based movement working in various areas to advance ecological populism and . . . Green values' (Charlene Spretnak, 1986).

Common Ownership
[1951]
Any business in which all the people who work in the business own its capital resources and share its profits. *See also* COLLECTIVE, COMMONWEALTH, COMMUNITY BUSINESS, COOPERATIVE, EMPLOYEE STOCK/SHARE OWNERSHIP PLAN.

Commons
[1968 in this sense. *L communis*, common, general, universal]
Any NATURAL RESOURCE which is freely available (at least in theory) to anybody who wants to use it (known to economists as a 'common property resource' — common land in the UK is an example, as is the

ATMOSPHERE outside 'national air space', the OCEANS outside 'territorial limits', and the ability to reproduce — *see* REPRODUCTIVE RIGHTS). Whenever GROWTH and COMPETITION are the ethical basis of a human society, rather than SUSTAINABILITY and COOPERATION, the commons are constantly under threat, as the biologist Garrett Hardin elegantly showed in a 1968 *Science* article called 'The Tragedy of the Commons': 'The tragedy of the commons develops in this way. Picture a pasture open to all. It is to be expected that each herdsman will try to keep as many cattle as possible on the commons. Such an arrangement may work reasonably satisfactorily for centuries because tribal wars, poaching, and disease keep the numbers of both man [*sic*] and beast well below the "carrying capacity" of the land. Finally, however, comes the day of reckoning, i.e. the day when the long-desired social stability becomes a reality. At this point the inherent logic of the commons remorselessly generates tragedy. As a rational being each herdsman seeks to maximise his gain. Explicitly or implicitly, more or less consciously, he asks: "What is the utility *to me* of adding one more animal to my herd?" This utility has two components: 1. A positive component, which is a function of the increment of one animal. Since the herdsman receives all the proceeds from the sale of the additional animal, the positive utility is nearly +1. 2. A negative component, which is a function of the additional overgrazing created by one more animal. But since the effects of overgrazing are shared by all the herdsmen, the negative utility for any particular decision-making herdsman is only a fraction of -1. Adding together the component partial utilities, the rational herdsman concludes that the only sensible course for him to pursue is to add another animal to his herd. And another; and another . . . But this is the conclusion reached by each and every rational herdsman sharing a commons. Therein is the tragedy. Each man is *locked in* to a system that compels him to increase his herd without limit — in a world that is limited. Ruin is the destination toward which all men rush, each pursuing his own best interest in a society that believes in the freedom of the commons. *Freedom in a commons brings ruin to all.*' 'To bring about the tragedy of the commons it is not necessary that men be bad, only that they not be actively good' (William Ophuls, 1977).

Common Sense

[16c]

Sound, obvious and appropriate reflection and action, unhampered by excessive sophistication. Ecology has been called 'the common sense approach': 'During the industrial age, our confidence in the omnipotence of science and technology has led us increasingly to divert from the path that would have been dictated by the common sense embodied in our traditional culture and so admirably reflected in its proverbs.

Ecology, seen as an approach rather than as a scientific discipline, provides the rationale for a return to common sense. It is in terms of this approach that we should consider the basic problems that our society faces today' (Eugene Odum, undated). 'Academic and aristocratic people live in such an uncommon atmosphere that common sense can rarely reach them' (Samuel Butler (1835-1902), quoted in Rudolf Flesch, 1968).

Commonwealth

[15c. 'Shared wellbeing']

Commonly-shared WEALTH. 'Commonwealth' or 'common weal' describes any self-reliant and democratic community, though by official use of the word it has come to be used mostly in relation to the British Commonwealth of Nations, a loose affiliation of independent states and dependencies with a history of British rule, which was established in 1931 (*see* COLONIALISM). The term has also been used to describe various COMMUNITY (sense (2)) and COOPERATIVE projects, such as the Scott Bader Commonwealth, an early WORKERS' COOPERATIVE established in Northamptonshire, England, in 1951. The constitution of the commonwealth included undertakings concerning the maximum size of the business, maximum wage differentials, the role of workers as partners, full accountability of the directors to the workforce, allocation of a minimum proportion of profits as wage bonuses and donations to charity, and a commitment not to engage in war-related business.

Communality

[1901. *L communis*, common]

A sense of group solidarity, particularly associated with communal groups (*see* COMMUNE). 'Communality is the key element in a communal situation, and it is best grasped intuitively and inductively. Although it can be described as an intention in the mind of someone who is a member of a group to behave in a co-operative, sharing and perhaps loving way towards the other members of that group, there is no one clear and standard definition of communality. There are an infinite number of degrees of communality, springing from the individual and the group's level of commitment, emotional and environmental circumstances, personalities, means, etc.' (Clem Gorman, 1975).

Commune

[*c*.1800 in this sense. *L communis*, common]

A group of people with shared interests, living in the same place or area; thus very close in meaning to COMMUNITY (senses (1) and (2)). 'Communes' are the French equivalent of the British parish or US county, the level of real local government. Since about 1963 'commune' has been used to describe a group of people who decide to live together in an

ALTERNATIVE way, sharing property and being committed to each other's welfare. 'Between 1965 and 1970, more than two thousand communal groups were established [in the USA]. Only afterward was it called a movement. At the outset, it was the gut reaction of a generation. Hippie groups living a few country miles apart were unaware of each other's existence and equally unaware of the other utopian experiments in American history. They thought theirs was unique and unprecedented and scarcely knew what names to go by. Some were called tribes; others nests, affinity groups, collectives, intentional communities or simply families. Eventually most answered to commune, a term to which this generation would give new and broader meaning' (Robert Houriet, 1971). Since about 1970, more and more people throughout the world have decided to live in this way: 'Living communally has become almost commonplace in the United States, both in rural and urban areas. People are getting better at it, more systematic, clearer about why they do it' (Peter Woodrow, *Communities* magazine, 1981).

Communication
[*L communicare*, to make common, make known]
(1) [early 16c] Using words, sounds and body language in a clear way to share important needs and ideas. Any two human beings are capable of sustaining very real and meaningful communication given a willingness to believe that ATTENTION and careful LISTENING are an intelligent and humane way of conducting our affairs. There is in fact no other way of learning in depth and detail about experiences different from our own. Green-thinkers believe that communication is just as important in the non-human world too, where different species have evolved many ways of communicating which we may not acknowledge, let alone understand (*see*, for example, FOREST). 'Inter-species communication', which fascinated many people particularly in the 1960s and 1970s, is the exploration of ways in which human beings can communicate directly with other species, particularly apes and dolphins. *See also* HUNDREDTH MONKEY, SYNCHRONICITY.
(2) [17c] A mechanical or electronic [*c*.1900] way of transporting people, things or ideas (*see* INFORMATION, TRANSPORT).

Community
[*L communis*, common]
(1) [*c*.1600] A group of people who live in close proximity to each other, with some degree of interaction and mutual involvement in local events and affairs. Green-thinkers see community as an important antidote to the isolation and alienation felt by many Westerners, especially those who live in urban areas. 'Community has to be seen as a necessity of everyday life, not something to be artificially contrived. It will be the

work of generations to make real communities again. Mere decentralisation will not be enough, for that is a quantitative concept. It is from quality, rather, that community stems: from the rich diversity of life's forms (not its technical complexity): from human variety, not our uniformities. Community, it might be said, comes from the sharing of qualities' (Maurice Ash, 1980). 'Living in a small community therefore makes every kind of sense to me: living closer to other people, living more lightly on the land, using less, wasting less, becoming more attuned to the earth's rhythms, learning to be less dependent on the dominant society's economic institutions and so less attached by necessity to its values and demands — all these things taken together begin to form a picture for me of what life is supposed to be all about' (George Clark, *Communities* magazine, March/April 1971). Hence 'community action', 'community centre', 'community development'.
(2) [1844] A group of people who live together by choice; often called an 'intentional community' (*see also* COMMUNE). 'The Federation of Egalitarian Communities is a group of intentional communities spread out across North America. . . Because we share so much, and because our vision of commuunity is not limited to our individual groups, we have joined together in a functioning network which cooperates on conferences, publications, industries and a variety of other mutually supportive activities' (*Communities* magazine, May/June 1978). *Communities* is a magazine linking people with an interest in communal living, founded in the USA in 1973. There have been several 'come-unity' gatherings in the USA, the first in 1977, for people to share their experiences of communal life.
(3) [1883] A grouping of plants or animals occupying a HABITAT.

Community Business
[*c*.1970]
A small-scale community-based and community-controlled economic project. More than 500 Community Development Corporations are now operating in the USA, particularly among black and Hispanic groups, and there are more than 80 community businesses in Britain, 'usually trading organisations owned and controlled by the community, creating local jobs, providing local services and other schemes of community benefit' (Gemma Nesbitt and Andrew Tonks (ed), 1986). *See also* COOPERATIVE.

Community Ground Rent
(*see* LAND TAX)

Community Land Trust
[1970]
A community-owned and community-controlled trust which acquires

LAND to be held in perpetuity, then rents it out on long-term, low-cost leases, usually with conditions about its use which ensure the land's long-term ecological health. There are now more than fifty CLTs operating in the USA, which 'stands as concrete evidence that not even Americans need to *own* their land individually to care about it, to work it, and to build on it, knowing that the fruits of their labor ultimately go not only to their own posterity but to the posterity of the larger community as well' (Kirkpatrick Sale, 1985). *See also* LAND OWNERSHIP.

Community Levy
[1974]
A system of financing alternative projects from a fund created by a voluntary levy on people's income. 'As part of this self-conscious identification with the growing counter-cultural movement for an alternative society, *Peace News* began to publish the CLAP catalogue. This "Community Levy for Alternative Projects" was an experiment in alternative economics — a kind of mail-order catalogue of alternative projects which people were invited to support with donations by means of a "community levy" on their incomes' (Andrew Rigby, in Gail Chester and Andrew Rigby (ed), 1986).

Companion Planting
[*c.*1970]
The planting of certain crops alongside others to the mutual benefit of both. A form of gardening which has been practised for centuries, but which has only recently been named and received widespread recognition. *See also* INTERCROPPING, MIXED CROPPING, POLYCULTURE.

Compassion
[14c. *L compati*, to suffer with, sympathise]
An awareness of the hurt inflicted on another person or living thing, together with a desire to help to alleviate it if possible. In recent years it tends to have become associated with the suffering of ANIMALS in medical research and intensive farming. 'Mostly whoever advocates compassion for animals doesn't do so in the belief that it is more important than to advocate compassion for humans, but because animals have neither voice nor vote, because the foulness is too deep, the hypocrisy is too shameful for the human race. And at the end it will emerge that by helping the animals we shall also have helped [hu]mankind' (Hans Ruesch, 1983). Compassion in World Farming is 'an organisation to promote the introduction of non-violence into our relationship with farm animals, wildlife, the plant kingdom, and the soil itself' (Michael Barker, 1986).

Competition
[*L competere*, to strive together]
(1) [*c*.1600] Striving for the same thing. Used in ecology [1905] to describe organisms which need something which is not in adequate supply for all of them. In an environment in which the different elements of an ecosystem are balanced (*see* STEADY STATE, SUSTAINABILITY), 'competition' literally means 'striving together', in the sense that although some individuals will perish — and occasionally some species may become extinct — the dynamic equilibrium of nature does look after its continued overall wellbeing. When one element of the system, however, starts to dominate the rest at the expense of the whole, 'competition' takes on its usual anthropocentric definition of 'striving against', a race which some will 'win' and others will 'lose' (*see* sense (2)). This understanding of 'competition' now dominates our view of both the natural world (*see* EVOLUTION, NATURAL SELECTION) and human society (*see*, for example, PROGRESS, RACE, SOCIAL DARWINISM, WEALTH). Human beings have created technologies which allow them to live out of balance with the available resources (*see* DRAWDOWN), and have brought us to a situation where there are *not* enough resources for an ever-increasing human POPULATION, particularly if we think of human needs being at the level of AFFLUENCE which the West now enjoys rather than in terms of BASIC NEEDS. The competitive ethic which accompanies this growing realisation, though believed by most people to be part of HUMAN NATURE, in fact benefits nobody. The 'losers' cannot fulfil their basic needs, and the 'winners' find that staying 'at the top' is stressful, insecure and lonely. By making themselves different from the masses they lose the recognition they sought to gain, and become outsiders, both to society as a whole and to the planetary ecosystem which ultimately supports them. 'Competition' in human society is a travesty of its green meaning, and simply perpetuates OPPRESSION by dividing human beings from each other and preventing the SOLIDARITY that leads to real CHANGE. *See also* COOPERATION.
(2) [1618] An event organised such that one person will 'win' and all the others 'lose', both of which concepts green-thinkers would like to replace. *See* EXCELLENCE, GAMES, NEW GAMES, NON-COMPETITIVE, RACE.

Complacency
[mid 17c. *L complacere*, to please greatly]
Misplaced self-satisfaction in the face of problems which threaten to engulf you. It is vitally important to be positive and visionary, *and* realistic. 'I understand the attraction of Murray Bookchin's world [of "social ecology" and its naive faith in the goodness of "individual self-consciousness" (Murray Bookchin, 1980)]. This is the world my friend

spoke of as "being here already" — interdependent, non-hierarchical, diverse, gently transcending, viable, harmonised, tailored artistically to the ecosystem, the world we inhabit in leisure hours with our friends, our affinity groups. Colonel North and President Reagan live somewhere else in another world — with Mrs Thatcher, Norman Tebbit, Rupert Murdoch *et al.* But that world is *not* somewhere else' (Penny Newsome, *Green Line*, April 1987).

Complementarity
[1911. *L complere*, to fill up, complete]
A relationship between two things or ideas in which each complements the other to the mutual advancement of both. 'Living organisms display another pair of complementary dynamic phenomena that are essential aspects of self-organization. One of them, which may be described loosely as self-maintenance, includes the proceses of self-renewal, healing, homeostasis, and adaptation. The other, which seems to represent an opposing but complementary tendency, is that of self-transformation and self-transcendence, a phenomenon that expresses itself in the processes of learning, development, and evolution. . . . To understand this phenomenon, therefore, two complementary descriptions will be needed. One will have to include many aspects of neo-Darwinian theory, such as mutation, the structure of DNA, and the mechanisms of reproduction and heredity. The other description must deal not with the genetic mechanisms but with the underlying dynamics of evolution, whose central characteristic is not adaptation but creativity' (Fritjof Capra, 1982).

Complementary Medicine
[1981]
The range of healing practices and systems which can be distinguished from mainstream scientific medicine by their belief in the vital importance of the SELF-HEALING capabilities of the human body, and their general (though not universal) belief in the importance of a HOLISTIC approach to HEALTH. 'The aggregate of diagnostic and therapeutic practices and systems which are separate from and in contrast to conventional scientific medicine' (Stephen Fulder, 1984). 'There is a subtle difference of emphasis between complementary medicine and the other widely used labels, alternative, fringe medicine or the more quasi-technical natural therapeutics. Each in its way points to the otherness of the therapies grouped under the headings which are, to a greater or lesser extent, distanced from conventional medicine according to their methods or underlying philosophies. . . . The idea that these therapies are part of a broader medical canvas, then, is implicit in the

term complementary medicine' (David Harvey, 1986). In 1984 an Institute for Complementary Medicine was founded in London.

Complexity
[1790. *L complexus*, entwined]
The quality of a SYSTEM which has very many components, all intricately linked with each other. The atomistic approach of scientism ('let's cut it up and look at it in detail') oversimplifies, and ignores the quality of SYNTHESIS within a complex system. The alternative holistic approach accepts complexity as a valuable quality of healthy systems, and interferes with those systems as little as possible. It is well-established within ecology that complex systems are far more dynamically stable than simple ones, and this applies to human systems too. *See also* NETWORK, WEB.

Compost
[late 16c. *L compositus*, put together]
A mixture of ORGANIC leftovers which is allowed to break down by the action of micro-organisms and then used as a fertiliser. An essential element of organic gardening, and a good example of RECYCLING. Describing the work of Fritz Schumacher in a radio talk in 1987, Tony Benn characterised it as 'the philosophy of the compost heap'. 'To encourage local townships to establish composting programmes, the Broome County landfill in upstate New York banned leaves from its premises effective September 1, 1986, and is considering banning all vegetative wastes from the landfill by 1988. In New Jersey, a program of state-sponsored economic incentives has spurred more than 80 municipalities to develop leaf composting and mulch programs' (*Worldwatch*, 1987).

Compromise
[16c. *L compromissum*, the mutual agreement to abide by a negotiated decision]
A concession to a policy or course of action known not to be ideal, but which appears to be attainable in the circumstances. Currently a great source of concern among green-thinkers, especially in West Germany, where the question of compromise has caused something of a rift between the FUNDAMENTALISTS and the REALISTS.

Computer
[*c*.1955 in its modern sense. *L computare*, to reckon together]
A small programmable electronic device capable of many complex mathematical, word-processing and control functions; thought by some people to be capable of almost anything, and by others to be potentially

the most dangerous of recent inventions. 'The first and most favoured response offered by the technologist is that the computer is simply a neutral machine that can be used for either good or evil . . . The assertion is irrelevant and misleading' (David Burnham, 1983). Green thinkers find computers invaluable for many purposes, from producing information sheets and printing address labels to computer models of atmospheric circulation which predict the distribution of acid rain and the assessment of pollution levels in seawater. Many computer systems, however, are developed especially for weapons control, 'intelligence' operations, for use by price forecasters in multinational corporations and by generals under Cheyenne Mountain. Several aspects of micro-technology concern green-thinkers:

— computers are fallible, both in terms of what they are programmed to do and the way they are programmed to do it, and (though engineers will often deny it) in their internal workings. To prove the point you only need to disrupt the power supply or poke a pointed instrument among the microchips.

— overdependence on computers often has people reaching for the calculator to do a simple multiplication, and facing queues at the airport terminal or bank counter because 'when the system's down we can't do anything'.

— computers provide those in authority and control with immediate access to a great deal of INFORMATION about our 'private' lives which, despite data protection legislation, can be used — usually without our knowledge — to discriminate against us, decide our credit rating, check up on our health record, and a host of other information both accurate, inaccurate, and inferred.

— like other TECHNOFIXES, microsystems involve the use of quantities of non-renewable resources. The popular myth is that before long computers will be able to build themselves, but a computer will never be able to heal itself as a living organism does. Microtechnology will never free us from the NET ENERGY PRINCIPLE, though it may well use less energy than other methods to achieve the same results (we must always question, however, whether we actually *need* those results).

— just like any other technology, appropriateness is the key. Green-thinkers use computers when — with everything taken into account — they attain given ends with the least use of resources, the least harm, and the least effort. While profit remains the engine of microtechnology, appropriateness will always take a back seat: 'The electronic office? It's a bit like seeing the helicopter as a convenient way of dropping fodder to the cavalry horses in the battlefield' (Michael Bywater, *Observer*, May 1986).

Concerned Investment
(*see* SOCIALLY RESPONSIBLE INVESTMENT)

Conflict Resolution
[*c*.1965]
Nonviolent ways of dealing with practical matters of disagreement between individuals, groups and nations. Some green-thinkers see conflict as unnecessary in an ideal world, others see it as an essential part of life, 'a needed struggle for growth' (Cheris Kramerae and Paula Treichler (ed), 1985) (*see also* STRUGGLE). A great deal depends upon who defines the conflict and the terms of engagement, but where the conflict is resulting in violence there is obviously a need for nonviolent resolution. *See* MEDIATION, NEGOTIATION.

Confrontation
[17c. *L confrontare*, to border on, from *frons*, forehead]
Dealing with something head-on, face-to-face. Confrontation is sometimes an important and effective way of forcing something to happen, as for example in the confrontation of missile carriers by peace campaigners or the confrontation of whaling ships by Greenpeace activists. Confrontation, however, often implies AGGRESSION, BLAME, accusation and negative CRITICISM.

Connection
[14c. *L connectere*, to bind together]
A link between people, organisms, things or ideas; one of the most important green ideas, since it is by linking things together that new insights are gained, and it is by people making connections that new understandings emerge. 'Connections are made slowly, sometimes they grow underground./You cannot tell always by looking what is happening./More than half a tree is spread out in the soil under your feet./ . . . Weave real connections, create real nodes, build real houses./ . . . Live as if you liked yourself, and it may happen:/Reach out, keep reaching out, keep bringing in' (Marge Piercy, 1985).

Consciousness
[mid 17c. *L conscius*, sharing knowledge]
A state of immediate AWARENESS, CLARITY and INSIGHT, which often results in new UNDERSTANDING of what is really happening in the world around you. 'I regard consciousness as fundamental. I regard matter as derivative from consciousness. We cannot get behind consciousness' (Max Planck, quoted in Kenneth Walker, 1966). Some people talk about 'levels of consciousness'; in general, green-thinkers prefer to think in terms of a unified consciousness, but different degrees of awareness. 'Consciousness is painful. It robs me . . . of all the comfortable day-

dreams about the future . . . Consciousness leaves me with a void so big I could spend my life trying to fill it. But it has cleared some of the shit out, hasn't it. And made room' (Su Negrin, 1972).

Consciousness-Raising
[1971]
The process of sharing personal experiences in a small group of similar people which meets regularly over a long period of time. The purpose of the group is to raise awareness of people's different life experiences, and thereby to gain solidarity and become effective as agents of political and social change. Consciousness-raising (or CR) evolved within the women's movement in the USA in the early 1970s and spread rapidly, both within the women's movement and to other (mostly oppressed) groups. Feminist CR groups are now more often called 'women's groups'. 'Usually the CR group consists of between five and fifteen women who meet weekly for a specified period . . . Discussions may be helped by a facilitator, or the women may take it in turns to lead. Topics — for example, childhood experiences, mother-daughter relationships, marriage, sexuality, images of femininity — are usually decided in advance, and all the women are expected to speak from their own experience. Understanding rather than advice or criticism is the aim, and every woman's experience is equally valid and important' (Lisa Tuttle, 1986). *See also* CONSCIOUSNESS, EXPERIENCE.

Consensus
[1861 in this sense. *L consensus*, feeling together]
A group decision supported by all the members of the group. 'Should decisions at meetings be made by a majority, or by unanimous vote only? Or should a consensus be aimed at, where nobody objects strongly enough to veto a proposal, although not everyone may be absolutely in favour? . . . Consensus decisions are probably the best compromise since they embody the spirit of communality, yet do not involve a majority rough-riding over a minority' (Clem Gorman, 1975).

Conservation
[*c*.1870 in this sense. *L conservare*, to preserve]
The thoughtful use of RESOURCES (including natural resources both biotic and abiotic, and important parts of our historical heritage) in order to ensure that no unnecessary harm is done to them. Before 1955 'conservation' usually had the more limited sense of ensuring the continued survival of a particular resource, often an area of land or a species of wildlife. In 1956 the International Union for the Protection of Nature changed its name to the National Union for Conservation of Nature. In the 1960s many links were made between different aspects of resource use: conservation as an urban planning concept arrived in

1961, to be enshrined in the 'conservation areas' of the UK Civic Amenities Act of 1967; energy conservation appeared as an idea in about 1962 and was well-established by the mid 1970s. When Friends of the Earth was founded in 1969, 'conservation', its meaning not now requiring explanation, was claimed as one of its main concerns. 'Conservation' is a difficult idea to pin down because it has been used as the foundation for many conflicting views on resource use; like GREEN it has political and commercial appeal, and its use needs careful monitoring. 'There are three main kinds of conservation. First, to many, conservation is essentially the preservation and protection of those features of the environment thought to be of amenity value, such as fine buildings, landscape, wildlife, clean air and water . . . Some foresee the pollution of air and water reaching levels where our very existence is threatened and they regard the maintenance of environmental quality as much more a necessity than an amenity. . . .To others conservation means the planned use of resources to ensure their continuing supply, or at least their eking out until substitutes can be found' (Bryn Green, 1981). 'The briefest definition runs: Conservation is wise use, but this implies acceptance of the sophisticated assumption that non-use may be an acceptable type of use' (Max Nicholson, 1970). 'One of the most enduring myths about conservation is that it is apolitical. Nothing could be further from the truth' (Charlie Pye-Smith and Chris Rose, 1984). 'Conservation begins precisely where the pain and destruction of modern development are most keenly felt — in the parish, that indefinable territory to which we feel we belong, which we have the measure of' (Richard Mabey, 1980). The World Conservation Strategy was launched in 1980 by the International Union for the Conservation of Nature and Natural Resources, the World Wildlife Fund, and the United Nations Environment Programme: 'The World Conservation Strategy is based on three main objectives: (a) To maintain essential ecological processes and life-support systems; (b) To preserve genetic diversity, which is being dangerously impoverished; (c) To ensure the sustainable use by us and our children of species and ecosystems' (The Conservation and Development Programme for the UK, 1983). The Conservation Society is a UK organisation set up in 1966 to monitor conservation issues. *See also* PRESERVATION, PROTECTION.

Conservatism
(*see* NEW RIGHT, REACTIONARY)

Conservatory
(*see* PASSIVE SOLAR)

Conspicuous Conservation
[1977]
Making it clear that you live your life using ecologically-sustainable tools and techniques — solar panels on the roof, a good compost heap, carefully separated rubbish (*see also* CONSPICUOUS THRIFT, VOLUNTARY SIMPLICITY).

Conspicuous Thrift
[1964]
Making it clear that you have dressed yourself and furnished your home from second-hand shops, scavenging and making things yourself. The idea is the antithesis of 'conspicuous consumption' [1899], and was first coined by Nicholas Tomalin (1964). Now it is used mostly in relation to clothes: 'Today's Conspicuous Thrift has more to do with actual survival. The tendency now is for Conspicuous Thrifters to create an illusory effect of wealth and style while working almost entirely within the confines of old, secondhand and antique clothes that cost next to nothing. This takes persistence and knowhow' (Carolyn Chapman, 1984).

Consumer
[1745 in this sense. *L consumere*, to devour]
A person who buys goods and services, often assumed to have little, if any, direct control over economic policies, and therefore limited to choosing between the goods and services readily available. A concept open to a great deal of abuse. We all buy goods and services, so we are all consumers. Being a consumer is one of the essential roles we play, and we should demand certain rights as consumers, such as information about the different choices we can make, safeguards against dangerous goods, protection against misrepesentation, and the right to challenge the supplier if goods or services prove to be faulty. Yet 'consumerism' — the belief that the more we consume the better off we are — is anathema to green-thinkers. Capitalist enterprise justifies its activities by clinging to the myth of consumer sovereignty — 'we have to provide what the consumer wants', but the myth fails on several counts:
— people don't know what the real differences are between different products.
— with most items, there is very little real choice anyway, most of the apparent choice being in packaging and cosmetic differences.
— many products contain substances which can be harmful to human and environmental health, about which the consumer is given little if any information.
— the pressure from advertising and business is so pervasive that people often don't know the difference between what they need and

what they want.
— people often don't have the time or mobility to check out all the 'choices' that are theoretically available.
— the things people really need are often not part of the choice. The emphasis is always on 'value for money' rather than cooperation and conservation: 'Consumer advertising comprises a persistent series of invitations and imperatives to the individual to look after him [or her]self and his [or her] immediate family: self-interest becomes the social norm' (Fred Hirsch, 1977). Green consumers are beginning to make their real needs felt in many markets — why else would chemical additives be phased out, bulk-buy facilities be available in supermarkets, and lead-free petrol be increasingly available? We are all consumers, and combined consumer power is considerable. *See also* ADDITIVE, ADVERTISING, CHEMICAL, CONSUMPTION, GROWTH, PACKAGING, RECYCLING, WASTE.

Consumption
[early 16c in this sense. *L consumere*, to devour]
The amount of a particular RESOURCE used in a given period; by extension, the general concept of using large quantities of resources to produce large quantities of goods and large quantities of WASTE. As well as impoverishing the earth's resource base and prising the gap between rich and poor wide open, the worship of consumption has turned weapons manufacture, drug production and nuclear development into 'healthy growth'. There are, however, signs that things are beginning to change, largely because many consumers are becoming better informed, relatively poorer, and more discriminating.

Contact
[*L contingere*, to have contact with]
(1) [1834] Getting or keeping in touch. Contact between people, and contact between a person and their physical surroundings, are thought by many people to be basic and crucial human needs (*see also* TOUCH).
(2) [1931] The person in a group or ACTION who has the role of keeping the rest of the group informed.

Contamination
[*L contaminare*, to defile]
(1) [17c] The addition of TOXIC or dangerous substances to food, air or water (*see also* ADDITIVE, CHEMICAL).
(2) [1913] To make something RADIOACTIVE by the accidental discharge of radioactive material.
See also POLLUTION — the two are often used interchangeably.

Contraception
[1886. *L contra-* + [*con*]*ception*, against conception]
The deliberate prevention of impregnation during sexual intercourse. Often used synonymously with BIRTH CONTROL, though the distinction is made by some people (especially women, who are often tacitly assumed by men to be looking after themselves and therefore to have 'made arrangements') between pragmatic short-term contraception, and longer-term birth control, which includes male vasectomy.

Contributory Livelihood
[*c.*1975]
An economic lifestyle based on work that contributes to the wellbeing of the world while providing satisfaction to the person doing it. 'Our relationship with our work is enormously simplified when our livelihood makes a genuine contribution both to ourselves and to the human family. It is through our work that we find opportunity to develop our skills, relate with others in shared tasks, and contribute to the larger society. If our work is directly contributory, it can be a source of great satisfaction and great learning' (Duane Elgin, 1981).

Control
[15c. *Old French contreroller*, to regulate]
Having POWER over someone or something. Green thinking stresses the distinction between appropriate power-over — being in control of yourself, your actions and the tools you use, and oppressive and exploitative power-over — manipulating and forcing other people to do your bidding, or needlessly destroying and hurting the environment. *See also* AUTHORITY, BUREAUCRACY, EXPLOITATION, LAW AND ORDER, STATE.

Conversion
[*c.*1940 in this sense. *L conversio*, turning around]
Using the resources of weapons and ARMS industries to make SOCIALLY USEFUL PRODUCTS, thus ensuring continuity of employment and skills without the perpetuation of the means of mass destruction. 'The conversion approach towards disarmament stresses the potential common interests between peace and labour groups in diverting resources from military to civilian or social use' (Tom Woodhouse, in Gail Chester and Andrew Rigby (ed), 1986). 'Conversion specialists . . . help defense-oriented factories and businesses develop "alternative use planning" by encouraging the formation of joint committees of workers and management. They discuss switching from the production of weapons to that of products such as light rail vehicles, commuter aircraft, and alternative energy systems' (Fritjof Capra and Charlene Spretnak, 1984).

Conviviality
[17c. *L convivium*, living together, banquet]
Living and working together, and enjoying and being fulfilled by it. An idea which made a comeback with the appearance of Ivan Illich's influential though rather stodgy *Tools for Conviviality* (1973): 'People need not only to obtain things, they need above all the freedom to make things among which they can live, to give shape to them according to their own tastes, and to put them to use in caring for and about others. Prisoners in rich countries often have more access to things and services than members of their families, but they have no say in how things are to be made and cannot decide what to do with them. Their punishment consists in being deprived of what I shall call "conviviality". They are degraded to the status of mere consumers. I choose the term "conviviality" to designate the opposite of industrial productivity. I intend it to mean autonomous and creative intercourse among persons, and the intercourse of persons with their environment; and this in contrast with the conditioned response of persons to the demands made upon them by others, and by a man-made environment. I consider conviviality to be individual freedom realized in personal interdependence and, as such, an intrinsic ethical value. I believe that, in any society, as conviviality is reduced below a certain level, no amount of industrial productivity can effectively satisfy the needs it creates among society's members.' Hence 'convivial economy', 'convivial society', 'convivial tools' (*see also* TOOLS).

Cooperation
[1817 in this sense. *L cooperari*, to work together]
Working together to a common end. A fundamental green idea with strong ecological implications: 'There's no question about cooperation being the underlying principle of non-human life forms. . . There's also not very much question about cooperation having been the underlying principle of all early human societies' (Kirkpatrick Sale, 1985). 'Cooperation', perhaps surprisingly, is very close to COMPETITION in its literal and green senses, though in general use, 'cooperation' and 'competition' are seen as antithetical, as in practice they so often are. Green-thinkers believe that cooperation is basic to our HUMAN NATURE, and that competition is learned behaviour, a result of an ethical stance based on mistaken ideas about GROWTH and PROGRESS. 'Cooperation' is often used to describe a cooperative way of working together (*see* COOPERATIVE). 'The history of co-operation in Britain starts at the end of the 18th century, when groups of working men in various parts of the country set up co-operative corn mills to break the monopoly of the millers. Early in the following century Robert Owen showed at New Lanark that it was possible to run a large cotton mill at a profit without the total

exploitation and degradation of the workforce which was almost universal at that time' (*Workers' Co-operatives*, 1980). 'Cooperation' is a word which needs to be used carefully in an age when civil rights protestors are asked to 'cooperate' with the police and unfairly-dismissed workers to 'cooperate' with management.

Cooperative
[1883. *L cooperari*, to work together]
A group project operated for the benefit of all the members of the group, owned and directly controlled by those members. 'Cooperative' is usually qualified by a description of the nature of its operations — thus 'workers' cooperative', 'neighbourhood cooperative', 'community cooperative', 'marketing cooperative' and FOOD COOPERATIVE. In the USA the usual distinction (because they come under different federal and state laws and regulations) is between 'consumer coop', 'producer coop' and 'worker coop' — 'worker coop' is virtually synonymous with COLLECTIVE. For Britons the word 'cooperative' is most commonly associated with the Co-operative Wholesale Society (the Co-op), a movement rooted in the early experiments in cooperative working and trading (the first 'equitable pioneers' society' was formed in 1844), but which became very different in spirit and purpose through the years: 'By the mid-1950s the Co-op Movement, comprising the Co-operative Wholesale Society and more than 400 retail societies, was operating a system which has been called, perhaps unfairly, consumers' capitalism. Whatever it may be called, and whatever view may be taken of its merits, it bears little relation to the intentions of the Movement's founders in Rochdale, which somehow came to be ignored, or perhaps forgotten, as the movement developed' (*Workers' Co-operatives*, 1980). The International Cooperative Alliance was founded in 1966, and has outlined the most important principles of cooperatives:
— membership should be voluntary and non-discriminatory, open to all who can make use of its services and accept its responsibilities.
— the affairs of cooperatives should be run democratically, with equal rights in voting and participation.
— share capital should only receive a strictly limited rate of interest.
— the economic results of the enterprise should be shared fairly among its members.
— an important aim of any cooperative is the ongoing education of its members.
— cooperatives should wherever possible work with and encourage other cooperative ventures.
The cooperative movement is growing extremely quickly all over the world, especially in France, Italy and Spain, which have long traditions of cooperative ventures (*see* MONDRAGON). 'Coops which can attain both

economic and non-economic goals will succeed. They will in fact be a model for the new world where cooperation can be a strong, viable force' (*We Own It*, 1982).

Co-Ownership
(*see* COMMON OWNERSHIP)

Cop-Out
[1940s. US underworld slang for 'escape'; first used in the following sense around 1963]
The refusal, usually because of FEAR, to accept an important responsibility, take a stand where necessary, or to follow through a chosen course of action. Telling someone they are copping out is too often used as a way of blaming them, when what is really needed is active SUPPORT and SOLIDARITY.

Coppicing
[early 16c. *Old French copeiz*, from *Medieval L colpus*, blow, cut]
A method of conserving woodland resources, in which the young shoots growing from the stump (more properly called the stool, to distinguish it from a dead stump) of many varieties of deciduous tree can be cut on a regular basis for hundreds of years. 'Coppice and wood pasture husbandry of woodland are a means of maintaining a regular supply of firewood, charcoal, hurdles, fencing, chair legs and a wide variety of purposes which were once vital to rural industries. Undershrubs such as hazel, and most trees, will send out a mass of shoots from the stump or stool if first cut when young, and will continue to do so for many hundreds of years on rotations of 10-25 years depending on the species and thickness of poles required' (Bryn Green, 1981). *See also* POLLARDING.

Core
[*Middle English coor*, core]
(1) [*c*.1870] The central part of the earth.
(2) [1949] The central and most radioactive part of a nuclear reactor. *See also* ACCIDENT, CHINA SYNDROME, NUCLEAR ENERGY, RADIOACTIVITY.
(3) ('ice core' [*c*.1960]) Parts of the polar icecap which have been frozen for thousands of years, and which by chemical analysis can give us some idea of changes in terrestrial and atmospheric conditions over long periods of time.
(4) ('core group' [*c*. 1975]) A small group of people chosen to coordinate and make decisions on behalf of a larger group.

Cornucopian Vision
[1979. *L cornu copiae*, horn of plenty]
A view of the future in which, despite all the signs to the contrary, the

earth can continue to supply ever-increasing amounts of whatever human beings might desire: 'A view that sees our earth as a boundless horn of plenty that can never be depleted of its treasures. . . The prospect of indefinite material abundance is alluring to many and is an article of faith to such prominent futurists as Herman Kahn and Daniel Bell. . . The challenge, then, becomes to manage indefinite economic growth, rather than to prepare for imminent decline. . . The view . . . founders on the law of diminishing returns. [It] is an illusion born of abundance' (W. Jackson Davis, 1979). *See also* ABUNDANCE.

Cost-Benefit Analysis
[1963]
A technique evolved by economists which attempts to provide a 'rational' basis for decision-making by weighing up the VALUE of the cost of each alternative against the value of the benefits thus gained. The question of the siting of the third London airport in the early 1970s was one of the first attempts to use cost-benefit analysis on a large scale; during the investigation economists and planners tried to measure the economic and social benefits that would come from building a new airport on different sites, and the environmental, economic and social costs of each alternative. Economists frequently argue that using this technique to evaluate projects is at least better than using a technique that does not take both costs and benefits into account, but there are several important shortcomings to be considered. The most important criticism is that in order to be included in the calculation, both costs and benefits have to be measured, usually in money terms, which raises the question of value. During the London airport investigation, planners had to assess the 'value' of several medieval churches and a number of unique wildlife habitats — an impossible task (*see also* SOCIAL COSTS AND BENEFITS). A second criticism of cost-benefit analysis is that it appears to many people to provide a rational basis for decision-making, when in fact many of the 'facts' can be manipulated to provide the basis for any decision that those in power wish to take. Thirdly, and most importantly in many cases, cost-benefit analysis supposes that anything is negotiable, without seeing that some resources are finite and some costs completely unacceptable. For example, if a government proposes to base nuclear missiles in an area which contains the only known habitat for a particular sensitive plant, the whole concept of the usefulness of cost-benefit anyalysis only makes sense if you believe that nuclear weapons have any value at all, and if you believe that a price can be put on the extinction of a species. 'Cost-benefit' is sometimes widened in sociology and psychology (and in daily life) to 'risk-benefit', an analysis of human behaviour that depends on the assumption that human beings consciously 'weigh up' everything they choose to do: 'That a "benefit-

versus-risk" mentality has become the common coin of everyday discourse attests to the all-pervasiveness of a market economy. . . There is a cruel, indeed, ironic justice to this calculation. Each risk that a benefit incurs, each "lesser evil" bought at the expense of a principle, ultimately yields a universe of risks and evils that by far surpasses the original pair of choices that led us to this ill-conceived strategy' (Murray Bookchin, 1986).

Cottage Industry
[1921]
Work which is done in the worker's own home; usually refers to HOME-WORKING which is done in rural or semi-rural areas. Cottage industry can be either a liberation or a form of economic oppression.

Counselling
[1915. *L consulere*, to consult]
The usual definition is 'The giving of advice on personal, social, psychological, etc., problems as an occupation' (*OED Supplement*); although often trained in this role, many marriage and relationship counsellors, crisis counsellors, and work and vocational counsellors now see their role much more as that of an attentive and supportive friend while the CLIENT sorts out their own problems. The green definition of 'counselling' sees SUPPORT and ATTENTION as more important than advice, and might run 'Giving attention to a person for a set period of time while they explore their problems, and if appropriate express their feelings, thus enabling them to think more clearly about the matter in hand'. This is certainly the key to 'co-counselling', an important therapeutic and self-empowering technique developed initially in the USA in the 1950s, and now used by many green-thinkers in dealing with their feelings of powerlessness and thinking clearly about how the world may be changed for the better. The basic technique involves two people taking turns to give attention to the other; the client uses the time to explore issues, discharge the DISTRESS (which enables them to think clearly about the issue), and appreciate (*see* APPRECIATION) both themself and the insights gained. This emphasis on new insight ('re-evaluation') is acknowledged in the usual name for this technique, 're-evaluation counselling'.

Counteraction
[1971 in this sense]
Action which involves adopting clearly different solutions to those proposed by the mainstream, and which assumes that SOLIDARITY and COOPERATION are vitally important. Some green-thinkers see this as an important way of achieving the consistency of approach necessary for radical change: 'If every move, every action great and small, is based on

the same counteractive principle, it will be an element in a realistic revolution with room for everyone sharing the same basic outlook' (Erik Dammann, 1984). But who decides on the basic outlook?

Counterculture
[1968]
A culture which rejects many of the economic, social and moral values of mainstream culture. An idea brought to prominence by Theodore Roszak in his controversial book *The Making of a Counterculture* (1969), and picked on by the media as convenient shorthand to cover the vast range of people opting out of various aspects of the mainstream. It seems to have declined in popularity as a label in the last ten years, possibly for the same reasons as the demise of the HIPPIE, perhaps because the distinction between mainstream and counterculture has blurred: 'To a significant degree, the counter culture has become less visible over the last decade only because it has dissolved into its surrounding social medium' (Theodore Roszak, 1979).

Counter-Economy
[*c*.1971]
Alternatives to the mainstream economy; a very general term covering the COOPERATIVE movement, the HOUSEHOLD ECONOMY, APPROPRIATE TECHNOLOGY, VOLUNTARY SIMPLICITY and many other ideas and experiments involving a new approach to ECONOMICS. 'There is, after all, a very appropriate personal trade-off between striving for greater secular power and wealth and ego gratification, and taking the path toward expanded consciousness. Those of us in the counter-economy have opted for the latter — and consider it a bargain' (Hazel Henderson, 1978).

Counterintuitive Behaviour
[1968]
Behaviour which is the result of acting blindly to cure a symptom, without bothering to look for and deal with the underlying problem: thus we see traffic jams and think 'More roads!', or see increasing cancer rates and think 'More hospitals!'.

Country
(*see* STATE)

Countryside
[1727]
Areas of land where urban development is not immediately apparent. Most people who live in urbanised and semi-urbanised areas tend to think of countryside as not-town, forgetting that most of the world is countryside and most of its inhabitants country-dwellers; this is

particularly noticeable in the media which, being almost entirely urban-based, tend to view anything rural as second-rate, quaint, and eminently ignorable. This is oppressive to rural people, and overlooks how central land and the life it supports is to continued human existence. The countryside is where the people live who really keep human affairs going, those who grow the food and stay more or less in touch with the natural world: 'City people cannot live without country people. But they can certainly live without *knowing* them. Country people are usually behind glass: seen through a car or train window or on the odd farming programme on the TV' (Herbert Girardet (ed), 1976). Increasing pressure from urban development led to planning legislation in many Western countries immediately after the Second World War; the impetus for much of this legislation was that the countryside was at risk. In the UK, the first 'Countryside in 1970' conference was held in 1963, resulting in the Countryside (Scotland) Act 1967 and the Countryside Act 1968, which brought the Countryside Commission into being. 'Countryside' is often used synonymously with 'agricultural landscape'; thus the UK Scott Committee Report of 1942 stated that 'the land of Britain should be both useful and beautiful, and . . . the two aims [agriculture and countryside] are in no sense incompatible. The countryside cannot be "preserved" . . .; it must be farmed if it is to retain those features which give it distinctive charm and character.' This is not the view of most green-thinkers, especially as the nature of farming has changed so radically in the last forty years. *See also* ACCESS, AGRICULTURE, AMENITY, TRAVEL, WILDERNESS.

Couple
[13c. *L copula*, bond, link]
Two people, usually assumed to be a woman and a man, in a tight and exclusive RELATIONSHIP. Being a couple is seen in conventional terms as the 'natural' way for people to live their lives. But many green-thinkers question the benefits of this way of relating, especially when it creates a rift between coupledom and the increasing number of people who choose or are forced to live alone (*see* SINGLE). 'Couplism' [*c*.1980] has been coined to denote the oppression of single people by a society in which coupledom is the 'norm'.

Courage
[14c. *L cor*, heart]
The STRENGTH and confidence to think and act in a righteous cause. 'Have the courage to live. Anyone can die' (Robert Cody, in Lawrence Peter (ed), 1977).

Cowboy Economy
[1966]
A system of economics which sees resources as limitless, and the solution to all our problems just over the next hill. 'The closed earth of the future requires economic principles which are somewhat different from those of the open earth of the past. For the sake of picturesqueness, I am tempted to call the open economy the "cowboy economy", the cowboy being symbolic of the illimitable plains and also associated with reckless, exploitative, romantic, and violent behaviour' (Kenneth Boulding, in Henry Jarrett (ed), 1966). Often contrasted with the 'spaceman economy' (*see* SPACESHIP EARTH).

Craft
[*Old English cræft*, power, skill]
(1) [before 12c] A particular skill; more especially, a manual or healing skill. This use of the word has sometimes led to a distinction between craft and 'art': 'art' is what artists make, while 'craft' is reserved for more mundane (literally 'earth-related') products and services. 'A term used by men to demote, from fine art, the work of women who use fabric and stitches rather than paint' (Marsha Rowe, in Cheris Kramerae and Paula Treichler (ed), 1985). Many green-thinkers are concerned with the loss of craft skills as a result of mechanisation and DESKILLING: 'The breakup of craft skills and the reconstruction of production as a collective or social process have destroyed the traditional concept of skill and opened up only one way for mastery [*sic*] over labour processes to develop: in and through scientific, technical and engineering knowledge. But the extreme concentration of this knowledge is in the hands of management' (Harry Braverman, 1974).
(2) [13c] Involvement with witchcraft, often referred to as 'the craft'. *See* WITCH.
(3) [*c*.1900] A product, usually hand-made, of a COTTAGE INDUSTRY (often in rural areas), and sold mostly to tourists. Hence 'craft guild', 'craft industry', 'craftwork'.

Creative Simplicity
[1977]
Another name for VOLUNTARY SIMPLICITY.

Creativity
[1875. *L creare*, to produce, make]
The quality of receptivity and FLOW that allows a person to make or work at something with zest and imagination. 'We have been hoodwinked somehow into believing that creativity is in a separate category from the simple acts of daily life. Art is something you do in a crafts studio or

a writer's workshop. We dispatch our housework as swiftly as mechanization and frozen dinners will let us so that we can hustle off to a class to get recharged with a few hours of "creativity." Meanwhile, to support this pattern of life, we Westerners are consuming the lion's share of world resources, and time is ticking out for the poor people of the world — and, just a little more slowly, for ourselves. Surely our "creativity" need not have so high a price. Why compartmentalize our lives so that art is a thing apart? There is an artistic way to carry out even the simplest task, and there is great fulfilment to be had from finding out that way and perfecting it' (Laurel Robertson, Carol Flinders and Bronwen Godfrey, 1976). 'Creativity in adults stems from the same sources and has the same motivations as the creative play of children. It stems from the desire for pleasure and the need for self-expression. It is marked by the same serious attitude that characterizes children's play. And like children's play, it is productive of pleasure' (Alexander Lowen, 1970). It is sometimes asserted that women do not produce important art because their creativity goes into having babies and looking after them. Women do produce important art despite the strictures of PATRIARCHY — having it acknowledged is another matter.

Crèche
[1854. *French*, from *Germanic krippja*, crib]
A day NURSERY or CHILDCARE facility, usually for pre-school children, to enable the parents (most often the mother) to work, shop, or take part in an event. The strictly accurate spelling is crèche, though creche and crêche are also found.

Credit Union
[*c*.1920]
A small cooperative banking organisation, formed by a group of people living or working in the same area, which encourages its members to save regularly and lends money to its members at low interest rates. The first credit unions took the form of 'people's banks' in Germany in the 1860s, though it was in the 1920s and 1930s that credit unions became vitally important, especially in the USA during the Depression years; most Western countries now have specific legislation to cover credit unions. Poorer people often find it hard to obtain credit at low interest rates, and credit unions provide this service at the same time as keeping local savings within the community.

Crisis
[*Gk krisis*, turning point, decision]
(1) [15c] A vitally important or decisive point in time. As H. Fowler points out in his book *Modern English Usage*: 'The proper meaning of the word is a state of affairs in which a decisive change for better or

worse is imminent. Used loosely for any awkward, dangerous, or serious situation it is a slipshod extension'. 'Crises, be they of a global or personal nature, can either be seen as times of extreme danger and even destruction of life, or they can herald the birth of new beginnings. A time of crisis can be an opportunity to learn from our past mistakes and make the move into a more mature relationship with life' (Michael Lindfield, 1986).
(2) [*c*.1965] A decisive point in the history of the world due to the pressures being made upon the planet's resources, hence 'environmental crisis', 'population crisis', 'crisis management' and 'ecocrisis'. 'At the beginning of the last two decades of our century, we find ourselves in a state of profound, world-wide crisis, whose facets touch every aspect of our lives — our health and livelihood, the quality of our environment and our social relationships, our economy, technology and politics. It is a crisis of intellectual, moral, and spiritual dimensions; a crisis of a scale and urgency unprecedented in recorded human history. For the first time we have to face the very real threat of extinction of the human race and of all life on this planet' (Fritjof Capra, 1982).
(3) [*c*.1978] A critical time in a person's life; more specifically, one that is brought about by physical or mental abuse, hence 'crisis centre', 'crisis counselling'.

Criticism
[*c*.1600. *Gk krinein*, to separate, choose, discern]
FEEDBACK designed to help people to assess themselves and their achievements, given out of respect and careful discrimination; by extension, the careful evaluation of something which a person has created. While it can be extremely useful to know what someone else thinks of you, your actions or the things you have created, criticism can be negative, oppressive and even vicious. 'Critique' is better, implying some acknowledgement that what is being said is the critic's opinion rather than something intrinsically wrong with what is being assessed; 'feedback' is even better, allowing both parties to distinguish between valid and helpful criticism, invalid criticism which is often in fact projection, and straight putdown. For many people, criticism implies rejection, a feeling which often stems from childhood experiences. When these feelings have been expressed, however, and critical feedback can be handled in a creative and loving way, criticism can be a very powerful tool for change: 'Instead of feeling unloved, you can experience criticism as a gesture of regard rather than attack. You can understand that criticism need not stem from someone's low opinion of you — that it can stem from respect or compassion, from a wish to reach out and make contact, from a desire to improve communication and deepen understanding. Criticism can provide a demonstration of

someone's clear and loving regard for you as a person in your own right' (Anne Dickson, 1982).

Crop
[14c. *Old English cropp*, cluster, bunch, ear of corn]
(1) Plants grown for human or animal consumption, hence 'food crop'; sometimes also used to describe animals.
(2) The amount of living material in a part of an ecosystem, usually termed 'standing crop'.

Culture
[15c. *L colere*, to cultivate]
The values and lifestyle of a particular group of people, hence 'Western culture', 'American culture', 'hippie culture', 'counterculture'. A vague term, but there is no useful equivalent. 'We need to rediscover our roots and our histories, and to learn from those cultures which are more in harmony with their environment than we are. We must stop imposing our values on native peoples as though we had all the answers for them — we don't. Through our imperial efforts we have forced people to abandon ways of life which were often more satisfying than we can ever imagine' (British Green Party, 1987).

Cure
[14c. *L cura*, care, charge, healing]
A course of action which leads to a return to HEALTH. Such a definition, of course, depends upon your definition of health — many medical practitioners (and patients) tend to see a 'cure' as something that simply gets rid of symptoms, and disregard the underlying cause of the DISEASE. It is central to holistic HEALING that any cure ultimately depends upon the CLIENT, and that it is unrealistic to expect any practitioner to be able to cure you without your active involvement in the healing process.

Cybernetics
[1948. *Gk kubernetes*, pilot]
The theory and practice of control systems, especially of self-regulating control systems and the way that information is conveyed around such systems, both natural and artificial. Central to the GAIA hypothesis is that the Earth's atmosphere is part of an integrated self-regulating BIOSPHERE: 'It appeared to us that the Earth's biosphere was able to control at least the temperature of the Earth's surface and the composition of the atmosphere. *Prima facie*, the atmosphere looked like a contrivance put together co-operatively by the totality of living systems to carry out certain necessary control functions. This led us to the formulation of the proposition that living matter, the air, the oceans, the land surface were part of a giant system which was able to control

temperature, the composition of the air and sea the pH of the soil and so on as to be optimum for survival of the biosphere' (James Lovelock, 1979). Some green-thinkers have pointed out that cybernetics can become just as mechanistic as the more mechanical models it replaces: 'That it could be regarded as another form of mechanism — electronic rather than mechanical — seems to have eluded most of its acolytes. . . A deadening vocabulary of "information," "inputs," "outputs," "feedback," and "energy" has replaced such once-living terms like "knowledge," "dialogue," "explanation," "wisdom," and "vitality," a substitution that has occurred in blissful ignorance that cybernetic technology was largely born with wartime research into radar and servo-mechanisms for military guidance systems' (Murray Bookchin, in Michael Tobias (ed), 1985).

Cycle
[14c. *Gk kuklos*, circle]
A series of events that recurs regularly, returning to a similar 'starting point' after a particular length of time. The natural world works in many cycles — seasonal, lunar, diurnal (daily); birth, death, decay and rebirth; the flow of nutrients and elements in the biosphere. In Western society cyclicity has often been driven underground, especially in urban communities, so that menstruation has become a dangerous and embarrassing taboo, the SEASONS an annoying irrelevance, and day and night virtually indistinguishable in terms of human activity. 'In the Circle of Life every being is no more, or less, than any other. We are all Sisters and Brothers. Life is shared with the birds, bears, insects, plants, mountains, clouds, stars, sun. To be in harmony with the natural world, one must live within the cycles of life' (Stan Steiner, 1976). Some processes that are called 'cycles' are not true cycles, but an attempt to pretend that human beings can beat the NET ENERGY PRINCIPLE — thus 'energy cycle' and 'nuclear fuel cycle' and, to a large extent, RECYCLING. *See also* BICYCLE, BIOGEOCHEMICAL CYCLE, HYDROLOGICAL CYCLE, NITROGEN CYCLE.

Dd

Dance
[14c. *Old French danser*, to dance]
A series of patterned movements over time, usually referring to movements of the human body accompanied by music or rhythm, but by extension used to describe dance-like qualities found in nature, from particle physics to the movement of heavenly bodies, with the whole flow and movement of nature in between. Thus 'sacred dance' or 'circle dance', dancing which consciously acknowledges the links with the earth and between people. 'We are dancing on the brink of our little world of which we know so little; we are dancing the dance of life, of death; dancing the moon up in celebration of dimly remembered connections with our ancestors; dancing to keep the cold and darkness of a nuclear winter from chilling our bones; dancing on the brink of ecological awareness; dancing for the sake of dancing without analyzing and rationalizing and articulating; without consciously probing for meaning but allowing meaning in being to emerge into our living space. Dancing has always been part of living for primal peoples. For us, the dance may be a Ghost Dance for all that is lost: condor, bison, redwood, watershed, wolf, whale, and passenger pigeon. Or it may be the dance of a new revelation of Being, of modesty and Earth wisdom on the turning point' (Bill Devall and George Sessions, 1985).

Death
[before 12c. *Old English death*]
The transition between the complex activity we think of as LIFE and the state in which an organism has no clearly separate identity (usually thought of as being 'dead'); part of a basic and vital natural CYCLE: 'But everything must die, or nothing would be renewed' (Margaret Elphinstone, 1987). A clear definition of death is virtually impossible in biological terms; as Lyall Watson pointed out in *The Romeo Error* (1974): 'Ask most biologists to define death and you learn that it is "an

absence of life". Ask for a definition of life and you get almost as many answers as there are practising biologists.' He concluded 'that the two states are almost indistinguishable, that they exist together in varying proportions along a sliding scale with no fixed points. . . . I am becoming convinced that it no longer makes biological sense to even try to discriminate between life and death at any level.' This may seem difficult to square with green-thinkers' emphasis on the importance of life — the group 'Women for Life on Earth' being one example — but this would be to misunderstand the meaning of 'life' in green terms, which is far more than the mere absence of death. 'I want nothing left of me for you, ho death/cxcept some fertilizer/for the next batch of us/who do not hold hands with you/who do not embrace you/who try not to work for you/or sacrifice themselves or trust/or believe you, ho ignorant/death, how do you know/we happened to you?' (Judy Grahn, quoted in Susan Griffin, 1984). *See also* ABORTION, DEATHING, EUTHANASIA.

Deathing
[1984]
An aware and sensitive approach to your own or somebody else's DEATH (by analogy with BIRTHING). 'I propose a modern craft of dying — a right and conscious way of dying — which I call "deathing". Right deathing is a method, an attitude, a collection of certain concepts. It is a technique acquired through concentrated preparation and practice before the death moment. Ordinarily when people die they are unprepared and uninformed; probably they are bewildered or frightened, especially if they are alone. Deathing can offer a way to free up dying people so that they can utilize the highest potential of the transition called death and experience it as a peak moment, a culmination of life' (Anya Foos-Graber, 1984).

Debt Crisis
[1985]
A situation in which a region, a country, or a large sector of the population of a country find it increasingly difficult to repay money lent to them; this in turn leads to economic difficulties among lenders. Most often used to describe the debt problems faced by Third World countries. 'The principal obstacle to Third World progress, one caused in part by ecological degradation, is mounting external debt. International financial institutions have been reluctant to recognize that scores of developing countries have crossed their debt-servicing thresholds. Private banks fear they will have to write off so many bad loans that it will greatly reduce their earnings and even threaten their solvency. Nonetheless, a substantial share of the Third World's $800 billion external debt will never be repaid' (*Worldwatch*, 1986). It is not only the Third World, however, that faces a debt crisis. Many observers

predict that a large proportion of the US farm debt (money lent to farmers) of more than $200 billion will never be repaid, and with the growth of consumer credit coupled with rising unemployment, an increasing number of people are finding it hard to service their personal debts. 'Not only will the Third World debt bomb be detonated by the next recession, but consumer credit, corporate debt, and various level government debts, now receiving much less attention than their dangers merit, may also explode and the detonation of any one of them can explode any or all of the others and accelerate the development of the next recession' (André Gunder Frank, 1984, in Victoria Brittain and Michael Simmons (ed), 1987). *See also* AID, DEVELOPMENT.

Decentralisation
[1846]
(US: 'decentralization')
The movement of people, businesses, functions and services away from the centre. 'To facilitate greater participation by citizens, the Greens [die Grünen] advocate decentralizing and simplifying administrative units with a greater share of government revenues going to states, regions, counties, towns and neighbourhoods' (Fritjof Capra and Charlene Spretnak, 1984). Decentralisation involves both movement away from the urban centre of an area, and the dispersal or delegation of functions within an organisation or NETWORK.

Decision
[15c. *L decidere*, to cut off, determine]
A conscious CHOICE to take (or not to take) a particular action or set of actions. 'Moral intelligence demands a nearly endless exercise of the ability to make decisions: significant decisions; decisions inside history, not peripheral to it; decisions about the meaning of life; decisions that arise from an acute awareness of one's own mortality; decisions on which one can honestly and willfully stake one's life' (Andrea Dworkin, 1983). 'It is better to stir up a question without deciding it, than to decide it without stirring it up' (Joseph Joubert, quoted in Rudolf Flesch, 1968). *See also* RESPONSIBILITY.

Decommissioning
[1926]
Taking a large piece of machinery or industrial plant out of active use. The decommissioning of nuclear power stations is of particular concern; because of the residual radioactivity, dismantling a nuclear power station involves far more than simply demolishing it. 'Nearly four decades and 350 power plants into the nuclear age, the question of how to safely and economically dispose of nuclear reactors and their wastes is still largely unanswered. . . . Not a single large commercial unit has

ever been dismantled. Nuclear engineers have been attracted to the exciting challenge of developing and improving a new technology, not in figuring out how to manage its rubbish. But as a growing number of plants approach retirement age, the problem of dealing with reactors that are no longer usable will demand attention. Not one of the countries currently relying on nuclear power is adequately prepared for this challenge' (*Worldwatch*, 1986).

Deduction
[16c in this sense. *L deducere*, to lead away, derive]
Drawing conclusions from general or universal premises (as opposed to INDUCTION, where conclusions are drawn from experimental observation).

Deep Ecology
[1973]
A profound wisdom and awareness of the connectedness of NATURE; sometimes contrasted with 'shallow ecology' (though the distinction is often a very hazy one), and the basis of GREEN philosophy. 'The essence of deep ecology is to ask deeper questions. The adjective "deep" stresses that we ask why and how, where others do not' (Arne Naess, 1982, quoted in Bill Devall and George Sessions, 1985). 'Deep Ecology concerns those personal moods, values, aesthetic and philosophical convictions which serve no necessarily utilitarian, nor rational end. By definition their sole justification rests upon the goodness, balance, truth and beauty of the natural world, and of a human being's biological and psychological need to be fully integrated within it' (Michael Tobias, 1985). The basic principles of deep ecology vary from writer to writer, but include some or all of the following:
— harmony with nature is always better than dominance over nature.
— all forms of life have value in themselves, and do not depend on human evaluation of their worth.
— all forms of life have an equal right to existence and wellbeing (*see* BIOCENTRIC EQUALITY).
— human beings have no pre-ordained right to reduce the richness and diversity of nature.
— simplicity, sufficiency, sustainability and appropriateness should be the basis of human livelihood.
— resources should be cared for, harvested sensitively, and used only for essential needs.
— the basis of working both with nature and in human society should be naturally-defined regions (BIOREGIONS).
— quality of life should replace 'standard of living' in evaluating human wellbeing.
— human beings are individually and collectively responsible for

making the changes necessary to implement the perspective of deep ecology.
'The foundations of deep ecology are the basic intuitions and experiencing of ourselves and Nature which comprise ecological consciousness' (Bill Devall and George Sessions, 1985). *See also* ECOLOGY.

Defence
[14c. *L defendere*, to strike against, ward off]
(US: 'defense')
Looking after yourself — though many people believe it has no green meaning beyond taking care of your own integrity (*see* ASSERTIVENESS, SELF-DEFENCE, TRUST) and ensuring that other living things are not hurt unnecessarily (*see*, for example, COMPASSION, ECODEFENCE). In mainstream usage 'defence' means getting ready to attack (*see* ARMS, DETERRENCE, NUCLEAR WAR, NUCLEAR WEAPONS, NUKESPEAK, VIOLENCE, WAR). Some green-thinkers use the term SOCIAL DEFENCE to describe nonviolent ways of looking after the interests of yourself and your community (*see also* NONVIOLENCE); SELF-DEFENCE is learning to protect yourself from personal physical attack while hurting your assailant as little as possible. 'Defensiveness' is a reaction (more common in men than in women) to CRITICISM which involves actual or imagined verbal attack. It results from FEAR and ANGER, which if not dealt with creatively can result in AGGRESSION and VIOLENCE. 'De-fencing' involves taking down the fences around military and nuclear installations: 'De-fencing is the removal of barriers that divide us and thereby accommodate conflict' (Barbara Harford and Sarah Hopkins (ed), 1984).

Defoliation
[*c*.1940 in this sense. *L de-* + *folium*, leaf removal]
The destruction of the leaves of plants, particularly trees, thus causing them to die. The defoliation may be very deliberate, as in the use of defoliants during the Vietnam War, or it may result from POLLUTION or OVERGRAZING.

Deforestation
[1874]
The destruction of large areas of trees. Each year an area the size of England is deforested, most of this loss (though by no means all) being in the tropics, and deforestation is thought by many conservationists to be the most critical element of environmental degradation in many parts of the world. Many factors contribute to deforestation, including industrial timber production (*see* FORESTRY), clearance for agriculture (two thirds of Costa Rica's forests have been cleared to provide pasture for beef, most of which goes to the USA for hamburgers), plundering for fuelwood, fire, drought, strip mining, pollution (*see* WALDSTERBEN), urban development and warfare (*see* DEFOLIANT). Trees are essential to

the planetary ecosystem (*see* FOREST, RAINFOREST), stabilising the world's climate by soaking up radiation and water, and helping to maintain the oxygen/carbon dioxide balance. They hold soil in place and prevent flooding, and maintain ecological diversity within a GENE POOL of unimaginable proportions. The destruction must stop, and following successful campaigns by environmental pressure groups some small action is now being taken to conserve this vital resource, including an $8 billion investment in tree planting coordinated by the World Resources Institute. *See also* REAFFORESTATION.

Delinking
[*c*.1980]
Breaking the links of DEPENDENCY with neocolonial powers; an option being considered and acted upon by an increasing number of THIRD WORLD countries.

Demand
[*L demandare*, to commit to, entrust]
A claim to something as a right (or something thought to be your right).
(1) [13c] A claim to something known to be your right both as a human being with BASIC NEEDS and as part of a group of people with specific needs. Thus the 'Seven Demands of the Women's Liberation Movement': equal pay; equal opportunities and education; free contraception and abortion on demand; free 24-hour community-controlled child care; legal and financial independence for women; an end to discrimination against lesbians; freedom for all women from intimidation by the threat or use of male violence.
(2) [*c*.1600] An unaware and insensitive claim made on somebody else's time, attention and resources. Dealing creatively with demands of this sort depends upon clear communication and assertive response.
(3) [1711] A myth of economics, suggesting that 'demand' is the sum total of what CONSUMERS are willing and able to pay for a particular product or service. Thus 'demand for electricity' is measured by how much people are actually using, regardless of how much is being wasted and how many old people are dying of hypothermia. 'Future demand' is an even more questionable concept (*see* PROJECTION).

Demi-Veg
[1981]
Someone who eats very little meat and has a largely VEGETARIAN diet; also used to describe such a dietary regime.

Democracy
[16c. *Gk demokratia*, government by the people]
Giving everybody an equal say in how things are organised. This is not, however, what democracy means in its more usual sense, if it means

anything at all: 'Democracy is the most valued and also the vaguest of political terms in the modern world' (David Robertson, 1985). As it works in contemporary society, democracy is passive in the extreme; it gives people the 'freedom' to complain if they don't like what is going on — not that anyone will necessarily listen. True democracy is active participation: 'Freedom to complain about what's wrong in our society without the power to do anything about the problems is virtually meaningless. Thus, *freedom from* interference is only part of what democracy means. We must also have *freedom to* achieve what makes life worth living — the freedom to have safe and satisfying work; the freedom to enjoy security in the form of food, housing, and health care; the freedom to share in decisions affecting our workplace, community, and nation; and the freedom to share in the responsibility of protecting our resources for coming generations' (Frances Moore Lappé, 1980). 'The choice is more democracy or much less. The effective participation of people in making the decisions that most directly affect them is the precondition for economic, political, and spiritual liberation. Until people can play a direct role themselves in shaping their own physical and economic environment they are not fully alive' (Richard Barnet, 1980). *See also* PARTICIPATORY DEMOCRACY, REPRESENTATIVE DEMOCRACY.

Dependence

[15c. *L dependere*, to hang from]

Relying on somebody or something else for support, acknowledgement, or continued existence. Dependence means recognising connection while acknowledging self-reliance, understanding how we can provide each other with the attention, the warmth and the support that we need without believing that our well-being and happiness rely on the actions of someone else. Green-thinkers usually prefer to call this 'interdependence' rather than dependence, because it describes more accurately how we can fulfil our needs without becoming overdependent. The varieties of dependence include:

(1) The dependence of one organism or life form upon another (though it is important to remember that the relationship is rarely one-way).

(2) The dependence of a very young, ill or disabled individual upon an older, healthy or able-bodied one (and again, the relationship is rarely one-way). Hence the demographic concept of 'dependent', which relies heavily upon the assumptions that only wage-earning activity counts, and that dependents are automatically a liability, which is oppressive towards non-wage-earners.

(3) Unaware clinging to another person, relying on them for identity and approval. 'Dependents' are often put in this role (then blamed for being dependent); people in power do it just as much but pretend they don't.

(4) Physical and chemical dependence upon an addictive substance (*see* ADDICTION).

Dependency

[*c*.1976 in this sense. *L dependere*, to hang from]

The situation that THIRD WORLD countries find themselves in when they want to move towards greater SELF-RELIANCE, but find that COLONIALISM and NEOCOLONIALISM have made such a break extremely difficult. Not only are the tentacles of neocolonialism strong and widereaching; dependency has also undermined the locally-based alternatives to a point where there is often little to build on: 'Once colonialism has raked over a country, there is no such thing as a "traditional" culture left for economic planners to push into the present' (Frances Moore Lappé, 1980). 'Dependency' can all too easily overlook the fact that all transactions are two-way: 'Interdependence in the days of John F. Kennedy used to mean, as the President once put it, "the burden will be completely on us"; the American debt to the rest of the world was barely acknowledged. Dependency ran one way only. But in the 1970s the steep rise in the cost of imported oil, the growing dependence on imported minerals, and the enormous importance of foreign markets to the US economy dramatized how crucially dependent the US has become upon the rest of the world. The rediscovery of biological dependence was even more unsettling' (Richard Barnet, 1980).

Depletion

[17c. *L deplere*, to empty]

A reduction in the amount or quality of a resource to the point where a RENEWABLE RESOURCE cannot easily recover, or where a NON-RENEWABLE RESOURCE is used up.

Depression

[*L deprimere*, to press down]

(1) [*c*.1800] A period of extreme economic hardship. Economists like to think of it as 'a severe trough in the business cycle', which conveniently assumes that there will always be an upturn. 'In the United States, where depression was deepest, GNP fell from $104 billion in 1929 to $56 billion in 1933. Unemployment soared from 1.5 million to 12.8 million, one person in four was out of work. Nine million savings accounts were lost as the banks collapsed. $30 billion in financial assets vanished when the stock market crashed. One in five of all Detroit schoolchildren was officially registered as undernourished by 1932' (Robert Lekachman, 1981).

(2) [1803] A period of extreme emotional hardship which can take many forms, but usually involves feelings of DESPAIR, isolation, helplessness and defeat. More than twice as many women as men experience

periods of depression, mirroring the fact that 'women are depressed by their life experiences in greater numbers than men' (Kathy Nairne and Gerrilyn Smith, 1984). With the world being in the state it is, you don't need to look far for the roots of depression, and as Kathy Nairne and Gerrilyn Smith point out: 'We need to ask not "Why am I depressed?" but "How do I manage *not* to be depressed?" '.

Deprivation
[15c. *L deprivare*, to deprive]
Being denied access to basic human needs (*see* BASIC NEEDS); usually it is the most oppressed who are the most deprived. A useful word, since it is one of the few descriptions of OPPRESSION which is both 'media-acceptable' and clearly implies that somebody is doing the depriving (though this is not always a conscious link).

Depth
[14c. *Middle English depth*]
(1) An idea or approach which attempts to look more than superficially at an issue, hence 'depth psychology' [1927], an approach which acknowledges the importance of the unconscious mind, and DEEP ECOLOGY [1973] (and it would be surprising if more 'deep' studies didn't follow).
(2) The level of DESPAIR felt by many people when they let themselves feel the pain of their personal and planetary predicament. At such times it is worth thinking about the link between the different meanings of 'depth'.

Dereliction
[c.1960 in this sense. *L derelictus*, abandoned]
Large areas of land, previously used for industry (and sometimes housing), which have been abandoned and left to decay without any effort being made to rehabilitate them. 'Stewart Udall [in *The Quiet Crisis*, 1963] has warned "We are no more than brief tenants of this planet. By exercise of choice, or by careless default, we shape the land legacy of our descendants." . . Our grandfathers tore wealth from this land, willing us a prosperity devalued by dereliction. Are we to do the same for our grandchildren? If we do they will curse us and they will be right to do so' (John Barr, 1969).

Deschooling
[*c*.1970]
The belief (and resultant practice) that SCHOOLS as they are organised at present should be replaced with more broadly-based EDUCATION, integrated with rather than separated from society in general, based more upon what young people want to learn and more in harmony with

the real needs of the planet. The protagonists of deschooling believe that schools frequently do children far more harm than good, actually teaching them how to fail, taking away their freedom and creativity, and teaching them how to conform with an oppressive social, economic and political system. 'All over the world the school has an anti-educational effect on society . . . The failures of school are taken by most people as a proof that education is a very costly, very complex, always arcane and frequently almost impossible task' (Ivan Illich, 1971). 'Most children in school fail. . . . They fail because they are afraid, bored and confused' (John Holt, 1965). The whole deschooling movement has a distinct sexist bias, as Theodore Roszak (1979) points out: 'It occurs to me that there seem to be very few women among the . . . experimental educators. . . . Yet, the classrooms of the world have long been one of women's major professional provinces. What explains their absence among the voices of radical discontent?' Well, you could start with Ivan Illich's influential 1971 book, *Deschooling Society*, which ends as follows: 'We need a name for those who love the earth on which each can meet the other . . . I suggest that these hopeful brothers and sisters be called Epimethean men.'

Desertification
[1974]
The process by which land (mostly though not exclusively in arid or semi-arid areas) is stripped of its vegetation, usually by DEFORESTATION, OVERGRAZING, and inappropriate agricultural and irrigation policies. SOIL EROSION intensifies, and the area eventually becomes barren desert. 'A decline in the diversity of plant and animal communities marks the onset of desertification. This in turn leads to a reduction of soil organic matter, a decline in soil structure, and a loss of water retention capacity. It also lowers soil fertility, reduced further by increasing wind and water erosion. Typically the end result is desert: a skeletal shell of soil consisting almost entirely of sand and lacking in the fine particles and organic matter that makes soil productive' (*Worldwatch*, 1987). 'Of the Earth's ice-free land area, over one-third is already affected or likely to be affected by desertification' (Norman Myers (ed), 1985). 'Desertification proper is confined to arid and semi-arid areas of the world. But it is part of a much larger picture of soil erosion . . . Desertification spreads slowly from small nuclei until it eventually lays waste large areas. It feeds upon itself, creating arid areas where previously rainfall was plentiful. Treatment in the early stages has a good chance of success. But if no action is taken, either because people are too poor or because of a lack of political will, halting desertification becomes increasingly expensive. Eventually recovery may be impossible' (Alan Grainger, 1982).

Design

[late 16c. *L designare*, to mark out]

The envisioning of structures, networks and facilities for the benefit of human beings. 'The planning and patterning of any act towards a desired, foreseeable end constitutes a design process' (Victor Papanek, 1974). The problem with much design is that it has inappropriate goals, usually financial ones. Green design — 'design for the real world' (Papanek's phrase) — is intimately linked with appropriate technology and 'design with nature' (the title of a book by Ian McHarg (1971)). Some green-thinkers see 'design' as an alternative to 'planning': 'Planning refers to the attempt to produce the outcome by actively managing the process; [design] refers to the attempt to produce the outcome by establishing criteria to govern operations of the process so that the desired result will occur more or less automatically without further human intervention' (William Ophuls, 1977). Several further aspects of design concern green-thinkers:

— design is too often one compartmentalised role in the production of an item, often coming long after the overall outline has been developed. Thus specialist designers are not involved in the political decisions about appropriateness, and are too often asked to add the finishing touches (if not to cover up the mistakes!).

— the best designer is often the user, and there should at least be continuing dialogue between designer and user about the appropriateness of any design.

— design is far too often limited by what has gone immediately before, and despite apparent change we often continue to use wasteful and inefficient designs simply because ingenuity and inspiration have been held back to conform with artificial standards of 'good design'. This is particularly true of the design of living spaces and TRANSPORT systems.

Desire

[13c. *L desiderare*, to yearn for]

Passionate longing for something; often used (in the absence of a better word) to imply the longing for fulfilling and non-oppressive sexual experiences. 'Desire' has become the preferred word among many feminists (especially in the USA) to describe the search for what SEX is really all about, though there is still heated debate about whether there will be anything left to search for if oppression is overcome. 'Desire is ever renewed — still, in sexual satisfaction, we find moments of rest and vision' (Ann Snitow, Christine Stansell and Sharon Thompson (ed), 1983). 'Although the erotic relationship may seem to exist freely, on its own terms, . . it is, in fact, the most self-conscious of all human relationships, a direct confrontation of two beings whose actions in the bed are wholly determined by their acts when they are out of it' (Angela Carter, 1979). Can they both be right? *See also* PASSION.

Deskilling
[*c*.1980]
Replacing the use of individual crafts and skills by increasing automation and technology, thus depriving many people of meaningful work. While many skills are unnecessarily (and very shortsightedly) being done away with, some deskilling is inevitable if economic activity is to become less specialised and people add more skills to their 'portfolio' (*see* PORTFOLIO JOB). Where this is happening, deskilling needs to be accompanied by 'reskilling' — providing the opportunities for a person who has specialised skills in an area where they are not currently needed to broaden their skills so that their experience can be used to their own and others' benefit.

Determinism
[1846. *L determinare*, to set boundaries]
A philosophy based upon a belief that events have fixed, immutable and necessary results. A Victorian idea that has a nasty habit of surfacing in the policies of reactionaries the world over.

Deterrence
[1954 in this sense. *L deterrere*, to frighten from]
A military strategy based on the belief that if you can blow the world up more times than your ENEMY can, they will be more frightened of starting a WAR than you are, and therefore will not dare to attack you. A very dangerous situation when you realise that both 'sides' are doing it. '"Deterrence" is not a stationary state, it is a degenerative state. Deterrence has repressed the export of violence towards the opposing bloc, but in doing so the repressed power of the State has turned back upon its own author. The repressed violence has backed up, and has worked its way back into the economy, the polity, the ideology and the culture of the opposing powers' (E.P. Thompson and Dan Smith (ed), 1980). 'Deterrence . . . is a vague, esoteric theory, which holds that the possession of nuclear weapons will prevent nuclear war. This argument is frequently presented to me as a reason why war has not occurred in Europe for thirty-seven years. I am often reminded of a patient who appeared in the casualty department of a hospital some twenty years ago. He was an old man who said he had been driving all his life and had never had an accident, but this night he appeared with a broken neck, having had an accident for the first time. Obviously, driving for so many years had not deterred him from having an accident' (Helen Caldicott, 1984). *See also* NUKESPEAK.

Development
[1756. *Old French desveloper*, to unwrap]
CHANGE for the better; healthy GROWTH. 'Development' has been used in so many contexts and with so many implications that it has often become almost meaningless; hence it is often best avoided unless you want to end up in interminable discussions involving shades of meaning. 'Urban development', 'regional development' and 'industrial development' are children of the post-war planning boom, and were picked up with alacrity by building contractors and 'land developers', who devastated great tracts of land in the name of 'development'. To green-thinkers, development conjures up the bulldozers at nuclear dumping sites and airport extensions, the countryside under threat, rainforest disappearing at an unprecedented rate. Then there are 'research and development', 'development departments', 'development boards', 'development commissions', 'housing development', REDEVELOPMENT, 'animal development', 'plant development', 'child development' — the list is endless. The relationship between green-thinkers and 'development' is an uneasy one: the influential (and, most people would consider, radical) magazine *New Internationalist* exists 'to bring to life the people, the ideas and the action in the fight for world development', with articles on 'agricultural development' and 'Third World development'. The phrase 'development issues' means to many the web of concerns facing the 'developing world' and its relationship with the 'developed world', usually through 'development agencies'. The successes to date however, though sometimes locally encouraging, have been very limited: 'The past three decades have been called "International Development Decades" — at least, the first two were. Since they didn't work, the name of the third was changed to "International Development Strategy Decade". It still doesn't work' (Manfred Max-Neef, in Mary Inglis and Sandra Kramer (ed), 1985). 'Although a lot of effort and many words have been spent in the attempt, the term "development" has never really been defined to anyone's satisfaction. Most citizens of the North, if they think about it at all, tend to see development as a way of making Southerners more like Northerners, making them more "modern" ' (Lloyd Timberlake, 1987). Then there is 'personal development', though the term is now losing some of the vogue it had in the 1970s (*see* HUMAN POTENTIAL MOVEMENT, PERSONAL GROWTH). A Resource for Human Development offers a weekend course on 'Self Development through Creative Imagery' with a leader trained in 'physical and personality development' (Amethyst Centre brochure, 1987). What a word! Yet despite its bewildering and frustrating overuse, it is always possible to analyse development in terms of who or what stands to benefit from it. If development is ecologically sound (*see* ECODEVELOPMENT), SUSTAINABLE, APPROPRIATE to the needs of the people

who are to use it, and encourages SELF-RELIANCE, then it is the sort of development that Greens can endorse. If it exploits nature, puts wealth in the pockets of the rich at the expense of the poor, and encourages further DEPENDENCE, it should be denounced at every opportunity. '"Development" must be redefined, here and in the third world, not merely in terms of more production or consumption, but first and foremost in the changing relationships among people. Development must be the process of moving towards genuine democracy, understood as the ever more just sharing of political and economic power' (Frances Moore Lappé, 1980). 'I believe we have now reached the point where humanity has to find a new stable life-form in which its forward development is an inward journey rather than an external expansion' (Rudolf Bahro, 1984).

Diagnosis
[mid 17c. *Gk diagnosis*, discernment]
The skill of identifying the reasons why something or someone is not as healthy as they could be; usually used in relation to the HEALTH of a human being. In conventional medical terms, diagnosis is almost always used to mean 'finding out what is wrong', with the tacit assumption that something is. Unless they have undertaken a radical rethinking of what they mean by 'health', very many doctors, in the company of a large number of their patients (not to mention many therapists and practitioners of 'alternative medicine') have a vested interest in finding something wrong. 'Though theoretically at the first encounter the physician does not presume that his patient is affected by a disease, through a form of fail-safe principle he [or she] usually acts as if imputing a disease to the patient were better than disregarding one. . . . Trained to "do something" and express his [or her] concern, he [or she] feels active, useful, and effective when he [or she] can diagnose disease' (Ivan Illich, 1976).

Die-In
[*c*.1983]
A mass ACTION in protest against WAR, specifically against the mass destruction caused by nuclear war, in which everybody taking part lies down on the ground for several minutes to symbolise the universally destructive power of present-day weaponry. 'March, rally and die-in in Cardiff highlighting the nuclear weapons role of the Royal Ordnance Factory at Llanishen near Cardiff' (*Womens' Peace Alliance Newsletter*, 1986). 'Dying to live' (Barbara Harford and Sarah Hopkins (ed), 1984).

Diet

[13c. *Gk diaita*, manner of living]

What we eat and drink. Diet is very much a question of our traditions and taboos about FOOD, and currently of great concern, because we are gradually becoming aware that the diet of most Westerners is actually making us ill. Most adults have grown up with the myth of the 'balanced diet' (protein/carbohydrate/vegetable), and have ended up eating far more fat, sugar and salt than was good for them, and far too little fibre (*see also* NUTRITION). Trying to get rid of the excess fat (or what is thought to be excess), more than 50% of women and 10% of men go on 'diets', though feminist and other green writers have shown that most dietary régimes cannot in themselves change attitudes towards eating. 'Diets rarely help a woman lose weight or reeducate her eating habits. Under the guise of control they bring havoc in the food area and frequently increased poundage. Diets turn "normal eaters" into people who are afraid of food' (Susie Orbach, 1982). Most people are agreed, however, that we in the West eat too much (*see* OBESITY). Yet there is a real danger in seeing a change in diet as the answer to all our food problems: 'A change in diet is not an *answer*. A change in diet is a way of experiencing more of the *real* world, instead of living in the illusory world created by our current economic system, where our food resources are actively reduced and where food is treated as just another commodity. . . A change in diet is a way of saying simply: I have a choice. That is the first step. For how can we take responsibility for the future unless we can make choices now that take us, personally, off the destructive path that has been set for us by our forebears?' (Frances Moore Lappé, 1980).

Difference

[14c. *L differens*, differing]

The qualities that help us to distinguish between people and things. As with so many of our perceptions of the universe, the DUALISM we have inherited tends to make difference and SIMILARITY two opposite extremes, when in fact all qualities are to be found in every possible degree and combination. Every aspect of the universe is both unique and part of the whole, and this describes human beings and their activities as much as it does anything else. 'What is the use of attempts at social, political, economic or any other action if the mind is caught up in a confused movement in which it is generally differentiating what is not different and identifying what is not identical? Such action will be at best ineffective and at worst really destructive' (David Bohm, 1980) (*see also* MASCULINE). When difference is stressed at the expense of SOLIDARITY and COOPERATION, perceived differences become the basis for PROJECTION and BLAME, thus providing the 'rationale' for OPPRESSION.

Differences such as skin colour and sexual physiology, relatively unimportant of themselves in a non-oppressive society where common humanity is paramount, become magnified to be seen as *the* important differences, and through a process of encouragement, discouragement and imitation, the imagined differences become all too real. 'Difference produces great anxiety. Polarization, which is a theatrical representation of difference, tames and binds that anxiety' (Jane Gallop, 1981, quoted in Cheris Kramerae and Paula Treichler, 1985). Green-thinkers see connection and uniqueness as vital and complementary qualities in an interdependent world — 'Different therefore equal'.

Differently-Abled
[*c*.1980]
A relatively non-oppressive adjective to use instead of DISABLED; others are 'physically (or mentally) challenged'; 'physically different'.

Digger
[1649]
Someone who — without 'permission' — carefully and productively uses LAND that would otherwise remain unused by its 'owner'. As the enclosure of land continued apace in England in the seventeenth century, ordinary people challenged the fencing and privatisation of land in many ways. This movement, known as LEVELLERS, included a small group in Surrey which called itself 'The Diggers', led and encouraged by a local tradesman, Gerard Winstanley. Before being forced to abandon their communal experiment, they had planted crops and built communal houses. In the 1970s the digger philosophy (the right to till land and the belief in the strength of communal activity) was seen as a historical precedent by many people who wanted to return to the land, and the Digger Carol, with its stirring 'Stand up now, Diggers all, stand up now!', has become part of the repertoire of several folk groups and street bands. *See also* LAND OWNERSHIP.

Diminishing Returns
[1815]
A rate of YIELD which decreases in proportion to the additional resources you use to try to boost it. Thus adding COMPOST to land will help to increase your cabbage crop, but only a certain amount will actually be beneficial — after that you start drowning your cabbages in nutrients and wasting compost. The same principle holds good in any agricultural, economic or human system — more QUANTITY does not automatically produce more QUALITY, and in many cases the addition of resources is — particularly in the long run — counterproductive, particularly when those resources are NON-RENEWABLE.

Direct Action
[*c*.1955]
An ACTION organised to take place at a place and time when it can directly affect or interrupt the oppressive behaviour of those in power. 'During the last ten years some environmental groups have adopted an increasingly belligerent stance against what they see as the Machiavellian policies of governments and industries. Direct action — action outside and beyond the ordinary channels of political protest — rather than compromise and cooperation is now coming to the forefront' (Charlie Pye-Smith and Chris Rose, 1984). *See also* NONVIOLENT DIRECT ACTION.

Direct Knowing
[1981]
The immediacy of communication and knowledge which is possible when things are seen as a whole, without having to go through the process of thought and analysis demanded by Western scientism to prove the truth of something. 'Direct knowing gets us out of the system. It is the awakening. It reveals the context that generates our lesser vision. The new perspective alters our experiences by changing our vision' (Marilyn Ferguson, 1981). *See also* AWARENESS, CONSCIOUSNESS, INTUITION.

Disabled
[1581]
Somebody who finds it difficult to live and work to their full potential in an environment designed primarily for people who are physically and mentally agile. 'Disabled' is one of the distinctions that 'normal' people make which easily leads to OPPRESSION — in this case HANDICAPPISM or NORMALISM (the preferred term) — though it becomes clear from the definition that 'disability' is a continuum of experience which nearly everybody experiences at some time in their life. 'The woman who can't walk is, as it happens, a gifted mathematician. The man who can't count is a competent swimmer. Both of them have their quota of other gifts as well. But somehow, they are no longer seen as able in some situations and un-able in others. Instead, a blanket description is thrown over them. They are "disabled". . . . By turning a description of a condition into a description of people, we are saying that this is all we really need to know about them. We confirm their "abnormality"' (Ann Shearer., 1981). 'Some people, particularly those whose "physical differences" are different than those conventionally considered "disabilities" or "handicaps" by society, and who have never really identified themselves as such before, will not want to identify as "disabled." For this reason, as well as to deal with our definition problems, I suggest that we consider

ourselves as consisting both of people with disabilities (or disabled people) and people working on physical distress. . . We might make it a general rule-of-thumb that by "disabled" we mean someone experiencing either ongoing oppression or needing ongoing accommodation in their life' (Marilyn Golden, *Complete Elegance*, 1983). 'We are disabled by society, not by ourselves or our "disabilities"' (*Spare Rib*, October 1982).

Disarmament
[1795]
The partial or complete reduction in the weaponry of an armed force (*see* ARMS). In the age of NUCLEAR WEAPONS, the form of disarmament uppermost in people's minds is nuclear disarmament, the most important demand of many green-thinkers. 'It is . . . time to change our way of thinking about arms control. I prefer not to use this phrase at all. Let's talk about rapid bilateral nuclear disarmament. It must be rapid because even if we achieve a freeze we still have 50,000 nuclear weapons; even if we move down to 5,000 within five years, that is still ample to kill most people in the world' (Helen Caldicott, 1984). 'Nuclear weapons are truly an evil obsession . . . They degrade us. They soil us. It is unfortunately true that in a world of unarmed deterrence we would still be relying for our defense on terror — relying for our safety on the threat of terrible crimes. Yet we would have succeeded in pushing the terror and the crimes into the background of our affairs. We would have withdrawn them from the center of the stage, thereby clearing a space into which the peaceful, constructive energies of humanity could flood. . . . It would not resolve the nuclear predicament, yet the day that the last nuclear weapon on earth was destroyed would be a great day. It would be a day for celebrations' (Jonathan Schell, 1984). 'Worldwide, there are just a few hundred people, outside foreign offices, working full time on disarmament issues. Regrettably, far more attention is paid to other major world problems — such as energy, the environment, development, population, and so on. A relatively large fraction of the few hundred disarmament scholars is Soviet. In the non-Communist developed countries disarmament is not a popular subject for study' (Frank Barnaby, *New Scientist*, 1977).

Discharge
[*Old French deschargier*, to unload]
(1) [*c*.1830] The continuous flow of toxic WASTE or EFFLUENT into the environment, usually from an industrial or agricultural source. *See also* POLLUTION.
(2) [*c*.1955] Another name for CATHARSIS; the point at which somebody allows themself to express repressed FEELINGS, thereby preparing themself for clear thinking and action.

Discrimination
[*L discriminare*, to divide, distinguish]
(1) [*c*.1814] The aware understanding of the many aspects of a situation and the important differences between them.
(2) [*c*.1866] The differential treatment of people and groups of people according to characteristics including race, sex, class and religion, which in an ideal world would be irrelevant in terms of HUMAN RIGHTS. Equal opportunities legislation in many countries has had little impact on underlying oppressive beliefs (*see* OPPRESSION), which need to be tackled at personal, community and social policy levels (*see* ADULTISM, AGEISM, CLASSISM, HETEROSEXISM, NORMALISM, RACISM, SEXISM). For deep ecologists and animal rights supporters the issue of discrimination goes further, to describe the way human beings constantly discriminate against other species (*see* BIOCENTRIC EQUALITY, SPECIESISM).

Disease
[14c. *Middle French desaise*, unease]
A feeling experienced by most people from time to time that everything is not as it should be; taken over with a vengeance by the medical profession in the late nineteenth century to mean (*Collins English Dictionary*) 'any impairment of normal physiological function affecting all or part of an organism, especially a specific pathological change caused by infection, stress, etc., producing characteristic symptoms.' This widely-accepted definition makes several assumptions about 'normality', 'pathology', 'stress' and 'symptoms' which have been fundamentally questioned by many healers, some of whom now prefer to hyphenate the word, 'dis-ease', in order to emphasise its wider meaning. An alternative approach to the 'disease' model is the WELLNESS model of PREVENTIVE HEALTH: 'Traditionally, Western medicine has tended to view disease as something "out there", beyond our power and influence. When it struck, the remedy was to be found in an attack upon the illness or disease symptoms. Leading the attack were the doctors, while we were often uninvolved bystanders. . . . Here the patient expects the doctor "to do it for him" [*sic*]. In the wellness model responsibility is assumed by the individual. When illness occurs, it is not perceived as a random and meaningless event in isolation from an individual's lifestyle. Instead, it is seen as a positive life force, a signal to examine the physical, mental, emotional and spiritual needs. In short, it is an invitation from within to look at your energy needs balance — and to arrange to have your 'whole person' needs met' (John Travis, undated). Ease, rather than dis-ease, is the principle by which green-thinkers prefer to live their lives: 'We should impart our courage and not our despair, our health and ease, and not our disease' (Henry Thoreau, 1854).

Disempowerment
(*see* EMPOWERMENT)

Disestablishment
[*c*.1600]
The dismantling of bureaucratic and oppressive systems of social control. *See* BUREAUCRACY, DECENTRALISATION, DESCHOOLING.

Disinformation
[1981]
Official LIES made to sound like the truth by embroidering them with detail and planting them in the media; the spreading of false information with the purpose of hurting someone. 'It is hard to think of any other form of government secrecy of such dubious benefit to individual societies, yet so capable of damaging nations collectively. All states would benefit from a de-escalation of such activities; each has the strongest reasons for submitting its own role in this respect to public oversight' (Sissela Bok, 1986).

Disintermediation
[1967]
Getting rid of middle-people. Most people who have heard the word will have seen it used to describe the way in which stocks and shares can now be sold by companies to the public without using the services of an underwriter, but disintermediation is at work throughout the Western economy, bringing producers into direct contact with consumers, and thus increasing efficiency, appropriateness of service, and face-to-face contact. 'Disintermediary livelihoods can be described as activities that cut across . . . narrowness and specialization. . . In education and medicine, an example of disintermediation exists in the magazine *Medical Self-Care* [which] assists people in gaining greater control over their lives, health, and doctor bills. . . *Medical Self-Care* estimates that 80 per cent of our existing medical expenses are avoidable. . . Without doubt, disintermediation is most easily accomplished in small businesses and organizations . . . Disintermediation is increasing dramatically in every sector of the economy' (Paul Hawken, 1983).

Dissipative Structure
[1980]
Another name for an open SYSTEM, stressing the way in which it remains in EQUILIBRIUM by constantly renewing itself. '[Ilya] Prigogine's [the Belgian chemist who won the 1977 Nobel prize for chemistry] term for open systems is dissipative structures. That is, their form or structure is maintained by a continuous dissipation (consumption) of energy. Much as water moves through a whirlpool and creates it at the same time,

energy moves through and simultaneously forms the dissipative structure. All living things and some nonliving systems (for instance, certain chemical reactions) are dissipative structures. A dissipative structure might well be described as a flowing wholeness. It is highly organized but always in process' (Marilyn Ferguson, 1981). The human body is one such system.

Distortion
[*c*.1600. *L distortus*, misshapen]
Something between BIAS and an outright LIE, perfected by people determined to maintain control over others.

Distress
[14c. *L districtus*, divided in mind]
An excessive amount of PAIN and suffering. When inflicted on a human being, it often results in an inability to behave intelligently; such distress needs to be discharged and reassessed so that intelligent behaviour can follow. In the name of 'research', pain is frequently deliberately inflicted upon animals (*see* VIVISECTION), and in the name of progress and profit pain is inflicted upon the earth, though from an anthropocentric standpoint human beings frequently refuse to acknowledge that ecosystems can feel pain and suffering.

Distress Pattern
(*see* PATTERN)

Distribution
[14c. *L distributus*, a sharing out]
The spread of things within a system. Many of the gross inequalities in the human world are the result of the maldistribution of the available resources, but green-thinkers are divided when it comes to saying how many. 'There is no more popular argument on the issue of whether the world is overpopulated than that which starts "if only food were equitably distributed there would be more than enough for everyone". Such arguments depend too much on assumptions that are either hypothetical or unsustainable or basically unattainable. . . The argument does have the merit of spotlighting the grotesque distortions in the pattern of what is produced and distributed. However, it is important, when considering what needs to be done, to conceive of population optima in terms of human beings as they now behave, and to strive for a world where everyone has the requisites of life in spite of the unequal distribution of goods, [whilst] efforts [are] made to reduce those inequalities' (Paul Ehrlich, Anne Ehrlich and John Holdren, 1977).

Diversity

[14c. *L diversus*, turned in different directions]

The measure of different varieties of ideas, things or organisms within a system. A widely-used term in ecology, and subsequently used to express the need to counteract trends towards uniformity in matters social and cultural; hence the popular green slogan, 'unity in diversity'. 'One of the hallowed tenets of modern community ecology is that diversity causes stability' (Charles Krebs, 1972). 'The old [*sic*] idea of the balance of nature, with the multiple interactions between species and their environment creating stable and efficient ecosystems, has been influential in the development of ecology. . . In terms of the maintenance of such functional properties as energy flow or production in the face of disturbance, diverse ecosystems are . . . more stable than species-poor ecosystems; for, although changes in environmental conditions may restrict or preclude the operation of some species, there are always others to compensate for them' (Bryn Green, 1981). Deep ecologists know that every species has an equal right to wellbeing (*see* BIOCENTRIC EQUALITY), and that ecological diversity is crucial, especially at a time when human activities are causing the extinction of species at a growing rate: 'The human population has reached almost five billion people by, in essence, "burning its capital" — destroying and dispersing a one-time bonanza of fossil fuels, minerals, deep soils, water, and biological diversity. It is the loss of biological diversity that may prove the most serious; certainly it is the most irreversible' (Paul Ehrlich, in Norman Myers (ed), 1985). *See also* DIFFERENCE.

Doctor

[*c.*1600 in this sense. *L docere*, to teach]

Originally meaning a TEACHER, 'doctor' is now almost exclusively used to describe somebody whose main work is in MEDICINE, supposedly HEALING but frequently doing little more than prescribing. A doctor often has important skills and experience to share, but must be willing to be flexible, sensitive and honest. 'I think that physicians in primary care will be cautious [of SELF-CARE]. Once you empower people to make their own decisions, some people will make decisions other than the one their doctor would have preferred. . . . Doctors need to identify situations in which it is appropriate for them to say, "I can't deal with this effectively," and perhaps suggest that they make lifestyle changes or involve themselves with a self-help group' (Lowell Levin, in Tom Ferguson (ed), 1980). Doctors usually work within a medical framework of beliefs and practices which militate against a sensitive and CARING approach, though many are now exploring the possibilities of COMPLEMENTARY MEDICINE. In Western-style medicine, doctors tend to be considered (and too often consider themselves to be) high-status professionals, a cut above lowly nurses, using their role as EXPERT to distance themselves from their PATIENTS — they are, despite recent advances in the recruitment of women, usually male. *See also* BAREFOOT DOCTOR, HEALTH, IATROGENESIS, PRIMARY HEALTH CARE.

Do-It-Yourself
[1952]
SELF-HELP: a phrase with a variety of meanings depending upon how generous you are. While reactionary governments talk about self-help, meaning 'go and do it yourself because we're not going to help', and multinational companies sell plastic do-it-yourself kitchens in 'home-care centres', many green-thinkers believe passionately in self-empowerment, where the only way in the end is to do it yourself. A campaigning guide from Friends of the Earth makes it clear that 'If you want something done, do it yourself' (Jonathon Porritt (ed), 1987). *See also* EMPOWERMENT.

Domination
[14c. *L dominus*, master]
Excessive CONTROL; EXPLOITATION; TYRANNY. The way in which many people believe they have the god-given right to use other people and resources exactly as they wish. Distorted ideas about PROGRESS and WEALTH encourage such behaviour. Some Jews and Christians justify such domination from scriptural sources: 'Thou hast given him dominion over the works of thy hands; thou hast put all things under his feet' (*The Bible*, Psalm 8:6). Many more, however, acknowledge that domination is no way to relate to any living thing, preferring to use ideas like STEWARDSHIP and TRUSTEESHIP in relation to the earth, and RESPECT in relation to other people.

Double Standard
[1951 in this sense]
Standards of behaviour which are applied differently to different groups of people; most often used to describe differences of expectations of women and men, or differences of approach towards women and men. '"You are not married," the well-known abolitionist Samuel May once said to Susan Anthony. "You have no business to be discussing marriage." "You, Mr May, are not a slave," she retorted. "Suppose you quit lecturing on slavery."' (*Faber Book of Anecdotes*, 1976). 'Some of the ecological, communal and human potential movements are deeply affected by a type of romantic escapism which could all too easily recreate woman's role as the servant of male culture. As an English feminist once said "We don't want an ecological society where men build windmills and women silently listen, bake bread and weave rugs"' (Petra Kelly, 1984).

Drawdown

[1949]

Borrowing from capital to fund current needs; by extension, using non-renewable resources to fuel economic growth. 'Drawdown is the process by which the dominant species in an ecosystem uses up the surrounding resources faster than they can be replaced and so ends up borrowing, in one form or another, from other places and other times. For our age, though the examples of such depletions are numerous, the most vivid is that of fossil fuels' (Kirkpatrick Sale, 1985). 'Unfortunately, this breakthrough we call industrialism differed in a fundamental way from earlier breakthroughs. It was based on a shift from takeover [of new territories and their resources] to draw-down; its increase of opportunities resulted from using substances that are not replenished in an annual cycle of organic growth' (William Catton, in Michael Tobias (ed), 1985).

Dream

[13c. *Old Norse draumr*, dream]

A creation of the IMAGINATION and the SPIRIT, usually taking place as we sleep, and believed by many to be a way of experiencing everything which is repressed and forbidden in our 'real' lives. To put Lyall Watson's (1979) theory in a nutshell, possibly the main function of sleep is to give us space to dream: 'Sleep is therefore not a suspension of consciousness, but a continuation of it under slightly different control. . . . Dreaming seems to be a continuous process in its own right, carrying on parallel to consciousness, and it is probably quite wrong to assume, as some have, that it is an altered state of consciousness.' Dreams give us the opportunity of experiencing our wildest fantasies; those who believe they have the right to dominate the earth too often believe they have the right to enact their dreams in the real world: 'He is conqueror. . . He has pierced the veiling mountains, ridden the rivers, spanned the valley, measured the gorge: he has discovered. Now nothing of this place is unknown, and because of his knowledge, this land is forever changed. This was his dream' (Susan Griffin, 1984). Many dreams are well worth translating into the real world — Martin Luther King's dream ('that one day the [children] of former slaves and the [children] of former slave-owners will be able to sit together at the table of brotherhood [and sisterhood]'), and Connie Ramos's utopian dream in Marge Piercy's *Woman on the Edge of Time* (1976) — but dreams cannot be forced on the world, and some dreams are a way of experiencing the horror of a world we do not want: 'In one dream I am with my friend, and we are standing with crowds of people outside, and we are all watching the sky. . . We all know the bomb is going to drop, but can do nothing about it' (Wendy, in Alice Cook and Gwyn Kirk,

1983). Native Australians accept the parallel reality of the 'dreamtime' without question; why can we not sometimes accept our dreams as sufficient reality in themselves? Perhaps our world is too changed for dreams to help us, but perhaps too they are our only salvation. *See also* VISION.

Drop-In

(1) [1958] Another name for a community centre, advice centre or refuge (sense (2)); hence 'drop-in centre'.

(2) [1969] A positive response to being labelled a drop-out. 'We don't think of ourselves as drop-outs, but rather as drop-ins. We believe we are the pioneers in a movement that will soon have to include most of civilization' (Alan, in Robert Houriet, 1971).

Drug

[*Middle English drogge*, drug]

(1) [14c] A healing REMEDY.

(2) [14c] An ingredient of a MEDICINE; a substance which gets rid of SYMPTOMS you don't like and enables you to 'get on with your life'. In this sense, drugs are chemicals which boost or suppress reactions within the human body. Most — including tranquillisers, painkillers (*see* PAIN), antihistamines, beta-blockers (heart relaxants) and anti-arthritics — are 'suppressants'. They literally prevent part of the body from functioning in the way it would naturally, thus preventing you from 'hearing' what your body is saying. On the other hand, some drugs used in appropriate circumstances are undoubtedly life-enhancing — insulin in diabetes, for example, vaccines for diseases like tetanus, and painkillers for acute pain. But do we really need all of the £2000 million worth of drugs consumed in Britain every year, or the $18 thousand million in the USA? 'If you have an ailment, the most important thing is to understand what's going on and how it relates to the rest of your life. First, try to understand the problem, its causes, its signs and symptoms. Then you can go on to possible ways of treatment, with drugs being just one possible kind of treatment' (Joe Graedon, in Tom Ferguson, 1980). Many drug companies also manufacture food ADDITIVES, agrochemicals (antibiotics, vaccines, hormone preparations, etc. for agricultural use), PESTICIDES, and chemical weapons for the armed forces. They also attempt, often successfully, to sell dangerous, inappropriate and expensive drugs to Third World countries. 'The poor are not going to get the drugs they need unless Third World governments can count on widespread support in implementing what may be seen as unpopular controls on the free market. . . . The support of WHO [World Health Organization], of rich world governments, and of professional and public opinion worldwide is now essential for the successful implemen-

tation of new health-centred drug policies throughout the Third World. This cooperation and understanding is vital to protect the health interests of millions of the world's poor' (Dianna Melrose, 1982).
(3) [1883] An addictive substance (*see* ADDICTION) which is (arbitrarily, since only some such substances are covered) outlawed by law. By extension 'drug' can mean anything taken in large quantities, like television or religion ('the opiate of the people' — Karl Marx). For clarity's sake, many green-thinkers reserve 'drug' for an addictive substance (remembering how many prescription medicines are addictive, not to mention alcohol and nicotine, caffeine and tannin), and use 'medicine' or 'remedy' otherwise. The drug industry, both 'legal' and illegal, is massive and multinational, with many traffickers reaping vast profits. Opium and marijuana are financially-important CASH CROPS in many Third World countries, especially in Central and South America — as long as such lucrative markets exist so the trade will continue. The only effective way to deal with addictive drugs is to deal with the roots of addiction.

Dual Economy
[1978]
An economy divided in two by officially-recognised definitions of WORK into the FORMAL ECONOMY (regular paid employment) and the INFORMAL ECONOMY (unpaid and voluntary work, together with unrecorded cash transactions). 'Many new practical tasks face us as we begin to take this new direction into the future. At the personal level these will involve learning to do many things for ourselves and other people which we have become incapable of doing during the industrial age. For society as a whole, the new tasks will focus on helping a benign dual economy to emerge out of the current crisis of the industrial way of life. By a benign dual economy I mean the economic arrangements for a fair, well-integrated society, in which all citizens participate and live their lives on equal terms in both the formal and the informal economy. Such a benign dual economy will contrast with another kind of dual economy — the divisive dual economy of a two-tier society whose superior and more fortunate members monopolise the activities of the formal economy and exclude the rest of us from it' (James Robertson, 1978).

Dualism
[1794. *L duo*, two]
(*also* 'mind-body division', 'mind-body split', CARTESIAN PARADIGM)
The belief, dating from the publication of René Descartes' *Discourse on Method* in 1637, that MIND and BODY are two distinct attributes of humanity. This belief, which has had numerous philosophical, scientific and social repercussions, is seen by many as the main reason why such

a large number of people find it difficult to make connections between intelligent thought and effective action. 'The Cartesian division between mind and matter has had a profound effect on Western thought. It has taught us to be aware of ourselves as isolated egos existing 'inside' our bodies; it has led us to set a higher value on mental than [on] manual work; it has enabled huge industries to sell products — especially to women [popularly seen as having less of a mind] — that would make us owners of the "ideal body"; it has kept doctors from seriously considering the psychological dimensions of illness, and psychotherapists from dealing with their patients' bodies. In the life sciences, the Cartesian division has led to endless confusion about the relationship between mind and brain, and in physics it made it extremely difficult for the founders of quantum theory to interpret their observations of atomic phenomena' (Fritjof Capra, 1982). By extension, 'dualism' has come to cover any questionable polarity, including male/female, left/right and scientific/artistic (*see*, for example, MASCULINE).

Dumping
[*Middle English dumpen*, to drop, fall, plunge]
Dropping something in a place it shouldn't be.
(1) [*c*.1800] Discarding rubbish, usually in large quantities, in out-of-the-way places where you hope you won't get caught (*see* POLLUTION, WASTE).
(2) [*c*.1860] Selling things you don't want very cheaply, often to poor and unsuspecting customers, in order to get rid of them. The sale of DDT (an extremely persistent pesticide) to Third World countries after it was banned in most parts of Europe and North America is a clear example of dumping. Another is the sale of Depo-Provera, an injectable birth control drug which is banned in the USA but sold widely in the Third World; its side-effects can include permanent infertility, irregular bleeding, and cancer.
(3) [*c*.1970] Another word for unaware 'clienting' (*see* CLIENT, sense (2)).

Duty
[13c. *Old French deu*, due]
Doing what you know to be right; RESPONSIBILITY. 'It is the duty of every generation to leave a better world to its successors' (Aurelio Peccei, 1981). For many people, 'duty' has become confused with what Fritz Perls calls 'shouldism': 'I'm sure that you are very familiar with this game. One part of you talks to the other part and says, "You should be better, you should not be this way, you should not do that, you shoudn't be what you are, you should be what you are not" ' (Fritz Perls, in Joen Fagan and I.L. Shepherd (ed), 1972). This version of 'duty' (along with

disempowering ideas about, for example, 'national patriotism' and 'always doing what you are told') is a result of the oppressive use of AUTHORITY, resulting in feelings of guilt which help nobody.

Dynamic

[1827. *Gk dunamikos*, powerful]

An all-purpose word, meaning virtually anything to do with movement and vitality. When it was first used by John Watt in the 1820s it meant 'the force or energy created by movement', and 'dynamics' became 'the study of moving objects', contrasted with 'statics'. 'Population dynamics' became part of ecological exploration in the 1960s; Bhagwan's 'sanyassins' started doing 'dynamic meditation' in 1972, involving much abandoned movement; and by the 1980s anything new, fast and exciting could be labelled 'dynamic'. As well as being used adjectivally, 'dynamic' is often used as a noun to refer to the power of relationships between people; hence 'group dynamic', 'psychodynamic'.

Dystopia

[1868 *Gk dys- + utopia*, a bad UTOPIA]

A wretched and miserable vision of the future. Examples of dystopias include George Orwell's *Nineteen Eighty-Four* (1947), Anthony Burgess' *A Clockwork Orange* (1962), the dystopian sections of Marge Piercy's *Woman on the Edge of Time* (1976) which are powerfully contrasted with a utopian vision, and Zoe Fairbairns' *Benefits* (1979).

Ee

Earth

[11c. *Old English eorthe*, earth]

The PLANET of which we are part. 'We are part of the earth and it is part of us. . . . The earth does not belong to man [*sic*]; man belongs to the earth. This we know. All things are connected like the blood which unites one family' (Chief Seathl, 1855). 'Because we know ourselves to be made from this earth. Temporary as this grass. Wet as this mud. Our cells filled with water. Like the mud of this swamp. Heather growing here because of the damp. Sphagnum moss floating on the surface, on the water standing in these pools. Places where the river washes out. Where the earth was shaped by the flow of lava. Or by the slow movement of glaciers. Because we know ourselves to be made from this earth, and shaped like the earth, by what has gone before' (Susan Griffin, 1978). 'Earth community' has become increasingly used to stress that human beings share the planet with all other forms of life: 'The evolutionary process finds its highest expression in the earth community seen in its comprehensive dimensions, not simply in a human community reigning in triumphal dominion over the other components of the earth community' (Thomas Berry, 1982). 'Earth Days' are celebrations of the earth, with special events, presentations and festivities — the first Earth Day was held in the USA on 22 April, 1970. Earth First! is an organisation (and newspaper with the same name), based in Arizona but with international links, passionately committed to the protection of the earth, using any 'creative means of effective defense against the forces of industrial totalitarianism' (*Earth First!*, 1986): *see also* MONKEYWRENCHING.

Earth Mother

(*see* MOTHER EARTH)

Earth Mysteries
[1968]
(*also* 'earth forces', 'earth magic')
An acknowledgement that we do not know all there is to know about the EARTH and its previous inhabitants. 'Most branches of Earth Mysteries research finally reach out to the fundamental question: is there some as yet undesignated form of natural energy at certain prehistoric sites? . . . If the answer is positive . . . then it means that at some point in prehistory there was a practical, if instinctive, knowledge of a form of natural science related to the planet, the surrounding cosmic influences and, perhaps, the human mind itself' (Paul Devereux and Ian Thomson, 1979). While drawing attention to what we do not know, and to the fact that our human ancestors often had a better understanding of the earth and its cycles than we do, 'earth mysteries' is too often drawn down ridiculous avenues of oppressive mysticism and scientistic pseudo-knowledge, ignoring the obvious and creating deliberate misinformation. Yet neither does 'science' have all the real answers, as many sceptics of earth mysteries have claimed. Read *The Ley Hunter: The Magazine of Earth Mysteries* and decide for yourself.

Earth Shelter
(*see* UNDERGROUND BUILDING)

Eco-
[*Gk oikos*, home]
A prefix widely used since about 1970 to qualify anything even vaguely to do with environmental issues. ECODEVELOPMENT, ECOFEMINISM, ECOLOGY, ECONOMICS, ECONOMY, ECOSPHERE and ECOSYSTEM warrant their own entries, otherwise my collection of 'eco-'s to date is:
Ecoaccident (John Cairns (ed), 1986) (*see* ACCIDENT).
Ecoact (Phyllis Ford, 1983) (*see* ACTION).
Ecoactivist (Michael Allaby, 1971) (*see* ACTIVIST).
Ecoantic (Mabel Hammersmith and Laura Watkins, 1974) (*see* ANTIC, GAME).
Ecobore (*Green Anarchist*, June/July 1986).
Ecocatastrophe (Paul Ehrlich, 1969, in John Barr (ed), 1971) (*see* CATASTROPHE).
Ecocentrism/Ecocentrics (David Pepper, 1984).
Ecocide (Michael Adelstein and Jean Pival (ed), 1971; Clifton Fadiman and Jean White (ed), 1971).
Ecocity (Andrews and Fein, 1981).
Ecocommunity (Murray Bookchin, 1986) (*see* COMMUNITY, ECOSYSTEM).
Ecocook (Friends of the Earth, 1975).

Ecocrime/Ecocriminal (Ernest Callenbach, 1980) 'Outrages against the environment.'
Ecocrisis (Cecil Johnson, 1970) (*see* CRISIS).
Ecoculture (UK conservation body, established in 1981).
Ecocycle (Geoffrey Yates, 1980) (*see* CYCLE).
Ecodeath (William Watkins and E.V. Snyder, 1972).
Ecodecentralism (Michael Marien, *Resurgence*, May/June 1983) (*see* DECENTRALISATION).
Ecodefence (Dave Foreman (ed), 1985) (*see* MONKEYWRENCHING).
Ecodynamics (Kenneth Boulding, 1978).
Ecoelegy (Margaret Stucki, 1981).
Ecoethics (Robert Lee, 1981) (*see* ETHICS).
Ecofactor (Lee Durrell, 1986).
Ecofarming (*also* 'biofarming') (Bernhard Glaeser (ed), 1984) 'An ecologically oriented agricultural technology that uses the soil . . . more rationally than do conventional agricultural methods.'
Ecofascism (David Pepper, 1984).
Ecofiction (John Stadler (ed), 1971).
Ecoforum (*Ecoforum* magazine, 1975 onwards).
Ecofreak (Stephanie Mills, 1974, in Art Kleiner and Stewart Brand (ed), 1986).
Ecofund (*Green Line*, April 1987) A grant system operated by the Green Party (die Grünen) in West Germany.
Ecogenetics (Edward Calabrese, 1984).
Ecogeography [*c*.1977].
Ecogreen (Fritjof Capra and Charlene Spretnak, 1984) (*see* GREEN).
Ecoguerrilla (David Day, 1987) (*see* ACTIVISM, MONKEYWRENCHING).
Ecoheretic (Richard Willson, in Edward Goldsmith (ed), 1977).
Ecohuman (*Getting Together*, 1986).
Ecohydrodynamics [*c*.1980].
Ecohysterics (Peter Beckmann, 1973).
Ecoindustry (Bernhard Glaeser (ed), 1984).
Ecointeraction (Albert Eiss, 1973).
Ecojustice (*Joint Strategy and Action Committee*, 1984, quoted in Charlene Spretnak, 1986) (*see* JUSTICE).
Ecolate (Garrett Hardin, 1972).
Ecoliberal (Rudolf Bahro, 1986).
Ecologic (W. Jackson Davis, 1979).
Ecologics (Jonathon Porritt, 1984).
Ecologistics (Patrick Howden, undated).
Ecologue (*The Guardian* column, 1985 onwards).
Ecomanagement (Bernhard Glaeser (ed), 1984) (*see* ECODEVELOPMENT, MANAGEMENT).

Ecomaniac (Lord Rothschild, 1978, quoted in Jonathon Porritt, 1984).
Ecomarxism (*The Leveller*, July 1978; Erik Dammann, 1984) (*see* MARXISM).
Ecomuseum (Barbara Dinham and Michael Norton, 1977).
Econergy (Robert Bowers, 1982).
Econews (Northcoast Environmental Centre journal, California, 1984; British Green Party magazine, 1986).
Econiche (John Allen and Mark Nelson, 1986) (*see* NICHE).
Econut (Lord Rothschild, 1978, quoted in Jonathon Porritt, 1984).
Ecopacifism/Ecopacifist (Rudolf Bahro, 1984) (*see* NONVIOLENCE).
Ecoparasite (Michael Allaby, 1983) 'A parasite adapted to a specific host'.
Ecoparty (Richard Willson, in Edward Goldsmith (ed), 1977).
Ecopeace/Ecopax (Philip Berrigan, quoted in Petra Kelly, 1984; Rudolf Bahro, 1984 and 1986) 'Eco-peace means standing up for life, and it includes resisting any threat to life'.
Ecophene [1922] The varieties of one species found within an ecosystem.
Ecophilosophy (Henryk Skolimowski, 1981) 'Ecophilosophy is life-oriented, as contrasted with contemporary philosophy, which is language-oriented'.
Ecophysics (James Wesley, 1974).
Ecophysiology [*c*.1977].
Ecopoiesy (*Biosphere Catalogue*, 1986) 'How to make a planet habitable for life'.
Ecopolitics (Karl Deutsch (ed), 1977; David Pepper, 1984).
Ecopornography (Jonathan Holliman, 1974).
Ecoreactionary (Sandy Irvine, *Green Comment*, 1986).
Ecoreformism (Rudolf Bahro, 1986) (*see* REFORMISM).
Ecoregion (Nick Albery and Yvo Peeters (ed), 1982; Kirkpatrick Sale, 1985) (*see* BIOREGION, REGION).
Ecoscience (Paul Ehrlich, 1977).
Ecosketch (Russel Bachert (ed), 1976).
Ecosocial (Karl Deutsch (ed), 1977).
Ecosocialism (Stephen Croall and Kaianders Sempler, 1980; David Pepper, 1984) (*see* SOCIALISM).
Ecosociety (Robert Hart, 1984).
Ecosolutions (Barbara Woods (ed), 1972).
Ecosophy (Arne Naess, quoted in Bill Devall and George Sessions, 1985) (*see* DEEP ECOLOGY).
Ecospace (*New Internationalist*, May 1987).
Ecospasm (Alvin Toffler, 1975).
Ecospeak (Winnipeg Pollution Probe magazine, 1982 onward).

Ecospecies [1922] A subdivision of a species of which the individual members are infertile.
Ecospiritual (Michael Lindfield, 1986) (*see* SPIRITUALITY).
Ecotactics (J. Mitchell and C. Stallings, 1970) 'The science of arranging and maneuvering all available forces in action against enemies of the earth'.
Ecotage (Sam Love and David Obst (ed), 1972) 'eco[logical sabo]tage' (*see* MONKEYWRENCHING).
Ecotech (Robert de Ropp, 1975) (*see* APPROPRIATE TECHNOLOGY).
Ecotechnics [*c*.1973].
Ecotecture (Richard Faust Register, 1978) 'eco[logical archi]tecture'.
Ecotone [1904] A transition zone between two ecological communities.
Ecotopia (Ernest Callenbach, 1970).
Ecotoxicity/Ecotoxicology [*c*.1979] (François Ramade, 1987) The study of pollutants in ecosystems.
Ecotrade (*Econews*, 1986).
Ecotype [1922] A subdivision of an ecospecies adapted to a particular habitat.
Ecovillage (Richard Faust Register, 1978) (*see* VILLAGE).
Ecovirtue (Sandy Irvine, *Green Comment*, 1986).
Ecowisdom (Bill Devall and George Sessions (ed), 1985) (*see* DEEP ECOLOGY).
Further sightings gratefully received.

Ecodevelopment

[1975]
Approaches to land MANAGEMENT and international DEVELOPMENT which include an ecological perspective; as with 'development', 'ecodevelopment' has a tendency to become all things to all people. 'An approach to development aimed at harmonizing social and economic objectives with ecologically sound management' (Ignacy Sachs, 1978). 'A strategy that flows with the natural processes of a specific bioregion and leaves vast areas free as untrammelled wild places' (Gwen Bell, 1976, in Bill Devall and George Sessions, 1985). The title of two books on the subject: Robert Riddell, *Ecodevelopment: Economics, Ecology and Development, An Alternative to Growth Imperative Models*, 1981; Bernhard Glaeser (ed), *Ecodevelopment: Concepts, Projects, Strategy*, 1984.

Ecofeminism

[1972]
A recognition of the links between ECOLOGY and FEMINISM, and of what the green movement can learn from feminism (and to a lesser extent vice versa). 'Françoise d'Eaubonne started an "Ecologie-Féminisme" movement in France in 1972, declaring that the destruction of our

planet was inevitable if power remained in male hands, and Mary Daly made a similar connection in *Gyn/Ecology* (1978). But although feminists have recognised the claims of the ecology movement, the male-led ecology movement has too often cut itself off from the women's movement by insisting that women subordinate their interests to that of a greater cause, whether it be saving whales or rainforests' (Lisa Tuttle, 1986). One of the pioneers of ecology in North America was Ellen Swallow, the first woman to obtain a degree from the Massachusetts Institute of Technology.

Ecology
[1858. *Gk oikos* + *logos*, study of the home]
The study of the interconnectedness of NATURE, including human beings and their activities. Purist scientists sometimes like to point to the dictionary definition, 'the study of the relationships between living organisms and their environment', but that has long been superceded, even in ecology textbooks: 'Because ecology is concerned especially with the biology of groups of organisms and with functional processes on the lands, in the oceans, and in fresh waters, it is more in keeping with the modern emphasis to define ecology as the study of the structure and function of nature. It should be thoroughly understood that [hu]mankind is a part of nature, since we are using the word nature to include the [whole] living world' (Eugene Odum, 1963). 'Ecology has taught us that the entire earth is part of our body and that we must learn to respect it as we respect ourselves. As we feel for ourselves, we must feel for all forms of life . . . the whales, the seals, the forests, the seas . . . The tremendous beauty of ecological thought is that it shows us a pathway back to an understanding and an appreciation of life itself' (*Greenpeace Newsletter*, quoted in Jon Wynne-Tyson (ed), 1985). Hence 'ecological accounting' in terms of efficiency and energy rather than money, 'ecological politics' — 'those measures that understand human beings and our environment as being part of nature' (die Grünen, quoted in Fritjof Capra and Charlene Spretnak, 1984), 'ecological understanding', 'ecological age' (Thomas Berry, 1981). DEEP ECOLOGY questions the ANTHROPOCENTRIC basis of scientific ecology, proposing an ECOWISDOM based on BIOCENTRIC EQUALITY; *see also* HUMAN ECOLOGY. The number of book titles called *The Ecology of . . .* has rocketed since the early 1970s, and include *The Ecology of Man* (Robert Lee Smith (ed), 1972), *The Ecology of Imagination in Childhood* (Edith Cobb, 1977), *The Ecology of Walls*, (Arnold Dartington, 1981) and *The Ecology of Freedom* (Murray Bookchin, 1981). 'Ecology is the one science that possesses the ability to recapture the experience of personality in nature. And it comes into its own as a profession at exactly the same time that an intense awareness of

personhood enters our political life. We have begun to liberate the Earth from her false identity — the mechanistic-reductionistic image which has made nature into an object of unfeeling manipulation — just as we begin to fight our way free of the false identities which have made human beings the object of social power' (Theodore Roszak, 1979).

Economics

[1792. *Gk oikonomos*, household manager]

The exploration of WEALTH, VALUE, and the distribution and management of resources. An important strand of green thinking about economics is Fritz Schumacher's (1973) concept of 'buddhist economics': 'the systematic study of how to attain given ends with the minimum means [and] . . . the smallest possible effort'. Mahatma Gandhi called this the 'economics of PERMANENCE'. 'The most important truth about ourselves, our artefacts and our civilisation is that it is all borrowed, even the molecules in our face and body. We are forever borrowing from the environment to create and maintain the totality of our way of life. Everything we transform eventually ends up back in nature after we have appropriated whatever temporary value we can from it. . . Borrowing had built-in limits. . . A civilisation should only borrow what it can pay back' (Jeremy Rifkin, 1985). 'The mistake . . . was to assume that there was a difference, even a separation, between economics and ecology, and that the economy could go where it pleased uninhibited by ecological constraints until the whole economic order broke down. But the last few years have made it clear that the economy is heavily influenced by ecological factors, especially by the onset of scarcity' (Warren Johnson, 1979). The green economics of the late 1980s is torn by the same dilemma as the green movement in general: is it possible to reform the existing system, or do we have to ignore the present system and start again from scratch? It is probably within the field of economics that green philosophy departs most drastically from current mainstream practice; the issues involved are EXPLOITATION, GROWTH, OPPRESSION, POWER, PROGRESS, value and wealth (to name but a few), and important though it may be to change the system, the system will almost certainly only change voluntarily in ways that do not threaten its fundamental PRIVILEGE; the concepts of VOLUNTARY SIMPLICITY have little place in that world except to be seen as 'failure'. Part of the problem is that business executives have learnt the right language: 'From being mindless and faceless bureaucracies where individual needs for self-realisation and growth are discounted, [corporations] must become something like cooperatives of free people, willingly collaborating within a given framework and pooling their efforts to achieve a common aim' (John Harvey Jones, Chairman of ICI, quoted in *Findhorn Foundation Prospectus*, 1987). In 1981 ICI had to withdraw Grofas, a medicated feed for pigs and poultry, after it was found to be toxic; ICI takes whole-page adverts to sell Estrumate, a synthetic prostoglandin tested on laboratory animals, as 'Just a little better than Mother Nature provided'; ICI dumps chemical effluent in the English River Mersey, threatening to close plants if they have to comply with river board proposals; ICI exported £635 million of pesticides from Britain in 1984, including the controversial herbicide Paraquat. Do we take account of words or of actions? One of the most difficult problems that green-thinkers have with economics is finding anybody who understands them yet who has not been taken over by the system; but perhaps we don't need to understand them, perhaps we are being blinded by economists' jargon and pseudo-expertise. How much of conventional economic theory and the existing economic establishment will be needed in a green society? 'Ever since the start of the Industrial Revolution, politicians and economists have worried themselves silly about supply and demand, productivity levels, the balance of payments, government spending or the international debt. . . It is no longer realistic to go on as we do now, ignoring basic human needs and deliberately destroying the planet in the process' (Jonathon Porritt, 1984). 'Conventional economics is a form of brain damage' (Hazel Henderson, quoted in John Elkington, 1987). 'Paradoxically, growth economics has been both too materialistic and not materialistic enough. In ignoring the ultimate means and the laws of thermodynamics, it has been insufficiently materialistic. In ignoring the Ultimate End and ethics, it has been too materialistic' (Herman Daly, in V. Kerry Smith (ed), 1979). *See also* BASIC NEEDS, DEVELOPMENT, INFLATION, MONEY, NEW ECONOMICS, PROFIT, SOCIAL WAGE, TAXATION, UNEMPLOYMENT, WORK.

Economy

[*c*.1530. *Gk oikonomia*, household management]

The fair distribution and wise use of RESOURCES. The antithesis of what most politicians and industrialists call 'the economy'. Some green-thinkers, following Donald Worster's example (*Nature's Economy: The Roots of Ecology*, 1977), see ecology as 'nature's economy', thus stressing that economic sustainability must be based on ecological sustainability. *See* ECONOMICS.

Ecosphere

[1953]

Another word for BIOSPHERE.

Ecosystem

[1935. From 'eco[logical] system']

The complex web of interactions within and between a COMMUNITY (sense (3)) and its environment. 'One refers to an ecosystem when it seems desirable to emphasize the physical, chemical and biological relationships that bind communities and their physical surroundings into more or less functional units. The ecosystems of the world are linked by movements of energy, chemicals and organisms into one global ecosystem, often called the biosphere or ecosphere' (Paul Ehrlich, Anne Ehrlich and John Holdren, 1973).

Edible Landscaping
[1982]
Using edible plants in domestic gardens instead of plants which are solely for display, thus producing more food and relying less on agri-business and imports. 'If only one out of every ten United States citizens planted just two fruiting trees, the world would be richer by nearly 6 billion pounds of fruit!' (Rosalind Creasy, 1982).

Education
[*c.*1530. *L educere*, to lead forth]
The opening up of opportunities for creative learning. Too often used to mean limiting and institutionalised systems set up by the STATE. 'The generation graduating from high school today is the first generation in American history to graduate less skilled than its parents' (John Naisbitt, 1984). Greens think rather differently: 'Learning is a lifelong process, and undertake at any age and any level it should explore and fulfil the potential of the learner. Education should cater for our creative, physical and spiritual needs, as well as the intellectual. It should encourage us to think independently, to work cooperatively, and to contribute positively and creatively to our communities. Responsible citizenship and techniques of peaceful conflict resolution are important aspects of learning. We need the basic skills of literacy and numeracy, but we also need very practical life and manual skills, environmental education, and a real understanding of the global situation' (UK Green Party *Manifesto*, 1987). 'A politics of meaning . . . would not necessarily entail the end of schooling. Rather, it would envisage an education in which the community itself was the school: in which education was determined by the place, rather than (as now) the place being the residue of whatever the Education Authority allows it to be. In such a school, the community would be the classroom' (Maurice Ash, 1980). 'The kids work with us. We try to share what we have learned and what we don't know . . . I think maybe growing up is less mysterious with us since the adult world isn't separate. What better place to learn anatomy than in a clinic? What better place to learn botany than a field of corn? What better place to learn mechanics than a repair shop?' (Marge Piercy, 1976). *See also* DESCHOOLING, SCHOOL.

Efficiency

[1633. *L efficere*, to bring about]

A measure of the ENERGY coming out of a system compared with the energy being put in. Thus a heating system in a house which is properly insulated and draughtproofed is more efficient than a heating system in a barn; eating potatoes with their skins on is more efficient than peeling them and throwing the peel into the dustbin; getting on with the important task in hand is more efficient than waffling around wondering what to do next. 'How much primary energy we use — the fuel we take out of the ground — does not tell us how much energy is delivered at the point of end use . . . for that depends on how efficient our energy supply system is' (Amory Lovins, 1977). A useful idea in many situations, but only if you use appropriate indicators, and only when you take into account where the energy is coming from and where it is going to. Conventional ECONOMICS, which usually uses money value as an indicator, talks about 'business efficiency', 'industrial efficiency' and 'agricultural efficiency' when it doesn't mean efficiency at all — it means making as much profit as you can. José Lutzenberger (in Mary Inglis and Sandra Kramer (ed), 1985) tells of the introduction of chemical peeling in a fruit canning factory in southern Brazil. It made hundreds of women redundant with no unemployment benefit, polluted the nearby river, and halted the supply of feed to the local pig-farming industry. '[The manager] who decided to introduce this new technology acted according to conventional ideology. He introduced an increase in efficiency: now two or three people with a machine can do what it took hundreds of women to do by hand. He was probably convinced that his decision was a purely technical one — nothing to do with ethics or politics. . . So we lost jobs, a river and the pigs. And who made a profit? Only the industry.'

Effluent

[1930 in this sense. *L effluere*, to flow out]

The flow of industrial and agricultural pollutants into the environment; usually used of liquid waste. *See also* POLLUTION, WATER.

Ekistics

[1942 *Gk oikistike*, relating to villages]

The integrated study of human settlements; a very popular idea amongst urban planners from about 1965, which seems to have subsided in recent years. 'Only the new science of ekistics can embrace the whole study of human settlements and their planning, in all their manifold elements' (*New Society*, 1968). Akin to ARCOLOGY; both possibly being ideas which have been overtaken by events.

Elders
[13c. *Old English eldra*, elder]
An alternative title for old people, used in many traditional societies, which emphasises their experience, wisdom and importance within the community.

Elegant
[*c*.1970 in this sense. *L elegans*, tasteful]
A simple and intelligent solution to an apparently difficult challenge. Previously only used in this sense in the mathematical sciences, but too useful a word to leave to them alone.

Elitism
[1947. *L eligere*, to elect]
The belief that some people are intrinsically better than others, and should therefore be the ones to tell everybody else what to do. A state of affairs which green-thinkers sometimes fall over themselves to avoid, confusing a belief in egalitarianism (anti-élitism) with a fear of effective leadership. 'In the early days of the US women's movement, individual women or small groups of women were sometimes charged with elitism by their sisters, who perceived they were taking too much leadership upon themselves, gaining too much prominence, . . or obtaining privileged knowledge . . . One proposal to guard against elitism was that "No member of Women's Liberation, so far as it is practicable, shall take on so much of a task or duty that no other member could take her place" ' (Sheryn Kallaway, undated, quoted in Cheris Kramerae and Paula Treichler, 1985).

Embrace
[14c. *Old French embracer*, to take in both arms]
To hug, cherish, LOVE, encircle, enclose, welcome. An expression of unity, power and inclusiveness. 'Embracing the base' is an ACTION in which the participants surround and symbolically transform a military base.

Emergence
[*c*.1700. *L emergere*, to rise up from]
One of the first visible expressions of healthy GROWTH; the first blades of green in the spring, the first fully aware solution; the first group of people to dare to be different.

Emotion
(*see* FEELING)

Empathy
[1904. *Gk empatheia*, passion]
Being able to understand somebody else's situation without becoming emotionally involved in that situation yourself (thus similar to COMPASSION). 'In 1979, [Carl] Rogers described empathy as the ability of a person to perceive the situation of another as if it were his [or her] own, without ever losing the "as if" quality of the perception. It involves an active process of trying to enter the perceptual world of another as accurately and sensitively as possible in order to understand the other's thoughts, feelings and behaviour from his [or her] point of view. It involves adopting an accepting and non-judgmental attitude to the client and to his [or her] experiences, enabling the confirmation and validation of his [or her] self, which in turn enables his [or her] negative self-concept to change' (Sue Walrond-Skinner, 1986).

Empiricism
[1657. *Gk empeirikos*, practised]
The belief that you can only understand something from direct EXPERIENCE, and that 'theory' as a thing in itself does not exist. Direct observation is what is important, and facts 'speak for themselves'. Empiricism has its roots in the seventeenth century writings of John Locke, George Berkeley and David Hume. Green-thinkers sometimes sit uneasily with the 'scientific' balance of theory and observation, tending towards the belief that while theory can be useful, the uniqueness of every situation needs careful discrimination and individual attention. Be careful of the fine distinction between 'empirical' ('based on direct observation') and 'empiricist' ('denying the importance of theory').

Employee Stock/Share Ownership Plan
[1975]
(*also* 'ESOP')
An arrangement by which the workers own shares in the company they work for indirectly through an employee's trust. This form of ownership, most common in the USA because of tax advantages, is often the result of the taking over or refinancing of an existing privately-owned company. ESOP does give employees a financial stake in the company, but rarely permits the involvement of workers in management decisions; thus although it is sometimes touted by industry as a form of industrial democracy, ESOP is most frequently used as a form of tax-favoured reinvestment.

Empowerment
[17c. *L in- + Middle English pouer* giving power]
Supporting and acknowledging a person's STRENGTH to the point where they are able to take control of their own lives and be effective in the

world. Ultimately this realisation has to come from that person themself through a process of 'self-empowerment'; many green-thinkers see this as a process of RECLAMATION (sense (1)) and talk of 're-empowerment'. 'Empowerment is what we have to be about — getting people to the river to bathe in the changes that expanding consciousness provokes' (Steven Wineman, 1984). 'The gravest single illness of our time is disempowerment' (Murray Bookchin, 1986).

Enabling
[15c. *L in-* + *habilis*, giving expertise]
Giving a person ACCESS to the information, materials, tools and so on which they can use to improve their life and thus the lives of others and the state of the planet. A useful word (in moderation), as it serves to overcome the sometimes patronising implications of 'helping'. Most often used in DEVELOPMENT issues and in PSYCHOTHERAPY.

Encounter
[1914 in this sense. *Old French encontrer*, to come up against]
A meeting of two or more people involving a deep level of SHARING, participation and openness. 'Encounter' is frequently used as an abbreviation for 'encounter group', a type of therapy group developed in the 1960s to provide participants with an intensive group experience designed to put people closer in touch with themselves and with other people. 'Encounter can help us to learn to express our feelings towards others more directly and can break through or burst some of our more manipulative and self-destructive patterns. It gives us practice in acting in the world in new and often exciting ways' (Sheila Ernst and Lucy Goodison, 1981).

Endangered Species
[*c.*1970]
A species of plant or animal under threat of EXTINCTION from overexploitation or loss of habitat. The US Endangered Species Act of 1973 distinguishes between 'endangered' and 'threatened' species, and the international Convention on Trade in Endangered Species (CITES), signed by over 90 countries since 1973, lists 87 plants and nearly 400 animal species as 'threatened with extinction' and prohibits trade in those species. Many ecologists believe the numbers of endangered species, especially of plant and insect species in species-rich habitats, to be much higher than this, and that many species will become extinct without our ever having been aware of their existence.

Enemy
[13c. *L inimicus*, unfriendly]
A person or people perceived (at least potentially) to be the cause of

your suffering, or to be threatening your freedom. An unknown and faceless 'enemy' is seen by many people as the perfect example of projection of your bad feelings about yourself onto something external, which can then be 'punished'. 'I asked him [Ronald Reagan] if he thought they [the Russians] were all evil, but he declined to answer. I also asked him if he had met a Russian, and he said, "No, but we hear from their émigrés." ' (Helen Caldicott, 1984). 'We have to stop thinking and feeling in terms of enemy figures. We must learn at last to distinguish in our thoughts, feelings and speech between person and role, between régime and population. "Enemies" are people with weaknesses and faults, with friendliness and strengths like ours. They are fathers and mothers, daughters and sons, members of clubs, students, workers, who are glad and sad, who quarrel and make up, who can be incited and who can put up resistance, who obey and doubt, and who, like us, want to live in peace' (die Grünen, 1983). 'The hatred of the enemy, whether it be in the form of pornography, sexism, racism, anti-semitism, is fundamentally, in its genesis, a form of self-hatred. . . The hatred of the other is a kind of suicide' (Susan Griffin, *Resurgence*, Nov/Dec 1983). When somebody is very obviously hurting you, the green concept of enemy sometimes becomes less persuasive: 'The countering phrase "men are not the enemy" [a phrase used in therapeutic circles to underline the belief that it is the system of patriarchy, not individual men, which needs to be destroyed] dismisses feminism and the reality of patriarchy in one breath and overlooks some major realities. If we cannot entertain the idea that some men *are* the enemy . . . then we will never be able to figure out all the reasons why, for example, we are being beaten up every day, why we are sterilized against our wills, why we are being raped by our neighbours, why we are pregnant at age twelve, and why we are at home on welfare with more children than we can support or care for' (Barbara Smith, 1979, in Cheris Kramerae and Paula Treichler, 1985).

Energy
[*c*.1600. *Gk energeia*, coined by Aristotle from *energes*, active at work] Vigour, vitality, the force underlying LIFE and movement. One of the commonest words to be heard in green circles; often used as a catch-all when more useful synonyms would improve communication, its subtle variations in meaning confounding clarity in even the most aware company. The original meaning is 'force or vigour, exertion, activity, liveliness, the efficient exercise of power'. In 1807 it was first used by Thomas Young to refer to the 'doing of work' by physical means, and was later divided into the categories so beloved of physics teachers: kinetic, potential, heat, light, chemical, and so on. It is now used in nuclear physics to distinguish between four main kinds of 'force' found

in the universe — gravitational, electro-magnetic, weak nuclear and strong nuclear. In economic resource terms (and its usual meaning in everyday use) it means the amount of transportable power, usually in the form of electricity, gas and oil, produced and consumed within a particular area and time-scale: 'Our ever increasing energy needs reflect the general expansion of our economic and technological systems' (Fritjof Capra, 1982). 'Viewed from a militaristic perspective, energy is a "strategic resource". It can replace manpower; it can be the source of incredibly destructive forces; it can be utilised to kill people and preserve buildings or tanks; and it can provide a research and development façade for military wants' (Rosalie Bertell, 1985). 'Power' is often used as a synonym for this definition of 'energy', though it is usually only substituted where to do so would not be confusing; thus 'solar power' is as frequently used as 'solar energy', while 'power crisis' with its implications of short-term disruption is not normally viewed with the same concern as an 'energy crisis'. 'Energy' in this sense has several important implications for green-thinkers:

— energy is a much more realistic and useful measure for assessing the EFFICIENCY of a system — even an economic or social system — than money. 'Energy accounting' can be used to understand both natural and human systems (*see also* CYBERNETICS, GENERAL SYSTEMS THEORY), yet energy accounting, closer though it is to reality than money accounting, is still a simplification and abstraction of any system.

— energy is available and can be used in very different ways. Our oil and electricity-based economy has given us a mentality which says that anything will work as long you can plug it in or put petroleum in it. This way of using energy is invariably very wasteful — coal-fired electricity generating stations rarely supply more than 35% of the potential energy of the fuel used; when all the energy input is calculated, nuclear power stations probably represent a net energy loss (*see* NUCLEAR ENERGY). Even when electricity is delivered to the consumer, the energy loss is again enormous: we use high-grade energy (energy capable of producing high temperatures) to heat space to no more than 25°C and keep water in hot water systems far hotter than we can ever use it, then lose up to half the heat thus produced to the atmosphere because of poor insulation and draughtproofing. 'Sustained development is unlikely without energy efficiency as fossil fuel supplies dwindle and the environmental impacts of fuel use worsen' (William Chandler, *Worldwatch*, 1987).

— wherever possible, we should use energy from RENEWABLE sources. We are still racing through our one-off bonanza of FOSSIL FUELS, impervious to the fact that whatever the economic forecasters predict, we shall not have them in such apparent abundance for much longer (*see*

OIL CRISIS). 'If just 0.005% of . . . solar energy could be captured with fuel crops, specially designed buildings, wind and water turbines, solar collectors, wave energy converters and the like, it would supply more useful energy in a year than we get from burning coal, oil and gas. Unlike fossil fuels, renewable energy cannot be exhausted' (Michael Flood, 1986). *See also* BIOMASS ENERGY, GEOTHERMAL ENERGY, HYDRO-ENERGY, SOFT ENERGY, SOLAR ENERGY, TIDAL ENERGY, WAVE ENERGY, WIND ENERGY.

— energy should be used appropriately, and with as little WASTE as possible. Enormous energy savings can be gained from using energy appropriately — using low-level (low-temperature) energy for space heating (*see also* CO-GENERATION), using solar energy directly rather than using up fossil fuels (using 'primary energy sources' rather than 'secondary energy resources'), and implementing energy conservation strategies wherever possible.

The idea of 'energy' is used in other areas of green interest in many different ways. Nutritionists (*see* NUTRITION) use 'energy' in combinations like 'energy-giving', 'energy foods' and 'energy intake' — foods which provide the body with heat energy, usually measured in calories [one calory is the amount of heat needed to raise 1 gramme of water by 1 degree centigrade]. 'In the *Recommended Daily Allowance of Food Energy and Nutrients in the UK* [the Department of Health and Social Security] recommends specific amounts of food energy and nutrients . . .' (*Great British Diet*, 1985). In HEALING, THERAPY and SPIRITUALITY 'energy' has a more universal application. It describes the FLOW in the human body which links our physical bodies with the flow of the universe, an idea frequently found in Eastern healing traditions (*see also* LIFE FORCE). 'Chinese and Indian . . . systems of medicine [are based] on the assumption that a primal energy system pervades the universe . . . The individual's ability to use this life force is believed to be the key to health and also to the process of spiritual growth' (David Harvey, 1986). 'When I use the word energy I am thinking of the Japanese *ki*, the Chinese *chi* and the Sanskrit *prana*. All these words point to a certain cosmic energy or vital force which courses through the whole universe, linking all things together' (William Johnston, 1978). 'Other people can be toxic to you as well as food, for we also assimilate finer, less tangible, but nevertheless real forms of energy' (Swami Anand Samarpan, 1983). In this vein, 'energy' can easily become a filler expression, being used whenever the precise word needed is not immediately to hand: 'Marin's this high-energy trip with all these happening people' (Cyra McFadden, 1977). 'I learnt a lot of new words at Findhorn — some Californian jargon, some dubious pseudo-religious language which reminded me of my Sunday-school days, a variety of ways of hiding what people really wanted to say behind vague and apparently safe platitudes. "I feel the energy isn't flowing between us" often meant "I wish you would go away" ' (John Button, 1985). When one word can mean so much, do make sure that it says what you mean it to say!

Enoughness
[*c.*1975. *Old English genog*, sufficient]
Another word for SUFFICIENCY: 'When the resources of the entire planet are considered, our view of what is possible changes. An "economics of enoughness" takes the place of an economic accounting system based on fear of scarcity' (Susan Campbell, 1983). 'Enoughness' appeared at about the same time as WELLNESS (an alternative word for HEALTH); similar terms are probably lurking just over the green horizon.

Enthusiasm
[*c.*1600 *Gk enthousiazein*, to be inspired by a god]
Excitement about life and its possibilities. An important aspect of a GREEN lifestyle, assisted by being able to spend your time doing worthwhile and fulfilling things, supported by likeminded friends and colleagues.

Entropy
[1868. *Gk en-tropein*, to change into]
A measure of the degree of disorder within a system. The second law of THERMODYNAMICS states that the entropy of a closed system must always increase with time; thus hot drinks cool to room temperature, and children's bedrooms frequently sink to a level of general chaos. What is more, however efficient we become at recycling ENERGY and materials, the only answer in the end is to use less of them: 'The entropy law tells us that recycling energy is always a losing proposition, and that recycling materials can never be one hundred per cent complete. Depletion and pollution are inevitable costs that should be minimized but can never be eliminated' (Herman Daly, in Michael Tobias (ed), 1985). Some green-thinkers have shown clearly how ignoring the entropy principle has led to the current impasse in economics and society: 'Most Americans believe that the world is progressing toward a more valuable state as a result of the steady accumulation of human knowledge and techniques. . . That is the power of a world view. Its hold over our perception of reality is so overwhelming that we can't possibly imagine any other way of looking at the world. . . [Yet] according to the Entropy Law, whenever a semblance of order is created anywhere on earth or in the universe, it is done at the expense of causing an even greater disorder in the surrounding environment. . . Today's inflation is tied directly to the depletion of our nonrenewable energy base. . . Inflation

. . . is ultimately a measure of the entropy state of the environment' (Jeremy Rifkin, 1980). Any society — like ours — which consistently ignores the entropy principle can be described as being in an 'entropy state' as opposed to a STEADY STATE: 'Simply put, the entropy state is a society at the stage when complexity and interdependence have reached the point where the transaction costs that are generated equal or exceed the society's productive capabilities' (Hazel Henderson, 1978). Natural systems are rarely closed, however, and where what we call LIFE is at work, systems almost invariably become more complex with time — though it should always be remembered that this can only be sustained by new energy from the sun, which is itself subject to the entropy law. Entropy has also been defined as the likelihood of finding rare molecular distributions within a system; as James Lovelock points out: 'It may seem at first obscure, but it . . . implies that wherever we find a highly improbable molecular assembly it is probably life or one of its products, and if we find such a distribution to be global in extent then perhaps we are seeing something of Gaia, the largest living creature on Earth' (1979).

Environment
[*c*.1600. *Old French en-viron*, within a circle]
The surroundings and context of something or someone; a much-used, much-abused word, almost impossible to define: '"The environment" proves an elusive concept. It is everything, bar something' (Maurice Ash, 1980). Until about 1950 it was used in a fairly 'neutral' way to describe the physical and social setting of a place or person. Increasingly from then on it was used to draw attention to what human beings were doing to their surroundings: 'Along with the possibility of the extinction of [hu]mankind by nuclear war, the central problem of our age has . . . become the contamination of [our] total environment with such substances of incredible potential for harm — substances that accumulate in the tissues of plants and animals and even penetrate the germ cells to shatter or alter the very material of heredity upon which the shape of the future depends' (Rachel Carson, 1962). Concern about the environment grew during the 1960s, culminating in the United Nations decision to hold a conference on the 'human environment' in Stockholm in June 1972. By now it was clear that 'environment' meant the human environment, the environment as it affects and is affected by human beings, almost as if 'environment' could not exist without human intervention. A book called *Man and Environment* [*sic*] (Robert Arvill, 1967) starts: 'This book is about people; about their impact on land, air, water and wildlife, and the environment they create; about the damage and destruction they cause and the measures they take as a society to remedy this. Above all it is about the possibilities they now have to

reshape and create an environment that fits their highest aspirations.' And again: 'To survive on the earth, human beings require the stable, continuing existence of a suitable environment. . . The environment makes up a huge, enormously complex living machine that forms a thin dynamic layer on the earth's surface, and every human activity depends on the integrity and proper functioning of this machine' (Barry Commoner, 1971). Paradoxically, at the same time as stressing the importance of the environment for human reasons, a great deal of ENVIRONMENTALISM tends to ignore the human element, concentrating on wildlife and resource CONSERVATION: 'Most books about the environment describe the ecological costs of modern society. Yet they often neglect the very human social cost. Every single day over 40,000 children, under the age of five, die because of hunger and poverty' (Joe Weston (ed), 1986). For Greens, 'environment' must involve an awareness of the interconnectedness of all these issues if it is to be at all useful. The perspective of DEEP ECOLOGY makes it clear that concern for the environment must stem from a clear understanding that 'the environment' is an anthropocentric concept — we cannot 'save the environment' either for ourselves or without the knowledge that we are an integral part of it. We are all in it together.

Environmental Impact Assessment
[1967]
(*also* 'EIA')
A detailed evaluation of the potential impact of any building project on its natural and social ENVIRONMENT. Since it was first made a legal requirement of all large proposed development in the USA, the use of EIAs has spread to several other countries. 'Each statement has to involve a wide range of considerations: the environmental impact of the proposed action, any adverse consequences which could not be avoided if the proposal were actually implemented, any irreversible resource commitment that might ensue, alternative strategies, and the relationship between local, short-term use of the environment and the maintenance of long-term productivity' (Andrew Goudie, in R.J. Johnston (ed), 1986).

Environmentalism
[*c*.1957 in this sense]
Awareness of and concern for the total ENVIRONMENT. The roots of modern environmentalism are to be found in the first unfavourable reactions to the industrial revolution and the exploitation of the land by industry and the needs of an industrial society. Since about 1960, however, there has been a sustained and growing concern about environmental issues, marked by an increasing questioning of capitalist

economic and social values. Politicians and industrialists periodically like to suggest that interest in the environment is waning again, but then contrive to produce a Seveso or Chernobyl to ensure the growing ranks of the environmentally concerned. Self-reflection is always a valuable exercise; as well as the concerns about the most useful approach to 'environment' outlined above, several other aspects of environmentalism have concerned green-thinkers:

— environmentalism tends to be thought of merely as dealing with one CRISIS after another. 'Classic environmentalism has bred a peculiar negative political malaise among its adherents. Alerted to fresh horrors almost daily, they research the extent of each new life-threatening situation, rush to protest it, and campaign exhaustively to prevent a future occurrence. It's a valuable service, of course, but imagine a hospital that consists only of an emergency room. No maternity care, no pediatric clinic, no promising therapy: just mangled trauma cases' (Peter Berg, quoted in Bill Devall and George Sessions, 1985). To be fair, this is a favourite media projection (campaigns being newsworthy and subtler changes not), but it does have more than a grain of truth.

— environmentalism tends to concentrate on small changes to the system which, while they might be very necessary, can cloud the need for radical change (this approach has been called 'reform environmentalism' — *see* REFORMISM).

— environmentalism tends to be élitist, proposing reforms which will make life more pleasant for the already-privileged but overlooking social and economic oppression and inequality. 'What we need now is a social environmentalism which can have real meaning and relevance to the mass of people, an environmentalism which is not held static by ideological dogma or "party loyalty" but recognises the full implications of an environmental perspective' (Joe Weston (ed), 1986).

— environmentalism tends to assume that the best we can do is survive, overlooking the potential for a very different but very real symbiosis between the human and natural worlds — which are after all the same world. 'Environmentalism, as I use this term, tends to view the ecological project for attaining a harmonious relationship between humanity and nature as a truce rather than a lasting equilibrium. . . Environmentalism does not question the most basic premise of the present society, notably, that humanity must dominate nature; rather, it seeks to *facilitate* that notion by developing techniques for diminishing the hazards caused by the reckless despoliation of the environment' (Murray Bookchin, 1981). This is a harsh judgement, and not entirely justified, but it does stress the need for environmentalism to look deeply into the causes of our current predicament, accepting only radical change, not temporary alleviation, as the ultimate goal.

Equality

[15c. *L aequalis*, level, equal]

The basic belief (and the practice that follows) that all human beings are equally important, that each person should be respected in their own right, and that resources and opportunities should be easily available to anybody who needs them. The two areas of equality that have been uppermost in people's concern have been racial equality and sexual equality. 'We [German] Greens see the many immigrant workers and their dependents as an important part of the population in our country, with equal rights to anyone else. . . The aim of the Greens is a humane society built on complete equality of the sexes in the context of an overall ecological policy' (die Grünen, 1983). Many people, particularly feminists, have pointed out the mistake of confusing equality with sameness and uniformity, and 'Different, therefore equal' has been a useful slogan.

Equal Opportunity

[*c*.1965]

A campaign or policy designed to prevent DISCRIMINATION against people on the grounds of sex, race, age, religion or physical difference. Despite legislation in many countries, including the USA and the UK, differentials and divides between the opportunities available to different sections of the community have generally widened rather than narrowed. 'Equal opportunity' is considered by many people to be an empty official phrase with little real meaning.

Equal Pay

[*c*.1920]

The principle that people should receive the same wages for the same amount of work done, regardless of their sex; it became the first demand of the Women's Liberation Movement. Despite Equal Pay legislation in the USA in 1963 and the UK in 1970, wage differentials between men and women are as great now as they were when the legislation was passed, with women receiving on average only about 60% of equivalent male earnings. With current redefinitions of WORK, employment and VALUE, the question of equal pay has widened into areas such as the need for a SOCIAL WAGE and economic SELF-HELP networks.

Equal Rights

[*c*.1860]

The belief that all human beings have the same CIVIL RIGHTS, regardless of sex, race, religion, age or physical ability. This is a complex area since so many different oppressive practices work against equal rights.

Some groups, particularly feminists and blacks, feel it is more important to work for women's rights and black rights than for nebulous 'equal rights'. In the USA, 'equal rights' is often linked to the Equal Rights Amendment, an unsuccessful attempt made between 1972 and 1982 to amend the US Constitution in such a way that it would be illegal to discriminate on the grounds of sex. As the ERA campaign gathered strength, so the male backlash grew stronger, and when Ronald Reagan and the Republicans changed tack in 1980 and declared themselves against the ERA, the amendment was effectively killed.

Equilibrium
[1608. *L aequilibrium*, equal balance]
A perfect BALANCE. In ecological terms it describes a system in which inputs and outputs are finely balanced (though not statically — hence 'dynamic equilibrium'). In economic theory, equilibrium is seen as that perfect but somehow unattainable state in which supply and demand are perfectly in balance, fair and affordable prices being the 'equilibriating mechanism'.

Erosion
[1830 in this sense. *L erodere*, to gnaw at, eat away]
The wearing away of the ground surface, particularly soil, by water and wind. This occurs when agricultural land is left uncovered by crops or ground cover, and as more detailed measurements reveal the extent of the damage, it has become a matter of great concern the world over. *See also* SOIL EROSION.

Erotic
[1651. *Gk eros*, love]
Relating to LOVE, particularly sensual love (*see* DESIRE, SEX). Seen by many green-thinkers as an area of our lives too often privatised, denied, exploited and divided, and as an important aspect of human experience to be explored and celebrated. 'Creative attention to the form and force of our own eroticism is disappearing fast, and relationships have lost much of their excitement. Setting up as a couple can be a grave mistake when a selfish need for security means that one partner stands in the way of change and development. Love is not an isolated romantic act between two people; love and life are indissolubly linked with one another. Love must be an integral part of all areas of society, so that it can halt the forward march of isolation, separation and a hostile social order' (Petra Kelly, 1984).

Ethical Investment
(*see* SOCIALLY RESPONSIBLE INVESTMENT)

Ethics

[14c. *Gk ethos*, moral, custom]

Deciding what is acceptable behaviour and what is not; by extension, deciding on self-imposed restraints on human activities for the common good. 'The reinstatement of an ethical stance beomes central to the recovery of a meaningful society and a sense of selfhood, a realism that is in closer touch with reality than the opportunism, lesser-evil strategies, and benefit-versus-risk calculations claimed by the practical wisdom of our time. Action from principle can no longer be separated from a mature, serious, and concerted attempt to resolve our social and private problems. The highest realism can be attained only by looking beyond the given state of affairs to a vision of what *should* be, not only what *is*' (Murray Bookchin, 1986). Hence LAND ETHIC [1933], 'conservation ethic' [1961], 'environmental ethics' [1970], 'bioethics' [1971] and 'ecoethics' [1981]. 'What we must now face up to is the fact that human ethics cannot be separated from a realistic understanding of ecology in the broadest sense' (Van Rensselaer Potter, 1971). Deep ecologists go even further, believing that nature itself holds the answer to appropriate behaviour, if we are aware enough to hear it: 'Nature seems to be writing its own natural philosophy and ethics' (Murray Bookchin, in Michael Tobias (ed), 1985). *See also* LIFEBOAT ETHICS.

Ethnic

[*c.*1960 in this sense. *Gk ethnos*, race]

Originally meant relating to a particular RACE of people; has come to mean any aspect of a (generally THIRD WORLD) culture — clothes, furniture, music, dance — introduced into the West, often hand-made, colourful and exotic. 'Ethnic . . . has come to mean foreign, or un-American, or plain quaint' (*Sun* magazine, 1965). While it can be a useful word, it is sometimes used in ways which are close to being racist.

Ethnic Minority

[1945]

(*also* 'ethnic group' [1935])

A group of people with a common cultural heritage living in an area where they form a small part of the population. 'Consistent support for the needs of minorities in our society is a major concern of the Greens. The prejudice and discrimination which still exist in many laws and regulations are based on a combination of ignorance and deliberate oppression of marginal groups' (die Grünen, 1983).

Ethnomedicine

[1964]

Any system of MEDICINE traditionally used within a particular culture;

such remedies are often folk remedies. Ethnomedicine is particularly important in the Third World, where natural local remedies are very much cheaper, and often as effective, as imported Western drugs.

Etiology
(*see* AETIOLOGY)

Eugenics
[1883. *Gk eugenes*, well-born]
Ways of supposedly 'improving' the human race by selective breeding and the use of REPRODUCTIVE TECHNOLOGY. An example of a TECHNOFIX — 'if we can do it, then as scientists we have a duty to do it' — and another way of maintaining the supremacy of patriarchal beliefs about medical expertise and REPRODUCTIVE RIGHTS. Is it a coincidence that when amniocentesis is used in India to ascertain the sex of an unborn child, more than 99% of subsequent abortions are of female foetuses? 'Whether "old" or "new", these procedures have in common that they represent an artificial invasion of the human body — predominantly the female body. Increasingly, more and more control is taken away from an individual's body and concentrated in the hands of "experts" — the rapidly — and internationally — growing brigade of "technodocs": doctors, scientists and pharmaceutical representatives (most of them male, white, and of Euro-American origin) who fiercely compete with one another on this "new frontier" of scientific discovery and monetary profits' (Renate Duelli Klein, in *Man-Made Women*, 1985).

Euthanasia
[1742. *Gk eu- + thanatos*, good death]
Allowing or helping somebody (usually somebody who is terminally ill) to die peacefully, without excessive pain or medical intervention. Though strictly illegal in most Western countries, many people believe that we have a right to decide how and when we want to die, and euthanasia is practised anyway, by medical 'experts' if not by trusted friends and relatives. '[Having taken all the objections into account] I still think that every human being has as much right to die as to live' (Mary Stott, 1981). *See also* DEATH, DEATHING.

Eutrophication
[1946. *Gk eutrophos*, well-nourished]
The overenrichment of a body of water, from the addition of sewage or agicultural or industrial effluent, to the point where algae grow very rapidly, consume all the oxygen in the water, and thus make it impossible for other life to live in it. The growth of algae in this way is sometimes called 'algal bloom'. 'The cessation of eutrophication of water bodies is clearly an immense task both technologically and institution-

ally; but failure to achieve it will result in the loss not only of biologically significant elements of diversity but also in the diminution of an important element of environmental quality for humans' (Ian Simmons, 1974). *See also* POLLUTION, WATER.

Evaluation

[1842. *Old French evaluer*, from *L valere*, to be strong, be worth something]

Assessing different possibilities before deciding on an appropriate course of action, and checking during or afterwards whether it is having the desired effect. Traditionally, 'evaluation' has meant 'cash evaluation' or COST-BENEFIT ANALYSIS; rejecting the idea of value in money terms, green-thinkers see evaluation in more general and far-reaching terms, as not having to give everything a precise value before taking it into account. Evaluation can be a very useful consciousness-raising exercise, but it is important to remember that any evaluation which is made in order to prove the rightness of one particular course of action is certain to be biased, and that over-prolonged evaluation can be an excuse for inaction.

Evapotranspiration

[1938]

The part of the HYDROLOGICAL CYCLE in which water evaporates from the earth's surface and is transpired from plants; thus the total amount of water being transferred from the earth back to the atmosphere.

Evolution

[1622. *L evolutio*, an unrolling]

A long process of CHANGE or unfoldment; more specifically the belief that varieties of plant and animal life evolve gradually from each other over long periods of time, adapting themselves to their environment in the process. Green-thinkers are concerned that human beings have forgotten that they too are part of evolution (*see* HUMAN EXEMPTIONALISM), and believe themselves to be outside and above the web of NATURE, with a right to dominate (and destroy) other life forms in the process. 'The long evolutionary history of the biosphere has made it a near-perfect superorganism, in which individual species are fit to survive, in which the populations of plants and animals are co-adapted to fit into steady-state ecosystems, in which individual ecosystems are adapted to fit into the biosphere as a whole. . . It runs as beautifully as a well-made watch (and never needs repair). . . In the course of evolution, nature, like the watchmaker, has tried many other possible designs and found them wanting. If one pokes at this arrangement carelessly, there is a strong likelihood that it will suffer damage' (William Ophuls, 1977). 'Evolution is slow and wasteful but it has resulted in an infinity of working, flexible compromises, whose success is constantly tested by life itself. Evolution is in large measure cumulative, and has been running three billion years longer than our current efforts. Our most glittering improvements over Nature are too often a fool's solution to a problem that has been isolated from context, a transient, local maximisation that is bound to be followed by mostly undesirable counter-adjustments throughout the system' (David Ehrenfeld, 1981). 'The concept of material progress implies that [we are] free to determine [our] own evolution. . . So long as we remain imbued with the aberrant world-view that leads us to mistake biospheric degradation for development, anti-evolution for evolution, and progress for regress, so long must we continue to mistake the causes of our problems for their solution, and thereby deploy all our energy and ingenuity into assuring their further aggravation' (Edward Goldsmith, *The Ecologist*, 1981). The scientific theory of evolution is usually traced to Charles Darwin's *The Origin of Species by Natural Selection* (1859); though Darwin himself was aware of the importance of cooperation in nature, this was immediately translated into the popular Victorian epithet 'the survival of the fittest' (*see* COMPETITION). 'Darwin's cosmology sanctioned an entire age of history. Convinced that their own behaviour was in consort with the workings of nature, industrial men and women were armed with the ultimate justification they needed to continue their relentless exploitation of nature and their fellow human beings without ever having to stop for even a moment to reflect on the consequences of their actions' (Jeremy Rifkin, 1984). 'The so-called stuggle of life, and survival of the fittest, should be interpreted in the sense of the ability to coexist and cooperate in complex relationships, rather than the ability to kill, exploit, and suppress' (Arne Naess, *Inquiry*, 1983).

Example
[14c. *L eximere*, to take out]
Providing a model for other people by practising the green ideas you preach. 'We cannot do it by force of arms; we must do it by example' (Walter Cronkite, quoted by David Brower in Dennis Paulson (ed), 1986).

Excellence
[14c. *L excellere*, to excel, raise up]
Aiming always to do your best. The conventional definition — 'being the best' — is rejected by green-thinkers because of its competitive and hierarchical implications. 'Commitment to excellence as a way of life would mean each one of us, adults and children, being all we could be, developing our abilities to the fullest. . . It would mean supporting and appreciating one another as we grapple with the challenges of life and the tasks we take on. With a deep commitment to excellence, a respect

and reverence for life would gradually emerge and become a basis for daily living and a foundation for meaningful, rewarding learning experiences' (Marta Harrison, in Stephanie Judson (ed), 1977).

Existentialism
[1930. *L ex(s)istere*, to come into being]
A philosophy, especially popular between about 1940 and 1960, based on the idea that individual existence must be the starting point of any belief system: the universe in itself has no fixed or pre-ordained meaning, and human beings must decide what to do without any certainty of being right or wrong. The basis of existentialism is that meaning always follows existence, and that things only have meaning when they matter to us. Some people see the existential point of view (particularly as set out by Jean Paul Sartre, who was also a left-wing activist) as one of the important roots of the alternative movement of the 1960s. The emphasis that existentialism puts upon individual RESPONSIBILITY and EXPERIENCE fits well with green thinking, but the idea that only human intervention can give true meaning to nature is anathema to green-thinkers, especially to deep ecologists.

Expectation
[16c. *L ex(s)pectare*, to look out for, look forward to]
Looking forward to something, all too often with a fixed idea about how it will be. Confounded expectation leads to disappointment; cynics say that the only way to cure disappointment is to have no expectations, but a green perspective allows for expectancy and flexibility — facing the FUTURE with excitement and openness. *See also* ASSUMPTION, TRUST.

Experience
[late 16c. *L experiri*, to try, test]
One person's direct and unique relationship with the circumstances of their life. A person's experiences, however they perceive them, need to be respected; it is often the denial of experience that leads to alienation and oppression (the denial of incest when reported by a child, for example, or the denial by some members of extreme right-wing organisations that the Nazi-perpetrated holocaust of the Jews ever really took place). There is also a link between the denial of individual experience and the growth of authoritarianism, which projects its own (inevitably false) model of 'normality': 'Society highly values its normal man. It educates children to lose themselves and to become absurd, and thus to be normal. Normal men have killed perhaps 100,000,000 of their fellow normal men in the last fifty years. Our behaviour is a function of our experience. We act according to the way we see things. *If our experience is destroyed, our behaviour will be destructive.* If our experience is destroyed, we have lost our own selves' (Ronald Laing, 1967).

Expert

[1825. *L experiri*, to try, test]

Someone who has specialist and detailed knowledge of a particular subject; conventionally only used of a person if they can convince others of their expertise by virtue of their qualifications, sex, dress and social standing. Thus a woman who has tended a cottage garden for sixty years will generally not be thought an expert on her local environment, while a college-trained official in a suit who has spent a few hours in the place will. 'Expert advice' or 'expert opinion' is a convenient way of not having to prove your point (or even say who you really are) — 'Experts say radiation not a risk'. The green perspective allows anybody to ask important questions — and to answer them: 'When you ask big questions, it is impossible to be an "expert" in everything that you study. But instead of being paralysed by that realization, I try to keep in mind the advice of a wise friend: "If you ask a big question you may get something wrong," [she] told me. "But if you ask a small question — as most narrow academics do — it doesn't matter if you're wrong. Nobody cares!"' (Frances Moore Lappé, 1980). 'Instead of remaining the "outside expert" trying to resolve the conflicting needs of the low-middle-high-income metropolis, or simply "helping the poor", we can become participants in our own community's search for new family structures or other changing patterns of association, and participants in the process of creating physical settings which would foster these ways of life — in effect, we become a part of, rather than an expert for, cultural change' (Robert Goodman, 1972).

Explicate Order

[1980]

A model of the universe in which the constituent parts are not seen as enfolded within each other, and in which the whole system, while extremely complex, can be understood part by part. *See* IMPLICATE ORDER.

Exploitation

[*Old French exploit*, accomplishment]

(1) [1803] The use of raw materials; usually used by economists and industrialists to imply 'reasonable' use, but 'exploitation' very often means unaware and excessive use of resources.

(2) [1844] Using another person for your own selfish purposes. This can either be in economic terms, where a consumer takes advantage of sweated labour to buy cheap goods, or may manifest itself as emotional manipulation, where someone may be persuaded to do something they do not really want to.

Exponential Growth
[1704]
A compound rate of GROWTH, in which the amount added during each period of time grows larger every time. Particularly of concern to green-thinkers because this is the pattern of population growth in many parts of the world. Thus with a 2% annual growth rate (and many countries exceed this) a population will double every 35 years. A curve of exponential growth against time traces the shape of a 'J', and is sometimes called a 'J-curve'.

Exterminism
[1980. *L exterminare*, to drive out]
A belief that we will all die in a nuclear holocaust regardless of what we try to do to prevent it. A widely-held belief which is important to name in order to be able to deny it. '"Exterminism" was coined by E.P. Thompson, one of the leading theorists of the European peace movement, to refer to the fact that the arms race is no longer a rational contest between the superpowers, but owes its existence in large part to the functioning of huge, self-aggrandizing, and out-of-control bureaucracies . . . in both countries' (Fritjof Capra and Charlene Spretnak, 1984). Some green-thinkers take the concept further: 'This exterminism is in no way confined to the danger of nuclear war. It is equally to be found in the absolute impoverishment to which the capitalist model condemns half of humanity. . . Not least, and inseparably connected with military and economic aggression, exterminism is expressed in the destruction of the natural basis of our existence as a species' (Rudolf Bahro, 1982). *See also* VITALISM.

Externalities
[*c*.1960 in this sense]
Any part of a system, particularly an economic or industrial system, which can conveniently be overlooked because it is not the obvious and legal responsibility of the person or business that benefits from the system, or because it cannot easily be given a cash value. Thus the cost of repairing roads is an externality to car users; the stress from noise of people living close to an airport is an externality for air passengers. Economists recognise the existence of externalities when they can be quantified in financial terms, but many externalities are impossible to value in this way — what is the cost of a sleepless night, for example, or the cost of the last sand lizard in Britain? *See also* COST-BENEFIT ANALYSIS.

Extinction
[15c. *L ex(s)tinctus*, quenched]
Complete destruction, particularly of a species of plant or animal.

'There are possibly as many as ten million species of plants and animals making up the biosphere today, and it is estimated that if present trends in planet mismanagement continue, up to 20% of these could become extinct by the year 2000' (Lee Durell, 1986). Some people use the evidence of extinction over the millennia of evolution — such as that of the dinosaurs — as proof that we shouldn't worry overmuch about continuing extinction, but 'The crucial point [about the extinction of the dinosaurs] is that they became extinct at a time when evolutionary processes were capable of replacing them with mammals . . . Earth's inventory of millions of species is the product of two biological processes — speciation and extinction. . . It is as if speciation were a tap running new species into a sink and extinction were a drain . . . Humanity has become the major agent of extinction, opening the drain ever wider, . . at the same time . . . inhibiting the long-term compensating process: speciation' (Paul and Anne Ehrlich, 1981). The complete destruction of many species (though not all) by nuclear holocaust is another extinction threat which faces human beings in particular (*see also* ANNIHILATION): 'Morally, however, human extinction is unlike any other risk. No conceivable human good could be worth the extinction of the race, for in order to *be* a human good it must be experienced by human beings. Thus extinction is one result we dare not — may not — risk' (Robert Seeley, 1986).

Extreme

[15c. *L extremus*, completely outside]

An argument or system of beliefs continued *ad absurdum* beyond the limits of reason or intelligence. Extremism arises largely from a person's inability to listen to anybody else, their certainty of their own 'rightness', and their willingness to die for their cause. Extremists are mostly white men, though they often take their 'dependents' with them: 'Every accommodation that women make to this domination, however apparently stupid, self-defeating or dangerous, is rooted in the urgent need to survive somehow on male terms. Inevitably this causes women to take the rage and contempt they feel for the men who actually abuse them, those close to them, and project it onto others, those far away, foreign, or different' (Andrea Dworkin, 1983). A favourite counter by real extremists is to call their opponents 'extremist' in return.

Ff

Facilitation
[*c*.1960 in this sense. *L facilis*, easy]
Providing the skills and resources conducive to the smooth running of a project or meeting; a useful alternative to 'leadership' in a non-hierarchical setting. Hence 'facilitator'. *See also* FOCALISATION, LEADERSHIP.

Fact
[early 16c. *L factum*, something done]
An event or circumstance which is known (at least by its observers) to have happened. Thus a fact is very different from an interpretation, and it is extremely common for interpretations to colour 'facts'. *See also* ASSUMPTION, REALITY, TRUTH.

Factory Farming
[1890]
Livestock farming where animals are treated as production belts for food. In many cases animals are kept indoors in cramped conditions, plied with artificial feed supplements, and dosed with hormone injections. 'It would seem to me to be taking our domination of the animal world beyond moral limits to cause ill health to an animal simply to produce pale flesh, the only attribute of which is the fulfilment of a snob requirement. Veal calf producers talk readily enough of cruelty, even admit that some of their methods are inhumane, but offer you the flimsy excuse that they are only producing what the public wants' (Ruth Harrison, 1964). 'The inescapable fact is that the consumer, led by his [or her] supermarket, has come to expect the kind of low cost, apparently attractive food which can only be produced by resorting to the chemistry set of antibiotics, hormones and pesticides' (James Erlichman, 1986). *See also* AGRIBUSINESS, AGRICULTURE, FOOD.

Fall-Out
[1946]
RADIOACTIVE particles giving out ionising RADIATION, carried as dust on the wind as the result of a nuclear explosion, and falling to the ground either as the dust reaches the ground, or in rain.

Family
[15c. *L famulus*, servant]
A group of people with a special RELATIONSHIP to each other, traditionally a 'blood' relationship; now the word is often used to describe any close-knit group of people. For many people, their family provides them with a great deal of love and support, though by no means all families are close-knit and loving. The myth of the ever-happy family creates expectations which can put an intolerable strain on its members to behave in a particular way — the 'mother' to keep things nice and tidy, the 'wage-earner' to earn wages, the 'children' to do what they're told. The privacy of the family can also allow extremes of violence and oppression to go unchecked (*see* INCEST). 'The family — what holds us, what hurts us' (Lois Helmhold and Amber Hollibaugh, in Steve Shalom (ed), 1982). 'It is the belief that kinship, love and having nice things to eat are naturally and inevitably bound up together that makes it so hard to imagine a world in which "family" plays little part. This mythologized unity must be picked apart, strand by strand, so that we can understand its power and meet the needs of its separate elements more fully. In part, this can be done by analysis and discussion, . . but it must also be done by experiments in new ways of living and by political campaigns to transform not the family — but the society that needs it' (Michèle Barrett and Mary McIntosh, 1982). *See also* NUCLEAR FAMILY.

Famine
[14c. *L fames*, hunger]
Extreme scarcity of food in a large area, affecting many people. While food may be very scarce in some areas, especially when harvests fail, Westerners often (and conveniently) assume that somehow 'nature' is to blame, rather than pressure from OVERPOPULATION, WAR, inappropriate agricultural and development policies, and human greed. 'Studies carried out for the ILO [International Labor Organization] suggest that in Ethiopia and Bangladesh in the 1970s it was not so much the famine that caused poor people to starve, but rather the inability of poor people to purchase what was available. Most at risk were the landless' (Norman Myers (ed), 1985). 'An analysis of famine that puts the blame on an "encroaching desert" will never come to grips with the inequalities in power at the root of the problem. . . Drought is a natural phenom-

enon. Famine is a human phenomenon. Any link that does exist is precisely through the economic and political order of a society that can either minimize the human consequences of drought or exacerbate them' (Frances Moore Lappé and Joseph Collins, 1980).

Fantasy
[14c. *Gk phantazein*, to make visible]
Using your IMAGINATION to make your DREAMS more accessible. Fantasy is often considered to be an escape from reality, but it can equally be considered an escape to reality from the absurdities of the world we live in (*see also* VISION). At the same time, many fantasies are the result of cultural expectations (romantic fantasy, for example), yet even here it is generally better to be aware of the power of fantasy, if only to free yourself from its clutches. 'We can open up the private world of dream and fantasy to share it and use it in positive, creative ways. We can move from a situation where dreams frighten us, fantasies dominate our waking lives and anxieties cut us off from the world, to a situation where we have more of our own inner power available to live our lives creatively in the present' (Sheila Ernst and Lucy Goodison, 1981).

Fast
[12c. *Old English fæstan*, to fast]
Abstaining from eating FOOD (or most foods) for a period of time, either for health reasons, to express solidarity with people in the world who do not have enough to eat, or to protest against your own ill-treatment (more usually called a 'hunger strike'). *See also* ANOREXIA.

Fast Breeder
(*see* BREEDER REACTOR)

Father
[before 12c. *Old English fæder*]
A male PARENT, co-creator of new life. Patterns of parenting are changing rapidly, and fathers are now in general much more involved with their children than they were only twenty years ago — unemployment has helped in the process. Many men are very good with babies and children, and most green-thinkers would question the myth that mothers naturally make better parents than fathers, but many fathers still absent themselves almost entirely from the domestic scene. When problems arise, fathers still tend to show their patriarchal colours, fighting for the custody of children they might have had little interest in before the divorce and not paying the maintenance they have agreed to. While many women welcome the increase in sharing of childcare, some women choose to bring up a child without its father's help, some choose to share parenting but not to live as a conventional family, and some are

concerned about men being involved in childcare at all, given the evidence that men can be potential rapists. There are also an increasing number of single parent households where a man is living with his children. Most green-thinkers, however, believe that the relationship between father and child is important and unique: 'It is not enough to argue the father's need of his children, his right to have a relationship with them, or the need of children for two parents, like some interchangeable circus double act or elegant variation in a child's life. The indispensability of the father in the full and healthy development of the child, and the tragic consequences of his frequent absence, have got to be fully recognised. Until they are, the real cost cannot be counted. Fathers are not simply stand-ins for mothers' (Mary Ingham, 1984).

Faustian Bargain
[1876. After Johann Faust, 16c magician and astrologer]
Sacrificing spiritual values for material gains — Faust sold his soul to the devil in exchange for knowledge and power. 'For us the lessons of Chernobyl are clear. The Faustian bargain of nuclear energy has been lost' (Austrian Foreign Minister, quoted by Christopher Flavin, *Worldwatch*, 1987).

Fear
[12c. *Old English fær*, danger, sudden calamity]
A feeling of distress or alarm resulting from imminent (real or perceived) danger. For many people fear is ever-present; if we did not sometimes feel fearful as a result of what is happening around us we would be fooling ourselves. Fear is a well-known product of OPPRESSION: 'As women, we learn fear as a function of our so-called femininity. We are taught systematically to be afraid, and we are taught that to be afraid not only is congruent with femininity, but also inheres in it. We are taught to be afraid so that we will not be able to act, so that we will be passive, so that we will be women — so that we will be, as Aristotle put it so charmingly, "afflicted with a natural defectiveness"' (Andrea Dworkin, 1976). Several collections of children's writing about the world they live in show that fear is not just an adult preoccupation: 'I am afraid./I'm afraid of what Future will look like./I'm afraid of the unknown, afraid of poverty and suffering, afraid of war and nuclear power./I'm afraid of the dirty houses, the cars and littering, afraid of all pollution./I don't know what the world will look like in a hundred years. If the world will still exist then./I believe that all children are just as frightened as I am. I am afraid' (Karin Norlander, in Helen Exley, 1985). *See also* THREAT, VIOLENCE.

Feedback

[1920]

A response to the effectiveness of a system which can then be used to make the system more effective. Originally a term used in electronics, later [*c*.1940] in CYBERNETICS, ecology and psychology. In the computer age, the 'feeding back' of information in order to refine a computer model is now commonplace, and the speed with which predictions can be made about complex systems makes it possible to see links that are not immediately apparent. Since about 1965 'feedback' has also been used to mean the reactions of a group or audience to a speaker or leader's 'performance', usually arranged in such a way that the feedback helps that person to improve the effectiveness of their presentation.

Feeling

[12c. *Old English felan*, to feel]

(*also* 'emotion')

The body's response to the things that happen around it. A signal for the body to do something, though because feelings are frequently repressed, the appropriate action (shouting, laughing etc.) has often been 'forgotten'. Because of the mind-body split, feelings are often thought to be 'emotional' rather than physical, when they are clearly both. The vocabulary of feeling is useful because it is small and international, but many therapists appear to believe that the expression of feelings is the raison-d'être of THERAPY, when it is just one (albeit an important) step on the way to self-empowerment: 'There are Institutes for Feeling Therapy, Centres for Feeling People, and therapists who continually talk about the importance of feelings. [As a therapist] I, too, see a lot of deep feelings expressed, and believe that to be a very important part of the whole process in which clients are engaged. But somehow there is falsity about saying that feeling is more important than sensing, thinking, intuiting, imagining, desiring, and so forth . . . The truth of the matter seems to be that in therapy what we are trying to do all the time is to encourage the real person to come out, and this means the whole person. . . A one-sidedly feeling person would be just as much a monster as a one-sidedly thinking person. What we are helping the client towards in therapy is integration, not [simply] feelings' (John Rowan, *Self and Society*, Jul/Aug 1985). 'Feeling' is also used to mean a person's total involvement in something that matters to them (*see also* CONNECTION, UNITY), in which case the feeling is more of a reminder of what is important in the world than a signal for action.

Feminine

[14c. *L femina*, woman]

While 'feminine' literally means 'relating to women', the cultural setting of oppression and false gender distinction has made the word almost worthless. 'Terms like masculinity and femininity . . . have become so overlaid with societal dogmas setting forth what women and men "should" be like as to have lost almost all meaning. Whose "should" are we talking about, and how do we know from one use to the next what subjective cast these sex-linked words are intended to convey?' (Casey Miller and Kate Swift, 1981). 'Feminine' is usually used to imply weakness, passivity, failure and dependency: 'If in the beginnings of history the feminine woman was defined by her physical dependency, her inability for reasons of reproductive biology to triumph over the forces of nature that were the tests of masculine strength and power, today she reflects both an economic and emotional dependency that is still considered "natural", romantic and attractive' (Susan Brownmiller, 1984). The notions of 'masculine' and 'feminine' seem to have a particular attraction for many people interested in spirituality — in searching for a balance between supposed innate 'masculine' and 'feminine' qualities they can overlook the importance of common humanity and the stranglehold of patriarchal attitudes. *See also* ANDROGYNY, GENDER, MASCULINITY, SEX, SPIRITUALITY, WOMAN, YIN/YANG.

Feminism
[1895]
The belief that discrimination against women (SEXISM) is intolerable and must be ended, thus radically changing the position of women in society. Since it is women who suffer from sexist OPPRESSION, women are more likely than men to recognise the importance of feminism, though an increasing number of men are coming to see that feminism is a vitally important strand of a holistic view of the world. A belief in feminism is unlikely to be effective without corresponding action: 'Feminism has only working definitions since it is a dynamic, constantly changing ideology with many aspects including the personal, the political and the philosophical . . . Feminism is a call to action. It can never be simply a belief system. Without action, feminism is merely empty rhetoric which cancels itself out' (Donna Hawxhurst and Sue Morrow, 1984, quoted in Lisa Tuttle, 1986). Despite many attempts to pin feminism down to definitions, and to divide feminism into constituent parts (radical feminism, socialist feminism, humanistic feminism, marxist feminism, lesbian feminism, separatist feminism . . .), the achievements of feminism as reflected in a marked shift of social and political attitudes over the past twenty years give the lie to what some people see as a stultifying fragmentation of contemporary feminism. 'The feminist movement is calling for a positive transformation and change in our consciousness. This change is not towards a state of static equalisation, but towards the full manifestation and vital interplay

of the balance of life's energies' (Stephanie Leland, in Léonie Caldecott and Stephanie Leland (ed), 1983). *See also* WOMAN.

Fertility
[15c. *L fertilis*, fertile, from *ferre*, to bear, carry, produce]
The ability to produce healthy and abundant GROWTH. Soil fertility is of particular concern to ecologists, as it is clear that despite 'enrichment' by artificial fertilisers, erosion and exploitative agricultural techniques are decreasing soil fertility in many parts of the world: 'As the topsoil layer is lost, subsoil becomes part of the tillage layer, reducing the soil's organic matter, tilth and aeration, and adversely affecting other structural characteristics that make it ideal for plant growth. This overall deterioration in soil structure is usually accompanied by a reduced nutrient retention capacity, which lowers productivity further. Additional chemical fertilizer can often compensate for the loss of nutrients, but the deterioration of soil structure is difficult to remedy' (*Worldwatch*, 1984). For human fertility *see* BIRTH CONTROL, CONTRACEPTION, POPULATION, REPRODUCTIVE RIGHTS.

Finite
[15c. *L finitus*, limited]
Only existing in limited amounts, as is the case with many of the planet's NON-RENEWABLE RESOURCES, including oil, metals, and ultimately water, air and land.

First World
(*see* THIRD WORLD)

Fitness
[16c. *Middle English fitten*, to arrange]
Another word for 'appropriateness' (*see* APPROPRIATE).

Flexibility
[late 18c in this sense. *L flectere*, to bend]
Willingness to adapt to changing circumstances. 'The golden rule is that there are no golden rules' (George Bernard Shaw, 1942).

Flow
[before 12c. *Old English flowan*, to flow]
Moving freely, as water in a stream or river. Many physicists now see universal flow or flux as fundamental to an understanding of the interconnectedness of the physical universe: '[This] can perhaps best be called undivided wholeness in flowing movement. This view implies that flow is, in some sense, prior to that of the "things" that can be seen to form and dissolve in this flow . . . There is a universal flux that cannot be defined explicitly but which can be known only implicitly, as indi-

cated by the explicitly definable forms and shapes, some stable and some unstable, that can be abstracted from the universal flux' (David Bohm, 1980). This idea of flow appears in Eastern religions, particularly in Taoism, which Alan Watts called 'The Watercourse Way', and also in humanistic psychotherapy: 'We all have experiences of wholeness and connectedness, times when the barriers dissolve between us and not-us, between us and another person, between us and the landscape of which we are part. We often call that experience love, and with love comes the rush of realization that we are part of a larger whole, an immediate knowledge of the connections between us and our environment, a sense of flow rather than struggle' (John Button, 1985). Energy flow is a useful way of understanding what is happening in a system, and emphasises the dynamic quality of systems rather than the static 'atomistic' point of view: 'In spite of many unresolved problems and differences in methods, the mapping of flows of energy is coming to be viewed as a more reliable method for macroeconomic analyses than conventional monetary approaches' (Fritjof Capra and Charlene Spretnak, 1984).

Focalisation
[*c*.1970 in this sense. *L focus*, hearth (the centre of the house)] (US: 'focalization')
Being the person in a group who takes on the responsibility of leadership in a non-hierarchical way, sharing decision-making with the group yet acting as the 'focus' for the group's activities. *See also* FACILITATION, LEADERSHIP.

Food
[before 12c. *Old English foda*, food, fodder]
A substance ingested by living organisms containing chemical energy and other nutrients, which can be converted and used for growth and energy; most often specifically used to describe human food, a matter of great concern in terms of human health, the health of the land the food is grown on, and equity for everybody living on the earth. Having enough nutritious food to eat is a basic human need and a basic human right. Contrary to popular (and convenient) mythology, there is enough food and of the right sorts to provide all earth's inhabitants with a healthy diet; although an increasing POPULATION will naturally stretch available food resources, the reason why more than ten per cent of the world's population goes to bed hungry every night is much more to do with greed, environmental degradation and unequal distribution than because the planet cannot provide enough food. In particular, several recent trends in AGRICULTURE have undermined food production, especially in the THIRD WORLD, taking the control of food supply out of local

hands and into the thrall of big business:
— traditional agricultural methods have been replaced by short-term rapid-return MONOCROPPING, which cannot be sustained and puts enormous pressure on LAND which is often agriculturally marginal.
— farmers have been encouraged to use massive inputs of machinery, fertilisers and pesticides, and both farmers and their land have become addicted to this inefficient and dangerous way of producing food. 'Modern agriculture . . . has become unrelated to food supply. In fact, modern agriculture's main export is famine, and its main local product is malnutrition. Its byproducts are worldwide soil erosion and the poisoning of soils, water and air. Modern agriculture feeds a commodity market, where the subsidised food purchased is not available to the poor or the hungry, so it is totally unrelated to its purported aims' (Bill Mollison, *Resurgence*, May/June 1985).
— MULTINATIONAL food companies have increasingly become land-owners, thus controlling food production, processing, marketing and pricing from field to supermarket, and leaving little for the local population to eat except the expensive imported food they can buy with their inadequate wages.
It is important to recognise how much our traditions, habits and taboos about food can shape and limit our eating patterns. Even in Western countries there are many wild crops we could eat but don't (*see* Richard Mabey's *Food for Free*, 1972); in demanding particular sorts of food, presented in particular ways, we seldom eat as holistically as we might if we were more flexible and less fussy. Appearance — often at the expense of flavour and nutritional value — is still what most consumers demand; so producers continue to wax, spray (*see* CHEMICAL), fortify, flavour, colour (*see* ADDITIVE), shrinkwrap, precook, advertise prodigiously, and generally overprocess and overpackage. And we, mostly willingly, pay the price. While a tenth of the world starves, the privileged often overeat, feeling guilty but addicted to the unreality of food and what it has come to represent (*see* DIET). Green-thinkers often talk about the need to eat more WHOLEFOODS — natural, ORGANIC foods with no chemical additives and the goodness left in. Wholefoods are important, both for human and ecological health, but we need to be careful not to be dogmatic, purist or judgemental. Frozen peas and dehydrated mashed potatoes are very nutritious and have kept many poor families healthy through a hard winter, when only the privileged could afford expensive wholefoods. The same is true with VEGETARIANISM and VEGANISM: both mean living more lightly and compassionately on the planet, but they do not justify insensitive criticism of people who are on their own way to discovering how they can help the earth and themselves to be healthier. Then there is the food we WASTE

— nearly a third of domestic Western waste is organic, much of which could be eaten if we could forget what we had learned about only eating the nicest bits. At least we should compost the rest. Finally there is the food that the West cannot eat, the surpluses created by robbing the land and paying already-rich farmers to produce more while small farmers go broke. Sometimes we deign to give some of it away as AID: it may be cheaper than paying to store it in warehouses, but it should be seen as the DUMPING exercise it is — food aid is invariably unwanted surplus. It does little to encourage Third World self-reliance, and we should not be surprised when we receive muted thanks in return. *See also* NUTRITION, HEALTH.

Food Chain

[1926]

The way that nutrients and other substances pass through an ecological system, usually by one type of organism eating another. Food chains are sometimes thought of as 'pyramids', since the amount of BIOMASS at each 'level' is considerably less (typically by 10% and often by as little as 1%) than at the previous level. Some ecologists now prefer to think in terms of 'food webs', which better describe the complexity of flows in an ecosystem. One major environmental concern is that numerous herbicides and pesticides do not break down as they pass through the food chain (they are known as 'persistent'), with the result that concentrations of these pollutants can become toxic at the end of the food chain — not the least important concern being that at the end of many food chains are human food consumers.

Food Cooperative

[*c*.1970]

A group of people who together organise the buying and distribution of food to the members of the group. The advantages are that the food can be bought in bulk from reliable sources (who can in turn rely on a market), quality can be monitored more easily, and items obtained (organic or wholefoods, for example) which might otherwise be difficult to buy.

Forest

[13c. *L forestis (silva)*, outside (wood)]

A large area of trees. Covering 30% of the earth's land surface, forests are crucial to the health of the planet, yet trees — particularly in the world's RAINFORESTS — are being felled at an ever-increasing rate. About a fifth of these rainforests were felled between 1950 and 1975, and at present rates another two-fifths could be lost by the end of the century. Temperate forests in Europe and North America are suffering the effects of acid rain. 'Not only are forests powerhouses of basic biospheric processes, notably photosynthesis and biological growth, creation of fertile humus, and transfer of energy, but their exceptional contribution to the biosphere goes much further. They play major rôles in the planetary recycling of carbon, nitrogen and oxygen. They help to determine temperature, rainfall and various other climatic conditions. They are often the fountainheads of rivers. They constitute the major gene reservoirs of our planet, and they are the main sites of emergence of new species. In short, they contribute as much to evolution as all other biomes' (Norman Myers, 1985). 'The way we stand, you can see we have grown up this way together, out of the same soil, with the same rains, leaning in the same way towards the sun. . . You know we have grown this way for years. And to no purpose you can understand. Yet what you fail to know we know, and the knowing is in us, how we have grown this way, why these years were not one of them heedless, why we are shaped the way we are, not all straight to your purpose, but to ours. And how we are each purpose, how each cell, how light and soil are in us, how we are in the soil, how we are in the air, how we are both infinitesimal and great and how we are infinitely without any purpose you can see, in the way we stand, each alone, yet none of us separable, none of us beautiful when separate but all exquisite as we stand, each moment heeded in this cycle, no detail unlovely' (Susan Griffin, 1984).

Forestry
[1823]
The cultivation of trees for the use of human beings. A sustainable renewable resource if used wisely, trees provide construction materials, pulp for paper, food crops, and shelter for wildlife and ground crops. But most forestry is not conducted as wisely as it could be. The monocropping of softwoods for maximum short-term financial return ('agroforestry') is what forestry is all about in most Western nations, regardless of the acidification of soils, vulnerability to disease and pollution, visual intrusion and impoverishment of ecosystem diversity. While softwood monocultures spread across marginal agricultural land, hardwood forest continues to decline throughout the world, both in temperate and tropical areas. Britain has lost more than half of its mixed woodland since 1933; since 1960 one third of Costa Rica's forests have been felled to provide grazing land for cheap beef. Green-thinkers see forestry as the careful harvesting of a valuable resource, which with good management in mixed ecosystems can fulfil a variety of functions. Many of the problems of modern commercial forestry are the same as those of agriculture, and require similar solutions: increasing species variety; using more native species; restricting the use of chemicals; stemming the amassing of enormous tracts of land by forestry business-

es and putting more land under community control; and encouraging the aware and efficient use of forestry products. *See also* CLEAR-FELLING, COPPICING, DEFORESTATION, FOREST, PERMACULTURE, POLLARDING, RAINFOREST, REAFFORESTATION.

Formal Economy
[*c*.1980]
An economy in which the only 'real' work is paid employment. 'The orthodoxy of the industrial age has been that the formal economy is the only real economy, and that respectable thought and action on economic and social questions should concentrate only on those activities that have a money tag attached. It has come to be assumed that the only real work is the work which is done in the formal economy — in other words, that paid employment is the only really valid form of work' (James Robertson, 1985). *See also* INFORMAL ECONOMY.

Fossil Fuel
[1835]
A carbon or hydrocarbon fuel — oil, gas, coal, shale or peat — formed by the decomposition of prehistoric organisms. Fossil fuels are among the world's most rapidly-exploited NON-RENEWABLE RESOURCES, and the present period of rapid fossil fuel consumption has been called the 'fossil fuel age' (sometimes contrasted with the coming 'solar age'). While we more or less contentedly burn our one and only fossil fuel heritage, few people ever stop to think just what a finite heritage it is: 'If all fossil fuels in the earth's crust could be burned, it would provide the equivalent of only a few weeks of sunlight' (Herman Daly, in Michael Tobias (ed), 1985). *See also* ENERGY.

Fourth World
[*c*.1965]
The sum of people who see themselves as part of a world of small-scale enterprises, social groupings and economic projects rather than as part of any multinational bloc. ' "Fourth World" embraces small nations, groups working for their autonomy and independence at all levels from the neighbourhood to the nation, minority groups whether ethnic, linguistic, cultural or religious, and those in the fields of peace action, ecology, economics, energy resources, women's liberation and the whole spectrum of alternative movements, who are struggling against the giantism of the institutions of today's mass societies and for a human scale and a non-centralised, multi-cellular, power-dispersed world order' (Nicholas Albery and Yvo Peeters, 1982).

Freedom
[12c. *Old English freodom*]
Being able to do what you want to, either as an individual or as a group of people. Historically, the earliest ideas of freedom were associated with racial or national freedom, and this is still vitally important for many oppressed cultural groups. Individual freedoms, CIVIL LIBERTIES, are (in theory at least) a fundamental part of the constitution in most 'democratic' countries. Freedom, however, depends not only on theoretical permission to do what you want, but on access to information and resources. Experience of freedom is empowering, and it is extremely important to recognise the difference between taking personal power and taking power over other people. Thus the often-heard claim that men should be 'free' to buy pornography ignores the actual and implicit oppression inherent in the production and consumption of pornography; the 'freedom' to wear fur coats ignores the exploitation of wild animals.

Freelance
[*c.*1900 in this sense]
A way of working which involves offering your professional services to a number of clients. While it does not offer the same security as full-time employment, it has a flexibility and freedom which is attractive to many people, and an increasing number of employers find it convenient to take on freelance staff as and when they need their skills.

Free School
[*c.*1962]
A SCHOOL which operates outside the constraints of the state school system. The free school movement started in the USA in the 1960s, and the first British free school opened in 1971 (though A.S. Neill's famous Summerhill School, founded in Suffolk, England, in 1921, was in many ways a model for free schools). A free school aims to be free, not only in terms of being non-fee-paying, but also by providing a free, non-authoritarian, non-hierarchical, voluntary and participatory learning environment. Other names for free schools include 'community schools', 'alternative education centres', and 'free centres'. Free universities have also been proposed, one such project having been started in Birmingham, England, in 1986. *See also* EDUCATION.

Freeze
[1979]
(*also* 'nuclear freeze')
The proposal — originally put forward by a group of people in the USA — that it would be a realistic first step in nuclear arms control if both superpowers could agree to stop deploying and testing new nuclear

weapons. 'The way to end the nuclear arms race, to borrow the late senator Thomas Aitken's proposal for terminating the Vietnam war, is for each side to declare itself the winner and just stop racing. This is not a wholly facetious suggestion, and it is the basic idea behind a bilateral nuclear freeze. However simplistic the freeze might at first appear, it is entirely consistent with the basic considerations that must govern a satisfactory arms control agreement between the United States and the USSR' (Union of Concerned Scientists, 1982). 'While the freeze is fully defensible as a measure in its own right, virtually none of the advocates of the freeze present it as the final goal of their efforts. . . They all regard it only as "a first step". [However], the freeze answers the urgent need to head off the next advance in the arms race, which promises to be a particularly perilous one' (Jonathan Schell, 1984).

Friend
[12c. *Old English freond*]
A person with whom you have a special bond of love and trust; a word that needs to be reclaimed. A concept often distorted by ideas about sex roles and the distinctions made between FAMILY, 'lovers' and 'friends', in which 'just good friends' usually come fairly low on the list. Marge Piercy (1976) makes a useful distinction between ordinary friends, hand-friends and pillow-friends. The idea of friendship was consciously extended to the planet when Friends of the Earth was founded in 1969. FoE is now a major international pressure group for green thinking and action, with groups in 28 countries worldwide.

Frugality
[early 17c. *L frugalis*, virtuous, worthy, related to *frux*, fruit]
Living without excessive consumption or possessions, and producing as little waste as possible. 'In this book, [frugality] will be used in its original meaning — to suggest economic conditions in which society is obliged by the force of circumstances to make full and "fruitful" use of all its resources' (Warren Johnson, 1979). *See also* SIMPLICITY, VOLUNTARY SIMPLICITY.

Frustration
[16c. *L frustrare*, to disappoint, frustrate]
The feeling of dissatisfaction and anger arising from not having your needs fulfilled. A very common feeling when you are held powerless and told to waste your time doing things which are meaningless.

Fundamentalism
[*c.*1980 in this sense. *L fundare*, to lay the foundation]
The belief that things can only be changed effectively by holding fast to your basic beliefs rather than compromising them for short-term

political advantage. Specifically, one of the main groupings within the German Green Party which rejects coalition with the major political parties: 'Those Greens who feel that the integrity of their positions would be compromised and eventually destroyed by a general coalition are called the "fundamental oppositionists" or simply "fundamentalists"' (Fritjof Capra and Charlene Spretnak, 1984). 'What is fundamentalism? Externally it puts ecology before economics, and fundamental long-term interests before immediate short-term ones' (Rudolf Bahro, 1986). The German Greens often shorten 'fundamentalists' to 'fundis', in contrast with the 'realos'. 'Fundamentalism' is also another name for a reactionary brand of Christianity currently suffering a worrying resurgence, particularly in the USA (*see* NEW RIGHT). *See also* REALISM.

Future
[14c. *L futurus*, about to be]
What lies ahead of us in time, which is to a large extent created every moment by us in the present. A common hope of all green-thinkers is that the future will be radically and very pleasantly different from the present. 'One delightful aspect of reality is that the future can never be predicted precisely, that it will always contain surprises. Our fears have longed for complete predictability, but this is only our fears. Boredom is a worse fate than terror, and boredom would be our lot if the future were completely predictable' (Harvey Jackins, 1973). 'Our dreaming muscles may be atrophied, but we can exercise and develop them. For the future is not out there in front of us, but inside us. Like the moth in the caterpillar's cocoon, it is hidden in us' (Joanna Macy, 1983). '"The future" is not something that will "happen" to us. We make the future every moment we live' (Jessica Lipnack and Jeffrey Stamps, 1986). *Future Shock*, the title of an influential book by Alvin Toffler (1970), describes the inability of human beings to adapt to the ever-increasing rate of change in technological and cultural innovation. The Future In Our Hands is an international movement for global awareness and equality, founded in Norway in 1977 — it has become an important voice for radical change in the Scandinavian countries, with connections with other green groups worldwide. *See also* UTOPIA, VISION.

Gg

Gaia
[*c.*1969 in this sense]
(*also* 'Gaea')
The Greek name for mother earth, '"the Deep-breasted One", called Oldest of Divinities' (Barbara Walker, 1983). Used by James Lovelock (at the suggestion of William Golding) as an appropriate name for the complex, sensate, living 'being' of the earth's biosphere. 'We have since defined Gaia as a complex entity involving the Earth's biosphere, atmosphere, oceans and soil; the totality constituting a feedback or cybernetic system which seeks an optimal physical and chemical environment for life on this planet' (James Lovelock, 1979). 'The "Gaia hypothesis" suggests that the earth and its atmosphere can best be looked at not as a lifeless physico-chemical construct, but as a living entity with the equivalent[s] of senses, intelligence, memory and the capacity to act. . . Gaia is non-human. She is the earth spirit, she is life, the ground, the air, the water and the interaction between all their inhabitants. Within the fabric of Gaia, the earth organism or the earth spirit, whichever term you prefer, there is an interwoven and intelligently driven web which searches for balance, continuity and stability' (Kit Pedler, 1979). People differ as to how 'Gaia' should be pronounced; most say 'guy-ah', though Kirkpatrick Sale (1985) claims that the Greeks pronounced it 'jee-ah', a pronunciation which also links it with other words from the same root like 'geography' and 'geology'. The renewed association between the 'body' of the earth and the body of a goddess presents many fruitful and frightening parallels (*see* BODY, EXPLOITATION, MOTHER EARTH, RAPE).

Games
[12c. *Old English gamen*, amusement, sport]
Time and energy diverted temporarily from the 'serious' business of

living to play, laugh, and remember how creative and spontaneous we can be — a very necessary part of all green-thinkers' lifestyle. 'Games are really important. They are an opportunity to build a sense of community and trust . . . Children joyfully "play games" inside and out, with energy, laughter and seriousness. . . [Adults] need to play as much as children do. . . There may be resistance to initiating a game because Western society has taught us to think of games as foolish, silly and a waste of time. However, hundreds of grownups have played these activities among themselves in a variety of situations and have enjoyed them tremendously. They have brought people together through laughter, offered alternatives to competition, and established new, more human lines of communication' (*For the Fun of It*, 1975). Since the mid 1970s, several groups of people have developed a range of non-competitive or NEW GAMES, in which spontaneity, cooperation and ingenuity are valued more than competition, force and manipulation. In group therapeutic situations the role of games — drama, roleplay and new games — is now an important one. In the therapy known as transactional analysis, developed by Eric Berne in the early 1960s, the name 'games' was used to describe the stereotyped exchanges between people playing set roles in their lives; this is a use of 'game' which underlines the relatively predictable nature of most organised, competitive games. Good games, however, always include lightness, spontaneity, laughter and insight: 'Good games flow quickly and have a monkey element to them' (Jenny James, 1985).

Garbage
(*see* WASTE)

Garden
[13c. *Old High German gart*, enclosure; *Old North French gardin*, yard]
An area of land, usually fairly small and surrounding a house, used for the cultivation of vegetables, fruit, herbs, trees and ornamental plants. Gardening is the one activity that brings a large number of people in Western society into contact with plants and the soil; in subsistence cultures gardening is an absolute necessity. The distinction between farming and gardening is partly to do with scale, partly with landownership, and partly with the amount of labour needed to look after the land; it is well-established that in terms of sustainable yield, small garden plots are far more productive than large agricultural units. 'I can think of no better form of personal involvement in the cure of the environment than that of gardening. A person who is growing a garden, if [they are] growing it organically, is improving a piece of the world' (Wendell Berry, 1972).

Gay
[*c*.1930 in this sense. *Old French gai*, merry]
Enjoying the company and close friendship of people of your own sex, and rejecting universal culturally-ordained heterosexuality. 'In the 1920s and 1930s the word gay surfaced in the underground homosexual subculture as a term of identification among homosexual men. Expressions such as "You're looking gay tonight", or "That's a gay tie you have there" were used to establish mutual identity in social situations. Finally, in the late 1960s, the term gay was taken up by the Gay Liberation Movement in its attempt to affirm "a truly joyous alternatve lifestyle" and throw off the sexually objectifying term "homosexual"' (Jeanna Cordova, 1974, quoted in Cheris Kramerae and Paula Treichler, 1985). While 'gay' is used more by men to describe themselves, in the USA it is also used by and of many gay women — in Europe 'lesbian' is the commoner term for a gay woman.

Gender
[14c. *L genus*, race, kind]
Popularly used as a synonym for SEX ('femaleness' and 'maleness'), but more specifically used by contemporary writers about sexual politics to mean the socially-imposed differences between women and men — between FEMININE and MASCULINE. 'Whereas sex refers to the biological, anatomical differences between male and female, gender refers to the emotional and psychological attributes which a given culture expects to coincide with physical maleness or femaleness. "Masculine" and "feminine" are gender terms, and although individuals born male are expected to develop a masculine gender identity as a natural course of events [and women a feminine gender identity], it is widely recognised that sex and gender may not always coincide' (Lisa Tuttle, 1986). Some feminist thinkers believe that gender must be eradicated if a truly egalitarian society is to evolve; others believe that the important thing is to be able to choose freely your own gender preferences.

Gene
[1911. *Gk genea*, race, generation]
Part of the DNA (deoxyribonucleic acid) structure found on a chromosome in the nucleus of a cell which transmits hereditary characteristics from parent to offspring. Of particular concern at present because of deterioration of genetic quality as a result of RADIATION and other pollutants, and because of recent developments in BIOTECHNOLOGY. 'Many geneticists believe that [human] genes constitute [our] most precious heritage, and that a deterioration in gene quality can result in a corresponding decrease in the quality of life. Steady progress in the control of infectious diseases, lengthening human life spans, and

improved procedures for identifying genetic disorders have revealed an important residue of genetic disease in human populations. An impressive proportion of hospital admittances, for instance, are now recognized as reflecting genetic disabilities. The prospects for directly curing the resulting genetic diseases, in contrast to merely alleviating their symptoms, are poor, and not likely to improve in the near future' (*Science*, 1975, quoted in Art Kleiner and Stewart Brand, 1986).

Gene Pool
[1970]
The vast variety of genetic material in the biosphere or in one part of it. Most ecologists are extremely worried about the erosion of the gene pool by human activities, particularly the destruction of natural habitats and the rapidly increasing use of unified hybrid species (which carry identical genes). The *reason* for maintaining the diversity of the gene pool, however, is still seen primarily as its potential resource for human beings — 'we never know how much *useful* genetic material we are destroying'. Green-thinkers know that the gene pool must be conserved for itself, and that human genes — themselves part of the pool — are ultimately as much at risk as any other (*see* BIOTECHNOLOGY, GENE).

General Systems Theory
[1951]
The recognition that all SYSTEMS have many of the same characteristics. This recognition makes it possible to draw useful analogies between different sorts of system, and to represent complex systems by making MODELS of them. On the other hand, scientists and social scientists in the 1960s and 1970s tended to see general systems theory as an answer to everything, and its overly-mechanistic approach often fails to take into account the important differences between different systems, considerations of scale and oversimplification, and, perhaps above all, anything that cannot be measured.

Genetic Engineering
[1969]
Another name for BIOTECHNOLOGY or REPRODUCTIVE TECHNOLOGY.

Genotoxin
[*c*.1976]
A general term for a substance which causes the mutation of the DNA code in chromosomes. 'If you hear that something is a mutagen, it is also probably a carcinogen. And vice versa. They can both be called "genotoxic"' Stewart Brand, 1979, in Art Kleiner and Stewart Brand, 1986). *See also* CARCINOGEN, MUTAGEN.

Gentleness
[14c. *Old French gentil*, noble]
Behaviour characterised by CARING, sensitivity, NONVIOLENCE and non-exploitation. 'Gentleness' is too often used to imply weakness; in women it is expected and belittled; in men it is often scorned, hence: 'Gentleman: a contradiction in terms' (Laura X, 1984, quoted in Cheris Kramerae and Paula Treichler, 1985). 'Planting saplings at Gorleben [the site of a planned nuclear installation in southern Germany] seems ridiculous, given that the bulldozers are ready and waiting to plough up the earth. We are not armed and we make easy targets, but we will not cut ourselves off from life. We have gentleness, force of numbers, freedom from domination on our side, and the solidarity to overcome all divisions. Our motto is, "Be gentle and subversive"' (Petra Kelly, 1984).

Geodesic
[1950 in this sense. *Gk ge + daiein*, to divide the earth]
A structure, usually curved or dome-shaped, made of light elements in tension; popularised in the late 1950s by Buckminster Fuller, who designed many dome-shaped structures: hence 'geodesic dome'. They are used as greenhouses, dwellings and public buildings, though such structures are often relatively short-lived.

Geothermal Energy
[1875. *Gk ge + therme*, earth heat]
Heat and power generated from the internal heat of the earth, especially when sources of such heat are found at the earth's surface. A very important source of energy in some areas, for example in Iceland, northern California and parts of New Zealand. 'Geothermal energy is another growing source of electricity. Where high-pressure steam is near the surface, geothermal power generation is already a bargain. . . Central America, parts of Southeast Asia, and the western United States have the potential for major reliance on geothermal energy. Prime sites also exist in parts of southern Europe and East Africa' (*Worldwatch*, 1986). Although usually thought of as a 'renewable' energy source, this is not strictly the case, since the heat below the earth's surface is subject to the same entropy laws as anything else. If not carefully controlled, geothermal energy can cause HEAT POLLUTION, though the development of underground heat transfer systems can alleviate this problem.

Gestalt
[1922. *German gestalt*, form, shape; from *Old High German stellen*, to place]
A pattern or structure which can be seen as an integrated whole, although this SYNERGY may not be obvious from examining any of the

parts in isolation; by extension (and its more common usage), a form of individual or group THERAPY based on the belief that the healthy human being must be seen as a whole, not as separate parts, and that the present experience of the client is more important than trying to understand the intricacies of the past. The aim of gestalt is to help people to become aware of and integrate their fragmented parts, to acknowledge and celebrate their own experience, and not to be limited by the expectations of others. Based largely on the pioneering work of Frederick Perls in California, gestalt techniques are now used by many therapists along with techniques drawn from other therapeutic disciplines. 'I do my thing, and you do your thing./I am not in this world to live up to your expectations/and you are not in this world to live up to mine./You are you and I am I,/And if by chance we find each other, it's beautiful./If not, it can't be helped' (Frederick Perls, 1969).

Ghettoisation
[1936. Possibly *Italian getto*, foundry, as the first Jewish ghetto was founded in 1516 on the site of a foundry in Venice]
(US: 'ghettoization')
The segregation and isolation of an oppressed minority group, usually in the slum area of a city. Until about 1900 'the ghetto' meant almost exclusively the crowded Jewish quarter of a city, crowded because of punitive anti-semitic legislation limiting the area available to Jews. 'Ghettoisation' now refers to any policy (or lack of policy) which forces people to live in slum conditions, frequently under conditions of extreme economic and social exploitation.

Gift
[13c. *Old Norse gift*]
Something which is freely given with no expectation of reciprocation. 'A glacial lake is a beautiful gift and it comes about but once in a million years' (Michael Tobias, 1985).

Global
[late 17c. *L globus*, globe]
Covering the whole PLANET; a recognition that we are all connected. 'Given the urgency, scope, and complexity of the challenges before us, the efforts now underway around the world fall far short of what is needed. An era of unpecedented global cooperation and commitment is essential (*Global 2000*, 1982). 'There are . . . many signs that a global view is developing, not least in public opinion. In all rich countries during the sixties and seventies, countless grassroots movements and groups have arisen with global solidarity as their primary objective' (Erik Dammann, 1984). 'For many who watch and listen, globalism is

more important than capitalism or socialism; the human problem more important than the political party' (John Holliday, 1986). 'Acting locally, thinking globally' (Hazel Henderson, 1978). Thinking on the large scale is vitally important, as human activities do affect the whole globe; but it is equally important not to become engulfed by the globality of everything to the point where we become so guilt-ridden and overpowered that we cannot act. Surrounded by books and projects bearing titles like *Sisterhood is Global*, *The Global 2000 Report to the President*, *Global Change: An International Geosphere/Biosphere Program* and *Global Possible*, it can be hard to see where we fit in. 'Global' is in danger of joining PLANETARY as a distant and inaccessible concept, taken over by anonymous bureaucracy.

GNP
(*see* GROSS NATIONAL PRODUCT)

Goal
[early 17c. *Middle English gol*, boundary, limit]
A specific objective for the FUTURE towards which efforts can be directed. If you don't know where you are going it is very difficult to know which direction to start out in: 'The first few steps in the process of deliberation consist in *seeing clearly*, in posing the problem plainly, in formulating the alternatives with which we are faced, and in considering the path and the outcome that will follow each alternative. This approach applies to deliberating about different goals or about a single goal. In the latter case, the alternatives can pertain to different possibilities for realizing that goal, or simply to whether to pursue it or not. This clear posing of alternatives seems obvious, but very often it is not done' (Roberto Assagioli, 1974).

Good
[*c.*1850 in this sense. *Old English god*, good]
Another name for a product with a money value; typical of the way that the capitalist mentality has taken over our most fundamental ethical choices. The resultant confusion between 'goods' and 'good' leads us to compare different aspects of what is good as if they were lined up on a supermarket shelf: 'The habit of separating the different kinds of good from each other is entirely a consequence of a deformed social order, in which rational intelligence has so often to try to justify emotionally unacceptable or repulsive actions' (Raymond Williams, 1985).

Good Work
[*c.*1975]
Useful, meaningful and fulfilling human activity. 'If we see work as nothing but an unpleasant activity, it is no use talking about good work,

unless we mean *less* work. Why put any goodness into our work beyond the absolute minimum? Who could afford to do good work? What would be the point of making something perfect when something imperfect would do as well?' (E.F. Schumacher, 1980). *See also* WORK.

Gradualism
[1835 *L gradus* step]
Achieving change by small steps; another name for INCREMENTALISM: '[Bioregionalism] has the virtue of gradualism. It suggests that the processes of change — first of organizing, educating, activating a constituency, and then of reimagining, reshaping, and recreating a continent — are slow, steady, continuous, and methodical, not revolutionary and cataclysmic' (Kirkpatrick Sale, 1985).

Graffiti
[1851. *Italian graffito*, a little scratch]
A popular response to the large blank spaces provided by much contemporary architecture, and to the immense advertising images displayed on hoardings. Graffiti frequently consists of colourful and witty commentaries on the state of society.

Grassroots
[1880]
Taking account of the wishes and opinions of everybody affected by political, social and economic policies, especially those who currently have little say, and involving them in direct decision-making. An important strand of green politics: 'Grassroots-democratic politics means an increased realization of decentralized, direct democracy. We start from the belief that the decisions at the grassroots level must . . . be given priority. We grant far-reaching powers of autonomy and self-administration to decentralized, manageable grassroots units' (die Grünen, quoted in Fritjof Capra and Charlene Spretnak, 1984).

Green
[*c*.1978 in this sense]
A set of beliefs and a concomitant lifestyle that stress the importance of respect for the EARTH and all its inhabitants, using only what resources are necessary and appropriate, acknowledging the rights of all forms of LIFE, and recognising that all that exists is part of one interconnected whole. The concept of being 'green' arose in the late 1970s, though since the 1950s 'green' had been used as a qualifier for environmental projects such as The Green Front, a tree-planting campaign initiated by The Men of the Trees in 1952, and GREENING was already in use in the late 1960s. The Green Alliance, an ecological pressure group, was founded in Britain in 1978; at this time 'green' was used to describe an

ecological perspective, and many of the social and economic implications of such a perspective had yet to be looked at. The rise of die Grünen (the Greens) in West Germany and their first parliamentary success in 1983 brought the word 'green' to many people's attention. By this time die Grünen had formulated many far-reaching policies, and the publication of the party programme in English late in 1983 attracted the interest of people throughout the alternative movement. To many people — and to most politicians — 'green' still means 'environmental', which is fine as far as it goes, but to green-thinkers being 'green' goes much further: 'For me personally, *the minimum criteria for being green* would run roughly as follows: a reverence for the Earth and for all its creatures; a willingness to share the world's wealth among *all* its peoples; prosperity to be achieved through sustainable alternatives to the rat race of economic growth; lasting security to be achieved through non-nuclear defence strategies and considerably reduced arms spending; a rejection of materialism and the destructive values of industrialism; a recognition of the rights of future generations in our use of all resources; an emphasis on socially useful, personally rewarding work, enhanced by human-scale technology; protection of the environment as a precondition of a healthy society; an emphasis on personal growth and spiritual development; respect for the gentler side of human nature; open, participatory democracy at every level of society; recognition of the crucial importance of significant reductions in population levels; harmony between people of every race, colour and creed; a non-nuclear, low-energy strategy, based on conservation, greater efficiency and renewable sources; an emphasis on self-reliance and decentralized communities' (Jonathon Porritt, 1984). 'Such a politics is "green" because it speaks of a new spring, when all things start afresh' (Maurice Ash, 1980). 'If there is an immediacy to Green politics, there is also a deep optimism that we have taken the first steps. .. The future, if there is to be one, is Green' (Fritjof Capra and Charlene Spretnak, 1984).

Green Ban
[1972]
The refusal by construction and other workers, usually with trade union support and always with the support of local residents, to take part in projects which are likely to cause environmental damage. An idea which has been most fully developed in Australia, especially in Sydney, where green bans have saved natural bushland, woodland and parkland from unnecessary and harmful development. Green bans and similar actions have taken place in Belgium, Britain, France, Italy, The Netherlands, Norway, Sweden, the USA and West Germany.

Green Belt

[1943]

An area of COUNTRYSIDE around a town or city in which urban expansion is carefully and strictly controlled in order to ensure open space for agriculture, wildlife and recreation. The first official green belt was that set up around London in 1947, now under extreme pressure from developers and the threat of acquiescence to this pressure.

Greenhouse Effect

[1937]

Excessive heating of the earth's surface due to an increased amount of carbon dioxide pollution which hinders the reflection of solar heat back into space. 'If the world continues at the present rate to increase its demand for energy, and for fossil fuels in particular, then the "natural" concentration of carbon dioxide in the atmosphere will double by about AD 2025. Many climatologists agree that such a change will, by enhancing the "greenhouse effect" that keeps the surface of the Earth warmer than if there were no atmosphere, increase mean temperatures over the globe by 2-3°C. The increases would be greatest at high latitudes and there would be associated shifts in rainfall patterns. It is impossible to predict exactly how the climate will change, but several analyses of the differences between warm and cold years of the recent past suggest that regions that would be both warmer and drier include the grainlands of the US, Europe and the USSR, while the changes in some parts of the Third World could benefit agriculture. This realisation has added a new dimension to the debate about the carbon dioxide "threat", emphasising its global nature and highlighting the differences between the "rich North" and the "poor South"' (John Gribbin, *New Scientist*, 1981).

Greening

[*c*.1963]

The process of 'going green'. 'Greening' first reached general recognition with Charles Reich's *The Greening of America* (1970): 'The extraordinary thing about this new consciousness is that it has emerged out of the wasteland of the corporate state, like flowers pushing up through the concrete pavement. . . For one who thought the world was irretrievably encased in metal and plastic and sterile stone, it seems a veritable greening of America.' Now almost anything can be greened, from deserts and cities to people and institutions.

Greenpeace

[1971]

An important international DIRECT ACTION campaigning group, started in Canada and now with an active membership in ten countries. Its name combines two important green ideas, and Greenpeace is synonymous in many people's minds with environmental action. Greenpeace's principal campaigns are against commercial whaling and sealing, the dumping of toxic and radioactive waste at sea, and the testing of nuclear weapons.

Green Revolution
[1968]
The enormous short-term increase in grain yields made possible by high-yield crop varieties, pesticides, fertilisers and mechanisation. Hailed by manufacturers of the products which made it possible as the solution to the world's food problems, but the short-lived 'green revolution' has created far more problems than it has solved. 'For the farmers the immediate effect of the new farming methods was a spectacular improvement in agricultural production, and the new era of chemical farming was hailed as the "Green Revolution". Soon, however, the dark side of the new technology became apparent, and today it is evident that the Green Revolution has helped neither the farmers nor the land nor the starving millions. The only ones to gain from it were the petrochemical corporations' (Fritjof Capra, 1982). It is very clear that only farmers who were already relatively rich have benefited: 'Where nothing is done to alleviate inequalities, the Green Revolution is guaranteed to worsen them. . . The university "development" sociologists and economists on our side of the world have been studying the everyday lives of people benefiting from — in their terms — the Green Revolution, with a view to dealing with them should they express discontent. Meanwhile, the poor have been carrying out research on their own everyday lives and have found them wanting. . . The Green Revolution is increasing their misery to what may . . . become an intolerable level' (Susan George, 1976).

Greens
[*c.*1980]
People who advocate and participate in green politics, particularly in West Germany, where the green party is called die Grünen — the Greens. 'The Greens introduced a new style of politics into the electoral system. While other politicians spoke with pompous and evasive rhetoric, the Greens used simple, direct language and coined new phrases. The conventional parties were all led by men; the Greens had a striking proportion of women in leading positions. The old-style politicians dressed in suits and ties; the Greens wore casual clothes. . . The Greens proposed an integrated approach to the current ecological, economic and political crises, which they stressed are interrelated and global in nature. They spoke of the "spiritual impoverishment" of industrialized societies. They asked questions that neither of the major

parties nor the government could answer and they amplified with playful humor the ironies that resulted' (Fritjof Capra and Charlene Spretnak, 1984). The German Green Party has several identifiable factions: visionary/holistic Greens, eco-Greens, peace-movement Greens and radical-left Greens. Jonathon Porritt (ed, 1987) has also coined the distinction between 'light Greens' (the reformers or 'realists' — in the German Green sense of advocating compromise to get things moving) and 'dark Greens' (the radicals or fundamentalists).

Gross National Product
[1947]
(*also* GNP)
The sum of all the goods and services provided through the 'market' within one state, including government expenditure; the shrine of growth economics. When GNP goes up the politician and economists cheer; when it goes down they fall silent. As a measure of a truly healthy economy (one that is ecologically sound and sustainable), GNP is a useless indicator of wealth — it only counts things that have a money value, it makes no distinction between money spent on totally different things, and it says nothing at all about sustainability. 'Because GNP is a "gross" figure it measures *everything* purchased and makes no distinction between a car, a Coke, and a cremation' (Paul Hawken, 1983). If you spend a lot of money creating pollution and then a lot more cleaning it up, both amounts go towards GNP; the more you make people ill and then spend money making them well again, the higher the GNP. 'The social costs of a polluted environment, disrupted communities, disrupted family life, and eroded primary relationships may be the only part of GNP that is growing' (Hazel Henderson, 1981). Many alternative indicators to GNP have been devised which take EXTERNALITIES, SOCIAL COSTS AND BENEFITS and SUSTAINABILITY into account. They include:
— ALP (Adjusted Local Product) (Paul Ekins (ed), 1986).
— ANP (Adjusted National Product) (*ibid*).
— BHN (Basic Human Needs) (J. and M. McHale, 1979).
— GNC (Gross National Cost) (Michael Tobias, 1985).
— MEW (Measure of Economic Welfare) (W.D. Nordhaus and J. Tobin, in M. Moss (ed), 1971).
— NRU (Natural Resource Units) (Westman and Gifford, *Science*, 1973).
— PQLI (Physical Quality of Life Indicator) (David Morris, 1982).

Group
[late 17c. *French*, from *Italian gruppo*, knot]
A number of people working together on a common project or towards

a common goal. Many different sorts of group exist — women's and men's groups, AFFINITY GROUPS, peace groups, etc. 'Groups' has recently become shorthand for therapy and similar groups. 'Group dynamics' or 'group process' describe the interactions within a small group of people; 'groupwork' or 'group therapy' is therapeutic work which is done in a small group of people.

Growth
[late 16c. *Old English growan*, to grow]
An increase in size or number. NATURE produces abundant growth wherever LIFE can gain a foothold, and in general does it best without human interference. Economic 'growth' is the guiding light of most economists and politicians who believe, despite mounting evidence to the contrary, that more is always better. 'Notwithstanding the fact that bringing the Jerusalem of economic growth to England's green and pleasant land has so far conspicuously reduced both the greenness and the pleasantness, economic growth remains the most respectable catchword in the current political vocabulary' (Edward Mishan, 1967). The influential book *The Limits to Growth*, published in 1972, explained in detail how unrestrained exponential growth, particularly of population and technology, could not be sustained: 'Every day of continued exponential growth brings the world system closer to the ultimate limits to that growth. A decision to do nothing is a decision to increase the risk of collapse' (Club of Rome, 1972). Most economists have still not yet seen the light: 'Growth economists and the politicians they advise still assume that economic growth on an indefinite basis is both possible and desirable, and hasten on towards environmental bankruptcy' (Paul Ekins, 1986). 'The mind-set that always puts growth in first place — the attitude that there is no such thing as enough, that cannot conceive of too much of a good thing, . . is the paradigm upon which rest the models and policies of our current political economy . . . [It] begins with the theological assumptions of indefinite wants . . . with redemption vouchsafed by the omnipotent saviour of technology. . . The first commandment is to produce more and more goods for more and more people, world without end. And that this is not only possible, but desirable' (Herman Daly, *The Ecologist*, 1979). Green-thinkers know that such growth cannot be sustained, and have put forward radically different models for sustainable and responsible consumption — *see* STEADY-STATE. 'If you are expansion-oriented . . . a drop in growth is a cause for pessimism. If you are contraction-oriented, then growth is a cause for pessimism' (Rudolf Bahro, 1986). For growth in a therapeutic sense *see* PERSONAL GROWTH.

Guaranteed Basic Income
[1978]
Another term for SOCIAL WAGE, preferred by the British Green Party.

Guilt
(*see* BLAME)

Guru
[*c.*1965 in this sense. *Hindi guru*, teacher]
The leading figure in a hierarchical charismatic movement (though originally 'guru' meant specifically a Hindu or Sikh religious teacher). A position open to a great deal of abuse and manipulation, and a situation wide open to projection — it is no coincidence that most gurus are men. Very many people in the alternative movement have at some point in their lives chosen a guru and considered them to be their spiritual teacher; they may have learned a great deal, but the handing over of your power to another person which this usually entails is anathema to many green-thinkers. *See also* SPIRITUALITY.

Hh

Habitat
[1796. *L habitare*, to dwell]
The place or type of environment where a plant or animal usually lives. 'Ecologists use the term habitat to mean the place where an organism lives, and the term ecological niche to mean the role that the organism plays in the ecosystem; the habitat is the "address", so to speak, and the niche is the "profession"' (Eugene Odum, 1963). A major concern of environmentalists is the destruction of certain types of habitat, which denies a home to the species that live there, hence 'habitat loss', 'habitat destruction' and 'habitat protection': 'As habitats have been damaged or destroyed, so individual species of flora and fauna have suffered in parallel' (*Countryside Conflicts*, 1986). Habitats are often subdivided according to their characteristic geology, vegetation and location, hence 'wetland habitats', 'woodland habitats', 'heathland habitats', 'grassland habitats', 'mountain habitats', etc.

Handicappism
[*c.*1980]
The systematic OPPRESSION of DIFFERENTLY-ABLED people by those who can move, speak and think easily; also (and less pejoratively) called NORMALISM. *See also* ACCESS, DISABLED.

Harassment
[17c. *Old French harer*, to set a dog on someone]
Constantly and deliberately hurting someone in relatively small but oppressive ways; 'harassment' is most often used as shorthand for 'sexual harassment at work': 'repeated, unreciprocated and unwelcome comments, looks, jokes, suggestions or physical contact that might threaten a woman's job security or create a stressful or intimidating working environment' (Ann Sedley and Melissa Benn, quoted in Elizabeth Wilson, 1983). Traditionally seen by men as 'just a bit of fun',

sexual harassment is seen by feminists as the thin end of the wedge of sexual violence (*see also* RAPE). 'Remember: Sexual harassment at work *is* a serious issue (men can *afford* to joke about it); To complain about it is not over-reacting; it is perfectly reasonable; it does cost women jobs, health and peace of mind; you have the right to work in an environment that is free from hassle and problems of this kind; there is no reason why any woman should have to "put up with it" ' (London Rape Crisis Centre, 1984).

Harmony
[14c. *L harmonia*, concord of sounds; from *Gk harmos*, joint]
The joyful unity achieved when different sounds, people or ideas are woven together in such a way that they maintain their own integrity and at the same time create a single composition.

Hazardous Waste
(*see* WASTE)

Healing
[*Old English hælen*, to heal; akin to *hal*, whole]
(1) [*c*.1890] Helping people to be healthy by so-called 'paranormal' means; hence 'charismatic healing', 'hand healing', 'faith healing', 'spiritualist healing'. 'Healing simply makes use of a sort of empathy as the main source of healing power. If the healer or patient believes that some sort of supernatural being gives this healing power it can be called faith healing, but the spiritual healers . . . do not demand that their patients believe in anything' (Andrew Stanway, 1980).
(2) [*c*.1970; a gradual extension of sense (1)] Helping people to be healthy in a holistic way, providing an alternative to MEDICINE and thus allowing them to move away from a drugs-and-surgery approach to HEALTH. 'Over the years there have been many theories of healing, but there has never been one comprehensive theory, a single unified structure which adequately explains healing to everyone's satisfaction. As we explore the concept of holistic healing, it will become clear that an all-embracing theory of healing is almost certainly neither possible nor desirable. In practice, no system of medicine can produce healing, much less curing, on its own and in every case. Whatever we believe about healing and being healed, we cannot ultimately deprive death of its due' (Jan Resnick, 1986).

Health
[12c. *Old English hœlth*; akin to *hal*, whole]
The state of well-being of living things; the word can refer to any organism, but is most often used of human beings, when it implies fulfilment and a zestful enjoyment of LIFE. This is not, however, the implicit view of

many 'health-care professionals', who tend to see 'health' as an almost impossible state which can only be achieved when DISEASE has been completely destroyed: 'Nothing has changed so much in the past twenty-five years as the public's perception of its own health. The change amounts to a loss of confidence in the human form. The general belief these days seems to be that the human body is fundamentally flawed, subject to disintegration at any moment, always on the verge of mortal disease, always in need of continual monitoring and support by health-care professionals' (Lewis Thomas, 1977, quoted in Lawrence LeShan, 1982). Many green-thinkers have stressed the importance of reclaiming health not only as a right and a virtue, but as the basic condition of being alive. 'To be in good health means not only to be successful in coping with reality but also to enjoy the success; it means to be able to feel alive in pleasure and in pain; it means to cherish but also to risk survival. . . A world of optimal and widespread health is obviously a world of minimal and only occasional medical intervention. Healthy people are those who live in healthy homes on a healthy diet in an environment equally fit for birth, growth, work, healing and dying; they are sustained by a culture that enhances the conscious acceptance of limits to population, of ageing, of incomplete recovery and ever-imminent death. Healthy people need minimal bureaucratic interference to mate, give birth, share the human condition, and die' (Ivan Illich, 1976).

Health Food
[1882]
FOOD and food supplements which are sold as being more nutritious than other foodstuffs. 'Twenty years ago, in the early stage of the natural foods movement in this country, the "health food store" was the principle type of alternative food outlet. This enterprise, however, actually sold very little food. Shelves were crowded with vitamins, nutritional supplements, "natural" medications, and various potions and elixirs. . . The health food store still exists, but for the most part it has been superceded by the natural foods store, . . where the primary aim is to provide whole, unadulterated staple foods, organically produced if possible and sold at competitive prices' (Ronald Kotzsch, *East/West* magazine, September 1985). Green-thinkers now usually reserve 'health food' to describe commercially packaged foods for the 'health market', using WHOLEFOOD to mean really healthy food.

Heart Politics
[1986]
A politics based on the power, creativity and potential of every human being; an idea expounded by Fran Peavey in her influential book of the

same name. 'The challenge of *Heart Politics* is that it doesn't ask for our approval. It doesn't try to convince us that Fran's choices are noble, or *the* way to change the world. It doesn't tell us which risks to take. Rather, *Heart Politics* challenges us to look at our own choices with fresh eyes and ask: Of what am *I* capable that I thought perhaps I did not have the courage to attempt?' (Frances Moore Lappé, in Fran Peavey, 1986).

Heat Pollution
[*c*.1960]
The contamination of the atmosphere or bodies of water with large amounts of waste heat, usually from power stations. 'The demand for power has meant that in Canada, for example, waste heat from thermal power generation is predicted to rise 14 times in the period 1966-90, and by AD 2000 the amount of waste heat reaching Lake Ontario in January will be equivalent to 8 per cent of the solar energy input in that month. Most of the heat is carried away as hot water and this produces distinct changes in biota. A body of water at 30-35°C is essentially a biological desert' (Ian Simmons, 1974). The pocket of heated air over a city is called an 'urban heat island'. *See also* CO-GENERATION, WASTE.

Heat Pump
[1894]
A device which extracts heat from a source only slightly warmer than its surroundings, delivering it at a higher temperature. This is done (as in a refrigerator but with the opposite result) by compressing a suitable fluid into a vapour in the lower temperature area, then condensing it back into a fluid in the higher-temperature area where the heat is needed. Thus heat can be extracted from industrial cooling water, or from air in the roofspace of a house for domestic heating.

Heat Storage
(*see* THERMAL STORAGE)

Heavy Metals
[*c*.1860]
Metals with a high specific gravity, such as mercury, lead and cadmium, which are poisonous to living organisms and persist when dumped or emitted into the atmosphere. 'The release of untreated industrial waste into rivers and the sea has contributed to the build-up of heavy metals such as mercury and cadmium in water and fish. Heavy metals crop up regularly elsewhere. Lead, for example, is found not only in emissions from motor vehicles, but in domestic water pipes, paint and food. Cadmium is used in several industrial processes and is also found in phosphate fertilizers' (John McCormick, 1985). *See also* POLLUTION, WASTE.

Hedgerow

[12c. *Old English hecg + raw*, hedge-row]

A long line of specially-planted and regularly-maintained shrubs and trees growing along a bank, acting as a land division, windbreak, source of food and refuge for wildlife. Hedgerows are an important part of the landscape of Britain, northern France, Ireland and New England, but many hedgerows have been destroyed in the last forty years as fields have been enlarged to accommodate ever larger machinery: 'Farmers removed a quarter of the hedgerows in England and Wales between 1946 and 1974, about 120,000 miles in all, or 4,500 miles a year' (Marion Shoard, 1980). Hedge removal has caused considerable concern among conservationists in Britain: 'Loss of hedgerows, depending upon their state of maintenance and the amount of woodland in the locality, can result in the loss of an important wildlife sanctuary at the field margin . . . About 250 plant species are basically hedgerow plants, [and] 21 of 28 species of mammals, 65 of 91 species of birds and 23 of 54 species of butterflies breed in hedges, though none is confined exclusively to this habitat. However, if both the woodlands and a large proportion of hedgerows in an area are removed, the consequences . . . can be devastating' (*Countryside Conflicts*, 1986). The rate of hedge removal has slowed down in recent years, partly as a result of public concern, partly because fields are now big enough to take large machinery, and partly as farmers recognise the ecological advantages to retaining hedgerows: 'There are good agricultural, as well as conservation, arguments in favour of the retention of boundary hedges. Properly maintained, they are still immeasurably better barriers to stock and people than any kind of fence. And the raised banks they usually stand on form ideal refuges for the insects that play such a crucial role in the pollination of cultivated flowering crops, particularly clover and fruit trees' (Richard Mabey, 1980).

Hedonism

[1856. *Gk hedone*, pleasure]

The belief that PLEASURE is the most important goal of human existence. Whether or not this squares with green thinking depends upon your definition of 'pleasure', but for many Westerners it means the accruing of ever more material possessions. *See also* UTILITARIANISM.

Herb

[13c. *L herba*, herb, grass]

A small non-woody plant that dies back at the end of each growing season; more specifically such a plant (and this includes some woody plants) that also has recognised medicinal or culinary qualities. The use of herbs in medicine has a long history, and more than half of the drugs used in mainstream medicine come originally from plants. The traditional wisdom of herbalism is again becoming popular as faith in allopathic medicine declines, though there have recently been several backlash attempts to control the use of 'dangerous' herbs.

Heritage
[*c*.1930 in this sense. *L heres*, heir]
Something important from the past which is part of our tradition and inheritance, and thus deserves special attention and STEWARDSHIP. The word has been used in so many contexts in recent years that 'heritage' is in danger of becoming an all-purpose advertising tool and losing its useful meaning. 1975 was European Architectural Heritage Year 'to awaken the interest of the European peoples in their common architectural heritage' (quoted in Alan Dobby, 1978); British Heritage is the new name given in 1985 to the Ancient Monuments Commission; and there has been a proposal for the reclassification of British conservation areas into three categories, the most important of which would be 'heritage sites': 'Heritage sites would be areas with special and irreplaceable nature conservation qualities (of wild or semi-natural vegetation) and/or highly prized landscape beauty' (*Countryside Conflicts*, 1986). *See also* CONSERVATION, PRESERVATION.

Heterosexism
[1975]
The OPPRESSION of anybody who chooses not to conform to the conventional standards of heterosexual relating; the GAY and LESBIAN experience of oppression.

Heterosexuality
[1892. *Gk heteros* + *L sexus*, other sex]
Preferring to share sexual experiences with people of the other sex than the one you belong to. Many feminists, particularly lesbians, see the institutionalisation of heterosexuality ('compulsory heterosexuality' — Adrienne Rich, 1980) as the basis of patriarchal oppression, and question whether it is ever possible for women to have relationships with men which are not oppressive: 'Any woman who takes part in a heterosexual couple helps to shore up male supremacy by making its foundations stronger' (Leeds Revolutionary Feminist Group, 1981). Other feminists question whether complete sexual disengagement is the answer, and many find the whole issue confusing. In general, however, all are agreed that men need to change very radically: 'Both men and women have choice and what I want is for men to start "choosing" to change. . . I'm convinced that they won't give anything up until they really begin to feel the draught' (Pat, in Leeds Revolutionary Feminist Group, 1981). 'Heterosexuality should not be proscribed as politically

incorrect, but it must, always, be questioned and criticized. . . It should be possible to criticize the institution of heterosexuality without banning the enjoyment of it' (Liza Tuttle, 1986).

Heurism

[1821. *Gk heuriskein*, to discover]

Solving problems by trying out different solutions rather than resorting to theory, and using what is learnt to build up a picture of the situation. An experiential way of learning, which very often produces appropriate results faster than more analytical methods of learning.

Hierarchy

[14c. *Gk hierarkhes*, high priest]

A social structure in the form of a 'pyramid' with the mass of the 'lower classes' at the bottom and a 'hierarch' at the top. A form of society which green thinking sees as being at the root of OPPRESSION, denying the importance and uniqueness of individual human beings, concentrating wealth at the upper levels, and being kept in place by force. It is often suggested that the hierarchy of society only reflects similar hierarchies in nature, but the perception of apparent hierarchy in nature can always be traced to an anthropomorphic approach which sees what it wants to see: 'Stratification and hierarchy within specific subgroups in the animal world is extremely rare, and almost all "evidence" of it is anthropomorphic carelessness' (Kirkpatrick Sale, 1985). 'The seemingly hierarchical traits of many animals are more like variations in the links of a chain than organized stratifications of the kind we find in human societies and institutions' (Murray Bookchin, 1981). Ecologists use the term 'hetarchy' to denote species and individuals with distinctive roles and features which are complementary rather than which constitute a hierarchy of dominance — this mirrors the feminist epithet of 'different therefore equal'.

Hippie

[1953. *American slang hip*, trendy, informed — origin unknown]

Someone who has chosen to opt out of mainstream society, usually living more or less communally, wearing unconventional and brightly-coloured clothes, and often letting their hair grow long. The word was originally used by hippies themselves to describe a lifestyle which was at its height in San Francisco in the early 1960s. It was not long before the exploiters moved in and the 'flower children' started to move out: 'The flower children had begun to flee San Francisco where . . . they had planted the first seeds of a community. For a while it flourished, and elsewhere small hippie ghettoes were rising in other slum-torn centres . . . But in the Haight, as elsewhere, the influx of hippies was followed by pushers, junkies, speed freaks, prostitutes and the Mafia. When the police came on the scene, the flower children were pushed off the streets, which had become unsafe for anyone, hip or straight' (Robert Houriet, 1971). Hippiedom in the 1960s had a positive and joyful character, but as in San Francisco so elsewhere the reactionary backlash took the word and used it as a weapon against the alternative movement: 'To me the true meaning of the term "hippy" is to be found in those 60s ideals [of] an "alternative" society based on peace and love, sharing and cooperation. . . Unfortunately, "hippy" has since acquired a whole wealth of new meaning. It has become a key word to summon up prejudice and emotions of fear and loathing, and its original meaning has been lost. The San Francisco hippies could see this happening way back in 1967. In Haight Ashbury they held a mock funeral for "Hippy", whose good name had been murdered by the media. Now, almost 20 years later, it is surely time to give the word a decent and final burial' (*Green Line*, July 1986). 'Hippies', 'hippy convoys' (*see* TRAVELLER) and 'hippy troublemakers' are the invention of frightened politicians looking for scapegoats, unwilling to acknowledge the right of everybody to their own choice of non-exploitative lifestyle. 'Peter had a beard and Jesus-eyes, and was referred to by the local children as a hippie. But then they'd call anyone a hippie who, if a woman, wore skirts longer than mid-calf, and, if a man, wore an earring' (Fay Weldon, 1987).

Hippocratic
[1620. After Hippocrates, 4th-century BC Greek physician]
Pertaining to the teachings of Hippocrates, often called 'the father of modern medicine', but in fact a healer who had his roots in the holistic 'Hygieian' tradition of Pythagoras, and whose methods had little in common with modern allopathic MEDICINE. While the 'Hippocratic Oath' [1747] is still upheld by doctors, many holistic practitioners believe that few doctors understand its real meaning, especially when it exhorts doctors 'never to injure or do wrong, never to give poison or allow it to be given'. 'Until recently, all medical students took the "Hippocratic Oath" before practising medicine. Modern medical knowledge has largely replaced Hippocratic wisdom, but for all its progress it can hardly claim to have unravelled the mysteries to which Hippocrates refers. Hippocrates' emphasis on "not harming or wronging" reflects his deep humility in the face of what he does not know. Do we know any better today what we do not know?' (Jan Resnick, 1986). 'For a wide range of conditions, those who are treated least probably make the best progress. "For the sick," Hippocrates said, "the least is best"' (Ivan Illich, 1976).

History
[14c. *Gk histor*, a learned person]
The PAST, and what we can learn about it which will help us to understand the present and plan for the future. 'Behind us lies the wealth of history itself, the treasure-trove of knowledge — of successes laden with promise and failures laden with fault. We are the heirs of a history that can teach us what we must avoid if we are to escape immolation and what we must pursue if we are to realize freedom and self-fulfilment' (Murray Bookchin, 1986). 'We are living in what is, by all odds, the most tumultuous type of historical epoch. Ever since the invention of the city some six or seven thousand years ago and the quick advance of urban societies into the habit of empire-building, the periods of collapse between imperial systems have been, without exception, the times of greatest violence, uncertainty, and confusion — and yet of potential creativeness. . . It is not to be supposed that history is being canceled for us. The same disruptions can be discerned — uncertainty of power at the apex, changes in ideologies and concepts, the sense of confusion, the search for a changed vision of the good life. But to these are added a number of new elements which bring wholly new dimensions of uncertainty to what is, by all historical tradition, an uncertain age. . . This is the first time in history that the ending of one imperial system has been attended not by an uneasy expectation of a successor, but by the passionate proclamation of the principle that imperialism itself is impermissible' (Barbara Ward, 1979).

Holism
[1926. *Gk holos*, whole]
The belief that systems can only be properly understood when seen as a unified whole rather than as a sum of their separate parts. 'In the 1920s Jan Christian Smuts, the Boer general who was twice Prime Minister of South Africa, formulated a brilliant concept that anticipated many scientific breakthroughs of the late twentieth century. In *Holism and Evolution*, Smuts called attention to an invisible but powerful organizing principle inherent in nature. If we did not look at wholes, if we failed to see nature's drive toward ever higher organization, we would not be able to make sense of our accelerating scientific discoveries' (Marilyn Ferguson, 1981). Since the mid 1970s the word 'holistic' has taken off in a big way, especially in relation to health and healing, spurred by such books as *The Holistic Health Handbook* (Berkeley Holistic Health Center, 1978) and *Holistic Health* (Lawrence LeShan, 1982). *The Holistic Health Lifebook* (Berkeley Holistic Health Center, 1981) lists in its index: holistic education, holistic healing, holistic health, holistic heath centers, holistic health practitioners and holistic medicine. 'At a minimum, holism, as applied to the health of individuals,

requires us to recognise that they are whole people, with cognitive, physiological, emotional and spiritual qualities. Furthermore, individuals and populations must be understood in their social, economic, political, and philosophical contexts. This point of view is dramatically different from the premises underlying the existing medical model' (Rick Carlson, in Berkeley Holistic Health Center, 1981). *The Holistic Herbal* (David Hoffmann, 1983), *The Holistic Cook* (Janet Hunt, 1985) and *The Holistic Gardener* (Margaret Elphinstone and Julia Langley, 1987) relate the concept of holism to their particular field of interest. One fascinating aspect of holism is the paradox of scale — whatever you start to look at or think about, a holistic perspective always involves going further and deeper: 'Holistic thinking is essentially paradoxical. Whenever we consider wholeness it is always only part of a bigger whole, it is ultimately beyond what can be described. . . [Yet] while the ultimate holism includes everything in infinite expansiveness, the holistic view paradoxically works best on the smallest scale' (Jan Resnick, 1986).

Hologram
[1949. *Gk holos* + *gramma*, recorded as a whole]
A three-dimensional image recorded on photographic plate by a split laser light, and recreated by the illumination of the interference patterns thus recorded. Such an image has the property of being able to recreate the whole image from any part of the photographic plate. David Bohm (1980) uses the hologram as an illustration of the way that everything in the universe is contained or enfolded within everything else (*see* IMPLICATE ORDER): 'The value of the hologram . . . is that it may help to bring this new notion of order to our attention in a sensibly perceptible way; but of course, the hologram is only an instrument whose function is to make a static record . . . of this order.'

Holomovement
[1980]
The intangible flux within the universe that supports order. 'To generalize so as to emphasize undivided wholeness, we shall say that what "carries" an implicate order is the holomovement, which is an unbroken and undivided totality. In certain cases, we can abstract particular aspects of the holomovement (e.g., light, electrons, sound, etc.), but more generally, all forms of the holomovement merge and are inseparable. Thus, in its totality, the holomovement is not limited in any specifiable way at all. It is not required to conform to any particular order, or to be bounded by any particular measure. Thus, the holomovement is undefinable and immeasurable' (David Bohm, 1980).

Holonomy
[1980. *Gk holos + nomia*, the law of the whole]
The premise that you must take the whole into account when looking at complex systems. 'In sufficiently broad contexts . . . analytic descriptions cease to be adequate. What is then called for is holonomy, i.e. the law of the whole. Holonomy does not totally deny the relevance of analysis. . . However, any form of relative autonomy . . . is ultimately limited by holonomy, so that in a broad enough context such forms are seen to be merely aspects, relevated in the holomovement, rather than disjoint and separately existent things in interaction' (David Bohm, 1980).

Home
[12c. *Old English ham*, village, home]
A safe place where you can relax and be yourself. A basic human need that many people do not have, while others have far more in the way of a 'home' than they need. For many, too, especially women, home is a domestic prison. Home can be the place where important ideas breed — 'the revolution begins at home'. The earth as our collective home has been an attractive idea for many writers: 'Attractive detached residence' says a Friends of the Earth postcard over a view of the planet from space. Yet we often treat the earth as we would never treat our home: 'If we do not feel perfectly at home here, that may after all have something to do with the way we have treated the place. Any home can be made uninhabitable' (Mary Midgley, 1978).

Homeopathy
[1826. *Gk homoios + patheia*, similar suffering]
(*also* 'homoeopathy')
The maintenance of health by treating disorders with minute amounts of remedies which produce similar effects to those of the disorder (as opposed to ALLOPATHY, which prescribes remedies to 'oppose' the disorder). Since its formal establishment by the German physician Samuel Hahnemann at the end of the eighteenth century, homeopathy has remained one of the more acceptable of the alternative healing techniques. In recent years several writers have made the link between personal and planetary healing in homeopathic terms, using Samuel Hahnemann's phrase 'Like cures like' to suggest remedies for environmental 'diseases'.

Homeostasis
[1929. *Gk homoios + stasis*, consistent standing still]
A state of dynamic BALANCE in a SYSTEM, regulated by internal and external FEEDBACK in order to maintain STABILITY both within the system and in the system's relationship to its wider environment. 'Fluctuations

play a central role in the dynamics of self-maintenance. Any living system can be described in terms of interdependent variables, each of which can vary over a wide range between an upper and a lower limit. All variables oscillate between these limits, so that the system is in a state of continual fluctuation, even when there is no disturbance. Such a state is known as homeostasis. It is a state of dynamic, transactional balance in which there is great flexibility' (Fritjof Capra, 1982).

Homeworking
[1902 in this sense]
Working at home; specifically doing piecework for an employer who can save money by paying homeworkers — often women with small children — very low wages while incurring minimal overheads. More than 90% of the 300,000 homeworkers in Britain are estimated to live below the poverty line: 'In few cases is homeworking a freely-chosen, life-enhancing option. On the contrary, in almost all cases it is a poor alternative to working outside the home, selected only because the homeworker's domestic commitments prevent her from going out to work' (Liz Bissett and Ursula Huws, 1985). *See also* COTTAGE INDUSTRY, FREELANCE.

Homosexuality
[1892. *Gk homos* + *L sexus*, same sex]
Preferring to share sexual experiences with people of the same sex as yourself. *See* GAY (the term generally preferred by homosexual men) and LESBIAN (the term generally preferred by homosexual women). *See also* HETEROSEXUALITY.

Honesty
[14c. *L honestus*, honourable]
Straightforwardness, CLARITY, and being true to yourself in relating to others; the only real way for people to relate. *See also* LIE, SECRET, TRUST.

Hope
[before 12c. *Old English hopian*, to hope]
Looking forward to something with the belief that it can happen. 'This conspiracy [the AQUARIAN CONSPIRACY] belongs to all of us, . . those who belong to it in spirit but have not yet known how many others share their sense of possibility, and for those who despair but are willing to consider the evidence for hope. Like the charting of a new star, naming and mapping the conspiracy only makes visible a light that has been present all along but unseen because we didn't know where to look' (Marilyn Ferguson, 1981).

Hospice

[*c.* 1970 in this sense. *L hospes*, guest]

A home or centre for people who are terminally ill, providing for the residents' medical, social and emotional needs. 'There is a vigorous growth of the hospice movement [in Britain], made widely known through the work of Dame Cicely Saunders at St Christopher's Hospice in Surbiton, and St Joseph's Hospice, Hackney. . . Dame Cicely estimated at the beginning of 1980 that there were no fewer than fifty hospices about the country' (Mary Stott, 1981). Until recently, most hospice beds were taken up by terminal cancer sufferers, many of whom were relatively old; since the advent of AIDS, hospice facilities for AIDS sufferers have been provided in North America, and it is likely that similar facilities will be provided in Europe in the near future.

Household Economy

[1975]

That part of the INFORMAL ECONOMY which comprises what is usually done in people's homes: domestic work, cooking, gardening, maintenance, childcare and so on. It has never been thought of as part of the 'real' economy, largely because so much of it is 'women's work', though 'if this work were charged for, it might be equivalent to 40 per cent of the formal economy' (Charles Handy, 1985). 'Home has always been seen as the basic consumption unit and we are now beginning to see [it] as a production unit, the way it used to be before the industrial revolution' (Hazel Henderson, 1981).

Housing

[early 19c in this sense. *Old English hus*, house]

Buildings for people to live in; used (particularly in Britain) to mean the provision of homes on a large scale in areas where only residential buildings can be built. Green-thinkers believe this to be a divisive and anti-social policy, and advocate the sensitive juxtaposition of buildings for residential, commercial, light industrial and social activity. 'In planning policy the Greens demand: a pro-people, socially and environmentally benign architecture; . . . no more skyscrapers must be built; no destruction of housing stock in good condition; renovation to take precedence over demolition and new construction; . . . a complete end to the expulsion of the residential population from old established urban districts; . . . the creation of ghettoes . . . must be avoided by planning a mixture of different types of housing' (die Grünen, 1983). 'When dwellers control the major decisions and are free to make their own contribution to the design, construction or management of their housing, both the process and the environment produced stimulate individual and social well-being. When people have no control over, nor responsibility for key decisions in the housing process, on the other hand, dwelling environments may instead become a barrier to personal fulfilment and a burden on the economy' (John Turner and Robert Fichter (ed), 1972). 'Social breakdown, like charity, begins at home' (Alice Coleman, 1985). *See also* ARCHITECTURE, PLANNING.

Housing Cooperative
[*c*.1965]
A non-profit-making association formed by a group of people with the purpose of building or improving housing, usually for its members. Many countries, including the USA and Britain, have specific legislation covering housing cooperatives; assistance is available from public funds and such associations now provide a substantial and growing proportion of new and improved accommodation. In Britain a 'housing association' [1957] is similar to a housing cooperative, though usually larger and involving less active participation from the people who live in the housing; its main function is to provide rented accommodation at reasonable prices, particularly for people with special needs.

Hug-The-Trees Movement
[1973]
A grassroots action by the Chipko people of northern India — mostly women and children — to stop the felling of publicly-owned forest, thus saving the trees, stemming further soil erosion, and safeguarding local employment. 'Failing in their effort to elicit any response from the central government, villagers took matters into their own hands. Whenever the timber merchants entered the local communities, people literally gathered about the trees and hugged them. During the years since 1973, the Chipko movement has spread throughout northern India. More important, it has forced the central government to revise forest policies to benefit local communities. In addition, the Chipko movement has sparked extensive voluntary reforestation efforts that are often superior to those designed by the government' (Lester Brown, 1981).

Human
[14c *L humanus*, human being]
Having the characteristics and qualities of a free human being (*see also* HUMAN NATURE). One of the problems in relation to 'human' is acknowledging that all human beings are in fact human: dictionaries right up to the current (1986) editions of Websters (US) and Collins (UK) define 'human' as 'relating to man or mankind' (or similar phrases), this ruling out half of the world's population. 'Human' and 'humanity' are powerful and important words, useful antidotes to MAN and MANKIND.

Human Ecology
[1910]
An approach to human affairs which acknowledges the importance of ecological principles; the study of human beings within their living environment. A term particularly favoured by geographers to describe their field of interest.

Human Exemptionalism
[1980]
The erroneous belief that human beings are somehow above and beyond the LAWS OF ECOLOGY, that 'humans are quite unlike all other animal species, [that] social and cultural environments are the crucial context for human affairs and the biophysical environment is largely irrelevant, . . and that culture is cumulative. . . We do not deny that humans are "exceptional", [but we do deny that this] exempts us from ecological principles and from environmental influences and constraints' (William Catton and Riley Dunlap, *American Behavioral Scientist*, 1980).

Humanistic Psychology
[*c*.1960]
Any approach to THERAPY which stresses the importance of the whole person and explores the range of possibilities open to them. Humanistic psychology has been described as a 'third force' in PSYCHOTHERAPY, alongside the older disciplines of behaviourism and psychoanalysis. 'Humanistic psychology emphasises . . . those experiences that foster self-actualisation, spontaneity, personal responsibility, worth, creativity, valuing, openness, being authentic, transcendence' (Association of Humanistic Psychology leaflet, 1986). 'While they might differ in methods and techniques, the new humanistic therapies shared the conviction that overcoming psychic and emotional blocks was not an end in itself but a step towards a more rewarding existence' (David Harvey, 1986).

Human Nature
[1745]
How green-thinkers believe human beings might behave in a world where green ideas held sway. Not a topic that many have explored in any detail, although some ideas have widespread acceptance and others have been widely rejected. Most green-thinkers believe, for example, that VIOLENCE is learned and not innate; that human beings are disposed to prefer COOPERATION, CARING and COMPASSION; and that given the opportunity, people have abundant CREATIVITY and IMAGINATION. So many models of 'human nature' have been created by philosophers and social scientists over the years that it is important to remember the

vested interests of those creating the models, and that the idea of 'natural' itself is highly suspect (*see also* NATURE). 'Humans are by nature unnatural. We do not yet walk "naturally" on our hind legs, for example: such ills as fallen arches, lower back pain, and hernias testify that the body has not yet adapted itself completely to the upright posture. Yet this unnatural posture, forced on the unwilling body by the project of tool-using, is precisely what has made possible the development of important aspects of our "nature". . . Man-made [*sic*] and physiological structures have thus come to interpenetrate so thoroughly that to call a human project contrary to human nature is naive: we are what we have made ourselves, and we must continue to make ourselves as long as we exist' (Dorothy Dinnerstein, 1977). Does this excuse such 'human projects' as nuclear tests and genetic engineering? 'I think it is illuminating to see many of the disputes in the various human sciences as grounded ultimately in competing conceptions of what it is to be human. . . To attribute the divisions within the human sciences to the lack of a generally accepted conception of what it is to be human is not to diagnose the problem, but to re-state it. Yet I think that this restatement has heuristic value because it leads us to focus attention on the whole notion of a theory of human nature. What questions should a theory of human nature be designed to answer, what are the methods by which it might discover those answers and what are the criteria for determining the adequacy of the answers offered?' (Alison Jaggar, 1983). Several schools of therapy have looked in some depth at the question of human nature, since what is the point of therapy if you have no idea of what it might lead you to? In general they agree that human beings are by nature intelligent, creative, and have a positive outlook on life. 'Our concept of the basic, underlying integral nature of the human being is primarily based on the assumption of a very large amount of flexible intelligence, of the ability to come up with new, accurate, successful responses. . . The nature of the human is integral, wholesome. The natural feeling of a human being is zest, the natural relationship with other human beings is love and cooperation. We assume this is the inherent nature' (Harvey Jackins, 1973). 'Human nature is not something fixed and immovable for all time; it's a collection of potentialities, a seed that will flourish or wither according to where it's planted. And at the moment we expect people to grow out of very stony ground, nurtured on images and models of violence, greed, envy and exploitation. The Green movement is not talking about changing human nature, but changing the environment in which the seed grows' (Peter Bunyard and Fern Morgan-Grenville (ed), 1987).

Human Potential Movement
[*c*.1960]
An umbrella term for a group of humanistic therapeutic approaches including psychodrama, GESTALT, transactional analysis, BODYWORK, encounter groups, and other individual, group and transpersonal approaches to PSYCHOTHERAPY. What these approaches have in common is that 'in contrast to most other approaches to psychotherapy, where the primary emphasis is the eradication of pathology, the human potential movement encompasses all those methods which help to fulfil the individual's potential by expanding his [or her] awareness and creativity and raising his [or her] level of functioning in either the cognitive, affective, behavioural or spiritual spheres. . . The human potential movement shades into and is often used synonymously with humanistic psychology. The term human potential movement, however, is somewhat broader and encompasses the "fringe" methods in addition' (Sue Walrond-Skinner, 1986).

Human-Powered Vehicle
[*c*.1980]
A vehicle based on a BICYCLE, but with a sturdier construction and a body shell which gives protection from the weather.

Human Rights
[1791]
Another term for CIVIL RIGHTS, given quasi-official status in such documents as the United Nations Charter of Human Rights and the European Declaration on Human Rights. 'Human Rights . . . are those rights and privileges held to belong to any man' (David Robertson, 1985) — no wonder Cheris Kramerae and Paula Treichler (1985) add: 'In reality, men's rights'. For green-thinkers, human rights are synonymous with BASIC NEEDS.

Human Scale
[*c*.1970]
A small SCALE of physical and social environment which reflects the physical size of human beings and their need to live in surroundings in which they feel comfortable. 'The other possibility for the new age to which we are moving lies in exactly the opposite direction [to TECHNOFIX]: towards the decentralization of institutions and the devolution of power, with the slow dismantling of all the large-scale systems that one way or another have created or perpetuated the current crisis, and their replacement by smaller, more controllable, more efficient, people-sized units, rooted in local circumstances and guided by local circumstances. In short, the human-scale alternative' (Kirkpatrick Sale, 1980).

Humour
[late 17c in this sense. *L humor*, moisture]
(US: 'humor')
Something that makes you laugh; the ability to laugh at things. 'Yes, the danger is real, and we may not get through it. But instead of cowering in the face of doom, I choose to face the mushroom cloud and roar with laughter. The laughter slices into the nuclear silence and penetrates even my own numbness' (Fran Peavey, 1986). Some green jokes: ' "What's the difference between ignorance and apathy?" "I don't know and I don't care" ' (Joanna Macy, 1983). 'After his first encounter group, Bob went to the library to find a book about getting close to other people. He was lucky. Almost the first volume he laid eyes on was called *How to Hug*. It wasn't until he got home that he found he'd checked out Volume 7 of the *Encyclopedia Britannica*' (anon). 'Technology is the answer! (But what was the question?)' (Amory Lovins, 1977). 'As part of a campaign to publicise the position of American Indians, a Cherokee arrived for a convention in New York dressed in full Indian costume. He decided to book in at a very exclusive hotel. The clerk looked at him doubtfully, but finally handed him a registration card. "Just put your X on the top line." The Indian carefully marked an X; then put another X alongside. "What's the other X for?" the clerk demanded. "That's my PhD from Harvard." ' (Greg Benton and Graham Loomes, 1976). In the hands of an oppressor, humour can be a sadistic tool of OPPRESSION. Sexism, racism and the other oppressions are not intrinsically funny, and to be told that you have no sense of humour because you refuse to laugh at a putdown of yourself is the final insult.

Hundredth Monkey
[1973]
A story which shows how small changes can eventually build up to a point where important CHANGE seems to happen spontaneously; first told by Lyall Watson in *Supernature* (1973), and subsequently embroidered into a parable for our nuclear times by Ken Keyes in *The Hundredth Monkey* (1981). Sceptics have questioned the veracity of the original source, but that doesn't detract from the story: 'Observing the learning habits of monkeys on a remote Japanese island, anthropologists scattered sweet potatoes for them to eat. One day a monkey dropped a sweet potato in the water and, retrieving it, found it tasted better when washed free of dirt and sand. She proceeded henceforth to wash her sweet potatoes and taught her sisters to do the same. The practice spread throughout the colony. When the hundredth monkey began to wash his [*sic*] sweet potato in the sea, the practice appeared simultaneously on another island colony of monkeys' (Joanna Macy, 1983).

Hunger
[before 12c. *Old English hungor*]
Weakness and ill health brought about primarily by lack of FOOD; the permanent condition of more than a tenth of the world's population. 'The real block to the solution of world hunger is the sense of powerlessness we are made to feel: that the enormity of the problem is outside our control and that it should be entrusted to others. In truth, however, the solution to hunger is firmly within all of our hands' (Frances Moore Lappé and Joseph Collins, 1980). *See also* FAMINE, MALNUTRITION.

Hydroenergy
[1827]
(*also* 'hydroelectricity', 'hydropower']
Conversion of the potential energy of falling water into ENERGY which can be used by human beings, usually in the form of electricity. 'Falling water is the source of one quarter of the world's electricity. Whether harnessed by a slowly turning wooden water wheel on a tiny stream in Nepal or by a hundred-ton steel dynamo at Aswan on the mighty Nile, all hydropower comes from the ceaseless cycle of evaporation, rainfall and runoff set in motion by the sun's heat and the earth's pull. By harnessing water in one step of this cycle, as it flows back to the sea, water wheels and turbines convert this natural and endlessly renewable energy into a usable form' (Daniel Deudney, 1983). 35 countries obtain more than two-thirds of their electricity from hydroenergy; in Ghana, Norway and Zambia the proportion is more than 99%. The biggest problem with hydropower is the social and ecological disturbance associated with the dams and reservoirs required to provide the heads of water for large hydro schemes, often in wilderness areas where ecological factors tend to count for little, though there are recent signs that public outrage can prevent the most devastating schemes such as the proposed Gordon-below-Franklin dam in Tasmania. Apart from the loss of land, vegetation and human habitation, dam and reservoir building often plays havoc with water-tables and increases the incidence of water-borne disease; reservoirs frequently silt up much faster than predicted, and dams prevent life-bringing annual flooding downstream of the dam, as has happened with disastrous consequences downstream of the Aswan High Dam on the Nile. Many different types of hydroenergy installation have been constructed, and even more proposed. One type, the 'pumped storage scheme', pumps water to an upper reservoir during off-peak periods and then generates electricity from that head of water during peak periods; there have also been proposals to use melting ice in Greenland and to turn a major Siberian river system southwards. An important alternative to large-scale hydro

schemes is the small 'mini-hydro' project. China has around 88,000 small hydro installations, which demonstrates that with rapid improvements in microprocessor-controlled systems and little need for large-scale dam construction, small-scale hydro stations could supply many rural communities with electricity cheaply and efficiently.

Hydrological Cycle
[*c*.1945]
The movement of WATER in the biosphere from the earth's surface to the atmosphere (through evaporation and evapotranspiration) and back again (through precipitation). The cycle is in fact far more complex than this, with many pathways and branches, but this simplified definition does emphasise the constant FLOW of water within the biosphere, and the importance of this flow to the life of the planet.

Hydroponics
[1937. *Gk hudor* + *ponos*, water work]
Growing plants without soil, usually in beds of sand saturated with nutrients in solution. Such a method requires considerable attention and care, but can produce high yields in arid areas, and is particularly important in places like Israel and southern California.

Hydrosphere
[1887. *Gk hudor* + *sphaira*, sphere of water]
The watery part of the BIOSPHERE, including rivers, lakes and oceans, together with the water vapour in the atmosphere. A useful concept when looking at the HYDROLOGICAL CYCLE, but it is important to remember that WATER is vital to life everywhere, and that in practice it is virtually impossible to distinguish easily between the hydrosphere and the biosphere.

Hyper-Expansionist
[1978]
(*also* 'HE')
The belief that society can break out of its present problems by using science and technology, including space colonisation, genetic engineering and microtechnology to the full. 'This view appeals to optimistic, ambitious, competitive people for whom economic and technical achievement is more significant than personal and social growth. They are often male' (James Robertson, 1978). Several green-thinkers have contrasted a 'HE' future with a SANE/HUMANE/ECOLOGICAL 'SHE' green future.

Iatrogenesis
[1924. *Gk iatros* + *genes*, created by a physician]
Ill health induced by the actions of doctors, and encouraged by current beliefs about HEALTH and MEDICINE. In a time when we are encouraged to see 'health' as a constant battle against encroaching DISEASE, the medical and pharmaceutical professions have produced an armoury of weapons with which to fight the battle. More than 50% of Britons and nearly 80% of Americans take some sort of DRUG every day: 'some take the wrong drug; others get an old or a contaminated batch; and others a counterfeit. . . Some drugs are addictive, others mutilating, and others mutagenic . . . In some patients, antibiotics alter the normal bacterial flora and induce a superinfection, permitting more resistant organisms to proliferate and invade the host. . . Subtle kinds of poisoning thus have spread even faster than the bewildering variety and ubiquity of nostrums. . . The pain, dysfunction, disability, and anguish resulting from technical medical intervention now rival the morbidity due to traffic and industrial accidents and even war-related activities, and make the impact of medicine one of the most rapidly spreading epidemics of our time' (Ivan Illich, 1976). Illich makes the distinction between 'clinical iatrogenesis' (ill health induced directly by medical practices) and 'social iatrogenesis' (ill-health induced by societal attitudes towards disease and medicine).

Idea
[14c. *Gk idea*, idea, model, pattern]
A creative, intelligent and practical thought or concept. Some green-thinkers believe that the emphasis of Greens should be on spontaneous action, and that there is too much thinking within the movement: 'We do not mainly need new, exciting ideas for actions. Our ideas need to be more connected with our core, our feelings, our hearts really. Out of

this connection creative action springs forth spontaneously' (Michael Trust, letter to *Peace News*, January 1987). While this exhortation not to become too cerebral is useful, it may be missing the distinction between having ideas and excessive theorising (*see* THEORY): 'I would rather talk about women of ideas than women theorists. The word theory does not have a good feminist history. What theory has been a friend to women?' (Dale Spender, 1984, quoted in Cheris Kramerae and Paula Treichler, 1985).

Identification
[1900 in this sense. *L identitas*, identity]
Recognising similarities between yourself and other people (especially people who have had a formative influence upon you), and between yourself and the wider world. 'A form of internalisation by which the individual can model aspects of his or her self upon others' (Sue Walrond-Skinner, 1986). 'The process of identification is sometimes expressed in terms of loss of self and gain of Self through "self-less" action. Each new sort of identification corresponds to a widening of the self, and strengthens the urge to further widening, further Self-seeking' (Arne Naess, in Michael Tobias (ed), 1985). Being very close to both empathy and projection, over-identification can be dangerous: too complete an identification sees a person giving away their power to another. Recognising the links between people, however, is an important step towards UNDERSTANDING and COMPASSION.

Ideology
[1813. *Gk idea + logos*, words about ideas]
A system of beliefs about human nature and society; often used to suggest that such a system is characterised by inflexibility and an unwillingness to listen to other points of view.

Illness
[1500. *Old Norse illr*, bad]
Not feeling well. The concept of 'illness' is very much part of the DISEASE model of health, and most green-thinkers prefer to use the more descriptive 'disease' for an unhealthy state, balanced against HEALTH or WELLNESS to describe the normal healthy state.

Image
[13c. *L imago*, representation]
(1) A visual representation, such as a picture, sculpture or photograph. Any image shows what its creator wants to show, incorporating his or her own values, and we see that image through the filter of our own particular experience. 'An image is a sight which has been recreated or reproduced. It is an appearance, or a set of appearances, which has

been detached from the place and time in which it first made its appearance and preserved — for a few moments or a few centuries. Every image embodies a way of seeing, [and] our perception and appreciation of an image depends also upon our own way of seeing' (John Berger, 1972).
(2) Our perception of ourselves ('self-image').
(3) Another word for SYMBOL.

Imagination
[14c *L imaginari*, to picture to yourself]
The capacity to think and act creatively and spontaneously, without being unnecessarily limited by psychological or social constraints. 'The real world is hidden . . . by the wall of imagination' (George Gurdjieff, quoted in P.D. Ouspensky, 1969).

Impact
[1781. *L impingere*, to dash or strike against]
The influence of an event or development upon its surroundings; usually referring to a situation where such influence is likely to be considerable. *See also* ENVIRONMENTAL IMPACT ASSESSMENT.

Imperialism
[1851. *L imperium*, command, empire]
Another word for COLONIALISM, but with the added assumption of unquestionable superiority by the empire-builder. Sometimes used to describe a condescending approach taken by people who should know better: 'Many Third World women reject [the] leadership of the West. . . They accuse American and European feminists of being obsessed with sexual issues and of paying too little attention to poverty and national liberation. They see the Western initiatives as another example of high-handed missionary zeal among the supposedly unknowing, and they resent what they see as feminist imperialism' (Soon Young Yoon, 1984, in Victoria Brittain and Michael Simmons (ed), 1987).

Implicate Order
[1980]
A model of the universe based on the idea that every part of what exists is enfolded within every other part. 'There is the germ of a new notion of order here. The order is not to be understood solely in terms of a regular arrangement of objects . . . or as a regular arrangement of events . . . Rather, a total order is contained, in some implicit sense, in each region of space and time' (David Bohm, 1980).

Import Substitution
[1963]
The use of locally-produced products rather than products which are

transported long distances. While this might reduce choice, it can save enormously on fuel and boost the local economy; on the other hand, both the product and the production method must be appropriate to the local economy, or surpluses of unwanted goods or large capital debts can result. The economic and political power of the MULTINATIONALS must also be taken into account. In the early 1970s, several THIRD WORLD countries consciously set out along the road of import substitution, with varying success. 'Industrialization policies concentrated on "import-substitution", setting up local industries to produce essential goods that had previously been imported. This involves keeping out foreign competition until the industry has captured the domestic market, and while it worked well enough in countries like India or Brazil, which possessed both large potential markets and considerable natural resources, it often led to excess capacity in small, resource-poor countries. In any case, substitution is very difficult in genuinely essential goods (which by definition cannot be done without, even temporarily). Thus, because such industries are subsidized, they tend to produce inessential goods inefficiently and expensively' (Christopher Pick, 1983).

Impossible

[14c. *L impossibilis*, not possible]

Something which is, or which appears to be, without a solution or a way of dealing with it. 'Be reasonable — demand the impossible!' was a common catchphrase in the early 1970s (it was first used during the 1968 Paris student demonstrations), and to live more greenly we must believe that seemingly impossible things can in fact be done, and take note of the fact that things which previously seemed impossible now seem only difficult: to a certain extent 'impossibility' is a mental and psychological block. On the other hand, it is important to know what is impossible in the circumstances, or to rephrase it in a more powerful way, what we choose not to tackle in the circumstances.

Incest

[13c. *L incestus*, impure, unchaste]

Technically, sexual intercourse between two members of the same family; in practice almost always the sexual exploitation of a child by an older relative, an important aspect of child abuse. Almost all incest is done by an adult male to a young female, often father to daughter. A recent American study showed that in cases of child sexual abuse, 92% of the children were girls and 97% of the assailants adult heterosexual men. 'The nature of male power in families means that there is always a possibility of sexual assault on any girl, because men and society regard families as places in which men do as they choose. The girls it happens to are not any different from those who are not assaulted — rather some escape because the men who are our fathers, guardians or friends choose not to abuse their power. Men see "their" children as belonging to them — not primarily as individuals with feelings and needs and rights but as servicers of their emotional, sexual and domestic needs' (London Rape Crisis Centre, 1984). *See also* FAMILY, RAPE, VIOLENCE.

Income Sharing
[*c*.1960]
The financial arrangements made by a group of people who live together, pool their money, and pay all communal bills from the common pool. A basic principle of many communal groups, though the organisational details vary widely.

Incrementalism
[1966]
A belief in economic and political change by small degrees; also known as GRADUALISM.

Independence
[1640]
Deciding for yourself what to do, and having the freedom to do it. Discovering the power and ability to be independent is a crucial part of finding your true identity: 'I have learned that freedom and independence can't be wrested from others — from the society at large, or from men — but can only be developed, painstakingly, from within. To achieve it, we will have to give up the dependencies we've used, like crutches, to feel safe. Yet the trade-off is not really so perilous. The woman who believes in herself does not have to fool herself with empty dreams of things that are beyond her capabilities. At the same time, she does not waver in the face of those tasks for which she's competent and prepared. She is realistic, well-grounded, and self-loving. She is free, at last, to love others — *because* she loves herself. All of these things, and no less, belong to the woman who has sprung free' (Collette Dowling, 1981). The same is also true of communities and cultures, though here the FREEDOM aspect of independence is often more difficult to achieve, given the tangled web of COLONIALISM, the MULTINATIONALS, and NEO-COLONIALISM. While stressing the importance of SELF-DETERMINATION and SELF-RELIANCE, which are often used synonymously with 'independence', many green-thinkers prefer to think in terms of INTERDEPENDENCE, which acknowledges the uniqueness and importance of an individual or culture, together with an awareness of mutuality and interconnection.

Indeterminacy
[1928 in this sense]
Another name for the principle of UNCERTAINTY in the NEW PHYSICS.

Individual
[17c. *L individuus*, not divisible]
One human being, unique and important, and at the same time inextricably linked with every other person and every part of the universe. 'Individuality' and 'individualism' can be difficult ideas: a basic tenet of green thinking is the FREEDOM of the individual, and our right to express our creativity in our own unique way, yet it is very easy to let individual freedom become so important that our freedom limits unnecessarily the choices open to other people. When upheld from a position of PRIVILEGE, the principle of 'individuality' can be very dubious. 'In today's overcrowded, urbanised, interdependent America, individualism as an ideology creates needless conflict and exacerbates loneliness and alienation. . . Joseph Mazzini pointed out in 1835 in referring to the ideas of the French Revolution that declarations of human *rights* alone would not build a society, since they did not take account of our social interdependence' (Hazel Henderson, 1978).

Induction
[mid 16c in this sense. *L inducere*, to lead in]
The belief that adequate conclusions can be drawn about something by looking at particular occurrences of it (as opposed to DEDUCTION) (*see also* HEURISM). Virtually synonymous with the 'scientific method' (*see* SCIENCE), whereby given enough testing and sampling the scientist can become 'sure' of something. Induction tends to ignore the role of the observer and the values of the society within which the method is being used. 'The traditional view of scientific knowledge has two parts, I think. One was the idea that scientific knowledge grows by accumulation; the other was the idea that the success of science has a particular source in the so-called "scientific method". This latter idea goes way back. Newton was sufficiently impressed by the ideas of the philosopher Bacon to describe his own method as "induction"; and ever since Newton the idea has been present that there exists something called "inductive logic", or the inductive method, and that the sciences can be characterised by the fact that they employ this method deliberately and consciously' (Hilary Putnam, in Bryan Magee, 1978).

Industrial Democracy
[*c.*1970]
The participation of the employees of a company in decision-making within the company. In the UK, the Labour government of 1974-79 commissioned a report on industrial democracy, *The Bullock Report*,

which was published in 1977. It recommended employee participation in all large private-sector businesses, with employee representatives being elected through trade union channels to a flexible single-tier management and supervisory board. With the change in government in 1979 both *The Bullock Report* and a government paper with specific recommendations on industrial democracy sank without trace. In the absence of any specific industrial democracy legislation in the UK or North America, the cooperative movement is gaining strength; other countries, such as Yugoslavia and West Germany, do have specific legislation.

Industrialism

[1831. *L industria*, skill, diligence]

A society in which manual labour, large-scale production and the amassing of capital are paramount. An industrialist philosophy maintains the supremacy of material (and particularly technological) PROGRESS, MASS PRODUCTION, anonymous labour, CONSUMPTION, COMPETITION, the scientific method (*see* SCIENCE) and utilitarian values (*see* UTILITARIANISM). Many green-thinkers see industrialism as the chief source of our current ills. Socialist Greens tend to believe that it is CAPITALISM rather than industrialism which is primarily responsible for environmental degradation, but others point out that in terms of industrialism, socialism and capitalism have much more in common than their philosophies and adherents might suggest. *See also* SUPER-INDUSTRIALISM.

Infinite

[14c. *L infinitus*, not finite]

Without LIMITS or boundaries. A two-edged concept: many economists and industrialists behave as though the resources of our planet are infinite (classical economic theory depends upon the premise), when they clearly are not. On the other hand, a useful concept when it comes to looking at the repercussions of our actions: 'We say that there is no end to any act. The rock thrown in the water is followed by waves of water, and these waves of water make waves in the air, and these waves travel outwards infinitely, setting particles in motion, leading to other motion and motion upon motion endlessly. We say the water has noticed this stone falling and has not forgotten' (Susan Griffin, 1978). *See also* ABUNDANCE, FINITE.

Inflation

[1838 in this sense. *L inflatus*, to blow into]

Having more money in an economy than things to buy with it, so that the ensuing SCARCITY pushes prices up. The concept of MONEY with no real value is a very recent one, and with many non-renewable resources noticeably beginning to run out and the slices of the world resource cake getting thinner all the time, Greens see inflation as the inevitable result of ignoring the planet's true WEALTH and the implications of the ENTROPY principle. 'The Exploratory Project for Economic Alternatives, a Washington think tank, recently undertook a detailed study of the basic causes of inflation. It concluded, in its final report, that in the four basic consumer necessities — energy, food, housing, and health care — the rising prices were tied to the increased costs associated with the transforming and exchanging of energy. While this seems obvious enough, most establishment economic thinking continues to centre on secondary effects like wages or fiscal and monetary policy' (Jeremy Rifkin, 1980). Not being able to afford the basics of living makes poor people feel the pinch of inflation long before the index-linked rich. It also helps the poor to recognise some of the reasons for inflation before the rich, as they hunt for firewood and scavenge for food. It has been suggested that inflation may ultimately be the mechanism for controlling population growth, though it can just as easily be the cause of famine.

Informal Economy
[*c.*1980]
Those parts of our life where we work for ourselves or for other people without money changing hands; some people extend it to include the BLACK or UNDERGROUND ECONOMY. We live in a society where the only 'real work' is paid work, but much if not most of useful human activity, especially that done by women and children, is unpaid and frequently unacknowledged (*see also* DUAL ECONOMY, FORMAL ECONOMY, MONEY, WORK). 'I use the term "informal economy" to include activities which people do for themselves and one another without being paid, as contrasted with the "formal economy" in which work takes the form of paid employment. In practice, the distinction is often blurred' (James Robertson, 1978).

Information
[14c. *L informare*, to give form to]
Knowledge about somebody or something. To have appropriate information is to have power; to have inappropriate information is to have power over. 'The currency is information' (John Todd, *New Age Journal*, November 1984). This is why green-thinkers believe it to be vitally important that we know what information other people have about us ('freedom of information'), and that important information is made as widely available as possible. 'What does it mean that ten thousand merchants all over the country [the USA] are able to obtain a summary fact sheet about any one of 86 million individual Americans in a matter

of three or four seconds from a single data base in southern California? What does it mean that a handful of federal agencies, not counting the Pentagon, have at least thirty-one separate telecommunications networks stretching all over the United States?' (David Burnham, 1983). Ours is a society based on information — far too much of it for most of us, pushing us into 'information overload' (Alvin Toffler, 1970) and persuading us that information, even information for its own sake, always has value: 'When Susan assigns a paper, her students immediately run home and feed all the key words into their machines, which are hooked up to various data banks and library resources, and proceed to string all this information together' (Maurice Berman, *Journal of Humanistic Psychology*, Spring 1986). 'We are drowning in information but starved for knowledge' (John Naisbitt, 1984).

Informative Economy
[1983]
An economy in which physical resources are increasingly replaced by the resources of human creativity and intelligence; an economy contrasted with the 'mass economy' of high physical input. 'The informative economy requires more intelligence from everyone — management, labor, consumers, governments. Those who do not become learners again, regardless of age or rank, will find themselves at an increasing disadvantage as the informative economy takes root. . . One of the reasons US business is slow to grasp the kind of changes necessary to make the shift from a mass to an informative economy is that no one can buy what is needed to make the transition' (Paul Hawken, 1983).

Inner Health
[*c.*1975]
An acknowledgement of the role of MIND and SPIRIT in HEALING. 'Inner health focuses on the way we conceptualise, form images and belief systems, respond intuitively and creatively — and tap into the life force that sustains each of us' (Nevill Drury, 1985). Since the publication of Timothy Gallwey's *The Inner Game of Tennis* in 1975, the 'inner game' of human activities — particularly sport — has increasingly been recognised: 'The forgotten secret is the power of the unconscious mind to teach and guide the body' (David Harvey, 1986).

Inner Limits
[1975]
The recognition that LIMITS exist not only 'out there' in the biophysical world, but within our own physiology and psychology as well; such limits include our capacity to accept and adapt to change, tolerance of stress, patience with bureaucracy, and having sufficient stimulus for

our creativity. *The Inner Limits of Mankind* [*sic*] is the title of an influential book by the philosopher Erwin Laszlo (1979).

Inorganic

[1794. *L in- + Gk organikos*, not serving as a tool]

A substance which does not have the conventional characteristics of being alive or being derived from living organisms (as opposed to ORGANIC). The usual criterion is that the substance does not contain carbon atoms in the long rings and chains associated with organic compounds, though with the discovery and creation of more complex substances, the distinction is becoming increasingly blurred. Inorganic substances are commonly called simply CHEMICALS. *See also* ABIOTIC, BIOTIC.

Input/Output

[1914]

The flow of energy and materials across the boundaries of a SYSTEM; providing a way ('input/output analysis') of assessing the EFFICIENCY of the system. First used in engineering and mathematics, the idea reached economics in 1953, and ecology and energy studies in the 1960s. In economic systems the unit of measurement is usually money value; in ecology and energy studies energy input and output are more often substituted.

Insight

[13c. *Old English insihthe*, internal sight]

Being able to understand a situation clearly and intuitively: 'The term carries implications of depth and suddenness and, as in lateral thinking, it has an unexpected quality. Hence gaining insight involves seeing beneath the surface of a person or situation, perhaps for the first time' (Sue Walrond-Skinner, 1986). *See also* INTUITION, KNOWING.

Inspiration

[15c. *L inspirare*, to breathe into]

Stimulation and excitement which often lead to spontaneous CREATIVITY and inspired action; such stimulation often comes from a particularly moving experience — talking to somebody special, seeing something particularly significant, reading a passage which seems remarkably apt.

Institution

[*c*.1860 in this sense. *L instituere*, to set up]

An established organisation, often set in its bureaucratic and hierarchical ways, and therefore highly resistant to change.

Insulation
[1870 in this sense. *L insula*, island]
A substance which resists the flow of heat (such as fibreglass, mineral fibre or polyurethane), thus retaining heat where it is needed. Because a great deal of heat generated in buildings is lost to the atmosphere without giving any benefit to the occupants, there has been an emphasis in the last twenty years on adequate insulation of buildings, particularly dwelling houses. 'Insulation is now built into most new houses, both in roof-space and cavity walls. Coupled with double-glazing, such methods significantly cut the energy needed to keep a northern house comfortable from the current requirement of 12-20 kilowatts to an efficient and cost-effective 5 kilowatts' (Norman Myers, 1985). As well as keeping the heat in, good insulation also keeps the cold out, though insulation is only completely effective if it is undertaken alongside other energy-efficient measures, like draughtproofing and using efficient heat sources. Double glazing is a popular form of insulation; the technology is improving rapidly, but again double glazing is only really effective as part of an overall insulation and efficiency plan. Some 'super-insulated' houses now need very little active heating (*see* ENERGY, PASSIVE SOLAR).

Integration
[17c. *L integrare*, to make complete or whole]
Putting the parts of something together to make a unified whole. Economics has 'vertical integration' (one firm becoming involved in every stage of the production of a particular item; one way of achieving monopoly) and 'horizontal integration' (another word for 'merger', and another way of achieving monopoly). 'Integrated environmental design', 'integrated agricultural policies', 'integrated rural development programmes' and 'integrated education systems' involve bringing together ideas and expertise from a range of sources. 'Structural integration' or 'postural integration' is a form of BODYWORK (also called 'rolfing') which liberates the physical structure of the body, allowing it to reintegrate into a healthier posture; 'primal integration' (*see* BIRTH TRAUMA) is a powerful form of PSYCHOTHERAPY. Despite its misuses, the idea of integration has a sound basis in ECOLOGY, NEW ECONOMICS, HEALING and HUMANISTIC PSYCHOLOGY.

Integrity
[15c. *L integritas*, wholeness, purity; from *integer*, whole]
Thinking and acting with full and unimpaired awareness. 'Integrity has no need of rules' (Albert Camus, quoted in Laurence Peter (ed), 1977).

Intellect
[14c. *L intellegere*, to perceive, choose between]
The capacity to understand things clearly. 'In a sense intellect is the combination of literacy and intelligence: literacy disciplines intelligence and intelligence expands the uses of literacy; there is a body of knowledge that changes and increases and also a skill in acquiring knowledge; there is memory filled with ideas, a storehouse of what has gone before in the world. Intellect is mastery of ideas, of culture, of the products and processes of other intellects. Intellect is the capacity to learn language disciplined into learning. Intellect must be cultivated: even in men, even in the smartest' (Andrea Dworkin, 1983).

Intelligence
[14c. *L intelligentia*, intelligence]
The innate ability of human beings to comprehend situations and respond to them in a creative, flexible and self-empowering way. Limited by some educational psychologists to mean a narrow range of mental skills, and frequently distorted by those in power to mean a way of thinking which they and only they possess (*see also* REASON), intelligence is a gift we all have. 'Intelligence is a form of energy, a force that pushes out into the world. It makes its mark, not once but continuously. It is curious, penetrating' (Andrea Dworkin, 1983). Andrea Dworkin goes on to speak of moral intelligence (as opposed to morality) and sexual intelligence: 'Moral intelligence must act in a public world, not a private, refined, rarefied relationship with one other person to the exclusion of the rest of the world. Moral intelligence demands a nearly endless exercise of the ability to take decisions. . . Sexual intelligence . . . would be active and dynamic; . . . it would pose not buttocks but questions, answers, theories, ideas . . . It would be in the body, but it could never be in an imprisoned, isolated body, a body denied access to the world.'

Interconnectedness
[1922. *L inter + connectere*, to link or bind among each other]
A concept which recognises the many links between different elements of any system, situation or environment (*see also* CONNECTION).

Intercropping
[1898]
Planting two or more different crops in alternate rows in order to increase diversity, to let the plants help each other (*see* COMPANION PLANTING), to increase ground cover, and often to increase yield. *See also* MIXED CROPPING, PERMACULTURE, POLYCULTURE.

Interdependence
[1822]
Mutual giving and receiving at every level. The example of interdependence presented to human beings by natural systems is often overlooked, and we can easily forget that we too are part of the biosphere. Interdependence also recognises that each of us shares a common history and destiny with all the other human beings in the world: 'The word interdependent has been much thrown around, driven into battle, vanguarded on the pillar of ecological tribute. Does it really matter to Americans whether millions of sub-Saharan nomads die out? What are the political ramifications, the destabilizing regional and global effects of local extinctions?' (Michael Tobias, 1985). *See also* DEPENDENCE, INDEPENDENCE, WEB.

Intergenerational Equity
[1977]
Ensuring the wellbeing of all generations to come, and not just our own. 'Future generations . . . have nothing they can exchange to the present generation, and . . . there is no way to represent their interest adequately . . . If afflicted by the actions of the present generation, future generations can do no more than curse their fate' (Victor Lippit and Koichi Hamada, in Dennis Pirages (ed), 1977). 'There is now a deeper conflict than ever between the long- and short-term interests of one and the same human being. What people have to do today to pay off the mortgage on their house can cost the lives of their own children tomorrow' (Rudolf Bahro, *Green Line*, February 1986).

Intermediate Technology
[*c.*1960]
A scale of industrial and commercial activity somewhere between that of the heavily capital-intensive West and the capital-starved Third World, such that it can provide products and services with a balance of low equipment cost, substantial involvement and control by the local workforce, ease of operation and repair, and appropriateness to the local situation. 'Such an intermediate technology would be immensely more productive than the indigenous technology [in the Third World] . . . but it would also be immensely cheaper than the sophisticated highly capital-intensive technology of modern industry. . . The intermediate technology would also fit much more smoothly into the relatively unsophisticated environment in which it is to be utilised. The equipment would be fairly simple and therefore understandable, suitable for maintenance and repair on the spot' (E.F. Schumacher, 1973). Although originally envisaged as a TECHNOLOGY suitable for the THIRD WORLD, intermediate technology is also of great interest to many

people in the industrialised countries. An Intermediate Technology Development Group was founded in London in 1965; it provides information and publishes books on a wide range of aspects of intermediate technology. *See also* APPROPRIATE TECHNOLOGY.

International Company
(*see* MULTINATIONAL)

Interpretation
[14c. *L interpres*, interpreter, negotiator]
Ascertaining your own understanding of somebody's actions, words, or creative work. Interpretation is always coloured by the amount of information you have, your previous experience, and your beliefs and opinions. In nearly every situation (and particularly in complex situations) there are as many interpretations as there are participants.

Interruption
[15c. *L inter- + rumpere*, to break in]
Getting in the way of something or someone. Most commonly used when one person breaks into what another is saying in order to silence them and put across his (usually) or her own point of view. 'In their study, Don Zimmerman and Candace West found that 98 per cent of interruptions in mixed sex conversations were made by males. In no case did they find females thought this was "out of order" or sufficient reason for protest; on the contrary, females tended to be silent after being interrupted by a male' (Dale Spender, 1980). On the other hand, interruption can be a useful and important course of action, as for example when the Greenham Common Peace Camp women interrupt manoeuvres of the Cruise missile convoy, or Greenpeace interrupt the dumping of nuclear waste. 'Interruption' is also used in some therapeutic techniques, notably co-counselling, to describe the way in which destructive and self-defeating patterns of behaviour can be sensitively 'poked' by the therapist, resulting in catharsis and reappraisal of the situation by the client.

Intervention
[15c. *L intervenire*, to come between]
Interference with the actions of another person; usually used to imply that the interference is unwanted and often unjustified, thus 'military intervention', 'police intervention'. In some client-centred therapeutic situations the client may ask the therapist to intervene as she or he feels appropriate.

Intimacy
[17c. *L intimus*, innermost, deepest]
A useful word to describe closeness between people who are special to each other. It may (but need not) include physical closeness.

Into
[*c*.1969 in this sense]
A catchword from the HIPPIE era meaning 'particularly interested in' something: 'First I was into Zen, then I was into peace, then I was into love, then I was into freedom, then I was into religion. Now I'm into money' (*New Yorker*, September 1971).

Intuition
[15c. *L intueri*, to look at or towards, contemplate]
Immediate KNOWING, spontaneous INSIGHT, instantaneous clear thinking. Intuition has frequently been derided as being inferior to the analytical reasoning beloved of philosophers and scientists. 'Even when we [women] display our power to think in terms men have validated, to follow their arguments and reach their conclusions, we will rarely receive 'credit' for it. . . For the consensus will invariably be that it was not *reason* that we used to arrive at our conclusions, but a much inferior, capricious and lucky process — *intuition*' (Dale Spender, 1982). Intuition, however, is a vital aspect of human intelligence, both female and male. 'We use "intuition" . . . to mean the very swift, untrammelled, unchecked-out operation of human intelligence. I don't think it's a different process that takes place; it's just that the intuition or intuitive leap is where we allow the mind to operate flexibly and freely without being suspicious of each step and checking on it so carefully' (Harvey Jackins, 1983).

Ionising Radiation
(*see* RADIATION)

Irradiation
[*c*.1960 in this sense. *L irradiare*, to shine forth]
The sterilisation of food with low doses of RADIATION. Irradiation is yet another way of passing off second-rate food as being of high quality, using the wonders of a potentially dangerous technology: 'Critics argue that irradiation can damage vitamins and other nutritional elements of food. It could lead to more food poisoning from salmonella if people grew complacent in the mistaken belief that irradiated food would remain germ free. And the danger would always exist that human error or faulty equipment could make our food "radioactive"' (James Erlichman, 1986).

Irrigation

[1618. *L irrigare*, to direct water towards]

Supplying crops with water. Providing crops with enough water is crucial for healthy growth, though large-scale irrigation projects have created correspondingly large-scale problems of DESERTIFICATION and SALINISATION (*see* TECHNOFIX). 'Badly built and maintained irrigation systems also turn good land into wet, salty deserts, wasting not only the land but the large sums of money spent on the irrigation systems in the first place. Irrigation has waterlogged some 11,500 square miles of Indian farmland, and big canal projects cost £14 million ($21 million) per square mile. Bad irrigation can therefore be a very expensive form of desertification' (Lloyd Timberlake, 1987).

I-Thou

[1937]

A relationship which acknowledges the conscious and empathetic link between one person and another or between a person and their environment. I-Thou is a translation of the German *Ich-Du*, the title of an influential book by the German theologian Martin Buber (1923), and symbolises the difference between a cold impersonal 'I-It' relationship and a warm involved 'I-Thou' relationship. 'William Steiger, chairman of the department of medicine of Virginia hospital, told a group of physicians that their empathy is what Martin Buber called I-Thou and the necessary objective examination and testing is I-It. He quoted Buber's statement that "knowledge is an autopsy upon the corpse of real living". If you count something, Steiger said, it goes away. "The I-It is a monologue, the I-Thou is a dialogue. They're complementary." When a medical problem persists, the doctor usually pursues more I-It, more lab tests, when what is needed at that point is a deeper human understanding, more I-Thou' (Marilyn Ferguson, 1981).

Jargon
[mid 17c in this sense. *Old French jargoun*, meaningless utterances]
Obscure, pretentious and often meaningless LANGUAGE indulged in by self-styled EXPERTS. Sadly, would-be green-thinkers too are not always models of clarity and straightforwardness. 'Cosmic evolution irrevocably intent upon completely transforming omnidisintegrated humanity from a complex of around-the-world, remotely-deployed-from-one-another, differently colored, differently credoed, differently cultured, differently communicating and differently competing entities into a completely integrated, comprehensively interconsiderate, harmonious whole' (Buckminster Fuller, 1981).

J-Curve
(*see* EXPONENTIAL GROWTH)

Jealousy
[13c. *Gk zelos*, zeal]
A myth of possessive ROMANCE which provides a rationale for being upset and getting violent when a third party 'takes' somebody who you thought was 'yours'. 'All lovers do well to leave the doors of their love wide open. When love can come and go without meeting a watchdog, jealousy will rarely take root because it will soon learn that where there are no locks and keys there is no place for suspicion and distrust, two elements upon which jealousy thrives and prospers' (Emma Goldman, 1979).

Job-Sharing
[*c.*1975]
(*also* 'job split')
An arrangement by which two people share one position of paid employment, each of them working part-time, and thus allowing more

flexibility to each of them. This type of arrangement is more common in the public services than elsewhere. *See also* WORK.

Joy

[13c. *L gaudere*, to rejoice]

Expression of the feelings evoked by well-being, fulfilment and real success. In a society where feelings are suppressed, there is rarely sufficient opportunity to express joy. 'I suppose it all started when Ethan was born. . . He is joyful and he gives joy. He wakes up each morning eager for new adventure. Maybe today it will be a piece of string, or the toilet plunger, or the telephone, or pots and pans, or — more rarely — a new toy. Ethan is joy. He enjoys each aspect of his life with his whole being. He gives joy to those near him. His joy is contagious. But will something happen to Ethan as it does to us all? Where will his joy go?' (William Schutz, 1967).

Judeo-Christian Tradition

[1899]

The TRADITION that has its roots and precedents in both Jewish and Christian theology and practice. It is believed by some cultural ecologists to be the source of many of our anthropocentric and destructive environmental practices: 'Our daily habits of action . . . are dominated by an implicit faith in perpetual progress which was unknown either to Greco-Roman antiquity or to the Orient. It is rooted in, and is indefensible apart from, Judeo-Christian teleology. . . Christianity inherited from Judaism not only a concept of time as nonrepetitive and linear but also a striking story of creation. By gradual stages a loving and all-powerful God had created light and darkness, the heavenly bodies, the earth and all its plants, animals, birds and fishes. Finally, God had created Adam and, as an afterthought, Eve, to keep man from being lonely. Man named all the animals, thus establishing his dominance over them. God planned all of this explicitly for man's benefit and rule: no item in the physical creation had any purpose save to serve man's purpose. And, although man's body is made of clay, he is not simply part of nature: he is made in God's image. Especially in its Western form, Christianity is the most anthropocentric religion the world has seen' (Lynn White, *Science*, 1967). In recent years, however, there has been a very noticeable change as both Jews and Christians begin actively to see the human role as STEWARDSHIP rather than dominion: 'Only during the past few years, under pressure from outside, have there been any signs within the [Christian] churches of interest in evaluating and reviving vital elements in Christian tradition which have been increasingly neglected since the days of St Francis of Assisi. . . Only when the churches reawaken to their positive duty to the environment will they be able to see in perspective their errors in working against the limitation of human numbers' (Max Nicholson, 1970). There are now Christian Ecology Groups and a Jewish Vegetarian Society; Monsignor Bruce Kent has become a leading light in the British Campaign for Nuclear Disarmament and many churchgoers have become involved in peace actions like PLOUGHSHARE; but many Greens wonder if there can be any meaningful integration of organised religion and a truly green philosophy. *See also* ANTHROPOCENTRISM, DOMINATION, HUMAN EXEMPTIONALISM, RELIGION, SPIRITUALITY.

Judgement
[13c. *L judicare*, to judge]
(*also* 'judgment')
Being able to discern important aspects of a situation in order to understand it and decide what to do next (*see also* CRITICISM, DISCRIMINATION). Unfortunately 'judgement' is frequently used to decide how someone else should behave, and to criticise them if they disagree. This always involves a belief that you know better than they do what they should do or should have done, denies the validity of their choice, shows a lack of respect, and is unlikely to lead to real change. Not judging does not mean withholding your opinion, but it can never be more than 'If I were you I would . . .'.

Justice
[12c. *L justitia*, justice]
Ensuring the RIGHTS of living things to enjoy access to the means of fulfilling their BASIC NEEDS, without unnecessary interference and outside control; most often used with reference to the rights and needs of human beings, though green-thinkers would include the rights of all species, and of the earth itself. In its human aspect, 'justice' is preferred to LAW AND ORDER, and includes the mechanisms by which communities regulate and POLICE themselves. 'Every human being has a responsibility for injustice anywhere in the community' (Scott Buchanan, quoted in Laurence Peter (ed), 1977).

Kk

Knee-Jerk Reaction
[1951]
Giving an opinion before you have thought about the issue, a favourite ploy of politicians. Green-thinkers advocate careful thought and appropriate action, even if this means working with paradox and admitting that you don't know all the answers.

Knowing
[14c. *Old English cnawan*, to know]
A deep sense of UNDERSTANDING and AWARENESS; sometimes used by green-thinkers rather than KNOWLEDGE, which has overtones of superiority and unfounded certainty. 'But in a moment that which is behind naming makes itself known. Hand and breast know each one to the other. Wood in the table knows clay in the bowl. Air knows grass knows water knows mud knows beetle knows frost knows sunlight knows the shape of the earth knows death knows not dying. And all this knowledge is in the hearts of everything, behind naming, before speaking, beneath words' (Susan Griffin, 1984).

Knowledge
[14c. *Old English cnawlæcan*, knowledge]
One aspect of KNOWING, that which conventionally comes from 'study, investigation, observation or experience' (*Websters*, 1986). Knowledge comes both from direct EXPERIENCE and from INFORMATION provided by others. Some psychologists discern three types of knowledge: 'Propositional knowledge is knowledge of facts or truths as stated in propositions; it is entirely language-dependent. Practical knowledge is knowing how to do something, as exemplified in the exercise of some special skill or proficiency. Experiential knowledge is knowing some entity by direct face-to-face encounter with her/him/it; it is direct discrimination of what is present in relation with the knower' (John Heron, 1981,

quoted in John Rowan, 1983). 'If you know what you are doing, you can do what you want' (Moshe Feldenkrais, 1986). *See also* FACT, TRUTH.

Ll

Labels

[1853 in this sense. *Old French label*, a slip of paper or cloth attached to something to describe or identify it]

General and impersonal names given to a person or group of people with the supposed purpose of defining or identifying them, but more often used as way of stereotyping people and thus limiting them. Sometimes used by people to describe themselves, but this again provides the basis for expectations: 'One woman said she was an anarcha-rad-fem with (practical) experience of the I.M.G., the T.S., W.R.P., C.P. and the Catholic Church, IN THAT ORDER, born white anglo-saxon but into almost anything that isn't, at the moment considering going ORANGE, celibate with bisexual TENDENCIES and five kids . . . emotionally VEGAN but eats meat during CHRISTIAN festivities' (Fanny Tribble, undated). Whenever a 'health professional' makes a diagnosis she or he runs the risk of unnecessarily labelling the client; this is particularly the case with 'mental illness'. 'It is rather like the old wives' tale about "if your eyes are crossed when the wind changes, you'll get stuck like it". You can cross and uncross your eyes many, many times and be none the worse for it, but if you get caught at the wrong moment, that's it — there is no going back. The implication of this is that if we refused to label people, they would drift into and out of mental states often regarded as "neurotic" or "psychotic" without ever losing their status as citizen, friend, child, human being or whatever. And this is precisely it' (John Rowan, 1983). 'The world is riddled with -isms and -ologies and -anities; with specialists and experts; with divisions, categories and compartmental thinking; and so with barriers, suspicions, ignorance, antagonisms, jealousies, strife, cruelty, wars and a sad array of stupidity and suffering. . . I believe that if there is one -ism worth hanging on to, it is eclecticism' (Jon Wynne-Tyson, 1976).

Labour
[14c. *L labor*, hard work]
(US: 'labor')
Originally meaning hard and often difficult work, 'labour' was adopted by economists in the 1880s to mean 'the productive services embodied in human physical effort, skill, intellectual powers, etc.' (*Penguin Dictionary of Economics*, 1972), and limited to work done for money. Not all paid work is thought of as labour, however — the often-used distinction between 'labour' and MANAGEMENT shows who is actually doing the productive work. Calling the human input of production 'labour' conveniently overlooks the enormous variety of human skills, the suffering that can result from some kinds of WORK, and all the work that is done without financial reward.

Labour Credits
[1967]
(US: 'labor credits')
A system of evaluating different sorts of work in a communal or community setting, thus ensuring that what work there is to be done — including cooking, cleaning, childcare, etc. — is fairly shared between the members of the group. 'Established in 1967, Twin Oaks [a community in Virginia, USA] has a highly-structured system of "labor credits" to organize work more equitably. Members work about forty-five hours a week in community jobs such as cooking, farming, childcare, or in the hammock factory (which is the community's main support)' (Corinne McLaughlin and Gordon Davidson, *East/West* magazine, April 1986).

Land
[12c. *Old English land*, the solid part of the earth's surface]
The two-fifths of the earth's surface not covered by water, and the most precious RESOURCE of all terrestrial life. 'We must . . . uphold the basic rights of the land. It is our duty to leave the land at least as healthy and fertile as we found it. The land is part of our common wealth. Land is life!' (*Politics for Life*, 1983). 'The linchpin of world trade is not oil, nor plastics, but land, and with it, agriculture. Land is always the last word, the true politic, our final comfort' (Michael Tobias, 1985). 'In new global and local conditions, people and institutions are recognising the need to adapt to changing economic fortunes, but they have not seen an equivalent need to adapt their perceptions and use of land. . . It is more difficult to expose and evaluate the land issue in the rich countries than it is in the poor. Yet it can be argued that it lies at the heart of human life and wellbeing, and is central to social and economic progress. . . The land has become a passive, secretive, and often regressive recipient of social and economic policies rather than an active force in securing future wellbeing' (John Holliday, 1986).

Land Ethic
[1933]
(*also* 'land partnership ethic')
The obligation to treat the environment carefully and sensitively, as you would treat yourself and the people close to you. 'All ethics so far evolved rest upon a single premise: that the individual is a member of a community of interdependent parts. . . The land ethic simply enlarges the boundaries of the community to include soils, waters, plants, and animals, or collectively: the land. . . A land ethic changes the role of *Homo sapiens* from conqueror of the land-community to plain member and citizen of it' (Aldo Leopold, 1949). *See also* ETHICS, LAND.

Landfill
[1952]
A way of disposing of WASTE materials by filling hollows or reclaiming land from water-covered areas with the waste, then covering it with soil. If the waste is inert this can be a useful way of 'reclaiming' land, but toxic wastes have frequently been buried in landfill sites with inadequate precautions against leakage, thus causing widespread and long-lasting pollution. While this is of concern all over the world, especially following incidents such as the Love Canal site in the USA where houses and a school were built on a toxic landfill site and later had to be evacuated, some authorities seem determined not to take it seriously: 'The (UK) Hazardous Waste Inspectorate discovered evidence of an unacceptably casual attitude towards the reception and disposal of drummed waste at landfills. For example, HWI has witnessed the deposit of a trailer load of [about 80] sealed 45-gallon drums of waste on a landfill site where the operator had no idea of the contents and made no attempt at inspection' (*Waste Management Papers*, quoted in Edward Goldsmith and Nicholas Hildyard (ed), 1986). *See also* RECLAMATION sense (2).

Land Loss
[c.1950]
The loss of agricultural LAND and WILDERNESS to urban, industrial and commercial use. Around 150 million hectares of cropland will probably be lost to urban and industrial development between 1986 and 2000 (Norman Myers, 1985). Official statistics of land loss always underestimate, partly by deliberately choosing deceptive categories and inaccurate surveying techniques, and partly because there is a good deal of land around towns and cities which, while technically 'agricultural', is in fact unused due to vandalism (both public and private) and pollution.

Land Ownership

[12c]

Assuming the sole right to use a piece of land, and denying that right to anybody else; one of the main reasons for inequalities in WEALTH. Green-thinkers question the whole concept of land ownership, believing that land is a common asset. 'Title deeds to the ownership of land are records of theft from the community' (Robert Waller, in Herbert Girardet (ed), 1976). 'Land ultimately cannot be *owned* by anybody. Land is constant while human life is transient on it. It is the duty of every generation to leave the land at least as vigorous and fertile as they found it, in order not to diminish the chances of future generations' (Herbert Girardet (ed), 1976). 'The present system denies people their natural birthright of access to the land, and is incompatible with the ecological emphasis on stewardship rather than ownership, on recognizing the land as a common heritage to be cared for on behalf of the community and future generations. The monopoly control of land ownership must be brought to an end, not through the fossilized notion of nationalization, which might well make things worse rather than better, but through measures of radical *communal* reform' (Jonathon Porritt, 1984). 'In most countries where people are hungry, large landowners control most of the land. A study of 83 countries showed that slightly more than 3 per cent of all landholders, those with 114 acres or more, control a staggering 79 per cent of all farmland' (Frances Moore Lappé and Joseph Collins, 1980). Most traditional societies had no concept of land ownership: 'The Great Chief in Washington sends word that he wishes to buy our land... How can you buy or sell the sky, the warmth of the land? The idea is strange to us. We do not own the freshness of the air or the sparkle on the water. How can you buy them from us?' (Chief Seathl, 1855).

Land Reform

[1846]

A policy designed to achieve a more equitable distribution of the appropriate use of LAND, particularly agricultural land. 'You can do anything [by way of development], but if you don't touch land you are not doing much. The chaos and anarchy of human settlements in developing countries are simple consequences of the unlimited private ownership of land' (Enrique Penelosa, quoted by Andrew Lycett, in Herbert Girardet (ed), 1976). Those involved in agricultural development have believed that the parcelling out of land will make for effective reform, but without careful and enforceable monitoring of the situation, this is usually only successful in the short term: 'The history of land reform reveals that parcelling the land out to the people in equal shares never works, however just it seems; the land always makes its way back into the hands of the landlords . . . To divide land out equally is like dividing a ship into separate parts. The ship would sink' (Robert Waller, in Herbert Girardet (ed), 1976). Green land reform involves community ownership and management, and the recognition that land cannot be owned by human beings, however 'fair' the distribution may seem. *See also* LAND OWNERSHIP, LAND TAX, PROPERTY.

Landscape
[early 18c in this sense. *Dutch landschap*, region]
Originally used to describe a painting of inland scenery, 'landscape' is now used to describe either a view or a vista, or, more commonly, the overall characteristics of a piece of LAND.

Land Tax
[1879]
(*also* 'community ground rent')
A fiscal mechanism which ensures that any money obtained directly from the use of land (as opposed to that which arises from human effort) goes to the community, following from the recognition that land cannot be owned, only nurtured and harvested. 'What Henry George [*Progress and Poverty*, 1879] proposed was that all land should be embodied in the people, the community, but that the land would belong to nobody. It would not even be owned by the community, but the community would have the constitutional right to a land tax based on site valuation. Throughout history private interests have been able to usurp this right of the community to a share in the wealth produced on its land, the yield of the land and the land's natural resources. Land as such has no [human-defined] value until labour is applied to it' (Robert Waller, in Herbert Girardet (ed), 1976). Land tax would also prevent land speculation, and ensure that land was used in the most ecologically appropriate way, since (as proposed, for instance, by the British Green Party), 'the nearer the land is to its original state, the lower the Community Ground Rent will be' (British Green Party, 1987). *See also* LAND, LAND OWNERSHIP, LAND REFORM, TAXATION.

Land Use Survey
[*c*.1930]
(*also* 'land utilisation survey')
A survey, more or less detailed, which looks at the way in which particular areas of LAND are being used. Detailed land use surveying started in the UK in the 1930s, and was done by independent academics; in recent years, however, less detailed government surveys have replaced these independent surveys which, while costing less, are often wildly inaccurate and capable of the same fudging as official unemployment statistics. 'It is difficult to avoid the conclusion that all these surveys

were designed, consciously or unconsciously, to conceal information rather than reveal it, which may reflect that the department responsible for advising on land-use policies . . . also designs the surveys that might expose the adverse consequences of its advice' (Alice Coleman, in Edward Goldsmith and Nicholas Hildyard (ed), 1986).

Language
[13c. *L lingua*, tongue]
The words, intonations and gestures we use to communicate our experiences, ideas and needs to each other. Language is not neutral; it is the way each of us constructs our REALITY according to our individual perceptions. 'Language is our means of classifying and ordering the world: our means of manipulating reality. In its structure and in its use we bring our world into realization, and if it is inherently inaccurate, then we are misled. If the rules which underlie our language system, our symbolic order, are invalid, then we are daily deceived' (Dale Spender, 1980). While we might speak of our 'mother tongue' (and children do receive most of their early language skills from their mothers), the arbiters of 'correct' language are mostly highly-educated white men: 'Every language reflects the prejudices of the society in which it evolved. Since English, through most of its history, evolved in a white, Anglo-Saxon, patriarchal society, no one should be surprised that its vocabulary and grammar frequently reflect attitudes that exclude or demean minorities and women. But we are surprised' (Casey Miller and Kate Swift, 1981). In acknowledgment of the importance of an awareness of this inbuilt linguistic bias and the need to reconstruct parts of our language without losing its spontaneity and accessibility, several sets of guidelines for non-oppressive language have been written, particularly in the area of non-sexist language. Not surprisingly there has been resistance to and scorn for such changes, but such usages as 'he or she', or 'humanity' rather than 'mankind', are rapidly gaining ground. Other oppressive bias in language has received less attention, but the absolute correctness of correct English in the face of perfectly acceptable alternatives is in question: 'Ain nothin in a long time lit up the English teaching profession like the current hassle over Black English' (Geneva Smitherman, *Black Scholar*, 1973). A relatively recent addition to the ways in which we receive language are the mass MEDIA which, while at least tacitly purporting to relate the truth, often simplify and distort language at the same time as introducing BIAS and DISINFORMATION. 'Mass communication communicates massively: its language lacks precise articulation and avoids demanding terms; it argues for the kind of behaviour in life which will make a "good programme" . . . Television writes our scripts and it thus gives us back our language in a verisimilitudinous recension, docked of amateurish or

embarrassing passions or obsessions which might cause our audience to switch off. If, lacking TV, you want a phrasebook of the prevailing television cant, why not simply turn on a friend?' (Frederic Raphael, in Leonard Michaels and Christopher Ricks (ed), 1980). An important goal in green thinking is SELF-DETERMINATION for MINORITY GROUPS, an important aspect of which is the right of such people to use their own language, facilitated by the provision of educational and official assistance; this applies both to minority groups living in their traditional areas within nation states, and immigrant minority groups. Green-thinkers have vital things to say, and the way we say them is crucial to our cause: 'The need today, as always, is to be in command of language, not used by it, and so the challenge is to find clear, convincing, graceful ways to say accurately what we want to say' (Casey Miller and Kate Swift, 1981).

Laterisation
[1903. *L later*, brick, tile]
(US: 'laterization')
The production of a hard layer of metallic oxides below the surface of tropical SOILS as a result of the removal of vegetation and the leaching of these minerals down through the soil. The laterite forms an impermeable membrane which makes it useless for agriculture.

Law And Order
[1598]
'Whose law and what order?' (John Lea and Jock Young, 1984). Many green-thinkers prefer to use JUSTICE rather than 'law and order', with its implications of state control and institutionalised violence. It is important to distinguish between different sorts of 'crime': Greens recognise that many of the actions of multinationals in the Third World, pesticide-spraying farmers, the nuclear industry and repressive military regimes, though not strictly 'illegal', are just as criminal as many 'real' crimes. Yet given that, officially-recognised crime is an issue that must be addressed, and it is the roots of the problem that must be worked with, not merely its symptoms: 'In our time, relative deprivation and discontent have increased. This, combined with unemployment and community breakdown, has not allowed such discontent to be channelled into political forms. Instead, the most obvious solution is that of crime. Meanwhile, community breakdown facilitates crime by drastically undermining the informal processes of social control. The same forces which make for the increase in crime fuel a moral panic about crime. That is, the real fear about crime is intimately related to the moral hysteria about crime' (John Lea and Jock Young, 1984). Dealing with the root of the problem means helping people to find meaning and

fulfilment in their lives, including GOOD WORK and real PARTICIPATION, COOPERATION and COMPASSION. Otherwise, the process of officially-sanctioned oppression and disempowerment can only lead to further violence and destruction: 'This process is a deforming, a deviation, of all the energies that might have gone into the collective struggle for change . . . If there is violence, wrecking, arson and looting in the places where the poor live, it doesn't really matter. The cargo of tormented humanity which the ambulances and police wagons fetch each day out of North American ghettos piles up in vain' (Jeremy Seabrook, *New Society*, April 1983). *See also* ECODEFENCE, MONKEYWRENCHING, POLICE, STATE.

Law Of The Minimum
[1863]
The minimum requirement of plants for certain crucial mineral salts (also known as 'micronutrients'); even if the soil contains the other nutrients necessary for growth, the plants will not grow if this minimum requirement is not present. 'We mislead ourselves by concentrating too much on the abundance of sunshine, or of some other useful commodity. . . Instead, according to a principle of agricultural chemistry formulated in 1863 by German scientist Justus von Liebig, whatever necessary resource is *least* abundantly available determines an environment's carrying capacity' (William Catton, in Michael Tobias (ed), 1985). *See also* LIMITING FACTOR.

Laws Of Ecology
[1971]
An informal statement of the basic principles of ecological thinking, formulated by Barry Commoner in *The Closing Circle* (1971):
The first law: Everything is connected with everything else.
The second law: Everything must go somewhere.
The third law: Nature knows best.
The fourth law: There's no such thing as a free lunch.

Leaching
[1828. *Old English leccan*, to moisten]
The removal of the soluble parts of a SOIL by water. Leaching is an important aspect of soil formation, but if soil is left bare, especially in areas of high rainfall, leaching can remove excessive amounts of valuable NUTRIENTS, thus impoverishing the soil.

Leadership
[1821. *Old English lœdan*, to lead]
The function of one or more people in a group to bring out, draw attention to, and focus the power and creativity of everyone in the group.

Leadership as a flexible role or function, rather than as more or less absolute power vested in one person, is sometimes difficult to grasp when we are more used to definitions of leaders and leadership which run something like: 'Leadership is a quality which . . . signifies the ability of a person . . . to persuade others to act by inspiring them and making them believe that a proposed course of action is the correct one' (David Robertson, 1985). Such leaders — and most leaders accept this definition of leadership — almost invariably come from a background of privilege. One aspect of green thinking has been to encourage leadership within oppressed and minority groups by people from those groups, often against pressure for leadership by the privileged: 'Many [neighbourhood] organizations have started when women get together under a streetlight because a child was hit by a car or something. They demonstrate, start a little group, apply for money. The group gets bigger. But when the money comes in, women's roles diminish, and most of the time a man will step in as president. Eventually, the women disappear. If local communities are to be the base of women's power, women must run the organizations they begin. Our goal is to train women as leaders in neighbourhoods. And because most of us have been so hurt by the abuse of power, we have to develop new leadership forms' (Annie Cheatham and Mary Clare Powell, 1986). 'Leadership may be intuitive, subtle, unrecognized, untitled, but at least one person in a group activity must assume the responsibility of thinking about the group and its goals and progress as a whole for such a group to function well. . . The job of a leader is not to do all the thinking for the people in the group which he or she leads, but rather to call forth, note and assemble the . . . thinking from all members of the group, . . to produce a complete and consistent program from the brilliant though sometimes fragmented thoughts of the people he or she listens to, and then communicate this integrated theory back to all the members of the group and secure their acceptance and their support for it' (Harvey Jackins, 1973). Many green groups prefer to think of themselves as networks rather than as organisations, and distribute leadership functions within the group as appears appropriate; on the other hand there are groups which have not resolved the challenges of leadership and in which a large amount of time and effort is spent dealing with members' feelings about authority, a process which can be enormously counterproductive to effective action. *See also* FACILITATION, FOCALISATION.

Lead-Time
[1944]
The length of time between the planning of a project and its completion. 'Prompt and vigorous changes in public policy around the world are needed to avoid or minimize these problems before they become

unmanageable. Long lead times are required for effective action. If decisions are delayed until the problems become worse, options for effective action will be severely reduced' (*Global 2000*, 1982).

Left

[1837 in this sense. *Old English left*, weak; akin to *Middle Dutch luft*, useless]

A RADICAL or progressive political grouping which questions traditional or reactionary points of view, so called because in the post-Revolution government in nineteenth-century France those in opposition to the crown sat on the left of the assembly building. In most Western countries, 'the left' today equates roughly with SOCIALISM, egalitarianism and anti-capitalism, but has often itself become fossilised in outmoded beliefs about the real distribution of wealth and power, locked into a static and seemingly immovable political structure. 'Left and Right are . . . ultimately empty slogan-words in modern politics. . . The whole idea of the Left/Right dichotomy assumes one can put political life onto a one-dimensional framework, and reduce judgements to a simple schema' (David Robertson, 1985). *See also* NEW LEFT, PARTY.

Left Brain/Right Brain

(*see* RIGHT BRAIN/LEFT BRAIN)

Leisure

[14c. *L licere*, to be permitted]

The freedom we experience when we are allowed (or allow ourselves) to stop working. This raises the question of what WORK is, since without being clear about what constitutes work it is hard to know when we have finished it. It also suggests that 'leisure' is not-work, a concept which the mother with three children at the playground or the allotment gardener breaking up new ground might find difficult. We also need to ask who it is that is allowing us to stop working, and what rights 'they' have over our time. 'A change of direction towards ownwork and the SHE [SANE/HUMANE/ECOLOGICAL] future will involve a shift of emphasis away from leisure industries and services to leisure organised for people by themselves. The dividing line between ownwork and this kind of leisure will often be difficult to draw. People will make use of their leisure — the increasing amount of time at their own disposal — to do useful work on their own account, on their own interests and on their own projects. Leisure activities will then shade into a much wider range of work and activity options than most people have today, when for most [*sic*] people leisure is what they have when not at work, and the two main options are either to work or to be unemployed' (James Robertson, 1985).

Lesbianism
[1870. From the Greek island of Lesbos, the home of the Greek poet Sappho, who is thought to have been a lesbian]
The lifestyle of women who reject limiting male-defined models of sexual relationships, and choose to put their time and effort into deep and loving relationships with other women, relationships which may or may not include physical intimacy or sexual sharing, depending upon their definition of lesbianism. A complex and potentially divisive issue, in which both lesbians and their critics have frequently been forced into extreme positions. 'Feminists . . . cannot agree on its meaning or its importance. Some consider it a matter of sexual preference, . . others play down the erotic aspects and emphasize lesbianism as a political choice' (Lisa Tuttle, 1986). The 1971 (American) National Association of Women conference approved a resolution calling for 'a woman's right to define and express her own sexuality and to choose her own life-style'. While a great deal remains to be done to make this practically possible for many women, and despite the feelings this statement brings to the surface for many women and men, the freedom to choose for yourself in all aspects of your life is fundamental to green-thinkers. *See also* FEMINISM, GAY, WOMAN.

Less Is More
[*c.*1975]
Another way of stating the principle of VOLUNTARY SIMPLICITY. 'Within the United States, the Stanford Research Institute estimates that some four to five million adult Americans practise the philosophy of "less is more", and an additional eight to ten million Americans have accepted at least some of its tenets' (Lester Brown, 1981).

LETS
(abbreviation for 'local exchange trading system', *see* LOCAL CURRENCY)

Leveller
[1598]
Someone who opposes established values, in particular the privilege of aristocracy and the private appropriation of land. Levellers were particularly active in Britain in the seventeenth and early eighteenth centuries: 'Evictions by landowners in rural Galloway in the 1720s, for instance, gave rise to the Levellers' Rising in which people dispossessed of their right to graze animals ripped out the enclosers' low turf walls or dykes, maintaining that the landlords had no right to turn them off "their" land' (Marion Shoard, 1987). *See also* DIGGER. *The Leveller* was an investigative and radical magazine, founded in Britain in 1976.

Liberation
[15c. *L liberare*, to free]
The removing of obstacles to FREEDOM and the state of being free; freedom from OPPRESSION of any kind. Liberation and the overthrow of oppression requires action from both oppressor (the giving up of CONTROL and PRIVILEGE, often not achievable without drastic measures) and oppressed (a realisation of personal power). Nobody can or should trust anybody else to liberate them; it is rarely in the oppressors' immediate interest to do so. It is always, however, in their long-term interest, and it is important for oppressed groups to have allies in the oppressor group. Nobody can be completely liberated until all are liberated — green thinking calls for freedom and full human rights for all human beings.

Liberation Theology
[*c*.1970]
A political Christian theology originating in Latin America, which stresses the rights of the individual and the need for radical political reform. 'Its basic premise is that theological reflection cannot be neutral or universal, but is confined by the contemporary social and political context' (Christopher Pick, 1983).

Lie
[before 12c. *Old English leogan*, to lie]
A statement made by somebody who knows it to be untrue or not the whole truth, often with the intention of manipulating or controlling the person it is said to. Green philosophy emphasises the importance of HONESTY, being honest both to ourselves and to each other. 'To lie habitually, as a way of life, is to lose contact with the unconscious. It is like taking sleeping pills, which confer sleep but blot out dreaming. The unconscious wants truth. . . This is why the effort to speak honestly is so important. Lies are usually attempts to make everything simpler — for the liar — than it really is, or ought to be' (Adrienne Rich, 1980). *See also* REALITY, SECRET.

Life
[12c. *Old English lif*, life]
A quality that green-thinkers uphold as sacred, usually without needing to define it. The Penguin *Dictionary of Science* and the Macmillan *Dictionary of the Environment* both ignore it; *Websters* has 'the quality that distinguishes a vital and functional being from a dead one; a principle or force that is considered to underlie the distinctive quality of animate beings; an organismic state characterized by capacity for metabolism, growth, reaction to stimuli, and reproduction.' A green definition of life must include the whole of the web of life on the planet,

and taking the GAIA hypothesis into account, must also question the absolute distinction between the BIOTIC and ABIOTIC elements of the biosphere, and the arbitrary distinction between life and DEATH. Such a definition would need to acknowledge that life, particularly human life in this context, is much more than mere SURVIVAL, and that FREEDOM is crucial to fulfilled and healthy living. 'All life is one. This is not a cliché, but a biological reality' (Norman Myers, 1985). 'Everyone has the right to life, liberty and the security of the person' (United Nations *Declaration of Human Rights*, 1948). 'The question of the worth of each individual human life, like the question of the worth of [hu]mankind, also poses the question of what life might be "for" — if, indeed, it is right to say that life is "for" anything — but with the crucial difference that while the individual can sacrifice his [or her] own life "for" others, [hu]mankind cannot do the same, since it includes all possible others within itself. . . Human beings have a worth — a worth that is sacred' (Jonathan Schell, 1982). 'Life' also means 'animation' and 'vitality', qualities important in any green activist.

Lifeboat Ethics

[1968]

The moral dilemmas raised when trying to work out appropriate solutions in a crisis, at the same time dealing with the vested interests of the participants. 'To resolve our conflict, one appealing answer has emerged: "Lifeboat ethics" — the simple notion, popularized by scientist Garrett Hardin [*BioScience*, 1974], that the earth now constitutes a lifeboat in which there is not enough food to go around. Isn't it then only logical that food should go to those most likely to survive, that you do not risk the safety of all by bringing new passengers on board? "What happens if you share space in a lifeboat?" asks Dr Hardin. "The boat is swamped, and everyone drowns. Complete justice, complete catastrophe"' (Frances Moore Lappé and Joseph Collins, 1980). The earth *is* a closed system, but beyond that the lifeboat analogy fails, since lifeboat survivors hope for rescue from an outside agency and the earth has no external air-sea rescue service. And who are privileged Americans to decide who should survive, indeed to decide that there is not enough to go round? 'The ethics of a lifeboat denies the existence of a community and guarantees the persistence of discrimination' (Timothy O'Riordan, 1976). Several 'lifeboat ethics' solutions have been mooted, including Garrett Hardin's own 'triage', in which aid is withheld from starving populations whose situation is deemed 'hopeless', and The Environmental Fund's 1976 campaign against food aid to any country not proven to be tackling contraception. Such ideas have generally since been abandoned by their proponents as oversimplistic, but strains of the lifeboat ethic linger on.

Life-Cycle Costing
[1980]
Ensuring that the costs and benefits of any technology throughout the period of its operation are taken into account; thus the meaningful balance sheet of a nuclear power station, for example, must include the full costs of nuclear waste disposal and eventual decommissioning.

Life-Enhancing
[1896]
Anything that improves the true quality of a person's life without hurting them, anyone else, or their environment. Open to materialist and capitalist manipulation — large cars and unnecessary drugs are but two products which have been advertised as 'life-enhancing'.

Life Expectancy
[1935]
The number of years someone of a particular group may be expected to live, based on the average recorded lifespan of people in similar circumstances. Life expectancy is one way of ascertaining the results of health policies, diet, and living circumstances on keeping people alive, though it is important to remember that life expectancy says nothing at all about quality of life.

Life Force
[1896]
(*also* 'bioenergy', 'chi', 'life energy', 'orgone energy', 'prana', 'vital energy', 'vital force')
A creative energy that maintains healthy life. 'The term "energy", as used in the unorthodox healing traditions, is rather problematic from the scientific point of view. "Life energy" is often thought of as some kind of substance which flows through the organism and is transferred between organisms. According to modern science, energy is not a substance but rather a measure of activity, of dynamic patterns. To understand the models of "energy medicine" scientifically it would seem, therefore, that one should concentrate on the concepts of flow, fluctuation, vibration, rhythm, synchrony and resonance, which are fully consistent with the modern systems view. Concepts like "subtle bodies" or "subtle energies" should not be taken to refer to underlying substances but as metaphors describing the dynamic patterns of self-organisation' (Fritjof Capra, 1982). 'George Leonard has termed this force "the silent pulse", in his inspiring book by the same title. In Gregory Bateson's [*Mind and Nature*], it is called "the pattern which connects"' (Susan Campbell, 1983). A common idea in alternative healing techniques, martial arts, and NEW AGE spirituality, though too often associated with wishy-washy notions about 'energy', and some-

times in danger of having the 'life' idea taken over by the 'force' — 'May the force be with you' and other calls to destroy the ENEMY. 'It is by replenishing the rich reservoirs and deep wells that sustain, and by carefully stewarding the earth that bears and gives forth the fruits of life, that we live on. Our own life force, then, does not die' (Jeremy Rifkin, 1985).

Lifestyle
[1929]
The way in which a person chooses to live their life; by extension, the way groups of people choose to live. 'The transition from an unsustainable society to a sustainable one will lead to materially different life-styles. In the former, life-styles are centred more around the pursuits of self-interest and gratification, but in the latter they will be infused with a sense of action and of common purpose' (Lester Brown, 1981).

Light
[12c. *Old English liht*, light]
A brightness in which we can see clearly; a symbol of life, awareness and lucidity. 'We say we are brilliant with light from the stars that began millennia ago and now burn in our minds' (Susan Griffin, 1984).

Limit
[15c. *L limes*, border, boundary]
(*also* 'threshold')
A boundary or restraint; a point beyond which you know you are taking risks. 'The closer any human activity to the limit of the earth's ability to support that activity, the more apparent and unresolvable the trade-offs become' (Club of Rome, 1972). 'Contrary to the implication of some economic growth models, the best evidence from geographers is that the diameter of the earth in fact does *not* grow at a rate equal to the rate of interest!' (Herman Daly, in Michael Tobias (ed), 1985). 'The word "limit" has a negative connotation, but the virtue of limits is that they are part of the self-regulating process that leads to community homeostasis' (William Ophuls, 1977). In PERSONAL GROWTH, which is subject only to the limits of individual imagination, exploration of the territory on and beyond the limits can be exciting and rewarding. Each person, however, must decide their own limits for themself: 'We have our own individual limits. However much you may look from the outside at someone else's situation and say "I don't know how you put up with it, I'd have left ages ago", each person will take what they want and decide on their own limits. We move if and when we are ready' (Anne Dickson, 1982). *See also* CHOICE, INNER LIMITS, LIMITING FACTOR.

Limiting Factor
[*c*.1930]
An aspect of the environment, such as soil temperature or availability of water, which restricts the distribution or activity of a species or population of living things. *See also* LAW OF THE MINIMUM.

Limits To Growth
[*c*.1970]
The acknowledgement of the existence of a vast range of current and potential constraints to continuous economic and physical expansion. The concept was brought to worldwide attention by the 1972 Club of Rome report *The Limits to Growth*: 'We are convinced that realization of the quantitative constraints of the world environment and of the tragic consequences of an overshoot is essential to the initiation of new forms of thinking that will lead to a fundamental revision of human behaviour and, by implication, of the entire fabric of present-day society.' The list of potential limits to growth is a long one: it includes physical limits of space, time, energy supply and physiology; ethical and social constraints; technological limits; and INNER LIMITS.

Linear
[1706. *L linea*, line; from *linum*, flax]
Seeing systems and situations in terms of simple one-way correspondences; as opposed to an ecological approach.
'*Linear System*
* Energy flows in straight lines.
* Made up of components with separate, specialized functions.
* High entropy, low information.
* Memory stored in centralized, specialized compartments.
* High rate of energy flow and material loss.
* Single channels for energy flow.
* High waste and pollution: resources out of place.

Ecological System
* Energy flows in loops.
* Made up of components with overlapping functions.
* Low entropy, high information.
* Memory stored in all components.
* Low rate of energy flow and material loss.
* Multiple channels for energy flow.
* No waste: the output of one channel is input for another'

(Sim Van der Ryn, in Berkeley Holistic Health Center, 1979). 'Linear' can be used to describe ways of thinking which run along narrow and prescribed channels (also called 'sequential thinking').

Listening

[12c. *Old English hlysnan*, to listen]

Paying attention to what somebody or something is saying to you; half of the process of COMMUNICATION, as important as speaking but less practised and relatively ignored as a skill, especially by those who speak the most and listen the least. 'Is it coincidence that listening is something which women do more than men, something which is less 'visible', and which has therefore (mistakenly) been associated with passivity? . . . Is there any connection between the devaluation of women and the devaluation of listening? I suspect that there might be. I suspect that women may be more familiar with and more appreciative of the "art of listening" (which is perhaps a more appropriate description than the "art of conversation") and perhaps even more skilled at it. It would seem reasonable to assume that, from the perspective of the dominant group, listening may well be a skill which can be overlooked' (Dale Spender, 1980). Learning to listen to other people is the only way we can fully understand their experience, but it does mean unlearning competitive ways of communicating that we have all learnt with more or less 'success': 'In most conversations, we are formulating a reply when the other person is talking, so as to be ready when he or she finishes; we are going back and forth between what is being said and our reply, so that we never really hear properly all that is said' (John Rowan, 1983). As well as listening to other people, we do well to take the time to listen to our own bodies, and to the natural sounds of the planet — hearing is a vital sense to those of us gifted with it.

Litter

[*L lectus*, bed]

(1) [*c*.1860] Plant debris (leaves, stalks etc.) covering the soil, protecting new plants and providing a habitat for ground-dwelling insects and other small animals. Brought into ecological use *c*.1930.

(2) [*c*.1890] Rubbish which is thrown away with little regard for where it falls. 'The mess we make is no longer confined to our living areas — we are itinerant polluters of our countryside, shedding litter like loose hairs wherever we go. And since modern packaging is deliberately indestructible the litter is now part of our landscape — tins and tinfoil, glass, waxed paper, plastics of all kinds, as well as the deluge of more perishable paper' (Nan Fairbrother, 1970). Good Greens never litter.

Living Lightly

[1973]

Following a lifestyle which takes as little from the land and puts back as much as possible (*see also* VOLUNTARY SIMPLICITY). A popular phrase in the north-western states of the USA (Washington, Oregon and northern

California), where several 'Living Lightly Associations' have been formed to link people and organisations with similar aims.

Local
[15c. *L locus*, place]
Something which is found in or comes from a particular small area. Before the advent of mass communications, almost all of a community's needs had to be met from what was available locally. The choice of diet, products, services and entertainments was thus limited, but the environmental cost was minimal. The aim of many green-thinkers is to live as far as possible within the constraints of what the local environment and economy can provide, though there are many practical and moral considerations to take into account. In urban areas it is difficult (though not impossible) to grow some of your own food; much of the food we currently eat cannot be grown in wet northerly climates. The vicissitudes of the world economic system are such that it appears to be cheaper to buy things made by low-paid workers in Taiwan or Korea than to buy the same thing made by a craftsperson in your own neighbourhood. Perhaps above all we are aware, unlike the medieval villager, of the extent of the planet we live on and are part of. Knowing what human beings have made of the world means that a head-in-the-sand reaction is entirely inappropriate. Thus the Planetary Citizens slogan (attributed to both René Dubos and Hazel Henderson): 'Thinking globally, acting locally'. *See also* HUMAN SCALE, LOCAL CURRENCY, NEW LOCAL ECONOMIC ORDER.

Local Currency
[1976]
(*also* 'local exchange trading system', 'LETS')
A currency or exchange arrangement which operates in a small area, thus keeping wealth and decisions about its use and distribution within the community, preventing speculation in MONEY, and providing an accessible, flexible and understandable currency which is available to everybody. There have been many experiments with local currencies, one of the more recent and successful being a LETS scheme established in Comox Valley, British Columbia, in 1983: 'A LETSystem is a self-regulating economic network which allows its members to issue and manage their own money supply within a bounded system. Its essential characteristics are: 1. The agency maintains a system of accounts in a quasi-currency, the unit being related to the prevalent legal tender; 2. Member accounts start at zero, no money is deposited or issued; 3. The network agency acts only on the authority of a member in making a credit transfer from that member's account into another's; 4. There is never any obligation to trade; 5. A member may know the

balance and turnover of another; 6. No interest is charged or paid on balances; 7. Administrative costs are recovered in internal currency from member accounts on a cost-of-service basis' (Landsman Community Services, quoted in Paul Ekins (ed), 1986). One of the problems with local currency systems is that they are usually outlawed by national banks, though if no 'real' money is changing hands such systems are generally legal.

Lorry
(*see* TRUCK)

Love
[12c. *Old English lufu*, love]
An acknowledgement of the links between us and others, and between us and aspects of our surroundings, which fills us with a joy which is difficult to express in words. Also a much-perverted idea; love in our exploitative society has been given a money value just like everything else: '"Eros Centres" in Frankfurt, Amsterdam and Copenhagen are frightening, impersonalized places where men use women to fulfil their exploitative fantasies. When video pornographers produce *Lovebirds* and *Teenage Love*, "love" has become the degradation of human closeness, a monotony of stereotyped sexual activity' (John Button, 1985). Yet however much people may deny the importance of love in the 'real world', it is the 'real world' with its lack of love that must be questioned, not the importance of love: 'In a culture which denies spirituality outside the confines of established religion, falling in love may have become unusually important as one of our few routes to an experience of the transcendent. It has been understood as a distortion of a deep urge to love the world which through social pressures gets funnelled into one person. In this, falling in love typefies the contradictory nature of our experiences under capitalism and patriarchy, our efforts to be human in a world organised along inhuman lines. . . The first step may be to accept and know our own experience better, and to move outwards from there. We may be able to make the first step towards transforming our love from bewildering passion for one person to a deep-rooted lust for all of life. We can at least try' (Lucy Goodison, in Sue Cartledge and Joanna Ryan (ed), 1983). 'We need a moral philosophy in which the concept of love, so rarely mentioned now by philosophers, can once again be made central' (Iris Murdoch, 1970). DEEP ECOLOGY makes it clear that our relationship with the earth must also be one of love, matching the love we seek for ourselves and other people: 'We seek a renewed stirring of love for the earth/ . . . We urge that all people now determine/that a wide untrammelled freedom shall remain/to testify that this generation has love for the next./If we want to

succeed in that, we might show, meanwhile, a little more love for this one, and for each other' (Nancy Newhall, 1961).

Mm

Macrobiotic
[1936. *Gk macro-* + *biotikos*, large-living]
A dietary regime based on a very limited range mostly of vegetarian foods, which is believed to provide a 'balance of energies' within the body. As with VEGETARIANISM, a reduction in the intake of animal products can reduce pressure on land and promote human health. While some proponents of macrobiotics stress the importance of locally-grown produce, the oriental roots of the discipline tend to emphasise rice and pulses as the basis of a macrobiotic diet, thus increasing dependence on Third World cash crops. 'Finding the right macrobiotic balance is complicated and many give up the search because it is too demanding. Those who become converts to the macrobiotic way of life can become extremely enthusiastic, even macroneurotic' (David Harvey, 1986).

Magic
[14c. *Gk magos*, sorcerer]
Ways of relating to the world which involve being totally in touch with the potential of the universe, and which to many people seem impossible or even 'supernatural'. 'When we practice magic we are always making connections, moving energy, identifying with other forms of being. . . Magic is art — that is, it has to do with forms, with structures, with images that can shift us out of the limitations imposed by our culture in a way that words alone cannot, with visions that hint at possibilities of fulfilment not offered by the empty world. And magic is *will* — action, directed energy, choices made not once but many times, . . . made up of hundreds of thousands of small decisions' (Starhawk, 1982). 'By "magic" . . . I do not mean sticking pins in dolls; I mean the affective, concrete and sensual experience of life. . . Magic is embodied in the way science is not; it emerges from the whole person, not just

from the intellect' (Maurice Berman, *Journal of Humanistic Psychology*, Spring 1986).

Male Supremacy
(*see* PATRIARCHY)

Malnutrition
[1862. *L male-* + *nutrire*, badly nourished]
Lack of an adequate healthy DIET; in many parts of the Third World the result of lack of FOOD, in the West due to an unhealthy diet often exacerbated by POVERTY. 'The truth is that though malnutrition is almost everywhere among the poor, the traveller in the Third World rarely sees people who are nothing but skin and bone. Only in extreme situations, in Biafra, Bangladesh or the Sahel, do these occur in large numbers. The everyday reality of malnutrition in the Third World is less dramatic. It is adults scraping through, physically and mentally fatigued and vulnerable to illness. It is children — often dying, not so frequently of hunger alone, as of hunger working hand in hand with sickness; but more often surviving impaired for life' (Paul Harrison, 1979). 'Commerciogenic malnutrition is a most malevolent export of the rich world to the Third World' (Geoffrey Yates, 1980). Malnutrition of a different kind — but with some of the same results — has recently been observed in the West, not a malnutrition of poverty, but of poverty of diet: 'Recently, the features of early beriberi were recognised in a group of otherwise healthy American children. . . The physicians suggested the lack of Vitamin B1 in their patients was due to their high consumption of junk foods' (*New Internationalist*, January 1986). Some nutritionists have even recognised 'muesli-belt malnutrition', supposedly the result of parental enforcement of a too strict wholefood diet, though others believe that what is being witnessed is a retreat from the 'norm' of overweight children.

Malthusianism
[1812. Named after the British economist Thomas Malthus, 1766-1834]
The belief that if unchecked, the human POPULATION will rapidly outstrip the resources capable of sustaining that population. In *An Essay on the Principle of Population* of 1798, Malthus presented a model of rapid population growth which put severe pressure on resources, an idea which was picked up with a vengeance by some ecologists in the 1960s (*see*, for example, CARRYING CAPACITY, COMMONS, LIFEBOAT ETHIC). His thesis was laced with a good deal of moralising, though it is important to remember the social climate in which he was writing. 'He certainly established the thesis that population was growing quickly and that people are biological as well as social beings. . . Yet he has been criticized, for example, for confusing moralist and scientific approaches and

for being a very poor prophet of events. . . It has also been argued that Malthus's reactionary views impeded the development of demography as a science' (Philip Ogden, in R.J. Johnston (ed), 1986).

Man
[12c. *Old English mann*, human being]
Originally meaning an adult human being of either sex, 'man' now means (more usually) an adult male person (see sense (1)), or (less commonly but nonetheless pervasively) all the human beings in a certain group, as in 'Western man' or 'economic man' (see sense (2)).
(1) A male human being, who takes on more or less of the role of 'man' as defined by others, and whose experiences are those of being so defined. In a patriarchal society men are primary, dominant, visible, taken notice of, respected. 'Men are the arbiters of human identity. From the time they are boys, men are programmed by the culture to refer exclusively to other men for validation of their self-worth. A man's comfort and well-being are contingent upon the labor and nurture of women, but his identity — his "knowledge of who he is" — can only be conferred and confirmed by other men. . . Under patriarchy, men are the arbiters of identity for both males and females, because the cultural norm of human identity is, by definition, male identity — *masculinity*. And, under patriarchy, the cultural norm of male identity consists in power, prestige, privilege, and prerogative *as over and against* the gender class women. That's what masculinity is. It isn't something else!' (Jon Stoltenberg, in Jon Snodgrass (ed), 1977). Some men — especially green-thinking men — have worked hard at a new awareness of SEXISM and what a POSTPATRIARCHAL society might be like, though there is still a long way to go: 'Men have been involved in a process of change for over a decade in response to the challenges of feminism but, in truth, little has changed. If anything there has been a vehement backlash against feminism and the demands for more equal relationships [of women] with men. Relationships seem to be changing for a younger generation, but this is difficult to assess. . . This is no easy task since it involves a challenge to our inherited sense of self, our dominant intellectual and moral traditions, and the ways in which we organise our daily lives. It will also mean facing the rage and resentments we often feel for women, though we are careful, sometimes, not to express this. These are feelings we will have to learn to deal with in our relationships with other men. This will bring us closer to our fear, including homophobia and the fear of showing our weakness and vulnerability to other men. This is part of the process of redefining masculinity. But it makes an enormous difference to know that we are not alone' (Vic Seidler, in Andy Metcalf and Martin Humphries (ed), 1985). 'The really major problem of writing about men is that the majority of men do not think

they have a problem' (Mary Ingham, 1984). While it may seem an insuperable challenge, the green future must be one in which men are willing to take the risk of 'unbecoming men' (*Unbecoming Men*, 1971) and becoming fully human. *See also* FEMININE, GENDER, MASCULINE. (2) All human beings, or everybody in a particular group; this use of the word is sometimes called 'the generic "man" syndrome'. The deep-seated oppression underlying this use of the word, and its derivations such as MANKIND and the use of 'he' as a generic pronoun, are neither necessary nor useful in our language; most green-thinkers attempt to avoid the ambiguity and invisibility thus created by using NON-SEXIST language (although using non-oppressive words is not always paralleled by similar attitudes and behaviour). 'It means the species: it also means the male of the species. If you write a book about man or conceive a theory about man you cannot avoid using the word, and you will use the pronoun *he* as matter of simple linguistic convenience. But before you are halfway through the first chapter a mental image of this evolving creature begins to form in your mind. It will be a male image and he will be the hero of the story . . .' (Elaine Morgan, 1972, quoted in Dale Spender, 1980). 'Man overlooks what he does not want to see — and so does woman. But males may have a greater vested interest in preserving the way things were than in acknowledging the way they are. If the word *man* were not so emotionally charged and politically useful, its ambiguity would have led long ago to its demise in any but the limited sense it immediately brings to mind. So the question for writers and speakers becomes, how can we get along without *man* in the old sense, that archaic crutch we no longer need but to which we have become habituated?' (Casey Miller and Kate Swift, 1980).

Management
[*c*.1600. *L manus*, hand]
The sensitive manipulation and use of a resource or system of resources; thus 'land management', 'resource management', 'wildlife management'. Management can easily edge over into control and exploitation, and this is certainly the case when 'management' overrides the needs and voices of the 'labour' it employs. In green terms, 'management' is close to CONSERVATION. When it comes to the management of human resources, HUMANISTIC PSYCHOLOGY offers a helpful range of approaches and techniques.

Mania
[*c*.1700 in this sense. *Gk mania*, madness]
An obsessional enthusiasm for something which blinds a person to other possibilities, thus 'growthmania', 'squandermania', 'technomania'.

Manipulation
[*L manipulus*, handful]
(1) (1828) Handling with skill.
(2) (*c*.1830) Encouraging a person to act (often against their own inclination) by devious means.
(3) (*c*.1920) Treating a person with your hands, as in MASSAGE or BODYWORK.

Mankind
[12c. *Old English manncynd*, people in general]
Everybody in the world. An ambiguous and oppressive word in its current usage (*see* MAN, sense (2)), preferably replaced by 'humanity', 'humankind' or 'human population'. 'Earthkind' has appeared in some NEW AGE publications.

Marginalisation
[*c*.1964. *L margo*, border]
(US: 'marginalization')
Being left on the edge, and in particular being kept out of decision making. Green policies seek the full and active involvement of all people, especially people from the minority groups who are so often marginalised. On the other hand, there are few green-thinkers who would wish to be central within mainstream society: 'Another general thing that can safely be said about the resources provided by marginality is that marginality opens the possibility of seeing structures of the dominant culture which are invisible from within it' (Marilyn Frye, 1983).

Mariculture
[*c*.1909. *L mare + cultura*, cultivation of the sea]
The cultivation of marine plants and animals for human use.

Market
[16c in this sense. *L merx*, merchandise]
A place for buying, selling and exchanging merchandise. In conventional economics, the market is where money is used to buy and sell goods and services: 'The market economy is the marketplace of society, where things and services are made and delivered for a price. Most of the market economy is privately owned but not all of it. The railways, coal mines and steel mills of the nationalized industries are part of the market economy because they trade for cash. Some schools and hospitals, the private ones, are there, as are all the businesses, shops and firms which fill the high street' (Charles Handy, 1985). Together with the state economy, the market economy constitutes the FORMAL ECONOMY. Some economists still have fond visions of a 'free market', in

which supply and demand are unhampered by tampering bureaucracies. Markets, however, are as often created as innate, and it can be difficult when in a market full of 'bargains' to distinguish between what you really want and what you are being persuaded to buy. *See also* CONSUMER.

Marxism
[1897. Named after Karl Marx, the German founder of modern communism, 1818-83]
Social and economic theory and practice which derive from the work of Karl Marx. Many strands of Marxism can be traced into the late twentieth century, often differing enormously in their analyses and proposals, but although there is much in Marx's (copious and often contradictory) writings which can be criticised from a green perspective, it is as well to remember that Marx's most far-reaching legacy is his way of examining society. In his theory of 'dialectical materialism' he saw human development through history as a constantly-changing interplay between the material/economic/labour base and the state/establishment 'superstructure'. This he interpreted as a constant class struggle between the owners of capital and the wage slaves, a struggle which is still all too obvious. As well as being a theorist, Marx was also a polemicist, and his proposals for the 'constant revolution' necessary to achieve a classless 'communist' society resulted in a variety of 'socialist' solutions from the 'national communism' of the USSR and Eastern Europe to the revolutionary views of Lenin and Trotsky. Many people now involved in green politics, particularly in Germany, have a Marxist-socialist background, and it is important to look at the links between 'red' and 'green'. 'To discuss a revolutionary transformation of our society without taking Marx into consideration would not only be meaningless, it would also make more difficult an open dialogue between freethinkers among Marxists and non-Marxists, who are often closer to one another than they realize' (Erik Dammann, 1984). Yet Marxism, despite its usefulness, usually embraces ideas which many green-thinkers cannot accept. In believing that all problems have their roots in economic organisation, Marx tends to belittle anything which cannot be given an economic value, including landscape, spirituality, beauty and wilderness, and modern Marxists often view the green approach as idealistic and bourgeois (sometimes with complete justification). While Marx wanted to see resources in the hands of the community rather than in those of capitalist entrepreneurs, he still saw nature as limitlessly abundant. On the other hand, his belief that change in society must come 'from below' still holds good. 'There are many particular elements in Marx that I still find useful, but the structure itself I have abandoned. For me Marxism is a quarry' (Rudolf Bahro, 1984). 'The Greens are to

Marx and Marxism what Einstein was to Newton and Newtonian physics — in short, a qualitative transformation of a worthwhile system whose time, however, is up' (Rudolf Bahro, quoted in Fritjof Capra and Charlene Spretnak, 1984). *See also* SOCIALISM.

Masculine
[14c. *L masculus*; diminutive of *mas*, male]
'Masculine' literally means 'relating to men', though like 'feminine' it has become so laden with sexist expectations as to be virtually meaningless (*see* FEMININE, GENDER). 'Masculine' has come to mean manly, virile, strong, aggressive and tough, and though some men are questioning this version of manhood (*see* MAN), macho masculinity is still the main model for those in power in today's world: 'Masculine society has insisted on seeing in sexuality that same sense of conflict and competition that it has imposed upon its relation to the planet as a whole. From the bedroom to the board room to the international conference table, separateness, differentiation, opposition, exclusion, antithesis have been the cause and goal of the male politics of power. Human characteristics belonging to the entire species have been crystallized out of the living flow of human experience and made into either/or categories. This male habit of setting up boundary lines between imagined polarities has been the impetus for untold hatred and destruction. Masculine/feminine is just one of such polarities among many, including body/mind, organism/environment, plant/animal, good/evil, black/white, feeling/intellect, passive/active, sane/insane, living/dead. Such language hardens what is in reality a continuum and a unity into separate mental images always in opposition to one another' (Betty Roszak, in Betty Roszak and Theodore Roszak (ed), 1969). *See also* ANDROGYNY, SEX, SPIRITUALITY, YIN/YANG.

Massage
[1860. Possibly from *Arabic massa*, to stroke; or *Portuguese massa*, dough, mass]
The manipulation by one person of the skin and underlying body structure of another, for pleasure and for health. In our society massage has often become associated with commercially-available impersonal sexual stimulation, mostly for men, but in many parts of the world, particularly the Pacific, eastern Asia and the Arabic countries, different massage techniques have been used in healing for centuries. 'The core of massage lies in its unique way of communicating without words' (George Downing, 1973). 'Massage is one of life's most compassionate moments' (Gordon Inkeles, 1980). Massage comes with a variety of qualifiers — 'healing massage', 'remedial massage', 'sensual massage', etc. Other forms of BODYWORK akin to massage include 'acupressure' and

'shiatsu' (which work on specific points), 'chiropractic', 'osteopathy', 'postural integration' and 'rolfing' (all deep manipulation techniques), 'Alexander technique' and 'Feldenkrais technique' (more gentle approaches to posture and movement), 'metamorphic technique' and 'reflexology' (foot massage), and 'cranial osteopathy' (head massage). With such a choice it can be difficult to know where to start, but basic massage techniques are easy to learn (it's second nature anyway), and exchanging massages with a friend you trust is an excellent way of keeping in touch and healthy. Massage can also be used to explore developing relationships without falling into the all-or-nothing trap of sexual involvement, though the healthy manipulation of massage can easily tip over into the unhealthy manipulation of unwanted and oppressive power play. *See also* TOUCH.

Mass Production
[1923]
The production of large quantities of identical products, usually on highly automated production lines. Thought for decades to be the industrialist's and economist's dream, since the economies of scale thus achieved increase turnover and profits, this process takes for granted the human suffering and boredom of assembly lines: to a large (though unacknowledged) extent, mass production is the ideal way to produce a mass worker, perfectly disciplined and unswervingly loyal. In fact, manufacturing industry is rapidly moving away from mass production as short-run technologies improve and people want a wider range of choice. 'We do of course continue to turn out cigarettes by the billion, textiles by the millions of yards, light bulbs, matches, bricks, or spark plugs in astronomical quantities. . . Yet these are precisely the products of more backward industries rather than the most advanced and today they account for only about 5 per cent of all our manufactured goods. . . What we are looking at, in effect, is custom tailoring on a high-technology basis. It is the reinstatement of a system that flourished before the industrial revolution — but now built on the basis of the most advanced, sophisticated technology. . . We are de-massifying manufacture' (Alvin Toffler, 1980).

Mass Trespass
[*c.*1930]
An ACTION in which many people simultaneously enter 'private' land in order to make a political point. Mass trespass has been used to establish rights of access to wild land (as in the famous Kinder Scout mass trespass of 1932 in the English Peak District), to protest against nuclear testing and dumping, to reclaim Greenham Common (the US air base in southern England), to squat unused housing, and to establish poor

people on land in Third World countries. *See also* ACCESS, ACTION, DIGGER, LEVELLER, SQUATTING.

Matrix
[15c. *L matrix*, womb]
The place from which something develops. A word often used by green-thinkers, but best avoided unless you really mean a mould for a casting, the rock surrounding a fossil, or a rectangular array of mathematical elements. 'Matrix is a conspicuous warning signal. . . It has a number of precise specialised meanings, [and] a conveniently hazy general meaning . . . as something within which something else originates, or takes form, or develops. . . But when somebody uses the word outside its jargons in general speech, it is a strident warning to listen suspiciously, because somebody may be showing off' (Philip Howard, 1978).

Mauve Economy
[1983]
Personal services and home businesses on the edge of the FORMAL ECONOMY. 'The respectable cousin of the black economy' (Charles Handy, 1985).

Mechanism
[1884 in this sense. *Gk mekhane*, machine]
The belief that the universe or any part of it behaves exactly like a machine, a view which in several respects is the antithesis of HOLISM. 'The principal feature of [the mechanistic] order is that the world is regarded as constituted of entities which are outside of each other. . . Each part is formed independently of the others, and interacts with the other parts only through some kind of external contact. By contrast, in a living organism, for example, each part grows in the context of the whole, so that it does not exist independently, nor can it be said that it merely 'interacts' with the others, without itself being essentially affected in this relationship' (David Bohm, 1980).

Media
[1923. *L medius*, middle]
'Media' started life as 'mass medium' (singular) and 'mass media' (plural), describing a channel or channels of communication reaching a large audience; now commonly used in the plural (often with a singular verb) to describe all such methods of communication. 'The industrial revolution, bringing with it the enormous elaboration of the mass media, thus alters radically the nature of the messages received by the ordinary individual. In addition to receiving uncoded messages from the environment, and coded but casual messages from the people around . . ., the individual now begins to receive a growing number of coded but

pre-engineered messages as well. . . The sea of coded information that surrounds [us] begins to beat at [our] senses wth new urgency. . . The waves of coded information turn into violent breakers and come at a faster and faster clip, pounding at us, seeking entry, as it were, to our nervous system' (Alvin Toffler, 1970). Satellite pictures can now reach us 'live' from the other side of the world, creating what Marshall McLuhan (1963) called the 'global village', in which 'the medium is the message. This is merely to say that the personal and social consequences of any medium . . . result from the new scale that is introduced into our affairs by each extension of ourselves or by any new technology' (Marshall McLuhan, 1965). Increasing 'coverage' of world events is seen as PROGRESS by most people, and an APPROPRIATE TECHNOLOGY of the media is difficult to pin down. Should Indian villagers really be subjected to episodes of *Dallas*, even if they and everyone with a vested interest in its wider distribution want it? A vital question in relation to the media is: who controls it? Appropriate media can inform, teach and stimulate an intelligent audience, but much of what is offered is stereotyped, biased, mind-dulling and manipulative. *See also* ADVERTISING, TELEVISION.

Mediation
[14c. *L medius*, middle]
Acting as a channel and catalyst for communication between two people or groups of people who have difficulties in communicating, such as parents and children, women and men, or people from different cultures. 'The most powerful thing about mediation is that you take control over your life. When people talk with each other, the success rate for resolving conflict is extraordinarily high. People say it changes their lives. Our biggest challenge is getting more cases, because people don't come to mediation voluntarily. We live in such a litigious society that we would rather deal indirectly with problems. The idea of sitting down with a third party, a community member, and talking about an issue is uncommon and scary' (Janet Rifkin, in Annie Cheatham and Mary Clare Powell (ed), 1986). *See also* NEGOTIATION.

Medicine
[13c. *L medicus*, doctor]
A substance used in HEALING, or a healing regime. With the ascendency of scientific medicine, medicine in the first sense is usually used synonymously with DRUG, and in the second with mainstream medicine. Green-thinkers often use 'alternative medicine' or COMPLEMENTARY MEDICINE to describe the practice of holistic healing, but tend to prefer REMEDY to 'medicine' when describing any substance used to help in the healing process, thus acknowledging HEALTH rather than illness as the normal state of a human being.

Meditation

[13c. *L meditari*, to reflect upon]

The focusing of attention and awareness in order to expand human consciousness, often leading to insights into the nature of existence. 'All meditations direct attention and alter states of awareness. In our usual thinking, we progress quickly from thought to thought — the mind races and attention is scattered. We usually think in words and then become inundated by our own continuous string of verbalizations. We seldom attend to only one thing at a time, or concentrate wholly on the action we're performing while performing it. In meditation, attention is focused and we become wholly engaged in a single behavior. . . Although meditations work by narrowing the focus of attention, the result is to enlarge the sense of being, and eliminate the subjective distinction between self and environment' (L. John Mason, 1980). There are many ways of meditating, from repeating a phrase or mantra over and over again, to watching a candle, to wild body movement, to sitting quietly on a hilltop. After meditating, people often feel more relaxed and at peace with their surroundings, though meditation can be used as an escape from the world: 'Meditation can be misused: it can be used as a way of "cutting-off" from other people or from emotions, for denying real problems and difficulties ("I'm spiritual, superior, and above all these petty concerns and feelings"). This danger should be watched for. Meditation should not be used as a way of kidding yourself that everything's O.K. when it's not, but rather as a way of gaining the space and strength to deal in a clear way with whatever you need to face' (Sheila Ernst and Lucy Goodison, 1981).

Meltdown

(*see* CHINA SYNDROME)

Mental Health

[*c*.1970]

A state of mental wellbeing, creativity and fulfilment. One important aspect of human HEALTH, yet like all health issues, firmly entrenched in the mainstream medical model which sees 'illness' as something which is 'wrong' with the patient and which needs to be cured. *See* MENTAL HEALTH SURVIVOR, MENTAL ILLNESS, SANITY.

Mental Health Survivor

[*c*.1979]

Someone who has been through the MENTAL ILLNESS system and re-emerged aware of their own power. 'No one has told us that our minds are capable of embarking on incredible journeys and different ways of being. . . I know now that most of our creative ways of expression get crushed very early on in our lives . . . I realize as well that my instincts led me to make many extreme changes in my situation. I'm a very changed person now — outspoken, volatile, and will fight with tenacity for *my* rights. I trust my selves, my visions, my dreams, my feelings — the biggest enemy is fear. We are fed with fear — fear takes us. We can take fear and change it — to survive' (Shirley Hall, in *Through the Break*, 1986).

Mental Illness
[*c*.1950]
A creation of professional psychiatrists from the mid-nineteenth century onwards to explain rebellious or 'anti-social' behaviour, usually called 'hysteria' until the 1950s and thought of as a predominantly female 'disorder'. In the last twenty years many people have questioned the legitimacy of the label of mental illness, and have criticised the way that those given the label are treated as second-class human beings. Green-thinkers prefer to take mental health or mental wellness as their starting-point, rather than framing the issue within the conventional and limiting terms of mental illness, disease or handicap. Some humanistic psychologists use the term 'mental distress': 'Humanistic psychology does not attach very much importance to diagnostic categories, and does not see mental distress as a medical problem' (John Rowan, 1976). Yet health care professionals, their patients, and the public have invested so much in believing that mental illness does exist that a person's mind and body frequently oblige by presenting very convincing symptoms, further confusing the question of whether or not there is such a thing as mental illness. 'The notion of a person "having a mental illness" is scientifically crippling. It provides professional assent to a popular rationalization, namely, that problems of living experienced and expressed in terms of so-called psychiatric symptoms are basically similar to bodily diseases. Moreover, the concept of mental illness also undermines the principle of personal responsibility, the ground on which all free political institutions rest. For the individual, the notion of mental illness precludes an inquiring attitude towards his [or her] conflicts which his [or her] symptoms at once conceal and reveal. For a society, it precludes regarding individuals as responsible persons and invites, instead, treating them as irresponsible patients' (Thomas Szasz, 1962). 'We must face the fact that much of what is called "mental illness" by the oppressive society is healthy and at least semi-rational rebellion against conformity, against submission to, or cooperation with, oppression. The "mental health systems" in our present societies are almost entirely instruments of oppression in spite of the good intentions and the basic humanness of the practitioners who act out their roles in the machinery. Mental health oppression is invoked and used to force submission, to enforce conformity, and to imprison and destroy

rebels and non-conformists' (Harvey Jackins, 1983). And of course it is still women who suffer the most, which is not unconnected with the fact that 86% of all US psychiatrists are men: 'In the mental health field, as in most other arenas of social life, it is largely men who have the power to define reality — to name the problem. . . The typical male Expert is likely to construe the . . . statistics to mean that women are psychologically sicker than men. The numbers may be taken as evidence of the problem of female mental illness. But is we look closer, this way of defining the problem is itself a part of the problem. For statistics also show that male doctors will diagnose women as neurotic or psychotic twice as frequently as they do men with the same symptoms: Man as Expert simply sees women quite differently than he sees men' (Miriam Greenspan, 1983).

Middle Way
[*c*.1937]
Living your life as a balance of all apparent opposites; part of Buddhist doctrine which was brought into green thinking by Fritz Schumacher in his book *Small is Beautiful* (1973): 'While the materialist is mainly interested in goods, the Buddhist is mainly interested in liberation. But Buddhism is "The Middle Way" and therefore in no way antagonistic to physical well-being. It is not wealth that stands in the way of liberation but the attachment to wealth; not the enjoyment of pleasurable things but the craving for them.'

Migration
[early 17c. *L migrare*, to migrate]
The mass movement of populations of animals, birds or human beings. Many species make a regular journey over long distances in order to take advantage of two or more different habitats, and there is as yet no international agreement safeguarding the freedom of any migratory species. 'In a crowded world, the seasonal movements of animals pose a problem. How can populations that cross national boundaries be protected without some form of international legislation?' (Lee Durrell, 1986). In a world where travel and transport have widened horizons, human migration in search of work, food, housing, freedom from oppression, or a better quality of life have radically affected population patterns throughout the world, putting pressure on natural resources in reception areas, creating social tension between newcomers and the existing population, and hardship in the homelands, since it is usually the people with marketable skills who leave first. Migration from poorer to more prosperous areas reinforces patterns of inequality, whether it be the 'brain drain' from Europe to America, the migration of Third World professionals to the West, or the movement of desert nomads into squatter camps.

Militarism

[1864. *L miles*, soldier]

The espousal by a STATE or those with power in a society of a doctrine and policy of armed VIOLENCE and extreme patriotism. While militarism is most easily seen in the aggressive words and behaviour of reactionary politicians and military men, it is deeply entrenched in any society where the support of militarism is accepted with little question. 'Back in 1983, when President Reagan first announced his "vision of hope for the future", we took it to be the optical illusion of an ageing man. To envisage the machinery of Star Wars actually placed in space was tantamount to seeing real shapes in clouds . . . The contradictory aspiration to render militarism obsolete by recourse to militarism remains — as it always will do — fantastical. Yet the "vision" itself has not dissolved away but rather gains in distinctness even as we watch and wait. . . Reagan's delirious whim, in being indulged, has also been made sanitary and reprocessed as rationality, thanks to its comforting association with ordinary people and their ordinary goings on in the common rooms of Heriot-Watt or the canteens of Plessey and British Aerospace. "What am I working on? — Fibre optics, well, yes, part of the SDI programme — want another coffee?"' (Kate Soper, in Dan Smith and E.P. Thompson (ed), 1987). *See also* ARMS, NUCLEAR WEAPONS, WAR.

Mind

[12c. *Old English gemynd*, memory, mind]

The 'part' of a human being which is traditionally seen as the location of mental processes — thinking, questioning, reasoning, working things out. The separation of BODY (physical) and mind (non-physical) is attributed to the seventeenth-century writings of Descartes, though it is deeply entrenched in the cultural and scientific milieu of his (and our) times. The further separation of mind (mental processes) and SPIRIT (transcendent and transpersonal processes) had also taken firm hold. HOLISM rejects these arbitrary distinctions, defining mind more as a corollary of life than as part of life: 'Gregory Bateson proposed to define mind as a systems phenomenon characteristic of living organisms, societies, and ecosystems, and he listed a set of criteria which systems have to satisfy for mind to occur. Any system that satisfies those criteria will be able to process information and develop the phenomena we associate with mind — thinking, learning, memory . . . As Bateson said, "Mind is the essence of being alive" [Gregory Bateson, 1979]. From the systems point of view, life is not a substance or a force, and mind is not an entity interacting with matter. Both life and mind are manifestations of the same set of systemic properties, a set of processes that represent the dynamics of self-organization. This new concept will be of tremendous value in our attempts to overcome the Cartesian division' (Fritjof Capra, 1982). 'I have a mind, but I am not my mind' (Roberto Assagioli, 1974).

Mind-Body Split
(*see* DUALISM)

Minichip
[1980. Abbreviation of 'mini c[ombined] h[eat and] p[ower]']
(*also* 'mini-CHP')
A small-scale CO-GENERATION installation, designed to provide heat and power for a large buildings or small district; if combined with a sewage works it can run on the sludge gas from the digesters. 'Mini-CHP schemes are almost three times as efficient as conventional power stations; can produce power at about two thirds the cost; and can be installed (or removed) in a fraction of the time' (Michael Flood, 1986).

Minimum Wage
(*see* SOCIAL WAGE)

Minority
[1921 in this sense. *L minoritas*, minority]
A group of people who have common social and cultural beliefs and traditions, forming a small part of a population the majority of which may hold very different beliefs and values. Minority groups are frequently the easy targets of DISCRIMINATION.

Minority Rights
[1924]
The acknowledgement and fulfilment of full HUMAN RIGHTS for all members of a MINORITY group; this may involve POSITIVE DISCRIMINATION to balance the disadvantage experienced by minorities.

Miracle
[c.1400 in this sense. *L miraculum*, object of wonder]
A source of wonder and an affirmation of connectedness. For centuries the almost exclusive property of the Christian church, 'miracle' in its original meaning of 'an object of wonder' has recently been repossessed by other wonderers, albeit in some questionable causes (including 'miracle drug' and 'miracle fertiliser'). Following the Christian tradition, we tend to think of miracles as events that happen very rarely and are somehow supernatural; in fact miracles are supremely natural, and happen all the time if we allow ourselves to be open to noticing them: 'Expect a miracle' (1970s badge slogan).

Mixed Cropping
[*c*.1940]
Planting two or more species together in the same field, usually species

of different heights or different growth cycles, so as to increase the biomass yield without adversely affecting either crop. Sometimes used synonymously with the term 'intercropping', but 'mixed cropping and intercropping are not quite synonymous since the latter implies the symmetrical cultivation of two crops in alternate rows, while mixed cropping refers to more of an asymmetrical arrangement' (Christopher Lewis, in Malcolm Slesser (ed), 1982). *See also* INTERCROPPING, POLYCULTURE.

Model

[*c*.1913 in this sense. *L modulus*, small measure]

An idealised and simplified representation of the real world (or a part of it), which attempts to explain how the real world works. 'Models can be viewed as selective approximations which, by the elimination of incidental detail, allow some fundamental, relevant or interesting aspects of the real world to appear in some generalized form' (Richard Chorley and Peter Haggett, 1967). Models, of course, are only as good (or bad) as the information they are based on and the assumptions used to manipulate that information, and in dubious hands can be made to prove almost anything. 'For the academic, the model may become more real than reality itself, and it may get in the way of an understanding of the multiplicity of alternative possibilities and contexts that the model excludes. Dogmatic belief in the model's validity can prevent the model thinker from seeing people and things in any other way than as the model describes them' (Erik Dammann, 1984). 'Looking for ideal models of human organization creates cynicism. There are *no* models; neither are there any ultimate solutions. . . Since there are no absolute answers . . , it is the development of a participatory, just *process* in which people can search and experiment that is the goal' (Frances Moore Lappé, Joseph Collins and David Kinley, 1980).

Mondragon

[1955]

'What must be the most successful producer cooperative in Europe, that based on Mondragon in the Basque Country of Spain, is constantly held up by ecocentrics as a shining example of how "alternative" lifestyles can succeed. Mondragon consists of over 60 industrial and 5 agricultural commercially viable cooperative enterprises, centred on a local cooperative bank. . . Mondragon's success is thought to be a function of the small-scale nature of most of the enterprises, and of the workers' financial and social interests being linked directly to the success of the enterprises' (David Pepper, 1984).

Money

[13c. *L moneta*, money, mint]

Anything which is generally accepted as medium of exchange. While often having very little intrinsic VALUE, money or the lack of it rules many people's lives. 'The argument is that, money being the calculus we use to measure value, it is vital that the money system should operate fairly and objectively. Money values should reflect the actual values and preferences that people have; for example, people's pay should reflect the value of the work they do. As things are, however, everyone knows that the money system does not work this way. Some people get highly paid for work of little value, while others get paid much less for work of much greater value. The people who run the money system — bankers, stockbrokers, and so on — do not run it professionally, with the aim that it should operate fairly and efficiently in the interests of society as a whole. They operate it in such a way as to cream off above-average incomes and capital gains for themselves and their clients. In this sense, the present money system is fundamentally corrupt' (James Robertson, 1985). 'Making money out of money — or more accurately making money out of debt — has become a massive industry, holding the world to ransom' (Green Party, 1987) (*see* DEBT CRISIS). Many Greens believe that our money system is beyond saving, so out of touch is it with real wealth and the real needs of people. While money can be liberating if used appropriately (never forgetting that is only symbolic of real wealth), green-thinkers see LOCAL CURRENCY, BARTER, OWNWORK and informal work largely taking its place. *See also* INFLATION, WEALTH.

Monkeywrenching

[1904]

Deliberate sabotage, specifically of projects which harm the earth and its living systems. Monkeywrenching received new impetus with Edward Abbey's novel *The Monkey Wrench Gang* (1975), in which a group of environmental guerrillas rampage through the American West, sabotaging bridge, dam and environmentally-destructive industrial projects. The action group Earth First! (*see* EARTH) use a monkey-wrench crossed with a native American tomahawk as their symbol. A book called *Ecodefense* (Dave Foreman (ed), 1985) contains many monkeywrenching schemes, from sinking metal spikes into trees to prevent them being felled, to instructions on exactly how to incapacitate a bulldozer. Marge Piercy's novel *Vida* (1979) shows clearly how deliberate sabotage brings up very contradictory thoughts and feelings in aware and sensitive people — green-thinkers never condone arbitrary violence and would never deliberately hurt or destroy living things, yet monkeywrenchers would prefer to have a grove of spiked trees rather than a chemical dump.

Monocropping
[*c*.1915]
(*also* 'monoculture')
The cultivation of a single crop (often a single genetically-engineered variety), over large areas of land. While this provides a uniform, easily-processed and readily saleable crop, it is a most unsound practice in ecological terms. 'Modern plant breeding, with its emphasis on inbred, uniform strains, has fostered a widespread trend towards large-scale monocultures. Whereas the traditional farmed landscape was genetically diverse, the emerging agricultural landscape is much more uniform. Most inbred strains of crop plant offer short-lived resistance to pathogens and pests. For example, the average lifetime of wheat varieties is only 5-15 years. As a result, plant diseases and pest infestations can sweep through monocultures like a prairie fire' (Norman Myers, 1985). *See also* AGRICULTURE.

Monopoly
[16c. *L monopolion*, sole selling rights]
The exclusive or near-exclusive provision of a product or service by a single supplier. A monopoly is able to dictate the conditions, including the price, under which it continues to supply its wares, especially in a highly-centralised capitalistic economy, and since monopolies tend to be large concerns, they often suffer from excessive bureaucracy. Free competition, which is the capitalist alternative to monopoly, is frequently even less satisfactory to the consumer than monopoly, since it tends to concentrate even more heavily on the most profitable areas of consumer demand. In a green economy, increased SELF-RELIANCE and more small-scale and COMMUNITY BUSINESSES, which really take the customers' needs into account, would increasingly remove economic power from monopolies and large-scale competitors altogether, and give it back to the people. *See also* MULTINATIONAL.

Morality
[15c. *L mos*, custom]
A system or doctrine of behaviour based on a set of values and beliefs. Personal morality is a question of personal choice, but is modified and manipulated by prevalent norms and rules. Morality is frequently invoked to prove the 'rightness' of a particular set of standards, and when systematised by a political or religious grouping, this sort of judgement is often called 'moralism'. 'Socialization creates the little person who accepts and demands authority. And morality reigns to check and inhibit any oversight in socialization' (Su Negrin, 1972).

Mother

[12c. *Old English modor*, mother; akin to *Gk meter* and *L mater*]
A female PARENT, co-creator of new life, and, for most Westerners, the person who in our early years kissed us better, kept us supplied with food and other necessities, and cleaned up after us. Women mother, but the institution of mothering, like that of the family, has largely been created by men. 'The glorification of motherhood is perhaps the most important aspect of capitalist ideologies of femininity. It justifies the restriction of women to the home and is interpreted as a rationale for every facet of husband- and home-work. More than this, the very sentimentalization of motherhood is a problem for women in becoming and being mothers, since it poses the insoluble dilemma of reaching perfection in imperfect circumstances' (Ann Oakley, 1981). The sweet and patient (and impossible) saintliness demanded of motherhood has been symbolised for Christians in the adoration of the Virgin Mary: 'The Virgin in the Catholic Church represents motherhood in its fullness and perfection' (Marina Warner, 1978). Mothering, however, is an ambivalent experience for many women, at the same time a vindication of their female creativity and a source of deeply-felt oppression: 'The lasting strength of the mothering literature is its powerful assertion of the contrast between the overwhelming importance of women's commitment to mothering and other types of caring, compared with the social undervaluing of such commitment. But this paradox of how to affirm the real value of women's mothering, while seeing how it also serves to perpetuate women's oppression, can also lead to a decreasing emphasis on the public responsibility for the adequate care of all dependent people' (Lynne Segal, 1987). Acknowledging mothering while sharing parenting is the basis of green thinking, though prejudices about parental roles, the family, and children's needs are so deeply ingrained that there is still a great deal of exploration of alternative patterns of caring to be done. 'We all became mothers. Every child has three. To break the nuclear bonding' (a vision of the future from Marge Piercy, 1976).

Mother Earth

[13c]
(*also* 'earth mother', 'mother nature')
The recognition of the earth as our collective birthplace. Though the image of the earth as a woman and as a parent is both powerful and fruitful in its associations, the symbolic link also opens the planet to the same oppressive abuse afforded to women in a patriarchal society. 'Herodotus said, "Three different names have been given to the earth, which is but one, and those derived from the names of women." Herodotus miscounted. Thousands of feminine names have been given to

the earth. . . Tacitus said the tribes of Europe regarded Mother Earth as "the all-ruling deity, to whom all else is subject and obedient"' (Barbara Walker, 1983). Many New Age and spiritual writers have used the earth mother image in their writing: 'You can throw yourself flat on the ground, stretched out upon Mother Earth, with the certain conviction that you are one with her and she with you' (Erwin Schrödinger, 1964, in Alan Watts, 1973). *See also* BODY, GAIA, RAPE.

Motor Car
(*see* CAR)

Mourning
[13c. *Old English murnan*, to be troubled]
The acknowledgement of the loss of something or someone important to you; the process of that acknowledgement. Generally accepted as a necessary part of bereavement, mourning for the loss or destruction of any important part of our environment is appropriate and needs to be respected. *See also* DEATH.

Movement
[1828 in this sense. *L movere*, to move]
A number of people working and acting together in a common cause and with a common goal, such as the the women's movement, the peace movement, the green movement, and the cooperative movement.

Muddling Through
[1959 in this sense]
A brave attempt to explore how we might survive our current situation by taking personal responsibility, making small changes, dealing with things as and when they arise, and remaining generally optimistic. The pros and cons of a 'muddling through' approach to green issues are set out very clearly in Warren Johnson's book *Muddling Toward Frugality* (1979).

Multinational
[1964 in this sense]
(*also* 'international company', 'multinational corporation' (MNC), 'multinational enterprise' (MNE), 'transnational', 'transnational corporation')
A large company with activities in many different states throughout the world. Being so large, widespread and diversified, these 10,000 or so companies are able to manipulate the world economy, labour market, and biosphere to their own advantage. Only 22 states have a larger national income than Exxon, the largest of the multinationals (Michael Kidron and Ronald Segal, 1981). 'The world economy has been in crisis for the past 15 years, [yet] the multinationals have profited from the

crisis. . . Their post-1973 annual growth has been 3.6 per cent, whereas domestic investment in the developed countries has risen by only 1.9 per cent per annum. [They have systematically off-loaded] the crisis onto other areas of the world economy: uninational firms, the Third World, and waged workers. The first strategy of the multinationals is one by which they control the technologies of the future. . . A second element . . . is that the multinationals take advantage of divisions within the Third World, divisions which they themselves provoke, and which they then aggravate to their own benefit. . . The multinationals' third strategy is to get tough on wages and conditions. . . These strategies give the multinationals a certain freedom in the recession. At the same time, they lay the ground for a capitalist way out of the crisis. As in any restructuring of capital, less competitive firms and sectors are going to go out of business, a process which nowadays takes place via the international centralization of capital. In these operations, the multinationals work hand in glove with banks which are themselves multinational. Together they map out the contours for a world economic order which is neither new nor progressive' (Wladimir Andreff, in *World View 1985*).

Multiple Use
[*c*.1950]
Using LAND for more than one thing at a time. In traditional societies land is nearly always used for more than one thing (*see* PERMACULTURE, POLYCULTURE). It is only with our Western attitudes towards land, LAND OWNERSHIP and land use that 'multiple use' has become a brave 'new' concept in the vocabulary of some land use planners. 'Multiple use' usually refers to agricultural or forestry land which is also used for recreational purposes.

Multiskilling
[*c*.1980]
Training someone to have a number of skills which can be put to use in the community, rather than becoming specialised in just one skill. *See also* PORTFOLIO WORK.

Murphy's Law
[1958. US origin]
Originally a military aphorism, now in common usage, which runs: 'If anything can go wrong, it will'. Sometimes used by green-thinkers to demonstrate how complex and vulnerable modern technologies are, and to counteract the technologists' bland assurances that a chemical or nuclear plant which has failed or caused massive pollution was built 'to every known standard'.

Music

[13c. *Gk mousa*, muse]

Sweet and pleasant sounds, usually made by human voices and musical instruments, though increasingly enhanced by computers and electronics. 'After silence, that which comes nearest to expressing the inexpressible is music' (Aldous Huxley, quoted in Laurence Peter (ed), 1977). *See also* HARMONY.

Mutagen

[1946. *L mutare* + *Gk -gen*, producing mutation]

A substance that causes genetic change in DNA, thus affecting both present and future generations of the mutated species; thus virtually synonymous with CARCINOGEN. 'Clearly, many more chemicals will be added to the current list of human mutagens and carcinogens. It has been estimated that over 50,000 chemicals produced in significant quantities are currently used in commerce and close to 1,000 new chemicals are introduced each year. Most of these — from flame retardants in our children's pajamas to pesticides accumulating in our body fat — were not tested for carcinogenity or mutagenicity before their use' (Stewart Brand, in Art Kleiner and Stewart Brand (ed), 1979).

Mutualism

[15c. *L mutuus*, exchanged, reciprocal]

Circumstances in which both or all of the people or organisms in a particular environment benefit in some way. Mutualism has been used as a synonym for SYMBIOSIS and COMMENSALISM in ecology, COOPERATION in economics, and COMMUNALITY in living arrangements.

Mutuality

(*see* RECIPROCITY)

Mystery

[14c. *Gk musterion*, secret rites]

Something which is beyond immediate (or even ultimate) understanding; something which we may not want or need to understand. 'This place. This place in which she breathes and which she takes into herself and which is now in her, sleeping inside her. What sleeps inside her? Like a seed in the earth, in the soil which becomes rich with every death, animal bodies coming apart cell by cell, the plant body dispersing, element by element, in the bodies of bacteria, planaria, and back to the seed, this that grows inside her and we cannot see. What does this body hold for us?' (Susan Griffin, 1984). *See also* EARTH MYSTERIES.

Myth
[1830. *Gk muthos*, fable]
A story or symbol which supposedly explains why something is the way it is; most commonly used in green thinking to mean some 'long-accepted truth' which is ripe for further questioning (*see*, for example, RAPE), though myth also has its uses in helping us to understand things that can only be told in parables. 'The healing process works on many levels. . . We may have to go inside before we can get outside of ourselves again to tell the story to the world, to be looked at and responded to from different perspectives. Personal myths which dwell in misery or seek forlornly for company may then be transformed into the active joys and sorrows of everyday living. The holistic process, in both its timely and timeless aspects, moves the myths inexorably towards healing' (Jan Resnick, 1986).

Nn

Naked

[before 12c. *Old English nacod*, naked]

Baring your skin to the world; a choice made by alternative and green people in appropriate situations — for swimming, in hot weather and so on. Yet we live in a clothed society, where shared nakedness is for most people a prelude to shared sexuality and all the fears and expectations that go with it. Nakedness for its own sensual and commonsense sake will continue to be beset by moralism and misunderstanding as long as sexual oppression and self-disgust hold sway, and as long as we continue to teach our children the limitations we have grown up with. 'The very fact that the law does not permit exposure of the sex organs is bound to give children a warped attitude towards the human body. I have gone nude myself, or encouraged one of the women on the staff to do so, in order to satisfy the curiosity of a small child who had a sense of sin about nakedness. On the other hand, any attempt to force nudism on children is wrong. They live in a clothed civilization, and nudism remains something that the law does not permit' (A.S. Neill, 1962). *See also* CLOTHES.

Name

[before 12c. *Old English nama*; akin to *L nomen; Gk onoma*, name]

The word or words by which something or someone is (sometimes uniquely) identified. Naming usually follows discovery or creation, and until a name is given it is easy to disregard or fear that which is nameless. 'These are the stories of estrangement, . . the structures that shape our thoughts, our images, our actions. We have named them now, and it is a magical principle that knowing something's name gives us power — not over it, but *with* it. What we name must answer to us; we can shape it if not control it' (Starhawk, 1982). Whoever does the naming, if they are not very careful, has and continues to have power over whatever is named. Thus the names given by colonisers continue to be used to name places, disregarding what the local population had called them for centuries — New Zealand (Aotearoa) for example — though the traditional names for some places have been restored. There is always the danger of thinking you know all about something once it is named, and naming can also divide what is named from the whole. Patriarchal standards dominate the naming of women, with many women still taking their husbands' name(s) on marriage. And 'names like Georgette and Georgina, Josephine, Paulette and Pauline, beautiful as they may sound, are diminutives. They are copies, not originals, and like so many other words applied to women, they can be diminishing' (Casey Miller and Kate Swift, 1976, quoted in Cheris Kramerae and Paula Treichler, 1985). In Western societies, people's first names, almost without exception, indicate their sex, thus allowing all the limitations of gender stereotyping.

Narcissism
[1899. Named after the mythical Narcissus, a beautiful youth who fell in love with his own reflection]
Excessive self-interest and self-congratulation. A favourite Freudianism, recently expanded and used by cultural historians (such as Herbert Marcuse, *Eros and Civilization*, 1958; Christopher Lasch, *The Culture of Narcissism*, 1980) to describe what they see as total self-absorption and a frantic search for fulfilment. There is a fine line between the true search for SELF, which does involve a great deal of self-seeking, and navel-gazing for its own sake.

Nation
[14c. *L natio*, birth, tribe]
Usually used as a synonym for STATE, though it is important to recognise that the inhabitants of culturally homogeneous areas which are not recognised as states may consider themselves to be part of a nation, albeit a nation which is considered second-rate because it is not a state, such as Scotland and Wales within the UK, or Quebec within Canada.

National Income Scheme
(*see* SOCIAL WAGE)

Nationalism
[1844. *L natio*, birth, tribe]
While it can be taken to acknowledge a shared cultural heritage and the right of people with a common culture to political autonomy (*see* NATION), nationalism today relates more often to the (frequently arbitrary) area within the borders of a nation state (*see* STATE), and the engineered patriotism created by politicians and generals to control its

citizenry. 'We cannot discuss nationalism without first defining the word "nation", and the only definition which covers the ground is "a community organized for war." A nationalist is thus a person who wishes to surround himself, and those who can be induced to conspire with him, with a closely and aggressively guarded military frontier, and incidentally to prevent as far as possible that cross-fertilization of ideas which always has been and always must be the sole insurance against the relapse into barbarism which perpetually threatens all human communities' (Aldous Huxley, 1937). 'Nationalism is a tough political power to replace. Throughout the twentieth century we have watched grudging efforts to modify the cruder forms of nationalism, and the continuing resistance to this process. This may explain the decade of U.N. conferences, where over a hundred governments have repeatedly voted in favor of resolutions on international action, but signally failed to do much to implement them. There is a curious tension between what governments subconsciously know to be the international realities and what they are prepared to accept in limitation of their own sovereign interests' (Barbara Ward, in Erik Eckholm, 1982).

National Park
[1872]
A large area of rural or wilderness landscape of outstanding ecological and aesthetic value which has been given some form of legislative protection. 'A national park is a relatively large area (a) where one or several ecosystems are not materially altered by human exploitation and occupation, where plant and animal species, geomorphological sites and habitats are of special scientific, educative and recreative interest or which contain a natural landscape of great beauty and (b) where the highest competent authority of the country has taken steps to prevent or eliminate as soon as possible exploitation or occupation in the whole area and to enforce effectively the respect of ecological, geomorphological or aesthetic features which have led to its establishment and (c) where visitors are allowed to enter, under special conditions, for inspirational, cultural and recreative purposes' (International Union for the Conservation of Nature and Natural Resources (IUCN), 1975). The first national park, Yellowstone in the USA, was so designated in 1872; in Britain, where because of the nature of the landscape national parks cannot be wilderness areas and must allow the continued occupation of their human population, the first national parks were established in 1949. In 1985 IUCN listed 3514 national parks or reserves covering over 400 million hectares, of which half had been established in the preceding 15 years. Despite (and often because of) the acknowledgement of their outstanding landscape and wildlife status, national parks are constantly under threat from pollution, mining and power projects, and

the sheer pressure of human visitors — there is often a pall of smoke over the Grand Canyon, and the silence that people seek to experience is punctuated by small aircraft carrying tourists over the gorge. *See also* WILDERNESS.

National Security
[1947]
Now most often used to mean 'keeping the outside enemy out, and the enemy within silent and harmless', the term was developed in the 1940s to refer to a greater control over postwar military matters by the US civilian administration. The 1947 National Security Act established the present US system of communications on defence issues, including the Central Intelligence Agency (CIA), and the National Security Council, set up to coordinate the State and Defense Departments of the US government. In 1952 a National Security Agency was established to monitor and coordinate US defence 'intelligence'. The whole concept of national security depends upon a firm belief in enemies and the need to keep secrets from them, concepts which green-thinkers in general do not accept. 'Terms such as "confidentiality" or "national security" . . . are used as code words to create a sense of self-evident legitimacy. They confront the questioner with what seems like a premise fundamental to an entire profession and hint that anyone who ventures to question the premise will have to question, in turn, the justification for the entire professional edifice built upon this foundation' (Sissela Bok, 1986). 'We could start by redefining "national security" to make the security of local communities a prime . . . goal' (Richard Barnet, 1980). 'We need a wider definition of national security, far beyond the narrow confines of military security, to embrace economic and ecological interdependence, and global environmental hazards. Our new definition will require new restrictions and new forms of co-operation, in the interests of all' (Gro Harlem Brundtland, in Lloyd Timberlake, 1987). *See also* SECURITY.

Native Peoples
[*c.*1925]
(*also* 'ecosystem peoples', 'indigenous peoples', 'inhabitory peoples') The peoples who were living in an area before being disinherited by the great European-based colonisation and appropriation of land from the sixteenth century onwards, right up to the present day, when native peoples like the Cree and Inuit in North America and the Sami in Scandinavia are being dispossessed of their lands to make way for mining and power projects. A preferred term for many Greens to 'natives' because it acknowledges that the original inhabitants are people with the full rights that go with that, and it emphasises the solidarity of such

peoples in different geographical areas. Thus the term 'native American' has replaced 'American Indian'; 'native Australian' 'aboriginal'. Many native peoples prefer to be known collectively by the name of their people — 'Navajo', 'Cree', 'Maori'. As a general guideline, green-thinkers prefer to call any native people whatever that people chooses to be called, usually a name of their own rather than one imposed by colonial settlers. The preferred native name sometimes replaces a partial and condescending label, thus for example 'Inuit' (literally 'the people') is used in place of 'Eskimo' (literally 'eaters of raw meat').

Natural
[13c. *L natura*, nature]
As found in NATURE; part of the living organism of the EARTH. Natural systems can be distinguished from artificial ones in that natural systems are self-maintaining and self-perpetuating. The third LAW OF ECOLOGY says that 'nature knows best', and by extension 'natural is best', though 'natural' has been so abused that it has become for most purposes an unhelpful and sometimes dangerous word, currently extremely overused. A flip through a 'new health' magazine yields: 'natural health products', 'the first totally natural skin renewal system', 'natural toffees', 'a natural way to reduce the effects of excess body water', 'natural herbs and roots', 'natural medicines', and even 'natural spray deodorants'. Nature has been so manipulated that there is much less 'natural' nature than might be imagined. Food crops have been highly bred, pollutants have found their way into every corner of the global environment, and many 'wild' landscapes are largely the result of human intervention. At best 'natural' is a relative concept, and more specific qualifiers ('no added sugar', 'organically grown') are far more helpful and accurate. In energy and resource terms, 'natural' can again be an unhelpful oversimplification. 'Renewable energy' is a more accurate term for 'natural energy', and 'natural gas' is just as finite a resource as gas made from oil or coal — why not 'natural oil' instead of 'crude oil'? 'Natural population increase' (another term for population growth) is far from patterns of population change found elsewhere in nature; 'natural resources' usually implies a right to exploit; and the economists' 'natural rate of unemployment' (the rate you might find in the non-existent monetarist free market) is a pure fiction. When it comes to human nature, the adjective is frequently worse than useless, and along with 'normal' is best dropped from a green vocabulary, though 'natural healing' (using non-intrusive physical techniques and as few manufactured drugs as possible) has taken on a life of its own: 'What is natural healing, exactly? It's not so much particular techniques as it is an attitude. It recognizes, first, that the human body is superbly equipped to resist disease and heal injuries. But when disease does take

hold, or an injury occurs, the first instinct in natural healing is to see what might be done to strengthen those natural resistance and healing agents so that they can act against the disease more effectively. Results are not expected to occur overnight. But neither are they expected to occur at the expense of dangerous side effects' (Mark Bricklin, 1983). *See also* NATURAL BIRTH CONTROL, NATURAL CHILDBIRTH.

Natural Birth Control
[*c*.1960]
(*also* 'natural family planning')
BIRTH CONTROL techniques which do not involve mechanical or chemical contraceptives, but rely on intercourse only happening during infertile periods of the woman's menstrual cycle, together with an increasing emphasis on body awareness and visualisation.

Natural Childbirth
[1933]
(*also* 'active birth')
A way of BIRTHING in which the mother and child are given as much support and information as they need, where the BIRTH is seen as positive and joyful rather than as an illness, and where the use of drugs and surgery is kept to the absolute minimum. There are different ideas about exactly what makes for the best conditions for birth. Many believe that wherever possible birth at home ('home birth') is best. Some women (and men!) favour a squatting position for the woman during birth, and some even suggest that birth under water is ideal, but most natural childbirthers stress peaceful and supportive surroundings, leaving the baby with the parents immediately after the birth, and a minimal use of tranquillisers. Above all, however, is the parents' (and particularly the mother's) right to choose the circumstances of the birth, and some people have criticised the natural childbirth movement for unnecessarily judging women who choose to accept painkillers and other aspects of a more mainstream approach to childbirth. 'The natural childbirth movement represents a reaction against the treatment of this, the most quintessentially creative human experience, as an impersonal and routine medical operation. Above all, the object is to restore the wonder of the act of giving birth and enable the mother to move through the whole experience of pregnancy to conception in a state of awareness and self-control. By the same token, the aim is to make the baby's emergence into the world as stress-free and safe as possible' (David Harvey, 1986). Natural childbirth, with its emphasis on the total involvement of the mother, puts childbirth back into the hands of women and takes it out of those of the male-dominated medical profession. The role of the female midwife is stressed, and some women choose not to have men involved in the birthing process at all.

Natural Pollutant

[*c.*1965]

A term used by some ecologists to describe any substance not created by human beings which is produced in large enough quantities to throw an ecosystem temporarily out of balance. Such substances include volcanic dust and ash, sea salt, smoke from forest fires, and sulphur dioxide such as was ejected from the Mount Agung volcanic eruption in Indonesia in 1963. Calling them 'pollutants' is misleading, since they are always short-term and non-persistent, and can be seen as part of necessary and beneficial change within the biosphere.

Natural Resources

(*see* RESOURCES)

Natural Selection

[1857]

The process, proposed by Charles Darwin, by which plant and animal individuals and species come to occupy the ecological niches best suited to them. The expansionist Victorians translated natural selection into 'survival of the fittest', red-toothed nature fighting for expansion, thus distorting the ecological principle of appropriateness of habitat. 'All living things have to be adapted to their surroundings in order to survive and reproduce their kind. Natural selection is the fundamental mechanism of this adaptation. But this phrase gives little idea of the infinite variety of stratagems by which living things come to occupy different "niches" and to produce the incredible variety of shape, colour, movement, patterns of courtship, of escape and challenge, which make up the richness of the biosphere. Natural selection involves, of course, conflicts for limited amounts of food and space. Competition in this sense exists all over nature. But it is not so sheerly ferocious as some nineteeenth-century thinkers made it out to be after the publication of Charles Darwin's *The Origin of Species*. Prudence, cooperation, indifference, parasitism all play a part' (Barbara Ward and René Dubos, 1972). *See also* COMPETITION, COOPERATION, EVOLUTION, SOCIAL DARWINISM.

Nature

[13c. *L natura*, nature]

One of the green ideas that philosophers and historians have had the most problem with: 'It is no surprise that A.O. Lovejoy could isolate some 66 different senses of the term "nature" and its cognate "natural" and C.S. Lewis could only narrow it down to 15' (David Livingstone, in R.J. Johnston (ed), 1986). 'Nature' is a convenient shorthand for a range of things and ideas from LANDSCAPE and COUNTRYSIDE to ENVIRONMENT and BIOSPHERE, from BEHAVIOUR and ETHICS to DUTY and RESPONSIBILITY.

The 'nature' of human beings is covered in this dictionary under HUMAN NATURE (always remembering that all living things are part of one planetary ecosystem). This entry will concentrate on the two commonest present-day meanings of 'nature':
(1) Plant and animal life as distinct from human beings and those parts of the landscape created by human beings. Because these are most obvious in countryside and wilderness areas, 'being in nature' for most people means being away from urban areas. 'Being in nature' does not necessarily, however, mean being in a 'natural environment' (if by this is meant a setting not made by human beings): 'Existing plant communities have largely been formed by the intervention of [human beings], but they are so old and so traditional that they have come to represent "nature"' (Anne Bülow-Olsen, 1977). Nor does an urban setting mean an absence of nature: 'If the ability of wildlife to survive literally on our doorsteps is remarkable, its persistence in the face of . . . ceaseless change is amazing. It is also, I find, amazingly cheering' (Richard Mabey, 1973).
(2) The complex web of LIFE that constitutes the biosphere, of which human beings are an integral part. There are always dangers of ANTHROPOCENTRISM when thinking about this aspect of nature, and it is important to recognise how much of 'nature' has been invented by human beings to justify their own actions. Parts of nature appear 'cruel', a red-in-tooth-and-claw reality-cum-myth sometimes used to justify human cruelty (*see* NATURAL SELECTION); parts appear peaceful and harmonious (and can be used to justify human 'decency'), until you become aware of the blackbird smashing the snailshell. In a rich urbanised society 'nature' means something different from what it would mean to a starving rural labourer; nature itself carries on regardless of the difference, simply doing its best to maintain the cycles of life and death. '"The Natural" is the meaning given by culture to nature; . . . it becomes the justification for whatever society approves and desires' (Judith Williamson, 1978).

Nature Knows Best
[1971]
The third LAW OF ECOLOGY: an acknowledgement that *any* major human change to an ecological system is likely to be detrimental to that system.

Needs
(*see* BASIC NEEDS)

Negative Feedback
[1934]
FEEDBACK which tends to stabilise a process when that process starts to fluctuate or expand in an unstable manner. Part of CYBERNETIC theory,

used both in the sciences and in psychology. Interestingly the term is used in groupwork in almost the opposite sense: giving a leader or participant 'negative feedback' consists of telling them what you felt went wrong (or in more green terms, what could have been better).

Negentropy
[1950. Abbreviation of 'neg[ative] entropy']
A measure of order or 'information' within a system. *See* ENTROPY.

Negotiation
[15c. *L negotiari*, to carry on business]
Dialogue between two people with the purpose of reaching AGREEMENT, ideally an agreement that benefits both parties. Green-thinkers generally believe that given openness and a willingness to communicate, listen and understand, anything can be negotiated. *See also* MEDIATION.

Neighbourhood
[15c. *Old English neahgeburhod*, a state of living nearby]
A small area in which most of the inhabitants live their everyday lives, which can be traversed easily by foot, and in which most of the human contact is face-to-face. Almost synonymous with COMMUNITY, though it implies a geographical area as well as its inhabitants. While most people like having such an area that they feel at home in, the reality in many places is that separation of home and work, increased mobility, and an emphasis on the inviolability of private property have led to a virtual breakdown of communication between people at a local level, other than in contractual relationships. In trying to 'create' neighbourhoods, planners and architects have sometimes caused more problems than they have solved.

Neocolonialism
[1961]
The way in which powerful states maintain economic and political control over THIRD WORLD countries, even though those countries are theoretically independent. In this way the powerful states maintain their dominance the world over. 'The strategy of neocolonialism can be said to have been based on three main principles. For one thing it was clear that the imperialist powers could no longer openly oppose the aspirations for development in the "Third World". What they could do, however, was to guide the development into capitalist tracks, to use the weak economic position of the underdeveloped countries in order to strengthen the power of their own monopolies in these countries. All the "aid" programmes, the Alliance for Progress, the Green Revolution, indeed the whole "Development Decade", were designed to promote the construction of conditions for a capitalistic development in the

underdeveloped countries. Secondly, given that a capitalist development had to be preferred to a maintenance of the old modes of production, neocolonialism was based on the idea that the emerging bourgeoisie would substitute or ally itself with the former internal supporters of the old colonial regimes. . . The third cornerstone of the neocolonialist strategy was the effort to coordinate the policies of the imperialist powers vis-à-vis the "Third World". . . Because of her exceptionally strong position the United States was able to act as a common leader of the capitalist world economy. The old colonial powers, with the partial exception of France, agreed to the hegemony of the United States in order to save part of their influence in their former empires' (Jan Otto Andersson, in *Third World Guide*, 1984). Some observers of the development scene believe that as a result of the increasing separation of Third World economies from the West, the West will increasingly find neocolonialism less attractive: 'Basically, a pro-South policy is hardly in "our" interest any more, because the neocolonial system is becoming less beneficial to us. It will be a liability in time, if it is not already, just as the colonial system became a liability after the Second World War' (Dudley Seers, 1982, in Victoria Brittain and Michael Simmons (ed), 1987). *See also* COLONIALISM, MULTINATIONAL.

Neomalthusianism

[1885]

A belief in the importance of BIRTH CONTROL, enforced if necessary, in preventing an unsustainable increase in the human POPULATION. A term introduced in the 1880s and considered old hat by the 1930s, but resurrected in the 1960s to describe the warnings of ecologists that continued rapid population growth ('the population bomb' in Paul Ehrlich's (1970) words) would bring catastrophe if global birth control were not implemented very soon. Just as Malthus has been criticised (and not without some reason), the neomalthusians have sometimes been accused of moralism and ecofascism. *See also* LIFEBOAT ETHICS, MALTHUSIANISM.

Net Energy Principle

[*c*.1970]

The recognition that when assessing the EFFICIENCY of a SYSTEM we always need to look carefully at both inputs and outputs. 'The true value of any energy source is the net energy available — the total energy available minus the energy used to find, concentrate and deliver the energy to the user' (G. Tyler Miller and Patrick Armstrong, 1982). Some systems use so much energy to create a different form of energy — NUCLEAR POWER, for example, or much commercial FOOD production — that their efficiency in ecological terms must be questioned.

Net Primary Production
[*c*.1950]
(*also* 'net primary productivity')
The amount of BIOMASS created by a plant community over a period of time, usually a growing season.

Network
[*c*.1940 in this sense. *Old English net*, net + *weorc*, act, deed, work]
A pattern of links between people, places or organisms. The networks that are crucial to many green-thinkers are networks of people with similar ideas and aims. 'Germinated in the uproar of the 1960s and born in the self-reflection of the 1970s, networks appear to be coalescing everywhere in the 1980s, an appropriate-sociology response to bureaucratic logjams. As potent and poignant antidotes to loneliness and fragmentation, networks link people of like minds, be they secondary school administrators in Minnesota, agronomists in Asia or doctors everywhere working to prevent nuclear war' (Jessica Lipnack and Jeffrey Stamps, 1986). 'Networks are cooperative, not competitive. They are true grass roots: self-generating, self-organizing, sometimes even self-destructing. They represent a process, a journey, not a frozen structure. . . a network is both intimate and expansive. . . Networks are the strategy by which small groups can transform an entire society' (Marilyn Ferguson, 1981). Instead of or as well as having a local community for support, acknowledgement and stimulation, people can rely on networks of friends for these crucial needs: 'A network differs from a group in that it exists beyond the constraints of space and time. It can stay intact even when long intervals elapse between meetings of its members and even though the whole network is never convened' (Sue Walrond-Skinner, 1986). Those involved even in the most exploitative activities use networks (such as the old boy network); the Aquarian Conspiracy has no monopoly. '(For the FBI agent who, inquiring about a sister, asked "Who is in her network?"): Who is in my network,/what links us, to be exact?/Better to ask the force/that cuts through rock the water's course/and binding like to like/makes also opposites attract./ Investigate the daisies for invasion of the lawn,/or the ivy for trespass where it wants to grow' (Susan Saxe, in Leonie Caldecott and Stephanie Leland (ed), 1983). For the transport aspect of networks *see* COMMUNICATION, TRANSPORT. *See also* HIERARCHY, WEB.

Networking
[1940]
The activity of participating in a NETWORK or networks. 'Networking is unbelievably strengthening. It makes you a whole person and gives you confidence in what you're doing, no matter what it is' (Elizabeth Wright

Ingram, in Annie Cheatham and Mary Clare Powell (ed), 1986). A growing number of people seem to do nothing but 'network' and call themselves professional networkers; this can be a dubious activity, akin to pretending that therapy is life. There are even some who actively manipulate the system: 'In essence [networking] is a magnificent concept, but I have so often seen it distorted by people taking advantage of others: someone knocks at a stranger's door, for instance, on the strength of a distant link with some group or mutual acquaintance and expects to be fed and entertained for several weeks' (Lionel Fifield, in Mary Inglis and Sandra Kramer (ed), 1985). You have been warned.

New Age
[mid 18c]
A new era which many people believe humanity to be entering, an era which will involve a radical shift in human awareness and relationships. 'It seems clear that future historians will mark a new age beginning somewhere within our lifetimes. The question is: what kind of new age will it be?' (Kirkpatrick Sale, 1980). Those who invoke a new age usually see it in spiritual, even mystical, terms, often relating this shift to the astrologers' claim that our planet is moving into the Age of Aquarius. This is not a new idea, having been elaborated by the poet William Blake in the eighteenth century, who in turn drew on the Swedish theologian Emanuel Swedenborg: 'Blake was indeed the first poet to speak of a New Age. That Age was neither his own nor that of the revolutions of his time (in which however he certainly read the signs of its advent) but the fulfilment of the prophecy of Emanuel Swedenborg, who had even given a date — 1757 — for its advent in "the heavens" (by which he meant the inner worlds of the mind)' (Kathleen Raine, 1979). Having been resurrected in the 1960s, 'New Age' rapidly hitched itself to an enormous range of alternative and esoteric activities: 'The vision of an emergent planetary culture involves the broadening and deepening of our individual and collective perspectives and assumptions so that we embrace ourselves as a species, as humankind, rather than as separate factions. . . Within this broadened context, our current different cultures can still exist. They are simply deepened to touch our human roots, not just our ethnic ones; they are expanded to embrace our planetary existence and our ecological interdependence rather than being confined to parochial interests. . . Anyone who moves into such a consciousness is stepping into a New Age. It doesn't matter whether they are living at Findhorn or whether they be anarchist, Baptist or Buddhist. If they seek to serve humanity in a way that we know inwardly will help the potential of humankind emerge, then essentially they have a grasp of what the New Age is' (David Spangler, 1973). Some are concerned by the exploitative and proselytising

aspects of New Age individuals and enterprises: 'Some individuals and organizations among these "New Age" movements have shown clear signs of exploitation, fraud, sexism, and excessive economic expansion, quite similar to those observed in the corporate world, but these aberrations are transitory manifestations of our cultural transformation and should not prevent us from appreciating the genuine nature of the current shift of values. As Roszak has pointed out [in *Person/Planet*, 1979] one must distinguish between the authenticity of people's needs and the inadequacy of the approaches that may be offered to meet those needs' (Fritjof Capra, 1982). *See also* TURNING POINT.

New Economics
[*c*.1980]
An ECONOMICS 'based on personal development and social justice, the satisfaction of the whole range of human needs, sustainable use of resources and conservation of the environment' (Paul Ekins (ed), 1986). The new economics drew a great deal of inspiration from two conferences organised by The Other Economic Summit to parallel the Economic Summit meetings held in London and Bonn in 1984 and 1985, and there is now a New Economics Foundation based in London. 'The new economists will set about inventing new criteria of efficiency, practicality and economic reality that will be grounded in the vocational needs of people' (Theodore Roszak, 1979). 'What work will people do in the future? How will it be paid for? How will the Earth sustain it? If the overall well-being of people is to be improved, the answers to these questions will entail new ways of organising work and meeting human needs, and of guaranteeing incomes; a new emphasis on local economic self-reliance, including local economic regeneration and the enrichment of poor countries and communities through self-reliant development; new awareness of ecological constraints, of human needs for survival, social justice and self-fulfilment; and new economic concepts to take these into account' (New Economics Foundation, 1987).

New Games
[1973]
A philosophy of NON-COMPETITIVE play, together with a large number of actual 'new games', developed in California and since spread to most parts of the Western world. 'New Games is a new concept in recreation. It is not only a series of basically non-competitive games that people can play. It is a whole philosophy about game playing and having fun. New Games is an outgrowth of two emerging play philosophies — soft war and creative play. Soft war is an alternative means for the physical release of aggressions. A game environment where one plays hard and fair with nobody hurt provides a safer and saner release for these

instincts than does war or violence or vandalism. Creative play implies a free-form environment which allows players to use their imagination by devising new ways to play and push their limits to achieve a sense of self and satisfaction' (Barbara Dinham and Michael Norton, 1977). *See also* COOPERATION, GAMES, PLAY.

New International Division of Labour
[1980]
(*also* 'NIDL')
The way in which the economies of THIRD WORLD countries are often dependent on a very small range of exports, even when they have developed an industrial exporting base. With independence, many Third World countries planned a programme of mixed industrial expansion in order to provide locally-needed products and reduce their dependence on imports. In a large number of countries, particularly in south-east Asia, such a programme has effectively been thwarted by the activities of MULTINATIONAL companies exploiting cheap labour to produce consumer goods for the West. Such production is specialised within countries or regions, thus creating export dependence on a limited range of manufactured products in countries which are often also dependent upon the export of a limited number of cash crops — all of which works to maintain the economic and political power of the multinationals. 'Only rarely do developing countries end up with the establishment of reasonably complex industrial branches . . . And even in the very few developing countries where such centres of partial industrialization have been established, there are no signs that they are being supplemented by a wider industrial complex which would enable them to free themselves from their dependency on the already industrialized countries for imports of capital and other goods, and for the maintenance of their industrial installations . . . Instead, industrial production is confined to a few highly specialized manufacturing processes . . . in world market economies . . . with no connection to the local economy except for their utilization of extremely cheap labour and occasionally some local inputs' (F. Fröbel, quoted in R.J. Johnston (ed), 1986).

New International Economic Order
[1972]
(*also* 'NIEO')
The collective demands of the THIRD WORLD for an equitable global economy in which the basic needs of local populations are provided for, natural resource bases are managed on a sustainable footing, and prices, wages and distribution of wealth are considerably more equitable than at present. Although some progress was made in the mid

1970s (in 1974 an action programme presented by 122 developing countries was approved by the UN General Assembly), the United States demolished the proposals in the late 1970s, supported by other Western countries in the light of growing economic recession. Since then the Western nations, led by the United States, have consistently vetoed measures for world economic reform and large increases in foreign aid. 'If things carry on as they are, the prospects for a new international economic order are nil. A genuinely new order can only be created out of the destruction of the old one. This the First World will never allow, because it owes its dominant wealth and power to the present structure of international relations. And this the Third World will never achieve, for the present order renders the poor countries too weak and vulnerable to destroy it. Third World nations thus have a choice. Either they continue within the present order, following the West's pattern of development (in which case they will always follow behind the West), or they attempt to attack the foundations of this order (failure in which enterprise would scarcely leave them worse off than they are already). . . The hunger, poverty and dependence of the Third World can only be ended by the Third World . . . Only where parties look to their own interests first can there arise a proper "mutuality" of interests; and only where they are able to stand alone can genuine "co-operation" between them occur. The absence of both these indices of freedom marks the present international economic order' (Michael Smith, in Christopher Pick (ed), 1983). *See also* DEVELOPMENT, ECONOMICS.

New International Information Order
[1980]
(*also* 'NIIO'; more fully 'The New World Information and Communication Order' or 'NWICO')
The collective demands of the THIRD WORLD for an equitable share in communications and information technology. In a world where INFORMATION is power, especially in the secretive spheres of economics and politics, the Third World has become increasingly concerned that nearly all the power (and the technology behind it) is in the hands of the West. In a state of post-war euphoria a 1948 UNESCO conference in Geneva established that the free flow of information was a simple extension of the right to free speech, but this ignored the basic questions of who possessed the information and who possessed the means of communicating it. 'For example, a French industrialist can obtain economic data [about a Third World country] more easily by subscribing to privately held specialized networks in the United States (which control 60-70% of the market for exporting information by computer and have a near monopoly on scientific-technological information) than

through national institutions' (Roberto Remo, in *Third World Guide*, 1984). A 1980 UNESCO conference in Belgrade adopted a resolution calling for a new information order, among other things calling for 'elimination of the imbalances and inequalities which characterize the present situation; elimination of the negative effects of certain monopolies . . .; freedom of the press . . .; the capacity of developing countries to achieve improvement of their own situations . . .; the sincere will of developed countries to help them attain these objectives; . . . respect for each people's cultural identity' (UNESCO, 1980, quoted in *Third World Guide*, 1984).

New Left
[1960]
A movement, mostly of young radical activists, who protested during the 1960s and 1970s against what were seen as the outdated ideas and structures of the 'old' left, particularly the hierarchical and rigid views of Stalinism. The New Left, often with Leon Trotsky and Chairman Mao as their heroes, concerned themselves particularly with campaigns of national liberation, women's issues and the Third World, but were heavily criticised for trying to tell the real poor of the world what to do from a position of privilege, and for concentrating on single issues without seeing the broader socialist vision. 'The driving force behind the New Left was an idealistic quest to overthrow "the system" and eliminate the sources of established power by direct action' (Lisa Tuttle, 1986). While green-thinkers can trace some of their revolutionary roots to involvement in the New Left, the red/green divide is still clearly visible (*see* MARXISM, SOCIALISM).

New Local Economic Order
[1984]
A recognition that LOCAL economies in Western countries are suffering from much the same sort of domination by MULTINATIONAL corporations as are Third World economies, that local control and awareness of local conditions are being completely disregarded in policy making, and that something must be done about it. 'In order for us to begin to live in harmony with ourselves, with the whole natural world and with the rest of the planet in a long-term sustainable way, I envisage the need for three new "Codes of Conduct" to which all enterprises in the local economy will have to adhere. . . (1) The relationship of the local enterprise with its work-force and the community as a whole, including its democratisation, an open accounts policy, provision for flexible working, and non-discrimination on any basis other than skill and ability to do the job. (2) The relationship of the local enterprise with the natural environment and other living creatures, including bans on the

import of endangered species of plants and animals into the local economy, strict curbs on pollution and animal experimentation, and incentives for conservation and positive ecological innovation. (3) The relationship of the local enterprise with other people and communities in the same country and abroad, including the guarantee of fair trading relations, of socially and ecologically sound investment, and a prohibition on the export of goods of a poisonous or socially destructive nature' (Guy Dauncey, 1984, in Paul Ekins (ed), 1986).

New Physics
[*c*.1960]
A SYSTEMS view of physics which is gradually replacing the exclusively mechanistic model which dominated physics until recently. Based on the findings of Albert Einstein, Werner Heisenberg and a number of other physicists, the formulation of what became known as 'quantum physics', a formulation which involves profound changes in the basic concepts of space, time, matter, and cause and effect, shook the foundations of the scientific establishment, or at least those members of it who took the new findings seriously. 'The violent reaction to the recent development of modern physics can only be understood when one realizes that here the foundations of physics have started moving; and that this motion has caused the feeling that the ground would be cut from science' (Werner Heisenberg, quoted in Fritjof Capra, 1982). The new physics, in adopting a systems approach which is shared by many other disciplines, has become part of knowledge, rather than the basis of it: 'In transcending the metaphor of the world as a machine, we also have to abandon the idea of physics as the basis of all science. According to the bootstrap or systems view of the world, different but mutually consistent concepts may be used to describe different aspects and levels of reality, without the need to reduce the phenomena of any level to those of another' (Fritjof Capra, 1982). Several writers (including Fritjof Capra, 1975; Gary Zukav, 1979; and David Bohm, 1980) have drawn the links between the new physics and spirituality, particularly ideas in Buddhism and Taoism.

New Right
[*c*.1980]
The reactionary reaction to both Old and New Lefts, and particularly to the hardships of economic recession. Traditionally conservative sections of the population, especially in the USA, are closing ranks and demanding a return to the ideals of competitive individualism, divinely-ordained inequality, moralism (*see* MORALITY) and the NUCLEAR FAMILY 'which made America (or Britain, or wherever) great'. A strong influence on these ideals, and again particularly so in the USA, is exerted by

the 'religious right' or 'moral majority', which controls vast communications networks and enormous financial resources. The New Right is a force for green-thinkers to reckon with, and it is difficult not to face their arguments with anger, ridicule and judgement, exactly the tools they themselves resort to. *See also* FUNDAMENTALISM.

New Settlers
(*see* BACK TO THE LAND)

NFZ
(*see* NUCLEAR-FREE ZONE)

Niche
[*L nidus*, nest]
Has two different but complementary meanings in ecology:
(1) [1917] The specific part of a HABITAT occupied by a particular species or individual.
(2) [1927] The role of a species or individual within an ecosystem.

NIDL
(*see* NEW INTERNATIONAL DIVISION OF LABOUR)

NIEO
(*see* NEW INTERNATIONAL ECONOMIC ORDER)

Night Soil
[1770]
Human excrement which is used as fertiliser; an important method of RECYCLING nutrients in many Third World countries. 'The collection of human wastes (known as night soil) for use as a fertilizer is a long-standing tradition in some countries, particularly in Asia. People use door-to-door handcarts to collect night soil in many of the older neighbourhoods of Seoul, South Korea, for recycling to the city's green belt. The World Bank estimated as recently as 1981 that one third of China's fertilizer requirements were provided by night soil' (*World-watch*, 1987). Recycling human waste has become more acceptable to some Westerners in recent years as the importance of recycling has been acknowledged. (*See also* COMPOST).

NIIO
(*see* NEW INTERNATIONAL INFORMATION ORDER)

Nitrogen Cycle
[1908]
The CYCLE of processes vital to life by which nitrogen is constantly recycled through the plants, the soil, and soil organisms. As farmers add

vast quantities of artificial nitrogen fertiliser to soils, there is the danger of throwing nitrogen cycles completely off balance, as well as causing the chronic pollution of groundwater and inshore parts of some of the world's oceans.

No-Dig
[1973]
(*also* 'no-till')
A method of cultivation where the SOIL is carefully mulched but not dug, thus saving energy and the unnecessary disturbing of soil structure and organisms. 'There are several reasons for not digging in the garden. If you bury manure or compost nine inches down in the soil you remove it from the oxygen and soil bacteria necessary to break it down into the nutrients which a plant can use. . . Capillary action bringing water up from the water table is disturbed by deep digging, and this can lead to the drying out of the top layers of the soil in spring and early summer. Another disadvantage of digging the soil is that every year new weed seeds are brought to the surface. It is also hard work' (Margaret Elphinstone and Julia Langley, 1987). 'No-till' is also used to describe a form of chemical agriculture where the ground is not ploughed, but is swathed in herbicides — the two meanings should not be confused.

Noise
[13c. *L nausea*, a feeling of sickness]
Unwanted and undesired sound; a phenomenon which all urban-dwellers and most other people, at least in the Western world, experience all the time. One of the most pervasive forms of pollution, since we can never — short of wearing earplugs — avert our attention from it as we can from visual ugliness. Traffic noise is the most common form of noise pollution; a 1978 British survey suggested that 78% of the population of Britain can hear fairly constant traffic noise when at home, and 18% are bothered by it (Stephen Plowden, 1980). Aircraft noise is limited by legislation in many countries, but the 110 decibel permitted roar of a jet taking off is louder than continuous gunfire. Even within the home automation creates a great deal of noise: 'A vacuum cleaner can register 80dB, the level of a noisy office; a spin drier 82dB, equivalent to a power drill. So far, relatively few British homes can rival the uproar of a typical middle-class American kitchen where, with ventilator fan (84dB), dishwasher (69dB) and garbage disposal machine (90+dB) all going at once the accumulated decibel level can be 100 or more, equal to the noise of a typical turbofan airliner taking off' (John Barr, 1970). Although noise legislation has been passed in several countries to regulate vehicle, aeroplane, and industrial noise, noise pollution continues to intrude, in some cases causing permanent physical damage: 'This

delicate sensing mechanism [the ear] is overwhelmed by the intensity of sound to which we customarily subject it, especially in cities. . . [The] damage begins at sound intensities around 85 decibels — a level often achieved by a vacuum cleaner, power saw, lawnmower, or motorcycle. Noise pollution is thought to be a substantial contributor to deafness rates and to hearing losses in the high-frequency ranges' (Ernest Callenbach, 1980).

Non-Competitive
[1906]
An activity, often a game or sport, which is designed such that there are no 'winners' or 'losers' in the usual sense, and in which the object is to enjoy participating rather than to prove you are better than everyone else. By extension, a way of relating to other people in which respect and equality are more important than always being right and in control. 'We need to rethink the concept of winning, when winning involves "beating" somebody else, who is then a "loser". . . When we experience love, and are able to stand aside from feelings of not being worthy of the experience, we know that we *are* winning, we know that we *are* right. These feelings of rightness and success are real and intense, and unlike the rightness of proving another person wrong or the success of beating other people in competition, rarely involve hurting or putting down somebody else. We can feel powerful without having any interest in having power over another person' (John Button, 1985). *See also* COMPETITION, COOPERATION, NEW GAMES, POWER.

Non-Directive
[1951]
A therapist-client or interviewer-interviewee setting in which the direction of the exchange is not controlled (or is minimally controlled) by the therapist or interviewer. Another term for 'client-centred'. Different amounts of direction or intervention are obviously appropriate in different situations, although in a non-directive setting the therapist or interviewer will refrain from giving advice and personal opinions, choosing rather to draw proposed solutions and actions from the client.

Non-Human Rights
[1974]
The right of living things other than human beings, and of the EARTH itself, not to be unnecessarily hurt or exploited (*see* BIOCENTRIC EQUALITY, DEEP ECOLOGY). A Conference on Non-Human Rights, held in 1974 at Claremont, California, was one of the first formal recognitions of the importance of environmental ETHICS.

Non-Intrusive
[1965]
Physical healing techniques which respect the integrity of the client or patient, and which limit the use of surgery and heavy manipulation to the absolute minimum. The physical equivalent of NON-DIRECTIVE.

Non-Nuclear Club
[1959]
Those countries which have consciously decided not to develop nuclear resources for either military or civil purposes, or (in the case of Sweden) to phase out nuclear plants as soon as possible. The club currently includes Australia, Austria, Denmark, Greece, Ireland, Italy, Luxembourg, New Zealand, the Philippines, Portugal and Sweden.

Non-Renewable Resources
[1956]
Materials contained in the biosphere and the earth's crust which cannot be recreated within a human timescale. When such RESOURCES (including FOSSIL FUELS, minerals, some groundwater and biotic reserves) are used they often undergo irreversible chemical change and cannot be used again in the same form. Current forecasts suggest that unless consumption is drastically reduced, oil will run out in about 30 years' time, tin, cadmium, lead and zinc in 40 years, and copper, antimony and nickel in about 70 years. Although these minerals will reach the end of their 'useful' lives, however, the second LAW OF ECOLOGY that says 'everything must go somewhere' suggests that simply 'using' these non-renewable resources does not mean we can then forget about them. *See also* POLLUTION, RENEWABLE RESOURCES, WASTE.

Non-Sexist
[1971]
Behaviour (and the society that results) which does not oppress women (*see also* POSTPATRIARCHAL, SEXISM); an important goal, though it is just as important to recognise how far we are from it. As far as our present efforts go, ANTI-SEXIST is usually a better adjective, acknowledging that we have more to unlearn than we can imagine. As yet there is no truly positive alternative to 'non-sexist' (though 'egalitarian', 'inclusive', 'progressive' and 'enlightened' go part of the way). Various guidelines for non-sexist language have been produced, such as Casey Miller and Kate Swift's *Handbook of Non-Sexist Writing* (1981): although the conscious use of non-sexist language is essential, we should never imagine that equal linguistic treatment automatically drives out deep-rooted sexism.

Nonviolence
[1920]
A refusal to resort to VIOLENCE, particularly physical violence, in order to achieve your goals. There have been examples throughout history of people who refused to fight or bear arms, not because of any lack of courage, but because they fervently believed that more can be achieved by negotiation than by force. The Quakers have acknowledged non-violence to be an integral part of their Christian philosophy since the seventeenth century; their peace testimony runs: 'We utterly deny all outward wars and strife, and fightings with outward weapons, for any end, or under any pretence.' In the twentieth century, particularly following the example of Mahatma Gandhi and Martin Luther King, many people have recognised that violence simply breeds violence, and that nonviolence is central to green philosophy and green politics. As Martin Luther King said: 'We no longer have a choice between violence and non-violence. The choice is either nonviolence or nonexistence' (quoted in Fritjof Capra and Charlene Spretnak, 1984). 'Non-violence does not mean doing nothing. It means making the enormous effort to overcome evil with good. Non-violence does not rely on strong muscles and devilish armaments; it relies on moral courage, self-control and the knowledge, unswervingly acted upon, that there is in every human being, however brutal, however personally hostile, a fund of kindness, a love of justice, a respect for goodness and truth which can be reached by anyone who uses the right means. To use these means is often extraordinarily hard; but history shows that it can be done — and done not only by exceptional individuals, but by large groups of ordinary men and women and even by governments' (Aldous Huxley, 1937). For many green-thinkers nonviolence is an absolute value, but then most are not faced with personal violence on a daily basis, and an under-standing of different perspectives on appropriate behaviour is im-portant if we are not to become judgemental. *See also* NONVIOLENCE TRAINING, NONVIOLENT DIRECT ACTION, NONVIOLENT REVOLUTION, PACIFISM, PEACE.

Nonviolence Training
[1969]
Techniques for nonviolent direct action developed in the USA and now used in many parts of the world. 'Initially, training focused very much on how to be able to carry through an action nonviolently — both responding nonviolently to police provocation and restraining violent elements among the protestors. But training also tried to provide structures of support for activists, where — in the safety of a "role play" — they could test their reactions and anticipate problems which might crop up in a situation' (Howard Clark, in Gail Chester and Andrew Rigby (ed), 1986).

Nonviolent Direct Action
[1965]
(*also* 'nonviolent action', 'NVDA')
An ACTION, often undertaken to emphasise some aspect of the military machine, in which an important principle is the avoidance of violence, even in the face of police or other institutional violence. 'The [British] Nonviolent Action Committee, with 200 demonstrators, blockaded the offices of Elliott Automation (involved in selling aircraft components to the Americans) in 1968, the first time that nonviolent direct action was supported officially by CND [the Campaign for Nuclear Disarmament]' (Diana Shelley, in Gail Chester and Andrew Rigby (ed), 1986). Some green-thinkers talk about 'considered nonviolent direct action', emphasising that such a course of action is carefully thought out.

Nonviolent Intervention
[1961]
An attempt to intervene and mediate in conflicts, using nonviolent methods. Examples of nonviolent intervention include the World Peace Brigade, formed in 1961, which had some success in Africa, particularly during the liberation of Zambia, and Witness for Peace, which attempted in the early 1980s to develop a nonviolent presence on the Nicaragua-Honduras border, and is still an important channel between North and Central America. 'Because this kind of nonviolent intervention is a new development, it is too early to evaluate its effects. The World Peace Brigade was probably unrealistic in hoping to recruit a standing nonviolent force [*sic*]. The Witness for Peace, on the other hand, was an ad hoc effort to which volunteers committed what time they could, without being on call for emergency intervention around the world. As such it may provide a realistic and workable model for future nonviolent intervention' (Robert Seeley, 1986).

Nonviolent Revolution
[1968]
A 'quiet revolution' of alternative and green ideas. '[Around 1968] the term "nonviolent revolution" began to appear, referring to a liberatory "movement of movements"... Nonviolent revolution entails taking back the power that has been taken from us, and refusing to exercise illegitimate power over anyone else, whether that power be domestic tyranny, economic exploitation or the threat of military force' (Andrew Rigby, in Gail Chester and Andrew Rigby (ed), 1986). Some green-thinkers have seen the connections between this way of thinking and the way that nature quietly 'takes over' when no-one is looking, the grass pushing up through the concrete and the birds nesting in the exclusion zone. *See also* REVOLUTION.

Normal

[*c.*1700 *L normalis*, conforming to the carpenter's square]

Conforming to what is expected. The perfect excuse for stereotyping, OPPRESSION, failure, and unwillingness to change, and an idea the green movement can do without. The ultimate threat of those in power is to declare anybody they see as a threat 'abnormal' and deprive them of their rights: the oppression of 'normality' (*see* NORMALISM) is a pervasive way of keeping all other oppressions in place (*see*, for example, MENTAL ILLNESS).

Normalism

[*c.*1982 in this sense]

The systematic OPPRESSION of DISABLED people by those who are physically and mentally agile ('normal'); 'normalism' is the generally preferred alternative within green circles to HANDICAPPISM.

North/South Dialogue

[1981]

The discussions and controversies which followed the publication of the report (*North-South: A Programme for Survival*) of the Brandt Commission on International Development Issues. On one hand the report recognised that the rich North has many reasons for being concerned with the poor South, and it brought development issues to the immediate attention of politicians world-wide, though interest varied from intense concern in parts of Europe to complete indifference in the USA. But 'not all reaction has been enthusiastic, for the Brandt Commission's analysis and programme can be criticized on a number of counts. First, the analysis fails to reflect the realities of political struggle: industrialized East and West are subsumed into an overall category "North", to which proposals are put as if all its countries shared similar positions in world trade, investment, etc. (this is undoubtedly why the North-South dialogue is taking place without the East); furthermore, the convenient notion of "nation (as a whole)" is pursued throughout, as if nations were not divided by antagonistic and exploitative class relationships. Second, it is difficult to see what "mutual interests" the rich and poor share in the present economic order, unless the desperation of the latter is so great that they cling to the present order lest even their present existence, meagre as it is, disappear. In fact, the real "mutual interests" connect the élites of both rich and poor countries. For this reason, the Brandt Commission's programme . . . aims to reinforce the structure of the international order by means of a number of apparently radical reforms. But these reforms amount to a massive shot in the arm for international capitalism, largely through the extraordinary proposal to use public funds to subsidize the western banks to the tune of an additional $20,000 million a year. It is difficult to see how the poor, who owe their destitution to the workings of the present international political economy, are to see an end to their misery through the further strengthening of that system' (Michael Smith, in Christopher Pick (ed), 1983). 'The Brandt Commission Report represents currently the most enlightened expression of establishment thinking about international economic matters, and, in particular, about the provision of so-called "aid" to developing countries. But it would be a mistake to think of its authors as primarily or exclusively concerned with the alleviation of poverty in those countries. They are, instead, primarily concerned with the preservation of the existing world economic order' (Teresa Hayter, 1981). *See also* AID, DEVELOPMENT, NEW INTERNATIONAL ECONOMIC ORDER, THIRD WORLD.

No-Till
(*see* NO-DIG)

Not In My Back Yard
[*c*.1980]
(*also* 'NIMBY')
The way in which people are happy to accept the benefits of technology, but object strongly to having factories, power plants, waste disposal sites and the other less desirable manifestations of modern technology in their neighbourhood. 'Local opposition to the disposal of radioactive wastes, for example, may be largely due to the NIMBY ("not in my back yard") syndrome, but it reflects judgment by many geologists that underground storage of wastes may one day lead to serious public health problems. The fact that the world has almost 400 nuclear power plants but not a single long-term waste disposal program yet in place must be considered one of the major failings of the nuclear era' (Christopher Flavin, in *Worldwatch*, 1987). Green-thinkers would prefer not to have such installations in anyone's back yard.

Not Man Apart
[1970 in this sense]
An unfortunately sexist quotation from a poem by Robinson Jeffers, used by Friends of the Earth in the USA for the title of its magazine. It does, however, stress that human beings are an integral part of the planetary ecosystem. The original poem runs: '. . . the greatest beauty is in organic wholeness,/the wholeness of life and things,/the divine beauty of the universe. Love that,/not man apart from that.'

Nourishment
[15c. *L nutrire*, to feed, to care for]
Anything which is truly life-enhancing. In relation to human beings

'nourishment' often refers to food and drink, though other forms of nourishment (ATTENTION, acknowledgement, beautiful surroundings) are also vital for real health. *See also* NUTRITION.

No War Toys
[1969]
A campaign to dissuade manufacturers and retailers from producing and stocking toy guns and other 'war toys', thus breaking the chain of socially-condoned violence engendered when boys are taught to be 'real men' by providing them with the means to be violent. In 1987 Finland became the first country to ban the manufacture and import of war toys, especially those imitating modern warfare. 'Take the toys from the boys' is a well-known slogan from the women's peace movement.

Nuclear
[1846. *L nux*, nut, kernel]
Relating to the nucleus (the dense core) of an atom; usually refers to either or both of NUCLEAR ENERGY and NUCLEAR WEAPONS — as the link between the two becomes ever clearer, people are realising that the 'nuclear debate' is about both. 'Would Britain have developed nuclear power so quickly or become so committed to its expansion without the earlier, exclusively military establishment of a nuclear programme? Would nuclear technology be spreading throughout the world if the giant nuclear construction industries of the West were economically viable domestically and did not actually *need* either subsidies from military research or export markets? "I doubt it" is my answer to both these questions' (Howard Clark, 1982).

Nuclear Arms
(*see* NUCLEAR WEAPONS)

Nuclear Chain
[*c*.1980]
An acknowledgement of the links between every aspect of nuclear technology, particularly between the so-called 'peaceful' uses of NUCLEAR ENERGY and the production and deployment of NUCLEAR WEAPONS. 'Stand up, women make your choice/Create a world without nuclear war./Now together we are strong/Break the nuclear chain' (Greenham Common Songsheet, 1984).

Nuclear Club
[1957]
Those nations (or more accurately their military forces) which possess NUCLEAR WEAPONS — 3 in 1952, 6 in 1974, thought to be 8 in 1987, and possibly 30 by 2000.

Nuclear Deterrence
[1955]
The dangerous belief that having more and bigger NUCLEAR WEAPONS will guarantee your safety, since your ENEMY will be too frightened to attack you because of the possible consequences of your retaliation. *See* DETERRENCE.

Nuclear Disarmament
[1958]
The call for all nations which have stockpiles of NUCLEAR WEAPONS to get rid of them, since they pose an intolerable threat to human and ecological survival. 'The Campaign for Nuclear Disarmament [was] formed in 1958 and, thanks in part to the Aldermaston March, had developed rapidly into a mass popular movement which organised Aldermaston marches on an ever larger scale in the subsequent five years' (Michael Randle, in Gail Chester and Andrew Rigby (ed), 1986). 'Nuclear disarmament today . . . involves many facets of society. It has drawn substantial support from doctors, nurses, the clergy, scientists, teachers, artists, musicians and even retired military officers. . . Without doubt millions of people in both East and West share a conscious desire for nuclear disarmament and an end to the cold war' (Joan Ruddock, 1987). With the agreement late in 1987 to dismantle a whole class of nuclear arms — intermediate-range missiles — it appears that after thirty years of nuclear deadlock, the states that have been holding the world to ransom have at last begun to listen to the myriad voices calling for nuclear disarmament. *See also* DISARMAMENT.

Nuclear Energy
[1930]
(*also* 'nuclear power')
A way of harnessing usable ENERGY (usually in the form of electricity, though large amounts of heat — usually too great to harness — are also generated) by releasing the binding forces in the atomic nucleus of certain elements by nuclear reactions. Because of the strength of these binding forces, vast amounts of energy can be released in a short space of time. There are two types of nuclear reaction used in the creation of nuclear energy — the fusion of light elements to form heavier ones, and the fission of heavy elements to form less heavy ones. Both types of reaction create large amounts of ionising radiation, which has to be very carefully contained. Many different designs of nuclear power stations have been built since the first US reactor in 1942, though the differences are mostly to do with the way in which the heat generated by the nuclear reaction is converted into electricity, rather than with the basic concept. Since the 1950s environmentalists, ecologists, doctors and

economists have questioned the safety and efficiency of nuclear power stations. The nuclear accidents at Windscale in Britain in 1957, Three Mile Island in the USA in 1979, and Chernobyl in the USSR in 1986, alerted public attention to the inescapable fact that nuclear power plants cannot be made safe, however much they are inspected and patrolled by armed guards to keep out terrorists; nor are they economic, even by the distorted standards of energy accounting. The country with most nuclear power plants, the USA, has cancelled 54 plants since 1977, the last year in which construction of a new plant commenced; more than a dozen countries (of the 31 who have plants in operation or under construction) have drastically reduced their nuclear power construction programmes in the last ten years. 'Over two thirds of the people in most countries are now against the construction of nuclear plants, a significant increase since Chernobyl. . . Nowhere does nuclear power command the enthusiastic assent of a large majority of the population . . . Nuclear power is a sick industry, not a mature one. Moreover, it is propped up by government subsidies and quickly losing the political life-support systems that have kept it going for the past two decades. Indeed, the global nuclear endeavor is like a cancer patient who has also suffered a heart attack — Chernobyl' (Christopher Flavin, in *Worldwatch*, 1987). *See also* BREEDER REACTOR, NUCLEAR, NUCLEAR WASTE.

Nuclear Family
[1947]
A sociologists' term for 'the basic family unit or group, consisting normally of father, mother, and offspring' (*Oxford English Dictionary: Supplement*). The 'normality' conferred by choosing the nuclear family as the 'basic' family unit is belied by the facts: in the UK only about 47% of families conform to the norm, and in cities like London and New York the proportion is less than 30% (*see* FAMILY). 'A nuclear family is a perfectly hermetically sealed little fascist state wherein all manner of atrocities occur daily without murmur or comment. . . The less nuclear a family is — the more neighbours, relatives, friends, other people's kids, even lodgers and home-helps are let in the doors, the healthier and sexier the family is likely to be — the more chance there is for breezes to blow away the mustiness of nuclear isolation, and the less likelihood there is of unseen atrocities occurring' (Jenny James, 1985).

Nuclear Freeze
(*see* FREEZE)

Nuclear-Free Zone
[1967]
(*also* 'NFZ')
An area in which a competent administration has declared a total prohibition on the manufacture, testing and deployment of NUCLEAR WEAPONS. Acknowledging the existence of the NUCLEAR CHAIN, some zones also cover any nuclear installation and the manufacture of nuclear-weapons-related products. The declaration of a NFZ does not in itself always make a de facto difference, since local authorities in most countries can be overruled by national governments 'in the national interest', but grassroots objection to nuclear weapons and nuclear power is clearly displayed in such policy-making. Both the Antarctic and much of South America are currently nuclear-free by treaty, and both Japan and New Zealand have successfully prevented nuclear-armed ships from entering their harbours. In Britain more than a hundred local authorities have refused to cooperate with government civil defence plans, and more than fifty, including Greater London and all of Wales, have declared themselves NFZs. Many towns in the USA, mostly in the North-East, have proclaimed themselves NFZs. 'A single nuclear free zone is small and unlikely by itself to have much effect. But many together could make nuclear strategy a near impossibility because they would make deployment and transportation of nuclear weapons extremely difficult. Administration spokespersons have actually expressed fears about the growth of the nuclear-free zone movement. Administration fears, in this case, are grounds for hope that the nuclear-free zone movement can be an effective tool against nuclear war' (Robert Seeley, 1986).

Nuclearism
[1982]
The beliefs and practices of pro-nuclear authorities in nuclear states. 'The [German] Greens maintain that nuclearism is devouring the very freedoms it is said to protect: they point to the new laws proposed in 1983 designed to keep citizens from assembling to protest deployment of the Pershing II and Cruise missiles. Richard Falk [1982] explains the dynamic in this way: "Being constantly ready to commit the nation to a devastating war of annihilation in a matter of minutes on the basis of possibly incorrect computer-processed information or pathological traits among leaders creates a variety of structural necessities that contradict the spirit and substance of democratic governance: secrecy, lack of accountability, permanent emergency, concentration of authority, peacetime militarism, extensive apparatus of state intelligence and police"' (Fritjof Capra and Charlene Spretnak, 1984).

Nuclear Mentality
[1980]
The state of extreme irresponsibility, engendered by patriarchy and its worst anti-life manifestations, which allows the development of nuclear technology to continue despite its potential to wipe out life on our planet. 'It is our belief that the tyranny created by nuclear activities is merely the latest and most serious manifestation of a culture characterized in every sphere by domination and exploitation. For this reason, the presence of the nuclear mentality in the world can only be viewed as one part of the whole, not as an isolated issue' (Susan Koen and Nina Swaim, 1980).

Nuclear Power
(*see* NUCLEAR ENERGY)

Nuclear Threat
[1946]
The power to blackmail, punish and destroy using NUCLEAR WEAPONS, which is 'enjoyed' by those who control them. It is a general numbing threat to every human being, and a more specific threat to the 'enemies' of the superpowers, and often used to 'explain' why deterrence 'has worked so well for so long'. 'The public record now reveals more than twenty cccasions when US presidents threatened to resort to nuclear war during crises' (Joseph Gerson, 1986)

Nuclear War
[1954]
'Nuclear war between the superpowers could occur at any time, triggered by computer accident or by design, as the Cold War escalates. It would take between thirty minutes and several hours to complete. One billion people would be dead with one billion more seriously injured, since there is no defense against strategic intercontinental nuclear weapons' (Helen Caldicott, 1984). *See* NUCLEAR WEAPONS, NUCLEAR WINTER.

Nuclear Waste
[1950]
Residual radioactive material produced by nuclear power stations. Being radioactive, often highly so, such wastes must be carefully contained if they are not to pose a major environmental pollution threat, yet nuclear waste disposal technology is years behind production technology, and many believe that there is no safe way of handling or disposing of the radioactive waste from nuclear power stations. 'The continuance of commercial nuclear technology in the USA and elsewhere depends on the creation of . . . nuclear waste depositories to

prevent the solid fission waste, especially strontium 90, cesium 137, carbon 14 and the trans-uranic elements like plutonium, from contaminating the environment. The repository must be stable for millions of years. A . . . repository has yet to be constructed and tested anywhere in the world with the possible exception of the USSR. There is no known way to prevent the escape of radioactive gases, tritium, or the uranium by-products' (Rosalie Bertell, 1985). *See also* RADIATION, RADIOACTIVITY.

Nuclear Weapons
[1948]
(*also* 'nuclear arms')
On 16 July 1945 the first nuclear bomb was exploded at Alamagordo in New Mexico. On 6 August ('Hiroshima Day') and 9 August the Japanese cities of Hiroshima and Nagasaki were devastated. Since then nuclear weapons have not been used in combat, though the threat of their use has never been far away (*see* NUCLEAR THREAT). There are now 50,000 nuclear weapons in the world, enough to destroy virtually all life as it exists today — the number of times they could kill each person ('overkill' in the jargon) is meaningless and ghoulish.

Nuclear Winter
[1983]
Severe and permanent damage to the biosphere which would result from a major NUCLEAR WAR. A major study of the probable environmental consequences of nuclear war, commissioned by the Royal Swedish Academy of Sciences and published in 1982 (*Nuclear War: The Aftermath*), showed that the massive clouds of smoke resulting from widespread fires would blot out sunlight from enormous areas for many weeks, resulting in atmospheric and climatic changes which would certainly result in a colder world climate, and might disrupt atmospheric and ecological systems irreversibly. 'If it came, the nuclear winter would have a devastating effect on living things. If the worst predictions were fulfilled, nuclear war and nuclear winter could wipe out most plants and animals in the Northern Hemisphere, severely damage life in the Southern Hemisphere, and threaten the survival of the human species' (Owen Greene, Ian Percival and Irene Ridge, 1985).

Nukespeak
[1982]
Official and media euphemisms for unthinkable nuclear activities, such as:

'Defence	=	Preparation for attack
Deterrence	=	A nuclear weapon
Limited Nuclear War	=	Much of Europe annihilated
Mutual Assured Destruction	=	Both superpowers bomb each other to pieces

To coin the term "nukespeak" itself is to make three main claims. First, that there exists a specialised vocabulary for talking about nuclear weapons and war together with habitual metaphors, and even preferred grammatical constructions. Secondly, that this variety of English is not neutral and purely descriptive, but ideologically loaded in favour of the nuclear culture; and thirdly, that this *matters*, in so far as it possibly affects how people think about the subject, and probably determines to a large extent the sort of ideas they exchange about it. . . Once you begin to look closely at nuclear language, you get the strong impression that in spite of the scientific background, in spite of the technical theorising, most talk about nuclear war and weapons reflects irrational, not to say superstitious, processes of thought' (Paul Chilton, 1982).

Number
[*c*.1965, probably from 'to have someone's number' [*c*.1850], to size someone up]
A manipulative attention-seeking ploy. 'A number is a bad and devious game: a way of attempting to get what you want without risk or energy or creativity or beauty. . . A successfully counteracted number turns like a boomerang back on the doer. An unsuccessfully counteracted number leaves you feeling done-to, ill, winded. A successfully perpetrated number works by virtue of the aggressor finding a "hole" in the victim: a weak spot, an Achilles heel, a vulnerability. Hence our work upon ourselves is to make ourselves whole, to heal ourselves' (Jenny James, 1985). *See also* INTERRUPTION, sense (2).

Nursery
[*c*.1500 (children); 1565 (plants). *L nutrire*, to nourish]
A place where new and growing life is nurtured. Used to describe a place where young plants can be bought ready to transplant into a garden, or an establishment, usually run by the state, which provides care for pre-school children. Parents (often one parent, and usually the mother) should not have to bear the sole responsibility for the care of pre-school children, especially if they want (or need) to work. 'It is a rare mother who never looks for somewhere or someone to leave the children with on a regular basis before they reach five [British school-starting age]. Anyone who has spent even twenty-four hours looking after a couple of toddlers and tried simultaneously to do ordinary things like shop, cook or clean, will understand why. At present, more than a quarter of us with children aged under four must find such an arrangement, because we want or are forced to go out to work. It would be reasonable to expect nursery provision to be part and parcel of our welfare state, which after all makes school attendance compulsory for our over-fives' (Michèle Cohen and Tina Reid, 1981).

Nutrient

[*c*.1880. *L nutrire*, to nourish]

A chemical which is necessary in small quantities for biological growth. Nutrients include vitamins and minerals, essential amino-acids and fatty acids. An excess of nutrients in an ecosystem can easily lead to damage to living things — this is particularly the case with the overuse of nitrates and phosphates as agricultural fertilisers.

Nutrition

[15c. *L nutrire*, to nourish]

The ways in which food and nutrients are used by living things; most commonly used when discussing the eating habits of human beings. As a science, nutrition is based in biochemistry and physiology, but because of its links with the FOOD industry and social policy-making, many people from community workers to food technologists, from health practitioners to agricultural economists, have an interest in the exploration of nutrition issues. 'We should be ready to consider new ideas and information about diet and health, but we should be wary when they are accompanied by extravagant promises. Good nutrition is not a matter of finding the single key, but of a balance among all the materials we need to live: water, proteins, fats, carbohydrates, vitamins, minerals, fiber' (Harold McGee, 1984). *See also* DIET, MALNUTRITION.

NVDA

(*see* NONVIOLENT DIRECT ACTION)

NWICO

(Acronym for 'New World Information and Communication Order'; *see* NEW INTERNATIONAL INFORMATION ORDER)

Oo

Obesity

[17c. *L obedere*, to eat up]

Weighing more than you should if you want to live a healthy life. As many as two thirds of Americans are overweight, carrying a grand total of 1.3 billion pounds of excess fat — this is the result of putting affluence before health, seeing food as an adequate alternative to fulfilment, eating foods (particularly fats) which are harmful in large quantities, and being cajoled by the food industry to eat more than is necessary. At the same time we are persuaded by the media — and often by the same companies that have an interest in gorging us (Weightwatchers, for example, is owned by Heinz) — that slim equals beautiful and happy. The idea is to make money out of the resulting confusion: 'Selling body insecurity to women (and increasingly to men too) is a vicious phenomenon' (Susie Orbach, 1982). Green-thinkers see diet, health and a fulfilling and sustaining lifestyle as interdependent: eating an adequate but not excessive amount (*see* DIET, FOOD) and relatively few animal products (*see* DEMI-VEG, VEGAN, VEGETARIAN), together with enough personal stimulation and acknowledgement, will automatically lead to physical and psychological health. Eating less, and eating further down the FOOD CHAIN, put less pressure on the environment, both at home and in the parts of the world that food is imported from to sustain Western obesity. At the same time, human beings come in a wide variety of shapes and sizes, and nobody should be made to conform with some acceptable 'norm'.

Objectification

[1836. *L obicere* (*ob-* + *jacere*), to throw against, oppose]

Seeing and treating people, particularly members of oppressed groups (women, children, blacks, people with menial service jobs) as objects rather than as equal human beings. Objectification leads to trivialisation, fetishism, and an emphasis on possession. The objectification of women is seen by many radical feminists as a fundamental means of sexist oppression: 'Objectification, carried out by the male not only as if it were his personal nature but as if it were nature itself, denotes who or what the male loves to hate; who or what he wants to possess, act on, conquer, define himself in opposition to; where he wants to spill his seed. The primary target of objectification is the woman. . . Female knowledge of objectification usually stops at a necessary but superficial understanding: beauty is rewarded and lack of beauty is punished' (Andrea Dworkin, 1981). By extension, objectification describes the way many people see nature and the earth as objects to be exploited rather than as living things with their own rights.

Obsolescence
[1847. *L obsolescere*, to wear out, grow old]
Something which is no longer useful, though in our THROWAWAY SOCIETY many products are designed and made to be instantly disposable, and the dictates of 'fashion' and an economic system that uses consumption as its chief indicator mean that very many products are thrown away or left unused not because they are no longer useful, but because something newer and even 'better' has taken their place. *See also* RECYCLING, WASTE.

Ocean
[13c. *Gk Okeanos*, the god of the outer sea which the Greeks believed encircled the world]
A vast expanse of salt water. Oceans cover more than 70% of the earth's surface, and play a vital part in the planetary ecosystem, yet human beings still treat the world's oceans as if they were a gigantic cesspit which nevertheless produces endless quantities of useful food and mineral resources. 'The oceans, those great expanses of deep blue sea, have far more to them than the capacity to dazzle an observer in outer space. They are vital parts of the global steam engine that transforms the radiant energy of the sun into the motions of air and water which in turn distribute this energy over all regions of the world. Collectively, the oceans form a reservoir of dissolved gases which helps to regulate the composition of the air we breathe and to provide a stable environment for marine life — about half of all living matter' (James Lovelock, 1979). The oceans receive the vast bulk of human wastes; at least 83% of marine pollution comes from land-based activities, and the problems of marine pollution are made worse because no single nation is responsible for them. There has been some progress since the early 1970s in legislation against dumping at sea and for international cooperation in monitoring and clean-up, but the costs of counteracting the decades-

old problem are high and governments (such as that of the UK) are slow to acknowledge and tackle marine pollution. Fish catches have been steadily declining since 1970 despite an increase in fishing effort, yet further proof of the vulnerability of what are often imagined to be limitless resources (*see* OVERFISHING). 'In its mysterious past [the ocean] encompasses all the dim origins of life and receives in the end, after, it may be, many transmutations, the dead husks of that same life. For all at last return to the sea — to Oceanus, the ocean river, like the ever-flowing stream of time, the beginning and the end' (Rachel Carson, 1951).

Official Secrets
[1889]
Supposedly legitimate ways of refusing to let people know what they have a right to know, maintaining absolute control over people and situations, disregarding public accountability, and achieving a false sense of self-aggrandisement. 'Secrecy, being an instrument of conspiracy, ought never to be the system of a regular government' (Jeremy Bentham, 1748-1832, quoted in Sissela Bok, 1986). *See also* SECRET.

Oil Crisis
[1973]
The period in 1973-4 when, because of OPEC (Organisation of Petroleum Exporting Countries) pricing policies, the price of oil rose very rapidly, forcing the large oil-importing countries to think seriously about their energy consumption. 'Until 1973, the world's oil consumers forgot — if, indeed, they ever knew — that they were spending energy capital accumulated over many millions of years. They forgot that they were exploiting Nature's literally "unrepeatable offer". OPEC had its own reasons for shocking its clients out of their complacency, but in doing so it did the world a long-term service' (Norman Myers, 1985). With increased efficiency and a short memory, oil supply no longer seems the crisis it did fifteen years ago, but because oil is a finite resource, the situation is of course much worse than it was then, the true 'energy crisis' even closer. Even if we only continue to use oil at present rates, known reserves will be depleted in about thirty years. As yet undiscovered reserves may extend this by a matter of decades, but at an ever-increasing cost.

One-Crop Economy
[1942]
A local or national economy which is dependent on one activity, usually a cash crop or export mineral resource, thus making it highly vulnerable to international price fluctuations and the policies of multinational companies. 'In 1978 crude oil made up over 90% of total exports for

Saudi Arabia, Iran, Iraq, Libya and Nigeria and over 50% for Algeria, Ecuador, Kuwait and Venezuela, among others. Copper represented 85% of Zambia's exports and 48% of Chile's. Iron ore led Mauritania's and Liberia's foreign sales with 69% and 50% respectively, while phosphates, uranium and diamonds made up over half of exports from Morocco, Niger and Sierra Leone. As for farm produce, over 60% of exports from Burundi, Colombia, Ethiopia and Uganda consisted of a single product, coffee. Cotton represented 50% of Sudan's foreign sales, cocoa over 70% of Ghana's and tobacco over 50% of Malawi's' (*Third World Guide*, 1984). One-crop local economies also dominate many regions of the West. *See* MONOCROPPING.

Oneness
[*c.*1600, but heavily revived *c.*1965. *Old English an*, one]
The recognition and direct experience of the essential unity of the universe and the connectedness of everything in it.

Ontology
[1721. *Gk einai* + *-genos*, to be born or produced]
Theories about the nature of being (the 'ontic' referring to a state of 'true being'), sometimes called metatheories. Within the framework of EXISTENTIALISM, 'ontology' is often used as a synonym for 'true being', and is at the heart of theories about existence. Ontological debate covers such areas as 'Is the world real or is it created by our experiencing it?'; 'Does the world consist of things, or structures, or events?'; 'Do things happen because we have identified them or would they happen even if we hadn't?'. In recent years 'ontology' has been also used as a synonym for PARADIGM or world-view: 'The haunting tradition of a nature-oriented ontology' (Murray Bookchin, in Michael Tobias (ed), 1985).

Open
[before 12c. *Old English open*, akin to 'up']
Free, available, accessible, flowing. Openness is an essential quality of any free and powerful human being, but it is easily forced, a sort of pseudo-openness which can be manipulative — and revealing: '["Open-minded" is a] liberal phrase that justifies noncommital and wishy-washy thinking. If you are open-minded, things tend to fall out — particularly those principles and convictions by which you define yourself' (Sue Yarber, 1985, in Cheris Kramerae and Paula Treichler, 1985). Openness is often extolled as a virtue by green-thinkers, though it is necessary to remember the element of choice: sometimes we need to protect ourselves. See also TRUST, VULNERABILITY.

Opportunity
[14c. *L opportunus*, seasonable (*ob-* + *portus*, towards harbour)]
Circumstances which are favourable for taking a decisive step. Too often used to mean the chance to exploit yet more valuable resources; too little used to mean equal opportunity for all living things to flourish.

Oppositionism
[1773. *L opponere* (*ob-* + *ponere*), to place against]
A belief that radical and fundamental.change in the policies of governments and organisations can only be achieved by clear and positive opposition, rather than by compromise. *See also* FUNDAMENTALISM.

Oppression
[14c. *L opprimere* (*ob-* + *premere*), to press against]
The widespread and systematic invalidation, in beliefs and actions, of the power and intelligence of one distinguishable group of people by another. To this end the oppressor group will maintain power over the oppressed group through laws, conventions and institutions, and will display an inflexible belief that they are right and justified in their actions. Oppression is clearly at work whenever anybody believes themself to be better than another person by virtue of their membership of a selfstyled 'superior' group. Obvious oppressions are the oppression of black people by whites, minorities by majorities, poor people by rich people, and women by men. Less obvious oppressions include the oppression of physically handicapped people in an environment designed only for the able-bodied, the oppression of children in an adult-centred world, and the oppression of people who live on their own in a society where 'the family' is the norm. Oppression is often described in terms of the nature of the oppression — sexism, classism, racism, ageism, adultism, normalism, speciesism. When an oppressed person comes to believe that they are in fact inferior, it is called 'internalised oppression'. When a person suffers as result of two or more oppressions (a black woman, for example), this is a case of 'multiple oppression'. 'Taken together, stratification *within* each oppressed group, divisions *between* oppressed groups, and the *overlapping* of oppressed groups create an enormously intricate and complicated maze of criss-crossing hierarchies. . . Very few people in our society "have nothing to lose but their chains"' (Steven Wineman, 1984). Counteracting oppression needs action by both oppressor and oppressed: any member of an oppressor group who wants the world to be different must learn to listen and not need to be right (*see* ALLY): 'I adopted a rule in those lessons that I have found useful many times since. I do not defend myself when someone points out an oppressive attitude or racist remark of mine. What I've said may be well-intended,

but that isn't really relevant when it has hurt another person. Of course, sometimes I felt unfairly accused or misunderstood, and often I felt confused, but I was learning. It was necessary to go through feelings like those in order to become a firm ally of black people' (Fran Peavey, 1986). And it needs oppressed people to recognise their oppression and refuse to be kept powerless: in order to do this, members of that group often choose to withdraw from the company of the oppressor group while they share their experience and identify their oppression (*see* SEPARATISM).

Optimism
[1759. *L optimus*, best]
A belief (at least some of the time) that things can change and improve, even when the world seems to be charging over the cliff of economic and ecological suicide. 'Greens . . . tend to be optimists by nature. For most every cause for hopelessness and despair, one can find a corresponding source of hope and encouragement that the necessary reversal of human priorities is beginning' (Brian Tokar, 1987). *See also* HUMOUR.

Organic
[1869 in this sense. *L organon*, implement]
Derived from plants and animals (more technically, relating to carbon compounds which form complex structures containing oxygen and other elements); by extension, 'organic' refers to any biological activity (especially farming and gardening) which uses only organic substances to enrich the soil and feed the plants and animals. This is supplemented by crop rotation and the recycling of animal wastes and plant residues. The British Organic Standards Committee has laid down detailed standards for foodstuffs that can be called 'organic' (similar standards have been established by other bodies). 'The soils upon which produce has been grown must have been treated in accordance with the following standards for a minimum of two years at the time of harvest:
—Soil enrichment products acceptable for use are only (a) organic matter products (composts, animal wastes, etc.) which have not been chemically fortified, (b) natural rock products, (c) beneficial bacterial and algae cultures.
—Although no standard is laid down, rotation is actively encouraged.
—Insect control may be achieved only by (a) predatory insects and insect disease cultures, (b) attractants, (c) sprays of plant origin.
—Weed control may only be done by (a) crop rotation, (b) mechanical or hand cultivation techniques, (c) thermal weeding.
—Fungal and bacterial disease may be controlled only by (a) plant and homeopathic sprays, (b) in extreme cases only, sulphur or copper fungicide, (c) for soil, steam sterilisation only.

—All chemical treatments such as growth regulators in cereals are prohibited.
—In storage, if fumigation is necessary, only diatemous earth may be used.
—In processing, all artificial flavourings, colourings, preservatives, antioxidants, etc. are prohibited'.
(Springhill Farm, 1986). Thought until recently to be a passing fad, demand for organic produce has led to many shops and supermarkets selling a range of organic produce. 'The organic movement has been plagued with what PR men describe as a twin image problem. Its devotees have been viewed as cranks — worthy crusaders in woolly hats and dung-covered wellies. And the food they grew, while wholesome and nutritious, was also wrinkled, stale, hard-to-find and expensive. . . A lack of apparent demand meant poor distribution and poor distribution brought only perished produce at premium prices to obscure greengrocers and health-food shops. There appeared to be no escape from this commercial straitjacket. Quite suddenly things [have begun] to change' (James Erlichman, 1986). Organic ranges of both home-produced and imported products have become widely available in the last few years as growers see the opportunity to produce ecologically-sound food economically, and the future for organic growing has never been brighter (*see also* FOOD, VEGANISM, VEGETARIANISM). 'Organics' is sometimes used as shorthand for 'organically-grown produce'. 'Organic' is also used to describe any process which grows and flows naturally, such as the growth of the green movement.

Orgone
(*see* LIFE FORCE)

Other
[before 12c. *Old English other*]
Being different. If 'other' is seen in the context of 'different, therefore equal', then individuality and uniqueness can be acknowledged, but 'otherness' can easily lead to separation and objectification. 'Otherness' was a concept central to existentialism, and used by Simone de Beauvoir to explain the oppression of women. 'The thesis is that woman has always been defined by man as the Other, the inessential, while man himself is defined as the One, the Subject, the being capable of transcendence — of free, independent and creative activity' (Mary Anne Warren, 1980, quoted in Cheris Kramerae and Paula Treichler, 1985). Used in psychology to indicate a person or people other than the client; thus 'other-directed' (doing what other people say) and 'significant other' (special relationship) — jargon which is best avoided.

Over-
[before 12c. *Old English ofer-*]
Too much. A favourite of proselytising doom-mongers, and a construction to be very careful of. 'Over-' implies LIMITS, and while these are sometimes obvious and real (OVERFISHING, OVERGRAZING, overkill, OVERSHOOT), some depend very much on circumstances (OVERSPECIALISATION, OVERURBANISATION), and some on point of view (OVERDEVELOPMENT, OVERPOPULATION). Green-thinkers need to be aware of the differences and be careful of unnecessary preaching on the 'over-' theme.

Overcapacity
[1928]
Having the factories and machinery capable of producing more than is needed. A widespread feature of the current world economic recession, especially in the THIRD WORLD, where the resources could have been deployed far more appropriately. 'One of the most ironic results of using rich man's technology in poor countries is that it lies idle much of the time, like a great whale stranded in a freshwater pond. . . Survey after survey has revealed the appalling waste of expensive plant in the Third World: Indian industry running at 75 per cent of capacity, West Pakistan's at 64 per cent, Afghanistan's textile mills at 43 per cent' (Paul Harrison, 1981).

Overdevelopment
[1869]
An economy whch has grown to the point where it cannot be sustained on ecological grounds. 'In addition to speaking of "underdeveloped" countries we must learn to speak of "overdeveloped" countries . . . The problem is not to convert underdeveloped into overdeveloped countries, but to convert both into steady-state economies at population and wealth levels that are sufficient for a good life and sustainable for a long future' (Herman Daly, in Michael Tobias (ed), 1985).

Overfishing
[1867]
Taking more fish out of the sea than natural population growth can sustain. 'Why has the steady increase in catch between 1950 and 1970, averaging 7 per cent per year, failed to continue? . . . The sad truth is that over-fishing is destroying our harvests. While the 1950s witnessed a few fishing failures, the 1960s and 1970s have seen more and more traditional fisheries collapse, some quite spectacularly, with a general reduction in stocks' (Norman Myers, 1985). Reasons for overfishing include a reluctance to limit catches, the difficulty of negotiating international conservation legislation, vacuum-cleaner-like fishing techniques, and an enormous growth in the amount of fish used as

animal feed (a third of the global catch is used for oil and fishmeal for this purpose). Some international legislation — particularly relating to whaling — has improved the situation slightly in recent years, but effective international action on catch size, appropriate equipment, and prohibited species has yet to be taken.

Overgrazing
[1919]
(*also* 'overstocking' [1844])
Keeping more livestock on a piece of land than the vegetation can sustain, leading to the degradation of vegetation and SOIL EROSION. In many arid and sub-arid parts of the world this is a result of inappropriate agricultural practices (often introduced from the West) leading to DESERTIFICATION, which drives pastoralist peoples onto marginal land that cannot support their herds, causing further overgrazing. The problem is often to do with introduced species — the native species of semi-arid areas invariably cause less damage to the land, and the sustainable harvest is often in excess of that obtained from domesticated species. In agriculturally marginal areas of temperate regions, overgrazing is often the result of misguided agricultural support policies, and can put severe pressure on fragile ecosystems. In the USA, for instance, the Bureau of Land Management gives grazing leases on public land to regulate grazing pressure, but many parts of the West are still sorely overgrazed.

Overkill
(*see* NUCLEAR WEAPONS)

Overnutrition
[1982]
Eating more than is healthy for you. People in the West on average take in around 40% more calories than they need for their physical well-being. Opinions vary about how much human beings need to eat to remain healthy yet not overnourish themselves; between 2,000 and 3,000 calories a day is the range that is usually given, though it depends very much on what activities you are involved in. *See also* MALNUTRITION, OBESITY.

Overpopulation
[1823]
More people than can be sustained by the resources available (*see also* POPULATION). 'A cornerstone of ecocentrism in the 1960s and 1970s was the appeal for global population stabilisation and even decline in the interests of controlling economic growth, pollution and resource depletion. Many saw "overpopulation" as the most fundamental cause

of environmental degradation' (David Pepper, 1984). Many green-thinkers still believe that drastic measures will be needed if world population growth is not to outstrip available resources and cause irreversible environmental degradation: 'The right to reproduce must no longer be treated as a "free good" — it should be regarded as a scarce asset, a legal right limited in total amount at a level corresponding to replacement fertility, or less' (Herman Daly, in Michael Tobias (ed), 1985). 'Overpopulation' is a concept that begs many questions: Why do people have children? Why are the resources not available? Who defines overpopulation? Why does it only appear to be the Third World that has an overpopulation problem? Who is to decide who can have babies? The doom-mongers can tend towards a moralistic stance (*see* LIFEBOAT ETHICS), but it is clear that continuing population growth is a crucial, if not the crucial, environmental challenge. The world is now divided by what has been called 'the demographic trap': on the one hand areas (including the West and countries with an active population policy like China) which have stabilised population growth and have adequate resources and a rising per capita income; on the other many parts of the Third World where population continues to increase rapidly, with resources becoming more and more stretched, and per capita income declining. Although resource distribution plays a large part in the creation of poverty and hunger, it is also clear that uncontrolled population growth in many subsistence economies is drastically degrading the ecological resource base to the point where widespread famine appears to be the only possible outcome. The Chinese one-child family programme, launched in the seventies, has succeeded in reducing population growth to 1% per annum and increasing per capita income to 58% per annum in the period 1980-86. 'In one Third World country after another, the pressure on local life-support systems is becoming excessive, as can be seen in their dwindling forests, eroding soils, disappearing farmland, and falling water tables. If other governments take a serious look at future population/resource balances, they may reach the same conclusion the Chinese did. And they may discover that they are forced to choose between a one-child family programme and falling living standards or, in some cases, rising death rates. Given the unprecedented numbers of young people who will reach reproductive age within the next two decades, a generation of one-child families may be the key to restoring a sustained improvement in living standards. Success in striving for an average of one child per family will bring problems of its own, including a severe distortion of age-group distribution, but it may be the price many societies will have to pay for neglecting population policy for too long' (*Worldwatch*, 1985).

Overproduction
[1822]
Producing more than is needed, a constant aspect of capitalist economics, and often resulting in vast stockpiles of unused goods and foodstuffs. The European 'food mountains', the result of ecologically and economically unsound financial support policies, are a prime example, unforgivable in a world of widespread hunger and environmental degradation.

Overshoot
[*c*.1972 in this sense]
Growth which continues beyond the point where it can be sustained by the environment, followed by collapse or crash. 'Overshoot is the inevitable and irreversible consequence of continued drawdown, when the use of resources in an ecosystem exceeds its carrying capacity and there is no way to recover or replace what was lost' (Kirkpatrick Sale, 1985). Some people think we have already reached this point as a species on a global scale, and that crash is now virtually inevitable: 'Nature must, in the not too distant future, institute bankruptcy proceedings against industrial civilization, and perhaps against the standing crop of human flesh, just as nature has done many times to other detritus-consuming species following their exuberant expansion' (William Catton, 1980).

Overspecialisation
[1931]
(US: 'overspecialization')
Knowing far too much about far too little, the result of the extreme compartmentalisation of further education, training, and work skills. With increasing unemployment, having a range of skills is far more appropriate and far less frustrating.

Overstocking
(*see* OVERGRAZING)

Overurbanisation
[1964]
(US: 'overurbanization')
Having a larger urban population than can be sustained by the resources available. More than 2 billion people, 40% of the world's population, now live in cities. While Western cities have either stabilised or declined in population, Third World cities are growing at an unprecedented rate, and often cannot provide even the most basic services of water and drainage. A 1979 survey of Lagos, for example, showed 75% of families living in a single room, 78% sharing kitchen facilities with another

family, and 87% without running water. As with overpopulation, 'overurbanisation' is a relative concept, and has to do with the unequal distribution of resources (all Third World cities have their rich suburbs, for example), yet it is clear that if uncontrolled growth continues some Third World cities will find it impossible to provide essential food, health and sanitation, resulting in widespread disease and death. 'There is no guarantee that vast cities with tens of millions of people — such as projected for Mexico City or Calcutta, for example — can be sustained or, indeed, should be sustained, if doing so requires heavy subsidies from the countryside' (*Worldwatch*, 1987).

Owner-Building
(*see* SELF-BUILD)

Ownwork
[1983]
Doing what you choose to by way of WORK rather than what you have to do in order to survive. 'Ownwork means activity which is purposeful and important, and which people organise and control for themselves. It may be either paid or unpaid. It is done by people as individuals and as household members; it is done by groups of people working together; and it is done by people, who live in a particular locality, working locally to meet local needs' (James Robertson, 1985). A useful idea insofar as it stresses individual autonomy and control, but not so useful for those for whom doing what you want is a seemingly impossible dream.

Ozone
[*c*.1840. *Gk ozein*, to smell]
A form of oxygen (0_3) arising from the recombination of oxygen by various photochemical and electrical processes in the atmosphere, in which the molecule consists of three atoms rather than two. Ozone is 'a blue gas with a distinctive odour familiar to anyone who has worked with electric sparks . . . Ironically, in view of its associations with health, vitality and fresh sea breezes — and its importance as a shielding layer in the atmosphere — ozone is toxic to humans at a concentration as low as one part per million in air' (John Gribbin (ed), 1986). Ozone levels in the atmosphere are causing concern in two ways — near the ground, ozone pollution is a major element in PHOTOCHEMICAL SMOG; in the upper levels of the atmosphere, the protective ozone layer appears to be thinning. First noted in California, ozone smogs are now commonplace in Europe during hot dry weather, when industrial discharges and car exhausts fill the lower atmosphere with nitrogen and sulphur oxides which react with sunlight to form photo-oxidants, ozone being the most dangerous. 'One calculation is that . . . current activities on the farm and on the autobahn will lead to a further doubling of the ozone in the air in

the next century. If this happens, it will have a "greenhouse effect", rather as carbon dioxide does, absorbing radiation from the sun and acting as a thermal blanket, warming the surface of the earth. It will also mean that all of Europe's plants become permanently exposed to concentrations of ozone that are known to cause damage. And it will mean that all of Europe's humans become almost permanently exposed to levels of ozone that are now considered unsafe for workers to be exposed to for a forty-hour week' (Fred Pearce, 1987). Since 1985, a severe periodic thinning of the ozone layer over Antarctica has been noticed, renewing concern about the effects of human activity on this vital feature of the atmosphere, which helps to protect the surface of the earth from harmful ultraviolet radiation. Among the possible threats to the ozone layer are the vapour trails of supersonic aircraft, the atmospheric testing of nuclear weapons, and the use of the chlorofluoromethane gases, widely used as propellants in aerosol sprays. *See also* WALDSTERBEN.

Pacifism
[1902 *L pacificus*, peace-making]
A strong belief in PEACE and NONVIOLENCE; more specifically a refusal to take up arms in wartime. A positive synonym for 'nonviolence', the term 'pacifism' seems to have fallen out of favour with the peace movement in recent years.

Packaging
[1934 in this sense. *Middle English pak*, pack]
The paraphernalia of paper, cellophane, card, polythene, rubber and plastic used to wrap up a product. The worst aspect of packaging is that it is specifically designed to become instant WASTE, and packaging makes up more than a third of all household waste in Western countries. 42% of paper products used in Britain are used for packaging, and are thrown away (and rarely recycled) once the thing inside the packaging has been unwrapped. Packaging constantly belies the products it covers up, being designed to make shoddy produce look attractive, and is a major weapon in manufacturers' ongoing campaign to cheat the customer. 'Buy as little junk in tubes and funny bottles as you can — the less you can buy, the less you'll be shafted. . . Even simple packages are often used deceptively to make things look better: thus carrots are packed in plastic which has thin orange stripes printed on it to make the carrots look more orange . . . Tell your supermarket manager that you think this is cheap deception and request that the store buy from other suppliers. . . Try to shop in a co-op grocery where such practices do not prevail — and you may even be able to buy many foods "in bulk", with no packaging at all' (Ernest Callenbach, 1981). As well as being deceptive, costly and wasteful, food packaging can be a health hazard, especially from the plasticisers in certain polythenes and PVC (polyvinyl chloride) clingfilms. *See also* RECYCLING.

Paganism

[15c. *L paganus*, a country dweller]

A religious or semi-religious faith rooted in the sanctity of the EARTH, its CYCLES and SEASONS. 'We consider as fundamentally Pagan all folk who hold the Earth sacred, who try to live in such a way that no living creature need suffer that they might live, regarding the plants and creatures as their kinfolk whose needs are to be treated with respect; who seek to prevent the exploitation and poisoning of our Mother Earth; who seek to re-establish a culture that will live lightly on the Earth, taking only enough for its needs, and living in peace and harmony towards the Earth, fellow creatures and other human beings' (Nicola Miles and Philip Cozens, undated).

Pain

[13c. *Gk poene*, penalty, punishment, grief]

What hurts; traditionally thought of as punishment for having fallen from grace. Pain in holistic terms is seen as a useful indicator of a physical or emotional injury or disease, and a condition that if experienced and worked through fully can lead to an awareness of what needs to be done to heal the hurt. 'In addition to alerting us to injury or disease, pain may serve a protective function, since it often causes us to guard or splint an injured or diseased area. . . Pain is a symptom and, as such, is not damaging to the body. However, the emotional stress that it may cause, as well as the lack of sleep, can cause actual physiologic damage. For this reason and others it is often important to relieve pain' (Mark Bricklin, 1983). Fear of pain has led to a growing market for 'instant relief' by strong drugs, which ignores the underlying cause of the pain and its appropriate treatment; some people believe that pain masked in this way is stored within the body and mind and can delay the real healing process. In several psychotherapeutic approaches it is believed that the only source of dysfunction in a human being is the experience of pain (often from the past), and that if the pain is fully experienced and dealt with, complete recovery is possible. In DESPAIR and EMPOWERMENT work this belief is taken into the realm of distress about the planetary crisis, particularly in the face of the nuclear threat. 'The feelings that assail us now cannot be equated with dread of our own individual demise. Their source lies less in concerns for the personal self than in apprehensions of collective suffering — of what happens to others, to human life and fellow species, to the heritage we share, the unborn generations to come, and our green planet herself, wheeling there in space. . . It is the distress we feel on behalf of or more precisely in connection with the larger whole of which we are a part. It is our pain for the world' (Joanna Macy, 1983).

Paradigm
[15c. *Gk paradeigma*, pattern, model]
A set of assumptions generally accepted by a particular society at a particular time. 'A "paradigm" has recently come to mean the way a whole culture sees itself: the thoughts, perceptions and values for forming its vision of reality' (Esalen Foundation, 1986). Since the early 1960s, when Thomas Kuhn used the idea extensively in his influential book *The Structure of Scientific Revolutions* (1962), 'paradigm' has become a favourite jargon word for scientists and social scientists, used as a filler whenever the more specific word needed is not to hand. Thus 'paradigm' can mean a MODEL, a world view, a cultural context, a CONSENSUS, a set of attitudes — almost whatever you want it to mean. As well as being a rather vague concept, the idea of paradigms has been criticised for being static, mechanistic, and overly generalised.

Paradigm Shift
[1962]
A radical reappraisal of your basic assumptions. Another Kuhnism (*see* PARADIGM), and the ultimate in green-tinted jargon, to be avoided whenever possible. To the uninitiated it sounds like a rather painful operation.

Paradox
[1540. *Gk paradoxos*, contrary to expectations]
Something that appears to be self-contradictory. The apparent paradoxes of the NEW PHYSICS troubled many physicists in the early years of this century, but concepts like indeterminacy (the UNCERTAINTY principle) and probability are now readily accepted, paradox and all. The necessary paradoxes in other aspects of HOLISM are now beginning to be explored, in healing for example: 'Perhaps the greatest paradox of medical practice is that, despite our immense knowledge of disease and its symptoms, every treatment, even the most apparently routine, is highly experimental. We do not and cannot know the outcome in advance, whether the treatment is orthodox or alternative. We can only be certain that the detailed results of treatment will be different for each patient. Even when the statistics show that a treatment has resulted in a particular outcome in 100% of cases, the next patient may be the exception. We are inevitably working from a position of uncertainty. . . Absolute certainty too often springs from a practitioner's unwillingness to admit what is not and cannot be known' (Jan Resnick, 1986).

Parallel Economy
[*c.*1980]
Another term for the BLACK ECONOMY, INFORMAL ECONOMY, or UNDER-

GROUND ECONOMY, emphasising the way in which it runs alongside the FORMAL ECONOMY.

Paranoia
[1811. *Gk paranoos*, distraught, demented]
Suffering from delusions. But then, what is real? And who makes the distinctions between delusion and vision? 'Far from a debilitating "mental disease", [paranoia] is strengthening and realistic dis-ease in a polluted and destructive environment' (Mary Daly, 1978). 'We say Their fear of us is paranoia. What about our fear of Them? Two paranoias facing each other, poisoning the present, destabilizing life, since for the first time ever the human race cannot be sure it will continue. An intolerable way to run the world' (Martha Gellhorn, 1986). 'Mutually stimulated paranoia is blinding all concerned to the way their opponent is likely to behave. The prophecies of aggression are self-fulfilling prophecies' (Church of England, 1982, quoted in Jonathon Porritt, 1984).

Parasite
[1539. *Gk parasitos*, one who lives at another's expense]
In ecology, an organism which obtains food at the expense of another, the host. In human society 'parasite' is usually a pejorative term applied to poor people who dare to question the unequal distribution of wealth. The negative connotations of 'parasite', and the growing recognition that all relationships in nature are reciprocal, have led many green-thinkers to drop the word from their vocabulary.

Parent
[15c. *L parere*, to bring forth]
A MOTHER or FATHER. In a society where the FAMILY, and especially the NUCLEAR FAMILY, is considered to be the ideal, parents are the adults who have by far the most influence and power over their offspring, making parenting at the same time an enormous responsibility and a potential source of great pleasure and stimulation for both parents and children. Under capitalism and patriarchy, parenting is seen very much as second-rate work, being both unpaid and done in the private and 'unimportant' world of the home. Parenting is often both unacknowledged and exhausting, turning what should be a joy into a prolonged agony, and leaving the 'primary parent' (almost always the mother) with no energy to do anything else. Green-thinkers view parents as an oppressed group, and consider it vital that the work of parenting is seen as at least as important as work done in offices and factories: 'Those mothers or fathers who devote themselves predominantly to their children, if need be giving up their other jobs to do so, are doing work of the utmost social importance' (die Grünen, 1983). 'If policy-makers . . . were truly

conscious of themselves and/or others as parents, instead of being encouraged to leave their parent-identity at home as secondary or "out of the action", our country's laws and public policies would take parents into account far more than they do at present. So, in the same way that people's eyes need to be opened to the role that society plays in shaping our experience of parenthood, we need to make it possible for the flow of our insights as parents to enter into our larger society's ethos. The public and private worlds cry out to be reintegrated, for the split between them is a destructive one' (Michèle Cohen and Tina Reid, 1981). The concept of 'parent' is used by green-thinkers to replace the conventionally-defined roles of 'mother' and 'father', with the acknowledgement that although dropping the limiting aspects of such well-established roles is not achieved overnight, mothers, fathers and children stand to gain a great deal from the active and as far as possible equal involvement of both parents. Yet the ideal of shared parenting (or 'co-parenting') is anathema to much of the society we live in: 'Men's involvement in childcare is an important goal to move towards, but it is hard to see how it could be fully realised by more than the privileged few, or the unemployed many, short of the abolition of the present capitalist market economy' (Lynne Segal, 1987). While the importance of parenting must be recognised, we also live in a society that expects people, and particularly women, to have children in order to be fulfilled, and 'not everyone is the better for having children. . . In a society which expects every "normal" person to have children, inevitably some will fall into parenthood when it isn't right for them' (Michèle Cohen and Tina Reid, 1981). As important as anything else is to respect a person's choice, and the decision whether or not to have a child must eventually rest with the prospective parents. *See also* CHILD.

Participation
[14c. *L participare*, to partake]
Having a part to play in a group activity or decision-making process. In the late 1960s and early 1970s there was a rash of reports looking at ways in which people might have more say in decisions which would affect their environment; one such was the British Skeffington Report of 1969, *People and Planning*, which defined participation as 'the act of sharing in the formulation of policies and proposals'. What was proposed, however, was little more than glorified public relations exercises, and the British public of the late 1980s is if anything even less interested in the planning process than at the time of *People and Planning*. True participation only works when the participants have real power, are listened to, and are taken seriously. 'If the majority see no real possibility of participating, then their feeling of powerlessness, and their consequent passivity, will be maintained. . . This is the most

crucial question for any movement for change, and for everyone who supports fundamental change. If no solution is found for the problem of majority participation, of communication between activist groups and the silent majority, then the affluent society's revolution will remain in the realm of theory' (Erik Dammann, 1984).

Participatory Democracy
[1968]
Government in which ordinary people can participate. Participatory democracy as it exists at present is neither participatory nor democratic. Under the parliamentary systems of the modern 'free' world, the holding of frequent referendums and public enquiries is the closest that national governments can get to citizen participation. It is only when decision-making is brought down to the local level where people can work face to face with each other that anything approaching true participatory democracy can be achieved. *See also* DEMOCRACY, PARTICIPATION.

Party
[1729 in this sense. *L partire*, to divide]
A group of politicians organised as a group with a name, which pursues the interests of its members and the people who voted for them, all the time extolling their own 'virtues' and the supposed failings of all other parties. The system of party politics which prevails in most of the West is highly divisive, competitive and simplistic, playing to the worst and most selfish aspirations of the electorate. Working within a party system is a challenge to green-thinkers, Green and Ecology Parties being an almost insuperable contradiction in terms. The German Green Party (die Grünen) has called itself the anti-party party, an alternative to the traditional parties: 'Neither right nor left, but in front'. *See also* PRESSURE GROUP.

Passion
[before 12c. *L pati*, to suffer]
Intense feeling, often the result of intense oppression, intense sympathy, and intense longing. Conventionally associated with sexual love, which can indeed be a wonderful and life-enhancing experience, but is as often the source of anger and disillusionment. 'I want to know why in the early morning I wake to see the dark blue light and cry in pain that the depths of passion and intimacy I once hoped would be mine are not mine but only flood my early-morning fantasy which by that evening will be transformed into a mature and moderate fatigue. And yet, when I find the very passion I had thought to seek and want so desperately, I feel myself cut from my moorings, wandering unclaimed, and I am

brought back to that tiresome and obsessive search for who, after all, I am' (Jane Lazarre, 1981). 'I . . . was unhappy about the flaccidity, the one-dimensionality, the lack of imagination, the lack of life in most of the men I saw around me. Where was their energy, their activity, their spontaneity? Where was their passion? The women I knew were filled with passion, not only sexual passion, although that too, but the passion for seizing life and shaping it, infusing it with the breath of an expansive humanity, an intelligent vitality. And they were gagging from the effort of repressing their desire for a truly human form of love' (Ingrid Bengis, 1973).

Passive Cooling
[*c*.1970]
Using SOLAR ENERGY to cool buildings, creating air movement through them by exploiting pressure differentials. A method often used in traditional architecture, especially in the Middle East, and now being revived as a cheap and ecologically-sound alternative to air conditioning.

Passive Resistance
[1883]
A pacifist or nonviolent stance; used in early pacifist literature to describe the peace-loving doctrine of Quakers and groups advocating similar beliefs and actions, and demonstrated in practical detail by Mahatma Gandhi (1869-1948), perhaps the greatest passive resister of all time.

Passive Solar
[*c*.1960]
The use of SOLAR ENERGY to heat buildings by trapping it within the structure of the building, from whence it can release the heat slowly throughout the building. A conservatory or greenhouse attached to the sun-facing side of a house is a passive solar device, as is the use of a body of water as a heat sink. 'The University of Saskatchewan Village House 1 — a passive solar structure — costs but $40 year to heat. There is no furnace, no scientific chicanery, merely good insulation' (Michael Tobias (ed), 1985).

Passivity
[14c. *L passivus*, having the capacity to suffer]
Doing nothing about what needs to be done, letting things happen to you rather than actively choosing, which, although it involves more effort, is also a lot more rewarding. 'Lack of emotionalism in discussions about nuclear war is not a sign of reason, but of a sick passivity' (Alice Cook, quoted in Joanna Macy, 1983).

Past
[14c. *Middle English passen*, to pass]
The time before now, which provides the lessons for the future without necessarily limiting the future in any way. *See also* HISTORY.

Pathogen
[1880. *Gk pathos* + *-gen*, causing suffering]
Any substance that causes or exacerbates disease; hence 'pathology', the study of the causes of disease. AETIOLOGY is preferred to 'pathology' by many holistic practitioners since it looks for general causes rather than specific 'culprits'; not that culprits do not exist, many of them the products and by-products of our technological society — pollutants like ozone and heavy metals, allergens in our food and water, and many of the drugs that are supposed to make us better.

Patient
[14c. *L pati*, to suffer]
A person receiving (and too often suffering from) medical care. Holistic practitioners prefer the term CLIENT, feeling that 'patient' implies 'being-done-to' rather than participation in the healing process.

Patriarchy
[1561. *Gk pater* + *archein*, father-rule]
(*also* 'male supremacy')
The institutionalised and internalised system by which men maintain their privilege at the expense of women; the social structure which fosters sexist oppression (*see* SEXISM). A fundamental concept, sometimes belittled by the unaware labelling of behaviour that hurts as 'patriarchal', when further exploration of the hurt and the behaviour that led to it would better help us to understand both the hurt and the elements of patriarchy. The apparent universality of patriarchy provides a convenient 'proof' for (mostly male) commentators that it is therefore the natural state of things, but green-thinkers believe strongly that 'biology is not destiny', and that despite the pervasiveness of 'patriarchal attitudes' (Eva Figes, 1978) it is possible, and very necessary, to interrupt oppression wherever it is found. The overthrow of patriarchy (a stated aim of many feminists) may seem an impossible task, but patriarchal attitudes and behaviour can be questioned and challenged in any and every social situation.

Pattern
[*L patronus*, patron, something to be imitated]
(1) [14c] A repeating set of structures or events; an ordered or arranged configuration. Human beings have always marvelled at and attempted to imitate the patterns of nature; scientists today who

attempt to reproduce those patterns without regard to ecological principles are in danger of destroying the beauty they seek to control. (2) [*c*.1947] Repetitive behaviour which has its origins in DISTRESS (past hurt which has not been dealt with) rather than in the clear appraisal of current circumstances (also called 'distress patterns' or 'patterned behaviour'); thus behaviour which is often inappropriate and ineffective. 'We draw a clear distinction between the person, good and wholesome in every respect, and the distress pattern, which appears to represent the person but which is actually a foreign element, parasitic upon the person' (Harvey Jackins, 1973).

Peace
[13c. *L pax*, peace]
Being at ease, free from conflict and disturbance; a setting and a state of mind in which human beings acknowledge their links with each other and their environment, and work for UNDERSTANDING and HARMONY. Our world is so far from being peaceful that peace has to be worked for simultaneously at many different levels and in many ways. First, peace means the cessation of armed conflict and the maintenance of a setting where people are not in fear for their lives; it is in this sense that 'peace' has been most subverted by militaristic organisations: 'Strategic Air Command, SAC (motto, "Peace Is Our Profession"; emblem, a mailed fist on a blue sky, three red lightning bolts and a green olive branch) was established in 1946 within the USAF as an elite nuclear strike force' (Jonathon Green, 1986). But 'peace is not simply the cessation of hostilities, [it is] a state of being in harmony with all of life. The peace we seek in the world and our own lives goes deeper than agreeing not to shoot at each other. Silencing the guns is a necessary first step' (Michael Lindfield, 1986). The distinction between 'peace' and 'defence' is important to acknowledge, since in many people's minds the two ideas are synonymous: 'Never before in the history of the planet has peace been needed as much and in the minds of some, never has it been a dirtier word. . . Why do people get so side-tracked onto matters of defence every time the word peace is mentioned?' (Vanessa Letham, *Social Alternatives*, Spring 1987). 'Peace' also means stillness and serenity, a rare experience for many people, but important to balance the actions and frustrations of being a peace campaigner. As well as the following entries, 'peace' is also used by green-thinkers in the terms 'peace education', 'peace manifesto', 'peace march', 'peace movement', 'peace research', 'peace studies' and 'peace walk'. Fundamental to green thinking are Gandhi's words: 'There is no way to peace; peace is the way' (quoted in Fritjof Capra and Charlene Spretnak, 1984).

Peace Camp
[1981]
A group of people camping just outside a military installation to draw attention to the iniquities of MILITARISM in general and the NUCLEAR MENTALITY in particular. Peace campers often undertake ACTIONS to attract publicity and concern. Following the example of the Greenham Common Peace Camp, several camps are for women only, where women have chosen to experience their own power in working for peace, forcing male military personnel to think in terms other than those of 'man-to-man' conflict. A similar group of people who travel round the country is sometimes called a 'peace convoy'; one such convoy was the butt of particularly brutal police violence in southern England in June 1985. There are currently about 24 peace camps in 11 countries.

Peace Campaigner
[1954]
A person who works actively for PEACE. 'The aims of peace campaigners can vary enormously, from the absence of organised forms of collective violence between nation states, to compelling visions of "Heaven on Earth", to the socialist commonwealth, or the anarchist society of small societies founded on co-operation and mutual aid' (Andrew Rigby, in Gail Chester and Andrew Rigby (ed), 1986).

Peace Tax
[1980]
An acknowledgement that much of the tax that people pay, even those who work for peace, is used for military purposes. As a result, a small but growing number of people are withholding that proportion of their taxes until they can be assured that it will be used for peaceful purposes. 'In America, 180 peace groups have refused to pay war tax in 1986. It's claimed that anything from 10,000 to 20,000 private US citizens are now openly disobeying the law by their refusal' (*Maggie's Farm* magazine, 1986). 'Surely it is time to insist that, in a period when £18 billion annually is spent on defence [in Britain], there should be some proportionate investment in peace. A Peace Fund (and perhaps such a fund would legitimate and encourage the payment of a peace tax) would do much to sustain a host of important projects which barely survive from year to year' (Tom Woodhouse, in Gail Chester and Andrew Rigby (ed), 1986).

Penetration
[1605. *L penetrare*, to penetrate deeply]
Going deeply into something. While 'penetration' can mean 'deep exploration', in its most common contemporary usage it implies forcing

your way into something, a favourite occupation (mostly of men) in a patriarchal socety. Mistakenly thought to be a necessary objective of sexual activity involving a man, penetration is being reconsidered by many people in the light of AIDS. 'It's a period where individuals are encouraged actually to learn about each other's pleasures, to find out about each other's bodies without the inevitable goal of penetration. Perhaps AIDS could be seen as a . . . pause . . . for people to find out about each other, less obvious pleasures, and a moment where sexuality could be redefined as something other than male discharge into any kind of receptacle. In this new context where penetration might literally spell death, there is a chance for a massive relearning about sexuality' (Ros Coward, *New Internationalist*, March 1987). 'Penetration aids: Devices added to the warheads in the re-entry vehicle of a nuclear missile' (Michael Sheehan and James Wyllie, 1986).

Perception
[1611. *L percipere*, to perceive]
(1) INSIGHT, INTUITION. 'If the doors of perception were cleansed, everything would appear . . . as it is, infinite' (William Blake, quoted in Gary Snyder, 1980).
(2) An individual's awareness of their environment, which affects the way they respond to it; by extension, a point of view. Thus your perception of an event will not necessarily be the same as mine, an important perception when it comes to letting go of absolute TRUTH.

Perfect
[13c. *L perficere*, to perfect an activity]
Entirely APPROPRIATE and excellent in all respects. A term, however, which is easily subverted to inappropriate ends — the drive for 'perfect' exploitation and 'perfect' oppression. Thus the 'perfect' housewife, the 'perfect' automobile and the 'perfect' nuclear power station cannot exist, despite the claims of market researchers and technologists.

Permaculture
[1978. Abbreviation of 'perma[nent agri]culture']
An integrated system of perennial agriculture, designed to enrich rather than destroy local ecosystems, which is as far as possible self-sufficient in energy needs. 'It is, in essence, a complete agricultural ecosystem, modelled on existing but simpler examples' (Bill Mollison and David Holmgren, 1978). Many of the techniques of permaculture have been developed at the Tagari Community in Tasmania, where the term was first used; there are now associations promoting permaculture ideas in several countries.

Permanence
[15c. *L permanere*, to remain throughout]
The awareness of continuity, and living and creating things in the belief that there is real value in traditions and artefacts that continue to be useful for a long time. By extension, refraining from activities that are certain to create hardship and imbalance in the future. 'A nonviolent economy would emphasise not conflict but co-operation, not conquest but harmony with nature. Gandhi called it the "economy of permanence". It was held together not simply by necessity and self interest, but by mutual trust and fellowship' (*Peace News*, 1976).

Persistence
[*L persistere*, to stand firm]
(1) [1546] Keeping going even when things get tough.
(2) [1962] The stability of a CHEMICAL. The more stable a chemical, the longer it will remain in an ecosystem before it breaks down and becomes relatively harmless. Many PESTICIDES and industrial wastes include very persistent ingredients which, although they may not be particularly toxic, do not break down in the biosphere. Traces of DDT (dichlorodiphenyltrichloroethane), a highly persistent insecticide theoretically banned in some countries, have been found in the fatty tissues of Antarctic penguins.

Personal Growth
[*c*.1958]
An expanding awareness of who you really are. There are many techniques of personal growth (*see* COUNSELLING, PSYCHOTHERAPY), but in general the term covers the psychotherapies which stress the rich potential of human beings as opposed to those which emphasise the detection and treatment of dysfunction. The range of personal growth techniques is sometimes referred to as HUMANISTIC PSYCHOLOGY or the HUMAN POTENTIAL MOVEMENT.

Personal Is Political, The
[1970]
The recognition that there is no necessary gulf between our private and public lives, and that our personal lives are the result of our political beliefs. We do not stop being political when the meeting or the action ends, and we can gain a great deal of political insight from sharing our personal experiences with other people. The phrase originated and was developed within the women's movement, and is at the heart of SEXUAL POLITICS. While accepting that a great deal of oppression operates at the personal level, 'the personal is political' has sometimes tended to become prescriptive, implying that the true radical has no right to PRIVACY and confidentiality. 'The original genius of the phrase "the

personal is political" was that it opened up the area of women's private lives to political analysis. . . However, opening up women's experience to political analysis has also resulted in a misuse of the phrase. While it is true that there are political implications in everything a woman *qua* woman experiences, it is not therefore true that a woman's life is the political property of the women's movement' (Anne Koedt, 1973).

Personality
[1795 in this sense. *L persona*, mask, character]
How we present ourselves to the world. This may or may not be the same as the person we know ourselves to be, and psychologists often make the distinction between the mask of our personality and our true SELF. One of the aims of HUMANISTIC PSYCHOLOGY is to reintegrate our self and our masks so that we become more aware of our behaviour. We often have more than one 'personality', 'a multitude of lives' (Piero Ferrucci, 1982): some therapies refer to these as 'subpersonalities'. The purpose of INTEGRATION is not necessarily to stop acting the parts of our different personalities, more to be aware of when we are acting and when we are not.

Perspective
[16c in this sense. *L perspicere*, to see through or into]
A point of view, one of many and all equally valid, even if mistaken. 'From a computer's perspective, human beings are on Earth merely to reorganize silicon into conductive chips. From the biosphere's perspective, the whole point of Homo sapiens is their armpits, aswarm with 24.1 million bacteria' (Michael Tobias, 1985).

Pessimism
[1815. *L pessimus*, worst]
A tendency to expect the worst, which means that the worst often obliges. The line between pessimism and being realistic is a very fine one. *See also* DEPRESSION, DESPAIR.

Pest
[1865 in this sense. *L pestis*, plague]
An insect or other animal (sometimes a human being) found in an inappropriate place at an inappropriate time. The place is usually among crops in a farm or garden, though if the crops are being grown according to ecological principles uncontrollable pest problems should be few and far between. Most crops, however, are not grown according to ecological principles, and large areas of MONOCULTURE are prime targets for hungry insects. 'Though it may sometimes appear that way, pests and diseases are not out to get gardeners. However much chemical companies may foster the idea, we are not engaged in a war within

our gardens, though nature is not going to do us any favours. When we have to kill something, the substance used does some other harm, however slight, so it is best not to use any poisons casually or as a preventative. Even a heavy water spray on roses or fruit trees, at the wrong time, may wash away large numbers of beneficial insects, and leave the plants susceptible to fast-breeding plant eaters. So we need to kill as little as possible, and try to create an ecosystem that works in our favour' (Margaret Elphinstone and Julia Langley, 1987).

Pesticide
[1925]
A substance designed to kill insects and other unwanted organisms, usually a manufactured chemical rather than a naturally-occurring one. A term that covers insecticides, herbicides (for vegetation), fungicides, nematicides (for worms), rodenticides and other killers. As long ago as 1962 Rachel Carson in her influential book *Silent Spring* made it clear that not only were the 'pests' becoming pesticide-resistant almost as fast as the agrochemical industry could create new killers, but that we were in danger of poisoning ourselves in the process. Nevertheless the pesticide market remains one of the fastest-growing in the economy. 'Today . . . around 4,000 different proprietary products . . . are in use in Britain. . . By the early 1980s, 97-9 per cent of all main crops, cereals and vegetables were sprayed at least once. Official figures for 1983 show that one crop of lettuce was dosed 46 times with four different chemicals' (Chris Rose, in Edward Goldsmith and Nicholas Hildyard (ed), 1986). Pesticide residues in food are causing growing concern despite bland official assurances that all is well: 'The organochlorine pesticides are lipid seeking. That means they lodge in fat tissues to reach concentrations 300 times higher than the level found in the blood. Enviro-Health Systems, which is run by Dr John Laseter, is not shy in its diagnosis of what these residues can do. It says: "Low-dose toxic exposure to common organic chemical compounds is implicated in an ever-broadening range of clinical illnesses"' (James Erlichman, 1986). Many pesticides are sprayed from the air, and there is mounting evidence that spray drift does considerable ecological damage, as well as endangering human health. Pesticides which are banned in Western countries are frequently dumped in the Third World, where as many as 10,000 people each year die from occupational pesticide poisoning and another 400,000 are made ill by it. Despite the growing mountain of evidence of the dangers of excessive pesticide use, very little national, never mind international, legislation has been enacted to limit pesticides. 'The whole system is geared to accommodating and nurturing the [agrochemical] industry's interest first, and anything else second. In an era when we realize that the capacity of the environment to absorb and

deal with toxic chemicals and pollutants is more and more exhausted, and as disease is increasingly linked to pollutants and diet, such a gross failure of [pesticides] policy is little short of catastrophic' (Chris Rose, *op. cit.*).

Phenomenology
[1797. *Gk phainesthai + logos*, the study of appearances]
A belief in the importance of things just as they are, without resorting to explanation, analysis or theory. Phenomenology rejects the distinction between subject and object, the observer and the observed. It also rejects expectation and presupposition, proposing instead that in simply concentrating instead on things and events just as they are, we begin to understand them from their own perspective. 'The sciences build upon the life-world as taken-for-granted in that they make use of whatever in it happens to be necessary for their own particular ends. But to use the life-world in this way is not to know it scientifically in its own manner of being' (Edmund Husserl, 1954). Objections to phenomenology include the fact that we can only experience things and events ('phenomena') as human beings, that we have to interpret to be able to understand, and that differing contexts may reveal different 'realities' (the field of study of 'constitutive phenomenology'). Insofar as it stresses openmindedness, receptivity, interconnectedness and the importance of direct experience, however, phenomenology is a useful philosophy in a green context.

Philosophy
[13c. *Gk philosophia*, lore of wisdom]
The exploration of wisdom and meaning; 'philosophy' has also come to mean the general attitudes and beliefs of a person or group of people. 'The Green philosophy is firmly grounded in the principle that the planet and its resources are finite, and its inhabitants interdependent, and this global perspective is shared by Green parties all over the world. All our policies stem from this' (Lindy Williams, in Edward Goldsmith and Nicholas Hildyard (ed), 1986). 'The thing to ask of any new philosophical statement . . . is only this: Does it take me into the things I fear most and wish to avoid, or does it make it easy for me to hide, to run away from them? Does it enable me to shut out the environment, ignore politics, remain unaware of my dream life, my sexuality, and my relationships with other people, or does it shove these into my face and teach me how to live with them and through them? If the answer is the latter, then I suggest to you we are on the right track. If the former, then it is my guess . . . that we are sinking into a sleep from which, in the name of enlightenment itself, there will be no easy awakening' (Morris Berman, *Journal of Humanistic Psychology*, Spring 1986).

Photochemical Smog

[1957]

A light haze occurring during hot dry weather, caused by the action of sunlight on hydrocarbon and nitrogen oxide pollution to form OZONE. The main causes of photochemical smog are industrial atmospheric pollution and vehicle exhausts; the most noticable effects are wilting (and sometimes death) of plants, and irritation of the eyes and lungs of animals, including human beings. Ironically, the cleaner atmospheric conditions resulting from anti-smoke legislation have increased the incidence of photochemical smog. It is now believed that ozone poisoning is an important contributory factor in the death of large numbers of trees in Europe and North America, originally thought to have ben due primarily to sulphur-laden rain (*see* ACID RAIN, WALDSTERBEN). Controls on vehicle emissions are planned for the 1990s in Europe and North America (with the notable exception of Britain), but this may be too late for many of Europe's dying forests.

Photosynthesis

[1898. *Gk phos* + *sunthesis*, putting together by light]

The way in which green plants create carbohydrates from atmospheric carbon dioxide and water, using sunlight as an energy source and chlorophyll to turn light energy into chemical energy, by a complex process that is not fully understood. Animals (including human beings) depend on plants for their essential carbon intake since they cannot use atmospheric carbon dioxide directly. For this reason, if for no other, the maintenance of healthy plant growth is essential to all forms of life.

Physically Different

[1963]

A relatively non-oppressive alternative preferred by some people to DISABLED, though used less in recent years. 'The term "physically different" . . . has increasingly been seen as yet another euphemism, like "children with special needs", which are vague and confusing to all of us, but especially able-bodied persons' (Marilee Thorne, *Complete Elegance*, 1983). Another alternative is 'physically (or mentally) challenged'.

Physics

(*see* NEW PHYSICS)

Pioneer Ecosystem

[1939]

A community of plants and animals which colonises or recolonises an area which has previously been barren, such as a derelict quarry or abandoned farmland.

Place
[13c. *L platea*, space]
A specific physical location with an identifiable character. In relation to human beings, a green approach to place stresses ecological principles, beauty, human scale and appropriateness for human activities over and above the profits of the developer — 'a centre of felt value' (Yi-Fu Tuan, 1977). It takes into account the unique ecology and history of the place, and its significance for the people who live there, so that when change is needed the best of what is there already is integrated with new elements which are sensitively designed and constructed. BIOREGIONALISM has been called 'the politics of place'.

Placebo
[1950 in this sense. *L placere*, to please]
An inert substance which is given to a patient in place of a drug, either to see how the reaction differs between the drug and the placebo, or because the doctor thinks the patient needs something to take in order to believe that improvement is possible. 'Magic works if and when the intent of patient and magician coincides, though it took scientific medicine considerable time to recognise its own practitioners as part-time magicians. To distinguish between the doctor's professional exercise of white magic from his function as engineer (and to spare him the charge of being a quack), the term "placebo" was created. . . A placebo pleases not only the patient but the administering physician as well' (Ivan Illich, 1976).

Planet
[13c, though 'planet earth' 1964. *Gk planasthai*, to wander]
A satellite of a star, though in green parlance it usually refers to the EARTH, the planet we inhabit. Thinking in terms of the planet as a whole is a relatively recent idea, but with ease of travel and communication the more affluent of the world's people are now used to receiving information about global events and trends. Ecologists have stressed the interdependence of the world's ecosystems, and scientists have proposed the GAIA hypothesis to explain how in many ways the planet behaves as one living organism. Since the first photographs showing the earth as a little blue marble in space were transmitted in 1972, the image of 'planet earth' has inspired many people with a new understanding of what SPACESHIP EARTH really means — a finite ecosystem with finite resources. 'As succinctly as I can put it, my argument is that the needs of the planet are the needs of the person. And therefore, the rights of the person are the rights of the planet' (Theodore Roszak, 1979). At the same time, this newly-available portrait of the planet has allowed it to be trivialised, used to advertise cars and jewellery, reproduced millions of times over as postcards and posters.

Planetary

[*c*.1951 in this sense]

Relating to the EARTH as a whole (*see* PLANET). 'Planetary' has become a favourite adjective in the last twenty years, in most senses synonymous with and certainly as ubiquitous as GLOBAL. Its uses range from the factual: 'planetary ecosystem', 'planetary life-support system', 'planetary pollution'; to the utopian: 'planetary peace' and 'planetary harmony'. The United Nations affiliated organisation Planetary Citizens was formed in 1974 to stress the common humanity of all the planet's human population; its founder, Donald Keys, is a planetiser par excellence: in the hundred short pages of *Earth at Omega: Passage to Planetization* (1982) he introduces us to 'planetary unification', 'planetary selfhood', 'planetary values', 'planetary village', 'planetary citizenship', 'planetary perspectives', 'planetary solidarity', 'planetary affairs', 'planetary consciousness', 'planetary revolution', 'planetary initiative' and 'planetary congress'. Watch out, Mr Spock.

Planning

[1748. *L planus*, flat; *plantare*, to plant]

Deciding what needs to be done and how best to do it. Used since about 1935 to describe a system whereby national and local government agencies make decisions about land use and related issues. Some control over land use is obviously needed in a capitalist economy, but who decides the criteria upon which a particular project can be allowed? Do the principles behind planning relate to sound ecological practice, some interpretation of human needs and rights, some sense of beauty and appropriateness? Planners often pretend that their task is to be rational and dispassionate, to take the stated goals of government policy and translate them into structures on the ground. This ignores the power of the planning process to dictate important aspects of people's lives, and the ways in which planning decisions tend to uphold the economic and social status quo. 'Contrary to popular mythology, planning did not bring socialism — in fact, it became a sophisticated weapon to maintain the existing control under a mask of rationality, efficiency and science. . . The problem, then, is not how to bring planners "closer to the people," as one familiar argument goes, but how to create the kind of cultural change where people are free of a dependency on such experts' (Robert Goodman, 1972). *See also* ARCHITECTURE, HOUSING.

Plant Variety Rights

[1985]

The right of plant varieties to a continued existence in the face of extinction. As with animal rights, it is important to remember that this is a right in itself, not only to be justified on the grounds of usefulness to human beings. 'Plant genetic resources should be considered part of common human [*sic*] heritage' (*Maggie's Farm* magazine, 1986).

Plastics
[1909. *Gk plassein*, to mould]
Materials which can be shaped or moulded by heat and pressure. Most plastics are polymers — made up of large molecules forming a repeating pattern. Plastics can be made from RENEWABLE RESOURCES like wood and cotton (cellulose plastics which are used to make film, cellophane, and textiles like rayon), or from NON-RENEWABLE RESOURCES, mostly petroleum (polyethylenes, polystyrenes and polyvinyl chlorides). While plastics are used in many products which are designed to be long-lived and would be difficult to make from any other material, around 25% of plastics are used in PACKAGING. As well as being wasteful, this leads to problems when it comes to WASTE disposal. Despite the claims of some manufacturers (especially of carrier bags) that their plastic is BIODEGRADABLE, some plastics which carry this claim release toxic chemicals into the soil as they degrade, especially if disposed of in large quantities. No plastics are known to degrade safely. Plastic containers are also difficult to recycle, although standardisation (anathema to most manufacturers) would reduce waste. Polyvinyl chloride (PVC) sometimes contains minute amounts of carcinogenic plasticiser, and so should be avoided for food packaging. 'When possible, you should avoid food that comes in "blister packs" . . . and don't store food or beverages in plastic containers or wrappings; use glass or ceramic containers, or waxed paper' (Ernest Callenbach 1981).

Play
[12c. *Old English plegan*, to play]
Enjoying yourself in an activity which is not essential to your livelihood. Acknowledged to be important for animals and children, but not for grown-ups, and thus thought by many adults to be childish, though most will readily join in with children when other adults are not looking. Playing games, having fun, having a good laugh, are essential to living a balanced life. 'As John Cage has written, purposeless play is "affirmation of life — not an attempt to bring order out of chaos, nor to suggest improvements in creation, but simply of waking up to the very life we're living" . . . Play has been abolished in contemporary society — except in children, until we knock it out of them — and in its place there is recreation — human maintenence' (Richard Neville, 1970). *See also* GAMES.

Playgroup
[1942]
Informal and short-period daycare for small groups of pre-school children, usually organised by parents on a rota basis. 'Play groups have blossomed all over the place since the 1960s, largely because mothers, desperate for some kind of social life for their kids and any kind of break for themselves, have got together to organise them. About half are run by parent committees . . . The rest are run by charities . . . and community organisations, such as a tenants' association. [In Britain] local authorities run 1 per cent of playgroups, but, quick to recognise a good, cheap (to the council) thing when they see one, give minimal grant-aid to others' (Michèle Cohen and Tina Reid, 1981). Playgroups fulfil an important function, but must be supplemented by nursery provision if parents (mostly mothers) want or need to work, and are seen by many politicians (if they ever think about them) as a useful way of passing the buck as far as the provision of pre-school care facilities is concerned. *See also* CRÈCHE, NURSERY.

Pleasure
[14c Old French 'plaisir', to please]
Getting what you want and giving other people what they want; sometimes (but mistakenly) limited to physical pleasure, pleasant though this is. 'Pleasure . . . is a state of heightened excitation, lumination, rhythmicity and self-awareness' (Alexander Lowen, 1970)

Ploughshare
[1980]
(US: 'plowshare')
An anti-nuclear campaign, originally started in the USA but now spread to Europe, involving the symbolic hammering of nuclear hardware and spilling of blood; the prison sentences given to some of the activists, who allow themselves to be apprehended, have been extremely harsh. The campaign is named after the passage from the *Bible* (Micah 4;3): 'They shall beat their swords into ploughshares, and their spears into pruning hooks; nation shall not lift up sword against nation, neither shall they learn war any more.'

Pluralism
[1965 in this sense. *L pluralis*, concerning many]
Different ethnic and cultural traditions existing alongside each other. Pluralism contrasts with assimilation in that it acknowledges the lifestyle and cultural needs of each community rather than demanding cultural integration. An acknowledgement of different needs often requires a great deal of education and understanding on the part of each of the groups making up a 'plural society'. 'We are all at the centre,

but we are different, and there is a possibility for coexistence among us . . . A plurality, an equality' (Johann Galtung, in Rudolf Bahro, 1986). *See also* DIVERSITY.

Poetry
[14c. *Gk poiein*, to make, create]
'The skilled and inspired use of the voice and language to embody rare and powerful states of mind that are in immediate origin personal to the singer, but at deep levels common to all who listen' (Gary Snyder, 1980). Many poets have written on the green theme, including Gary Snyder himself (*Turtle Island*, 1974), Marge Piercy (*Circles on the Water*, 1985), William Heinesen (*Arctis*, 1980), John Purser (*The Counting Stick*, 1976), Kathleen Raine (*Collected Poems*, 1981) and Elizabeth Jennings (*Collected Poems*, 1967). 'Mean while the Mind, from pleasure less,/Withdraws into its happiness:/The mind, that Ocean where each kind/Does straight its own resemblance find;/Yet it creates, transcending these,/Far other Worlds, and other Seas;/Annihilating all that's made/To a green Thought in a green Shade' (Andrew Marvell, 1681).

Poison
(*see* TOXIN)

Police
[16c. *L politia*, administration; from *Gk polis*, city]
Employees of the STATE who should act as careful arbiters when JUSTICE is miscarried, and who must be accountable to the people whose rights they protect. 'The paramount fact is that the police need the public and that the effectiveness of policing is dependent on the extent to which we transform, as Steve Bundred of the GLC [Greater London Council] Police Committee put it, "the police force into a police service". . . It is essential to impose a system of positive public accountability in which the needs of the community direct the activities of the police' (John Lea and Jock Young, 1984). Unfortunately this is not always how policing is carried out: 'At 7.30 the police arrived. A song began as more vans drew up and suddenly police were everywhere. Inside the fence and outside, more and more arrived. They began to remove the women. I watched as friends were dragged along the road and flung into the mud at the side of the banks. The clash between women and police began in earnest now. It terrified me. There was fear and violence in the air, shouts and cries, harsh orders and banshee wailing, a woman's scream and the thud of bodies flung on to the mud. Behind the fence a woman fell to the ground and two policemen rushed towards her. One, twisting his fingers into her hair, began to drag her through the gate. I saw his boot and heard the thud and suddenly I had to vomit. Police were dragging,

shoving, pulling, but women kept returning. Stronger now and even more determined. The fear was gone' (Barbara Harford and Sarah Hopkins, 1984). *See also* LAW AND ORDER

Politics
[1551. *Gk polites*, citizen]
The exploration of patterns of LEADERSHIP, POWER relationships, administrative structures and citizen PARTICIPATION. In the classical city-state ('polis') from which politics gets its name, 'politics' allows everyone who had a vote (free men, of course, not women, children or slaves) to take part in face-to-face negotiation. In modern society politics has come to mean 'what they do for (and to) us', and most people have very little say in policy-making and administration — those in power like to keep it that way, and do their best to hold intelligent people who ask difficult questions at arm's length: 'Politics appears to attract just the sort of person I would rather not vote for' (Peter Ashley, *The Guardian*, March 1987). The recognition that the PERSONAL IS POLITICAL alerts us to the dangers of supporting the status quo without question, and reminds us that each of us can be an agent for political change. 'In a world where "politics", for most people, means the proclamations of politicians and the petty squabbles among government officials, Greens promise to give the word a new meaning. Green politics embodies a new understanding of the public sphere as a forum for enhancing the living interrelationships among people and communities, not just a different way of administering the institutions of the state' (Brian Tokar, 1987).

Pollarding
[1670. *Middle English pol*, head]
Cutting the branches of a tree back to the head of the trunk in order to promote a dense and healthy head of foliage. One way (*see also* COPPICING) of extending the life of a tree and providing a continuous supply of young timber for firewood and carpentry.

Polluter Pays
[1972]
The idea that any operator who creates POLLUTION should bear the cost of dealing with and clearing up the pollution. If polluters were to bear all such costs, many environmentally-harmful technologies simply would not be profitable.

Pollution
[1877 in this sense. *L polluere*, to defile]
The contamination of the environment by substances which, because of their nature or quantity, cannot be readily absorbed by the ecosystem. When pollution first became an issue of public concern in the 1960s it

was often thought, despite the warnings of some scientists, to be a problem that only affected small areas following ACCIDENTS. This is still the mentality of many people even today, despite the appalling evidence — 52% of Germany's trees dead or dying, a quarter of Sweden's lakes acidified, an estimated 50,000 premature deaths in the USA every year caused by atmospheric sulphates and particulates, 675,000 American children with dangerously high concentrations of lead in their blood. The message is clear: the deliberate pollution of air, land and water is stretching ecosystems to (and in some cases beyond) the limits of stability; what we are risking is ecological collapse. 'Over the last two centuries — a mere instant of geologic time — industrial societies have altered the earth's chemistry in ways that may have staggering ecological and economic consequences within our lifetimes or those of our children. Three stand out as particularly threatening and costly to society: diminished food security from a changing climate, the demise of forests from air pollution and acid rain, and risks to human health from exposure to chemical pollutants in the environment. These consequences arise from everyday activities that collectively have reached a scale and pace sufficient to disrupt natural systems that evolved over millions of years' (Sandra Postel, *Worldwatch*, 1987). 'In sum, environmental pollution is not to be regarded as an unfortunate, but incidental, by-product of the growth of population, the intensification of production, or of technological progress. It is, rather, an intrinsic feature of the very technology which we have developed to enhance productivity. Our technology is enormously successful in producing material goods, but too often is disastrously incompatible with the natural environment systems that support not only human [and all other] life, but technology itself' (Barry Commoner, 1969, in Robert Disch (ed), 1970).

Polyculture
[1915. *Gk polus* + *L cultura*, cultivating many kinds]
Growing and rearing a number of different crops together, both plants and animals. 'There is yet another level of ecological complexity in agriculture that has tremendous potential on a decentralized scale, but which is as yet to be fully explored. This is the idea of the polyculture farm. The concept is borrowed from practices of the rice-vegetables-fish-livestock economies of southern and eastern Asia. Adapted to current information about ecological principles and a holistic science, modern polyculture farms would link several artificial ecosystems in a balanced and relatively self-sufficient complex of renewable energy systems, mixed crops, aquaculture, plus livestock and insect husbandry' (John Todd, in Richard Merrill (ed), 1976).

Population
[1612. *L populus*, the people]
All the people living in a particular place; taken into biology [1889] to refer to numbers of any organism in a given area, thence into ecology. Many ecologists, following in Malthus's footsteps (*see* MALTHUSIANISM, NEOMALTHUSIANISM), believe that population (meaning human population growth) is not only the biggest environmental problem we now face, but that 'it is a problem in its own right and one that multiplies all others' (Paul Ehrlich, 1970). 'The emerging history of population is a story of disaster and denial' (Garrett Hardin, 1964). 'Those who drafted the UN statement implying that parenthood is a right . . . did not realise that if it is, population control is impossible. Only by making parenthood a privilege, to be enjoyed under specified conditions and to a specified extent, can society achieve population control' (Garrett Hardin, 1978). On the other hand, expectations too often colour facts, and as long as population growth is viewed with all the inevitability of a runaway train, the danger is that it will remain inevitable: 'Our 5 billionth inhabitant was born on Monday 7th July, 1986, according to estimates of the Population Institute. "It is a sobering symbol of the shocking rapidity at which the world's population is multiplying," an Institute spokesman said' (*Simply Living* magazine, Autumn 1986). While it is important to acknowledge the sheer quantity of the human population and the pressure this places upon RESOURCES, it is too easy to wring our hands in helpless despair. There are many complex issues related to population growth (*see* AGRICULTURE, EDUCATION, GROWTH, HEALTH, LAND OWNERSHIP, NEOCOLONIALISM, POVERTY, PROGRESS, TECHNOLOGY), and thinking in terms of 'population' rather than 'people' dehumanises the issue. It is both condescending and inaccurate to think that people in the Third World actively choose environmental degradation by 'refusing' to practise constraint. 'The runaway growth in many peasant populations today is more than the simple arithmetic of births for once swamping deaths because of modern medicine and hygiene. Heinrich von Loesch, an economist specialising in demography, lays the blame on "imported progress" which ". . . offered an unexpected chance for social and economic improvement to the people of poor countries. Wholly inexperienced in matters of progress they react in a logical way . . . by sacrificing personal mobility and consumption to have more children for the better future of their families". Von Loesch derides the current idea that peasants have increased the size of their families because they lack the psychological or physical techniques of constraint' (Peter Bunyard and Fern Morgan-Grenville (ed), 1987). Though green-thinkers may believe that the populations of most Western countries are too large for their resource base, most of these countries have reached a fairly stable

population, suggesting that populations can level out according to S-CURVE theory. The choice facing green-thinkers is a difficult one. Population growth is a vital issue which we often feel powerless to do anything about, but it is only by recognising the connections between population growth and the insidious ways in which Western actions and beliefs, particularly those of 'progress' and 'growth', affect the whole world that any hope can be offered. *See also* OVERPOPULATION.

Pornography

[1864. *Gk porne* + *graphein*, writing about prostitutes]
Depictions of naked or scantily-clad people, almost always women, which exploit and degrade them by lying about their true power, purpose and humanity. 'Pornography — hard or soft core — depicts women as limited beings with a restricted sexual presence subservient to apparently specific male desires' (Andy Moye, in Andy Metcalf and Martin Humphries (ed.) 1985). '[Pornography presents] women in one or more of the following ways: as dehumanized sexual objects, things or commodities; as sexual objects who enjoy pain or humiliation; as sexual objects who experience sexual pleasure in being raped; as sexual objects tied or cut up or mutilated or bruised or physically hurt; in postures of sexual submission or sexual servility, including inviting penetration; women's body parts — including but not limited to vaginas, breasts and buttocks — are exhibited, such that women are reduced to those parts; as whores by nature; being penetrated by objects or animals; in scenarios of degradation, injury, torture, shown as filthy or inferior, bleeding, bruised, or hurt in a context that makes these conditions sexual' (Catherine MacKinnon and Andrea Dworkin, in Cheris Kramerae and Paula Treichler, 1985). The link between pornography and VIOLENCE has been made by many feminists, and although the direct connection (pornography leads to violence against women) can be questioned, the oppressive OBJECTIFICATION common to both cannot be denied. It is important to recognise that the extreme right have their own definition of pornography — roughly 'any depiction of uninhibited nakedness or sexual activity' — which is not compatible with that of the women's movement. The relative importance of pornography in the OPPRESSION of women has recently threatened to create rifts in some parts of the women's movement: 'Pornography seems to me a very tricky issue merely from the point of view of tactics, and we might do well to direct our anger elsewhere, at least for a while. Not only is feeling about this issue very divided in the women's community, it's an issue that is bound to be misperceived by the culture at large as anti-sexual no matter how many declarations we make to the contrary . . . The best cure for pornography is sex — I mean autonomously chosen activity, freely engaged in for the sake of real pleasure, intense,

and unmistakably the real thing. The more we have experiences like this, the less we will be taken in by the confusions and lies and messes all around us' (Joanna Russ, 1985).

Portfolio Job
[1985]
A lifestyle and way of earning your living by doing a variety of paid and unpaid work instead of relying on one job and one source of income (should you be so lucky as to have one). 'Many people have shied away from the one-basket approach and have tended to put together a portfolio of activities and relationships, each of which makes its own contribution to the package of things we want out of work and life. Will the portfolio approach become more common as we are forced to be less dependent on fading jobs?' (Charles Handy, 1985).

Position
[14c. *L ponere*, to lay down]
A point of view with a nasty tendency to become a fixed opinion. PERSPECTIVE is more useful.

Positional Goods
[1976]
Things that have value to their owners only if they are not possessed or intruded upon by others — a cottage on an unspoilt beach, a Picasso, the managing directorship of a large firm. The idea of 'positional goods' contradicts (even in capitalist terms) the idea that more growth and consumption is always a good thing.

Positive
[14c. *L positivus*, dogmatic; from *ponere*, to lay down]
Believing that things can get better; affirming your power; tending to say yes rather than no. 'Opposition to the arms race, racism, sexism, injustice, and the centralised state must be coupled with the creation of positive alternatives. This means initiating and supporting moves for decentralisation and autonomy, such as local energy groups, shared child-care and education, self-help health groups, and workers' co-operatives. It means taking responsibility for our own lives, fighting our own sexism and racism, and our own dependence on the state' (*Peace News*, 1981).

Positive Discrimination
[1967]
(*also* 'reverse discrimination')
Choosing a person or people from an oppressed group for a job or a place in preference to members of a privileged group, even if the latter is better qualified (remembering that 'qualification' often comes with

privilege), in an attempt to redress the balance of opportunity. People who favour positive discrimination generally see it as a temporary measure which a more egalitarian society will render unnecessary, but an essential mechanism in a society in which privileged people will not readily give up their power. *See also* TOKENISM.

Positive Feedback
[1934]
FEEDBACK which tends to exaggerate a process; it can either lead a system to run out of control, or in a sluggish process it can stimulate renewed activity. The concept of part of CYBERNETIC theory, used both in the sciences and psychology. Using 'feedback' in the sense of helpful CRITICISM, 'positive feedback' implies compliments and congratulation.

Possession
[14c. *L possidere*, to own or occupy]
The belief that a person can own something and have complete control over it. Green-thinkers prefer to think in terms of STEWARDSHIP or TRUSTEESHIP, especially in relation to natural resources such as land and water. 'Every superfluous possession is a limitation upon my freedom' (Henry Thoreau, quoted in Rudolf Bahro, 1986). Possession is also implicit in the way human beings relate to each other: 'my wife', 'my husband' and 'my children' are often not so very different from 'my car' and 'my house'. Some humanistic psychotherapists (particularly those who take account of the work of Carl Rogers, known as Rogerian therapy) use the terms 'non-possessive warmth' and 'non-possessive love' to describe the strong links between two people who are important to each other and yet want to acknowledge their autonomy. *See also* AFFLUENCE, CONSUMPTION, LAND OWNERSHIP, PROPERTY.

Post-Industrial
[1947]
A society in which manufacturing industry no longer dominates the economy. This has the most profound effects in those areas of Western countries which since the nineteeenth century have been dependent on manufacturing, and where issues like high UNEMPLOYMENT and DERELICTION need to be acknowledged and addressed.

Postpatriarchal
[1984]
A vision of a society in which sexist oppression has been abolished or at least reduced to a minimum (*see also* NON-SEXIST, SEXISM): 'Since the [German] Greens oppose all exploitation of women in patriarchal society, their official programmes are unequivocally nonsexist, and the party is committed to the goal of a postpatriarchal future' (Fritjof Capra and Charlene Spretnak, 1984).

Potential

[14c. *L potentia*, power]

Something which is possible but has not yet happened; the possibilities latent within human beings and societies. It usually refers to positive and life-enhancing possibilities (as in 'human potential'), though it is important to remember that many futures which are possible are not desirable — 'potential for development' can go either way.

Poverty

[before 12c. *L pauper*, poor]

Having inadequate resources; being poor or in need. All poverty is relative, but whichever way it is viewed, the distribution of resources, both nationally and internationally, is desperately unequal — and the gaps are widening. 'Poverty is self-sustaining and self-generating, a trap that holds about one billion people, nearly a fifth of the world's population. In general, the poor in the North can at least survive, through a safety net of social services (although not all-embracing). Their poverty can be seen as "extreme social deprivation". In the South, however, the term "absolute poverty" is the only one applicable. Even if they survive a malnourished childhood, hundreds of millions will never have the opportunity to realize their full human potential. All the routes out of the trap are firmly shut, because of lack of education, technical aid or credit, employment, sanitation or safe water, access to health services, transport or communication' (Norman Myers, 1985). Even in a country like Britain the inequalities in WEALTH are enormous — before government subsidy the richest 20% of families in 1983 had an average income of 155 times that of the average of the poorest 20%; even after subsidies and taxes the average was 4 times as much — and these are averages (*Social Trends*, 1986). Figures for countries and income groups mask the fact that it is always women, children and old people who control fewer resources than men — more than a third of all households in countries as different as Denmark and Zimbabwe, Jamaica and Vietnam are single women with children, and they are almost invariably among the poorest. 'Poverty is rapidly becoming feminized' (Joni Seager and Ann Olson, 1986). When assessing poverty, it is important to keep in mind the idea of BASIC NEEDS; we live in a world where poverty is balanced against excessive AFFLUENCE, and Western observers can too easily over-react when faced with a traditonal society which is 'poor' in consumer goods yet extremely rich in other ways: 'The *force-vitale* of the whole human pageant made shocking nonsense of her preconception of the misery of poverty. In such places [the street markets of Lagos], poverty in monetary terms is an ever-present reality, widespread enough to be the general rule. But we must be careful not to fall into the western trap of equating everything with money, and giving every form of worth and wealth a monetary value' (Marcus Linear, 1985).

Poverty Trap
[1972]
The trap of being poor and never having enough resources to lift yourself out of it; more specifically, a situation that arises when means-tested government benefits cease when a person's income reaches a certain level, so that any increase in earnings is offset by a loss of benefit — a particular problem in Britain. Several suggestions have been made for schemes whereby benefits could be 'insulated' so they would not simply be taken away when income reached a certain level, but be decreased gradually as income increased. These suggestions have had little impact, despite the Conservative government's stated policy of reducing unemployment. 'Insulation of benefits might . . . cost very little if it did indeed encourage more people progressively to work themselves out of the benefit system. All it would require is a change of attitude, a change from thinking of "maintenance" to thinking of "investment", from "society's charity" to "the individual's right"' (Charles Handy, 1985).

Power
[13c. *L posse*, to be able]
The strength in us — too often suppressed and denied — to be in control of our lives, and having recognised our personal power, to have a real say in the decisions that affect us, our community, and the world we live in. 'Power' is also a synonym for 'control', 'power over', the meaning given to it by the oppressive regimes that presently dominate politics — some more despotically than others. The reclaiming of personal power is central to green thinking. This involves a growing awareness of power structures (politicisation), dealing with feelings of POWERLESSNESS, the conscious release of PRIVILEGE (though opinion varies as to whether this is possible), and the development of egalitarian processes and structures for group decision-making. Since every aspect of our lives is bound up in limiting power structures, the reclaiming of power leaves few stones unturned — becoming assertive can involve exploring everything from our body language to the way we play with children, from the way we deal with criticism to our involvement in political action. 'The old concept of power, in which most of us have been socialized, originated in a particular world view. This view . . . saw reality as composed of discrete and separate entities. . . Power came to be seen as a property of these separate entities, reflected in the way they could appear to push each other about. It became identified with domination, [or] power-over. . . It fosters the notion . . . that power

involves invulnerability. To be strong, to keep from being pushed around, defenses are needed. Armor and rigidity are needed, so as not to let oneself be influenced or changed. From the systems perspective, this patriarchal notion of power is both inaccurate and dysfunctional. . . Life processes are intrinsically self-organizing and evolve through the dynamic and symbiotic interaction of open systems. Power, then, which is the ability to effect change, works not from the top down, but from the bottom up. It is not power-over, but power-with' (Joanna Macy, 1983). 'Some women react to being called powerful with alarm — assuming that being powerful means being domineering or threatening. We confuse power with oppression, having power *over* someone else. The assertive meaning of power is not the power of intimidation but power that comes through finding and being yourself' (Anne Dickson, 1982). 'Power' also refers to ENERGY — both the sort of energy that lights our buildings and powers our machinery, and to the power of the universe, of which our personal power is part: 'The wealthiest magnate on Earth cannot make an apple no matter how he might stand in the sun or squat and contort his flesh. He does not have the power of an apple tree to make apples and neither does anyone else. He can own them. He can fence them, transport them, plant and prune them; he can bulldoze them, line them up in military formation, poison them, grind them up, bore them to death, set fire to them, graft them and use them; and this is *control*. He can never, from the substance of his body, make an apple as an apple tree can; this is *power*' (Judy Grahn, 1981, in Charlene Spretnak (ed), 1982).

Powerlessness
[17c. *Old English poerlas*, powerless]
Having your POWER denied; being oppressed. OPPRESSION leads to feelings of helplessness, and the mute fatalism that the ruling class prefers in underlings, despite their protestations of democracy and equality. 'To an overwhelming extent [powerlessness] is the result of the long-time systematic operation of the oppressive societies. These, in their nature, reserve *apparent* power only for a small number of rulers, slaveowners, nobles, owning-class people, but deny any *real* power to everyone. The ruling-class person, accepting the role of "pseudo-power" and resulting rewards, is as much a captive of the oppressive society's structure and conditioning as anyone. The societies systematically bludgeon any aspiration to power or even to protest out of the great majority of the population. It resorts to condemnation, persecution, imprisonment, or even death for those individuals whose hurts leave them with patterns of rigid rebellion instead of rigid cooperation' (Harvey Jackins, 1983). To break out of the cycle of powerlessness, those people who presently control resources must choose (or in

the minds of many, must if necessary be forced) to share decision-making, and we must refuse to accept powerlessness as a fact of life. 'We have two choices: to lend our weight to the forces that indoctrinate women to passivity, self-depreciation, and a sense of powerlessness; or consider what we have to work against. . . And this means, first of all, taking ourselves seriously . . . I would suggest that not biology, but ignorance of our selves, has been the key to our powerlessness' (Adrienne Rich, 1979).

Practice
[15c. *Gk prattein*, to do, practise]
What we actually do (which may or may not be what we believe, what we think we do, or what we think we ought to do). The integration of THEORY and practice is central to green thinking, remembering always that each person's actions are ultimately their choice and responsibility, and can be accepted and respected even when they seem not to correspond with their theory, or with our own theory and practice.

Pragmatism
[1864. *Gk pragma*, act]
Making decisions and acting purely on the basis of current considerations, without resorting to theory or dogma. Pragmatism involves INTUITION and FLEXIBILITY; if we are not aware of our motives it may mean acting from DISTRESS.

Prana
(*see* BREATH, LIFE FORCE)

Present
[14c. *L praeesse*, to be before one]
Now; the time we actually live in, the result of the PAST and the preparation for the FUTURE, and the only time in which we can affect things directly. Humanistic psychologists stress the importance of learning to live in the present, when many people (in the West at least, where the opportunity exists) tend to dwell on the past or save up for the future. Some see the experience of complete 'now-ness' as a rare but beautiful 'peak experience': 'ordinary ecstasy' (John Rowan, 1976). Unresolved hurt and PAIN from the past often stops us from being fully present, and it is only through CONSCIOUSNESS-RAISING and dealing with the FEELINGS associated with that pain that the past can be left behind. 'Presence' is also a synonym for ATTENTION.

Preservation
[17c in this sense. *L praeservare*, to make safe in advance]
Protecting; keeping safe from harm. In some senses, as in the preservation of buildings and other objects, 'preservation' is synonymous with

CONSERVATION, though 'preservation' often implies keeping things just as they are, which in natural systems ignores the importance of dynamic balance or HOMEOSTASIS — green-thinkers fighting to protect wilderness and habitat need to be aware of the distinction when accused of being 'preservationists' and not acknowledging the need for change. 'Preservation' of nature, although the basic concept behind the first national parks and nature reserves, has given way to 'nature conservation' along with the growing recognition that human beings must work within ecosystems and not from outside them, and that the purpose of conservation is as much for the sake of what is being conserved as it is for the human enjoyment of it.

Preservative
(*see* ADDITIVE)

Pressure Group
[1928]
A number of people with a similar concern (such as an environmental organisation, a trades union or an anti-nuclear group) who work together to influence politicians and administrators, providing information, proposing policies and legislation, and if necessary organising actions in order to communicate their concern. *See also* PARTY.

Preventive
[1870 in this sense. *L praevenire*, to come before, anticipate]
(*also* 'preventative')
Timely action which helps us to avoid problems. Used particularly in HEALING to describe steps that can be taken to avoid potential health problems, or to stop early symptoms becoming chronic. Bureaucratic administrative systems and accounting systems which count increased production of drugs, pollutants and clean-up machinery as 'healthy growth' militate against preventive action, which means that we are nearly always dealing with chronic ill health, whether it be of human beings or of ecosystems.

Pricing
[13c. *L pretium*, price]
Setting money values to goods and services, a privilege of those who control such resources. *See* MONEY, MULTINATIONAL, TRANSFER PRICING, VALUE, WORTH.

Primal
(*see* BIRTH, BIRTH TRAUMA)

Primary Health Care
[*c*.1960]
The provision of basic HEALING skills, remedies and equipment within the COMMUNITY or locality. An emphasis on drugs and medical technology means that primary care is often overlooked, a particular problem in the THIRD WORLD but of increasing concern elsewhere. 'Despite the large expenditures on health, and the technical feasibility of dealing with many of the most common health problems, efforts to improve health have only had a modest impact on the vast majority of the population in most developing countries. . . Health activities have overemphasised sophisticated, hospital-based care, mainly in the urban centres, while neglecting preventive public health programmes and simple primary care provided at conveniently located facilities' (Marilyn Carr, 1985). *See also* BAREFOOT DOCTOR, HEALTH.

Primary Productivity
[1953]
The total YIELD of growing plant organisms, which is globally estimated at around 160,000,000,000 tonnes per year. 44% is formed by trees, 35% in the oceans, 10% by grassland, 6% on cultivated land, 3% in fresh water and 2% in desert and semi-arid regions.

Prior Informed Consent
[1985]
Ensuring that the purchaser of a potentially dangerous product knows about the hazards before agreeing to buy; used particularly of PESTICIDES being exported to Third World Countries, a provision made in FAO (Food and Agriculture Organisation) guidelines in 1985: 'Under the proposed FAO scheme, exporting governments would prohibit shipments of a pesticide until they had received notice from the government of the importing state that it had not only received full information of the ecological and health implications of the chemical, and of the regulations governing its use in the country of manufacture, but that it still wanted the shipment to proceed' (Chris Rose, in Edward Goldsmith and Nicholas Hildyard (ed), 1986).

Priority
[1917 in this sense. *L prior*, previous]
Deciding the order in which to do things. Choosing what priority to give to things acknowledges that some things are more important than others, that some things are best done in a particular order, and that a clear sense of priorities makes it possible to concentrate fully on each thing as it arises.

Privacy
[15c. *L privatus*, withdrawn from public life]
Choosing when you want company, and when you want space and silence: a choice denied to most people most of the time, but essential for serious self-exploration. The problem is two-edged — how to be alone when you want, and how not to be alone when you want company. 'A precious ingredient of the past is in danger of rapid extinction: privacy, that marvelous compound of withdrawal, self-reliance, solitude, quiet, contemplation, and concentration' (Serge Chermayeff and Christopher Alexander, 1963). 'The privacy of the family is cast in a new light if we realize that a quarter of reported violent crime is wife-assault' (Michèle Barrett and Mary McIntosh, 1982).

Private Property
(*see* PROPERTY)

Privilege
[before 12c. *L privilegium*, the law relating to the rights of the individual]
Having what you need and, if you control those resources, making sure you continue to get what you need, even if it means depriving and manipulating other people, maintaining privilege by systematic OPPRESSION and denial of basic rights to the unprivileged. 'We are rare and precious, because we are alive, because we can think. We are privileged to live, to influence and control our future. I believe we have an obligation to fight for that life, to struggle not just for ourselves, but for all those creatures who came before us and to whom we are beholden, and for all those who, if we are wise enough, will come after' (Carl Sagan, in Dennis Paulson (ed), 1986). 'The oppressors do not perceive their monopoly of *having more* as a privilege which dehumanizes others and themselves' (Paulo Friere, 1970).

Problem
[14c. *Gk proballein*, to throw forward]
Something which is or appears to be difficult to deal with. In relation to current environmental and economic trends, 'problem' in the mouths of politicians usually means 'something we're thinking about but don't have any hope of changing'. Calling something a problem can make it one; some people prefer to think in terms of CHALLENGE, believing that there is an important lesson to be learnt from each 'problem' we face. 'The only fundamentally unsolved problem in this unsteady interregnum between imperial ages which may be dying and a planetary society which struggles to be born is whether the rich and fortunate are imaginative enough and the resentful and underprivileged poor patient enough to begin to establish a true foundation of better sharing, fuller

co-operation, and joint planetary work. . . In short, no problem is insoluble in the creation of a balanced and conserving planet save humanity itself' (Barbara Ward, 1979).

Process
[14c. *L procedere*, to proceed]
An overused and imprecise word, implying simply that whatever is happening is taking place over an extended length of time. In green and alternative parlance, it often means the interactions between members of a group (also called 'group dynamics' or 'group process'). 'The most serious internal problem the Green party faces is what humanistic psychologists have termed "bad process". In the American peace movement, for example, it is used to describe the dynamics of an affinity group that does not communicate well and function well together' (Fritjof Capra and Charlene Spretnak, 1984).

Production
[15c. *L producere*, to lead forward]
What is created by part of a system; thus a factory produces goods and its output is a product. An ecosystem produces biomass, and we call the end results which can be used directly by human beings agricultural products. In ecological or systems terms, however, this process is more usefully seen as transformation rather than production, turning one set of resources into another. By calling some things 'production', others 'by-products', others WASTE, and ignoring yet others completely, conventional economic accounting ignores — at its peril — the ecological principle that everything must go somewhere.

Productivity
[*L producere*, to lead forward]
(1) [1899] In economics, the 'efficiency' of a process measured in terms of the amount of input against amount of output. A concept that suffers from all the failings of economic accounting and ignores ecological principles. Thus 'productivity' increases if you can afford to ignore the destination of toxic waste, or if you employ one person to test for flaws rather than two. 'The vested interests in increasing productivity are tremendous, and for that reason the system *needs* people who have the following characteristics: they should be able to see the necessity of high productivity, but also be blind to the following: Point One: international politics; Point Two: history; Point Three: culture; Point Four: nature; Point Five: human beings. If you're blind on all these five but very perceptive on productivity, then you have the key to a career' (Johann Galtung, *Resurgence*, March/April 1981).
(2) [1908] In ecology, another name for YIELD (*see also* PRIMARY PRODUCTIVITY).

Profit

[14c. *L proficere*, to advance]

Ways of creating MONEY in a capitalist economy, usually by manipulating the money value of resources. Economics and accounting have various ways of assessing profit, from gross profit to super-normal profit, but they all depend on the assumption that money value really means something. It does, of course, in terms of what it will buy, but in ecological terms 'profit' in this sense has no meaning, and 'there's no such thing as a free lunch' applies with a vengeance. Ignoring the real value of things that have no price tag, the emphasis on money as the only real wealth keeps the stock exchanges rolling, making yet more imaginary wealth (profit) out of the imaginary wealth which is already enjoyed by the rich few, giving them yet more purchasing power and reducing the resources available to the majority of people yet further. Profit is sometimes justified on the grounds that all sustainable systems need a surplus for 're-investment'; the difference between 'profit' and the seeds of future security is easy to distinguish, however — 'profit' is the one that ends up in the pockets of the privileged. Many green businesses, recognising the iniquity and inequity of private profit, operate consciously as not-for-profit (more accurately 'non-profit-distributing') enterprises. *See also* DEBT CRISIS.

Progress

[*c*.1700 in this sense. *L progredi*, to advance]

Increasing awareness and understanding, change for the better. Green-thinkers need to be wary of the subversion of this important idea: 'progress' in our growth-oriented and materialistic culture is usually used in a very narrow sense. 'The typically Western concept of progress can be characterised as . . .: pragmatic because [it] is mainly preoccupied with material gains and practical improvements for the immediate future; empiricist because the world is viewed . . . as basically made of physical parts interacting in a mechanical fashion; scientistic because the laws of physical science are thought to be of supreme importance . . ; exploitative because the natural resources and subtle balances of the ecosystem have been taken for granted. . .; elitist because this progress has actually benefited very few at the expense of the very many, and at the expense of natural resources belonging to all' (Henryk Skolimowski, *The Ecologist*, 1979). 'No civilisation prior to the European had occasion to believe in the systematic material progress of the whole human race; no civilisation drove itself so relentlessly to an ever-receding goal; no civilisation was so passion-charged to replace what is with what could be; no civilisation had striven as the West has done to direct the world according to its will; no civilisation has known so few moments of peace and tranquillity' (W. Woodruff, 1967). 'The ultimate value judgement upon which technological society rests — progress conceived as the further development and expansion of the artificial environment necessarily at the expense of the natural world — must be looked upon from the ecological perspective as unequivocal regress' (George Sessions, *Journal of Environmental Education*, 1983). 'We reject all "progress" in the wrong direction' (Rudolf Bahro, 1986). 'Scientific and technological progress is cloaked in a kind of fatality. When states decide to make supersonic aeroplanes in order to gain three hours in the New York-Paris hop — even though the time saved might be lost in the bottleneck between the airport and the centre of town — those responsible in both the public and private sectors can only reply with the meaningless phrase, "You can't stop progress"' (Raymond Aron, 1968).

Project
[*L pro(j)icere*, to throw forth]
(1) [1916] A specific (usually practical) task undertaken by a group of people. 'Projects to undertake: . . . Make sure there are a variety of tasks for people to choose from — indoor ones such as fund-raising and research, and outdoor ones involving survey work' (Angela King and Sue Clifford, 1985). 'If twenty people are sufficiently committed to a project, they can draw in two hundred more. This is big enough for a self-managing, self-caring social community' (Rudolf Bahro, 1984).
(2) [1969] A large-scale engineering scheme; such schemes are often seen as great technological wonders (*see* TECHNOFIX), but usually create far more problems than they solve. It has been this sort of scheme that the rich countries have chosen to finance in the THIRD WORLD with 'foreign aid' (thus 'aid project'), knowing full well that such a project will need massive material and expert input from the West, and will continue to stimulate Western-style development for many years to come, requiring continuing and expanding economic dependence.

Projection
[*L pro(j)icere*, to throw forth]
(1) [1896] Transferring aspects of yourself that you find difficult to accept on to another person, thereby coming to believe that they actually possess these attributes. When the person involved is a therapist it is usually called 'transference'. 'Another way we often avoid taking responsibility for our own feelings is by projecting onto other people qualities or emotions which are in fact our own: "You're very competitive"; "You don't seem to like me"; . . In a therapy group, when you make remarks like this, people usually encourage you to "own" what you are actually feeling yourself and make some statement about yourself rather than about the other person. For example, if Ann says to

Betty "You're very competitive", what she should really be saying may be "*I* feel competitive with *you*". The woman who says "You don't like me" often really means "*I* don't like *you*"' (Sheila Ernst and Lucy Goodison, 1981). *See also* SHADOW.
(2) [1952] A forecast of future TRENDS, based on past and current experience and assumptions about the FUTURE. An unspoken law of economic projections is that the graph must always rise; only recently has the reality of recession begun to bite (*see* GROWTH). Population projections are a favourite of ecologists; those of human POPULATION show continued rapid increase for many parts of the world, but the fact that this is not universal, even in areas once thought to be heading for demographic disaster like China, shows that there is nothing inevitable about projections — they are indicators of what might happen, nothing more (and nothing less). The 1972 *Limits to Growth* report of the Club of Rome used computer modelling to make linked projections of a range of ecological concerns, and as such modelling has become more sophisticated, projections are able to take account of more complexity. It is still wise to bear in mind that useful though projections might be, they will almost always prove to be wrong.

Property
[*14c. L proprius*, your own]
In legal terms, something which you have 'the exclusive right to possess, enjoy and dispose of'. In green thinking a distinction is often made between STEWARDSHIP or TRUSTEESHIP (looking after something, being responsible for its careful use and being generous in sharing it) and ownership (having exclusive control of something and denying anybody else access to it). It is the latter sense that the nineteenth century French socialist Pierre Proudhon had in mind when he wrote in his 1840 pamphlet *What is Property?* that 'property is theft'. Many NATIVE PEOPLES have no concept of ownership of things beyond their own immediate belongings, particularly of LAND OWNERSHIP. In practical terms, the more and larger things that are owned, and particularly when ownership exceeds BASIC NEEDS, current Western ideas about property part company with green philosophy. It is bad enough that in a country like Britain, 54% of the marketable 'wealth' is owned by 10% of the population; viewed globally it is iniquitous that the *average* American owns (in money terms) sixty times as much as the average Bangladeshi. Green-thinkers are especially concerned about the 'ownership' of natural resources which are the common heritage of all living things, especially with the prevailing philosophy that once something is your property you can do whatever you want with it. Two thirds of the world's banana seed, for example, is 'owned' by one company; four individuals 'own' half a million acres (6%) of the Scottish Highlands.

The Economic Programme of the German Green Party (die Grünen) says very clearly that 'property in the hands of private individuals — as well as in those of the state — must no longer be permitted to result in control over human beings, the destruction of nature, and the direction of the economy, the society, and of politics. . . The problem is not necessarily surplus value or profit, but . . . control' (quoted in Fritjof Capra and Charlene Spretnak, 1984). 'Private property seems to me to be in a kind of crisis, because how can you expect people to defend the principle if they don't own any of the substance? What's private property to somebody who doesn't have any property?' (Wendell Berry, in Art Kleiner and Stewart Brand (ed), 1986). In general terms, green-thinkers favour decentralised community control of the use of resources considered to be common heritage, rather than the appropriation or nationalisation often favoured by socialists.

Proportional Representation
[1870]
An electoral system in which each party is represented in a legislative body according to the proportion of votes cast by the electorate. Although many systems follow the general principle, the term covers a wide variety of methods of translating votes into seats. In some (in Ireland for example) the system used is the single transferable vote, which enables the voter to choose which individuals she or he prefers; in others (such as West Germany and Israel) the voter votes for a party, and each party decides who will represent it. In general PR is a much more equitable system of representation than the first-past-the-post system used in countries like the USA and the UK, but still begs many questions in terms of real PARTICIPATION and REPRESENTATION.

Prostitution
[1553. *L prostituere*, to set out in public]
Selling your body for money, usually to fulfil the buyer's sexual fantasies. Most prostitutes are women, and virtually all 'clients' men, making it clear that prostitution typefies the subject-object relationship between men and women, and that men have the power to purchase and use women (*see* PORNOGRAPHY, POSSESSION). While a man who buys the services of a prostitute is operating from a distorted idea about human needs, he may have convinced himself that this is the only way to get what he wants, and some people (including many prostitutes) believe that if this is the case and he is willing to pay for it, it is one way of diverting wealth from those who have it to those who need it. This does not detract from the fact that prostitution is an enormous health risk, mostly for prostitutes, and that much of the money that changes hands goes into the pockets of male pimps and property owners. 'Sex

tourism' is a rapidly growing phenomenon, especially in South-East Asia, where it is a large part of the economy of cities like Bangkok: 'The women who are offered up for these sex tours are often kept in conditions of near slavery. . . Many of the prostitutes are children: there are an estimated 30,000 prostitutes in Bangkok under the age of 16' (Joni Seager and Ann Olson, 1986). Despite its 'acceptance' by PATRIARCHY, prostitution is more or less technically illegal in most countries, thus putting prostitutes out of the reach or help of the law.

Protection
[14c. *L protegere*, to cover the front]
Keeping something safe, including your own integrity (*see* SELF-DEFENCE, TRUST). Often used synonymously with PRESERVATION, or even CONSERVATION, as in the British Royal Society for the Protection of Birds (RSPB). Also, however, used to mean 'defence' and 'doing down the competition' (*see* PROTECTIONISM). In the USA, the term 'protected groups' means women, ethnic and racial minorities, veterans and differently-abled people who are the subject of equal opportunity programmes, and 'protective legislation' supposedly protects women from 'heavy work', thus bolstering the belief that women need protection because of their biological attributes, not support because of the excesses of patriarchy.

Protectionism
[1844]
The control of international trade (by way of tariffs and QUOTAS) in order to 'protect' domestic industry. Originally introduced to ensure continued home production in case foreign sources were cut off, later to protect the imaginary 'balance of payments'. Protectionism has started to backfire on the rich world as some Third World countries start a process of DELINKING their economies with those of the West. *See also* BOYCOTT.

Protest
[15c. *L protestari*, to make a formal declaration]
Making it clear that you don't like what is going on. Making a noise, singing, getting in the way (*see* ACTION). Yet protest, important though it is, is usually treated by authority as an attack, and the ensuing entrenchment rarely leads to change. 'We have protested and we have survived. But non-stop protest becomes exhausting, and mere survival is a poor fruit for "advanced" civilization to bear — a passing on of the present time's crisis unresolved to the next generation' (Dan Smith and E.P. Thompson (ed.), 1987). Effective protest includes honest COMMUNICATION, LISTENING as well as shouting, SUBVERSION, GAMES, PRACTICE that squares with THEORY, and above all, HOPE.

Psychiatry

[1846. *Gk psukhe + iatros*, doctor of the soul]

Medical approaches to psychological, emotional and mental health. Being part of mainstream medicine, psychiatry works on the 'dysfunction' model of health, attempting to find out exactly what it is that has 'gone wrong', and using drugs to 'cure' it (*see* MENTAL ILLNESS). Modern psychiatry is trying hard to adapt to a more eclectic and multidisciplinary approach, but non-medical PSYCHOTHERAPY is rapidly gaining ground. The developmment of groups like 'People Not Psychiatry' in London in the 1970s, a growing concern about legal definitions of 'diminished responsibility', and dissatisfaction with the arbitrary labelling and medicalisation of people who simply want to be listened to, have all led to the 'profession' of psychiatry feeling very threatened. On the other hand, a quick dose of a drug costs less than a course of psychotherapy, supressing problems takes less time than unearthing them, and in times of recession these considerations alone may guarantee psychiatry a future. In the USA psychoanalysts and even psychotherapists are sometimes popularly called 'psychiatrists', though there is an important difference in approach.

Psychology

[1653. *Gk psukhe + logos*, words about the soul]

The study of human behaviour. Psychology still likes to think of itself as a SCIENCE, and like other scientists, psychologists still mostly behave (even if it doesn't match with their personal experience and beliefs) as if their discipline were objective and value-free: 'Psychology, as one of the compartmentalised disciplines of the social sciences, isolates the individual from his or her social/historical/economic context and assumes that in so doing it can validly study the behavior of the individual in all societies for all times' (Miriam Greenspan, 1983). Since the area of study is human beings, this is even more nonsensical than similar beliefs held by physicists, chemists and biologists. This is not to deny the importance of the endeavour — seeing how people behave and understanding that behaviour — but it does question many of psychology's basic assumptions: the neutrality of the observer, the objective existence of norms, an emphasis on 'abnormality', and the usefulness of psychological tests. 'Thus our [feminist] endeavours to re-orient psychology are limited by the impoverishment of the discipline as traditionally practised. Feminists and non-feminists have churned out research (and to a lesser extent theory) which has had the result of making the psychology of women just another topic . . . This co-option . . . has diverted attention away from . . . the redefinition of both theory and practice, [which] would involve an assault on the nature of the scientific method as used by psychologists, a rejection of psychological practice which preserves the status quo in favour of a more flexible alternative' (Beverly Walker, in Dale Spender (ed.), 1981).

Psychotherapy
[1850. *Gk psukhe* + *therapeia*, attention to the soul]
Any or all of a range of techniques designed to give a person ATTENTION and to help them understand what is going on in and around them; often referred to simply as THERAPY. Since psychotherapy has its roots in PSYCHOLOGY and PSYCHIATRY it can suffer from excessive pseudo-objectivity parading as 'expertise', 'a Father Knows Best approach to psychotherapy' (Miriam Greenspan, 1983); this is not helped by the fact that the majority of therapists are men and the majority of clients women. Very many people (in the Western world at least) have nevertheless gained a great deal from psychotherapy, and if a technique and a therapist are chosen with care, it can be enormously beneficial in assisting a person to rediscover their power and creativity. *See also* COUNSELLING, SELF-HELP.

Public
[15c. *L populus*, the people]
Available (at least in theory) to everybody. 'Public' does not, however, imply that whatever is provided is what the public want or in the form they want it; 'the public interest' is usually defined by a vocal and persuasive elitist minority, a minority who can often afford to by-pass 'public services' and buy better private ones. This ever-widening split between minority and majority means that it becomes 'in the public interest' to dispense with public transport, to spend far less per child on public education (known as 'state education' in Britain) than on private education (known rather surprisingly in Britain as 'public schools'), and to treat public health problems as a thing of the past at the same time as pollution increases. In Britain, a 'public enquiry' is part of the planning process where large projects such as nuclear power stations and motorways are discussed to see whether they should proceed or not — though they often become show trials rather than real exercises in public PARTICIPATION. The question is, who decides what the public really wants, and do the public really have any say in the way that decisions are made?

Purism
[1803. *L purus*, untainted]
Rigid adherence to a particular belief or practice, guaranteed to blind you to other possibilities and to stifle communication with anyone who disagrees with you. Purism arises in green circles whenever a particular solution — whether it be vegetarianism or herbs or natural birth control — is seen as the *only* solution. The green line is always FLEXIBILITY together with APPROPRIATENESS.

Purpose
[13c. *L proponere*, to propose]
A conscious intention or GOAL; the answer to the important question 'Why are we doing what we are?' 'Purpose' is also a synonym for 'meaning', and green-thinkers believe that the universe — including the earth and the natural systems it comprises — has a deep purpose which we do not have to understand fully in order to recognise and appreciate it, since we are an integral part of it.

Putdown
[1926]
An oppressive and humiliating remark, often made in response to an important point. A way of communicating that has no place in green discourse, but still appears with alarming regularity.

Quality
[13c. *L qualis*, of what kind]
An essential part of the character of something or somebody, to be respected as such and not unnecessarily harmed. Around 1600 the word was being used to mean 'accomplishment', 'attainment', 'nobility', whence it became inextricably associated with superiority. 'Quality of life' (meaning overall fulfilment) was first used by the British writer J.B. Priestley in 1943, and the American politician Adlai Stevenson first contrasted the quality and quantity of American life in 1955. The two aspects of quality — the innate and the value-laden — still confuse current thinking. It is important to recognise that natural things (in the sense of things not made by human beings and their technology) have qualities and quality simply by virtue of their existence and interconnection. Human beings may see further qualities in them (usefulness, profitability), but to exploit those qualities in an unaware way is to have no respect for the innate qualities of nature. Ecological thinking recognises that there is often a trade-off between quality and quantity — with a given resource base you can either have a lot of poor-quality growth or a little high-quality growth; growth economists have been slow in learning that this applies to all systems.

Quantity
[14c. *L quantus*, how much]
An amount or number of something. Knowing how many and how much is a favourite human occupation, and often blinds us to the variety of the things we are counting, and to the purpose of counting in the first place. On the other hand, knowing how many and how much is crucial when it comes to acknowledging the damage we are doing to the biosphere. A balance between measuring and taking action is important in all campaigns. 'We play with numbers. Charming and sweet, we play

little games with them, these figures. They are pale reflections, without the gravity of being the potato, the glacier, the growth of lichen, the feather of an egret, the flecks in the iris of the eye, cracks in the dried clay of soil or the shed shell of a turtle, all of which they quantify, from which all they derive, the material forms whose awesome processes these numbers merely imitate, making simpler dramas with which we rest our minds, and in this bloodless theatre of mathematics our hearts are eased. We are able to see the inevitablity of process, count the days until our deaths, number the generations before and after, calculate the future colors of the eyes of our progeny, for numbers allow us, for moments, to objectify our own existence, which we know we cannot do to the potato or the glacier or the egret, the turtle nor the eye that meets us like our own with all its beautiful and its terrible knowledge of survival, the eye attached by ganglia and arteries through the brain's cortex down the spine even to the flesh of a foot that edges bare over the earth, feeling the hard outline of a crack on the clay surface' (Susan Griffin, 1984). 'We long ago accepted Descartes' picture of a mechanistic universe totally understandable in terms of mathematical logic. The only real difference . . . today is that we view life more appropriately as being made up of informational flows and computable programmes rather than mechanistic parts. We still remain convinced, however, that we can quantify our way to the truth of existence' (Jeremy Rifkin, 1985). We need to learn to use numbers so they cease to frighten us, but always to remember their limitations.

Quantum Theory
[1911]
The idea that sub-atomic particles (including the radiant energy of light) exist simultaneously both as waves and as particles, thus shattering the idea of atoms as fixed lumps of matter. Quantum theory, along with relativity theory, helped to bring physics from a mechanistic view of the world to a much more holistic approach; a view of the physical world in which the stress is on interconnectedness, and any hope for absolute scientific certainty has been banished for ever (*see* BOOTSTRAP APPROACH, NEW PHYSICS, PARADOX, REALITY, SCIENCE).

Queer
[1922 in this sense. Probably from *German quer*, crosswise, crooked]
Strange, different, threatening — hence used as an oppressive synonym for 'homosexual' (*see* HOMOSEXUALITY).

Question
[14c. *L quaerere*, to seek, ask]
Asking about something you don't know or don't understand; an obvious thing to do, but demeaned by the frequent insistence on giving

lies as answers, insulting the questioner, or refusing to answer. 'I feel myself clearly bigger than I used to. The difference is QUESTION EVERYTHING' (Su Negrin, 1972).

Quota

[1618. *L quota (pars)*, how large (a part)]

A carefully-worked-out share of an available resource or resources, designed to provide everybody with what they need while permitting the continuation of a sustainable yield. Several green-thinkers have proposed ecologically-sound quota systems for resources, including 'resource depletion quotas' (Herman Daly, in Michael Tobias (ed), 1985) and 'transferable birth quotas' (Herman Daly, 1977). The main problem with all quota systems is that they must be decided by the community as a whole, or they will always be subverted by those with more than their share of WEALTH and PRIVILEGE.

Rr

Race

(1) [12c. *Old Norse ras*, running]

Anything which involves speed and (usually) COMPETITION. Running — using your body to its capacity and getting somewhere quickly without immediately resorting to the car — is excellent excercise, but the competitive element in racing creates unnecessary tension and conflict. When the racing takes place in fast cars and speedboats, enormous energy and financial resources are diverted from the places they are most needed, not to mention the creation of noise and other pollution. One of the brightest hopes for the late 1980s is that — at last — the nuclear ARMS RACE is slowing down, one race which nobody can win though both competitors have been hell-bent on staying in the lead.

(2) [16c. *Italian razza*, group of people, generation]

A group of people with common ETHNIC and cultural traditions, often coming from one part of the world, and having distinguishable physical characteristics such as colour of skin and hair, and shape of face. Race, like sex (barring surgery), is immutable — it and its repercussions are with you until you die. Being immutable, race makes perfect candidacy for OPPRESSION, and centuries of mythology, colonial domination, brutalisation and OBJECTIFICATION of the races considered by those in power to be inferior have led to the most seemingly intractable divides within the human population. Beliefs about difference have resulted in real difference — in opportunity, respect, health, education, housing and standard of living. Following the protracted struggle of oppressed populations, particularly in the last thirty years, concern about RACISM has increased dramatically, and much important work is now being done to heal the rifts between races, but most people who as a result of their race have conventionally been considered inferior by those in power continue to suffer from POVERTY, DISCRIMINATION and miscarriage of JUSTICE.

Racism
[1936]
(*also* 'racialism' [1907], though 'racism' is more usual)
The OPPRESSION of the people of one RACE by the people of another — usually of non-white people by white people. 'Every black human being in the United States is a victim of oppression — a particular oppression based on racism and discrimination. Regardless of economic, political or other status; regardless of the fact that some blacks unawarely participate in the oppression of other blacks and profit by it; all blacks are oppressed and are victims of the general oppression directed against all black human beings in the United States. This oppression is vicious, open and blatant in many parts of the country and in many expressions of the culture. It is concealed, rationalized and "justified" in other parts of the country and culture' (Suzanne Lipsky and Harvey Jackins, 1978). The USA is not the only location, of course, in which racism rears its head, nor the oppression of non-whites the only form of racism — Chicanos, Poles, Jews, Irish and Chinese people (among many others) are all oppressed by racism. The perception of oppressed peoples being defined as the VICTIMS of racism can betray a degree of condescension: 'Racism is something that is first of all a white person's problem, not ours. We are subject to its effects, we have it directed against us, and the end result affects our lives. Yet we still retain a particular lifestyle, cultural forms and ideas which have their own autonomy quite apart from racism and our relationships with whites, and we can and do exist over and above racism. To perceive of us as victims does not credit us with the capability to exist for ourselves and to help ourselves, and ultimately perpetuates paternalistic attitudes by whites who wish to help' (Isiaka Amodu, 1987). The links between racism and other oppressions, particularly SEXISM, have been examined by many feminists: '[Racism is a] crucial issue for feminism because any analysis of oppression needs to include intersecting oppressions, because any analysis of women's situation needs to engage with the specificities of different women's conditions, . . because white women themselves partake of the privilege afforded white people in many Western societies, and because racism within the women's movement itself needs to be addressed if solidarity among women is to be fostered' (Cheris Kramerae and Paula Treichler, 1985). As well as direct oppression, both structural oppression and internalised oppression have an important role in maintaining racism, as does the widely-held myth that all blacks (Chinese, Mexicans, Turks . . .) look the same. In a multiracial society, which many parts of the world now are (though it is important to recognise that some are not), real communication and understanding between people of different races is crucial if racism is to be eliminated.

'For the white person who wants to know how to be my friend: The first thing you do is to forget that i'm Black. Second, you must never forget that i'm Black. . . In other words — if you really want to be my friend — don't make a labor of it' (Pat Parker, *Heresies*, 1982).

Radiation
[1896 in this sense. *L radiare*, to shine]
The emission and transfer of ENERGY through space, the atmosphere, and (with some kinds of radiation) through matter. Radiation can be in the form of heat, light, radio, infrared, ultraviolet, gamma, cosmic and X-rays ('electromagnetic radiation'), or in the form of a stream or cloud ('emission') of charged particles. Some types of radiation ('ionising radiation') — gamma, ultraviolet and X-rays, or a stream of high-energy electrons, alpha particles or protons — can cause changes in the structure of the atoms it passes through, dislodging electrons to create 'ions'. 'When ionizing radiation passes through a material it causes changes in the structure of the material — sometimes temporary, sometimes permanent, sometimes useful, sometimes harmful. . . The effects of ionizing radiation become particularly important if the radiation is passing through living matter; the delicate molecular arrangements of living matter can be easily upset by radiation' (Walter Patterson, 1976). Even low levels of ionizing radiation are known to affect the health of living things, including human beings: 'The gradual breakdown of human bio-regulatory integrity through ionising and breakage of the DNA and RNA molecules gradually makes a person less able to tolerate environmental changes, less able to recover from diseases or illness, and generally less able to cope physically with habitat variations. . . If the radiation damage occurs in germ cells, the sperm or ovum, it can cause defective offspring. . . Exposure to radiation is also known to reduce fertility, [and can] damage an embryo or foetus while it is developing within the mother's womb' (Rosalie Bertell, 1985). As nuclear experts are fond of telling us, 'natural background radiation' (ionising radiation from 'natural' sources) has always been with us; this is radiation from elements like uranium and potassium at the earth's surface. What they don't point out is that this 'natural' radiation is intensified by mining and processing operations, making it much easier for ionising radiation to be taken into ecological cycles. Natural radiation is estimated to contribute around three-quarters of the radiation to which we are exposed; as far as artificial sources are concerned, more than 90% of our combined radiation dose comes from medical X-rays. Natural radiation, however, is dispersed throughout the biosphere, and we can normally choose whether or not we want to expose ourselves to X-rays. Some of the highest short-term radiation doses have been received involuntarily as the result of nuclear

explosions and leaks from nuclear power stations, as the victims of Hiroshima, Nagasaki, the Rongelap Islands, Chernobyl and Sellafield (Windscale) know to their cost. RADIOACTIVITY which produces ionising radiation is carried by the wind on dust particles, which can fall (as 'fallout') hundreds of miles downstream, either as the dust reaches the ground or as the nuclei of raindrops. Especially following the Chernobyl explosion there has been much talk about 'safe levels' of ionising radiation — 'This many X-rays are safe' and 'That much fallout is acceptable'; the truth is that nobody knows how much radiation causes how much damage to each individual organism, and it varies enormously from organism to organism. What is known is that hugely increased levels of radiation — levels which in the wake of Chernobyl have destroyed the culture of the Sami people of Lapland through contamination of their food chain, and which may lead to 100,000 premature cancer deaths in Europe (*Worldwatch*, 1987) — are entirely avoidable, given what is known about the dangers and the alternatives. 'Radiation is oppression, the daily average/kind, the kind you're almost used to/and live with as the years abrade you,/high blood pressure, ulcers, cramps, migraine,/a hacking cough: you take it inside/and it becomes pain and you say, not/*They are killing me*, but *I am sick now*' (Marge Piercy, 1985).

Radical
[14c. *L radix*, root]
Going to the roots of an issue and examining it thoroughly, questioning everything and leaving no stone unturned. 'Radical' has unfortunately also descended, via 'radical reform' and 'radical change', to mean EXTREME, exactly the opposite of its useful meaning, and it is in this use that it has attracted the attention of frightened conservatism. Having examined the roots, radical thinkers usually find that standard explanations no longer work, whatever political hue they display, and that the only useful way of nurturing healthy social, economic and ecologically balanced plants is to grow them from seedlings and pull up the old dead plants by their roots. Several branches of the green tree have used the adjective 'radical' to describe a fundamentally new approach — 'radical education', 'radical feminism', 'radical politics' and 'radical technology' among them. 'Renewed radical politics are necessary whether or not they are "realistic", because there are no other realistic options. . . Radical politics rest on a refusal to despair; rest on stubborn faith in contrary possibilities' (Steven Wineman, 1984). 'The color of radicalism today is no longer red; it is green, and should be raised aloft boldly if the modern crisis is to be resolved' (Murray Bookchin, 1986).

Radioactive Waste
(*see* NUCLEAR WASTE)

Radioactivity
[1899]
(sometimes confused with RADIATION — meaning ionising radiation — and used interchangeably)
The ability of some elements (or more correctly, some isotopes of some elements; that is, atoms with different numbers of neutrons) to change spontaneously from one energy level to another ('decay') by releasing particles. Although this happens naturally on a small but widespread scale (or, in the centre of stars, on a massive scale), some of the most potentially harmful radioactive decay in the earth's ecosystem is triggered by artificially manufactured nuclear reactions, nuclear explosions either in the open biosphere, or in the 'controlled' setting of a nuclear power station. The radiation thus released must be contained, or it will spread into surrounding ecosystems and atmospheric circulations.

Railway
[1776]
(*also* 'railroad', 'rail system')
Long chains of containers, suitable for carrying people and goods, which run on wheels on a continuous permanent set of rails. In energy terms, railways are the most efficient way of carrying large loads and quantities of people: a train carrying 300 passengers can take a person 55km per litre of fuel used compared with 6km for one person in a large CAR. Yet in Britain in the 1960s, more than 30% of the rail network was abandoned; in the USA passenger use has fallen enormously in the last twenty years. Most new railway building in recent years has either been for economic exploitation (in Australia, South America and the USSR for example) or for urban rapid transit systems — the building rate is currently running at about 2 new systems and 5 extensions each year. In general, railway companies are now concentrating on freight and inter-city operations, having virtually abandoned local services (except in suburban areas), though some countries are investing in this area. Rail transport and its derivatives, particularly 'light rail', should have an increasingly important role in an energy-efficient world. 'The fact is that we have in many areas [in Britain] an overloaded road system that apparently we cannot afford to keep in a state of repair to match the annual increase in road usage. Alongside it, we have 10,500 miles of railway, nearly all of which is capable, with negligible outlay on improvements, of carrying greatly increased volumes of passsengers and freight. In other words we already have duplicates to the motorway network — but with rails instead of a tarmac surface, more productive, pollution free on electrified lines, vastly safer, and ready to carry more traffic' (Michael Bonavia, 1985).

Rainforest
[1903]
(*also* 'tropical rain forest')
Lush evergreen FOREST growing in areas of high rainfall (usually over 100"/250cm per year) and no marked dry season. Rainforests grow on fairly low ground around the equator, in Amazonia, the Congo Basin, and in Sumatra, Borneo, Papua New Guinea and the adjacent islands, and once covered 10% of the earth's surface. Over 40% of the rainforests have been felled in the last fifty years, and about 200,000 square km are being lost every year. About a quarter of this loss is due to forestry, but clearing for agriculture, firewood, roads, mining and dam projects affects enormous areas. The short-sightedness of such clearing becomes plain when you realise that although rainforest is an enormously diverse ecosystem, it thrives on land which is essentially barren, almost all the nutrients in the system being in the plant cover. Not only does the rainforest provide a home for half of the earth's known plant and animal species (over five million — the world's most important gene pool); the unique ecosystem supports an equally unique human population, peoples who have been decimated over the past five centuries and are still seriously at risk. In recent years ecologists have suggested that the degradation of the rainforest poses a global threat, since as well as destroying a vital ecological (and economic) resource, the forest is crucial in helping to maintain atmospheric and climatic balance. 'The destruction of the world's rainforests amounts to waging biological warfare against the planet' (Charles Secrett, undated).

Rape
[14c. *L rapere*, to seize]
Sexual assault on somebody else's body, almost always by a man on a woman's body; 'Rape occurs every time a man forces a woman to perform a sexual act against her will' (Frederique Delacoste and Felice Newman, 1981, quoted in Cheris Kramerae and Paula Treichler, 1985); 'It is all the sexual insults . . . that we all suffer in our daily contact with men' (London Rape Crisis Centre, 1984). Rape is the subject of more myths than almost anything else, myths which bely the reality of rape for any woman who has been raped: shock, nightmares, fear, shame, guilt, feelings of powerlessness and loss of control, repulsion, depression, anger. The rape myths include:
— 'women enjoy rape'
— 'you can't rape your wife'
— 'rapists are maniacs'
— 'only bad women get raped'
— 'rapists have an uncontrollable sex drive'
— 'women use the charge of rape to get at innocent men'

— 'rape is an aberration'

The facts put the lie to all these myths, yet they won't go away, because of the vested interest of patriarchy in 'dividing and deceiving women, disguising the real level of male violence and its significance to all of us . . . Once we see that rape is not an abnormal act, but part of the way men — not just strangers or maniacs but fathers, uncles, husbands, boyfriends, friends and professionals — treat us as women, we realise that we cannot make a distinction between "normal men" and rapists. The silence around rape and the myths that obscure the reality have prevented women from realising that rapists are not recognisable as such. While men may choose not to commit rape, they are all capable of it and know this. When women know this too, we can stop relying on men for protection, start being angry and begin to find our own strength' (London Rape Crisis Centre, 1984). Much discussion of rape has been generated in the green movement following several rapes at green gatherings and peace camps — particularly at Molesworth in England in 1986, exposing some further rape myths:

— 'women who go to alternative and green events are easier to lay than other women and, being the freedom-loving sort, enjoy it more'

— 'men who go to alternative and green events wouldn't dream of committing rape'

Rape metaphors ('the rape of the land', 'the rape of the environment', 'the rape of nature', 'the rape of our cities', even 'the rape of mankind') were commoner in the environmental movement of the 1960s and 1970s than they are now, the decline presumably being a result of increased awareness, but they still appear from time to time, highlighting the subject/object links between man and woman/earth-mother. *See also* INCEST, OBJECTIFICATION, PORNOGRAPHY, SEX, VIOLENCE.

Rarity

[1560. *L rarus*, sparce]

Something which only exists in small numbers or quantities; by extension, a species of plant or animal which has been reduced to or is only known in small numbers and whose continued existence is threatened. The International Union for the Conservation of Nature and Natural Resources distinguishes between ENDANGERED SPECIES (in immediate danger of EXTINCTION), 'vulnerable species' (rapidly-diminishing species at risk of becoming endangered), and 'rare species' (small populations which are not endangered, but are at risk). Another meaning of 'rarity' is 'something not widely known about'; biologists reckon that although human beings have catalogued about 1,500,000 animal species and 380,000 plant species, there may be another thirty million species that have not yet been identified — many of which will probably be destroyed without our ever having recognised their existence.

Rational
(*see* REASON)

Rational Needs
(*see* BASIC NEEDS)

Reactionary
[1840. *L reagere*, to react]
Reacting against change; ultraconservative. Often used as a pejorative term to describe anybody who is obstructing what you see as beneficial change, which begs the question of the usefulness of the change. 'The term came to popular usage through liberal thinkers in the nineteenth century, whose idea of the inevitability and desirability of progress was so strong that they felt it was possible to identify groups and institutions who were clearly attempting to hold back an unarguably good process' (David Robertson, 1985). In communist and maoist circles, the 'reactionary' is the despised opponent of the 'revolutionary' — thus Chairman Mao's denunciation: 'All reactionaries are paper tigers'. A useful and accurate word in danger of overuse.

Reafforestation
[1884]
(*also* (mostly US) 'reforestation')
Planting trees in areas where most of the indigenous forest has been destroyed, in order to save ecosystems from further degradation and to provide human beings with a sustainable harvest of tree products. Some countries, notably China, India and South Korea, have mounted extremely successful reafforestation programmes, using the resources of local communities ('social forestry' or 'community forestry') and state encouragement to plant large areas of land with both fast-growing fuelwood and native species. Despite widespread efforts at reafforestation, however, the world's trees are still being felled at a faster rate than they are being replanted, especially in tropical regions, and replanting is often done with non-native species which can have serious repercussions on ecosystems and wildlife habitats. *See also* DEFORESTATION.

Realism
[1817 in this sense. *L res*, thing]
Accepting that things are as they are; by extension, seeing the changes needed for a more ecological and harmonious existence in terms of a gradual shift from present circumstances rather than demanding radical reform, since the former approach appears more likely to achieve any change at all given present political realities. This choice of policy is currently at the centre of much green debate, especially in

West Germany, where the motives of the realists ('realos') have been questioned by those proposing less compromise and more radical and fundamental stances on important issues (the 'fundamentalists' or 'fundis'). *See also* FUNDAMENTALISM, INCREMENTALISM, PRAGMATISM, REFORMISM.

Reality
[1550. *L res*, thing]
The one word in this dictionary where definition is impossible. 'Real' and its derivatives 'really' and 'reality' mean an enormous range of things in different contexts: '["real"] serves to contrast the natural with the artificial, as when we ask whether a woman's [*sic*] hair is really red as opposed to being dyed; the natural with the synthetic, as when we talk of real as opposed to cultured pearls; the genuine with the spurious, as one might say of a picture that it was a real Van Gogh; what comes up to standard with what does not, in the sense in which I should say that I was not a real bridge-player; what is designed for a practical purpose with what is designed for a mimicry of this purpose, as in the contrast between a real and a toy trumpet, which, as my small son pointed out to me, also makes real noises, though not of the same volume or range. We speak of real as opposed to affected or merely superficial emotions, of real as opposed to ostensible reasons, and we also contrast the real with the imaginary or the fictitious, which is not quite the same as contrasting it with the apparent. . . We should . . . be hard put to say what was the real colour of the sun, or the real shape of a cloud' (A.J. Ayer, 1973). As far as green thinking is concerned, there seem to be two main related strands to the idea of the 'reality' of the universe, and two further (and also related) ideas about the nature of the real human being (though *see also* HUMAN NATURE):
(a) The belief that reality is all one interconnected network or system, with no meaningful distinction between the observer and the observed. This is not consistent with the scientific tradition that Westerners have grown up and been educated in: 'With the rise of modern science, whose golden age was the seventeenth century, the assumption entered our culture that total reality is divided between perceivers and perceived, or if you like between subjects and objects. There are humans (and perhaps God too) observing the world, and there is the world they are observing. This dualism, this assumption of a twofold division throughout the whole of reality, has become all-pervading in our thought, including our philosophy and our science. Yet, contrary to what most Western men and women probably suppose, it is a view of reality peculiar to the West and, what is more, peculiar to it only in the last three or four centuries' (Bryan Magee, 1978).
(b) The belief that reality just is; that it is BENIGN, wishing us no parti-

cular harm and doing us no particular favours. This again is not what our (this time religious) background has taught us. 'We must look underneath the crust of pseudo-reality: deep reality is everlasting and pure and shining and nourishing and beneficient and benign. The temporarily dangerous crust covering it, composed of patterns and oppression and misinformation, is shallow' (Harvey Jackins, 1983).
(c) The belief that there is for each person a 'real self', which almost always hides behind the masks created by pain and self-deception, but is nonetheless real and intimately interconnected with the larger reality (*see* SELF, TRANSPERSONAL PSYCHOLOGY).
(d) The belief that each person's perception of themself and their setting is equally real and valid, and thus that nobody can ever succeed in defining another person's reality. This might appear to contradict (a) and (b), but the 'fact' of an interconnected and benign universe that just 'is' doesn't preclude different perspectives — think of the cloud of the first quotation: it really does look like a map of Africa from one angle; from another it really does look like a cat. Thus the popular phrase 'creating your own reality' is true, as long as it is *you* creating it. Those who go further to suggest that we all deserve everything that happens to us are wading into dangerous oppression-infested waters.
The green version of 'reality' is very different from the dictionary's (*Collins*, 1986) 'state of things as they are or appear to be, rather than as one would wish them to be'. For most green-thinkers, real reality is the state of things as we wish them to be and know we can make them. 'There are children in school today who don't know where milk comes from, or what coal actually is. . . The real "real" world is made up of earth and rock and coal and water and crops and grass — in contrast to the phoney world of money markets, capital transfers and petro-dollars, of hollow promises, political myths and notional levels of economic growth' (Peter Bunyard and Fern Morgan-Grenville (ed), 1987).

Reason
[13c. *L ratio*, reckoning]
The innate human capacity for INTELLIGENCE, leading to APPROPRIATE action. PATRIARCHY has gone to even greater lengths than usual to subvert the idea of reason, redefining it to mean 'a cold and unemotional approach to decision-making', an approach that women (being 'emotional') are deemed incapable of undertaking. The righteous anger of women at being excluded is then conveniently interpreted as justification for their further exclusion (on the grounds of 'emotional insecurity'). Many people, including a number of feminist women, have turned against reason and logic with a will, proclaiming that what is needed is more sensitivity and understanding. This is to ignore the fact that what has been labelled 'logical' and 'reasonable' by those who

maintain power over other people is nothing of the sort. Crime, killing, aggressive defence policies, economic competition and pollution are the antithesis of rational behaviour; these antisocial and exploitative behaviours are the result of thoughtless and uncontrolled emotion, justified in the name of 'reason'. In a world where emotion has led us to the brink of disaster, it is time to reinstate reason as the creative spark for radical change. 'Though we would never be so foolhardy as to assume that reason alone is sufficient to build a caring, civilized society, the politics of ecology is none the less profoundly rational' (Jonathon Porritt, 1984). 'The essential point is that holistic, or ecological, thinking is not a retreat from reason; it is an enlargement of it to more comprehensive and hence more efficient means of analysis' (Charlene Spretnak, 1986).

Recession
[1929 in this sense. *L recedere*, to go back]
A time of economic crisis in which the rich generally stay rich and the poor are exhorted to cut back or lose their jobs; gradually coming to mean a period when the whole economic structure of the world begins to break down. The writing is already on the wall: apart from short-term fluctuations world trade has peaked and is declining, the debt crisis is coming to a head, unemployment (by current definitions) is rising sharply. 'The total wealth of the United States, from real estate to stocks, from gold fillings to the last piece of silverware, amounts to $7 to $8 trillion. It is also estimated that we now owe $5.2 trillion against that. If the United States were a business, it would have difficulty getting a loan' (Paul Hawken, 1983).

Reciprocity
[1776. *L reciprocare*, to move back and forth]
(*also* 'mutuality', 'mutual aid')
A system of mutual exchange between people or groups of people: a system of reciprocity operates, for example, in small agricultural communities where neighbours help each other at times like harvesting, when intensive communal work is the most efficient way of getting things done.

Reclamation
[*L reclamare*, to cry out]
(1) [1787] Rediscovering your strength; taking back your rights. 'Reclaim the night marches: particularly useful in areas in which there have been attacks on women recently are all-women demonstrations, bringing women together in a large group to walk carrying placards and torches, and chanting together' (London Rape Crisis Centre, 1984). 'Reclaim the Hills: Coulport Trident Trespass, October 4th, 1986'

(poster, 1986). 'Reclaim our lives, at Greenham Common Women's Peace Camp, on December 13th/14th' (*Women's Peace Alliance Newsletter*, December 1986).
(2) [1861] 'Improvement' of economically marginal land for human purposes, usually the draining of coastal wetlands and marsh for agriculture. What is seen as 'marginal land' to human eyes is often extremely important to wildlife. 'Destruction of coastal wetlands in industrialized countries is now due mostly to direct pollution and "reclamation"' (Lee Durrell, 1986). 'Since 1949, about 50% of lowland fens, mires and valleys [in Britain] have been destroyed or significantly damaged, mostly due to drainage and reclamation' (*Countryside Conflicts*, 1986). In the USA the 'Bureau of Reclamation' is responsible for dam building and the destruction of many unique wilderness habitats.
(3) [1937] A synonym for RECYCLING.

Recycling
[1926 in this sense]
Reclaiming materials for further use instead of throwing them away for mass WASTE treatment. It is wise to remember that according to the ecological law of 'everything must go somewhere', recycling happens whether we do it consciously or not. We don't decide whether or not to recycle things, we decide whether to recycle them in a more or less aware way. Nature has been perfecting recycling for millions of years, and if left to itself has got it just about perfect: 'The secret [of the lush growth of rainforests on barren soil] lies in the fact that these forests are virtual closed systems in which nutrients are perpetually recycled. They are highly efficient — studies in Venezuela have revealed that less than 1% of nutrients are lost through leaching' (Charles Secrett, undated). Would that human recycling were that efficient. Given the will and the (relatively inexpensive) facilities to deal with it, more than 80% of Western household waste and as much as 90% of industrial waste could easily be recycled — the only big problems are PLASTICS and toxic waste. At present even the best levels of recycling are pathetically low — Japan, the best, manages 10% of household waste — but many statutory and volunteer schemes are now underway all over the world. However efficient our recycling becomes, it must be subject to the NET ENERGY PRINCIPLE, so it is always more ecological not to use a resource than to recycle it, or to RE-USE rather than recycle — our aim should be to reduce THROUGHPUT to a minimum. Recycling is one aspect of ecological thinking that is easy to grasp, and 'the inevitable global transition from dependence on extractive industries to reliance on recycled materials has already begun' (*Worldwatch*, 1987).

Red
[1848 in this sense]
The colour associated with a revolutionary political approach (after the colour of the badges of revolutionary parties in Germany and Russia); by extension a general label for all socialist and communist political stances (*see* ANARCHISM, MARXISM, SOCIALISM). The juxtaposition of 'red' and 'green' politics has been explored by many authors on the fringes of both, including Rudolf Bahro in *From Red to Green* (1984) and the socialist/green essayists in *Red and Green* (Joe Weston (ed), 1986).

Red Data Books
[1983]
Detailed information about the conservation status of endangered species, published by the International Union for Conservation of Nature and Natural Resources (IUCN). 'Keeping track of the current status of endangered wildlife and environments is the vital task of the IUCN Conservation Monitoring Centre. . . This information is made available to all parts of the global conservation network in the form of special reports and the renowned series of IUCN Red Data Books, which have now become standard reference works in the conservation world' (Lee Durrell, 1986).

Redevelopment
[1873]
The rebuilding of large areas of inner cities; too often planners' dreams and people's nightmares. 'The core of northern Southwark is a much vaunted experiment in comprehensive redevelopment on a grandiose scale, which has become the most notorious ultra-Utopia in London and, according to some, in the whole of Europe. It was built in the early 1970s when the vogue for "streets in the sky" was at its peak, and . . . many residents say they live in a permanent state of fear and stress' (Alice Coleman, 1985). In North America redevelopment is more often called RENEWAL. *See also* HOUSING, PLANNING.

Redistribution
[1611]
Policies designed to achieve a fair distribution of resources. Redistribution is the basis of WELFARE policies, and while fairer distribution is undoubtedly necessary, green-thinkers prefer to see the issue in terms of the right to BASIC NEEDS, rather than relying on the grudging assistance of those with power and privilege.

Reductionism
[1943]
Taking things apart in an attempt to understand them better. The

danger in reductionism is the belief that it is possible to understand the whole by knowing how the parts work, the antithesis of HOLISM (*see also* SYNTHESIS). 'Although the reductionist approach has been extremely successful in biology, culminating in the understanding of the chemical nature of genes, the basic units of heredity, and in the unravelling of the genetic code, it nevertheless has severe limitations... The functions of a living organism that do not lend themselves to a reductionist description — those representing the organism's integrative activities and its interactions with the environment — are precisely the functions that are crucial for the organism's health' (Fritjof Capra, 1982).

Redundancy
[1601. *L redundare*, to overflow]
Being surplus to requirements. A uniquely human concept, begging the question of whose requirements — the answer being those who control the distribution of resources (*see also* OBSOLESCENCE, UNEMPLOYMENT, WORK).

Reforestation
(*see* REAFFORESTATION)

Reformism
[1904. *L reformare*, to form again]
Wanting to change things gradually, using the political and legal systems that are already in place; a close equivalent to GRADUALISM, INCREMENTALISM and REALISM. While accepting that slow and gradual evolution is entirely appropriate to natural systems, many green-thinkers believe that the human situation is now so critical that reformist change can no longer take us towards a sustainable future (*see* FUNDAMENTALISM, NONVIOLENT REVOLUTION, RADICAL): 'A complete change of direction is needed now, leading to a decline in the role of mass political parties, government agencies, business corporations and so on. It is quite unrealistic to expect a process of evolutionary reform, arising mainly from the interplay of political forces corresponding to the existing power structure, to bring about such a change of direction. Such a change will have to be initiated primarily by people outside the existing power structure, who identify with the new direction of change' (James Robertson, 1978).

Refuge
[*L refugere*, to escape]
(1) [1933] A wildlife sanctuary, often with the emphasis on birds, though with 'controlled hunting' at certain seasons, most refuges in the USA are the last place any bird would want to be. Money for the creation of refuges in that country often comes from hunting organisations.

(2) [1976] A place of safety for women who are the survivors of male violence in their homes.

Refugee

[1685. *L refugere*, to escape]

A person who has been forced to leave their home because of FAMINE, WAR, persecution, or other circumstances that have made their life intolerable. In the 1970s more than nine million people became international refugees, and more than two million more were displaced within their own country. Refugees frequently suffer some of the worst human deprivation, putting increased pressure on already overstretched resources in those places where they can find a temporary home. *See also* MIGRATION.

Regeneration

[1888 in this sense. *L regenerare*, to reproduce]

The creation of a new cycle of life. Used in ecology to describe the natural regrowth of an ecosystem that has been disturbed by human or natural intervention; taken into many aspects of green thinking and practice to denote any process that is capable of restoring the harmony of ecological and social systems and ensuring sustainable and self-perpetuating development, thus 'regenerative agriculture', 'regenerative systems', 'regenerative technology' and 'social regeneration'. *See also* REVITALISATION.

Region

[14c. *L regere*, to direct]

An area of land with a particular character. Regions are nowadays often simply an administrative convenience, following meaningless boundaries drawn by bureaucrats, but the idea of true regional identity is being reinstated by green-thinkers in the concept of BIOREGIONALISM. 'A region holds the power to sustain and join disparate people: old ground charged with common wholeness and forces of long-growing life. All people are within regions as a condition of existence, and regions condition all people within them' (Peter Berg, 1978).

Regionalism

[1881]

The awareness of inhabiting a particular REGION. An powerful concept for anyone with strong regional roots, and an important antidote in a world where big business and centralised government are doing their best to produce boring sameness across whole continents. 'Regionalism has always defined the American experience. . . Whether thought of as sectionalism, localism, separatism, or nullificationism, whether identified with Jeffersonians, Regulators, Agrarians, Grangers, or Statesrighters — and those are just *some* of the names by which it has gone in our history — regionalism has been recurrent in American life, in its political experience and social patterning as in its speech, food, housing, literature, religion, folk art, and sense of humour' (Kirkpatrick Sale, 1985). There is also a regionalist movement in Britain, 'advocating autonomy for historic national and regional territories within a quasi-federal Britain or, more radically, a Europe of the Regions' (David Robyns, *Green Options*, Spring 1987), and vocal regionalist movements exist throughout the world. 'Regionalism is about regional solutions to regional problems' (David Robyns, *op. cit.*). *See also* BIOREGIONALISM.

Relationship

[1944 in this sense. *L relatio*, narration, relation between two concepts]

A special connection with somebody or something; more specifically, a special friendship which involves some degree of intimacy, involvement and commitment. 'This book is for all those who want to create better, more meaningful relationships with the people in their lives. It presents proven principles and techniques that can help you create satisfying relationships with lovers and friends. These principles apply to all kinds of relationships, including family, work, social, and even political relationships' (Marc Allen, 1985). Despite efforts to widen its meaning, 'being in a relationship' usually implies the same exclusive (at least in theory) heterosexual living-with qualities of marriage, but without legal and religious sanction. The wider meaning may slowly be gaining ground, but 'being in a relationship' is still very different from 'being in relationship'. *See also* COHABITATION, FRIEND, RIGHT RELATIONSHIP.

Relaxation

[16c. *L relaxare*, to loosen up]

Letting TENSION out of the mind and body, often using specially-designed exercises. 'Relaxation is surprisingly difficult to achieve for people who are not naturally relaxed. Lying down is easy but a very great deal of tension will still remain in the body unless the mind too can be stilled. People "relax" in front of the television but the postures they take, and the tiredness they feel afterwards, demonstrates the opposite; that their physiology continues its state of sympathetic activation and arousal. True relaxation implies a profound shift in many physiological systems, the mind barely ticking over, a deep surrendering of the body to its supports and a slow and regular breath' (Stephen Fulder, 1984). 'Edmund Jacobsen said, "An anxious mind cannot exist within a relaxed body". Fifty years ago he developed a series of over 200 exercises designed to relax the muscles by teaching muscle awareness and relaxation through tensing individual muscles. . . [He] used the exercises to treat a wide variety of physical complaints, and his research forms the foundation for our understanding of the mind/body awareness processes, and the use of relaxation in healing' (L. John Mason, 1980).

Release

[14c. *L relaxare*, to loosen up]

Letting go. The appropriateness of release depends entirely upon you and your circumstances. Releasing the need to be right, releasing unreasonable expectations, releasing excessive privilege, and releasing tension (*see* RELAXATION) are all elements of green philosophy and practice. Releasing your basic rights only bolsters oppression. Releasing large quantities of sulphur and heavy metals from factories is ecological madness. Some spiritual practices advocate release (or 'surrender') as part of the spiritual path, but here it is vitally important to be clear about exactly what it is that you are choosing to let go of.

Religion

[13c. *L religio*, a bond between humans and the gods]

SPIRITUALITY which incorporates a belief in the power of god or a similar 'universal spirit' (a term used by Gallup opinion polls to establish the role of religion in modern American society); thus depending on what 'universal spirit' means to you, 'religion' can be virtually synonymous with 'spirituality', and it is used in this sense by some green-thinkers. In popular usage, however, 'religion' implies the ritual, dogma, and more or less hierarchical organisation of spirituality, for most Westerners synonymous with the JUDEO-CHRISTIAN TRADITION. While in its more reactionary elements it manages to combine paternalism, sexism, exploitation, and bureaucracy in a unique mixture, this tradition has been influential in changing attitudes and practice towards exploitation, especially in Third World areas with a powerful Christian presence (*see* LIBERATION THEOLOGY), and many people experience a special sense of community in being part of a local religious congregation which they cannot find elsewhere. The opinions of green-thinkers vary enormously as to whether religion (as distinct from spirituality) can be incorporated into a truly green philosophy. 'Unless major changes occur in churches, ecologists and all those working in ecology movements will feel very uncomfortable sitting in the pews of most American churches' (Bill Devall, quoted in Charlene Spretnak, 1986). *See also* PAGANISM, SANCTUARY (sense (3)).

Remedy

[13c. *L remederi*, to heal again]

A treatment used in HEALING. A word used by many holistic practitioners in preference to MEDICINE, which is inextricably linked in the popular imagination with DRUG. It is true that some remedies are also drugs, but unlike the vast majority of manufactured drugs, remedies used by complementary practitioners — where they involve taking any substance internally — are usually of natural origin.

Renewable Energy
[1971]
Sources of ENERGY for human use based on RENEWABLE RESOURCES. *See* BIOMASS ENERGY, GEOTHERMAL ENERGY, HYDROENERGY, SOLAR ENERGY, TIDAL ENERGY, WAVE ENERGY, WIND ENERGY. Renewable energy sources are sometimes just called 'renewables'.

Renewable Resources
[1956]
(*also* 'renewables')
NATURAL RESOURCES which can either be grown (timber, foodstuffs), regenerate over a relatively short period of time (water in water tables, some soils), or renew themselves continuously as the result of the input of SOLAR ENERGY (direct solar energy, wind and tidal energy, some water resources). Renewable resources are only renewable if they are used at the rate they need to accumulate, and in many cases they are being used much faster than they are being regenerated, leading to DEPLETION: 'Economist Lester Brown has summarized the evidence that the global per capita productivity of our four basic renewable resource systems has peaked and is now in decline. Forest productivity . . . peaked in 1970 at 0.67 cubic meters. Fisheries productivity . . . peaked in 1970 at 19.5 kilograms. Grasslands productivity is indicated by figures on wool, mutton, and beef. Wool peaked in 1960 at 0.86 kilograms; mutton in 1972 at 1.92 kilograms; and beef in 1976 at 11.81 kilograms. Croplands . . . peaked in 1976 at 346 kilograms' (Herman Daly, in Michael Tobias (ed), 1985).

Renewal
[1965. *L re- + Old English neowe*, to make new again]
The more common North American term for REDEVELOPMENT — the rebuilding of large areas of decaying inner cities. 'No war declared/No storm had flared/No sudden bomb so cruel./Just a need for land/A greedy hand/And a sign that said "urban renewal"' (placard, 1967, quoted in Robert Goodman, 1972).

Repercussion
[1536. *L repercutere*, to cause to rebound]
A consequence of an action, usually used to describe an unwanted consequence that 'wasn't foreseen' (because they didn't bother to think too hard about anything other than the task in hand). Thus we end up with the drastic repercussions of organic pesticides (a silent spring: *see*

PESTICIDE), organofluorides (OZONE depletion), and sulphur emissions (ACID RAIN).

Representation
[17c in this sense. *L repraesentare*, to exhibit]
Elected or nominated representatives acting on behalf of a constituency. However fairly this is done (*see* PROPORTIONAL REPRESENTATION, REPRESENTATIVE DEMOCRACY) it will always be second best to a system in which each person acts as far as can possibly be arranged on behalf of themself (*see* ANARCHY, DECENTRALISATION, DEMOCRACY, PARTICIPATION).

Representative Democracy
[1844]
A DEMOCRACY in which each person (if they can be bothered) elects one or more PARTY candidates to 'represent' them, frequently finds that the person they voted for has failed to win a seat, and then has no communication with the person who did win for the period that person is in office. In practice this is virtually the only form of democracy currently being practised, and a contradiction in both terms.

Repression
[16c. *L reprimere*, to hold back]
Suppressing or restraining something — information and anger are the two commonest candidates (*see* CENSORSHIP and FEELINGS). *See also* SUPPRESSION.

Reprocessing
[1956 in this sense]
Using the spent nuclear fuel rods from nuclear reactors to produce weapons-grade plutonium and fuel for breeder reactors. 'The remaining highly radioactive debris is stored as liquid in large carbon or stainless steel drums, awaiting some kind of solidification and burial in a permanent repository. Waste of lower radioactivity is buried in dirt trenches or — as in Windscale (Sellafield) in England — piped out to sea' (Rosalie Bertell, 1985). It is 'the Achilles heel of the nuclear industry' (Peter Bunyard, in Edward Goldsmith and Nicholas Hildyard (ed), 1986).

Reproductive Rights
[*c.*1971]
(*also* 'reproductive freedom')
The right to choose when and how you have (or do not have) children, taking all the circumstances into account and without pressure from other people or from institutions. Reproductive rights obviously affect women much more than men, and the concept arose within the women's movement, but it affects men as well whenever they consider CONTRACEPTION, conception and parenting: 'The flip side of the claim that

abortion is a woman's right is that it is no longer a man's responsibility' (Barbara Ehrenreich, quoted in Alison Jaggar, 1983). At a time when world population continues to increase rapidly, 'reproductive rights' must be balanced by a 'reproductive responsibility' to think very carefully before introducing new human life to the world (*see* OVERPOPULATION, POPULATION), though most green-thinkers believe that the individual right to choose should never be overridden by coercive population policies — people must be given all the information and assistance they need, and allowed to make their own decisions. *See also* ABORTION, AID, BIRTH, BIRTH CONTROL, PARENT, REPRODUCTIVE TECHNOLOGY.

Reproductive Technology
[1978]
An important and potentially frightening aspect of BIOTECHNOLOGY concerned with medical control over women's fertility, 'including developments in embryo transfer, *in vitro* techniques, cloning, ectogenesis (artificial wombs), sex predetermination, and related practices such as surrogate motherhood and artificial insemination. Although writers such as Shulamith Firestone and Marge Piercy have envisioned a brave new world in which women have been released from biological slavery through technology, and both sexes share equally in the creation and care of children, there is no sign in our own world that these new developments will be used for feminist aims' (Lisa Tuttle, 1986). 'Newspapers assure us that such new reproductive technologies . . . are merely "therapies" which kindly physicians provide for infertile women. Of course there is more to it than that. Through the years, with widespread use of the technologies, social institutions will be restructured to reflect a new reality — tightened male control over female reproductive processes' (Gena Corea, in *Man-Made Women*, 1985) (*though see* AID).

Research
[*c*.1600. *Middle French recerch(i)er*, to search, investigate]
Careful and detailed investigation. At one and the same time, the only way to find out useful information, and a method almost invariably flawed by adherence to 'scientific technique', a set of untenable assumptions about the nature of REALITY (*see also* SCIENCE).

Reservation
[1789 in this sense. *L reservare*, to save up, keep]
An area of land set aside for the use of a native people, supposedly without interference from the state, though such promises almost invariably come to nothing when land is 'needed' for minerals, power projects, or tourism. 'WARNING: No outside white visitors allowed. Because of your failure to obey the laws of our tribe as well as the laws

of your own this village is hereby closed' (sign outside Old Oraibi Hopi village, quoted in Wendell Berry, 1981).

Reserve
[*L reservare*, to save up, keep]
(1) [1912] The amount of a NON-RENEWABLE resource which has not yet been used. 'Proven reserves' refers to reserves which mining and drilling companies reckon are profitably exploitable; 'known reserves' or 'ultimately recoverable reserves' include virtually everything they might be able to lay their machinery on if the price made it worth it.
(2) [1915] An area of land or water set aside for wildlife, thus 'game reserve', 'nature reserve', 'wildlife reserve'.

Resilience
[1824. *L resilire*, to jump back, recoil]
The ability to recover quickly from a shock. Natural systems, being complex and having many interconnections, can usually recover quickly from natural interruptions; simplistic systems engineered by human beings — even though they may be technologically advanced — can often be destroyed by a simple failure, oversight, or 'act of god'. Thus in 1970 disease affected half the US corn crop — a handful of hybrid species fell prey to the first virus to thrive on them; Chernobyl may have been due to one person's mistimed action. 'The soft [energy] path (*see* SOFT ENERGY) appears generally more flexible — and thus robust. Its technical diversity, adaptability, and geographic dispersion make it resilient and offer a good prospect of stability under a wide range of conditions, foreseen or not. The hard path, however, is brittle; it must fail, with widespread and serious disruption, if any of its exacting technical and social conditions is not satisfied continuously and indefinitely' (Amory Lovins, 1977).

Resistance
[15c. *L resistere*, to take a stand against]
Being able to withstand the threat of danger and destruction. 'Ecological resistance is action from central principles of doing what is necessary, of witnessing nonviolently. It arises from a shift in consciousness . . . Deeply committed persons in the ecology movement sense the vulnerability of natural processes to human intervention, and the fundamental necessity of maintaining biological diversity. . . In a real sense, ecological resistance involves becoming friends with another species or a river or a mountain' (Bill Devall and George Sessions, 1985).

Resources
[1870 in this sense. *L resurgere*, to rise again]
The qualities and materials that we can draw on when we need them.

An idea subverted by the economics of greed to mean something 'that is available for supplying an economic want' (Michael Allaby, 1983); in capitalist economists' language, resources include human labour, capital, land, minerals, fuel — anything that can be used to make a profit. In green circles 'resources' has come almost exclusively to mean what the economists call NATURAL RESOURCES — materials and energy from the biosphere used by human beings. Natural resources are either RENEWABLE or NON-RENEWABLE.

Respect
[14c. *L respicere*, to look back, regard]
High regard for someone or something in the recognition of their uniqueness and importance in their own right. 'I have the right to be treated with respect as an intelligent, capable and equal human being' (Anne Dickson, 1982) (*see also* SELF-ESTEEM). 'Respect for nature really means respect for our own nature, for the full range of experience of which it is capable — and for its limitations as well. It is simply not possible (even if it were desirable) for our own social institutions to manage with sufficient care the full effects of large-scale ecological manipulation. We must recognise those limitations and try to live with them' (William Leiss, 1978).

Responsibility
[1787. *L respondere*, to promise in return, respond]
The capacity to manage our lives intelligently; responding appropriately to what happens around us and to the information we receive; recognising that we are here for a purpose; knowing that if we don't act we can't expect anybody else to do it for us. It is sometimes convenient to define things for which we are responsible and things for which we are not, but assigning BLAME is not a useful green activity. You and I both consume electricity, drive around in cars, buy things wrapped up in too much packaging; how can we say exactly who is responsible for acid rain? Even when we are doing our very best to live lightly we are still responsible. 'Responsibility or irresponsibility is one of the "yes-no" questions in our lives, like an "on" and "off" switch on a light. The light is either on or off — it is not a little bit "on". There are many questions which are gradual in our behavior. We can be tall or taller; we can push against an object with infinite variation in our pushing force. But we are either completely responsible or logically not at all, and our patterns deceive us when they attempt to set limits to our responsibility' (Harvey Jackins, 1973). 'We are each responsible for the conduct of our lives. Additionally, we are each unique. Thus, we are each uniquely responsible for our response to this time of transition and challenge. There is no one who can take our place' (Duane Elgin, 1981). Arbit-

rarily-assigned responsibility is one of the most useless guilt-trips of a divided society, and any green-thinker should be very clear about her or his motives for getting involved in green politics. We cannot protect trees because we feel sorry for them; they have as much right to be there as us, and it is our responsibility to respect that right. Most of us have been brought up on a diet of duty, obligation and commitment imposed on us from outside, and 'responsibility' fits neatly on the menu. It is good to remember that nobody else can define any of these things for us; true responsibility must start with individual awareness.

Retrofitting
[1975 in this sense. Abbreviated from 'retro[active re]fitting']
(*also* 'backfitting')
Installing low-energy low-waste ALTERNATIVE TECHNOLOGY systems in existing buildings.

Re-Use
[1959]
Using things again wherever possible, an even better conservation habit than RECYCLING. Many items can be used over and over again, particularly containers — bottles, bags and cartons. In Denmark the sale of non-refillable soft drinks containers is prohibited, and nine US states are now operating bottle deposit schemes to encourage re-use.

Reverse Discrimination
(*see* POSITIVE DISCRIMINATION)

Revitalisation
[*L re-* + *vita*, bringing in new life]
(US: 'revitalization')
Putting new life into something (*see also* REGENERATION). Seen by some green-thinkers as one response to the breakdown of civilisation, the other being stagnation. 'In order for revitalization to occur, a significant minority must be well prepared to cope with the difficult conditions of civilizational breakdown. In turn, the creative minority could provide many visible examples of a wide diversity of alternative ways of living and working. . . The coherent alternatives of the few could help to transform the chaos of the many into a revitalizing path of civilizational growth' (Duane Elgin, 1981).

Revolution
[1600 in this sense. *L revolvere*, to revolve]
The overthrow of a political regime by a large section of the population; by extension, any sort of overthrow of an existing system: 'There is a revolution coming. It will not be like revolutions of the past. It will originate within the individual and with culture, and it will change the political structure only as its final act. It will not require violence to

succeed, and it cannot be successfully resisted by violence. It is now spreading with amazing rapidity, and already our laws, institutions and social structure are changing in consequence. It promises a higher reason, a more human community, and a new and liberated individual' (Charles Reich, 1970). 'It is . . . a revolution from below that is now in the making. Not just a revolution *against* insanity, but equally a revolution *for* what we are lacking — for the right of all to act as fellow human beings in relation to one another, for the right of the disempowered to responsibility, for the ordinary person's right to take control from those who are too intelligent to understand the purpose of it all. . . This is what revolution in the affluent society means' (Erik Dammann, 1984). 'The environmental revolution' (Max Nicholson, 1970). Some green-thinkers call it a NONVIOLENT REVOLUTION; others are unhappy with the whole idea of revolution and its violent confrontational overtones: 'For many of us, the word "revolution" itself has become not only a dead relic of Leftism, but a key to the deadendedness of male politics: the "revolution" of a wheel which returns in the end to the same place; the "revolving door" of a politics which has "liberated" women only to use them, and only within the limits of male tolerance. When we speak of *transformation* we speak more accurately out of the vision as a process which will leave neither surfaces nor depths unchanged' (Adrienne Rich, 1980). 'Please don't sell me revolution when it's freedom I need' (Su Negrin, 1972).

Right
[before 12c. *Old English riht*; akin to *L regere*, to rule]
APPROPRIATE, fitting. 'A thing is right when it tends to preserve the integrity, stability, and beauty of the biotic community. It is wrong when it tends otherwise' (Aldo Leopold, 1949). *See also* RIGHTS and, for the political sense, NEW RIGHT, REACTIONARY.

Right Brain/Left Brain
[*c.*1965]
The apparent functional differentiation of the two hemispheres of the BRAIN. 'Since the mid-1960s a variety of psychological studies have shown that the left and right sides of our brain specialize in different types of activity. The left side of the brain appears to be more concerned than the right with rational, sequential thought, and with linguistic faculties such as reading, writing and speech. The right side of the brain seems to be more concerned with visual-spatial functions, aesthetic and emotional appreciation, and perhaps with intuitive thought. The general picture that has emerged is that the left is more analytic, processing in a step-by-step mode, while the right is more synthetic, processing more holistically. In addition, the left side has

been associated with active modes of thought, with "doing"; and the right with receptive modes of thought, with "letting things be"' (Peter Russell, 1982). Though widely questioned and disputed, the distinction has joined yin and yang (*see* YIN/YANG) in the popular mythology of DUALISM, complementing nicely the oppressive myth of the active male and the passive female. Even if there is any truth to the assertion, there is no evidence that left-brain/right-brain equates with biological sex differences — if it helps people to recognise the worth of traditionally female qualities then perhaps it has some value, but it is all too easy to fall into the trap of biological DETERMINISM.

Right Livelihood
[*c*.1900 in English: translated from the original Pâli, Sanskrit and Tibetan texts]
(*also* 'right living')
Harmonious and fulfilling ways of obtaining a living; appropriate economic activity. 'Right livelihood' is part of the Buddhist 'Eightfold Path' or 'Middle Way', popularised among green-thinkers by Fritz Schumacher following his discussion of Buddhist economics in *Small is Beautiful* (1973). 'The Eightfold Path begins with Right Views, a deep understanding of the basic principles of the Buddha's Teaching. Then comes the Buddhist version of True Morality, including Right Motive, Right Speech, Right Action and Right Livelihood with the foregoing. Then Right Effort must be developed to provide the will-power to the final stages, [Right Concentration and Right Meditation]' (Christmas Humphreys, 1974). A 'Right Livelihood Award' was inaugurated in 1980 by the Swede, Jakob von Uexkull, and is given annually to people and groups who have made a major contribution to the practice of right livelihood; while some attempt is made to celebrate a range of contributions, the vast majority of the recipients to date have been white men from the First World (even though a great many of them, like Jakob von Uexkull himself, have done useful work in the Third World). Always remember that RIGHT here means 'appropriate', not 'uniquely correct', as this humorous commentary points out: 'Right Livelihood: (1) Living with the assumption that you are always right. (2) Getting very lively when somebody suggests that they are right. (3) The name of an annual prize (sometimes called the Alternative Nobel Prize) set up by a Swedish stamp collector and awarded to the most successful person or group to assert their rightness' (Jeremy Slocombe, in *One Earth*, December 1986/January 1987).

Right On
[1925]
Originally an expression of approval and support, 'right-on' is now also

used as an adjective meaning politically sound and having a good understanding of a situation. It often verges on rigid 'political correctness' in the Marxist sense, and can lead to judgement, sarcasm and competitiveness, what has been called 'more right-on than thou'. 'I *am* angry. Recently I find myself getting more and more furious as a man with men. I no longer feel part of this very judgmental slagging-each-other-off according to the feminist book which is nothing but the age-old defensive competitiveness. . . *I'd* rather have it rough and open than gentle, subtle, right-on and round the back' (Michael Trust, *Peace News*, January 1987).

Right Relationship
[*c.*1975]
Being aware of the interrelatedness of life, and the practice this requires. One of the many 'rights' to appear in the 1970s as an extension of the model provided by the Buddhist 'Eightfold Path' (*see* RIGHT LIVELIHOOD). 'The emerging cultural value on right relationship with the Earth . . . includes . . . sensing one's interrelatedness with all of life . . . Respect for the carrying capacity of the land . . . Balancing wilderness preservation and diversity with cultivation . . . Reverence for the Earth and its creatures as living beings, and . . . openness to understanding the Earth as an "energy system" ' (Susan Campbell, 1983).

Rights
[before 12c. *Old English riht*]
The BASIC NEEDS of living things, which deserve to be respected and fulfilled wherever possible (*see* ANIMAL RIGHTS, CIVIL RIGHTS, EQUAL RIGHTS, HUMAN RIGHTS, NON-HUMAN RIGHTS, PLANT VARIETY RIGHTS, REPRODUCTIVE RIGHTS — 'land rights', of course, mean something completely different in our anthropocentric society). In green thinking everything has the right to be exactly what it is, though this always carries RESPONSIBILITY in equal measure to rights.

Risk
[17c. *Italian riscare*, to run into danger]
Taking courageous (or foolhardy, depending on your perspective) action in the knowledge that a safe outcome cannot be guaranteed; by extension, the process of making decisions that may involve danger ('risk assessment'). In PSYCHOTHERAPY and groupwork the taking of risks is often actively encouraged: 'People are encouraged to say what they really feel, and really feel what it is they are saying or hearing or doing, and generally to experience and share their own reality. This is very risky for most of us — we fear rejection, partly because there is so much of us that we reject in advance. If we have parts of ourselves that we want to reject and want to disown, it is no wonder that we do not

want to tell others about them. But the extraordinary thing is that if we take the risk, and do it properly and thoroughly, going where it leads, we find that it can make us feel much better about ourselves, not only in the group, but in our life generally' (John Rowan, 1976). This is taking risks with our own life; there are plenty of people taking risks with everybody's lives, if not all life. And economists and militarists have the audacity to calculate the 'risk' that life may be wiped out, *and* continue to manufacture and deploy the means of doing it. Not to mention the 'lesser risks' of ozone depletion, acid rain, nuclear waste dumping, pesticide pollution. Nature always builds very wide margins of error into its systems, human beings just hope that nothing will go wrong — until it does (*see* ACCIDENT). Those in charge of new technologies are constantly taking risks with us and our environment (*see*, for example, IRRADIATION, NUCLEAR WASTE, RADIATION); green-thinkers would like to see industrialists proving that their technology was ecologically sound *before* using it, rather than leaving it to the victims to prove that it isn't safe *after* it has done its dirty work. Risk always involves RESPONSIBILITY, and if you are taking risks with the environment, that is also where your responsibility lies.

Ritual
[1649. *L ritus*, rite]
A more or less formalised CELEBRATION which empowers its participants and affirms a sense of COMMUNITY. ACTIONS — particularly women's actions — often involve ritual. Rituals can include dancing, music, chanting, fire, holding hands in a circle, or standing in silence. 'Rituals are part of every culture. They are events that bind a culture together, that create a heart, a centre, for a people. . . In *ritual* (a patterned movement of energy to accomplish a purpose) we become familiar with power-from-within, learn to recognise its *feel*, learn how to call it up and let it go. . . Rituals create a strong group bond. They help build community, create a meeting-ground where people can share deep feelings, positive and negative — a place where they can sing or scream, howl ecstatically or furiously, play, or keep a solemn silence' (Starhawk, 1982).

Road
[*c*.1600 in this sense. *Old English rad*, from *radan*, to ride]
A continuous open way, usually paved, providing free passage from place to place. Frequently used in the plural to describe a complex network of roads, and almost always defining the area which is used by motor vehicles and therefore unsafe for living organisms not protected by a metal box to spend any length of time. Other places have not yet reached Los Angeles' impressive achievement, where more than 50% of

the city's land area is covered by roads and related uses, but it is clear that in a growth-is-everything economy enough CARS will always appear to render any road-building programme obsolete in a very short space of time. Roads are an extreme hazard to humans, animals, and ecological communities: '6,000 people a year are killed on Britain's roads, and more than a quarter of a million worldwide, not to mention the millions of non-fatal accidents. Many of these are children; more than 15% of child deaths [in Britain] are the result of road accidents' (Jonathon Porritt (ed), 1987). 'Hundreds of thousands of birds and small mammals are slaughtered needlessly every day by the cars that go crashing through our countryside. The toll is even worse with new roads because they often cut across traditional animal pathways' (John Seymour and Herbert Girardet, 1987). 'Covering an area with tar and concrete is one of the most effective ways of permanently extinguishing its wildlife interest [not to mention its wildlife]' (Charles Secrett and Victoria Cliff Hodges, undated).

Role
[1913 in this sense. *French rôle*, an actor's script]
(*also* 'rôle')
Stereotyped behaviour which follows an imaginary script; a part played in a social setting which is thought to be appropriate to a person's standing and circumstances. A great deal of stereotypical behaviour is related to OPPRESSION — both oppressor and oppressed do what is expected of them, often knowing that something is wrong but thinking that nothing can be done about it. Feminist studies have explored in great depth the sex-role system, and how from babyhood children are treated and educated to think of themselves first as girls and boys and second as human beings — a process known as sex-role socialisation. By the time they are adult, most people have learned their scripts so well that they are no longer aware of what is script and what is the real person, and find it hard to believe that the script they use is only one of many that they could choose to use if they wanted.

Roleplay
[1943]
A technique in PSYCHOTHERAPY, more specifically in psychodrama and ASSERTIVENESS training, in which either the therapist or the members of a group take on the roles of people who are influential in the life of a CLIENT in order to act out real or imaginary situations and explore the interactions. 'Role-play is borrowed from the traditional techniques of behaviour therapy. It helps the person to rehearse what she wants to say or do in a given situation. Another person takes the complementary role — for example, someone else might sit in for the shopkeeper, the

queue jumper, the restaurant manager, the child, husband, friend, parent, boss, and so on — so that the first person can practise handling the situation assertively. Without any learned skill, the person taking the complementary role can identify with the situation and will often surprise herself and everyone else by finding the right words to use, the correct intonation, and many subtle ways of making the role-play situation very real for the person who is practising' (Anne Dickson, 1982).

Romance
[13c. *L romanice*, in the Roman manner]
The subject of love stories; a myth created to keep women in their place, safely anaesthetised. 'The stake in the heart of women is romance' (Robin Morgan, 1982). 'I had a romance once but I don't think I will again. It was much too messy' (Andy Smart, *Just Seventeen*, 1986).

Rotation
[1778 in this sense. *L rota*, wheel]
A planned sequence of cropping in which crops are not grown in consecutive years on the same piece of land, thus providing a cycle of complementary nutrient needs and reducing the likelihood of large-scale pest damage. Many farmers have more or less given up rotations in favour of chemical fertilisers, but these can never replace the efficiency of natural soil fertility regeneration, and eventually lead to total dependence on agrochemicals and a decreasing yield.

Rubbish
(*see* WASTE)

Runoff
[1893]
Water which falls as rain and snow and runs over the ground surface to form streams rather than seeping through the soil. DEFORESTATION, vegetation clearance, and leaving agricultural land with no vegetation cover all encourage increased runoff, and thus hasten SOIL EROSION.

Rural Resettlement
[1977]
Moving into the countryside and living and working there with respect for the countryside, its traditions and inhabitants (even if they are all second home owners and fellow resettlers) — the usual British term for what in North America and Australia is more often called the BACK TO THE LAND movement. The Rural Resettlement Group, set up in Britain in 1977, publishes a *Rural Resettlement Handbook*. While rural resettlement in the West is a freely-chosen escape from urban living, in parts of the THIRD WORLD (Tanzania for example) it is a policy pursued by

governments and aid agencies to reduce OVERURBANISATION and encourage agricultural development, reversing a migration to the cities that would probably never have occurred if agricultural development had been taken seriously in the 1960s and 1970s. Though some resettlement schemes appear to be working, they will always be handicapped as long as the bulk of Third World resources continue to be allocated to urban areas.

Ss

Sacred
[14c. *L sacer*, holy]
A place or phenomenon deserving particular awe and respect. In the secular West 'sacred' is tied up with a particular brand of religious holiness and has been rejected by many people, but in acknowledging our connectedness with the earth and its inhabitants we have a great deal to learn about RESPECT (*see also* SPIRITUALITY). NATIVE PEOPLES like the Hopi in North America and the Aborigines in Australia still take their sacred sites very seriously, as a direct connection with the planet that gave them birth. Such 'shrines' have regularly been desecrated by the march of Western progress, but do now have some protection under legislation like the US Religious Freedom Act of 1978. 'All the earth is sacred, every step we make;/All the earth is sacred, every breath we take./Heal the people: we are one' (Sufi chant). 'The task is to acknowledge the miraculousness of life, the preciousness of life, and the vast beauty of what we do not know about life and the living. To treat life, our neighbours, our land, our green life, our architecture, as sacred at least teaches us to be careful, appreciative and sensitive — from here on it is up to each of us how we build' (Keith Critchlow, *Resurgence*, July/August 1984). 'I believe we must internalise the order of nature in order to transform the problems we experience among ourselves. Wind and water are powerful forces which transform Earth energy into balance. These forces are part of our spiritual nature [and] a deeper understanding of these environmental forces will give us greater insight into our spiritual nature. We have much to learn from the ancient cultures which still exist. They know that the Earth is alive and that it deserves peace and purification, and that this can only happen if we attune ourselves to its sacred order' (Joan Price, in Vance Martin and Mary Inglis (ed.),1984). '*Sacred* refers to that which helps take us out of our little selves into the larger self of the whole universe' (Gary Snyder, 1984).

Safety
[13c. *L salvus*, healthy, uninjured]
A setting in which people are free to live in a fulfilling way without having their physical well-being and self-respect threatened. In PSYCHOTHERAPY and groupwork the aim is to encourage self-exploration in a safe setting, where the client knows that whatever happens somebody will be there to catch them at the end. Social WELFARE systems are in theory supposed to do the same, but are almost invariably bogged down in hierarchy and BUREAUCRACY; the 'safety net' provided by social security is so full of holes that few people trust it. When it comes to our physical environment, safety clearly takes second place to convenience and commercial considerations unless public opinion and pressure groups can influence government policy, as has happened with road safety following the massive Ralph Nader campaign of the 1960s. Yet nuclear physicists still tell us that nuclear energy generation is safe; militarist politicians that the world is a 'safer place' thanks to nuclear deterrence. 'Dr Alice Stewart carefully collected information on children born in England and Wales and through rigorous analysis showed damage from radiation at levels . . . being assumed "safe" by the nuclear military-commercial establishment. By 1970 Dr Stewart had studied some 16 million children, and through her painstaking documentation and dogged persistence had moved the medical world to recognise the harmful effects of the medical X-ray during pregnancy' (Rosalie Bertell, 1985). *See also* SECURITY.

Salinisation
[1928. *L sal*, salt]
(US: 'salinization')
The accumulation of excessive salt in soil, often as a result of large-scale IRRIGATION schemes in semi-arid areas (*see also* TECHNOFIX).

Sanctions
(*see* BOYCOTT)

Sanctuary
[*L sanctuarium*, repository for holy things]
(1) [14c] A place reserved for worship and MEDITATION. An idea revived in the 1960s to denote a room (also 'meditation room') or outdoor location used specifically for meditation. 'The settlement comprises nine cottages, large vegetable gardens, animals, boats for fishing and recreation, craft studios for candle making, stained glass work, spinning and knitting, and a beautiful sanctuary which looks across the sea to the sacred isle of Iona' (Findhorn Foundation, 1987).
(2) [1879] An area of land or water set aside for the protection of wildlife, particularly of ENDANGERED SPECIES (from the idea of

'sanctuary' as a place of immunity from danger).
(3) [*c.*1975] The 'sanctuary movement' is a network of church groups in the USA which looks after thousands of Central American 'illegal' refugees fleeing WAR and FAMINE. In 1985 many of the movement's coordinators were convicted of harbouring illegal aliens and conspiracy, a case which has brought many people's attention to the issues surrounding REFUGEES and the integrity of the STATE.

Sane/Humane/Ecological
[1977]
(*also* 'SHE')
A vision of a future society in which these three sets of values are incorporated into people's lifestyles, in contrast to the 'HE' (HYPER-EXPANSIONIST) vision which results from an extension and exaggeration of currently-prevailing values. 'By contrast the "SHE" vision of the future foresees, not an acceleration along the same path of development we have followed during the industrial age, but a change in the direction of development . . . The breakthrough will be primarily psychological and social, not technical and economic. It will enlarge the human limits to human achievement. It will amplify our capacity to develop ourselves as human beings, together with the communities and the societies in which we live. Not only will it bring fundamental social and personal change, as the industrial revolution did, but that is what will be its main motive force' (James Robertson, 1985).

Sanity
[17c. *L sanus*, sane, healthy]
COMMON SENSE, INTELLIGENCE and REASON, the realistic antidotes to the insane 'reality' of the nuclear mentality and Western-style 'progress'. 'We are facing the ultimate insanity — destroying the world we live in. This insanity is the "real" world. Yet if women talk plainly about how this insanity affects their lives now, before the event, they are called mad themselves' (Alice Cook and Gwyn Kirk, 1983).

Scale
[17c in this sense. *Late L scala*, ladder]
The size of something relative to its function, specifically in relation to the size of a human being and human needs (*see* HUMAN SCALE). TECHNOFIX solutions are almost invariably conceived on an inappropriately large scale, ignoring the obvious fact that big solutions = big risks = big problems. 'No work of human ingenuity, however perfect otherwise, can possibly be successful if it is too small or, more to the usual point, too big, just as a door fails if it is too small, a doorknob if it is too large to grasp; just as an economy fails if it is too small to provide shelter as well as food, a government if it is too large to let all its citizens know about

and regularly influence its actions. At the right scale human potential is unleashed, human comprehension magnified, human accomplishment multiplied' (Kirkpatrick Sale, 1985).

Scarcity
[14c. *L excerpere*, to pick out, select]
An inadequate supply of something. In the 'science' of economics scarcity has the technical meaning of there being 'less of something than people would like to have if it cost nothing to buy' (*Dictionary of Economics*, 1972), a pointless definition, implying that the only things that aren't scarce are the things you can't buy, like air and sunshine (and by extension life and freedom). In the real world scarcity arises because resources cannot fulfil people's needs, usually because greed and market mechanisms are creating artificial scarcity rather than because the resources are literally insufficient. 'This is the realization of scarcity — scarcity of certain wild species and landscapes, scarcity of low-cost (or at least low-environmental-cost) energy, food, and other raw materials; scarcity of public amenity and a growing scarcity of reasonably priced private amenity. . . A pervasive uncertainty . . . has all but replaced the beguiling self-confidence which has characterized the ruling elite in western democracies ever since the industrial revolution' (Timothy O'Riordan, 1976).

Scavenging
[17c. *Old French escauwage*, inspection]
Using the surplus of natural systems and the 'waste' of human ones for life-enhancing purposes. In the West most of us automatically believe that 'new and bought' is best; in the THIRD WORLD (and increasingly in the 'rich' world) most people would never dream of buying something they might scavenge, and RECYCLING and the RE-USE of materials is a mainstay of the economy. 'One must draw some little part of one's livelihood from the breadth of the landscape: spotting downed trees for next year's firewood, gathering mushrooms or berries or herbs on time, hunting, fishing, scrounging' (Gary Snyder, 1980). 'There is a particular kind of enjoyment gained in salvaging from a junk pile something whose beauty or usefulness only you can appreciate' (Ernest Callenbach, 1981).

Schizophrenia
[1912. *Gk schizein + phren*, split mind]
A state in which a person appears to lose touch with their surroundings, seems unable to communicate in words about what is going on, and withdraws into 'another world'. Conventionally defined as a 'psychotic disorder' and a MENTAL ILLNESS, schizophrenia is seen by psychiatrists as a medical fact, though it can often be seen as a perfectly intelligent

response to a harsh and insane world. 'Though schizophrenia is only a concept and a methodological convenience, most psychiatrists treat schizophrenia as if it were a well-defined illness' (Eia Asen, 1986). 'In general, whenever people feel unable to prevail by means of ordinary speech, . . they are likely to shift their pleas to . . . weeping [and] body signs. We have come to speak of this . . . as "mental illness". As a result, instead of realizing that people are engaged in various types of communications . . . we construct — and then ourselves come to believe in — various types of mental illnesses, such as "hysteria", "hypochondriasis", "schizophrenia" and so forth' (Thomas Szasz, 1962).

School
[12c. *Gk skhole*, leisure spent in the pursuit of knowledge]
An institution or building in which young people are educated. Schooling (which is compulsory in many countries) varies enormously, and teachers often have a difficult task working within the system and maintaining their integrity and individuality. Partly because of these pressures, and partly because of lack of resources, a great deal of education limits children as much as it opens up opportunities. 'In most schools there is no contact, either with the real world, or real things, or real people. In these dull, ugly, and inhuman places, where nobody ever says anything either very true or truthful, where everybody is playing a kind of role, where the teachers are no more free to respond openly and honestly to the students than the students are free to respond to the teachers or each other, where the air practically vibrates with suspicions and anxiety, the child learns to live in a kind of daze, saving his [or her] energies for those small parts of his [or her] life that are too trivial for the adults to bother with and thus remain his [or hers]. . . It is a rare child who can come through his [or her] schooling with much left of his [or her] curiosity, his [or her] independence, and his [or her] own dignity, competence and worth' (John Holt, 1970). It is the institutional aspect of EDUCATION, where students have little say or choice, that concerns many green-thinkers: 'The institutionalisation of permanent education will transform society into an enormous planet-size classroom watched over by a few satellites. Only the labels will enable one to distinguish it from an enormous hospital ward, from a planetary mental home and from a penitentiary universe, where education, punishment, medical care and imprisonment are synonymous' (Ivan Illich and Etienne Verne, 1976). Although there is still much that can be done and there are still far too many dull, ugly and inhuman schools, there have been rapid changes in schooling in recent years in some Western countries, and many schools have become centres of community action and social and economic concern, limited only by resources and reactionary official policies. *See also* DESCHOOLING, FREE SCHOOL.

Science
[Late 17c in this sense. *L scientia*, knowledge]
KNOWLEDGE, WISDOM; an important part of relating to the natural world and of understanding that relationship. 'Science', however, has largely become a victim of Western DUALISM and the ideas of PROGRESS that go with it. From the early nineteenth century until recently, when there have been some glimmers of a hopeful alternative viewpoint, 'science' has been a way of looking at the world which only acknowledges the truth of something when and if it can be observed, measured, and operated on using 'the scientific method' [1854]. The scientific method makes several assumptions, which must be taken into account when considering the validity of any scientific approach. These include:
— That there is such a thing as objective reality, and that the purpose of science is to observe, measure and categorise it.
— That the subjects of scientific study exist independently of and are not influenced by the scientist.
— That science is value-free.
— That the more information that can be gathered about a subject, the better it will be understood.
— That the more we know about something, the better we are.
— That although women are grudgingly tolerated, most real science is done by men.
Many green-thinkers are convinced that a great deal of modern science, in the way it has been formulated and controlled, is antithetical to a holistic approach, and that the dichotomy is unbridgeable. 'Socially irresponsible science not only pollutes our rivers, air and soil, produces CS gas for Northern Ireland, defoliants for Vietnam and stroboscopic torture devices for police states. It also degrades, both mentally and physically, those at the point of production, as the objectivisation of their labour reduces them to mere machine appendages' (Mike Cooley, 1987). Some feminists, equating science with patriarchal power, have reached the same conclusion: 'Science *is* men's studies and cannot be modified, and . . . a "woman-centred science" would be so radically different that it would no longer be invested with the meaning of "science" as we know it" (Dale Spender, 1981). Some disagree, not necessarily with such an analysis, but with the degree to which the idea of science can be stretched: 'Can there be a science that is not based exclusively on measurement; an understanding of reality that includes quality and experience and yet can be called scientific? I believe that such an understanding is, indeed, possible. . . I am prepared to call any approach to knowledge scientific that satisfies two conditions: all knowledge must be based on scientific observation, and it must be expressed in terms of self-consistent but limited and approximate

models' (Fritjof Capra, 1982). Though many scientists either declare or imply that their science is intrinsically neutral, there is very little science which is not funded by concerns whose main interest is commercial viability, and a great deal of scientific research and development continues because MULTINATIONALS and militaristic governments fund it and because scientists choose to do it, not 'because it's there to be done'. 'His face was wreathed in a smile of almost angelic beauty. He looked as though his inner gaze were fixed upon a world of harmonies. But in fact, as he told me later, he was thinking about a mathematical problem, whose solution was essential to the construction of a new type of H-bomb. . . He had never visited Hiroshima and Nagasaki, even though he had been invited. . . To him research for nuclear weapons was just pure higher mathematics untrammelled by blood, poison and destruction. All that, he said, was none of his business' (Robert Jungk, 1956). Yet ecologists, meteorologists, nature reserve wardens, appropriate technologists, new physicists, and many of the green-thinkers who have drawn our attention to the perils of dangerous technologies are scientists too, and their careful skills are needed. Is it possible, knowing what we now know, to return science to its ancient status of wisdom and deep knowing? 'Science and technology cannot be humanely applied in an inherently inhuman society, and the contradictions for scientific workers in the application of their abilities will grow and, if properly articulated, will lead to a radicalisation of the scientific community' (Mike Cooley, *op. cit.*). *See also* TECHNOLOGY.

Scientism
[1877]
Complete yet ultimately mistaken faith in the scientific method (*see* SCIENCE); sometimes contrasted with HOLISM.

S-Curve
[1976]
A curve on a graph which shows accelerating growth, then slows down until it flattens out again against an upper limit, forming an elongated 'S'. Such a curve shows the sort of EXPONENTIAL GROWTH that is currently being experienced in, for example, global oil consumption or the human population of the planet, but slowing down as a limiting level of reserves or resources is reached; a slowing down which has already happened with, for instance, demand for electricity in Western Europe and the number of people in China. 'S-curve thinking' contradicts the pessimism of some OVERSHOOT and collapse theorists and is more in line with ecological principles: '[If] a living organism is introduced into a certain container, and if a constant steady stream of energy is supplied in the form of a steadily added nutrient, then the growth curve will start off

[showing a gradual but steady increase,] but instead of a sudden termination during its period of fastest growth, or an infinitely upward curving line, growth begins to slow after a certain point. . . Growth begins to decelerate, population increases more and more slowly until the maximum number of individual oganisms are held in equilibrium by the limits of the container and the steady flow of energy. . . The Earth, like a petri dish, is a finite container limited by gravity on one side, you could say, and the crust of the lithosphere on the other, while the sun's energy is a constant source of nutrition sustaining life' (Richard Faust Register, 1978).

Sea
(*see* OCEAN)

Seasons
[14c. *L serere*, to sow]
The annual CYCLE of nature; of growth, harvest, death and rebirth. A cycle underestimated by many Westerners, who have come to expect lettuce during the traditional hungry gap of late winter and the same length of working day year-round, cursing snow on the roads and shivering in midsummer air-conditioning. Many green-thinkers try consciously to be aware of the seasons, celebrating the equinoxes in spring and autumn and the solstices in summer and winter, like the many traditional societies who are directly dependent upon the seasonal progression. The Hopi, for example, take the heels off their shoes in the spring so as not to damage the pregnant earth. 'Turn and turn again and turn,/always rolling on with massive thumps/and sudden lurching dives, I am pinned/to the wheel of the seasons, hot and cold, sober and glad and menacing,/bearing and losing' (Marge Piercy, 1985). *See also* PAGANISM.

Secrecy
[15c. *L secretus*, concealed]
Deliberately hiding something so that nobody apart from those who are specially chosen can have access to it. A confusing idea because of its associations with FEAR, INTIMACY, MYSTERY, PRIVACY, SILENCE, furtiveness and deceit. A useful though necessarily arbitrary distinction for green purposes is between privacy (the basic right to be with whom you want and not with whom you don't want, to have a peaceful setting in which to do it, and to be silent when you choose) and secrecy (deliberate withholding in order to maintain power over someone). Hiding things is something we learn when we are very young, first as a game and then to have something that adults can't take away from us, making it difficult to distinguish between secrecy as choice and secrecy as defence. Secrecy as DEFENCE is an obvious reaction to OPPRESSION, as is the fear

of secrets being discovered by an ENEMY — in fact the whole concept of secrecy depends upon having enemies to hide things from. When there are people who can maintain their power over you by using INFORMATION you would rather withhold, it is important to keep those things from them, but the ultimate solution to an imbalance of power is the end of oppression, not ever-increasing secrecy. The whole spectrum of human behaviour is beset by secrecy. 72% of the men interviewed in the *Hite Report on Male Sexuality* (Shere Hite, 1978) who had been married for two years or more had had at least one affair, and 97% of them had kept it secret (19% had been found out). Secrecy is rife in industry, especially in those which really have something to hide like the nuclear industry, and at the level of national OFFICIAL SECRETS are whole communities of people who can never talk about their work for fear of the legal and personal repercussions. Fiascos such as Watergate and Irangate, the Belgrano scandal and the Rainbow Warrior sinking, all display 'democratic' governments employing a combination of LIES and secrecy on a grand scale. Then there are the vast amounts of information held about us by official and non-official institutions which in most countries — and the USA is in many ways a notable exception — is kept secret even from us, the people they purport to represent. 'If military or industrial secrecy prevents [the] exercise of citizenship then it undermines a . . . principle to which I hold very strongly, which is that secrecy should be anathema to any civilized community, . . no matter what its alleged justification' (Kathleen Lonsdale, 1950, in Rosalie Bertell, 1985).

Security
[15c. *L securus*, without care]
A travesty of SAFETY created by locks and bolts, armoured cars, star wars, massive nuclear arsenals, policemen with guns and riot shields, spies and counterspies. 'Do any of us seriously believe that the prospect of the Third World War recedes as the nuclear megatonnage builds up? If we cast our minds, not over the next decade or two, but over a hundred, two hundred years, then we must surely acknowledge that this frenetic accumulation cannot continue for ever, and there are really only two options facing us: extermination or an end to the Cold War and the relentless amassing of arms that goes with it' (Kate Soper, in Dan Smith and E.P. Thompson (ed), 1987). *See also* NATIONAL SECURITY.

Seed
[before 12c. *Old English sæd*]
The germ of new growth, containing all the potential for a fully-grown life-form. 'Thus seeds are portable dormitories in which repose unborn generations, provided with food when they wake from their sleep. If no

moisture gets near them they can remain in their cradles for years, even for centuries, still retaining their power to rise up. Seeds of the kidney bean have been known to sprout after sixty years at rest, while cornflower and raspberry seeds dug from the dry darkness of Celtic sepulchres have grown and flowered like the seeds of yesterday' (John Stewart Collis, 1973). 'Seed' is a potent symbol of the future possibility of healthy growth, used by green-thinkers in expressions like 'seed money', 'seedcorn project' and 'Johnnie (or Janie) Appleseed' — someone who plants appropriate seeds in appropriate places.

Self

[Late 17c in this sense. *Old English self*]

The individual uniqueness of a person; the person they really are as distinct from the personality they project and the games and roles they play. The idea of 'self' is central to most traditions within psychology and to most green thinking. It acknowledges that each person has a real and unique existence which provides a purpose for their presence, and which deserves respect and acknowledgement. 'Our prime aim, then, in humanistic psychology, is to enable the person to get in touch with their real self — to gain an actual experience of the true self. And so we encourage clients all the time to question all — all without exception — of the taken-for-granted images of themselves, having no respect at all for their defences' (John Rowan, 1983).

Self-Acceptance

[17c]

Accepting yourself as you are; loving yourself. Most green-thinkers know that it is extremely difficult to love anything or anyone else until you have learned to love yourself, accepting that you don't have to conform to anybody's ideas — including your own — about how you should be.

Self-Actualisation

[1969]

(US: 'self-actualization')

(*also* 'self-discovery')

Finding, integrating and becoming your SELF. 'The process by which a person becomes so sure and self-aware has been called by Maslow "self-actualization". It means becoming that self which you truly are. It means realizing all of what you have it in you to be. It seems clear that there can only be self-actualizing people, probably never any self-actualized people. It seems to be not a state but a process — a process of continually laying oneself on the line and being open to experience, so that one can genuinely meet it' (John Rowan, 1976).

Self-Appreciation
[*c*.1970]
(*also* 'self-validation')
Liking yourself; more specifically, saying something good about yourself in a therapy session or group. 'She glances at the clock and, in a second, she is sitting up and back to her normal consciousness. As she gathers her belongings, preparing to leave, I ask her to appreciate herself for something she did in the session. She groans a little with displeasure. Self-appreciations are a chore with her, as they are for most of my clients. "Okay. Let's see . . . I was able to really feel my anger and let most of it out" ' (Miriam Greenspan, 1983).

Self-Build
[1970]
(*also* 'owner-building')
Building your own SHELTER. Most people in the Third World have routinely built their own houses, but house-building in the West has become highly specialised and institutionalised, and the same inappropriate mass-production of housing is now appearing all over the world. An increasing number of people in the West are choosing to build their own houses, either individually or in groups as housing associations and cooperatives. 'Not only is new housing highly priced, but it is an inherently unsatisfactory product. Houses are often very poorly constructed, . . . they are expensive to run, . . they are poorly designed inside and out . . . So what is the answer to all this? Firstly, the costs can be reduced, and the owner-builder—along with other forms of self-building—enjoys substantial cost savings over the commercially available product. But secondly, the owner-builder can exert a large measure of control over the design, the building techniques and the building materials that are used to ensure that the house is designed to suit its location and environment and to provide effective, low-cost and sympathetically designed shelter for its occupants' (Michael Norton, 1980). *See also* ARCHITECTURE, HOUSING.

Self-Care
[*c*.1973]
Looking after our own HEALTH as individuals and communities. 'For self-care advocates, the problem is that most laypeople know far too little about (1) evaluating and improving their health *without* waiting until they get sick and (2) coping with illness — both through self-care and by making good usee of health facilities — when illness does occur. The self-care movement feels that we have depended too much on experts in health care and that with the proper training and self-study materials, laypeople would be capable of being their own paramedics' (Tom Ferguson, 1980).

Self-Defence
[17c]
(US: 'self-defense')
Ways of protecting yourself when physically attacked, preferably without hurting your assailant more than is necessary. Self-defence often has more to do with acknowledging and exploring your physical strength and intelligence as much as learning how to throw someone over your shoulder. As women are becoming aware that male violence can be interrupted, physically if needs be, self-defence classes have become increasingly popular: 'Developing your physical strength and using it to protect yourself in any way is undoubtedly valuable. A word or two of caution though. Self-defence techniques are sometimes misleadingly presented as instant and foolproof remedies for attack, [but] . . . only you are able to judge what you are able to do at that moment to endure and survive what is happening. . . If you choose not to fight, it does not mean you consent to rape' (London Rape Crisis Centre, 1984).

Self-Determination
[1911 in this sense]
The belief that a NATION or cultural group should decide its own policies without pressure from outside. *See* COLONIALISM, NEOCOLONIALISM.

Self-Esteem
[17c]
(*also* 'self-confidence', 'self-respect')
Being pleased with yourself. Not to be confused with arrogance, which is believing yourself to be better than other people, though self-esteem is a rare experience for many people, and you may have to deal with other people's feelings of anger and frustration because they are not pleased with themselves. 'Self-esteem is wrongly confused with conceit and arrogance. It is wrongly assumed to be dependent upon success. Self-esteem stems from a strong, rooted sense of self-worth which survives both failure and success; it survives mistakes, disappointment, and most of all self-esteem survives acceptance and rejection from others. . . Two of the major ingredients of self-esteem are the feelings of being accepted and being loved' (Anne Dickson, 1982).

Self-Healing
[*c*.1975]
Helping yourself to become and remain healthy; 'self-healing' usually refers to techniques such as AFFIRMATION, MEDITATION, RELAXATION and VISUALISATION.

Self-Help
[1891]
Helping yourself, either as an individual or within a group of people with similar interests. 'Self-help' in green parlance usually refers to groups in which the members help each other, either in practical or therapeutic ways (thus 'self-help group', 'self-help therapy'). 'The power of self-help mutual aid groups derives from the fact that they combine a number of very important properties. These include the helper-therapy principle, the aprofessional dimension, consumer intensivity, the use of indigenous support, and the implicit demand that an individual can do something for him or herself. Self-help groups show that people need not be passive, that they have power — particularly in a group that demands they do something for each other. . . They enable their members to feel and use their own strengths and their own power, and to have control over their own lives' (Alan Gartner and Frank Riessman, 1977, in Tom Ferguson, 1980). The rapid growth of the self-help movement has encouraged short-sighted reactionary governments to withdraw funding and resources from state-sponsored health care and education, the idea of 'self-help' fitting in very nicely with an 'each-for-their-own' philosophy (*see* NEW RIGHT). 'Self-help' is also sometimes used to mean 'self-improvement', not always in an unselfish way, as titles like *Think Yourself Rich* and *Banish Poverty-Consciousness* suggest.

Self-Reliance
[1833]
Looking after your own affairs without outside interference; most frequently used in green circles as a synonym for SELF-SUFFICIENCY, or to describe the policies of increasing self-reliance being adopted by some THIRD WORLD countries in association with a DELINKING of their economies with the West. 'But how would [delinking] help people in the Third World? One possible answer is that it would be a response to their increasing emphasis on "self-reliance". It would lessen the pressure of outside advice, and the cacophony of ideologies, theories and techniques we emit, which is so loud and persistent that those in the Third World can hardly hear themselves think' (Dudley Seers, 1982, in Victoria Brittain and Michael Simmons (ed), 1987).

Self-Respect
(*see* SELF-ESTEEM)

Self-Sufficiency
[1973 in this sense]
(*also* 'self-reliance' (though *see* SELF-RELIANCE), 'self-support')
Growing and producing as much as possible of what you need through

your own efforts. 'More and more city people will leave the big cities . . . and set up their workshops in pleasant places, and many of these people will eventually get the idea of being at least partially self-supporting . . . A surprising number of the more intelligent people who have passed through the big-city-industrial stage are reacting against it: they want to advance to a more interesting and self-sufficient kind of life' (John and Sally Seymour, 1973). Self-sufficiency has been, and to some extent still is, the vision of rural resettlers, though if carried to extremes it can be both ecologically unsound and antisocial. Green-thinkers see self-sufficiency in relative terms, and view communal, local and regional self-sufficiency, though still linked with the larger world, as more realistic and life-enhancing alternatives to self-sufficiency at the family level (*see* COLLECTIVE SELF-RELIANCE).

Self-Validation
(*see* SELF-APPRECIATION)

Separatism
[*c*.1960 in this sense. *L separare*, to separate]
Choosing, as a member or members of an oppressed group, to escape from the OPPRESSION in the company of your own people and without the help of the oppressor group; consciously-chosen segregation. It is important to distinguish between separatism and separateness — in green terms separatism is concerned with the celebration of DIVERSITY within the whole, and is a reaction against attempts to make all human beings conform to the same cultural standards and norms. The practice of separatism varies greatly, from holding closed meetings to ensuring complete avoidance wherever possible. Many black groups in the USA in the 1960s asked whites — however aware and well-intentioned — to leave them to organise their own lives and actions. Starting in the late 1960s many women took the same line. Though some feminist women see separatism as a necessary but temporary measure, many — some but not all LESBIAN — view separatism as the only way to deal with the excesses of patriarchy and to maintain their own power and sanity. 'The feminist separation can take many forms. Breaking up or avoiding close relationships or working relationships; forbidding someone to enter your house; excluding someone from your company, or from your meeting; withdrawal from participation in some activity or institution, or avoidance of participation; avoidance of communications and influence from certain quarters . . ; withholding commitment or support; rejection of or rudeness towards obnoxious individuals' (Marilyn Frye, 1983). The idea of conscious choice in separatism concerns some feminist women, who believe that non-communication as often results from fear and anger as from choice: 'I'm always being amazed to find

out how many apparent separatists aren't at all. We seem to have no language to express engagement with brothers, sons, lovers and male friends or workmates that doesn't also compromise their power. And so uncompromising feminists will stick to a separatist rhetoric which leaves out whole areas of their lives but at least declares "no surrender"' (Amanda Sebestyen, in Scarlet Friedman and Elizabeth Sarah (ed), 1982). 'The most radical extreme of separatism can be seen in the refusal of some lesbian feminists to ally with women who maintain any emotional connections with men, including male infants. At this extreme, separatism seems to be a dead end. It is retreat rather than a political response' (Lisa Tuttle, 1986). 'Separatism' also means the demands of a NATION or cultural group for SELF-DETERMINATION, separate from the STATE of which it currently forms a part: 'An exhaustive catalog of the identifiable separatist movements around the globe would be tedious, so numerous are they. Louis L. Snyer's comprehensive *Global Mini-Nationalisms: Autonomy or Independence* lists twenty-nine nations [states] with fifty-eight separatist strains and still fails to mention at least twenty other nations with forty-five other separatist groups and resistant minorities — and that is counting only the most vociferous and self-conscious movements, not even such identifiable but not explicitly antagonistic subpopulations as the Andalusians in Spain, the Ladakhis in India, or the Mohawks in the United States' (Kirkpatrick Sale, 1985).

Service Economy
[1970]
An economy in which the majority of the workforce works in the 'service sector' or the 'tertiary sector', rather than in the 'primary sector' (agriculture and the extraction and refining of raw materials) or the 'secondary sector' (manufacturing industry). 'Some futurists have suggested a service economy (i.e. one based on such things as recreation, education, health and social care, finance, law, public administration, etc.) as the model for post-industrialism. When we examine the ecological position of the service industries in the resource cycle, however, we are struck by their total dependence on the basic industries. The service industries function to circulate and redistribute capital that is generated ultimately by manufacturing and the more basic industries, much as the carnivores circulate and redistribute energy that is fixed ultimately by plants . . . A service economy, while an undeniable concomitant of industrialism at maturity, is not a feasible model for post-industrial civilization' (W. Jackson Davis, 1979).

Sex

[14c. *L sexus*, sex; akin to *secare*, to divide]

Possibly the only really useful meaning of 'sex' in a green vocabulary is the biological distinction between maleness and femaleness. The massive structure of convention, norms, behaviours and institutions which has been built on this distinction, the social construction of sexual differentiation, is better described, as many feminists distinguish it, as GENDER. This construction is responsible for the notions of MASCULINE and FEMININE, a polarisation so pervasive as to have been given a new lease of life in the ANDROGYNY and YIN/YANG of many green-thinkers, including some feminists. 'Unfortunately, as [some] recent feminism has become synonymous with the reclamation and establishment of a so-called female principle, it has come to reflect and reproduce dominant cultural assumptions about women' (Alice Echols, in Ann Snitow *et al* (ed), 1984). '"Masculine" and "feminine" are useless; or rather, they serve only and oppressively to naturalize cultural realizations and representations of human activity that should and must be analyzed as such, understood as part of the sexual fix. "Masculine" and "feminine" are "concepts" we need to learn to refuse' (Stephen Heath, 1982). The other meaning of 'sex' in common use is to describe 'sexual behaviour', which generally implies heterosexual (*see* HETEROSEXUALITY) intimate behaviour culminating in 'the sex act', or intercourse with PENETRATION. One function of intercourse is the conception of new life, a joyful event when chosen by the prospective parent (*see* BIRTH CONTROL, CONTRACEPTION, PARENT); most sexual activity, however, is more to do with shared love and pleasure than with conception. Sexual sharing — heterosexual, homosexual, or with yourself — can be extremely pleasant, but there is always the danger of using sexual behaviour to manipulate another person, as a substitute for the non-fulfilment of a different need, or because you are addicted to it: 'Sex — the new opiate of the people' (Germaine Greer, 1984) (*see also* DESIRE, EROTIC, INTIMACY, PASSION). The recent concern with 'safe sex' (*see* AIDS) has begun to bring it home to people that not only must they be entirely responsible for their own health and the fulfilment of their needs in the way *they* choose, but also that there are an enormous number of ways of giving and receiving physical pleasure (*see* BODYWORK, MASSAGE, TOUCH). Feminism has clarified the right for each person — especially for women — to define and choose their own sexuality; feminism has also traced the links between sex, PORNOGRAPHY and VIOLENCE. While accepting that these links have been created and are maintained by institutionalised SEXISM, green-thinkers are convinced that physical sharing is possible without either violence or degradation: 'The con game that's been practised on all of us has been the equation of sex with violence, as if we have to choose between being sexual and victims of violence on the one hand or no-violence-therefore-no-sex on the other' (Joanna Russ, 1985). 'The question of knowledge about sexuality is one very pressing reason why "sexual liberation" was not wholly a bad thing for women — in spite of the fact that it was men who mainly benefited from this freedom since they never had to bear the consequences of sex. The increased sexual freedom and possibility of choice and experimentation did give *some* women the possibility of knowing more and taking more control of their sexuality. The new need to communicate about sexual habits and practices is something which could greatly benefit girls since it would extend the information they have about sex. It seems to me that what is really at stake in the AIDS crisis is not whether we can preserve our existing freedoms but whether we can use the crisis to transform the balance of power between the sexes' (Ros Coward, *New Internationalist*, March 1987).

Sexism
[1968]
The OPPRESSION of women by men, considered by some people to be the basic oppression upon which the others are modelled. Although the word is now in common use, the most usual interpretation of sexism is 'discrimination against people (not women, note) on the grounds of sex'. This tends to be seen only in terms of tangible DISCRIMINATION — wage rates, job opportunities and so on: important though these are, they are only part of a system of oppression which pervades every aspect of social life. This interpretation also suggests that discrimination against men can be traced to sexist oppression: most green-thinkers are clear that while men may be oppressed, it is the structure of a patriarchal society (*see* PATRIARCHY), not women, which is oppressing them. As with other oppressions, the behaviours we have all learned as men and women often make it hard to recognise the more subtle forms of sexism when they arise; as yet, however, even the most blatant aspects of sexist oppression are all too common. The situation is unlikely to change until men themselves begin to understand the futility of oppression. Because men have no experience of being at the receiving end of sexism, only women are in a position to be the final arbiters of the relative oppressiveness of male behaviour. This makes suspect any man or group of men who call themselves ANTI-SEXIST, let alone NON-SEXIST, though that is no reason for men not to work against sexism in every aspect of their lives.

Sexual Politics
[1968]
The recognition that the POWER relationships between men and women

are just as political as any other, despite being ignored in conventional politics; a concept central to FEMINISM. 'When one group rules another, the relationship between the two is political' (Kate Millett, 1968).

Shadow
[1923 in this sense. *Old English sceadu*, shade]
That part of ourselves which we fear to confront. If our shadow is denied it can be projected (*see* PROJECTION) on to another person or people, who are then conceived of as enemies and treated as scapegoats. When this happens on a large scale, with great numbers of people feeding each other's PARANOIA, it is sometimes referred to as the 'collective shadow', or 'emotional plague'.

Shadow Work
[*c.* 1981]
(*also* 'shadow economy')
WORK which contributes directly to the mainstream economy and would not exist if that economy were not there, yet which is unpaid; the unique bondage upon which capitalism depends. 'It comprises most housework women do in their homes and apartments, the activities connected with shopping, most of the homework of students cramming for exams, the toil expended commuting to and from the job. It includes the stress of forced consumption, the tedious and regimented surrender to therapists, compliance with bureaucrats, the preparation for work to which one is compelled, and many of the activities usually labelled "family life"' (Ivan Illich, 1981). *See also* INFORMAL ECONOMY.

Sharecropping
[1923]
An agricultural arrangement whereby the landowner provides seed, equipment and other inputs on credit, and receives an agreed share of the crop in return. Sharecropping agreements vary, but in general the precarious and short-term leases preclude good land management and encourage a feudal society.

Sharing
[16c. *Old English scearu*, share]
Being generous; ensuring that other people get what they need, especially when you have more than enough; giving without expecting anything in return. In the 1960s 'sharing' became a favourite verb with the human potential movement; people didn't tell things to their group or therapist, they shared. 'Within the community, "sharing" had a special meaning. When anyone related [their] deeds, [they] "shared" [their] past. . . If a member was given insight into another's hangup,

[they] shared [the] insight out of love. "Sharing" was also the name of the general meeting during which such experiences and revelations were exchanged. The time was also used for group glossolalia [babbling in a non-existent language], if they were so moved, and to cure members' minor ailments' (Robert Houriet, 1971).

SHE
(*see* SANE/HUMANE/ECOLOGICAL)

Shelter
[Late 16c. Origin unknown, maybe from *Old English sceld*, shield] A structure providing safety and protection from inclement weather, usually for human beings. A word used by green-thinkers in two contexts: firstly, as an alternative word for HOUSING with its all conventional connotations; secondly, to refer to structures for human habitation in many different settings and circumstances, acknowledging that not everybody lives in 'houses'. 'Sheltered housing' is accommodation provided within a communal or semi-communal setting for old and disabled people, offering them a range of assistance appropriate to their needs.

Shifting Agriculture
(*see* SLASH-AND-BURN)

Silence
[13c. *L silere*, to be quiet]
(1) Utter stillness. A rare treat for many people, and thus often frightening when it is experienced, but sometimes necessary and a right that should be respected. 'In the conventional economics of our society, silence, of course, [has] no existence at all. It is not a commodity, a utility, a resource, a service . . . except perhaps in the form of soundproofing. But I have in mind the raw, original stuff of silence, as we would know it in the state of nature. Not sound blocked out, including wind and rain and bird song, but ourselves keeping quiet, subtracting our human clamour from the world, listening. . . If silence is the measure of permanence, noise is surely the measure of progress' (Theodore Roszak, 1979). *See also* NOISE.
(2) A refusal to speak. Another human right, protected in the US Bill of Rights, but often used as a weapon, especially when there are important things to be said (*see* SECRET).
(3) Preventing someone (someone who has been labelled a second-class citizen with no mind and no tradition) from speaking, writing, having an opinion or creating a work of art — and therefore, from having a visible history. 'The entire history of women's struggle for self-determination has been muffled in silence over and over' (Adrienne

Rich, 1979). Also, preventing the same someone from getting hold of whatever writing, opinions and works of art have managed to slip through the net. 'There is much, much more good literature by women in existence than anyone knows' (Joanna Russ, 1983).

Silviculture
[1880. *L silva* + *cultura*, the cultivating of woodland]
The care and cultivation of trees. *See* FOREST, FORESTRY.

Similarity
[17c. *L similis*, same]
A quality or characteristic held in common. It makes for problems that in English 'same' and 'similar' have the same root and many of the same connotations. 'Despite holding the same ideals for boys and girls, the parents in the study resisted a definition of non-sexist childraising that saw it as making girls and boys more similar. They did want to minimize the differences between the sexes imposed by sex-role stereotypes, but at the same time they did not want to talk about making boys and girls "the same" ' (June Statham, 1986). Green-thinkers celebrate similarity and uniqueness simultaneously, recognising similarity as the quality that overcomes difference and acknowledges interdependence.

Simplicity
(*see* VOLUNTARY SIMPLICITY)

Singing
[before 12c. *Old English singan*, to sing]
Making harmonious sounds with your voice, either on your own or with other people; a wonderful way to link directly with your power when you have overcome the fear that you can't do it properly, can't do it well enough, or can't do it at all. 'If you sing the same note it's unison; if you sing a different note it's harmony — there's no such thing as a wrong note' (Frankie Armstrong, 1985). Singing is an important part of PROTEST: 'We are singing, singing for our lives' (*Greenham Common Songsheet*, 1984).

Single
[17c. *L singulus*, individual]
Choosing to be your own person, which may include having no partner and living alone. In a society in which singleness is seen as an aberration, a punishment for bad behaviour, or an unfortunate mistake, it is hardly surprising that images of singleness have become so stereotyped, images that have a nasty habit of being forced into reality. 'Our patriarchal culture so denies and degrades the reality of aloneness for women, that it feels like travelling a new journey without a map. . . The models that do exist tend to reinforce the ideas of deprivation; the

single parent, struggling with little money or support; or, at the other extreme, the glamorous career woman, ruthless and self-assured, who sees sex as a desire to be satisfied regardless of feeling. Neither image suggests dignity and self-esteem' (Tricia Bickerton, in Sue Cartledge and Joanna Ryan (ed), 1983). *See also* COUPLE.

Sister
[1968 in this sense. *Old English sweostor*, sister]
A powerful WOMAN, especially as recognised in solidarity by another. The use of 'sister' in this way comes originally from black American speech, and for some black women the title feels inappropriate in white hands. 'Sisterhood' is a celebration of the links between all women.

Sit-In
[1937]
An ACTION involving a number of people refusing to move from a public place in order to draw attention to a particular injustice; used by black Americans in the 1960s to protest against segregated eating places, and widespread ever since. Hence 'lie-in', 'work-in' (*see also* DIE-IN).

Slash-And-Burn
[1939]
(*also* 'shifting agriculture')
A tropical agricultural practice in which areas of land are cleared and burned, then crops are grown for a few seasons until the nutrients in the soil are depleted, when the farmer moves on to a new area, leaving the original patch to regenerate. This has worked well in parts of the tropics for centuries, but pressure on land from rapidly-increasing numbers of people, many of whom are deliberately encouraged to move to the poorest areas, has created serious problems of deforestation, soil erosion and land degradation. 'Unlike indigenous tribal peoples, these lowlanders have little idea how the forest works or how to make it work for them. Invariably . . . the only option left when the soil fails, after a few years of subsistence farming, is to move deeper into the rainforest, clearing larger patches and leaving permanently degraded remnants behind' (Charles Secrett, undated).

Small Is Beautiful
[1973]
The belief, popularised by the British economist Fritz Schumacher, that generally the smaller an economic organisation or industrial enterprise the better: 'People can be themselves only in small comprehensible groups' (Fritz Schumacher, 1973). The plea was very much a reaction against the prevalent giantism of multinational corporations and vast corporate structures in which workers are merely cogs. 'Small is

Beautiful' caught on in a big way, and some industrialists even heeded its message and started to look at methods of involving their workforces in HUMAN SCALE group activities. Though it might be generally true of industry, 'small is beautiful' has been forced into contexts in which it is entirely inappropriate, and has probably outlived most of its usefulness. 'It's not simply a matter of size in quantitative terms, it's as much to do with the *quality* of scale. Whatever size it is that takes away our dignity, makes us passive recipients rather than active participants, makes us dependent rather than self-reliant, alienates us from the work we do and the people we live with — *that* is too big' (Jonathon Porritt, 1984). *See also* SCALE.

Smoke
[before 12c. *Old English smoca*, smoke]
A cloud of fine particles suspended in a gas, usually as the result of the incomplete burning of BIOMASS and FOSSIL FUELS. Smoke POLLUTION cuts out sunlight, leaves a deposit of soot on surfaces, and can be a major lung irritant. Partly for these reasons and partly because smoke pollution is so obvious, many countries now have anti-smoke legislation (though large parts of Eastern Europe, for instance, do not). Unfortunately the result of clean air legislation has been an increase in the new hazard of PHOTOCHEMICAL SMOG, as clear skies allow more sunshine to penetrate to ground level. *See also* GREENHOUSE EFFECT, NUCLEAR WINTER.

Smoking
[*c*.1600]
Placing a thumb-substitute in your mouth, poisoning your lungs, doing what peer pressure demands, and putting money in the hands of the government. While it is important to understand why people smoke and the pressure exerted by advertising and society, the facts are that smoking kills (90% of deaths from lung cancer, chronic bronchitis and obstructive lung disease are a direct result of smoking), smoking costs (£170 million a year to the British National Health Service), and five and a half million tons of nutrient-demanding tobacco each year are grown on land which could raise food crops. 'Anxious that their domestic markets may well shrink dramatically over the next few years, cigarette companies have . . . made the controversial move of promoting their sales abroad. Whilst one study showed that only 7% of an American university's students smoked, a comparable figure for Nigeria was 10 times that proportion' (Richard North, 1986). It is not only smokers who suffer from cigarette smoke: 'There is now evidence to suggest that the non-smoker who passively and involuntarily inhales "sidestream" smoke (from the end of the cigarette) in fact takes in a much higher

concentration of noxious substances than the smoker who actually inhales "mainstream" smoke. . . The spouse and children of a smoker also have a higher incidence of chest infections and cancers and, on average, die four years earlier than those who are not exposed to cigarette fumes' (Chandra Patel, 1987). Many public areas have now been declared no-smoking areas, and New York may soon become the first US state to forbid smoking in any public place.

Snowball
[1985]
An ACTION in which an ever-increasing number of people deliberately cause 'criminal' damage by symbolically cutting the wire around military and nuclear installations. The idea is to stretch the legal system to its limit in an attempt to have the arguments against NUCLEAR WEAPONS heard in court and reported.

Social Audit
[*c*.1970]
(*also* 'social accounting')
A form of accounting — not necessarily in money terms — which examines how well a business or project is deciding on and achieving its social goals. 'Social auditing and accounting goes far beyond simply planning for social benefit and measuring achievement; it is also a process of balancing financial profit and loss with social benefit and non-benefit' (John Pearce, in Mary Inglis and Sandra Kramer (ed), 1985). Social audit techniques are already being used by many public authorities in the planning of education, health, and similar facilities. *See also* SOCIAL COSTS AND BENEFITS.

Social Costs And Benefits
[1901]
The costs and benefits of a project or development to everybody who will be affected by it; in fact the only sensible way of conceiving of the cost/benefit equation, though to some economists 'social costs and benefits' mean the ones they can leave out of the calculations because no particular individual will come back to haunt them with litigation. *See also* COST-BENEFIT ANALYSIS, SOCIAL AUDIT.

Social Darwinism
[1887. Named after Charles Darwin, British naturalist, 1809-82]
The application of natural selection principles to human society, portrayed both as necessary conflict between human beings and between 'man' and nature (*see* EVOLUTION, NATURAL SELECTION). 'In its most vulgar form, social Darwinism is generally portrayed as the attempt "to justify the competetive ethos of Victorian capitalism in terms of the struggle

for existence" [P.J. Bowler, 1984]. . . More recently, with the rise of sociobiology, the legitimacy of transferring biological laws to the social order has again become the subject of debate' (David Livingstone, in R.J. Johnston (ed), 1986). The 'war against nature' rears its head in some unexpected places, including the spiritual dimension: 'The most sophisticated modern variety of this sort of thought is found in the works of Father Teilhard de Chardin, who claims a special evolutionary spiritual destiny for humanity under the name of higher consciousness. Some of the more extreme of these Spiritual Darwinists would willingly leave the rest of Earth-bound animal and plant life behind to enter a realm transcending biology' (Gary Snyder, 1980).

Social Defence
[1980]
(US: 'social defense')
The protection of large numbers of people from conventional military and similar threats of violence using nonviolent methods; NONVIOLENT DIRECT ACTION on a large scale. 'Social defense protects a population from foreign or internal attacks through active, nonviolent resistance and non-cooperation. It includes large-scale symbolic actions, economic boycotts by consumers and producers, social and political boycotts of institutions, strikes, overloading of facilities and administrative systems, stalling and obstructing, deliberate inefficiency, ostracism of persons, and numerous forms of noncompliance in all sectors of a society' (Fritjof Capra and Charlene Spretnak, 1984). 'People committed to nonviolence . . . have tried to connect nonviolent action as a form of protest with nonviolent action as a defence policy. The core concept is social defence. Social defence does not assume a national framework, but a framework of social struggle: protecting the environment, upholding certain values, defending a particular institution or people's rights. Its focus is not on what threats might arise, but on immediate situations. . . Lynne Jones has written about Greenham as a form of social defence. Its keynotes are flexibility and improvisation — precisely the qualities which would be needed in the event of military invasion or occupation' (Howard Clark, in Gail Chester and Andrew Rigby (ed), 1986).

Social Dividend
(*see* SOCIAL WAGE)

Social Ecology
[1984]
The exploration of human behaviour and institutions within an ecological context (*see also* HUMAN ECOLOGY). 'The broader applications of ecological thinking lead to "social ecology", the perception of societal structures and human interactions as an intricate web of dynamic

systems that are simultaneously interrelated parts and complete in themselves' (Fritjof Capra and Charlene Spretnak, 1984).

Socialism
[1839. *L socius*, comrade]
A label which covers many differing perspectives, but which has at its heart the belief that an egalitarian and humane society must ensure that the most important resources of that society are controlled by the community as a whole, and not by private capitalist entrepreneurs. Marx's belief in a sharing society — 'from each according to [their] ability, to each according to [their] need' — is also a central issue (at least theoretically) for most socialists. There are many brands of socialism, including those advocating ANARCHISM, communism, libertarianism, MARXISM, REFORMISM, revisionism and REVOLUTION. The NEW LEFT of the 1960s and 1970s, the breeding-ground of many green-thinkers-to-be, was in large part a reaction against the status quo both within society and within socialism, but in recent years the theoretical and practical distinctions between RED and GREEN have grown, partly as green thinking has developed and partly as socialism, with its backlog of historical impedimenta, has found it difficult to accept change. The socialist tradition of egalitarianism and the fight for basic human rights have given green politics more than is often credited, and many green-thinkers see the transformation of socialism as more productive than its complete rejection: 'Today there are stronger calls from socialist feminists and some male socialists for a renewal of that more democratic and participatory vision of socialism which reaches out to include all social relationships and to give people a sense of greater control over their own lives' (Lynne Segal, 1987). Yet perhaps socialism is too set in its ways to accept the need for radical re-examination, even of its most treasured beliefs: 'We must choose either between ecology, with its naturalism, its anarchistic logic of decentralization, its emphasis on humanly scaled alternate technologies, and its non-hierarchical institutions; or socialism, with its typically Marxian anti-naturalism, its political logic of centralization, its emphasis on high technology, and its bureaucratic institutions. Gorz [André Gorz, 1978] gives us neither alternative in the name of both and perpetuates a confusion that has already produced an internal crisis in every American and European ecology movement' (Murray Bookchin, 1980). 'The progressive, radical, libertarian thrust of socialism has been vitiated by its wholehearted commitment to materialist industrialism: one simply cannot cure today's problems with the means that have produced them' (Jonathon Porritt, 1984). Also working against the positive aspects of socialism is its popular image, an image created largely by its detractors, but not assisted for green-thinkers by the emphasis of socialist politicians on

economic growth and class conflict. The jargon used by some socialists does nothing to further the cause: 'Phrases like "the dictatorship of the proletariat" or the "labour theory of value" may mean something to those in the know but are likely to turn everyone else off' (*New Internationalist*, November 1985). 'The socialist concept, in theory and in practice, was tied to industrialism and statism. And since its theory is tied to the perspectives and historical practice of the disintegrating labour movement, it would be quite illogical to call myself a socialist. Like Marxism, socialism has become a quarry from which we can take various things, such as the concept of self-management which socialists have dropped in any case. The best and the permanent elements have been bequeathed to us' (Rudolf Bahro, 1984).

Socially Responsible Investment
[*c*.1980]
(*also* 'concerned investment', 'ethical investment', 'social investment', 'SRI')
Putting resources, usually money, into worthwhile projects such as cooperatives, inner city projects and community projects. More narrowly, SRI means putting your money into investments which will yield a financial return for you, but which do not support areas of business interest that you disapprove of, such as ARMS, tobacco, alcohol, APARTHEID, the violation of HUMAN RIGHTS, NUCLEAR ENERGY, VIVISECTION, RACISM, or DISCRIMINATION. In 1987, Marin County in California became the first US county to disinvest in the nuclear industry.

Socially Useful Products
[1973]
(*also* 'socially useful work')
Things made in factories which enhance life, often referring to the CONVERSION of factory facilities from military production. 'The Lucas workers proposed a new range of socially useful products which they and their company could produce, including a "hobcart" for children with spina bifida, a life-support system, energy-conserving products, a hybrid power pack, all-purpose power generation equipment for third world countries, a road/rail vehicle, kidney machines, and telechiric devices' (James Robertson, 1985).

Social Responsibility
[1970]
The recognition that TECHNOLOGY is not benign, and that those who develop it have a responsibility to society for the repercussions of its use (*see also* SCIENCE); by extension, the recognition that any economic programme must take into account the effects it has on all the people it involves. '"Social responsibiity" is understood by most [German] Greens

to mean social justice and an assurance that the poor and the working class will not get hurt by programmes to restructure the economy and our consumer society ecologically' (Fritjof Capra and Charlene Spretnak, 1984).

Social Wage
[1925]
(*also* 'basic income', 'citizen's wage', 'guaranteed basic income', 'minimum income', 'national income scheme', 'social dividend')
A cash sum paid to each person, regardless of status, which would guarantee everybody the basic necessities, and would to a large extent replace present complex social security systems. 'While a full national income scheme seems too big a step to take, the principle behind it is important — that a citizen is entitled to a livelihood as much as to education and health care, that the state is not a provider of last resort to those who cannot help themselves but a guarantor of basic rights' (Charles Handy, 1985). The introduction of a social wage obviously means a major upheaval of any country's TAXATION system, since the income must come from somewhere — the British Green Party would finance its basic income scheme from a series of taxation changes, including a LAND TAX. Be aware that this is not the only definition of 'social wage' — the British Conservative Party, for instance, uses the expression to mean the value of public money 'handouts' to claimants.

Society
[*L socius*, comrade]
(1) [16c] The interrelationships between people in a large population; the field of exploration of sociology. Green-thinkers consider the strength of any society to be (as in nature) diversity: 'What makes unity in diversity in nature more than a suggestive ecological metaphor for unity in diversity in society is the underlying fact of wholeness. . . Society, in turn, attains its "truth", its self-actualization, in the form of richly articulated, mutualistic networks of people based on community, roundedness of personality, diversity of stimuli and activities, an increasing wealth of experience, and a variety of tasks' (Murray Bookchin, 1986).
(2) [17c] An organised group of people with a common interest, goal or concern, as in Society Against Violation of the Environment (SAVE), or Society for the Protection of Ancient Buildings (SPAB).
(3) [1823] The fashionable set; 'important' people with whom you associate if you want to be 'important' too. A warning to any would-be green 'in crowd'.
(4) [1899] Another word for an ecological COMMUNITY.

Soft Energy
[1970]
(*also* 'soft technology')
Energy systems which use RENEWABLE RESOURCES and are kind to the environment; often used in the phrase 'soft energy paths'. 'There exists today a body of energy technologies that have certain specific features in common and that offer great technical, economic, and political attractions, yet for which there is no generic term. For lack of a more satisfactory term, I shall call them "soft" technologies: a textural description intended not to mean vague, mushy, speculative and ephemeral, but rather flexible, resilient, sustainable, and benign. . . These are defined by five characteristics: (1) They rely on renewable energy flows . . . (2) They are diverse . . . (3) They are flexible and relatively low technology . . . (4) They are matched in scale and geographic distribution to end use needs . . . (5) They are matched in energy quality [heat where heat is needed, electricity where electric power is needed, etc.] to end-use needs' (Amory Lovins, 1977).

Soil
[14c. *L solium*, seat; *solum*, base, ground]
Weathered material at or near the earth's surface, more or less mixed with organic debris by soil-dwelling organisms to create a firm, moist and nutritious foundation for plants. Soil is vital for food production and therefore for life, but this important resource, non-renewable except over a timespan of centuries, is being lost to the oceans in increasing quantities as a result of SOIL EROSION.

Soil Erosion
[1896]
Washing away of SOIL from unvegetated land by heavy rainfall; thought by some conservationists to be one of the most serious of environmental hazards we currently face. 'A sudden storm on a light sandy or sandy loam soil can have dramatic effects. On slopes of only two or three degrees, fields can be scarred by a dense network of well-defined channels or rills, 20 to 25 centimetres deep and 30 to 50 centimetres wide. The material washed out of these channels fills localised depressions in the landscape and covers the gentler sloping land on the valley floors, frequently burying crops. Where the material discharges into rivers, it is a pollution hazard, both from the sediment itself and from the chemicals adsorbed [sticking] to it' (R.P.C. Morgan, in Edward Goldsmith and Nicholas Hildyard (ed), 1986). 'Around one-quarter of a million tonnes of topsoil are washed off the deforested mountain slopes of Nepal each year, and a further sizeable amount from the Himalayan foothills in India's sector of the Ganges catchment zone. As a result, a

gigantic shallow is building up in the Bay of Bengal, covering some 5 million hectares. When this shallow breaks the surface of the sea, it will be claimed either by India as New Moore Island, or by Bangladesh as South Talpatty. Nepal, the country which contributes most to the phenomenon, is not even being consulted' (Norman Myers, 1985). The main cause of erosion is the elimination of ground cover, particularly by DEFORESTATION, together with the practice of leaving ground barren for long periods in winter, OVERGRAZING, destroying soil structure and the working of steep slopes without terracing. About 11 million hectares of arable land are lost to agriculture every year through soil erosion, a rate which, if unchecked, will mean losing 18% of the world's arable land in the next twelve years. A great deal can be done to prevent erosion if the will and resources exist to achieve it. The main protection is to keep land under vegetation and minimise soil disturbance: 'Erosion must be prevented by keeping a continuous ground cover, and by avoiding soil compaction from the use of machinery. Organic matter must be maintained by the use of mulch [a covering over the ground such as straw or grass mowings]. And leaching must be countered, as it is in the natural forest and in the long-fallow system of shifting cultivation, by deep-rooted trees or plants, which pump nutrients up into the foliage, from which they ultimately fall back into the soil' (International Institute for Tropical Agriculture, 1983, in *Worldwatch*, 1986). Although this advice is designed to conserve tropical soils, many temperate areas are losing soil at a rate which cannot be sustained by natural soil regeneration. Here the advice is the same — keeping ground cover maximised by reintroducing ROTATION with grass leys, increasing organic content by more organic farming methods, and keeping steep slopes under permanent vegetation. In the timescale of decades, soil is a non-renewable resource and should be respected as such.

Solar Energy
[1901]
(*also* 'solar power')
The source of energy which allows all life on earth to exist. Energy must constantly be added to the earth's planetary ecosystem to prevent ENTROPY leading to the rundown of all the planet's living systems, and it is the sun which provides this energy. More anthropocentrically, 'solar energy' is used to describe forms of solar radiation which can be converted into a form usable by human beings. Nearly all the energy we use is originally solar (with the possible exceptions of tidal energy, which is created primarily by the gravitational pull of the moon, and nuclear energy). FOSSIL FUELS are the result of prehistoric plant growth fuelled by photosynthesis; GEOTHERMAL ENERGY is solar energy stored from the earliest geological times; BIOMASS fuels are the product of

current growth cycles; HYDRO and WIND ENERGY come from solar-heat-driven atmospheric circulation. In fact, 'solar energy' usually means energy derived directly from sunshine, though wind and biomass energy are sometimes included, in which case sunshine conversion is called 'direct solar energy'. Because solar radiation arrives at the earth's surface at a fairly low temperature, sunshine is often thought of as low-grade energy and therefore unsuitable for heavy power applications. 'However, the nature of solar radiation is such that it can be upgraded for tasks where high-quality energy is indispensable. Streaming out from the sun, sunshine is not degraded as it travels through space, being instead simply dispersed as it streaks along its radial routes away from the solar reactor. . . A three-inch lens will gather enough light to produce a temperature of a few hundred degrees, and the huge parabolic mirror of the French solar furnace in the Pyrenees will gather enough to melt tungsten, at a temperature of nearly 6,000°F' (John Elkington, 1984). In fact we do not need high-quality energy for most of our energy needs — between 55 and 60% of the energy we use in the West is used for low-temperature heating (heating things to less than 100°C) and cooling — and solar energy is useful for both. Many individual solar energy systems have been built into new and existing buildings — they work either as a PASSIVE system with no moving parts or, more commonly, as an ACTIVE system incorporating some kind of pumping mechanism. As with other types of energy system, economies can be achieved by providing solar energy to whole neighbourhoods and communities from one solar scheme — such schemes are in operation for example in the Mojave Desert in California, where 1,800 mirrors reflect heat to a central boiler, providing energy for 2,000 homes (John Seymour and Herbert Girardet, 1987), and in northern Sweden, where efficient solar collectors heat water which is then stored in a vast underground cavern, providing space and water heating for a community of 550 dwellings (Michael Flood, 1986). A great deal of thought has been put into the design of 'solar houses' and 'solar architecture' — features which can be incorporated into solar architecture include 'solar panels' (collectors which use sunshine to heat water), photovoltaic systems (which convert light energy into electricity), conservatories and greenhouses, large south-facing and small north-facing windows (the other way round in the southern hemisphere!), sensitive control mechanisms to regulate heat, HEAT PUMPS and reservoirs, and good INSULATION. Much of the reason for solar energy being considered a 'second-rate source' is that the 'hard energy' industries prefer not to deal with competition, though many oil and electric companies are investing in the development of solar technology, and this is certain to continue as supplies of non-renewable energy resources dwindle (the apparent oil 'surplus' of the late 1980s being due solely to overproduction and bad forecasting). One fifth of the world's energy needs are already supplied by solar energy in the form of biofuels, mostly wood, used in the Third World: in most Western countries the use of biofuels is considered so second-rate that it isn't even included in energy statistics. Many green-thinkers are convinced that solar energies — 'the renewables' — are the key to our energy future, so much so that some describe the future as 'the solar age' (for example, Hazel Henderson, *The Politics of the Solar Age*, 1981). On the other hand, there are ecological limits and constraints to the use of solar energy just as with any other potential TECHNOFIX; small-scale solar technology may be preferable to most other forms of energy conversion, 'but it is ironic that solar energy enthusiasts criticize advocates of coal and fission for disregarding ecological costs and calculating only monetary costs, yet they glibly regard solar energy as "free" just because no corporation could bill us for the incoming sunshine. . . If 99.9% of the solar energy that reaches Earth's surface is not being captured by plants and fixed in organic molecules, this does not mean that solar energy is a "vast untapped reserve" awaiting man's [*sic*] exploitation. For [hu]mankind to try using even one-tenth of one percent would be to impose upon the energy system of the ecosphere an extra load comparable to the energy budget of the entire standing crop of organisms of all kinds! How colossal should we aspire to be?' (William Catton, in Michael Tobias (ed), 1985).

Solidarity
[1848 *L solidus*, firm]
The acknowledgement of a shared concern and the promise to support those who share it. Traditionally used almost exclusively in relation to class and race issues, but increasingly being used to give voice to shared OPPRESSION on a global scale. 'Work meaningfully, live in solidarity' (die Grünen, 1983, quoted in Rudolf Bahro, 1986). 'Solidarity' is also the name of the first legitimised Polish trade union, recognised in 1980 but outlawed from 1982 onwards.

Space
[*L spatium*, space, distance]
(1) [17c] The universe beyond the earth's atmosphere; a favourite setting for patriarchal pseudo-utopian technological visions. 'The future of man and biospheres will expand in time to areas throughout our Solar system in micro-gravity orbit, and on the surfaces of planets, moons, and asteroids just as Biosphere I life seeks ever to expand and fill new econiches' (John Allen and Mark Nelson, 1986). *See also* TECHNOFIX.

(2) [15c] A physical place in which you feel comfortable, sometimes bounded by walls or fences but sometimes simply visualised as the fulfilment of a psychological requirement. The need for space is not always respected, a circumstance not helped by the fact that many people have no space to be themself in. 'We need a lot more empty space in our minds and in our feelings' (Rudolf Bahro, 1986).
(3) [1976] A word often loosely used to describe a state of mind, as in 'Leonard had a lot going for him, and Kate liked the space he was in' (Cyra McFadden, 1978).

Spaceship Earth
[1966]
A metaphor for our planet which recognises that it is to all intents and purposes a closed system, receiving and giving out energy in the form of radiation, but otherwise finite and exhaustible if its systems are stretched beyond their limits. 'Our little Spaceship Earth is only eight thousand miles in diameter, which is almost a negligible dimension in the great vastness of space. . . Spaceship Earth was so extraordinarily invented and designed that to our knowledge human beings have been on board it for two million years without even knowing they were on board a ship' (Robert Buckminster Fuller, 1971). 'Spaceship Earth' is a concept which has been heavily criticised by DEEP ECOLOGISTS as excessively ANTHROPOCENTRIC — the idea that human beings are at the 'steering wheel' is simply an extension of HUMAN EXEMPTIONALISM and ELITISM, and 'Spaceship Earth' (like the LIFEBOAT ETHIC) ignores the fact that all the 'passengers' do not have the same requirements. 'The dominant metaphor of the rocket age is "spaceship earth". Such a metaphor is the ultimate arrogance of humanism — the expansion of a machine metaphor to include the whole earth' (Bill Devall, in Herman Daly (ed), 1980).

Speciation
[1906]
The formation of new and distinct species in the course of EVOLUTION. Over the long lifespan of the earth, speciation is the principle which counteracts natural EXTINCTION.

Speciesism
[1975]
(*also* 'specism')
Treating other species as secondary and inferior to human beings; the OPPRESSION and exploitation of animals and plants, though most generally used in relation to ANIMALS. 'To say one species has a *right* to exploit the others is to be guilty of the prejudice of speciesism, just as to argue that one race has the right to subordinate another is racism'

(Richard Ryder, 1974). 'The racist violates the principle of equality by giving greater weight to the interests of his [*sic*] own race when there is a clash between their interests and the interests of those of another race. The sexist violates the principle of equality by favouring the interests of his own sex. Similarly the speciesist allows the interests of his own species to override the greater interests of members of other species. The pattern is identical in each case' (Peter Singer, 1977). While green-thinkers would unite in agreeing that all species have rights and should be respected, many would argue that it can be dangerous to see speciesism as a direct parallel to the oppressions of people by other people, since such a view can lead to the anthropomorphisation of animals. One of the rights of any animal is to be distinguished from a human being: 'Sir, Could we have a moratorium on the use of the phrase "they behaved like animals" to describe any especially nasty form of human brutality? . . Do we hear of dolphins torturing other dolphins, gorillas cutting, or biting, bits off other gorillas, elephants inflicting prolonged periods of terror on other elephants, or indeed on any other animal? Rather should dolphins left to die in nets, gorillas killed in order that their dried heads should be sold to tourists, elephants dying in agony from poisons for the sake of their tusks, exclaim, in condemnation of acts of savagery (should these ever occur) committed by members of their own species: "They behaved like humans"' (Elspeth Huxley, 1984, quoted in Jon Wynne-Tyson, 1985). On the other hand, speciesism differs from all other oppressions in that none of the oppressed can answer back (or at least not in a way that human beings will acknowledge); therefore it is the ALLIES of animals who must protect their rights. *See also* ANIMAL RIGHTS, FACTORY FARMING.

Spiral

[17c. *L spira*, coil]

Anything with a shape that curves away from a centre, sometimes in a precise geometrical form, sometimes more generalised; also used to describe things with a form like a loosely-coiled spring. The spiral form is found throughout the natural world, from galaxies to weather circulations, eddies in water to seashells; it is also found in traditional buildings and land use patterns. Many green-thinkers are now rediscovering the spiral — as a building form and garden layout (Bill Mollison, 1979); as a form of spiritual ritual (Starhawk, 1979); and in theoretical constructions of cultural history and psycho-social development: 'Jung was a pioneer in the psychology of the soul and his work, together with that of the humanistic and transpersonal schools that have flourished in recent years, has brought the study of consciousness full circle and onto another turn of the evolutionary spiral' (Michael Lindfield, 1986); 'What [Charles] Hampden-Turner [1977] says is that [human development] can be seen as a spiral of experience, such that at any one time we are either moving up the spiral towards full humanness or down the spiral towards alienation and anomy' (John Rowan, 1976). While the spiral may be a useful metaphor, it must be used carefully — some metaphors veer heavily towards the pre-green idea of PROGRESS: 'the further up the spiral the better you are'.

Spirit
[13c. *L spiritus*, breath, spirit; from *spirare*, to breathe]
ENERGY, LIFE FORCE, the essential nature or distillation of something or someone. 'Some of the most spiritual people would never talk about "spirit" or even necessarily understand intellectualization about the spirit. Some people who would consider themselves very religious are obedient to the external authority of a church, but miss the essence of the spirit, while others use their religion as a form through which a certain kind of spiritual contact can be made. By "spirit" I do not mean anything hushed or holy, I mean the power of life, the life force. . . You can feel your spirit on a mountain, in a movement of music, doing exercises, having sex, preparing a meal, or in a moment of human contact. There is no prescribed road to the spirit' (Richard Gillett, 1987). In Christianity, the religion many Westerners have grown up with, 'spirit' implies the holy spirit; 'spirit' is also a synonym for 'ghost' and 'hard liquor' — the implications of the word need to be taken into account when using it, since your listeners may not hear what you intend to convey.

Spirituality
[14c. *L spiritus*, breath, spirit; from *spirare*, to breathe]
The acknowledgement and direct experience of a dimension to existence beyond the material and the directly tangible. 'My own working definition of spirituality is that it is the focusing of human awareness on the subtle aspects of existence, a practice that reveals to us profound interconnectedness' (Charlene Spretnak, 1986). 'Spiritual or mystical experience . . . is the mirror image of science — a direct perception of nature's unity, the inside of the mysteries that science tries valiantly to know from the outside' (Marilyn Ferguson, 1981). Western culture and philosophy, in general unlike that of the East, has felt the deep and lasting effect of separating the material and spiritual aspects of human experience, a legacy which green-thinkers often find very hard to accept and unravel. Whether we like it or not, we live in a world where even the green/ alternative/radical/new age community is often split down the middle, the mystical/meditating/crystal-reading/esoteric/ earth-mysteries/guru/Findhorn/yin-yang/astrology people on one side, the radical/green-politics/peace-action/self-sufficiency/ecology/solar-

energy/Friends-of-the-Earth/Worldwatch/wilderness people on the other. There is also a great deal they have in common — wholefoods, therapy, holistic healing, meetings — and there are groups and philosophies which bridge the divide with some success — ECOFEMINISM and DEEP ECOLOGY stand out particularly. In the last few years there have been notable advances in the integration of material and spiritual concerns, but we would be fooling ourselves if we did not recognise that the integration of mind, body and spirit has hardly begun in the West, and is unlikely to get very far until we are willing to question our most fundamental beliefs about reality and human nature. It is crucially important to remember that whatever the spiritual questions, the answers lie within us and our own experience of flow and connectedness. Searching for outside answers, whether from GURUS, the mystical East, the fundamentalist West, Esalen or the Western Buddhist Order, the tarot or the *I Ching*, will never on its own provide proof of a 'spiritual plane' — they can provide clues, but it is too easy to take one of them as *the* spiritual truth. All 'teachings' have skeletons in their cupboards — Buddhist elitism, Hindu suttee, fundamentalist militarism, the misuse of the tarot in black magic — and therefore careful discrimination is essential. It is also important to forget about spiritual planes, dimensions and levels. HIERARCHY (invented by human beings, usually male ones) pervades current versions of spirituality, and anyone who suggests that the payment of large sums of money and giving away your power (RELEASE or 'surrender') to another human being is part of a spiritual path has to be suspect. Spirituality is about connectedness inclusiveness and integration of all experience, especially that which is usually denied in our materialist culture. 'The spiritual context of Green politics — which unfortunately is not expressed, and is almost opposed, in the party structure — means understanding how everything is connected and understanding your relationship with planet Earth in daily life. We've become so divorced from our ties with the Earth that most people don't understand what the Greens are fighting for. With the holistic sense of spirituality, one's personal life is truly political and one's political life is truly personal. Anyone who does not comprehend within him- or herself this essential unity cannot achieve political change on a deep level and cannot strive for the true ideals of the Greens' (Petra Kelly, quoted in Fritjof Capra and Charlene Spretnak, 1984). If many 'political greens' are encamped on one side of the divide, there are just as many 'NEW-AGERS' on the other: 'In this new equilibrium, I realize that it is as mistaken to take refuge in the spirit and despise matter as it is to attach oneself to matter and deny the spirit. To live the life of the body as fully as that of the spirit now seems essential' (Gitta Mallasz, *Resurgence*, September/October 1982). There is also an uneasy link between spirituality and RELIGION: some sort of distinction can be made if religion is thought of as 'organised spirituality', but this is only a definition of convenience. When someone asks 'Are you religious?' it is likely to be because our culture has no other acceptable label for someone who recognises the importance of the non-material. *See also* PAGANISM, WOMEN'S SPIRITUALITY.

Squatting
[*Old French esquatir*, from *L cogere*, to compress]
(1) [15c] Sitting in a crouching position with bent knees and the weight on the feet. Many native peoples squat rather than sitting on chairs, which holistic health practitioners recommend for improved posture and internal body functioning; it is also generally thought to be a healthy position for defecating, as the low incidence of piles in non-Western countries suggests; and for childbirth, where it is central to the practice of some methods of NATURAL CHILDBIRTH.
(2) [1880] Moving on to land or into a building that is not currently being occupied and taking up residence (*see also* DIGGER, LEVELLER). In capitalist societies squatting is usually considered by those in power to be theft, though the squatting of land in Australia and New Zealand involves legal rights dating from the nineteenth century and still in force. In the Third World every city has its squatter settlements — 'bidonvilles', 'gourbevilles', 'favelas', 'colonias paracaidists': 'In Lima and La Paz, for instance, the tin-and-tarpaper shacks of the urban poor are found in the shadow of tall, modern office buildings. Mexico City has gained notoriety for the large number of people living in makeshift burrows in a hillside garbage dump' (Lester Brown and Jodi Jacobson, *Worldwatch*, 1987). As many as half a billion people in the world are squatting around the cities of Africa, South and Central America, and Southern Asia. In the West, squatting of empty houses began on a large scale in the late 1960s, and many countries now provide limited rights to squatters. 'Since 1968, over a quarter of a million people in Britain have walked into an uninhabited house owned by someone else and proceeded to set up home, without seeking permission and without paying rent. By doing so, they have become squatters. Some have been thrown out within hours. Others have stayed for months, even years, before being evicted by bailiffs or leaving under threat of a court order. A few have managed to establish permanent homes' (*Squatting*, 1980). A similar state of affairs prevails throughout most of Western Europe; in the USA, where the police have powers of immediate eviction, squatting is rare except as a short-term political action.

Stability

[15c. *L stabilis*, steady]

Being flexible enough to last for a long time; an apparent contradiction in a culture where stability implies rigidity and absolute security. 'The dictionary meanings of the word "stable" include "fixed", "not fluctuating", "unvarying" and "steady", all of which are inaccurate to describe organisms. The stability of self-organizing systems is utterly dynamic and must not be confused with equilibrium. It consists in maintaining the same overall structure in spite of ongoing changes and replacements of its components' (Fritjof Capra, 1982). *See also* STEADY STATE.

Standard Of Living

[1898]

Having the material comforts and possessions that commercial and peer pressures suggest you should have; enshrined in some countries in a 'standard of living index' which includes average spending on food, products and services including tobacco, alcohol, toiletries, leisure and recreation. Green-thinkers believe QUALITY of life to be at least as important as quantity of possessions.

State

[16c in this sense. *L status*, manner of standing]

(*also* 'country', NATION, 'nation state')

An arbitrarily-defined part of the earth's surface, occasionally having a human population with a common culture and language, which is more or less cut off from all other parts of the world and forms the geographical base for centralised and hierarchical control of its human population by powerful elites. The division of the world into states is a condition taken so much for granted that we almost never stop to think why we have states at all, why we need them, and what the world might be like without them. Yet the very notion of the state is antithetical to green thinking. 'The nation-state makes us less than human. It towers over us, cajoles us, disempowers us, bilks us of our substance, humiliates us — and often kills us in its imperialist adventures' (Murray Bookchin, 1986). The idea of arbitrary division and rigid boundaries is totally unecological, the concept of centralised elitist control contrary to individual empowerment, yet every aspect of our lives is controlled by the fact of our citizenship of one of the world's 229 nations. Many green-thinkers have looked at the practicalities of decentralising government to more ecologically-meaningful regions (*see* BIOREGION), but few have taken on the concept of 'state' itself; this may be because in Europe the division into nations does after many centuries fairly accurately represent cultural distinctions, and in North America the USA is large enough to embrace whole bioregions. In Africa the situation is very different: 'Under colonial rule people of widely differing cultural and religious backgrounds were often lumped together in highly centralised artificial states. Tribes were arbitrarily divided between two or more states, without regard to their ethnic heritage. Herein lie the roots of today's troubles' (Jimoh Omo-Fadaka, in Nick Albery and Yvo Peeters (ed), 1982). Why does the state exist? Many of the reasons are historical, but the legacy has hardened into seemingly-intractable rigidity — international borders have changed less in the last ten years than in any previous decade since 1800. Part of the confusion is that every human being needs places to feel at home in; the mistake is to confuse 'home' with 'patriotism'. What does the state do? Green-thinkers would see the function of the state being to maintain the status quo by a combination of social control, threat, and structural violence: 'The state acts to contain the political repercussions of the socio-economic system' (Michael Dear, in R.J. Johnston (ed), 1986); 'The State means . . . the set-up of authoritative and legitimately powerful roles by which we are finally controlled, ordered and organized' (David Robertson, 1985). 'The nation-state is caught in the middle. It is neither large enough to plan on a global scale, nor small enough to be accountable to people where they live' (Richard Barnet, 1980). But where are the visions of an alternative? 'My country is the whole world' (Virginia Woolf, 1938).

Steady State
[1928]
A SYSTEM in which the balance between inflow and output of energy is constant over time; a system in dynamic EQUILIBRIUM. A concept used in ecology and astronomy, and recently [1976] taken into economics to describe an alternative to conventional GROWTH theories. 'A steady-state economy is an economy with constant stocks of artefacts and people. These two populations are constant but not static. People die and artefacts depreciate. Births must replace deaths [*sic*] and production must replace depreciation. These "input" and "output" rates are to be equal at low levels, so that life-expectancy of people and durability of artefacts will be high. . . The economy maintains itself by this throughput in the same way that an organism maintains itself by its metabolic flow' (Paul Ekins (ed), 1986). 'A growth economy and a steady-state economy are as different as an airplane and a helicopter. An airplane is designed for forward motion — if it cannot keep moving it will crash. Likewise our growth economy cannot be still without crashing into unemployment' (Herman Daly, in Michael Tobias (ed), 1985). 'If the earth must lose that great portion of its pleasantness which it owes to things that the unlimited increase of wealth and population would extirpate from it, for the mere purpose of enabling it to support a larger

but not a better or a happier population, I sincerely hope, for the sake of posterity, that they will be content to be stationary, long before necessity compels them to be' (John Stuart Mill, 1861).

Stewardship
[15c. *Old English stigweard*, keeper of the hall]
Looking after something and taking care of it; a concept preferred by green-thinkers to that of ownership, especially where land and other natural resources are concerned. 'Stewardship' is also term used in Christianity (after one of the parables of Jesus), and is useful when looking at ways that Christians might approach ecological issues.

Stocks
[17c in this sense. *Old English stocc*, tree trunk]
Readily-available reserves of RESOURCES which have been harvested but not yet used. They are often kept in large 'stockpiles' where they are useless both to the natural system they were taken from or the human system they are intended to enhance. *See also* RESERVE (sense (1)).

Strength
[12c. *Old English strengthu*, strength]
Power-from-within, as opposed to power-over (Starhawk, 1982). The connection between strength and flexibility is perhaps one of the hardest for Westerners to understand: TAOist philosophy has several useful metaphors which make it clear that real strength is a result not of rigid resistance, but of being willing to bend and flow with the circumstances, like the reed in a storm. While trees and buildings fall around it, the reed bends with the wind and is still standing when the storm abates.

Stress
[14c. *Old French estresse*, narrowness; from L *strictus*, strict]
Physical force; by extension, outside influences on the human body which cause TENSION and, if not acknowledged and dealt with, DISTRESS and DISEASE. 'Stress is inherent in every healthy form of life . . . People cannot maintain an erect posture without the tension of opposing muscles that balance each other and keep the skeletal system erect. Eating puts some stress on the digestive system; active exercise puts stress on the cardiovascular system. Your immunological system is constantly killing off bacteria in your body' (L. John Mason, 1980). But most people in the West live in a world of excessive stress — caused by NOISE, POLLUTION, glare, rapid movement, COMPETITION, FEAR, the whole paraphernalia of life in the fast lane — and don't have the time or knowledge to deal with the results. Thus the well-known 'stress diseases' [1948] — cancer, heart disease, ulcers — plague our society, killing over

half of the American population prematurely (36% of deaths due to heart disease compared with 6% in Japan; 21% from cancer compared with less than 0.5% in Burma) (*Third World Guide*, 1985). Holistic medical practitioners and therapists use a range of techniques to cope with stress, from breathing and YOGA to MEDITATION and jogging. Most underline the importance of letting go of the symptoms of stress (holding the breath, rigid muscles etc.) as quickly as possible, so that everyday 'healthy' stress does not become chronic stress. The best advice, however, must always be to remove yourself as far as possible from the sources of stress, problematic though it might seem. Other organisms experience stress too, resulting in disease and premature death — the forests of central Europe are but one victim (*see* WALDSTERBEN).

Strokes
[1961 in this sense. *Old English strac*, stroke]
Apart from killing far too many Westerners ('stroke' = obstruction of an artery in the brain) and being pleasant forms of TOUCH (*see* MASSAGE, SEX), 'strokes' is another word for 'recognition'. Introduced by Eric Berne as an integral part of a therapy called 'transactional analysis' in the early 1960s, 'strokes' is now an essential part of growth movement jargon. 'Strokes may be either positive or negative, and although positive strokes are much to be preferred, negative strokes (for example, criticism or punishment) are better than no strokes at all. Strokes can also be either unconditional (strokes for being) or conditional (strokes for doing)' (Sue Walrond-Skinner, 1986).

Structural Violence
[*c*.1975]
VIOLENCE against people which is built into the oppressive nature of society, the STATE, and the international situation. 'A third of the 2,000 million people in the developing countries are starving or suffering from malnutrition. Twenty-five per cent of their children die before their fifth birthday. . . Less than 10 per cent of the 15 million children who died this year had been vaccinated against the six most common and dangerous children's diseases. Vaccinating every child costs £3 per child. But not doing so costs us five million lives a year. These are classic examples of "structural violence"' (Petra Kelly, 1984).

Struggle
[14c. *Middle English struglen*, to struggle]
Constantly striving for your rights; an activity involving faith and frustration. 'Struggle' is a favourite word of the NEW LEFT, and drops too easily from socialist lips. It *is* a struggle for oppressed people to keep demanding their rights, but 'struggle' sometimes implies a resignation to the inevitability of oppression, a feeling that it will never

end until we are all dead. Less passive labels — ACTION, CAMPAIGN, PROTEST — are useful alternatives.

Subsistence

[17c in this sense. *L subsistere*, to stand firm, remain standing]
Having just enough resources to fulfil your needs. In most traditional societies (as in nature), a subsistence economy means that everybody gets sufficient to fulfil their basic needs with the minimum amount of work, minimal THROUGHPUT, and minimal ecological disruption. 'As long as peasant economies remain free of outside market forces, they also appear to generate their own stability. . . Subsistence [is] a goal and not the result of deprivation, which has often been the modern interpretation' (Peter Bunyard and Fern Morgan-Grenville (ed), 1987). In the green sense, 'subsistence' is close to SELF-RELIANCE, but in common use 'subsistence' is usually equated with POVERTY, and in many parts of the THIRD WORLD with the unattainable vision of having enough to eat — the result of a world economic order in which the resources nurtured and harvested by the poor are systematically siphoned out of traditional economies for the benefit of the rich.

Substitution

[1902. *L substituere*, to substitute]
The replacement of one product by another which performs a similar function. Substitution should not be confused with the deliberate manipulation of demand or the empty promises of the TECHNOFIX merchants. The first says 'This de luxe electric carving knife is a useful and equivalent substitute for your old hand-held one', the second 'Let's not worry about oil running out, we're sure to have invented a replacement by then.' Intelligent substitution can be enormously beneficial to both the consumer and the environment, though there are always limits to substitution, and the costs of substitution can be high. Thus despite starry-eyed enthusiasm in the late 1970s about endless deposits of exploitable oil shale ready for when the oilfields ran dry, nonetheless the amount of waste rock produced, the amount of water needed to keep everything cool, and in the end of course the amount of cash investment needed, have all thankfully scared the oil companies off — for the time being.

Subtopia

[1955. Abbreviation of 'sub[urb' + 'u]topia']
The boring and visually depressing landscape of many Western suburbs. 'The world of universal low density masses . . . an even spread of . . . fake rusticity, wire fences, traffic roundabouts, gratuitous notice boards, car parks and things-in-fields' (Ian Nairn, 1955).

Subversion

[14c. *L subvertere*, to turn upside down]

Encouraging change by questioning and manipulating the basic structures and beliefs of society. 'Subversion' is often used by mainstream politicians to mean 'perceived threat' or 'minor irritation'; but for green-thinkers the original meaning of 'small-scale but highly effective change from the grassroots' is central to green philosophy. In an influential book, Paul Shepard (1969) called ecology 'the subversive science', and subversion can come into play every time we have an opportunity to use deadening systems to life-enhancing ends. A good example is the 1970 anti-Vietnam-war 'comply-in', when a clause in the draft law which required that registrants 'inform the draft boards within ten days of any change in address or status, meaning changes in religion, mental attitude and everything else' (quoted in Gene Sharp, 1973) was taken literally by hundreds of draftees, inundating and incapacitating the draft office with thousands of postcards.

Succession

[1860 in this sense. *L succedere*, to follow closely, go after]

The way in which ecological associations succeed each other in a particular area. Successive stages may bear little resemblance to the community that eventually inhabits the area (the CLIMAX) — a typical succession in a temperate area might be grassland, shrubs, pine forest, hardwood forest, and each stage would have its typical plants and animals. The first stage of colonisation on a barren site is called the primary succession; further major changes are called secondary succession.

Sufficiency

[15c. *L sufficere*, to suffice]

A philosophy of having just enough for your needs, rather than always wanting more; 'the shift from surfeit to sufficiency — from the politics of more and more towards the politics of enough' (Jonathon Porritt, in Mary Inglis and Sandra Kramer (ed), 1985).

Sun

[before 12c. *Old English sunne*, sun]

The star at the centre of our solar system, the source of the energy which feeds the earth's life support system, and an important symbol of life and light. *See also* SOLAR ENERGY.

Sunrise/Sunset Industries

[1980]

A distinction between up-and-coming light and service industries and old-and-dying heavy manufacturing industry. A 'sunrise' concept among journalists and economists, who are in danger of being enchanted by a new but just as unsustainable growth-trip. Sunrise and sunset industries are rarely found in the same areas, thus creating major economic dislocation.

Supply-Side Economics
[1976]
An approach to economic analysis which emphasises the role of the supply of resources, unlike most economic theory, in which the customer (demand) is king. Partly a response to 'crises' like massive oil price rises and raw material shortages, the increasing discussion of supply-side economics is possibly one of the first signs that economists are realising that resources are finite. Not surprisingly the idea was almost instantly subverted by the establishment to 'prove' that reducing tax rates, especially among the rich, would increase investment and thereby stimulate supply — a complete misunderstanding of the process of real wealth creation.

Support
[14c. *L supportare*, to carry, convey]
Providing assistance for somebody who needs it, and in general who has asked for it. Hence 'support group', 'support network', 'support person'. 'Form your own personal support group — not an official organization, but friends and colleagues you can call on at any time to share frustrations, fears, depressions, and even hopes and fantasies. It should be a group that celebrates and reinforces your successes and gives you encouragement for the future' (Neil Wollman (ed), 1985). 'Once, when I was chairing a meeting with a group of blacks, whites, Spanish, Poles, Italians, and Irish, I knew I was going to be attacked. I was very uncomfortable until I looked round the room and saw five women from my Italian-American support group. Suddenly, I felt very strong. The dispute turned out to be a small thing that I could have handled by myself, but having my friends there felt great' (Sally Martino Fisher, in Annie Cheatham and Mary Clare Powell (ed), 1986).

Suppression
[15c. *L supprimere*, to press down]
Banning or restraining something (*see* CENSORSHIP, FEELINGS, SILENCE). 'Suppression' and REPRESSION are virtual synonyms, though 'supression' tends to be used to describe the quelling of citizen actions, while 'repression' more often refers to a state of continual restraint.

Survival
[*c.*1600 *L supervivere*, to outlive]
Living through difficult circumstances and coming out at the other end.

Survival means very different things in different circumstances. 'It is learning how to stand alone, unpopular and sometimes reviled, and how to make common cause with those others identified as outside the structures, in order to define and seek a world in which we can all flourish. It is learning how to take our differences and make them strengths' (Audre Lorde, 1981, quoted in Cheris Kramerae and Paula Treichler, 1985). '[After a nuclear war] it would be a survival of some of your people and some of your facilities, but you could start again' (Ronald Reagan, quoted in Helen Caldicott, 1984). 'Survival is a poor fruit for "advanced" civilization to bear — a passing on of the present time's crisis unresolved to the next generation' (E.P. Thompson, in Dan Smith and E.P. Thompson (ed), 1987). Many people prefer to use 'survivor' rather than VICTIM, especially when talking about the results of OPPRESSION, in order to stress that nobody is 'natural victim', but that we are all 'natural survivors'. 'When the buffalo are all slaughtered, the wild horses are tamed, the secret corners of the forest heavy with the scent of many men, and the view of the hills blotted by talking wires, where is the thicket? Gone. And where is the eagle? Gone. The end of living and the beginning of survival' (Chief Seathl, 1855).

Sustainability
[1971. *L sustinere*, to hold up]
The capacity of a system to maintain a continuous flow of whatever each part of that system needs for a healthy existence. Thus 'sustainable yield' means taking no more from an ecosystem than it can create and at the same time remain healthy, diverse and self-perpetuating. The concept of sustainability applies to all ecosystems, including ones with human beings in them, though lack of ecological wisdom has led us to degrade and destroy so many systems that some people doubt our ability to learn the crucial lesson before the global ecosystem becomes non-selfsustaining. 'A sustainable way of life is one which recognizes that all Earth's resources are finite and that there are limits to the growth of all living systems. These limits are finally dictated by the finite size of the Earth and the finite input of energy from the sun. We humans need to attend to how much traffic the Earth can bear and still nourish a quality of life fitting for continued human unfoldment' (Susan Campbell, 1983). 'From our side of the divide it's clear that all industrial nations are pursuing an unsustainable path. Every time we opt for a "conventional" solution, we merely create new problems, new threats. Every time we count on some new technological miracle, we merely put off the day of reckoning' (Jonathon Porritt, 1984).

Symbiosis
[17c. *Gk sumbiosis*, living together]
A close and long-term relationship between two species which is beneficial to both; by extension, any such mutually beneficial relationship. 'The occurrence of cellulose-digesting protozoans in the guts of wood-eating cockroaches and termites is a symbiotic relationship, as the insects cannot digest cellulose unaided, and the protozoa cannot live independently' (Michael Allaby, 1983).

Symbol
[15c. *Gk sumbolon*, token for identification]
Something which represents something else; often a small physical object, drawing, pattern or movement representing some larger reality (*see* CIRCLE, SPIRAL). In a materialistic culture, material and status symbols replace more universal ones; changing status symbols reflect changing values.

Symptom
[16c. *Gk sumptoma*, occurence, phenomenon]
A noticeable indication that a system is not working as it should. In human healing, mainstream MEDICINE starts from a recognised set of symptoms, from which 'illnesses' are diagnosed. This assumes that the existence of a symptom proves the existence of an ILLNESS, which is a prime candidate for medication. Holistic healing, on the other hand, treats symptoms as important indicators rather than as part of the disease, often suggesting preventative treatment for the whole body rather than just 'curing' the obvious symptoms. Trying to cure symptoms without recognising the underlying imbalance is a favourite occupation of a dualistic culture, ignoring all systems and ecological considerations. Green-thinkers look deeper: 'Inflation is not so much an economic disease, to be cured by control of wages or of the money supply, as a symptom of much deeper problems' (Jonathon Porritt, 1984). *See also* PAIN.

Synchronicity
[1953 in this sense. *Gk sunkhronos*, simultaneous]
Events occurring within a short space of time which are linked in the mind of the observer and often seem to bring good fortune, but which appear to have no causal relationship. 'Strange as they might sound, such coincidences are not uncommon. Alan Vaughan, in his book *Incredible Coincidence* [1979], details many such instances. He tells, for example, of a lady who had locked herself out of her house, and was busy trying to find another way in, when the postman arrived with a letter from her brother returning a spare key he had borrowed. Another typical case is of the person who accidentally got off the New York

subway at the wrong station, realised his mistake when he reached the exit, and was about to return to the trains when he bumped into the very person he was on his way to visit' (Peter Russell, 1982). Synchronicity of ideas is another element of the concept — it is fascinating to see how similar green ideas arise simultaneously in different places (*see* HUNDREDTH MONKEY). At a time when in the new physics 'causal relationships' are ceasing to have very much meaning, and when green-thinkers are emphasising the interconnectedness of the universe, synchronicity should come as no surmountable theoretical problem. While we constantly need to question our motivation and remember our responsibilities, 'going with the flow of the universe' — a favourite NEW AGE concept — should also see everything falling into place more easily, including the pattern of our own lives. The 'meantness' of things, as long as it doesn't veer into the oppressive and fatalistic version of 'creating your own reality' (*see* REALITY), is close to the ecological principle of APPROPRIATENESS.

Synergy
[17c. *Gk sunergos*, working together]
Working together in an integrated way; by extension, 'synergy' is sometimes used to describe how, in an integrated system, the whole system is much more than simply the sum of its parts. 'When we look at organisms that work — and just about every organism apart from human society does work — we find that there is one particular quality which they all share: the many components naturally and spontaneously function together, in harmony with the whole. This characteristic can be seen operating in organisms as different as a slime mould, an oak tree, or the human body. It is usually described by the word synergy' (Peter Russell, 1982). 'Synergy' is a useful but overused NEW AGE word: 'Everyone is recognized as having the ability to tune into the universal mind and offer his or her perspective and contribution to the government of the whole. This co-creative interaction leads to a government through synergy where individuals, knowing their own authority and power, are not threatened by each other but are working together to create a whole greater than the sum of its parts' (François Duquesne, in Findhorn Community, 1980). 'Synergy' also describes the way in which different toxic chemicals combine to form new 'pollution cocktails' with unpredictable consequences.

Synthesis
[*c*.1600. *Gk sunthesis*, putting together]
Seeing the whole picture; pulling all the strands together. Be careful of the link with 'synthetic', which in the late nineteenth century was used to denote 'man-made' (synthesised from chemicals), and by the 1930s had come to mean anything artificial.

Syntropy
[1978]
Another word for NEGENTROPY.

System
[17c. *Gk sustema*, a composite whole; from *sunistanai*, to cause to stand together]
A NETWORK of individual components and relationships between them. 'Systems theory' or 'systems thinking' differs from traditional science in that the latter is concerned almost entirely with simple causal relationships, while systems thinking recognises the overwhelming importance of complex interconnection and the danger of simplification. On the other hand, systems thinking is still very much limited by the concept of SCIENCE in which it has grown up, which constantly attempts to limit the usefulness of systems thinking by insisting on measurement and explanation to prove existence. While the inherent DUALISM of our culture is difficult to ignore, green-thinkers regard systems thinking as essential to our present understanding of the planet and its inhabitants. 'The systems view involves looking at the world in terms of relationships and integration. . . Examples of living systems abound in nature. Every organism — from the smallest bacterium through the wide range of plants and animals to humans — is an integrated whole and thus a living system. Cells are living systems, and so are the various tissues and organs of the body. The same characteristics of wholeness are exhibited by social systems—such as a family or community—and by ecosystems that consist of a variety of organisms and inanimate matter in mutual interaction. The specific structures of all these systems arise from the interactions and interdependencies of all their parts. Systemic properties are destroyed when a system is dissected, either physically or theoretically, into isolated elements. Although we can discern individual parts in any system, the nature of the whole is always different from the mere sum of its parts' (Fritjof Capra and Charlene Spretnak, 1984).

Systems Theory
(*see* GENERAL SYSTEMS THEORY)

Tt

Taming
[before 12c. *Old English tam*, tame]
Bending something or someone to your own will. Bending nature to the will of 'man' is central to the anthropocentric idea of PROGRESS characteristic of current mainstream Western culture, and is thus a concept deeply etched into the way we think and live. Feminism has traced the link between the taming of nature and the taming of women: 'He makes her his own. He encloses her. He encircles her. He puts her under lock and key. He protects her' (Susan Griffin, 1984).

Tao
[1900. *Chinese dao*, path, way]
Literally 'the way'; the fundamental nature and principle of the UNIVERSE, and at the same time 'that which is nameless' (*see* PARADOX). The concept of the tao is at the heart of the Chinese spiritual philosophy of Taoism, popularised in the West by John Blofeld and Alan Watts among others, and an accessible way of approaching SPIRITUALITY without the physical and psychological paraphernalia of organised RELIGION (though even Taoism embraces a sometimes oppressive moral code). 'Lao-tzû tells us that "Tao" is just a convenient term for what had best be called the Nameless. Nothing can be said of it that does not detract from its fullness. To say that it exists is to exclude what does not exist, although void is the very nature of the Tao. To say that it does not exist is to exclude the Tao-permeated plenum. Away with dualistic categories. Words limit. The Tao is limitless' (John Blofeld, 1973). To call a book *The Tao of . . .* is to appear very holistic; *The Tao of Physics* (Fritjof Capra, 1975) is probably the best-known, *The Tao of Pooh* (Benjamin Hoff, 1982) the most entertaining.

Taxation

[14c. *L taxare*, to appraise; from *tangere*, to touch]

MONEY taken from people and organisations by the STATE in order to finance whatever that state chooses to spend it on. In theory a way of redistributing WEALTH to create a more egalitarian society, in practice often the opposite. A major part of our money is spent on things that few greens would support, such as DEFENCE (*see* PEACE TAX), space technology, NUCLEAR ENERGY and major ROAD construction; more is spent dealing with issues in ways that Greens know could be improved on, such as AGRICULTURAL subsidies, EDUCATION, LAW AND ORDER, HEALTH services and public HOUSING. Even at the level of wealth redistribution through social benefits (*see* WELFARE), current taxation systems are failing abysmally. 'Despite widespread moaning about taxes, few people realize how unfair our tax system really is. Rich Americans [Britons, Germans, Australians . . .] often pay proportionally less of their income in taxes than you do, not more. Many millionaires pay no taxes at all, and the share of taxes paid by corporations has been steadily whittled away for decades. Our taxes as a whole are in fact "regressive", not "progressive" (they soak the poor, not the rich), partly because of loopholes in the tax laws and partly because sales taxes, phone taxes and gas [petrol] taxes all bear more heavily on poor people . . . In short, taxes are spent mostly to maintain the profits and privileges of the ruling class and to throw some sops to their middle-class supporters' (Ernest Callenbach, 1981). 'Pensions, national income schemes, benefits and taxation policies are, in the end, very technical matters. But they ultimately work or do not work because of the philosophies which underlie them. The Protestant ethic joined income and labour in line with St Paul's view that he who did not work should starve. That philosophy, however much it lingers on in the hearts and minds of many, cannot work where [paid] jobs cannot be guaranteed' (Charles Handy, 1985). Some green-thinkers have looked hard at current taxation systems, and come up with several alternative suggestions. As well as considering carefully what 'public' money needs to buy, most green taxation proposals relate directly to the need to reduce the use of NON-RENEWABLE RESOURCES and to encourage ecological practices. In the UK several 'conservation taxes' and 'resource taxes' have been proposed, including a tax on new housing to subsidise the conversion of existing buildings, selected import taxes to encourage SELF-RELIANCE, a luxury housing tax, and a LAND TAX. In general, however, they tend not to question the fundamental issues of VALUE, wealth, and HUMAN RIGHTS. In the USA, Paul Hawken has proposed a hefty oil tax: 'The kind of tax I am talking about is a big one: $1 per gallon at retail. Before people object vociferously, they might ask how Switzerland, with no oil resources, can pay such a tax and have a per capita income 50 per cent greater than our own. The initiation of such a tax would be painful, but not as painful as reduced Social Security benefits, high interest rates, or a collapsing economy. If America raised the price of oil by such a margin, it is my belief that we would quickly become world leaders in all phases of energy conservation and alternative energy generation' (Paul Hawken, 1983). Taxation is almost always seen as the concern of each individual state, which overlooks the need for the global redistribution of wealth; where such redistribution does take place it is always seen as charity (*see* AID) rather than as a RESPONSIBILITY: 'If we accept progressive taxation for the benefit of the disadvantaged in our own country, why can we not also accept a progressive taxation of the rich countries to the benefit of the poor countries? Why should levelling of this sort be regarded as charity in the international context, when nationally it is accepted as common justice?' (Erik Dammann, 1984).

Teacher

[14c. *Old English tœcan*, to show]

Someone or something you want to learn from; an inspiration. To some people 'teacher' is synonymous with GURU. 'To me, respect for a schoolteacher is an artificial lie, demanding insincerity; when a person really gives respect, he [or she] does so unawares. My pupils can call me a silly ass any time they like to; they respect me because I respect their young lives, not because I am the principal of the school, not because I am on a pedestal as a dignified tin god. My pupils and I have mutual respect for each other because we approve of each other' (A.S. Neill, 1962). 'Children [and grown-ups] are naturally drawn to learning if you can keep the spirit of the occasion happy and enthusiastic. Remember that your own enthusiasm is infectious, and that it is perhaps your greatest asset as a teacher' (Joseph Bharat Cornell, 1979).

Technocentrism

[1977]

The belief that TECHNOLOGY will solve everything. 'A "mode of thought" which recognises environmental "problems" but believes either unrestrainedly that man [*sic*] will always solve them and achieve unlimited growth (the "cornucopians") or, more cautiously, that by careful economic and environmental management they can be negotiated (the "accommodators"). In either case considerable faith is placed in the ability and usefulness of classical science, technology, conventional economic reasoning (e.g. cost-benefit analysis), and their practitioners' (David Pepper, 1984).

Technocracy
[1919. *Gk tekhne* + *kratia*, the power of the skilled]
A situation in which scientists and technologists are in control, where everything has a technological solution. Some green-thinkers believe that we are entering a post-technocratic period with the run-down of traditional industries (Alvin Toffler, 1970), but most are less optimistic, pointing to numerous occasions when environmentally unsound policy decisions are made on the basis of 'technical considerations'; in one public hearing about nuclear installations in the USA, 'pro-nuclear witnesses saw the use of technical expertise as a way to interpret and resolve issues — 80% of their testimony was "couched in terms of technical facts-and-figures" as compared to 17% for the anti-nuclear groups' (S. Del Sesto, 1980, quoted in David Pepper, 1984).

Technofix
[1970]
(*also* 'technological fix')
A technological solution designed 'once-and-for-all' to deal with an environmental or social problem without having to look at the root causes of the problem — a contradiction in ecological terms but a common technocratic ploy. Thus the 'solution' to OZONE pollution is seen as the universal use of catalytic converters on cars, rather than looking at alternative forms of transport. Many of our major disaster areas were once (and in some cases still are) seen as technofixes — NUCLEAR ENERGY, DDT, high-rise flats. Other technofixes are still gleams in the eyes of the technoaddicts: colonies on Mars, space wars, household robots. Unless nipped in the bud, technofixes have a nasty habit of being realised. 'When we fall into the trap of believing or, more accurately, hoping that technology will solve all our problems, we are actually abdicating the high touch of personal responsibility' (John Naisbitt, 1984).

Technology
[17c. *Gk tekhnologia*, the systematic study and use of skills]
Using our knowledge about the world to useful and non-harmful ends. This green definition is not, however, widely held; more common is 'the application of practical or material sciences to industry or commerce' (*Collins*, 1986). In the green version, technology predates SCIENCE by millennia, and belies the current practice always to link the two; the great debate about the 'usefulness' of technology hinges on its subversion by scientism and the scientific imperative, which since the nineteenth century has been intimately linked with CAPITALISM, centralisation, and the idea of PROGRESS. 'Western society has accepted as unquestionable the technological imperative that is quite as arbitrary as

the most primitive taboo: not merely the duty to foster invention and constantly to create technological novelties, but equally the duty to surrender to these novelties unconditionally, just because they are offered, without respect to their human [or environmental] consequences' (Lewis Mumford, quoted in Jonathon Porritt, 1984) 'John Thyme [1978] . . . describes a "technological imperative", by which environmentally-damaging technologies, such as motorways, SST aircraft, nuclear power stations or nuclear weapons, are advanced in an "unstoppable" (and therefore undemocratic) way' (David Pepper, 1984). Yet small-scale SOLAR ENERGY schemes, bicycle trailers and garden tools are also the results of technology, as are many of the more dubious but accepted-as-necessary aspects of everyday life in the West like telephones, electric power and TRANSPORT systems. The problem with technology is not the concept itself, but its interpretation. The questions for green-thinkers are: Which technologies are environmentally sound? Who is technology benefiting? Who is making decisions about which technologies are developed, and which not? 'Ecologists are not hostile to technology *per se*, and the use of advanced technologies of many kinds is essential to the development of an ecological society. . . It is a matter of choice whether technology works to the benefit of people or perpetuates certain problems, whether it provides greater equity and freedom of choice or merely intensifies the worst aspects of our industrial society. It is quite clear that in today's economy the introduction of labour-saving machinery strengthens the hand of a very small group of managers and technicians representing the interests of big business' (Jonathon Porritt, 1984). *See also* TOOLS.

Teleology
[1740. *Gk telos* + *logos*, words about the end]
The belief that there is evidence of PURPOSE in the UNIVERSE; by extension, the belief that there is some sort of 'designer'. For many green-thinkers it is enough that the universe exists (*see* DEEP ECOLOGY, REALITY); 'purpose' is a human creation and useful to human beings, but assigning purpose to anything beyond ourselves is prone to ANTHROPOCENTRISM, and trying to convince other people that we know that purpose better than they do is close to indoctrination.

Telephone Tree
[1980]
A way of getting a message to a lot of people over a large area very quickly; used by networks of people such as nuclear weapons surveillance groups. The person or group mobilising the action rings a small number of prearranged people, who then each ring another handful. In this way a message can be passed to a large number of people in a few

minutes, but to be effective the system must be well-organised and dependable, and does require members of the tree to own phones.

Television
[1907. *Gk tele + L visio*, seeing at a distance]
A machine which brings instant passive entertainment into most Western homes. While television programmes can be stimulating, useful and even subversive, most are not. Television replaces direct communication between people, often displays the worst features of our culture, is financed (especially in the USA) largely by multinational corporations whose main interest is profit, involves no physical exercise whatsoever, is addictive, and can be a health hazard (some people being highly sensitive to short-wave radiation and high-frequency flicker). 'Statistics vary and can't be depended on exactly; still, we know that most children in the United States watch television a great deal of the time. One study of preschool children said fifty-four hours a week, which is hard to believe since most preschool children are only awake a few hours more than that. On the other hand, in many households the TV is left on all day. It seems a fair conclusion, at any rate, that the average American child sees a great deal more of the TV than of either parents or friends' (Ernest Callenbach, 1980). In most homes the television is always on display, too easy to turn to. The recent development of facilities for low-cost programme-making has at least brought some degree of grassroots participation, but is no substitute for real face-to-face involvement.

Tension
(*see* STRESS)

Teratogen
[1903. *Gk teratogenes*, monster-born]
A MUTAGEN which can cause abnormalities in an unborn foetus; most mutagens are also known to be teratogens.

Theory
[*c*.1600. *Gk theasthai*, to observe]
(1) A MODEL or set of ASSUMPTIONS used to explain why something is the way it is.
(2) Something you believe, but may or may not have tried out. For green-thinkers the integration of theory and PRACTICE is vital, if not always easy to achieve; in fact the whole idea of dividing experience into 'theory' and 'practice' is dubious: 'Radical feminist theory is that theory follows from practice and is impossible to develop in the absence of practice, because our theory is that practising our practice is our theory. If this sounds like semantic hoop-jumping I am sorry' (Gail Chester, 1979).

Therapy
[1846. *Gk therapeia*, attendance]
Giving someone ATTENTION while they explore and heal themself. 'Therapy' is often used synonymously with PSYCHOTHERAPY, though it can be used to describe any healing technique. 'One person can help another to grow — and this doesn't depend on the other person having a problem. . . It is a kind of compassionate skill, a kind of love work' (John Rowan, 1983). Some green-thinkers, especially those with a Marxist or socialist background, question the effectiveness of therapy in a world where so much needs to be done 'on the outside' without all this 'navel-gazing'; most, however, are convinced that it is impossible to be effective in the world until you have explored your own inner world, the unnecessary baggage we all carry from the past which continues to weigh us down. On the other hand, some therapists and therapies seem to exist in a dreamworld of plush reception rooms and hefty fees, ignoring the realities of unemployment, oppression and nuclear threat. In order to keep themselves in business they get people hooked on long courses of expensive therapy, forgetting that the point is to heal, not to create therapy junkies. This is 'therapy for therapy's sake'. Access to therapy is an important political issue, as is the sort of therapy that people deserve access to. Green therapy must be about empowering people to be more effective in changing their lives and their world, not about keeping therapists in business.

Thermal Pollution
(*see* HEAT POLLUTION)

Thermal Storage
[*c*.1970]
(*also* 'heat storage')
Ways of storing low-grade energy (especially energy generated by methods which depend on cyclical sources, like SOLAR and TIDAL) so that it can be used when it is needed. Such storage methods include 'heat sinks' or 'thermal mass' techniques such as 'hot rocks' and large enclosed volumes of water, methods of using latent heat, and electrical phase change technology.

Thermodynamics
[1854. *Gk thermos* + *dunamikos*, the power of heat]
The exploration of ENERGY processes, especially those involving heat. Two principles which appear to be true for all energy systems are called 'the laws of thermodynamics'. These are:
(a) In a system with a constant mass, energy cannot be created or destroyed (the law of the conservation of energy).

(b) Apart from short-term and local aberrations, energy always moves from a hotter part of a system to a colder part (the law of increasing entropy). *See also* ENTROPY, NEGENTROPY, NET ENERGY PRINCIPLE.

They
[13c. *Old English tha*, they]
(1) Other people, especially the people who seem to be creating problems for us. Though 'they' very often are doing so (and are being paid to do it), most green-thinkers, most of the time, know that it doesn't help either to be confrontative or to act out a VICTIM role. It doesn't improve things to perpetuate the 'us and them' game, and it can be very disarming (as well as productive) to jump the divide and treat one of 'them' as one of 'us'.
(2) A pronoun that doesn't have all the sexist problems of 'he' and 'she' and is a completely acceptable alternative despite the complaints from old-fashioned teachers and editors. All the best writers have used 'they' as a third person singular pronoun — you will be in the company of Shakespeare, Goldsmith, George Eliot, Walt Whitman, John Ruskin, George Bernard Shaw, Elizabeth Bowen, Lawrence Durrell and Doris Lessing, to name but a few (Casey Miller and Kate Swift, 1981). Neither is there anything amiss with 'Each of them can choose for themself' — in ten years' time nobody will even notice it, and sexist language will have been dealt another blow.

Thinking
[before 12c. *Old English thencan*, to think]
Using your intelligence to the full. Some psychotherapies, like co-counselling, emphasise the importance of clear thinking in order to make the distinction between behaviour which is the result of intelligent thought and behaviour which is the result of distress. Clear thinking is the only reliable guide to appropriate behaviour, and it is important to trust it: 'Other people's thinking can be good information for you, but it can't replace your thinking. Your thinking is good. Depend on your thinking. This is your only guide to what you would like to do, what your best judgement is; not anybody's shoulds, or society's rules, or anything of the sort. You'll make some mistakes, of course, if you trust your own thinking; but if you make the mistake while trusting *your own* thinking, you'll be alert to the fact that the results aren't working and you'll correct it quickly. . . Trust your own thinking and it will work out fine' (Harvey Jackins, 1983)

Third Line/Third Sector/Third Wave/Third Way
[*c*.1980 onwards]
'Third' is a favourite green qualifier, usually indicating a (more or less) alternative approach to the polarity apparent in many aspects of human

behaviour and society. Thus 'third line medicine' — first line being basic care and second line specialist treatment — is 'that portion of the practice of medicine which is devoted to improving the state of health of patients whose illnesses continue to cause distressing symptoms following standard courses of treatment by medical specialists' (Melvyn Werbach, 1986). The 'third sector economy' — first sector being the formal economy and the second the 'unemployed' — 'covers a whole range of enterprises that are believed necessary for the re-building of the economy and the maintenance of what have hitherto been regarded as public and social services' (Nick Murgatroyd and Peter Smith, 1984). The 'third wave' — the first wave being the agricultural revolution and the second the industrial revolution — is the information revolution and everything that goes with it, a 'Third Wave civilization' (Alvin Toffler, 1980). 'West and East are no longer alternatives to each other. Against the status quo we pose our vision of a new third way which leads beyond confrontation' (Rudolf Bahro, 1986). *See also* MIDDLE WAY.

Third World
[1952]
The poorest countries of the world, mostly in Africa, South and Central America, and southern Asia. 'The expression "Third World" was first used by French demographer Alfred Sauvy in 1952, and immediately popularized in journalistic and diplomatic media. In the sense in which Sauvy used it, it was an allusion to the *tiers état* (third estate) of French society before the revolution of 1789, made up of people deprived of privileges — as opposed to clergy and nobility — including various social strata: merchants, civil servants, artisans, peasants and workers. This "third estate" was characterized by its political marginalization in the society of the period, and by the common interest in overcoming it. Thus the original sense — which remains valid — refers to all those countries, differing greatly among themselves, which are marginalized in the current international system' (*Third World Guide*, 1984). The 'three-world theory' developed rapidly, with the superpowers of the USA and USSR as the first world and the other industrialised countries as the second world. As an alternative to 'Third World', 'developing countries' is not only a downright lie in many cases, but it depends on a Western concept of DEVELOPMENT which is inappropriate in most Third World settings. Despite their diversity, Third World countries do have important characteristics in common — they have nearly all been colonies of foreign powers; they have all suffered from the exploitation of their natural and human resources; and they have all been subjected to cultural domination. The strength of the concept is that it underlines the fact that the Third World consistently comes bottom of the quality-of-life tables. One danger of the label is

that it fits neatly with the Western mentality that the first two worlds are intrinsically 'better' than the third, and that despite the ravages of COLONIALISM and NEOCOLONIALISM, the Third World doesn't deserve any help from the West: 'By and large, conventional politicians today have, despite a certain twitching of their conscience, dismissed the Third World entirely from their concern. They are in the business of winning power, so they pander to the majority of the electorate, who, to put it bluntly, don't give a stuff for the Third World' (Jonathon Porritt, in Mary Inglis and Sandra Kramer (ed), 1985). Then there is the problem of the Western EXPERT on the Third World, when the Third World can speak and act very well for itself, given the opportunity: the Third World is 'too important in many cases to be left to national or international policy-makers and far too important for the journalism of casual visitors giving the cursory once-over. It is an area whose myriad specialists are those who live there, usually unheard outside' (Victoria Brittain and Michael Simmons (ed), 1987). Perhaps the main problem with the concept, however, is that although there seems to be no useful alternative to 'Third World', the whole idea of a divided world is one we would be better off without: 'Anyone who is literate and in possession of their right senses knows that there is no "Third World". There is only one world, and that belongs to all of us, and it is the only one we have' (Gerald Durrell, in Lee Durrell, 1986). 'To native peoples, there is no such thing as the first, second, and third worlds; there is only an exploiting world . . . whether its technological system is capitalist or communist . . . and a host world. Native peoples, who occupy more land, make up the host world' (Winona LaDuke, 1983, in Cheris Kramerae and Paula Treichler, 1985). *See also* AID, APARTHEID, APPROPRIATE TECHNOLOGY, BOTTOM-UP, CASH CROP, DEBT CRISIS, DELINKING, DESERTIFICATION, ECODEVELOPMENT, FAMINE, FOOD, FOURTH WORLD, GREEN REVOLUTION, IMPERIALISM, IMPORT SUBSTITUTION, LAND OWNERSHIP, LIBERATION, MULTINATIONAL, NATIVE PEOPLES, NEW INTERNATIONAL DIVISION OF LABOUR, NEW INTERNATIONAL ECONOMIC ORDER, NEW INTERNATIONAL INFORMATION ORDER, NORTH/SOUTH DIALOGUE, ONE-CROP ECONOMY, OVERPOPULATION, OVERURBANISATION, POVERTY, PROGRESS, RACE, RACISM, RAINFOREST, RURAL RESETTLEMENT, SELF-RELIANCE, SQUATTING, SUBSISTENCE, TRADE, TRAVEL, TRICKLE-DOWN, WAR, WORLD.

Threat
[before 12c. *Old English threat*, oppression, use of force]
An indication of imminent harm, usually resulting from a refusal to comply with the demands of someone who is using their power in an oppressive and exploitative way. *See* NUCLEAR THREAT.

Threshold
(*see* LIMIT)

Throughput
[1922]
The amount of energy or resources passing through a system. In line with the second law of THERMODYNAMICS (the ENTROPY law), the more throughput passing through a SYSTEM the more energy it will lose in the process and the less efficient it will be (*see* EFFICIENCY). Natural processes (and the best human ones too) are very energy-efficient, and reduce throughput to a minimum — this is, of course, in direct contradiction to the 'more is better' attitude to PROGRESS and economic GROWTH. 'Throughput is the entropic physical flow of matter-energy from nature's sources, through the human economy, and back to nature's sinks. . . It is the final cost' (Herman Daly, 1977). 'Throughput is by no means a desideratum, and indeed is to be regarded as something to be minimized rather than maximized. The essential measure of the economy is not production and consumption at all, but the nature, extent, quality and complexity of the total capital stock, including . . . the state of human bodies and minds' (Kenneth Boulding, in John Barr (ed), 1971).

Throwaway Society
[1928]
A society (like the USA is now and Europe is increasingly becoming) where many of the everyday things we use — cutlery, food containers, razors — are designed to be thrown away after being used once, or for a very short period. While green-thinkers try to avoid things designed to be thrown away, we are constantly encouraged to consume more instantly-disposable goods, thereby saving ourselves the trouble of cleaning, mending and carrying things round with us. But who really benefits? 'Our enormously productive economy . . . demands that we make consumption our way of life, that we convert the buying and use of goods into rituals, that we seek our spiritual satisfactions in consumption. . . We need things consumed, burned up, worn out, replaced, and discarded at an ever-increasing rate' (N. Singh, quoted in Derek Wall, *Green Line*, November 1986). And what do we really want? 'If we look to moving day in 1999, we may well see a family loading their car with a few boxes full of art and craft objects, ceramics, hand-woven cushions and wall-hangings, books and cassettes, while nearly all of the so-called "hard goods" have either been returned to the lessor or thrown away, to be replaced by newly leased appliances and inexpensively purchased furnishings at the point of destination' (Victor Papanek, 1974). The general idea sounds fine, but you don't need to live in a throwaway world for this to work, just one where people have stopped clinging to 'their' possessions and are living much more lightly. *See also* PACKAGING, PROPERTY, RECYCLING, RE-USE, WASTE.

Tidal Energy
[*c*.1900]
Conversion of ENERGY from the rise and fall of the tide into forms useful to human beings. 'Tidal range energy' uses the difference between high and low water to power turbines or a waterwheel. The rising tide is used to fill a basin or reservoir (usually a natural inlet), then at high tide the sluice gates in the dam are shut, and as the tide falls the outrush of water turns the turbine to create electricity or the waterwheel to provide direct mechanical energy for grindstones and pulleys. 'Single effect' schemes only use the outflowing tide to produce energy; 'double effect' schemes are able to use both inflowing and outflowing tides, thus doubling the amount of time that energy can be generated from about 30% to about 60%. More complex schemes with more than one basin allow energy to be generated continuously, but are much more expensive to build. Large tidal range schemes are already in operation in France, China and the USSR. 'Tidal flow energy' uses the periodic tidal current through a narrow channel to generate energy; only small prototypes of this type of installation have yet been built. 'Tidal power . . . has an impressively long history, with notable schemes in ancient Egypt and another, incorporating four 6-metre (20-foot) reversible water wheels, installed under the arches of the medieval London Bridge in 1580 to pump water. These wheels lasted until 1824. As late as the Second World War, there were still scores of tide mills in operation around Europe. . . Even in the United States, tidal mills were still working well into the present century' (John Elkington, 1984). Large-scale tidal energy schemes can disrupt fragile ecosystems and habitats, especially vulnerable WETLANDS — as with all other technologies there is the constant danger of a TECHNOFIX mentality.

Time
[12c. *Old English tima*, time]
The non-spatial continuum within which events and processes take place; often thought of as a fourth dimension. Time is possibly the most precious of non-renewable resources, and unless we use it wisely it could be the resource that is running out the fastest. Like so much of what we take for granted, the late twentieth-century Western concept of time is by no means universal. Physicists generally agree that time is not uniform throughout the universe. In many Eastern belief systems, time is seen in terms of cycles rather than as a straight line from the big bang to the heat death of the universe. In traditional agricultural societies seasonal variation is the most important aspect of time, and shorter lengths of time are often measured in terms of everyday activities: 'In Madagascar, an accepted unit of time was called "a rice cooking"; a moment was known as "the frying of a locust". Englishmen

[and women?] spoke of a "pater noster wyle" — the time needed for a prayer — or, more earthily, of a "pissing while"' (Alvin Toffler, 1980). It is the demands of industrialised, highly organised, technologised society that force strict timekeeping on us, and like so many things we need to ask why we are doing it and who we are doing it for — it isn't healthy, and most of the time it isn't even efficient.

Tipi

[1835. *Dakota tipi*, dwelling]
A conical tent, traditionally used by many North American native peoples, now also found in communes, peace camps and peace convoys.

Tithing

[12c. *Old English teogetha*, one tenth]
Giving part of your income to a chosen cause on a regular basis. In many parts of the Christian world this was traditionally one tenth of each family's income given to the church; recently the idea has been revived to provide funds for worthwhile projects. In the USA members of a 2% club tithe 2% of their income to a fund which supports community and alternative projects; in the UK there is a 1% club with similar aims. *See also* COMMUNITY LEVY, PEACE TAX.

Tokenism

[1962. *Old English tac(e)n*, token]
Making only a token effort to involve oppressed or minority groups in mixed activities; having one black person or one woman on a committee or contributing to a book so you can say you've taken account of the 'minority' point of view. 'As a symbolic gesture, this can do more harm to women than straightforward exclusion. The presence of a few women in a male preserve — whether a university, a coal mine, or a board of directors — implies that institution offers equal rights, and allows it to get away with perpetuating sexism in working and hiring practices. The token woman becomes a weapon to be used by the male establishment' (Lisa Tuttle, 1986). While it is perhaps only to be expected, tokenism is alive and kicking in parts of the green movement too. Until the mid 1970s nobody thought it was important to include women's, black or third world voices in 'green' anthologies; in the late 1980s the record is not much better:
Deep Ecology, edited by Michael Tobias (1985) — 23 contributors, including one woman and one Philippino.
The New Economic Agenda, edited by Mary Inglis and Sandra Kramer (1985) — 17 contributors, including one woman and one Argentinian.
Red and Green, edited by Joe Weston (1986) — nine contributors, no women.
Green Britain or Industrial Wasteland?, edited by Edward Gold-

smith and Nicholas Hildyard (1986) — 28 contributors, including three women.
It's not that the books aren't good; it's simply that any claim to be representative rings hollow.

Tolerance
[15c. *L tolerare*, to sustain, bear]
Being able to endure hardship. Used in ecology to describe the range of conditions in which an organism can survive, and in everyday use to describe the limits to which people are driven by a generally inhuman world. 'The tyranny of tolerance dissuades women from tough-minded thinking, from responsibility for disagreement with others, and from the will to act. Worse, it allows oppressive values to surface without being rebutted. . . Tolerance is essentially a passive position' (Janice Raymond, 1986).

Tools
[before 12c. *Old English tol*, tool]
Useful equipment, skills, techniques and structures (*see* TECHNOLOGY). Traditionally meaning hammers and chisels, forks and spades, 'tools' is now often used to cover all the means by which a person can be in control of his or her own livelihood, including physical resources, bargaining and therapeutic skills, means of transport, legal procedures and land tenure systems. Part of 'being in control' is ensuring that the tools are tools that you choose and not ones that are forced on you — this is particularly important in the Third World, where the imposed technologies and institutions of the West are often totally inappropriate. 'Defense of conviviality [*see* CONVIVIALITY] is possible only if undertaken by the people with tools they control. Imperialist mercenaries can poison or maim but never conquer a people who have chosen to set boundaries to their tools for the sake of conviviality' (Ivan Illich, 1973).

Touch
[13c. *L toccare*, to strike a bell]
The sensation of feeling something against your skin, particularly another person's skin; touch is thought by many people to be the most fundamental of the senses, proving the reality of the real world — perhaps this is why we sometimes use 'touch' to describe anything which has really made CONTACT with us, as in 'it really touched me'. 'Touch means contact — relationship with what lies outside our own periphery, the ground beneath our feet. And for humans, as for other animals, touch is of vital importance. It gives reassurance, warmth, pleasure, comfort and renewed vitality. It tells us we are not alone' (Lucinda Lidell, 1984). Yet there has probably never been a society where touch — particularly human touch — was so denied as in Western culture.

Many people live long stretches of their lives without being touched, and we feel we have to apologise if we brush somebody by accident. Intimate touch is so bound up with sexual mythology that close physical contact for its own sake is virtually unheard of — in the popular press MASSAGE only means one thing. Frustration of such a basic need means that most people don't get what they want; oppressive beliefs about women and sexuality mean that most women get exactly the sort of physical attention they don't want (*see* CHILD ABUSE, HARASSMENT, INCEST, RAPE). Unwanted touch can easily arise in the most supposedly aware settings — in therapy for example: 'Permission to touch is often seen as one of the more liberating aspects of the growth movement . . . Like the so-called permissive society, and the sexual revolution, it has largely been developed on male terms and in male interests. . . Permission to hug, hold and touch is needed for people brought up to restrict such contact to sexual encounters or family rituals. However, the fact that these are the norms means that when a group leader feels free to put his arms around a woman, or when men in the group hug her, this is not necessaily going to be experienced straightforwardly by the woman herself. Being hugged by someone in authority, or by strange men, has a particular meaning for most women. . . Most men, however well-intentioned, have certain conditioned responses to touching women' (Shiela Ernst and Lucy Goodison, 1981). Yet we all deserve to have our need for physical contact met in a caring and respectful way, and despite the frustration and lack of communication that stand in the way, most green-thinkers see the fulfilment of that need as an achievable goal. 'Of course, we need to discriminate among the various kinds of touch for ourselves and for our children — touch that is kind, loving and comforting as opposed to touch which is intrusive, hurtful or damaging. That there are misguided individuals whose touch leaves scars is not a reason for us to stop touching altogether. We would only leave different scars' (Mirka Knaster, *Washington Post*, January 1986). *See also* BODYWORK, SEX.

Toxin
[1886. *Gk toxicos*, of a bow (*toxicon pharmakon*: the poison used on arrows)]
Another word for poison; more specifically an intensely poisonous substance produced by certain bacteria in the human body. The production of such toxins can sometimes be traced to the introduction of a particular artificial substance into the body — in recent years there have been a small but increasing number of cases, some fatal, of 'toxic shock syndrome', a disease which has been traced in many instances to the use by women of cellulose-based tampons. *See also* 'toxic waste' under WASTE.

Trace Elements
[1932]
Another term for NUTRIENTS.

Trade
[16c in this sense. *Middle Low German trade*, track, path]
Local and regional exchange and barter, designed to give people access to the full range of basic material needs. This is not, however, the usual meaning of 'trade'. In our world 'trade' has become a complex world-wide system of flows of money and goods designed to make rich and powerful people even more rich and powerful. The green equivalent is gradually to reduce unnecessary world trade to a minimum, organise what is essential in a socially responsive and ecologically sound way, and largely replace world trade with local and intra-regional trade. Economists and politicians still sometimes talk about free trade as an ideal, but free trade cannot exist where there are unfree people, and world trade today is often founded on the worst forms of exploitation, both of people and of the environment. With RECESSION (seen by many as the death of traditional economics) in the world's north, PROTECTIONISM is on the increase, adding to the already massively unfavourable terms of trade which have decimated the economies of many THIRD WORLD countries. What is to be done? In the Third World it is becoming increasingly clear that dependence upon trade to obtain income is a race against POVERTY that cannot be won, since the rich countries are refereeing the race and keep changing the rules. 'An open, trade-oriented strategy inevitably sucks countries into the trends of technology change, which are determined by the world technological leaders . . . As time passes, countries are forced to adopt increasingly capital-intensive technologies to maintain competitive standards. Consumption patterns tend to switch to more and more sophisticated goods for high income groups. There is a lack of availability of goods appropriate for low incomes: poor consumers tend to adopt lop-sided consumption patterns, with expenditure on inappropriate luxuries and inadequate expenditure on goods to meet basic needs' (Frances Stewart and Ejaz Ghani, in Paul Ekins (ed), 1986). Despite the pressure from the West, and especially from MULTINATIONALS, to invest in increasingly sophisticated production facilities, more and more Third World countries are seeing the wisdom of at least partially opting out of world trade (*see* DELINKING), and where possible of fostering trade between Third World countries, known as 'countertrade'. In the West, wealth and 'free trade' have given us the apparent advantage of being able to buy anything we want from anywhere in the world. This 'freedom' of choice ignores several fundamental inequalities between the 'north' and the 'south', and some important ecological considerations:

— we can buy cheaply only because the people who do the work are being massively exploited.
— we can buy cheaply only because much of the land in the Third World is being impoverished.
— we can buy cheaply only because the true cost of the NON-RENEWABLE RESOURCES being used to transport goods round the world is not taken into account, nor are the POLLUTION and other environmental costs. Some aspects of alternative lifestyles actually make things worse. Increasing vegetarianism in northern Europe, for example, means that many vegetarians are consuming less locally-produced food, eating instead rice from the USA, beans from Madagascar and China, dried fruit from Kenya and Australia, and nuts from Mozambique. Deciding how you trade as an individual consumer, as with everything else you do, has repercussions right down the line. Buy locally-produced goods wherever you can; buy Third World goods through trading cooperatives which encourage SELF-RELIANCE and buy directly from the producers; avoid the unnecessary consumption of anything. 'Exercising the right to choose what to buy and what not to buy, particularly when done collectively, makes it possible for individuals to shape both the type of product available and the manner in which it is produced' (Jonathon Porritt, 1987). *See also* CONSUMER.

Tradition
[14c *L tradere*, to hand over, transmit]
Handing important and valuable things and ideas down from generation to generation; a task we seem to be rather bad at, having forgotten what the important and valuable things are. *See also* CHILD, CULTURE, HERITAGE, INTERGENERATIONAL EQUITY.

Transcendentalism
[1803. *L transcendere*, to climb across]
A belief in the primary importance of the spiritual aspect of existence, often at the expense of the material. Transcendentalism takes many forms, perhaps the most obvious being a belief that we don't have to worry too much what humans do 'because god/nature/the universe will make it all right', another being that the beauty of nature is more important than its workings, a belief held for example by some nineteenth-century poets including Ralph Waldo Emerson.

Transference
[1910. *L transferre*, to carry over]
Transferring aspects of yourself that you find hard to accept (or aspects of people who have been influential in your life) on to your therapist, and believing that she or he really possesses those qualities. *See also* PROJECTION.

Transfer Pricing
[1969]
Arranging comparative but imaginary 'prices' between the different sections of a large company so that actual money does not have to change hands. Where this takes place between different national divisions within a MULTINATIONAL it bypasses international exchange rates and currency controls, thus giving such companies even more commercial advantage.

Transformation
[15c *L transformare*, to transform]
A complete and radical CHANGE, particularly the necessary change both in society and in individual consciousness which results from recognising that HOLISM and the GREEN approach make sense. 'Industrial civilization will be forced to make a rapid transition from its current business-as-usual growth ethic to a steady-state society. . . [This] great cultural transformation must be effectively completed within the next 50 to 100 years. If it is not, we shall experience this turning point in history as the greatest period of violence, suffering, and destruction ever known. Even if we are able to begin reversing current trends today, we shall not be able to escape the disorientation, confusion, and suffering implied by such an unprecedented cultural change' (Gary Coates (ed), 1981). 'In the area of personal and social relations, a truly transformative change is one which reflects not simply a shift from identification with one point of view to another, but rather an entirely new relationship between points of view formerly held in opposition to each other. This provides a new set of assumptions about how the world works and a larger, more inclusive context for decisions and actions' (Susan Campbell, 1983). 'The beginning of personal transformation is absurdly easy. We only have to pay attention to the flow of attention itself. Immediately we have added a new perspective' (Marilyn Ferguson, 1981).

Transnational
(*see* MULTINATIONAL)

Transpersonal Psychology
[1968]
Approaches and techniques in PSYCHOTHERAPY which emphasise the integration of the spiritual aspects of human awareness within a person's whole experience, stressing the importance of the UNCONSCIOUS and human existence beyond the physical body. Among such approaches are MEDITATION, some sorts of HEALING, and psychosynthesis, which uses VISUALISATION and FANTASY exercises to explore 'the transpersonal'. In fact the distinction between HUMANISTIC PSYCHOLOGY and transper-

sonal psychology is a fine one — many humanistic practitioners use transpersonal techniques and few would deny the importance of SPIRITUALITY, while almost all transpersonal therapists use techniques which are very similar to those used in COUNSELLING and GESTALT. 'Transpersonal' has also been taken into other green fields, particularly 'transpersonal education'.

Transport
[14c. *L transportare*, to carry across]
(US: 'transportation')
Ways of getting where you want to go; one of the aspects of human behaviour that has changed most radically in the last half-century. Buckminster Fuller has estimated that the average American in 1914 travelled 1,640 miles in year, 1,300 of them by foot. Today it is more like 16,000 miles a year (and perhaps 300 of them by foot). We take the provision of transportation facilities so much for granted that we rarely stop to think whether we really *need* to use them; wanting is quite enough. And because we almost always go for the easiest option — the private CAR — we end up with POLLUTION, NOISE, danger, dying trees and rapidly-dwindling oil reserves, and often we don't get there any faster than if we walked or used a BICYCLE. In central London the *average* traffic speed is 11 m.p.h. Transportation is a favourite target for the technofixers — supersonic aircraft that get less than 1% of air travellers there a couple of hours earlier, blasting sonic booms across the countryside and depleting the ozone that protects us from the sun's dangerous ultraviolet rays; motorways that generate more traffic than they can accommodate. Like all TECHNOFIXES, current transport policies are highly divisive — simply put, the poorest and most oppressed can't afford to go anywhere. Third World women still carry their harvest home on their heads; Western women suffer most from public transport cutbacks. The alternative is to use different forms of transport for the purposes they serve best, using the most efficient and least environmentally-damaging technologies available, and ensuring that everybody has access to the transport they need. At the same time we have to recognise that Westerners — especially rich ones — have been spoilt by having transport immediately to hand whenever it is needed. Though difficult to ask and difficult to answer, we have to question whether our journey is really necessary. As well as carrying us about, a large proportion of the world's transport system exists to carry freight and goods. The message here is simple — the less we use, the less needs to be carried. *See also* RAILWAY, ROAD, TRADE, TRAVEL, TRUCK.

Travel

[14c. *Old French travailler*, to exert yourself]

Journeying from one place to another; intimately connected with ease of TRANSPORT. Questioning motives is the key to aware travelling. Many people travel to get away from it all, when more long-term advantage might be gained from making here more like your fantasy of there (especially when you see what some of there looks like). When faced with images and descriptions of conditions in parts of the THIRD WORLD, an increasing number of people feel they want to go and help. Any Westerner should think very carefully before taking such a step. If you have a particular skill to share and are clear about why you want to go you may well be able to help, but some people go because they feel guilty, or frustrated, or that they have a duty. 'Always treat people respectfully and try to understand their lifestyle without being patronising. Even when you find local customs and lifestyles oppressive or limiting, observe sensitively, remembering that it is their land and culture, not yours. Self-styled teachers and liberators with little experience of the Third World will frustrate themselves and annoy their hosts. And of course, there's always the environment. Be it Greek islands or Himalayan peaks, it's often a threatened environment put under even more pressure because of tourists like you' (Jonathon Porritt, 1987). There have always been people for whom travelling is a way of life. The Romany (gypsy) tradition in Europe is an ancient one, rich in folklore and practical skills. In recent years other people have decided to become 'travellers', moving from place to place in converted trucks, buses and trailers, often providing music and entertainment as well as believing passionately in a green lifestyle. They sometimes have a hard time in a society that fears their creativity, and leaves no piece of land 'unowned' where travellers can legitimately stop and camp. Western concepts of LAND OWNERSHIP have always been inimical to people with nomadic lifestyles.

Tree

(*see* FOREST)

Trend

[1777. *Old English trendan*, to turn]

A general direction in which something is heading, usually used in relation to change through time. 'If present trends continue, the world in 2000 will be more crowded, more polluted, less stable ecologically, and more vulnerable to disruption than the world we live in now. Serious stresses involving population, resources, and environment are clearly visible ahead. Despite greater material output, the world's people will be poorer in many ways than they are today. . . [These

trends] do not predict what will occur. Rather, they depict conditions that are likely to develop if there are no changes in public policies, institutions, or rates of technological advance, and if there are no wars or other major disruptions. A keener awareness of the nature of current trends, however, may induce changes that will alter these trends and the projected outcome' (*Global 2000*, 1982). The word 'trend' is often used by politicians to mean the direction they would *like* things to be heading, as in 'the trend is upwards'. Trend-watching is big business, but the good news is that in general people appear to be way ahead of their politicians and administrators in terms of green thinking: 'trends are generated from the bottom up, fads from the top down' (John Naisbitt, 1984). Based on information from newspapers, magazines, newsletters and televison, John Naisbitt in his influential book *Megatrends* identifies ten major trends in present-day American society:
— from an industrial society to an information society.
— from forced technology to high tech/high touch [humane].
— from a national economy to a world economy.
— from short-term to long-term.
— from centralization to decentralization.
— from institutional help to self-help.
— from representative democracy to participatory democracy.
— from hierarchies to networking.
— from north to south [within the USA].
— from either/or to multiple-option.
Nearly all of these trends fit with a green philosophy, and nearly all are being ignored, or at best grudgingly acknowledged, by 'top-level' politicians and administrators. When will it strike home that over 60% of Americans want a nuclear freeze, 74% of Britons think the gap between rich and poor is too big (Charles Handy, 1985), and 70% of West Germans want to stop building nuclear power stations (*Worldwatch*, 1987). *See also* PROJECTION, sense (2).

Trickle-Down
[1944]
The belief that wherever you put resources into an economy, eventually there will be enough to seep through to the poor. No politician or economist has ever dared make trickle-down an official policy (it doesn't appear in the Penguin *Dictionary of Economics* (1984)), but it has been a common if unspoken theme of AID policies, first in the USA in the late 1940s and early 1950s, then, when it was rejected there, in relation to the THIRD WORLD from the 1950s onwards. Trickle-down only works if there are unlimited resources to pump in, and if the rich ever admit to having enough. 'Every time I hear that phrase, "trickle down", I'm reminded of those nineteenth-century cartoons of bloated industrialists

at groaning tables, usually with gravy dribbling down their chins and falling in thick gobbets on to starched table napkins, while drawn and emaciated workers look on and fill their bellies with dreams' (Jonathon Porritt, 1984). Green-minded economists use 'trickle-up' or BOTTOM-UP instead, acknowledging the fact that the most important changes happen at the GRASSROOTS level.

Trophic Level
[1942. *Gk trephein*, to feed]
A step in the FOOD CHAIN; thus green plants are considered to be the first level, the small animals that eat the plants the next, and so on. Though widely used as the basis for ecological fieldwork, 'trophic level' is not a particularly useful concept because it ignores the complexity of energy flows within an ecosystem, and in practice is virtually useless except at the smallest scale. A better alternative is 'trophic continuum' [1980].

Tropical Rainforest
(*see* RAINFOREST)

Truck
[1916 in this sense]
(*also* 'lorry', 'wagon')
A large and heavy ROAD vehicle used for carrying freight. Heavy freight traffic travelling long distances on roads is an environmental and economic nonsense. Apart from the question of whether we need the mountains of stuff they carry, heavy items should not be on our roads at all except to get them to their final destination — the only reason they are there is because roadbuilding and maintenance is so heavily subsidised by Western governments. Trucks often run empty when they return to base, and virtually identical products from different firms are constantly passing each other going in opposite directions. It may all add to gross national product, but it makes no sense at all. The green alternative is to consume as little as possible, buy local products where possible (*see* TRADE), and lobby for better rail services (*see* RAILWAYS) and the control of goods vehicles on the road.

Trust
[13c. *Old Norse traust*, confidence, firmness]
Believing that things can be how you want them to be. Trusting has to start with yourself, with self-empowerment: if you can't trust yourself it can be very difficult to trust other people. The main reason we don't trust is that we have never been allowed to trust ourselves, especially as we grew up. 'Trusting our kids as adults is an indispensable factor in being able to let them go. In fact, the ways we have let our trust in them grow, through the teenage years especially, stand by to help us when

they move away as adults' (Michèle Cohen and Tina Reid, 1981). 'Trusting other people' is a tricky concept, especially when it involves expectations — in the end you can only trust someone else to be themself, and this must involve openness and clear communication. Nowhere is this more true than where you trust yourself and another person enough to make love: 'Many of us find it difficult to trust and enjoy this intensely physical experience in our own unique way because it has become standardized, labelled and just another part of the outside reflection against which we rate and assess ourselves. Not even during these profound and private moments are we free from the need for outside approval' (Anne Dickson, 1985). Trusting other people while we drop our defences is an issue that often arises in groupwork: 'Remember that it takes *time* to build up enough trust to explore feelings in a self-help group. Anxiety and mistrust are bound to come up at the start of a new group, and it should not be seen as a failure' (Sheila Ernst and Lucy Goodison, 1981). While nature is organised to ensure the survival of life as an integrated system, it is important not to assume that we can trust it to ensure our continued individual existence. Some spiritual teachings suggest that all we need to do is 'trust the universe' — this can easily lead to unhealthy passivity and a suspension of DISCRIMINATION, when what is needed is awareness and action.

Trusteeship
[1730]
Being entrusted to use and look after something on someone else's behalf. 'Trusteeship', along with STEWARDSHIP, is sometimes used by green-thinkers as an alternative to ownership or POSSESSION. While some see it in terms of looking after 'god's creation', others see the trusteeship of the natural world in more general ecological terms — helping nature to look after itself and using it in ways that will enhance rather than harm it. 'The idea of trusteeship was crucial to Gandhi's view of economic relationships, and trusteeship meant that the wealth of the world came from God, and that it was therefore incumbent on those who had become wealthy to share their wealth with the rest of the community' (Tom Woodhouse, in Gail Chester and Andrew Rigby (ed), 1986).

Truth
[before 12c. *Old English treowth*, fidelity]
A green paradox. If 'true' means 'real', you have to question REALITY. If 'truth' means 'the facts' you are on slightly firmer ground, as long as everyone agrees on the FACTS, and as long as factual truth is seen only as a useful way of comparing experience, and not as a Universal Truth. Simply put, there is no Universal Truth, or at least not one that we can

expect to comprehend: 'truth is not one thing, or even a system. It is an increasing complexity. The pattern of the carpet is a surface. When we look closely, or when we become weavers, we learn of the tiny multiple threads unseen in the overall pattern, the knots on the underside of the carpet' (Adrienne Rich, 1980). For 'truthfulness' *see* HONESTY.

Turning Point
[1851]
A period of decisive and critical change and transformation, a metaphor used by several writers to describe the period of rapid cultural change we are currently passing through (notably Fritjof Capra in his useful though over-long book called *The Turning Point* (1982)). Turning Point is also the name of a British-based information network concerned with green issues. *See also* NEW AGE.

Tyranny
[14c. *Gk turannos*, tyrant]
A system of strict and oppressive regulation either literally or apparently imposed upon someone; by extension, a seemingly unchangeable state of affairs. *See also* BUREAUCRACY, STATE.

Uu

Uncertainty

[14c. *un-* + *L cernere*, not decided]

The belief that we cannot ever be sure of anything, nor that we need to be sure, since uncertainty is part of the nature of existence. The German physicist Werner Heisenberg proposed the 'uncertainty principle' in 1934: 'This showed that it was impossible to measure both a particle's position and its speed beyond a certain limit of accuracy. The more accurately you measured one aspect, the less accurately you could measure the other. . . Heisenberg had shown that the act of observation itself affects what is being observed' (Peter Russell, 1982). This holds true in the world at large, too. The one thing you can be certain of is that things will not happen exactly as you have planned them, which makes scientists' and politicians' claims of certainty ring very hollow. This is particularly true when it comes to the HEALING process, whether it is the healing of people or of the environment — we do our best as healers but we must have the humility of knowing that while we do our best, we may not be right. 'For many people in our culture, uncertainty produces feelings of fear and helplessness, and the practitioner cannot afford to collude with these feelings. Insecurity provides the counterbalance to the narcissism of being a healer' (Jan Resnick, 1986). 'Uncertainty is inevitable in this complex world, and besides it creates conditions for challenge and surprise which promote growth, discovery and the development of new potentials' (Susan Campbell, 1983).

Unconditional Positive Regard

[1967]

(*also* 'unconditional love')

Accepting and appreciating somebody for exactly who they are, with no demand or expectation that they be different. Though the concept grew out of the idea of client-centred therapy in the 1950s, it was pinned down by Carl Rogers as one of the 'core conditions' for therapists leading encounter work, where 'the therapist communicates to his [or her] client a deep and genuine caring for him [or her] as a person with human potentialities, caring uncontaminated by evaluations of his [or her] thoughts, feelings or behaviour' (Carl Rogers, 1967). The concept found its way into the spiritual fringes of the HUMAN POTENTIAL MOVEMENT in the early 1970s, being transformed into 'unconditional love' on the way. 'Handling your [emotional] addictions opens your heart to loving everyone unconditionally — including yourself' (Ken Keyes, 1979).

Unconscious

[1884 in this sense. *un- + L conscius*, not participating in knowledge] The knowledge and experience within us that we are not immediately aware of. The concept of the 'unconscious' was developed within psychoanalysis in its early years as a pseudo-scientific set of 'truths' about the mind, perpetuating the body/mind dualism which still pervades much psychoanalysis. Carl Jung developed the concept of 'unconscious' to include the 'personal unconscious' and the 'collective unconscious' [1917]: 'In his attempts to describe the collective unconscious, Jung . . . used concepts that are suprisingly similar to the ones contemporary physicists use in their descriptions of subatomic particles. He saw the unconscious as a process involving "collectively present dynamic patterns," which he called archetypes' (Fritjof Capra, 1982). The meaning of 'unconscious' has shifted within HUMANISTIC PSYCHOLOGY, from the implication of a subconscious mind somehow separated from conscious mind and physical function, towards a more pragmatic definition which simply acknowledges that we do not know everything that there is to be known, either about ourselves or about our links with other people and the world around us. 'To some extent all therapy is concerned with making the unconscious conscious — whether it is childhood memories, repressed emotions or unnoticed body sensations which we are bringing to light . . . through the language of dream, symbol and fantasy. The aim of this approach is not only to increase our self-awareness, but also to help us recognise and use our intuition or inner wisdom, and to reach a deeper sense of who we are beneath the conscious level of personality with which we normally identify' (Sheila Ernst and Lucy Goodison, 1981).

Underdevelopment

[1949]

A degree of material wealth and economic organisation considered to be inferior or lacking; a judgment about how other places and people *should* be, usually how the THIRD WORLD lacks PROGRESS and *should* be more like the West, which is followed up by a process of DEVELOPMENT.

'"Underdevelopment" is a much-discussed term seen by many as "neutral" description of the Third World situation. In fact it implies a "Western" interpretation of what constitutes development: that there are "stages" of development through which every country must pass, that underdeveloped countries remain at a backward stage of evolution and face the simple problem of finding a procedure for "takeoff". However, most Third World intellectuals and scientists question this view and propose a "different" kind of development with different goals. Many now talk about "maldevelopment" — a term applicable both to the Third World situation and to that of industrialized countries where the "lifestyle" meets growing opposition from those who find it essentially dehumanizing' (*Third World Guide*, 1984).

Underground Building
[*c.*1975]
(*also* 'earth shelter')
Building houses and other constructions either wholly or partly underground. The main advantages of earth shelter building are the use of the surrounding material as insulation and the potential for landscaping the structure into its physical setting.

Underground Economy
[1978]
Another and less pejorative name for the BLACK ECONOMY: cash transactions which are not notified to the state and are not therefore liable to tax or picked up in official statistics.

Undernutrition
(*see* MALNUTRITION)

Understanding
[12c. *Old English understandan*, to understand]
Seeing and taking account of people and situations as a whole. It is often difficult to believe that COMPASSION and understanding can exist between any two people, but the simple truth is that it can. What is needed is a willingness to learn how to listen and give clear ATTENTION, and the courage to trust that your EXPERIENCE is valid, important, and worth listening to.

Unemployment
[1888. *un-* + *L implicare*, to stop being involved]
Having no work to do: a concept which does not exist in green thinking, since in the very process of living their lives people are doing and making, and all have a right to the necessities of life. A grim reality, however, of the present economic situation in all industrialised societies. Here, unlike in traditional societies, 'unemployment' means not

having a 'real' job to provide your livelihood, and thus having to depend on WELFARE (if it is available), your savings or inheritance, or your wits. 'Unemployment' stems from several major misconceptions, fuelled by conventional economics:
— that continuous GROWTH is desirable and possible.
— that work is only real work if it is given a cash value (thus housework, childcare and all other 'voluntary' work is not 'employment').
— that you can have rapidly-increasing automation *and* not affect the amount of work done by human beings.
— that 'real work' is the most important asset in a real person's life.
It is abundantly clear to green-thinkers that this parlous state of affairs is largely a result of questionable economic theory which has only held sway for a century or so (see the date of the first use of 'unemployment') and which is now in a state of terminal decline, along with the oppressive attitudes which demean women's work and discriminate against anybody not considered to be fit for 'real' work. The only way out of the dilemma is a rapid and radical change of emphasis, involving redefinitions of most of the underpinnings of conventional economic theory, including WORK, VALUE, WEALTH and BASIC NEEDS. The official definitions of 'work' are the most insidious, turning people who don't have access to it into second-class human beings with little hope of a reasonable quality of life. Many sorts of employment are literally denied to them: 'Law and custom have dissuaded old, young and unemployed alike from doing useful work of an informal kind. Unemployed people have even been forbidden to commit themselves to voluntary work or to self-chosen courses of education and training, on pain of losing their unemployment pay' (James Robertson, 1985). Frightened politicians, knowing they are fighting a losing battle with the unemployment statistics, keep changing the criteria for the preparation of statistics in the vain hope that people won't notice that things are getting rapidly worse, but the reality is that there is no solution unless 'unemployed' people take issues of work, wealth and money into their own hands. The signs are that this is happening, and that ignoring official controls and regulations is becoming increasingly common. 'In addition to the some 11 million people who are officially unemployed in the United States, as well as the 1.7 million discouraged workers and 5.5 million part-time workers, there are others who long ago chose not to be employed in conventional ways. As they drop between the cracks of conventional government accounting, they are not even missed. And as they find alternate economic pathways that satisfy their need for income, support, and meaningful work, they expand the societal network and framework for this kind of economic behavior' (Paul Hawken, 1983). Eventually, perhaps, some enterprising government will recognise the

need to change their whole emphasis to one of providing a decent livelihood for everyone, beyond the narrow confines of 'employment' and 'unemployment' (*see* SOCIAL WAGE).

Unilateralism
[1802. *L unus* + *latus*, one-sided]
Deciding for yourself without needing a similar decision from anybody else. Choosing for yourself (as long as it doesn't harm anyone else) is central to green thinking; some people go so far as to believe that in any potential conflict it only needs one of the parties to be completely rational for a solution to emerge that will benefit both parties concerned. The concept of unilateralism is most often applied to NUCLEAR DISARMAMENT — do we have to wait until everybody agrees to disarm before one country chooses to? 'True reason coincides with morality. And our own chances of survival in Britain, which depend in the long term on the general disarmament which we might help to initiate, will scarcely be harmed even in the short term by the repudiation of nuclear arms to which morality impels us' (Martin Ryle, 1981).

Unity
[14c. *L unitas*, unity]
The recognition that we are all part of one universe, despite all the apparent divisions and distinctions we live with. *See also* DIVERSITY.

Universe
[*c.*1600. *L universus*, turned into one]
Everything that exists; a more concrete Western equivalent to the TAO of Eastern thought. It was only in the late eighteenth century that 'universe' was taken into scientific use and 'tamed', so that astronomers could start to think of it in specific and measurable terms, though even there the qualification 'the known universe' is often used. Greenthinkers, particularly those of more spiritual hue, usually use the word in its original meaning.

Urbanisation
[1888. *L urbs*, city]
(US: 'urbanization')
The creation of cities. 'Aside from the growth of world population itself, urbanization is the dominant demographic trend of the late twentieth century. The number of people living in cities increased from 600 million in 1950 to over 2 billion in 1986' (Lester Brown and Jodi Jacobson, *Worldwatch*, 1987). A growing population, land degradation in rural areas, and the attraction of urban wealth have resulted in massive urban growth in the THIRD WORLD, while in some Western cities urban decay (*see* ARCHITECTURE, HOUSING, REDEVELOPMENT, RENEWAL) and the

pull of the suburbs has had the opposite effect. The biggest problem with urbanisation is the provision of food and services for a large number of people in a small area. While rural FAMINE has been a feature of the 1970s and 1980s, this has to some extent been a result of the diversion of resources to urban centres. In a city there is usually something to beg or scrounge, and the underground economy is nowhere more rampant than in the cities of the Third World (*see also* OVERURBANISATION, SQUATTING). Urbanisation has led to a city-centred approach to environmental issues, and the centralisation of organisations and media (even of green ones), while understandable in terms of a limited version of efficiency, stands in stark contrast to many of the nature-centred issues of DEEP ECOLOGY, which stresses the importance of WILDERNESS, SILENCE, and a LAND ETHIC. 'At the same time, even as it heightens the fantasy life of people, the city isolates them from the basic ecological facts of life in such a way that they cannot clearly judge the difference between wants and needs, necessities and luxuries. . . By the very fact that they are locked away from the Earth in an artificial environment, urbanites lose sight of the planet as a living entity with whom they must maintain their organic reciprocity. . . As the cities become bigger, the sum total of practical ecological sensitivity in the population diminishes, until we are at last asking what is economically impossible of the planet' (Theodore Roszak, 1979). *See also* COUNTRYSIDE, VILLAGE.

Utilitarianism
[1827. *L utilis*, useful]
The belief that you can add up the pleasure and pain experienced by each person, and decide what to do on the basis of working out 'the greatest good for the greatest number'. *See* BENTHAMITE CALCULUS.

Utopia
[16c. *Gk ou-topos*, no place]
The ideal place where everything is just how you want it. Thomas More created the first 'paper utopia' in 1516, choosing the name carefully to signify that it did not really exist. Utopian visions are important because they offer a range of possible futures we might head towards, and those who knock utopias as naive rubbish would do well to remember that the FUTURE will one day be the present, and not having an idea of how we want things to be is to allow other people to decide our VISIONS for us. 'Utopia is more than a fishing picnic . . . Utopia is necessary' (Su Negrin, 1972). On the other hand, we can be fairly certain that the future will not conform precisely to any of our utopian visions — whatever we see for the future is always coloured by how we are in the present. 'A utopia is only a design for a time to come, tomorrow-in-genesis, the present articulation of the possible future' (Kirkpatrick Sale, 1985). Fascinating

'green' utopias have been explored by several authors, including Charlotte Perkins Gilman (1915), Marge Piercy (1976), Ernest Callenbach (1970 and 1981), Sally Miller Gearhart (1978), John Crowley (1979), Brenda Vale (1984), and Margaret Elphinstone (1987).

Validation
(*see* APPRECIATION)

Value
[15c. *L valere*, to be strong, worth something]
The intrinsic worth of something or someone. This green definition does not correspond with the more usual 'amount of money you could get for it', though the two are linked. 'We no longer believe that the products and services which people work to provide have objectively quantifiable *real* values, distinct from actual costs and prices. We no longer believe, however, that we can simply rely on the system of costs and prices that actually exist, to define our values for us. We make a distinction between value and price, and we regret that economics has lost sight of it. We know what Oscar Wilde meant when he said a cynic is someone who knows the price of everything and the value of nothing' (James Robertson, 1985). Some people prefer to use WORTH rather than 'value', in order to get away from limiting ideas about money value. The Values Party in New Zealand, founded in the late 1960s and now virtually defunct, was the first 'green party' anywhere in the world.

Values
[14c. *L valere*, to be strong, worth something]
Beliefs and opinions which colour the way we see the world. One of the most pervasive myths of DUALISM is that human beings and their fields of study can stand outside REALITY and thus be value-free. SCIENTISM is possibly the worst culprit, but claims of neutrality on anyone's part are immediately suspect — nobody is neutral, nobody is unbiased. This recognition does not mean that we should play down our beliefs, simply that it is crucial to recognise the variety of interests and points of view in any situation. 'Values' also incorporate a recognition of the things we value (*see* VALUE); most green-thinkers believe that a radical appraisal

of the things we value is essential in today's exploitative world: 'Nothing of any deep human significance changes in our world without there first being a change in our own values' (Guy Dauncey, in Mary Inglis and Sandra Kramer (ed), 1985).

Vandalism
[1798. Named after the Germanic peoples who overthrew the Roman Empire in the 5th century]
Deliberate destruction. Popularly thought to be perpetrated exclusively by bored youths in city streets, but seen on a much larger scale all over the world, with some contractors, architects and developers being among the biggest culprits.

Vegan
[1944. *L vegetare*, to enliven]
A diet which exludes all animal products, including eggs, fish, milk and milk products. Some vegans also avoid using animal products in clothing and other purchases. 'Veganic gardening' — using no animal products at all — is increasing as the demand for vegan products grows. The arguments for veganism are similar to those for VEGETARIANism, with an added stress on the exploitation of animals which are kept for their products and not just for their meat. There has been much debate in vegan circles about the need for additional vitamins B12 and D (these supposedly being unavailable from a vegan diet and lifestyle); small amounts of yeast extract (for vitamin B12) and large amounts of open-air activity (for vitamin D) will deal with all possible deficiencies.

Vegetarian
[1842. *L vegetare*, to enliven]
A diet which excludes meat and meat products, and usually fish (a diet which excludes all animal products is called VEGAN). There are several reasons why it is more humane and ecologically sound to eat little or no meat:
— You are eating further down the FOOD CHAIN, which means that the food you eat uses much less land and energy.
— You are not perpetuating the cruelty to which many farm animals are submitted (*see* FACTORY FARMING).
— A great deal of the grain and vegetable harvest of Third World countries goes to feed meat animals for the West, and in Costa Rica, for example, two thirds of the country's forests have been cleared for cattle ranches.
As well as the ecological reasons for vegetarianism, eating little or no meat costs a lot less in cash terms, and is much healthier than a high-meat diet. It used to be thought that vegetarians missed out on protein and vitamins by not eating meat: this has now been conclusively shown

to be inaccurate — a balanced vegetarian diet provides all the nutrients needed for health without the excessive fat intake of most meat-eaters. Vegetarians who eat no meat or milk products but do eat eggs are sometimes called 'ovo-vegetarians', those who eat milk products 'lacto-vegetarians'. Vegetarianism or near-vegetarianism (often called DEMI-VEG) is of necessity the basis of most Third World diets; in the West the proportion of vegetarians is between five and eight per cent and rising rapidly, and most restaurants now provide vegetarian alternatives. For every complete vegetarian in the West, there are many more people who have cut down enormously on their meat consumption. There is a danger — as with so many green issues — of excessive purism in vegetarian circles. 'The man [or woman] who takes a high moral attitude about not eating meat, and eats eggs, drinks milk or eats butter and cheese, wears shoe leather or wool, just does not have to be taken seriously at all. A cow won't give milk unless she has a calf every year, and every other calf she has, on average, is going to be a bull. What do you do with the bull? . . You can't hatch eggs to provide yourself with hens to lay more without hatching out as many cocks as hens. What do you do with the cocks?' (John and Sally Seymour, 1973). 'Proselytizing vegetarians should remember that for some environments, meat eating is an appropriate lifestyle. They should not compare the obscenities of Western beef and dairy mountains with the frugal and prudent pastoralism of the Third World. We have the luxury of being able to choose. We can adopt a varied and nourishing vegetarian diet. Elsewhere people do not have this option' (Ann Cullen, *New Internationalist*, June 1986). As in all other aspects of a green lifestyle, aware and responsible choice for yourself and non-judgement of others is paramount. *See also* FOOD, TRADE.

Victim
[15c. *L victima*, victim]
A person who is hurt, usually by the deliberate violence of an oppressor. A label rejected by some people, including many feminists, as a stereotype deliberately created by an oppressive society and its media which perpetuates an image of helplessness and keeps oppressed people 'in their place'; the better alternative for a person who lives through a time of violence is 'survivor' (*see* SURVIVAL). 'Surviving is the other side of being a victim. It involves will, action, initiative on the victim's part . . . To be defined as victim in the context of victimism is to deny that identity is ongoing and changing; it is to deny whole parts of our active self in the experience of surviving the assault or slavery; it is to deny that women construct ways of coping and dealing with that violence in its aftermath' (Kathleen Barry, 1979, quoted in Cheris Kramerae and Paula Treichler (ed), 1985). 'There is not a separate category of women who are "victims" just as there is no category of men who are

"rapists". Using the word "victim" to describe women takes away our power and contributes to the idea that it is right and natural for men to "prey" on us' (London Rape Crisis Centre, 1984). 'Blaming the victim' is an all-too-common practice which denies the reality of OPPRESSION and lets the oppressor off the hook. *See also* VIOLENCE.

Vigil
[13c. *L vigil*, watchful]
An ACTION in which a group of people stand or sit quietly in a public place for a period of time in order to draw attention to a cause. Handing out leaflets to passers-by and the holding of candles at night are both common features of vigils.

Village
[14c. *L villa*, farm]
A small COMMUNITY, together with its land and buildings. In villages is where more than half of the people in the world live, and the facilities that can be provided at the scale of the village furnish its inhabitants with a focus and a personal service. Urban and suburban dwellers often hanker after the sense of place that 'village' represents, and after the disastrous large-scale civic planning of the 1960s and 1970s, many architects and citizens' groups are rediscovering the human scale of the village. The concept of 'global village' (Marshall McLuhan, 1963) or 'planetary village' (Donald Keys, 1982) has been used by some authors, describing a worldwide network of village-like communities linked by high-tech electronics and similar POST-INDUSTRIAL concepts and technologies — while this has appealing possibilities of APPROPRIATE TECHNOLOGY, it is in grave danger of becoming another TECHNOFIX.

Violence
[13c. *L violare*, to violate; from *vis*, force]
The use of force and threat, often physical, to take and maintain control over another person or people. Violence is constantly portrayed to us as 'simply the way the world is', but green-thinkers know better. Violence is not an innate feature of human existence — it is a creation of competitive and divisive PATRIARCHY; it is men using culturally-condoned and learned AGGRESSION which, given will and faith, can be unlearned. In this light, conventional and limiting assumptions can be replaced with new insight: 'Men are aggressive' points to the obvious fact that most men have no other outlet for their strong FEELINGS, particularly their FEAR; if crying and screaming are disallowed, never mind joy and exhilaration, the only way that those feelings can be expressed is by using the energy to destroy. While most violence is done by men, women are frequently those most hurt: 'As women, nonviolence must begin for us in the refusal to be victimized. We must find alternatives to

submission, because our submission — to rape, to assault, to domestic servitude, to abuse and victimization of every sort — perpetuates violence. . . The refusal of which I speak is a revolutionary refusal to be a victim, any time, any place, for friend or foe. . . We will diminish violence by refusing to be violated' (Andrea Dworkin, 1983). Green thinking about how to reduce violence has followed several paths, including:
— recognising the difference between the important and necessary feelings of fear and ANGER and the destructive and senseless action of aggression.
— providing a safe space for the expression of pain, fear and anger (*see* THERAPY).
— helping children, especially boys, not to be frightened into violence, by rescuing them from frightening experiences and encouraging them to express their feelings.
— recognising the phenomenon of ADDICTION to violence, and stopping scaring ourselves unnecessarily. We can always turn the television off.
— exploring techniques of NONVIOLENCE and nonviolent action.
— exploring new ways of communicating with each other (*see* COUNSELLING, MEDIATION).
— providing easily-approachable channels through which people who have a problem with violence can seek help, such as refuges for battered women, support groups for the survivors of violence, and groups for men who want to look at their violent behaviour, such as the Violence Diversion Programmes in California (Daniel Jay Sonkin and Michael Durphy, 1982).

Vision
[13c. *L visio*, sight]
(1) Seeing clearly. 'There are many ways to speak about vision. Every meaning, however, is possessed of a certain tension . . . At one and the same time, vision means "the exercise of the ordinary faculty of sight" and "something which is apparently seen by other than ordinary sight". Another way of phrasing this tension is to ask how, indeed, it is possible to see with the ordinary faculty of sight, that is, to maintain a necessary realism about the conditions of existence, and to see beyond those conditions, that is, to "overleap reality"? . . An individual vision is based on two sights-seeing — near- and far-sightedness . . . [which] means not being crushed by the contrast between what the world is and the way it ought to be' (Janice Raymond, 1986).
(2) Imagining how you want things to be in the FUTURE (*see* the quotation under sense (1)). 'Her vision: Now she sees with her own eyes' (Susan Griffin, 1984).

Visualisation
[*c.*1970 in this sense. *L videre*, to see]
(US: 'visualization')
Using your imagination creatively in order to empower yourself. In the last twenty years 'visualisation' has covered a multitude of techniques, from self-hypnosis and biofeedback to MEDITATION and AFFIRMATION. In holistic healing it is now being extensively used in the self-treatment of many disorders, especially in the relief of cancer and AIDS. 'Visualisation therapy today is a form of auto-suggestion or self-hypnosis; an exercise in positive thinking on the assumption that if you start driving convinced that you will fail your test, you probably will fail it. Similarly, if you imagine vividly enough your immune system defeating your cancer, it may help to do so' (Kit Mouat, 1984). As well as being used in healing, 'creative visualisation' can be part of exploring what you want in your life, though there is always the danger of wandering into 'think yourself rich at someone else's expense' territory.

Vital Energy, Vital Force
(*see* LIFE FORCE)

Vitalism
[*L vita*, life]
(1) [1822] The belief that the phenomenon of life involves more than the scientifically observable processes of physics and chemistry.
(2) [1975] The belief that life will continue; used by some green-thinkers to contradict the EXTERMINISM practised by many military and governmental bureaucracies.

Vitamins
[1912. *L vita*, life]
Organic substances present in small quantities in unprocessed foods (and sometimes created within the human body) which are essential to healthy life. Doses of vitamins are thought by many people to be a good 'natural' diet supplement, but apart from the water-soluble vitamins B and C, excessive vitamins can easily reach toxic levels in the body. 'The vitamins differ from the three major kinds of nutrients [carbohydrates, fats and proteins] in that they are needed only in very small quantities, usually a few hundredths of a gram per day. Their function is not to provide energy or to become part of our physical structure, but rather to perform very specific roles in the metabolic processes that regulate growth, tissue replacement, and general cellular activity. To understand this basic fact is to understand why it is that vitamins are unlikely to be panaceas, and why excessive doses can be downright dangerous' (Harold McGee, 1984).

Vivisection
[1707. *L vivus* + *secare*, to cut the living]
The use of live animals in experiments, involving pain and cruelty. Something like 4-500,000 animals — mostly mice, rats and rabbits, but also dogs, cats, birds, fish and monkeys — are killed worldwide every day to 'test' drugs, cosmetics, food additives — or just to see what happens. And it isn't necessary. Nearly all of the most useful drugs used in healing, including chloroform, iodine, digitalis, quinine and aspirin (not to mention the milder herbal remedies) were discovered without experimenting on animals. It isn't even as though you can tell anything about how human beings will respond to a substance from the way an animal does — penicillin, for example, is toxic to guinea pigs, so if it had been tested first on animals we would not have its benefits now. Vivisection is inhumane, vicious, dehumanising and unnecessary, and wherever possible green-thinkers use products which have not been tested on animals. 'The little monkey . . . was clearly in agonizing pain. Its facial expression could have symbolized the sum of human sufferings through the ages. Half crouched, devoured by pain, it clung desperately with its little hand to the wiremesh of its cage. The lips looked thin and drawn very wide, in an agonized grin. The huge eyes, staring at an incomprehensible world, seemed lost, and looked enormous in the emaciated, fleshless face, its skin clinging to the bones. One foot, which had served for god only knows which "scientific" investigation, was bandaged, and clumsily so' (Hans Reusch, 1983).

Voice
[13c. *L vox*, voice]
Being allowed to speak and being listened to; speaking out. The human voice is much more powerful than most people think, capable of carrying for several miles in still air. United in a chant, or a song of protest, the sound of many voices in harmony is one of the most moving of human experiences.

Voluntary Poverty
(*see* VOLUNTARY SIMPLICITY)

Voluntary Simplicity
[1974]
(*also* 'conspicuous conservation', CONSPICUOUS THRIFT, 'contributory livelihood', 'creative simplicity', 'frugality', LIVING LIGHTLY, 'simple living', 'voluntary poverty')
Choosing a lifestyle which gives you what you need materially, intellectually and spiritually, while consuming as little as possible. 'A manner of living that is outwardly more simple and inwardly more rich; an integrative way of living that balances both inner and outer aspects of our

lives; a deliberate choice to live with less in the belief that more of life will be returned to us in the process; a path towards consciously learning the skills that enable us to touch the world ever more lightly and gently; a way of being in which our most authentic and alive self is brought into direct and conscious contact with every aspect of living; a way of living that accepts the responsibility for developing our human potentials, as well as for contributing to the well-being of the world of which we are an inseparable part; a paring back of the superficial aspects of our lives so as to allow more time and energy to develop the heartfelt aspects of our lives' (Duane Elgin, 1981). A philosophy which works if you have anything to give up, are clear about why you're giving it up, and are in a position to make a free choice — many people, and not only in the Third World, are forced into 'compulsory simplicity'. On the other hand, those who have don't find it so easy to give up. Will we end up with compulsory simplicity for all, or the 'liberation' of wealth for the many?

Vulnerability

[*c*.1600. *L vulnerare*, to wound]

Being open to the experience of PAIN and grief. A great deal of therapeutic work depends on the provision of enough safety to allow a person to be vulnerable, to feel their anguish without having it denied, and to work through the pain towards HEALING. Being vulnerable, however, is a very different experience for someone who is used to being in control than it is for someone who is used to being oppressed, and a blanket call (as some humanistic psychologists have made) for increased vulnerability — 'opening to experience' — can be dangerous. In our divided society there is a temptation to see vulnerability (the 'victim role') as innate to oppressed groups, especially women, children and old people, whereas the truth is that people are only made vulnerable by the existence of THREAT (*see* VICTIM). Choosing to be vulnerable is very different from being forced into vulnerability, and appropriate self-protection is just as important as appropriate openness (*see also* TRUST). People from oppressor groups, on the other hand, have a great deal to learn from being vulnerable, being open enough to hear what is said about and to them without being defensive. Being open to receiving energy from the sun and the cycles of nature, ecosystems are extremely vulnerable to human intervention: 'The vulnerability of a form of life is roughly proportional to the weight of influences from afar, from outside the local region in which that form has achieved an ecological equilibrium. This lends support to our efforts to strengthen local self- government and material and mental self-sufficiency' (Arne Naess, *Inquiry*, 1982).

Wagon
(*see* TRUCK)

Waldsterben
[1983. *German*, 'forest-death']
The rapid decline and death of large areas of trees, thought to be a result of OZONE pollution which damages the leaves of trees, resulting in stunted growth and an inability to regenerate. More than half of Germany's forests are affected, together with substantial numbers in Holland and Belgium, France, Britain, Switzerland, Austria, eastern Europe, southern Scandinavia, and parts of North America. 'The disease seems to be quite different from the lethal assault by high concentrations of sulphur dioxide that still occur in parts of Eastern Europe. It is more subtle and more difficult to explain. But it is spreading fast, all over western Europe' (Fred Pearce, 1987). The main cause is almost certainly vehicle exhausts, and the reason it has only just become so obvious is partly that it takes a little while for trees to reach their limit of tolerance, and partly that foresters have only recently started to look for the signs of waldsterben. By the time the signs are clear the trees are probably beyond saving, but that doesn't deter drivers from spewing out yet more toxic exhaust. Part of the answer is the fitting of catalytic converters to exhausts — the use of such converters in California has reduced nitrogen oxide fumes to less than 10% of what they were in 1975. Europe, however — and Britain is the worst culprit of all — is dragging its feet while the forests die.

Walking
[14c. *Old English wealcan*, to roll, toss]
The healthiest and most efficient and pollution-free way of travelling short distances — a healthy human being can easily cover a mile in twenty minutes. A quarter of all car journeys in Britain are less than 2

miles, 60% under 5 miles (Stephen Plowden, 1980) — and the proportions in other Western countries, where car ownership rates are higher, are probably even larger. One of the biggest nonsenses is getting up early to jog, then driving the couple of miles to work. 'Pedestrians make up the greater part of humanity. More than that — its best part' (Ilya Ilf and Eugene Petrov, quoted in Rudolf Flesch, 1968).

War

[before 12c. *Old North French werre*, war]

Armed conflict between two groups of people, almost always men. Until the advent of Western-style ARMS, warfare in traditional societies was ritualised; though bloody, it was waged by relatively few people, almost all of whom were actively involved. It was with the advent of trench warfare and the massive casualties of the 1914-18 war, followed by the gas chambers of the 1939-45 war (built to protect the soldiers from the horror of their actions), that war became dehumanised — no longer was it a question of hurting someone else by yourself at close quarters; pulling a lever would do the job more efficiently. As the technologies of MILITARISM have 'progressed', so war has increasingly become officially-sanctioned mass brutality, almost always involving civilians and the destruction of nature. 'By eleven o'clock the hamlet [of My Lai] had ceased to exist. The ditch was full of bodies. Between 450 and 500 Vietnamese civilians had been massacred. On the American side, not one death and no one wounded. Good clean work' (Seymour Hersh, 1970). Under PATRIARCHY, it is assumed that men will always rise to the call to 'prove themselves' by being prepared to lose their lives for their country: this method of oppressing men is so pervasive that few people have questioned the appropriateness of giving boys guns to play with (*see* NO WAR TOYS), cheering them as they go off to fight, or calling them cowards if they refuse. Wars have often been condoned on the grounds of the worse tyranny that might have befallen had they not been undertaken, and while this must be taken into account, such a position is far less tenable in an age of NUCLEAR WEAPONS, when retaliation could spell global annihilation. Green-thinkers believe that there must be a sane alternative to war and VIOLENCE; the lessons from the past are clear if they can be heeded. What causes war is the firmly-held belief that you have an enemy, someone who will take what belongs to you if you don't stop them by force — ENEMY, POSSESSION and force are all ideas which the green perspective refuses to endorse. *See also* NONVIOLENCE, NONVIOLENT INTERVENTION, NUCLEAR WAR.

Waste

[13c. *L vastare*, to lay waste]

Materials that human beings think they have no further use for and which are more or less indiscriminately fed back into ecosystems, usually in forms and quantities that cannot easily be reassimilated. 'In the closed model system of nature there is no waste. The residues of one are the resources of another. When Indians defecate in the forest, they are fertilising the trees. But when we of industrial society put dirt into the ground or a river, we are creating pollution, because we are putting it in the wrong place. Sanitary engineers see something fundamentally undesirable in garbage and industrial effluent, so they do things like build enormous dumps to bury it in, and then put trees over it. But it hasn't disappeared; it's just like sweeping dirt under the carpet' (José Lutzenberger, in Mary Inglis and Sandra Kramer (ed), 1985). The worst sorts of waste are NUCLEAR WASTE, which remains radioactive for millennia, and 'toxic waste' (collectively sometimes called 'hazardous waste'). Anything in large enough quantities in the wrong place is toxic, but industrialists continue to insist that the dumping of large quantities of HEAVY METALS and dangerous chemicals does no long-term harm — despite Love Canal and ten thousand other poisonings of human beings, animals and ecosystems. Then there is what we waste every day: 'Residents of New York collectively discard 24,000 tons of materials each day. This amalgam, considered trash by most of its contributors, contains valuable metals, reusable glass containers, recyclable paper and plastic, and food wastes high in nutrient value. It also contains ever greater amounts of hazardous waste — mercury from batteries, cadmium from fluorescent lights, and toxic chemicals from cleaning solvents, paints, and wood preservatives' (Cynthia Pollock, in *Worldwatch*, 1987). The US figure is twice and three times that of European countries, four times that of Third World cities, and almost immeasurably more than that of the Third World poor. We must — for our own and for our planet's sake — learn to RECYCLE and RE-USE, avoid unnecessary PACKAGING and PLASTICS, and in general use less of everything.

Water

[before 12c. *Old English wæter*, water]

The reactionary futurologist Arthur C. Clark has suggested that the name of our planet should be 'Water' rather than 'Earth', after the liquid skin that covers three-quarters of its surface. Water is essential to all life, and if used wisely is a constantly renewable resource available to all that need it. There is sufficient water almost everywhere in the world to supply the agricultural, industrial and domestic needs of the human population, but waste and inefficient use are widespread. The average Westerner uses 2-300 litres of water every day, compared with an Indian's 25 litres — nearly a third is flushed down the toilet. Because water is generally thought of as 'free' and is brought directly into most Western homes, it is easy to forget that it always 'costs' to use a resource, and that most water in the Third World has to be carried to where it is to be used, often several miles. Other factors add to the waste of water: some Western cities are losing as much as 50% of their water supply from leaks in the distribution network. The water used for industrial purposes (cooling, cleaning, etc.) can often be re-used many times: in the USA industrial water is used, on average, 8 times before becoming effluent, compared with 2 times in 1954. With improved technology and pollution control measures, it could be 17 times by 2000. Nearly three-quarters of the world's water supplied by human agency is used for AGRICULTURE. Much of this is currently being used at far less than maximum efficiency, though water-conserving agricultural technologies are being increasingly used in some areas like Israel and Texas (where the financial resources are available). In the 1950s and 1960s many large-scale IRRIGATION projects were built, often involving massive reservoirs. As well as creating environmental and social havoc, several of these projects, such as the Aswan High Dam in Egypt, have proved to be financial liabilities and ecological disasters, suffering among other things from rapid silting and EUTROPHICATION. 'The transition to a water-efficient economy will not be easy or painless. But it has begun, and it should be fostered. With the methods and technologies now available, even modest expenditures on conservation and efficiency could make unnecessary many of the inordinately expensive, ecologically disruptive water projects that have dominated water-planning agendas for decades' (Sandra Postel, *Worldwatch*, 1986). *See also* WATER POLLUTION.

Water Pollution
[1877]
The contamination of WATER, one of our most precious resources, nearly all of it more or less deliberate. 'Water, a supposed fount of life, kills at least 25 million people in developing nations each year, three-fifths of them being children' (Norman Myers, 1985). 'The [British] National Coal Board's Phurnacite smokeless fuel plant near Mountain Ash in South Wales discharges 30,000 cubic metres of effluent into the River Cynon every day. In 1982, 8 per cent of samples met the consent condition. In 1981 and 1983 no samples met the consent. But the Welsh Water Authority, like others, has virtually given up prosecuting firms that fail their consents' (Fred Pearce, in Edward Goldsmith and Nicholas Hildyard (ed), 1986). *See also* ACID RAIN, AGRICULTURE, OCEAN, POLLUTION.

Wave Energy
[1979]
Using the ENERGY in sea waves to generate electricity. There have been

many proposals as to how this might be done, and a few schemes have been successfully completed. Wave energy generation schemes include:
— the transformation of the movement at the water surface into a flow of air which can drive a turbine.
— the transformation of this same movement by using floating devices which rise and fall at different rates.
— the use of underwater devices which are activated by sub-surface movement.
— letting waves break over a barrier into a lagoon which is then used as a head for a HYDRO scheme.
'Realising wave energy's full potential would require a major research effort. Nevertheless, if the technical challenge can be met, even the lowest estimates suggest that wave energy could supply up to one fifth of current UK electricity' (Michael Flood, 1986).

Wealth
[13c. *Old English welthe*, well-being, riches]
ABUNDANCE, profusion, having everything you need for a full and healthy life. An important idea, though corrupted within a narrow materialist vision to mean anything that has a cash value. 'Wealth creation', which in green terms means 'sustainable yield', has come to mean the stock-piling of AFFLUENCE, living off the capital of the earth's rich biosphere rather than earning a fair living from its renewable harvest. Having given everything which can be bought and sold this new version of 'value', the rich of the world have proceeded to hoard it for their own use, denying the poor the SUBSISTENCE which had been negotiated with the environment over centuries. 'The people of the USA can build a holiday centre with vast lakes for fishing and boating in their deserts, while the people of Africa starve to death in theirs. The difference between them is not a difference of climate or, as environmentalists have tended to argue, of population size. The difference between them, the one thing which above all else determines their respective relation-ships with "nature", is their wealth' (Joe Weston (ed), 1986). 'In one world, as in one state, when I am rich because you are poor, and I am poor because you are rich, the transfer of wealth from the rich to the poor is a matter of right. It is not an appropriate matter for charity' (Julius Nyerere, 1972). Green-thinkers have proposed several methods for ensuring that wealth does not continue to pile up in the hands of the rich minority, including simple limits on the amount of wealth owned or earned by any individual: while this may appear to infringe individual freedom it is no more radical than the limit on the amount of Danish land which can be owned by any individual, and a necessary constraint in any society which recognises the importance of equity and finity of resources. 'In nature, whenever one element of an ecosystem multiplies

or grows out of proportion to its proper functioning relationship with the rest of the elements in the system, it robs other life forms of the . . . energy they need to survive. By doing so, it threatens the continued existence of the entire system. This is also the case in human society. When certain individuals or institutions capture an inordinate amount of the society's energy for themselves, their gross accumulation of wealth and power robs the rest of the members of society of the available energy they need to survive. History shows that whenever a society's energy (wealth) becomes so concentrated in the hands of a few individuals or institutions that the rest of society suffers energy deprivation so great as to imperil their own survival, the society either crumbles or moves to revolution or both. While nature relies on self-regulating biological laws to restore balance, society must rely on agreed-upon principles of economic justice to achieve the same ends' (Jeremy Rifkin, 1980).

Weapons
[before 12c. *Old English wœp(e)n*, weapon]
Physical objects used to threaten and control, too dangerous to leave in the hands of the powerful. 'The possibility of war increases in direct proportion to the effectiveness of the instruments of war' (Norman Cousins, quoted in Laurence Peter, 1977). *See also* ARMS, ARMS RACE, DETERRENCE, DISARMAMENT, FREEZE, NUCLEAR WEAPONS, PLOUGHSHARE, WAR.

Web
[*c*.1975 in this sense. *Old English web(b)*, anything formed by weaving]
A closely-woven NETWORK or structure; a widespread and useful metaphor for the interconnectedness of all things, used particularly by the women's peace movement: 'We are the weavers, we are the web' (quoted in Starhawk, 1982). 'Each link in a web is fragile, but woven together creates a strong and coherent whole. A web with few links is weak and can be broken, but the more threads it is composed of, the greater its strength' (Alice Cook and Gwyn Kirk, 1983).

Weed
[before 12c. *Old English weod*, weed, herb]
A plant which is thought by a human being to be growing in the wrong place, getting in the way of the crops and decorative plants put there by the farmer or gardener. 'It is important to remember that a weed is not a different kind of plant from our cherished garden crops, and it can tell us some very important things about our garden. . . A weed is simply a plant that does not fit in with our image of what our garden is to be' (Margaret Elphinstone and Julia Langley, 1987). *See also* PESTICIDE.

Welfare

[1904 in this sense. *Old English wel faran*, fare well]

Looking after your own and other people's well-being. In a healthy and self-reliant community, each member's needs are met through a constant awareness of what is needed and what is available, with flexible and appropriate mechanisms for the exchange and redistribution of resources. In a society — and on a planet — where material inequality between people is so extreme, 'welfare' has come to mean 'handouts by a grudging state-controlled bureaucracy to people who refuse to help themselves'. When universal welfare schemes were introduced in Western countries in the 1930s and 1940s (Roosevelt's 1935 New Deal in the USA; the 1942 Beveridge Report in Britain), they were seen as a way in which the 'welfare state' would ensure a basic provision of benefit to anybody who became unemployed. As UNEMPLOYMENT has grown and as the 'family with a wage-earner at its head' has become a minority of all households, many other 'residual' welfare schemes have been introduced, resulting in a vast array of welfare arrangements, ideal for bureaucratic inefficiency and arbitrary discrimination. 'One of the ways that the welfare state maintains political stability is by dividing an underclass of welfare poor from the middle-class and upper section of the working-class and creating structural conflict between them. . . The result is that many "middle Americans" who work hard for their wages feel (rightly) that they are taxed excessively, but are set up to blame this on the welfare poor' (Steven Wineman, 1984). As with POVERTY, welfare is highly feminised: 'Welfare's like a traffic accident. It can happen to anybody, but especially it happens to women' (Johnnie Tillmas, 1972, in Cheris Kramerae and Paula Treichler, 1985). While green-thinkers believe that everybody has a right to a basic level of resources — a right which rampant CAPITALISM cannot fulfil — state-operated welfare systems are by their nature not able to replace the need for community-based welfare where the real needs of individual people are taken into account (*see* BASIC NEEDS, SOCIAL WAGE, STATE, TAXATION). 'It's difficult to be a yuppie doleite. There's no place in your Filofax for your signing on card' (Yoobie fforti, *Women's Review*, April 1987).

Wellness

[1977]

Another word for HEALTH, used to emphasise that being healthy is the natural state of a human being, not just the fortuitous absence of DISEASE. There are several 'Wellness Centers' in the USA, and the idea of 'Well Woman Clinics' (and now 'Well Man Clinics' too) has spread to Europe and Australasia. 'We're not diagnosing, treating, or taking care of the person. We're serving as a consultant, to give them more information, teach them skills, to show them how to become more aware of their past, to see what's going on inside their bodies, how to visualize, how to communicate better, how to love and accept themselves' (John Travis, in Tom Ferguson (ed), 1980).

Wetlands
[1778]
Swamps, marshes and undrained coastal areas. 'Wetlands serve vital ecological functions, and teem with life. Yet we treat them as wastelands, suitable only for dumping rubbish and sewage or "reclamation"' (Lee Durrell, 1986). See also DUMPING, RECLAMATION, TIDAL ENERGY.

Whole
[before 12c. *Old English hal*, healthy]
Complete, entire, healthy. Sometimes used as a noun — 'the whole' — in a sense akin to TAO or UNIVERSE. 'Whole' has been incorporated into many green projects, such as *The Whole Earth Catalogue* and its offspring, a series of resource books started in California in 1968 (whence 'whole-earther' [1975] found its way into the vocabulary).

Wholefoods
[1960]
Whole, unadulterated, unrefined staple foods; sometimes confused with commercially-produced HEALTH FOODS.

Wholeness
[before 12c. *Old English hal*, healthy]
Taking everything into account. Used by some holistic healing practitioners to describe a state of health which incorporates physical, emotional, mental and spiritual wellbeing.

Wholism
[1939]
HOLISM spelt with a 'w', sometimes done deliberately to stress the link, both etymologically and semantically (in terms of origins and use), with 'wholeness'. Hence 'wholistic'.

Wild
[before 12c. *Old English wilde*, wild]
Things in their natural state, untamed, intense, untidy, reckless, joyful, unconventional, enthusiastic. The perfect antidote to control and boredom. 'In wildness is the preservation of the world. . . Life consists of wildness. The most alive is the wildest' (Henry David Thoreau, 1851). 'Let them be left, the wildness and wet;/Long live the weeds and the wilderness yet' (Gerard Manley Hopkins, 1877). *See also* TAMING.

Wilderness

[13c. *Middle English wildeornes*, wilderness; from *wildeor*, wild beast]

A large area of land which is essentially without human influence. The official US definition runs: 'A wilderness . . . is hereby recognized as an area where the earth and its community of life are untrammelled by man [*sic*], where man himself is a visitor who does not remain, . . an area of undeveloped Federal land retaining its primeval character and influence, without permanent improvement of human habitation' (quoted in Bill Devall and George Sessions, 1985). There are very few areas of real wilderness left in today's world, especially in the relatively densely-populated (by humans, that is) regions, though the often subconscious link between lack of human activity and 'wilderness' shows how anthropocentric our version is. 'Wilderness is a strictly civilized concept. The fact that we see natural areas as "wild" and call them wilderness is an indication of the extent to which we are removed from our own natural state. It must be completely unimaginable to indigenous people that we could call their life-sphere a "wild" place. Wilderness is a home. It's a home for whatever species are there and it's the original human home' (Roger Dunsmore, quoted in Jessica Lipnack and Jeffrey Stamps, 1986). To the multinationals and giant power corporations wildernesses represent one of the last 'big challenges' and 'major untapped resources'. Threatened by mineral working, reservoir building, clearfelling of natural forest and 'development' of tourist potential, the world's wildernesses are under siege. Other values must prevail: 'There is no quiet place in the white man's cities. No place to hear the unfurling of leaves in spring, or the rustle of insects' wings. But perhaps it is because I am a savage and do not understand' (Chief Seathl, 1855). And other values are beginning to prevail. In 1983, after a long battle, the Franklin River Dam scheme in Tasmania was rejected. In 1985 the Alaska Lands Conservation Act established 100 million acres of wilderness. But the losses are enormous. Only 13% of the USA is now wild compared with 100% 300 years ago. If current forest losses continue, Brazil, with the largest rainforest in the world, will be treeless in thirty years' time. Europe, with little wilderness left, is witness to the ways in which even 'protected' land is vulnerable when it comes to 'the public interest' — the German army break up the fragile soils of the Lüneberger Heide doing 'exercises', ski lifts dot the Swiss Alps, the Sami in the Scandinavian wilderness cannot eat their reindeer meat because of fallout from Chernobyl, the British government chooses to run a four-lane highway through an ancient forest in the Dartmoor National Park against all advice. To be wilderness at all, wilderness must be large: 'In big wilderness you learn how important size itself is to the viability of the wilderness. It needs enough buffer to keep its heartland essentially free from the pervasive influences of technology' (David Brower, 1968). 'In wilderness is the preservation of the world' (Henry David Thoreau, quoted in Laurence Peter, 1977).

Wildlife
[1933]
The way life would be if it weren't constantly controlled, manipulated and exploited by oppressive human beings; the more usual definition is 'wild animals and plants'. Seeing 'wildlife' as intrinsically different from 'tamelife' perpetuates the distinctions that make it 'okay' to continue the exploitation: 'after all, it's only a couple of hedgehogs and a few blades of grass'. ' "Wildlife" is . . . a concept that can never apply to any specific creature, and thus is always an image or translation of nature' (Judith Williamson, 1978). *See also* ANIMAL, TAMING, WILD.

Wind Energy
[1976]
ENERGY extracted from wind, which is used to drive the sails of a windmill to provide electricity or direct mechanical energy. Windmills have used the power of the wind for centuries, mostly pumping water and grinding corn. Modern wind generators are more efficient machines built on aerodynamic principles, using techniques developed in aeroplane and helicopter design. Large wind-energy installations are now operating in California, where there are several large groups of windmills ('wind farms'), and windmills are also providing electricity for national elctricity supply systems in France, Holland, Denmark, Britain (in South-West Wales, Devon, Orkney and Shetland) and several other countries, not to mention the thousands of small installations supplying the needs of isolated farms and houses. 'I can't think of any other energy source which has a smaller environmental effect. No chimney stacks spewing pollution, no waste material, and I couldn't care less if a bunch of terrorists were let loose among an array of windmills' (Peter Musgrove, quoted in John Elkington, 1984).

Wisdom
[before 12c. *Old English wisdom*]
Deep KNOWING, UNDERSTANDING, and connecting. 'Although ecology may be treated as a science, its greater and overriding wisdom is universal. That wisdom can be approached mathematically, chemically, or it can be danced or told as a myth. . . It is manifest, for example, among pre-Classical Greeks, in Navajo religion and social orientation, in romantic poetry of the eighteenth and nineteenth centuries, in Chinese landscape painting of the eleventh century, in current Whiteheadian philosophy, in Zen Buddhism, in the worldview of the cult of the Cretan

Great Mother, in the ceremonials of Bushmen hunters, and in the medieval Christian metaphysics of light. What is common among all of them is a deep sense of engagement with the landscape, with profound connections to surroundings and to natural processes central to all life' (Paul Shepard, 1969).

Wishywashyness
[*c*.1700]
Meaningless and often pretentious waffle; shallow and insufficiently thought out lines of argument; the opposite of CLARITY (sense (2)). A tendency all green-thinkers should constantly guard against. 'We have opted for the A5 format [for our magazine] as we feel this creates a sense . . . of community spirit . . . linking the parts into a greater supportive whole' (*The Mediator*, Spring 1986). 'We live in an increasingly global world' (Open Gate Centre, 1987).

Witch
[before 12c. *Old English wicce*, witch; *Anglo-Saxon witan*, to see, know]
A person skilled in healing and magic; now used of both women and men, but traditionally used almost exclusively to describe wise women, 'the scientists and healers of the people' (Barbara Ehrenreich and Deirdre English, 1973). Following a papal request of 1486, as many as 9 million women (and a much smaller number of men) were killed in the next three centuries, often brutally, the charge being involvement in witchcraft. Any woman involved in healing, indeed any strong or individualistic woman, was branded a witch, to be burned, hung or drowned. The fairytale version of the wicked witch is a direct result of the hatred and fear engendered by the church against witchcraft. A patriarchal, authoritarian and solemn Christianity could not tolerate the earthiness of the Celtic wicca-craft, with its emphasis on the power of women, lively ritual, recognition of the earth and the its seasons, and celebration of sexuality. The church neatly — but falsely — equated witchcraft with its own version of 'evil', resulting in a spate of horror stories laced with brutality and anti-woman violence. This propaganda still pervades current beliefs about 'the occult' (literally 'the mysterious'), to the extent that many of the women (and some men) who are actively involved in 'the craft' talk about 'wicca' or PAGANISM instead of witchcraft. Not surprisingly, there are also people involved in what they call 'witchcraft' who really do perpetuate the oppressive beliefs and practices of their wider society, watching *The Omen* on their video screens and acting out the role models which are there portrayed so vividly. *See also* WOMEN'S SPIRITUALITY.

Witness
[before 12c. *Old English witnes*, testimony]
Saying publicly what needs to be said; by extension any nonviolent ACTION. A term often used by Quakers involved in peace work (*see* NON-VIOLENCE). 'As a man I have been unable to take part in the witness at Greenham Common and I started work on [the peace passion, *The Gates of Greenham*,] with some trepidation. . . In writing it, however, I felt that I was supporting the women in the only way I could, as well as paying tribute to all who have suffered in the cause of a more peaceful world' (Tony Biggin, 1986).

Woman
[before 12c. *Old English wifmann*, female human being (*wœpmann*, male human being, was the equivalent term for 'man')]
A female human being, who takes on more or less of the role of 'woman' as defined by others, and whose experiences are those of being so defined. In a patriarchal society women are secondary, OTHER, lacking, invisible, marked: the basis of sexist oppression is the perceived and mostly artificially-created difference between women and men: 'Without the category "woman" feminism could not exist. Without the category "woman", feminism would not be necessary, for sexism could not exist' (Lisa Tuttle, 1986). Feminists and green-thinkers (and women who are both) know that women are powerful, intelligent and capable, even though the practical acknowledgement often lags behind the theory. Most are convinced that women have a great deal to teach, given their particular experiences; some believe that women have innate skills which men do not have (*see* WOMEN'S SPIRITUALITY). Some believe that 'female' and 'male' — like FEMININE and MASCULINE — are human (mostly patriarchal) constructions that we should reject if we are to explore fully our common humanity: 'The discovery is, of course, that "man" and "woman" are fictions, caricatures, cultural constructs. As models they are reductive, totalitarian, inappropriate to human becoming. As roles they are static, demeaning to the female, dead-ended for male and female both. . . We are, clearly, a multisexed species which has its sexuality spread along a vast fluid continuum where the elements called male and female are not discrete' (Andrea Dworkin, 1974). It is certainly true that what women understand by 'woman' and what men understand by it are not the same thing: 'My conception of woman is inevitably the feminine conception; a thing so entirely unlike the masculine conception of woman that it is eminently needful to define the term and make my meaning clear. . . By a woman . . . I understand an individual human being whose life is her own concern; whose worth, in my eyes (worth being an entirely personal matter) is in no way advanced or detracted from by the accident of marriage; who does

not rise in my estimation by reason of a purely physical capacity for bearing children, or sink in my estimation through a lack of that capacity' (Cicely Hamilton, 1909, quoted in Cheris Kramerae and Paula Treichler, 1985). Some feminists and green-thinkers prefer to use a form of the word that does not include the syllable 'man' or 'men', in order to stress that women are autonomous and should not be defined in relation to men — hence 'womon', 'wimmin' and 'womyn'. *See also* FEMINISM, GENDER, MAN, PATRIARCHY, SEX, SEXISM.

Women's Spirituality
[*c.*1970 as a name, though the concept is of course ancient]
(*also* 'spiritual feminism', 'womanspirit')
The recognition that male-defined forms of RELIGION and SPIRITUALITY have exactly the same oppressive limitations as every other aspect of PATRIARCHY, and that in their exploration of the vital spiritual aspect of their lives women need to reclaim and create other models, rituals and traditions. Women's spirituality takes many forms, including witchcraft (*see* WITCH), goddess-worship (*see* PAGANISM) and MEDITATION, all of which affirm the importance of the links between women, and between women, nature, and the earth and its cycles (*see* CYCLE, SEASONS). While more or less acknowledging the importance of women's spirituality, feminists and green-thinkers have questioned some aspects of current theory and practice. Some think it perpetuates the spiritual/material split that DUALISM has forced on us, turning spiritual feminists away from the 'real' political issues. Many have questioned the (often implicit) assumption that women are somehow naturally closer to nature than men, that they have 'holistic proclivities' (Charlene Spretnak, 1982). It is true that it is often women who have opened our eyes to aspects of the natural world and its oppression, and that 'those of us who are born female are often less severely alienated from nature than are most men' (Susan Griffin, in Léonie Caldecott and Stephanie Leland (ed), 1983), but is there really a 'cosmic essence of womanhood', as Adrienne Rich among others has suggested? 'It is a strange projection on to nature, of course, that nature is female; that it can be seen as gentle, sensual and nurturing rather than as brutal, ravaging and indifferent to individual life and survival. We have here an inversion of the sociobiology which is so popular on the right, where nature is "male". And bloody' (Lynne Segal, 1987).

Words
[before 12c. *Old English word*, word, command]
Ways of circumscribing REALITY, often thought to convey TRUTH. Words can be boring, pedantic and longwinded, or beautiful, concise and well-chosen, but they are still only words. *See also* LANGUAGE, POETRY.

Work

[before 12c. *Old English weorc*, physical or mental effort]

There is nothing wrong with the original meaning: physical or mental effort. To most people, however, work means something very different. To people with 'real' jobs, and to politicians and economists, work means 'paid employment in a trade, occupation or profession'. To most women it means unpaid drudgery and constant pettiness. To the 'unemployed' it means the grass on the other side of the hill. To most green-thinkers 'work' is an almost meaningless concept — to be alive is to work, and people are not lazy by nature. Given stimulation, the fulfilment of their basic needs and recogition of their basic rights, human beings do 'make an effort'. 'People need work not mainly for income, but for self-expression, for self-discipline and for a sense of participation in the human experience' (Susan Campbell, 1983). The problem is that most 'work' is boring, repetitive, geared to capitalist profit rather than individual purpose, and uninspiring. A great deal is also dangerous and destructive: 'It is extraordinary that we have people in this country fighting to preserve the right to crawl on their bellies underground hacking coal out of seams, particularly when their fathers were desperate to keep them out of the pits. But the reason why they are doing this is because we haven't yet offered any alternative to the employee society: they don't know any other way in which a decent able-bodied person can earn respectability [and money] and contribute to society' (Charles Handy, in Mary Inglis and Sandra Kramer (ed), 1985). The concept of meaningful work, GOOD WORK, is only part of the way to the answer — the green future depends on the breaking down of the basic concepts of work, employment and UNEMPLOYMENT. 'There is an old Haitian proverb which I think should be our watchword through this period, and it goes as follows: "If work were a good thing, the rich would have found a way of keeping it all to themselves"' (Barrie Sherman, in Mary Inglis and Sandra Kramer (ed), 1985).

Worker Cooperative

[1969]

(*also* workers' cooperative)

A business in which the workers are also the owners. In a worker cooperative people are not just cogs in a machine of some multinational entrepreneur's making; they cannot be bought and sold, or laid off at short notice. Worker cooperatives, being usually small and community-based, are more easily able to take account of local social and environmental needs. The COOPERATIVE movement is usually associated with SOCIALISM, though the self-help aspect appeals to some right-wing politicians. Important though worker participation is, it does not go far enough for many Greens, who believe that the whole concept of WORK versus non-work needs to be questioned. Some worker cooperatives have looked carefully at issues like CRÈCHE facilities, flexible working hours and JOB-SHARING — though there has been some success, the sheer pressure of earning a living often militates against radical experimentation.

Workshop
[1937 in this sense]
A short and intensive group activity which concentrates on a particular theme, topic or technique.

World
[before 12c. *Old English weorold*, human existence]
Originally meaning 'the sum of human existence', 'world' in common use is now most often synonymous with PLANET or EARTH, 'worldwide' with PLANETARY or GLOBAL. Particular uses in green matters include: The World Health Organization (a body set up in 1948 to monitor health conditions and promote human health); the World Wildlife Fund (founded in 1961); 'world farm' [1976] (an acknowledgement that agricultural production and distribution are now organised intenationally); the *World Conservation Strategy* (published in 1980, which stresses the links between natural resources and human wellbeing); and the designation of 'world heritage sites' by the International Union for Conservation of Nature and Natural Resources in 1985.

Worth
[before 12c. *Old English weorth*, worthy]
Another word for VALUE, preferred by many green-thinkers because it separates the idea of worth from that of money value. Some spiritual Greens would like to reinstate 'worship' — 'worth-ship' — in the green vocabulary.

XxYyZz

X-Rays
(*see* RADIATION)

Yield
[15c. *Old English gieldan*, to pay, reward]
The useful output of an ecological, agricultural or industrial system. In any system that is to remain in a STEADY STATE over time, the yield must be SUSTAINABLE. The important questions to ask when considering yield are: 'useful to whom?', 'for how long?' and 'with what side effects?'.

Yin/Yang
[1893. *Chinese yin*, shade; *yang*, sun]
The natural duality of the East, too often used to justify the unnatural DUALISM of the West. Day and night, light and dark, summer and winter, life and death are all aspects of the cyclical pattern of nature, and were captured by the ancient Chinese in the symbolism of yin and yang. There is every reason to believe that the male/female distinction so beloved of present-day spirituality was a much later connotation, one which fits very neatly into dualistic Western minds, both male and female. *See also* ANDROGYNY, FEMININE, MASCULINE, SPIRITUALITY, WOMEN'S SPIRITUALITY.

Yoga
[1820. *Sanskrit yoga*, union]
A Hindu philosophy, lifestyle and discipline, the goal of which is the union of the SELF with the UNIVERSE (often referred to as 'the supreme being'). In popular use 'yoga' has come to refer to any set of physical and mental exercises with this purpose, which usually include MEDITATION, breath exercises (prana), and body movements (asanas).

Young People
[*c*.1970 in this sense]
A term preferred by some green-thinkers instead of 'children', 'teenagers' or 'adolescents', stressing the fact that children are people with their own rights. For the same reason 'young adults' is also used to refer to older children and teenagers. *See also* CHILD.

Zen
[1902. *Japanese zen* and *Chinese chan*, from *Sanskrit dhyana*, meditation]
A Japanese philosophy of MEDITATION and reflection, popularised in the West from the 1870s onward, but especially in the 1960s by people like Alan Ginsberg, Jack Kerouac and Alan Watts. In many ways Zen is rather like Taoism, both being akin to Buddhism, and 'zen' is popularly used in the West in much the same way as TAO. Zen emphasises concentration on the task in hand, 'ordinarv miracles', and the creativity of PARADOX, as exemplified in the zen riddle or 'koan', the most famous being 'What is the sound of one hand clapping?'

Zero Population Growth
[1967]
(*also* 'ZPG')
An acknowledgement that relatively stable human population levels are now essential if the resources available are not to be stretched beyond their limits (*see* OVERPOPULATION, POPULATION). ZPG has virtually been reached by many Western countries, and by China, one of the countries that might have been written off by the population doomsters of the 1960s; rapid population growth, however, continues in much of the Third World, which many green-thinkers see as one of the most pressing of human concerns. ZPG is also the name of an organisation which works to bring the need for the stabilisation of world population to the notice of public and politicians. *See also* LIFEBOAT ETHIC, MALTHUSIANISM, NEOMALTHUSIANISM.

Zoning
[1912 in this sense. *Gk zone*, girdle, zone]
The designation by a competent authority of areas of land as suitable only for certain uses, in an attempt to control undesirable development. Zoning is a common practice in land-use PLANNING, though its implementation varies in detail from place to place. While the aims of zoning may be noble ones, it has proved to be as much of a hindrance as a benefit in many cases. Zoning tends to be static and inflexible, fossilising the interests of those who created the zones and ghettoising underprivileged groups. Green-thinkers would like to see more flexible guidelines drawn up with the participation of the people who live in an area, and more of a mix of housing, open space, workshops and services.

Sources

As explained in the introduction, only author, title and date of first publication are given in this list of sources quoted. This is partly to save space, partly because many of the books quoted are available in different editions in different parts of the English-speaking world; it should always, however, provide sufficient information to find a particular volume. Books with multiple authors are occasionally quoted by title and date only; journals and periodicals are quoted by title only.

Edward Abbey, *The Monkeywrench Gang*, 1975
Michael Adelstein and Jean Pival (ed), *Ecocide and Population*, 1971
Nick Albery and Yvo Peeters (ed), *How to Save the World*, 1982
Michael Allaby, *The Ecoactivists*, 1971
Michael Allaby, *Macmillan Dictionary of the Environment*, 1983
John Allen and Mark Nelson, *Space Biospheres*, 1986
Marc Allen, *Friends and Lovers*, 1985
American Behavioral Scientist
Amethyst Centre (Dublin), brochure, 1987
Isiaka Amodu, comments on *A Dictionary of Green Ideas*, 1987
Andrews and Fein, *The Urban Environment*, 1981
Architectural Review
Robert Ardrey, *The Territorial Imperative*, 1967
Frankie Armstrong, notes from a voice workshop, 1985
Raymond Aron, *Progress and Disillusion*, 1968
Robert Arvill, *Man and Environment*, 1967
Eia Asen, *Psychiatry for Beginners*, 1986
Maurice Ash, *Green Politics*, 1980
Graham Ashworth, *Encyclopedia of Planning*, 1973
Roberto Assagioli, *The Act of Will*, 1974
Association of Humanistic Psychology, leaflet, 1986
Margaret Atwood, *Dancing Girls, and Other Stories*, 1977
A.J. Ayer, *The Central Questions of Philosophy*, 1973

Rudolf Bahro, *Socialism and Survival*, 1982
Rudolf Bahro, *From Red to Green*, 1984
Rudolf Bahro, *Building the Green Movement*, 1986
Richard Ballantine, *Richard's Bicycle Book*, 1975
Michael Barker, *Directory for the Environment*, 1986
Richard Barnet, *The Lean Years: Politics in the Age of Scarcity*, 1980
John Barr, *Derelict Britain*, 1969
John Barr, *The Assault on Our Senses*, 1970
John Barr (ed), *The Environmental Handbook*, 1971
Michèlle Barrett and Mary McIntosh, *The Antisocial Family*, 1982
Gregory Bateson, *Mind and Nature: A Necessary Unity*, 1979
Peter Beckman, *Ecohysterics and the Technophobes*, 1973
Ingrid Bengis, *Combat in the Erogenous Zone*, 1973
Greg Benton and Graham Loomes, *The Big Red Joke Book*, 1976
Peter Berg, *Reinhabiting a Separate Country*, 1978
John Berger, *Ways of Seeing*, 1972
Berkeley Holistic Health Center, *The Holistic Health Handbook*, 1978
Berkeley Holistic Health Center, *The Holistic Health Lifebook*, 1981
Maurice Berman, *The Reenchantment of the World*, 1981
Thomas Berry, *The Riverdale Papers on the Earth Community*, 1981
Thomas Berry, *Teilhard in the Ecological Age*, 1982
Wendell Berry, *A Continuous Harmony*, 1972
Wendell Berry, *The Long Way Back to the Land*, 1978
Wendell Berry, *The Gift of Good Land*, 1981
Rosalie Bertell, *No Immediate Danger*, 1985
The Bible
Tony Biggin, *The Gates of Greenham* (record sleeve), 1986
BioScience
The Biosphere Catalogue
Liz Bissett and Ursula Huws, *Homeworking in Britain Today*, 1985
Black Scholar
John Blofeld, *The Secret and Sublime*, 1973
David Bohm, *Wholeness and the Implicate Order*, 1980
Sissela Bok, *Secrets*, 1986
Michael Bonavia, *Twilight of British Rail*, 1985
Murray Bookchin, *Toward an Ecological Society*, 1980
Murray Bookchin, *The Ecology of Freedom*, 1981
Murray Bookchin, *The Modern Crisis*, 1986
Kenneth Boulding, *Ecodynamics: A New Theory of Societal Evolution*, 1978
P.J. Bowler, *Evolution*, 1984
Harry Braverman, *Labour and Monopoly Capital: The Degradation of Work in the Twentieth Century*, 1974

Mark Bricklin, *The Practical Encyclopedia of Natural Healing*, 1983
Victoria Brittain and Michael Simmons (ed), *Third World Review*, 1987
David Brower, *Gentle Wilderness*, 1968
Lester Brown, *Pure Sociology*, 1903
Lester Brown, *Building a Sustainable Society*, 1981
Susan Brownmiller, *Against Our Will: Men, Women, and Rape*, 1984
Susan Brownmiller, *Femininity*, 1986
Anne Bülow-Olsen, *Plant Communities*, 1977
Peter Bunyard and Fern Morgan-Grenville (ed), *The Green Alternative*, 1987
David Burnham, *The Rise of the Computer State*, 1983
John Button, *Making Love Work: A Radical Approach*, 1985

John Cairns, *Ecoaccidents*, 1986
Edward Calabrese, *Ecogenetics*, 1984
Léonie Caldecott and Stephanie Leland (ed), *Reclaim the Earth: Women Speak Out for Life on Earth*, 1983
Helen Caldicott, *Missile Envy*, 1984
Ernest Callenbach, *Ecotopia*, 1970
Ernest Callenbach, *The Ecotopian Encyclopedia*, 1980
Ernest Callenbach, *Ecotopia Emerging*, 1981
Susan Campbell, *Earth Community*, 1983
Fritjof Capra, *The Tao of Physics*, 1975
Fritjof Capra, *The Turning Point: Science, Society and the Rising Culture*, 1982
Fritjof Capra and Charlene Spretnak, *Green Politics*, 1984
Marilyn Carr (ed), *The AT Reader*, 1985
Rachel Carson, *The Sea Around Us*, 1951
Rachel Carson, *Silent Spring*, 1962
Angela Carter, *The Sadeian Woman*, 1979
Sue Cartledge and Joanna Ryan (ed), *Sex and Love: New Thoughts on Old Contradictions*, 1983
William Catton, *Overshoot: The Ecological Basis of Revolutionary Change*, 1980
Carolyn Chapman, *Style on a Shoestring*, 1984
Annie Cheatham and Mary Clare Powell (ed), *This Way Daybreak Comes: Women's Values and the Future*, 1986
Serge Chermayeff and Christopher Alexander, *Community and Privacy*, 1963
Kim Chernin, *The Hungry Self*, 1985
Gail Chester, *I Call Myself a Radical Feminist*, 1979
Gail Chester and Andrew Rigby (ed), *Articles of Peace*, 1986

Paul Chilton, *Nukespeak*, 1982
Richard Chorley and Peter Haggett (ed), *Models in Geography*, 1967
Howard Clark, *Atoms for War*, 1982
Club of Rome, *The Limits to Growth*, 1972
Gary Coates (ed), *Resettling America*, 1981
Edith Cobb, *The Ecology of Imagination in Childhood*, 1977
J.M. and M.J. Cohen, *The Penguin Dictionary of Modern Quotations*, 1980
Michèle Cohen and Tina Reid (ed), *Ourselves and Our Children*, 1981
Alice Coleman, *Utopia on Trial*, 1985
Collins Dictionary of the English Language, 1986
John Stewart Collis, *The Worm Forgives the Plough*, 1973
Barry Commoner, *The Closing Circle: Confronting the Environmental Crisis*, 1971
Communities
Complete Elegance
Alice Cook and Gwyn Kirk, *Greenham Women Everywhere*, 1983
Mike Cooley, *Architect or Bee?*, 1987
Joseph Bharat Cornell, *Sharing Nature with Children*, 1979
Countryside Conflicts, 1986
Rosalind Creasy, *Edible Landscaping*, 1982
Stephen Croall and Kaianders Sempler, *Eco-Socialism in a Nutshell*, 1980
John Crowley, *Engine Summer*, 1979
Current History

Herman Daly, *Steady-State Economics*, 1977
Mary Daly, *Gyn/Ecology: The Metaethics of Radical Feminism*, 1978
Erik Dammann, *Revolution in the Affluent Society*, 1984
Ken Darrow and Rick Pam, *Appropriate Technology Sourcebook*, 1978
Arnold Dartington, *The Ecology of Walls*, 1981
Raymond Dasmann, *Wildlife Biology*, 1964
W. Jackson Davis, *The Seventh Year*, 1979
David Day, *The Whale War*, 1987
Rosalind Delmar, *What is Feminism?*, 1986
Daniel Deudney, *Rivers of Energy: The Hydropower Potential*, 1983
Karl Deutsch, *Ecosocial Systems and Ecopolitics: A Reader on Human and Social Implications of Environmental Management in Developing Countries*, 1977
Bill Devall and George Sessions (ed), *Deep Ecology*, 1985
Paul Devereux and Ian Thomson, *The Ley-Hunter's Companion*, 1979
Anne Dickson, *A Woman in Your Own Right*, 1982
Anne Dickson, *The Mirror Within*, 1985

Barbara Dinham and Michael Norton, *The Directory of Social Change: Education*, 1977
Dorothy Dinnerstein, *The Mermaid and the Minotaur*, 1977
Robert Disch (ed), *The Ecological Conscience*, 1970
Alan Dobby, *Conservation and Planning*, 1978
Collette Dowling, *The Cinderella Complex*, 1981
George Downing, *The Massage Book*, 1973
Ruth Draper, *A Class in Greek Poise*, 1913
Nevill Drury, *The Bodywork Book*, 1984
Nevill Drury, *Inner Health*, 1985
Lee Durrell, *The State of the Ark*, 1986
Andrea Dworkin, *Woman Hating*, 1974
Andrea Dworkin, *Our Blood: Prophecies and Discourses in Sexual Politics*, 1976
Andrea Dworkin, *Pornography: Men Possessing Women*, 1981
Andrea Dworkin, *Right-Wing Women: The Politics of Domesticated Females*, 1983

Earth First!, leaflet, 1986
Earthlife News
East/West
Erik Eckholm, *Down To Earth*, 1982
Ecoforum
Ecologist, The
Econews
David Ehrenfeld, *The Arrogance of Humanism*, 1981
Barbara Ehrenreich and Deirdre English, *Witches, Midwives and Nurses*, 1973
Paul Ehrlich, *The Population Bomb*, 1970
Paul Ehrlich, Anne Ehrlich and John Holdren, *Human Ecology: Problems and Solutions*, 1973
Paul Ehrlich, Anne Ehrlich and John Holdren, *Ecoscience*, 1977
Paul Ehrlich and Anne Ehrlich, *Extinction*, 1981
Albert Eiss, *Eco-Interaction*, 1973
Paul Ekins (ed), *The Living Economy*, 1986
Duane Elgin, *Voluntary Simplicity*, 1981
John Elkington, *Sun Traps*, 1984
John Elkington, *The Green Capitalists*, 1987
Margaret Elphinstone, *The Incomer*, 1987
Margaret Elphinstone and Julia Langley, *The Holistic Gardener*, 1987
Steve Elsworth, *Acid Rain*, 1984
James Erlichman, *Gluttons for Punishment*, 1986
Sheila Ernst and Lucy Goodison, *In Our Own Hands*, 1981

Esalen Foundation, 1986/87 Catalogue
Helen Exley, *Cry for our Beautiful World*, 1985

The Faber Book of Anecdotes, 1976
The Face
Clifton Fadiman and Jean White (ed), *Ecocide — and Thoughts Towards Survival*, 1971
Joen Fagan and I.L. Shepherd (ed), *Gestalt Therapy Now*, 1972
Zoe Fairbairns, *Benefits*, 1979
Nan Fairbrother, *New Lives, New Landscapes*, 1970
Richard Falk, *Indefensible Weapons*, 1982
Beatrice Faust, *Women, Sex and Pornography*, 1980
Moshe Feldenkrais, pamphlet, 1986
Marilyn Ferguson, *The Aquarian Conspiracy*, 1981
Tom Ferguson (ed), *Medical Self-Care*, 1980
Piero Ferrucci, *What We May Be: The Visions and Techniques of Psychosynthesis*, 1982
Eva Figes, *Patriarchal Attitudes*, 1978
Findhorn Community, *Faces of Findhorn*, 1980
Findhorn Foundation, 1987 Programme
Shulamith Firestone, *The Dialectic of Sex: The Case for Feminist Reform*, 1971
Rudolf Flesch, *The Book of Unusual Quotations*, 1968
Michael Flood, *Energy Without End*, 1986
Anya Foos-Graber, *Deathing: An Intelligent Alternative for the Final Moments of Life*, 1984
Phyllis Ford, *Eco-Acts*, 1983
Dave Foreman (ed), *Ecodefense: A Field Guide to Monkeywrenching*, 1985
For The Fun Of It (included as an appendix to Stephanie Judson (ed), 1977)
H.W. Fowler, *A Dictionary of Modern English Usage*, 1968
Michael Fox, *Agricide*, 1986
Scarlet Friedman and Elizabeth Sarah (ed), *On The Problem of Men*, 1982
Friends of the Earth, *The Eco-Cookbook*, 1975
Paolo Friere, *The Pedagogy of the Oppressed*, 1970
F. Fröbel, J. Heinrichs and O. Kreye, *The New International Division of Labour*, 1980
Erich Fromm, *To Have Or To Be?*, 1976
Marilyn Frye, *The Politics of Reality*, 1983
Stephen Fulder, *The Handbook of Complementary Medicine*, 1984
Buckminster Fuller, *Operating Manual for Spaceship Earth*, 1978
Buckminster Fuller, *Critical Path*, 1981

Timothy Gallwey, *The Inner Game of Tennis*, 1975
Sally Miller Gearhart, *The Wanderground*, 1978
Martha Gellhorn, *The Face of War*, 1986
Geographical Review
Henry George, *Progress and Poverty*, 1879
Susan George, *How the Other Half Dies*, 1976
Joseph Gerson, *The Deadly Connection*, 1986
Getting Together, 1986
Richard Gillett, *Overcoming Depression*, 1987
Charlotte Perkins Gilman, *Herland*, 1915
Herbert Girardet (ed), *Land for the People*, 1976
Bernhard Glaeser (ed), *Ecodevelopment: Concepts, Projects, Strategies*, 1984
Glasgow University Media Group, *Really Bad News*, 1982
Global 2000, 1982
Emma Goldman, *Red Emma Speaks*, 1979
Edward Goldsmith (ed), *The Doomsday Fun Book*, 1977
Edward Goldsmith and Nicholas Hildyard (ed), *Green Britain or Industrial Wasteland?*, 1986
Robert Goodman, *After the Planners*, 1972
Clem Gorman, *People Together*, 1975
André Gorz, *Ecology as Politics*, 1978
Alan Grainger, *Desertification*, 1982
The Great British Diet, 1985
Green Anarchist
Bryn Green, *Countryside Conservation*, 1981
Green Comment
Jonathon Green, *The A-Z of Nuclear Jargon*, 1986
Owen Greene, Ian Percival and Irene Ridge, *Nuclear Winter*, 1985
Greenham Common Songsheet, 1984
Green Line
Green Options
Green Party (British), General Election Manifesto, 1987
Greenpeace Newsletter
Miriam Greenspan, *A New Approach to Women and Therapy*, 1983
Germaine Greer, *Sex and Destiny*, 1984
John Gribbin (ed), *The Breathing Planet*, 1986
Susan Griffin, *Woman and Nature*, 1978
Die Grünen, *Programme of the German Green Party*, 1983
Die Grünen, *Peace Manifesto*, 1983
The Guardian

Peter Hall, *The Containment of Urban England*, 1973
Mabel Hammersmith and Laura Watkins, *Eco-Antics*, 1974

Charles Hampden-Turner, *Sane Asylum*, 1977
Charles Handy, *The Future of Work*, 1985
Garrett Hardin (ed), *Population, Evolution and Birth Control*, 1964
Garrett Hardin, *An Ecolate View of the Human Predicament*, 1972
Garrett Hardin, *Stalking the Wild Taboo*, 1978
Barbara Harford and Sarah Hopkins (ed), *Greenham Common: Women at the Wire*, 1984
Paul Harrison, *Inside the Third World*, 1979
Ruth Harrison, *Animal Machines*, 1964
Robert Hart, *Ecosociety*, 1984
David Harvey (ed), *Thorson's Complete Guide to Alternative Living*, 1986
B. Haurwitz and J.M. Austin, *Climatology*, 1944
Paul Hawken, *The Next Economy*, 1983
Teresa Hayter, *The Creation of World Poverty*, 1981
Stephen Heath, *The Sexual Fix*, 1982
William Heinesen, *Arctis*, 1980
Hazel Henderson, *Creating Alternative Futures: The End of Economics*, 1978
Hazel Henderson, *The Politics of the Solar Age*, 1981
Nancy Henley, *Body Politics*, 1977
Heresies
Seymour Hersh, *My Lai Massacre*, 1970
Fred Hirsch, *The Social Limits to Growth*, 1977
Shere Hite, *Male Sexuality*, 1978
HMSO (Her Majesty's Stationery Office), *Development Plans Explained*, 1951
Benjamin Hoff, *The Tao of Pooh*, 1982
David Hoffmann, *The Holistic Herbal*, 1983
John Holliday, *Land at the Centre*, 1986
Jonathan Holliman, *Consumer's Guide to the Protection of the Environment*, 1974
John Holt, *How Children Fail*, 1965
John Holt, *The Underachieving School*, 1970
Gerard Manley Hopkins, *Poems*, 1877
Robert Houriet, *Getting Back Together*, 1971
Philip Howard, *Weasel Words*, 1978
Patrick Howden, *Ecologistics*, undated
Martin Hoyles (ed), *Changing Childhood*, 1979
Keri Hulme, *The Windeater: Te Kaihau*, 1987
Charles Humana, *World Human Rights Guide*, 1986
Humboldt Journal of Social Relations
Christmas Humphries, *The Buddhist Way of Life*, 1974
Janet Hunt, *The Holistic Cook*, 1985

Edmund Husserl, *The Crisis of European Sciences and Transcendental Phenomenology*, 1954
Aldous Huxley, *An Encyclopædia of Pacifism*, 1937

Ideal Home, 1986
Ivan Illich, *Celebration of Awareness*, 1971
Ivan Illich, *Deschooling Society*, 1971
Ivan Illich, *Tools for Conviviality*, 1973
Ivan Illich, *Limits to Medicine*, 1976
Ivan Illich, *Shadow Work*, 1981
Ivan Illich and Etienne Verne, *Imprisoned in the Global Classroom*, 1976
Mary Ingham, *Men*, 1984
Mary Inglis and Sandra Kramer (ed), *The New Economic Agenda*, 1985
Gordon Inkeles, *The New Massage*, 1980
Inquiry
International Union for the Conservation of Nature and Natural Resources, *Threatened Protected Areas of the World*, 1975

Harvey Jackins, *The Human Situation*, 1973
Harvey Jackins, *The Upward Trend*, 1978
Harvey Jackins, *The Reclaiming of Power*, 1983
Wes Jackson, *New Roots for Agriculture*, 1985
Alison Jaggar, *Feminist Politics and Human Nature*, 1983
Jenny James, *Male Sexuality: The Atlantis Position*, 1985
Arthur Janov, *The Primal Scream*, 1970
Eric Jantsch, *The Self-Organizing Universe*, 1980
Henry Jarrett (ed), *Environmental Quality in a Growing Economy*, 1966
Elizabeth Jennings, *Collected Poems*, 1967
Cecil Johnson, *Ecocrisis*, 1970
Warren Johnson, *Muddling Toward Frugality*, 1979
R.J. Johnston (ed), *The Dictionary of Human Geography*, 1986
William Johnston, *The Inner Eye of Love*, 1978
Journal of Environmental Education
Stephanie Judson (ed), *A Manual on Nonviolence and Children*, 1977
Robert Jungk, *Brighter Than a Thousand Suns*, 1956
Just Seventeen

Petra Kelly, *Fighting for Hope*, 1984
Ken Keyes, *A Conscious Person's Guide to Relationships*, 1979
Ken Keyes, *The Hundredth Monkey*, 1981

Donald Keys, *Earth at Omega: Passage to Planetization*, 1982
Michael Kidron and Ronald Segal, *The State of the World Atlas*, 1981
Angela King and Sue Clifford, *Holding Your Ground*, 1985
Art Kleiner and Stewart Brand (ed), *News That Stayed News*, 1986
Anne Koedt, *Radical Feminism*, 1973
Susan Koen and Nina Swaim, *Handbook for Women on the Nuclear Mentality*, 1980
Arthur Koestler, *The Ghost in the Machine*, 1967
Cheris Kramerae and Paula Treichler (ed), *A Feminist Dictionary*, 1985
Charles Krebs, *Ecology*, 1972
Thomas Kuhn, *The Structure of Scientific Revolutions*, 1962

Ronald Laing, *The Politics of Experience and The Bird of Paradise*, 1967
Frances Moore Lappé, *Diet for a Small Planet*, 1980
Frances Moore Lappé and Joseph Collins, *Food First*, 1980
Frances Moore Lappé, Joseph Collins and David Kinley, *Aid as Obstacle*, 1980
Christopher Lasch, *The Culture of Narcissism*, 1980
Erwin Laszlo, *The Inner Limits of Mankind*, 1979
Jane Lazarre, *On Loving Men*, 1981
John Lea and Jock Young, *What is to Be Done about Law and Order?*, 1984
Robert Lekachman, *Capitalism for Beginners*, 1981
Robert Lee, *Faith and the Prospects of Economic Collapse*, 1981
Leeds Revolutionary Feminist Group, *Love Your Enemy? The Debate Between Heterosexual Feminism and Political Lesbianism*, 1981
William Leiss, *The Limits to Satisfaction*, 1978
Aldo Leopold, *A Sand County Almanac*, 1949
Lawrence LeShan, *Holistic Health*, 1982
Leveller, The
Lucinda Lidell, *The Book of Massage*, 1984
Michael Lindfield, *The Dance of Change: An Eco-Spiritual Approach to Transformation*, 1986
Marcus Linear, *Zapping the Third World*, 1985
Jessica Lipnack and Jeffrey Stamps, *The Networking Book*, 1986
Suzanne Lipsky and Harvey Jackins, *A Statement on Black Liberation and Re-evaluation Counselling*, 1978
Bernard Little and Stewart Biggar, *The Future of Agriculture in Britain* (unpublished paper), 1986
London Rape Crisis Centre, *Sexual Violence: The Reality for Women*, 1984
Konrad Lorenz, *On Aggression*, 1966

Sam Love and David Obst (ed), *Ecotage*, 1972
James Lovelock, *Gaia: A New Look at Life on Earth*, 1979
Amory Lovins, *Soft Energy Paths*, 1977
Amory Lovins, *The Energy Controversy*, 1979
Alexander Lowen, *Pleasure*, 1970
Alexander Lowen, *Bioenergetics*, 1975

Richard Mabey, *Food for Free*, 1972
Richard Mabey, *The Unofficial Countryside*, 1973
Richard Mabey, *The Common Ground: A Place for Nature in Britain's Future?*, 1980
Joanna Rogers Macy, *Despair and Personal Power in the Nuclear Age*, 1983
Bryan Magee (ed), *Men of Ideas*, 1978
Maggie's Farm
Herbert Marcuse, *Eros and Civilization*, 1958
Vance Martin and Mary Inglis (ed), *Wilderness*, 1984
Andrew Marvell, *Miscellaneous Poems*, 1681
Abraham Maslow, *The Farther Reaches of Human Nature*, 1973
L. John Mason, *Guide to Stress Reduction*, 1980
J. Masserman, *Principles and Practice of Biodynamic Psychotherapy*, 1980
Man-Made Women, 1985
John McCormick, *The User's Guide to the Environment*, 1985
Cyra McFadden, *The Serial*, 1977
Harold McGee, *On Food and Cooking*, 1984
J. and M. McHale, *Basic Human Needs: A Framework for Action*, 1979
Ian McHarg, *Design With Nature*, 1971
Marshall McLuhan, *The Gutenberg Galaxy*, 1963
Marshall McLuhan, *Understanding Media*, 1965
The Mediator
Dianna Melrose, *Bitter Pills*, 1982
Richard Merrill (ed), *Radical Agriculture*, 1976
Andy Metcalf and Martin Humphries (ed), *The Sexuality of Men*, 1985
Leonard Michaels and Christopher Ricks (ed), *The State of the Language*, 1980
Mary Midgley, *Beast and Man*, 1978
Nicola Miles and Philip Cosens, Pagans Against Nukes leaflet, undated
Rufus Miles, *Awakening from the American Dream*, 1976
John Stuart Mill, *Utilitarianism*, 1861
Casey Miller and Kate Swift, *The Handbook of Nonsexist Writing*, 1981

G. Tyler Miller and Patrick Armstrong, *Living in the Environment*, 1982
Kate Millett, *Sexual Politics*, 1968
Erik Millstone, *Food Additives*, 1986
Edward Mishan, *The Costs of Economic Growth*, 1967
Mission to South Africa: The Commonwealth Report, 1986
J. Mitchell and C. Stallings, *Ecotactics*, 1970
Bill Mollison and David Holmgren, *Permaculture*, 1978
Bill Mollison, *Permaculture Two*, 1979
Shirley Morahan, *A Woman's Place: Rhetoric and Readings for Combining Yourself and Your Prose*, 1981
Robin Morgan, *The Anatomy of Freedom*, 1982
David Morris, *The New City-States*, 1982
M. Moss (ed), *The Measurement of Economic and Social Performance*, 1971
Kit Mouat, *Fighting for our Lives*, 1984
Lewis Mumford, *Pentagon of Power*, 1970
Iris Murdoch, *The Sovereignty of Good*, 1970
Nick Murgatroyd and Peter Smith, *The Third Sector Economy*, 1984
Norman Myers, *The Sinking Ark*, 1979
Norman Myers (ed), *The Gaia Atlas of Planet Management*, 1985

Ian Nairn, *Outrage*, 1955
Kathy Nairne and Gerrilyn Smith, *Dealing With Depression*, 1984
John Naisbitt, *Megatrends*, 1984
Su Negrin, *Begin at Start*, 1972
John Neihardt, *Black Elk Speaks*, 1932
A.S. Neill, *Summerhill*, 1962
Gemma Nesbitt and Andrew Tonks (ed), *The National Directory of New Co-operatives and Community Businesses*, 1986
Richard Neville, *Playpower*, 1970
New Age Journal
New Economics Foundation, leaflet, 1987
Nancy Newhall, *This is the American Earth*, 1961
New Internationalist
New Left Review
New Scientist
New Society
New Yorker
Max Nicholson, *The Environmental Revolution*, 1970
Richard North, *The Real Cost*, 1986
Michael Norton, *The Directory of Social Change: Housing*, 1980
Julius Nyerere, *Appeal to the Socialists of Europe* 1972

Anne Oakley, *Subject Woman*, 1981
The Observer
Eugene Odum, *Ecology — The Commonsense Approach*, undated
Eugene Odum, *Ecology*, 1963
One Earth
Open Gate Centre, programme, 1987
William Ophuls, *Ecology and the Politics of Scarcity*, 1977
Susie Orbach, *Fat is a Feminist Issue 2*, 1982
Timothy O'Riordan, *Environmentalism*, 1976
Leonard Orr and Sondra Ray, *Rebirthing in the New Age*, 1977
George Orwell, *Nineteen Eighty-Four*, 1947
P.D. Ouspensky, *In Search of the Miraculous*, 1969
Oxford English Dictionary, 1933
Oxford English Dictionary: Supplement, 1972 to 1986

Victor Papanek, *Design for the Real World*, 1974
Pagan Parenting Network Newsletter
Chandra Patel, *Fighting Heart Disease*, 1987
Walter Patterson, *Nuclear Power*, 1976
Dennis Paulson (ed), *Voices of Survival in a Nuclear Age*, 1986
Peace News
Fred Pearce, *Acid Rain*, 1987
Fran Peavey, *Heart Politics*, 1986
Aurelio Peccei, *One Hundred Pages for the Future*, 1981
Kit Pedler, *The Quest for Gaia*, 1979
The Penguin Dictionary of Economics, 1972
David Pepper, *The Roots of Modern Environmentalism*, 1984
Frederick Perls, *Gestalt Therapy Verbatim*, 1969
Laurence Peter (ed), *Quotations for Our Time*, 1977
Christopher Pick (ed), *What's What in the 1980s*, 1983
Marge Piercy, *Woman on the Edge of Time*, 1976
Marge Piercy, *Vida*, 1979
Marge Piercy, *Circles on the Water*, 1985
Dennis Pirages (ed), *The Sustainable Society*, 1977
Dennis Pirages and Paul Ehrlich, *Ark II: Response to Environmental Imperatives*, 1974
Stephen Plowden, *Taming Traffic*, 1980
Politics for Life (British Green Party), 1983
Jonathon Porritt, *Seeing Green: The Politics of Ecology Explained*, 1984
Jonathon Porritt (ed), *Friends of the Earth Handbook*, 1987
Van Rensselaer Potter, *Bioethics: Bridge to the Future*, 1971
John Purser, *The Counting Stick*, 1976
Charlie Pye-Smith and Chris Rose, *Crisis and Conservation*, 1984

Kathleen Raine, *Blake and the New Age*, 1979
Kathleen Raine, *Collected Poems*, 1981
François Ramade, *Ecotoxicology*, 1987
Frederick Raphael, *The Language of Television*, 1980
Janice Raymond, *A Passion for Friends*, 1986
Richard Faust Register, *Another Beginning*, 1978
Charles Reich, *The Greening of America*, 1970
Jan Resnick, *Holistic Healing* (unpublished paper), 1986
Resurgence
Adrienne Rich, *On Lies, Secrets, and Silence*, 1979
Adrienne Rich, *Compulsory Heterosexuality and Lesbian Existence*, 1980
Jeremy Rifkin, *Entropy: A New World View*, 1980
Jeremy Rifkin, *Algeny*, 1984
Jeremy Rifkin, *Declarations of a Heretic*, 1985
Andrew Rigby, *Communes in Britain*, 1974
Rights of Women, *The Cohabitation Handbook*, 1981
Vicky Rippere, *The Allergy Problem*, 1983
David Robertson, *The Penguin Dictionary of Politics*, 1985
James Robertson, *The Sane Alternative*, 1978
James Robertson, *Future Work*, 1985
Laurel Robertson, Carol Flinders and Bronwen Godfrey, *Laurel's Kitchen*, 1976
Carl Rogers, *On Becoming a Person*, 1967
Robert de Ropp, *Eco-Tech: The Whole-Earther's Guide to the Alternate Society*, 1975
Betty Roszak and Theodore Roszak (ed), *Masculine/Feminine*, 1969
Theodore Roszak, *The Making of a Counterculture*, 1969
Theodore Roszak, *Person/Planet*, 1979
John Rowan, *Ordinary Ecstasy*, 1976
John Rowan, *The Reality Game: A Guide to Humanistic Counselling and Therapy*, 1983
John Rowan, *The Horned God*, 1987
Joan Ruddock, *CND Scrapbook*, 1987
Hans Ruesch, *Slaughter of the Innocents*, 1983
Joanna Russ, *How to Suppress Women's Writing*, 1983
Joanna Russ, *Magic Mommas, Trembling Sisters, Puritans and Perverts*, 1985
Peter Russell, *The Awakening Earth*, 1982
Richard Ryder, *Speciesism: The Ethics of Vivisection*, 1974
Martin Ryle, *The Politics of Nuclear Disarmament*, 1981

Ignacy Sachs, *The Salient Features of Development*, 1978

Kirkpatrick Sale, *Human Scale*, 1980
Kirkpatrick Sale, *Dwellers in the Land: The Bioregional Vision*, 1985
Swami Anand Samarpan, *The Feeling Good Book*, 1983
Jonathan Schell, *The Fate of the Earth*, 1982
Jonathan Schell, *The Abolition*, 1984
E.F. Schumacher, *Small is Beautiful*, 1973
E.F. Schumacher, *Good Work*, 1980
William Schutz, *Joy*, 1967
Science
Joni Seager and Ann Olsen, *Women in the World*, 1986
Chief Seathl, speech of 1855, quoted in full in Herbert Girardet (ed), 1976
Charles Secrett, *Rainforest*, undated
Charles Secrett and Victoria Cliff Hodges, *Motorway Madness*, undated
Robert Seeley, *The Handbook of Non-Violence*, 1986
Lynne Segal, *Is The Future Female?*, 1987
Self and Society
John and Sally Seymour, *Self-Sufficiency*, 1973
John Seymour and Herbert Girardet, *Blueprint for a Green Planet*, 1987
Steve Shalom (ed), *Socialist Visions*, 1982
Gene Sharp, *The Politics of Nonviolent Action*, 1973
George Bernard Shaw, *Maxims for Revolutionaries*, 1942
Ann Shearer, *Disability: Whose Handicap?*, 1981
Michael Sheehan and James Wyllie, *Pocket Guide to Defence*, 1986
Paul Shepard, *The Subversive Science*, 1969
Marion Shoard, *The Theft of the Countryside*, 1980
Marion Shoard, *This Land is Our Land*, 1987
Ian Simmons, *The Ecology of Natural Resources*, 1974
Simply Living
Peter Singer, *Animal Liberation*, 1977
Peter Singer, *The Expanding Circle: Ethics and Sociobiology*, 1981
Peter Singer, *In Defence of Animals*, 1985
Narindar Singh, *Economics and the Crisis of Ecology*, 1976
Burrhus Skinner, *Walden Two*, 1948
Burrhus Skinner, *Science and Human Behavior*, 1953
Henryk Skolimowski, *Eco-Philosophy*, 1981
Malcolm Slesser (ed), *Macmillan Dictionary of Energy*, 1982
Dan Smith and E.P. Thompson (ed), *Prospectus for a Habitable Planet*, 1987
Robert Lee Smith, *The Ecology of Man*, 1972
V. Kerry Smith (ed), *Scarcity and Growth Reconsidered*, 1979

Ann Snitow, Christine Stansell and Sharon Thompson (ed), *Desire: The Politics of Sexuality*, 1983
Jon Snodgrass (ed), *For Men Against Sexism*, 1977
Gary Snyder, *Turtle Island*, 1974
Gary Snyder, *Good, Wild, Sacred*, 1980
Social Alternatives
Social Trends
Daniel Sonkin and Michael Durphy, *Learning to Live Without Violence*, 1982
David Spangler, *The Laws of Manifestation*, 1973
David Spangler, *Revelation: The Birth of a New Age*, 1976
David Spangler, *Emergence: The Rebirth of the Sacred*, 1984
Spare Rib
Dale Spender, *Man Made Language*, 1980
Dale Spender (ed), *Men's Studies Modified*, 1981
Dale Spender, *Women of Ideas and What Men Have Done to Them*, 1982
Charlene Spretnak (ed), *The Politics of Women's Spirituality*, 1982
Charlene Spretnak, *The Spiritual Dimension of Green Politics*, 1986
Springhill Farm, *The Consumer's Guide to Organic Food* (pamphlet), 1986
Squatting, 1980
John Stadler (ed), *Ecofiction*, 1971
Andrew Stanway, *Alternative Medicine: A Guide to Natural Therapies*, 1980
Starhawk, *The Spiral Dance*, 1979
Starhawk, *Dreaming the Dark: Magic, Sex and Politics*, 1982
June Statham, *Daughters and Sons: Experiences of Non-Sexist Childraising*, 1986
Stan Steiner, *The Vanishing White Man*, 1976
Mary Stott, *Ageing for Beginners*, 1981
Margaret Stucki, *Eco-Elegia*, 1981
The Sun
Thomas Szasz, *The Myth of Mental Illness*, 1962

A.G. Tansley, *Introduction to Plant Ecology*, 1946
Third World Guide, annual volumes, 1984/85 onwards
Lewis Thomas, *Human Responsibility: Phenomenon of Change*, 1986
Henry Thoreau, *Walking*, 1851
Henry Thoreau, *Walden*, 1854
Henry Thoreau, *Yankee in Canada*, 1866
Threads
Through the Break, 1987

John Thyme, *Motorways Versus Democracy*, 1978
Lloyd Timberlake, *Only One Earth*, 1987
Michael Tobias, *After Eden: History, Ecology and Conscience*, 1985
Michael Tobias (ed), *Deep Ecology*, 1985
Alvin Toffler, *Future Shock*, 1970
Alvin Toffler, *The Eco-Spasm Report*, 1975
Alvin Toffler, *The Third Wave*, 1980
Brian Tokar, *The Green Alternative*, 1987
Nicholas Tomalin, *Man About Town*, 1964
F.E. Trainer, *Abandon Affluence*, 1985
John Travis, *Wellness Workbook*, undated
Fanny Tribble, *Heavy Periods*, undated
Yi-Fu Tuan, *Space and Place: The Perspective of Experience*, 1977
Colin Tudge, *The Famine Business*, 1977
John Turner and Robert Fichter (ed), *Freedom to Build*, 1972
Lisa Tuttle, *Encyclopedia of Feminism*, 1986

Unbecoming Men, 1971
Union of Concerned Scientists, *Beyond the Freeze*, 1982

Brenda Vale, *Albion*, 1984
Brenda and Robert Vale, *The Autonomous House*, 1975
Alan Vaughan, *Incredible Coincidence*, 1979

Barbara Walker, *The Woman's Encyclopedia of Myths and Secrets*, 1983
Kenneth Walker, *The Circle of Life*, 1966
Robert Waller, *The Agricultural Balance Sheet*, 1982
Sue Walrond-Skinner, *Dictionary of Psychotherapy*, 1986
Barbara Ward, *Progress for a Small Planet*, 1979
Barbara Ward and René Dubos, *Only One Earth*, 1972
Marina Warner, *Alone of All Her Kind*, 1978
Washington Post
William Watkins and E.V. Snyder, *Ecodeath*, 1972
Lyall Watson, *Supernature*, 1973
Lyall Watson, *The Romeo Error*, 1974
Alan Watts, *The Book on the Taboo Against Knowing Who You Are*, 1973
H.D. Watts, *The Branch Plant Economy: A Study of External Control*, 1981
Websters Ninth New Collegiate Dictionary, 1986
Fay Weldon, *The Heart of the Country*, 1987
We Own It, 1982

Melvyn Werbach, *Third Line Medicine*, 1986
James Wesley, *Ecophysics: The Applications of Physics to Ecology*, 1974
Joe Weston (ed), *Red and Green*, 1986
Richard Wilhelm, *I Ching, or Book of Changes*, 1951
Raymond Williams, *Towards 2000*, 1985
Judith Williamson, *Decoding Advertisements*, 1978
Elizabeth Wilson, *What is to Be Done about Violence Against Women?*, 1983
Elizabeth Wilson, *Adorned in Dreams: Fashion and Modernity*, 1985
Steven Wineman, *The Politics of Human Services*, 1984
Neil Wollman (ed), *Working for Peace*, 1985
Women's Peace Alliance Newsletter
Women's Review
Clive Wood, *Birth Control: Now and Tomorrow*, 1969
W. Woodruff, *The Impact of Western Man*, 1967
Barbara Woods (ed), *Eco-Solutions: A Casebook for the Environmental Crisis*, 1972
Virginia Woolf, *Three Guineas*, 1938
Workers' Co-operatives, 1980
World View 1985
Worldwatch, annual volumes, 1984 onwards
Donald Worster, *Nature's Economy: The Roots of Ecology*, 1977
Machaelle Small Wright, *Behaving as if the God in All Life Mattered: A New Age Ecology*, 1983
Jon Wynne-Tyson, *Food for a Future*, 1976
Jon Wynne-Tyson (ed), *The Extended Circle*, 1985

Geoffrey Yates, *Food: Need, Greed and Myopia*, 1980

Gary Zukav, *The Dancing Wu Li Masters*, 1979